W9-BFF-992

Adobe®
Creative Suite 2
ALL-IN-ONE DESK REFERENCE

FOR
DUMMIES®

Adobe® Creative Suite 2

ALL-IN-ONE DESK REFERENCE

FOR DUMMIES®

by Jennifer Smith and
Christopher Smith

WILEY

Wiley Publishing, Inc.

Adobe® Creative Suite 2 All-in-One Desk Reference For Dummies®

Published by
Wiley Publishing, Inc.
111 River Street
Hoboken, NJ 07030-5774
www.wiley.com

Copyright © 2005 by Wiley Publishing, Inc., Indianapolis, Indiana

Published by Wiley Publishing, Inc., Indianapolis, Indiana

Published simultaneously in Canada

No part of this publication may be reproduced, stored in a retrieval system or transmitted in any form or
by any means, electronic, mechanical, photocopying, recording, scanning or otherwise, except as permit-
ted under Sections 107 or 108 of the 1976 United States Copyright Act, without either the prior written
permission of the Publisher, or authorization through payment of the appropriate per-copy fee to the
Copyright Clearance Center, 222 Rosewood Drive, Danvers, MA 01923, (978) 750-8400, fax (978) 646-8600.
Requests to the Publisher for permission should be addressed to the Legal Department, Wiley Publishing,
Inc., 10475 Crosspoint Blvd., Indianapolis, IN 46256, (317) 572-3447, fax (317) 572-4355, or online at http://
www.wiley.com/go/permissions.

Trademarks: Wiley, the Wiley Publishing logo, For Dummies, the Dummies Man logo, A Reference for the
Rest of Us!, The Dummies Way, Dummies Daily, The Fun and Easy Way, Dummies.com, and related trade
dress are trademarks or registered trademarks of John Wiley & Sons, Inc. and/or its affiliates in the United
States and other countries, and may not be used without written permission. All other trademarks are the
property of their respective owners. Wiley Publishing, Inc., is not associated with any product or vendor
mentioned in this book.

LIMIT OF LIABILITY/DISCLAIMER OF WARRANTY: THE PUBLISHER AND THE AUTHOR MAKE NO REPRESENTATIONS
OR WARRANTIES WITH RESPECT TO THE ACCURACY OR COMPLETENESS OF THE CONTENTS OF THIS WORK AND
SPECIFICALLY DISCLAIM ALL WARRANTIES, INCLUDING WITHOUT LIMITATION WARRANTIES OF FITNESS FOR A PAR-
TICULAR PURPOSE. NO WARRANTY MAY BE CREATED OR EXTENDED BY SALES OR PROMOTIONAL MATERIALS. THE
ADVICE AND STRATEGIES CONTAINED HEREIN MAY NOT BE SUITABLE FOR EVERY SITUATION. THIS WORK IS SOLD
WITH THE UNDERSTANDING THAT THE PUBLISHER IS NOT ENGAGED IN RENDERING LEGAL, ACCOUNTING, OR
OTHER PROFESSIONAL SERVICES. IF PROFESSIONAL ASSISTANCE IS REQUIRED, THE SERVICES OF A COMPETENT
PROFESSIONAL PERSON SHOULD BE SOUGHT. NEITHER THE PUBLISHER NOR THE AUTHOR SHALL BE LIABLE FOR
DAMAGES ARISING HEREFROM. THE FACT THAT AN ORGANIZATION OR WEBSITE IS REFERRED TO IN THIS WORK
AS A CITATION AND/OR A POTENTIAL SOURCE OF FURTHER INFORMATION DOES NOT MEAN THAT THE AUTHOR OR
THE PUBLISHER ENDORSES THE INFORMATION THE ORGANIZATION OR WEBSITE MAY PROVIDE OR RECOMMEN-
DATIONS IT MAY MAKE. FURTHER, READERS SHOULD BE AWARE THAT INTERNET WEBSITES LISTED IN THIS WORK
MAY HAVE CHANGED OR DISAPPEARED BETWEEN WHEN THIS WORK WAS WRITTEN AND WHEN IT IS READ.

For general information on our other products and services, please contact our Customer Care
Department within the U.S. at 800-762-2974, outside the U.S. at 317-572-3993, or fax 317-572-4002.

For technical support, please visit www.wiley.com/techsupport.

Wiley also publishes its books in a variety of electronic formats. Some content that appears in print may
not be available in electronic books.

Library of Congress Control Number: 2005923191

ISBN-13: 978-0-7645-8815-0

ISBN-10: 0-7645-8815-X

Manufactured in the United States of America

10 9 8 7 6 5 4 3

1O/RV/QS/QX/IN

WILEY

About the Authors

Jennifer Smith is the founder and Vice President of American Graphics Institute (AGITraining.com). She has authored multiple books on Adobe products and is a technical writer for the Adobe Classroom in a Book series. Jennifer has worked in all aspects of graphic design and production including as an art director of an advertising agency. More than ten years ago, Jennifer took her experience and applied it to teaching. Under her leadership, AGI has grown into the largest training organization focused on print, Internet, video, and PDF publishing. Her teaching and writing style shows a clear direction that can only be achieved by someone who knows the industry and has experienced the Adobe applications in a professional workflow. She lives in the Boston area with her husband (who co-authored this book) and children.

Christopher Smith is President of American Graphics Institute and oversees curriculum content and delivery for Adobe's largest and oldest Certified Training Provider. An Adobe Certified Expert, he works as part of the Adobe Creative Team as the lead technical writer for the *Adobe Classroom in a Book* series for both Adobe Acrobat and Adobe InDesign. His more than ten other books include *Moving to InDesign, Teach Yourself Adobe Acrobat in 24 Hours,* and *Real World Adobe Acrobat.* Smith has served as an elected member of the School Board in his hometown in suburban Boston, Massachusetts, where he lives with his wife and children.

Dedication

To our parents, Ed and Nancy Smith; Mary Kelly and in loving memory of Jennifer's father, Joseph Kelly, the best teacher of all!

To our *perfect* children, Kelly, Alex, Grant Elizabeth, and soon to arrive baby Edward.

Authors' Acknowledgments

Thanks to all of our friends and colleagues at Adobe Systems for their support, encouragement, and faith in our work: Ali, Joe, Ron, Dave, Donna, Steve, Noha, Lynn, Adam, Christine, Jill, Jeffrey, Bagel, Carrie, and the many product team members who responded to our questions throughout the writing process.

Thanks also to the highly professional instructional staff at American Graphics Institute (AGI) who always provide great insight into the best ways to help people learn these software applications.

Thanks to all at Wiley Publishing. This book involves a lot of detail and information and it was up to acquisitions editor, Melody Lane and her "tough love" to make sure it got to the state it is now. Thanks to Colleen Totz and technical editor Cathy Auclair for the great insight.

Thanks to our family as they had to deal with parents who toiled away at the keyboard night after night.

Jennifer: thanks all the friends of my teenage daughter who gave rights for me to use their images.

Publisher's Acknowledgments

We're proud of this book; please send us your comments through our online registration form located at www.dummies.com/register/.

Some of the people who helped bring this book to market include the following:

Acquisitions, Editorial, and Media Development

Project Editor: Colleen Totz

Acquisitions Editor: Melody Layne

Technical Editor: Cathy Auclair

Editorial Manager: Carol Sheehan

Media Development Manager: Laura VanWinkle

Media Development Supervisor: Richard Graves

Editorial Assistant: Amanda Foxworth

Cartoons: Rich Tennant (www.the5thwave.com)

Composition Services

Project Coordinator: Adrienne Martinez

Layout and Graphics: Lauren Goddard, Denny Hager, Stephanie D. Jumper, Barbara Moore, Melanee Prendergast, Heather Ryan, Ron Terry

Proofreaders: Leeann Harney, Joe Niesen, Evelyn Still

Indexer: Richard T. Evans

Publishing and Editorial for Technology Dummies

Richard Swadley, Vice President and Executive Group Publisher

Andy Cummings, Vice President and Publisher

Mary Bednarek, Executive Acquisitions Director

Mary C. Corder, Editorial Director

Publishing for Consumer Dummies

Diane Graves Steele, Vice President and Publisher

Joyce Pepple, Acquisitions Director

Composition Services

Gerry Fahey, Vice President of Production Services

Debbie Stailey, Director of Composition Services

Contents at a Glance

Table of Contents

Introduction

*A*dobe software has always been highly respected for creative design and development. Adobe creates programs that allow you to produce amazing designs and creations with ease. The Adobe Creative Suite 2 is the company's latest release of sophisticated and professional-level software that bundles many separate programs together as a suite. Each program in the suite works individually, or the programs can be integrated together using Version Cue, Adobe's work management software that helps keep track of revisions and edits, and Adobe Bridge, an independent application that helps you control file management, with thumbnails, metadata, and other organizational tools.

You can use the Adobe Creative Suite to create a wide range of productions, from illustrations, page layouts, and professional documents, to Web sites and photographic manipulations. Integrating the programs in the Adobe Creative Suite extends your possibilities as a designer. Don't worry about the programs being too difficult to figure out — just come up with your ideas and start creating!

About This Book

The *Adobe Creative Suite 2 All-in-One Desk Reference For Dummies* is written in a thorough and fun way to show you the basics on how to use each of the programs included in the suite. You find out how to use each program individually and also how to work with the programs together, letting you extend your projects even further. You find out just how easy it is to use the programs through simple and easy-to-follow steps so that you can discover the power of the Adobe software. You'll be up and running in no time!

Here are some of the things you can do with this book:

✦ Create page layouts using text, drawings, and images in InDesign.

✦ Make illustrations using drawing tools with Illustrator.

✦ Manipulate photographs using filters and drawing or color correction tools with Photoshop.

✦ Create PDF documents using Adobe Acrobat or other programs.

✦ Create Web pages and put them online with GoLive.

You discover the basics of how to create all these different kinds of things throughout the chapters in this book in fun, hands-on examples and clear explanations, getting you up to speed quickly!

Foolish Assumptions

There isn't much that you have to know before picking up this book and getting started with the Adobe Creative Suite. All you have to know is how to use a computer in a very basic way. If you can turn on the computer and use a mouse, you're ready for this book. A bit of knowledge about basic computer operations and using software helps, but it isn't necessary. We show you how to open, save, create, and manipulate files using the Adobe Creative Suite so that you can start working with the programs quickly. The most important ingredient to have is your imagination and creativity — we show you how to get started with the rest.

Conventions Used in This Book

We use a few different conventions in this book. *Conventions* refer to particular formatting that is applied to some of the text you find in the chapters that follow.

Adobe Creative Suite 2 is available for both Windows and the Macintosh. We cover both platforms in this book. Where the keys you need to press or the menu choice you need to make differs between Windows and the Mac, we let you know by including instructions for both platforms. For example:

✦ Press the Alt (Windows) or Option (Mac) key.

✦ Choose Edit➪Preferences➪General (Windows) or InDesign➪Preferences➪ General (Mac).

The programs in Adobe Creative Suite 2 often require you to press and hold down a key (or keys) on the keyboard and then click or drag with the mouse. For brevity's sake, we shorten this action by naming the key you need to hold down and adding click or drag, as follows:

✦ Shift+click to select multiple files.

✦ Move the object by Ctrl+dragging (Windows) or ⌘+dragging (Mac).

The formatting conventions used in this book are listed here:

✦ **Bold:** We use **bold** to indicate when you should type something, or to highlight an action in a step list. For example, the action required to open a dialog box would appear in bold in a step list.

✦ `Code font:` We use this `computerese font` to show you Web addresses (URLs), e-mail addresses, or bits of HTML code. For example, you would type a URL into a browser window to access a Web page such as `www. google.com`.

✦ *Italics:* We use *italics* to highlight a new term, which is then defined. For example, *filters* might be a new term to you. The word itself is italicized and is followed by a definition to explain what the word means.

What You Don't Have to Read

This book is such a large text, you might wonder if you have to read it from cover to cover. You don't have to read every page of this book to discover how to use the Adobe Creative Suite. Luckily, you can choose the bits and pieces that mean the most to you and will help you finish a project you might be working on. Perhaps you're interested in creating a technical drawing and putting it online. You can choose to read a couple chapters in Book III on Illustrator, and then skip ahead to Book VI on GoLive, and just read the relevant chapters or sections on each subject. Later, you might want to place some associated PDF documents online, so then you can read a few chapters in Book V on Acrobat or Book II on exporting InDesign documents.

You don't have to read everything on each page, either. You can treat many of the icons in this book as bonus material. Icons supplement the material in each chapter with additional information that might interest or help you with your work. The Technical Stuff icons are great if you want to find out a bit more about technical aspects of using the program or your computer, but don't feel that you need to read these icons if technicalities don't interest you.

How This Book Is Organized

The *Adobe Creative Suite 2 All-in-One Desk Reference For Dummies* is split into six quick-reference guides or minibooks. You don't have to read these minibooks sequentially, and you don't even have to read all the sections in any particular chapter. You can use the Table of Contents and the index to find the information you need and quickly get your answer. In this section, we briefly describe what you find in each minibook.

Book I: Adobe Creative Suite 2 Basics

Book I shows you how to use the features in Adobe Creative Suite 2 that are similar across all the programs described in this book. You discover the menus, palettes, and tools that are similar or work the same way in most of the Adobe Creative Suite's programs. You also find out how to import, export, and use common commands in each program. If you're wondering about what shortcuts and common tools you can use in the programs to speed up your workflow, then this part has tips and tricks you'll probably find quite useful. The similarities in all of the programs are helpful because they make using the programs that much easier.

Book II: InDesign CS2

Book II describes how to use InDesign CS2 to create simple page layouts using text, images, and drawings. Hands-on steps show you how to use the drawing tools in InDesign to create simple illustrations, and also use other menus and tools to add text and pictures. Importing stories and illustrations into InDesign is an important part of the process, so you find out how this is done effectively as well. Book II shows you how easy it is to create effective page layouts using this powerful and professional design program.

Book III: Illustrator CS2

Book III starts with the fundamentals of Adobe Illustrator CS2 to put you on your way to creating useful and interesting illustrations. Check out this mini-book to discover how to take advantage of features that have been around for many versions of Illustrator, such as the Pen tool, as well as new and exciting features, such as vector tracing. See how to take advantage of the Appearance palette and save time by creating graphics styles, templates, and symbols. Pick up hard-to-find keyboard shortcuts that can help reduce the time spent mousing around for menu items and tools.

Book IV: Photoshop CS2

Book IV on Photoshop CS2 is aimed to help you achieve good imagery, starting with basics that even advanced users may have missed along the way. In this minibook, you find out how to color correct images like a pro and use tools to keep images at the right resolution and size, no matter whether the image is intended for print or the Web.

This minibook also shows you how to integrate new features in Photoshop, such as an improved Browse window, layer management, and a dynamic Histogram, into your workflow. By the time you're finished with this mini-book, you'll feel like you can perform magic on just about any image.

Book V: Acrobat 7.0

Adobe Acrobat 7.0 is a powerful viewing and editing application that allows you to share documents with colleagues, clients, and production personnel, such as printers and Web page designers. Book V shows you how you can save time and money previously spent on couriers and overnight shipping by taking advantage of annotation capabilities. Discover features that even advanced users may have missed along the way, and see how you can feel comfortable about using PDF as a file format of choice.

Book VI: GoLive CS2

Book VI shows you how creating a Web site in GoLive CS2 can be easy and fun. Take advantage of the tools and features in GoLive to make and maintain a very clean and useable site. After the fundamentals are covered, discover how to take advantage of improved CSS (Cascading Style Sheets) capabilities, as well as exciting rollover and action features that add interactivity to your site. In the past, these functions would require lots of hand-coding and tape on the glasses, but now you can be a designer and create interactivity easily in GoLive, no hand-coding or pocket protectors required.

Icons Used in This Book

What's a *For Dummies* book without icons pointing you in the direction of really great information that's sure to help you along your way? In this section, we briefly describe each icon we use in this book.

The Tip icon points out helpful information that is likely to make your job easier.

This icon marks a generally interesting and useful fact — something that you might want to remember for later use.

The Warning icon highlights lurking danger. With this icon, we're telling you to pay attention and proceed with caution.

When you see this icon, you know that there's techie stuff nearby. If you're not feeling very technical, you can skip this info.

You can use the Adobe Creative Suite programs all together in many different and helpful ways to make your workflow more efficient. Throughout this book, we explain just how you can implement integration wherever it's pertinent to the discussion at hand. We highlight these tidbits with the Integration icon — you won't want to miss this information.

Where to Go from Here

If you want to find out how to make page layouts for brochures, advertisements, books, and more, then skip ahead to Book II on InDesign. If you really want to start with drawings and illustrations, then go to Book III on Illustrator. Book IV on Photoshop is the first stop for you if you have images you want to manipulate by cropping or modifying, or by using color correction. Photoshop is also great for painting and drawing, so start here if you have creative ideas you want to express. If you want to create PDF documents, then you can skip ahead to Book V on Acrobat; however, if you want to create a page layout for your document and then export it as a PDF, you should start with Book II on InDesign instead. If designing for the Web is what you're most excited about, you should begin reading Book VI on GoLive. Book I is a great place to start reading if you have never used Adobe products before, or if you're new to design-based software. Discovering some of the common terminology, menus, and palettes can be very helpful for the later chapters that use the terms and commands regularly!

If you want to, you can start with Book I, Chapter 1 and progress through the book all the way to the end! The *Adobe Creative Suite All-in-One Desk Reference For Dummies* is designed so you can read a chapter or section out of order, depending on what subjects you're most interested in. It's also written in such a way that reading it in a linear fashion from cover-to-cover is beneficial. Where you go from here is entirely up to you!

Book I

Adobe Creative Suite 2 Basics

The 5th Wave   By Rich Tennant

"It says,' Seth - Please see us about your idea to wrap newsletter text around company logo. Production.'"

Contents at a Glance

Chapter 1: Introducing Adobe Creative Suite 2

In This Chapter

✔ Looking over InDesign

✔ Drawing with Illustrator

✔ Introducing Photoshop

✔ Getting started with Acrobat

✔ Going over GoLive

✔ Integrating the programs in Adobe Creative Suite 2

The diverse software in Adobe Creative Suite 2 enables you to create everything from an e-commerce Web site to a printed book of many hundred pages. Each piece of software in the Adobe Creative Suite works on its own as a robust tool. When you use different programs when working on a single project, however, you have more room for creativity and exploration, and you have a wider toolset to work with. The Adobe Creative Suite unites leading-edge software for Web and print production and allows you to integrate these tools to create powerful and engaging presentations.

In Book I, you discover how the Adobe Creative Suite functions and how you can use it. Many features are consistent among the programs, which makes the software much easier to use. If you're accustomed to using color in Illustrator, you will also feel comfortable dealing with color in Photoshop or InDesign. Opening and closing panels feels familiar in GoLive after you've used InDesign. Therefore, you can figure out the software quickly, more so than if you were working with a combination of programs from many different software companies. We explore these similarities throughout Book I, show you how to use the interface, and tell you what some of the common terminology means.

Introducing InDesign CS2

InDesign is a diverse and feature-rich page layout program. Using InDesign, you can create documents with rich typography and unique page layout and design, and you can execute complete control over your images and text. InDesign has many great features, including excellent integration with several other products in the Adobe Creative Suite.

InDesign, shown in Figure 1-1, allows you to accomplish the following:

✦ Use images, text, and even rich media to create unique layouts and designs.

✦ Export layouts for use in GoLive to create interactive Web sites.

✦ Import native files from Photoshop and Illustrator to help build rich layouts in InDesign.

✦ Export your work as an entire book, including chapters, sections, numbered pages, and more.

✦ Create interactive PDF documents.

✦ Create drawings using the basic drawing tools included in the software.

Toolbox

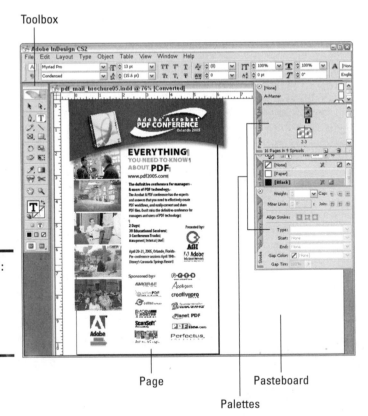

Figure 1-1:
Use InDesign to lay out pages or spreads.

Page

Pasteboard

Palettes

InDesign caters to the layout professional, but it's easy enough for even beginners to use. You can import tables (say, from Microsoft Excel) into your documents alongside existing artwork and images to create a layout. You can even easily import text from Microsoft Word, Adobe InCopy, or simply Notepad (Windows) or TextEdit (Mac). In a nutshell, importing, arranging, and exporting work is a common process when working with InDesign. Throughout this entire process, you have a huge amount of control over your work, whether you're working on a simple one-page brochure or an entire book of 800 pages.

Book II is all about how to get started with InDesign and use it to create and output simple but effective page layouts by importing a variety of media and using the built-in toolset.

Using Illustrator CS2 for Drawing

Adobe Illustrator is the industry's leading vector-based graphics software. Aimed at everyone from graphics professionals to Web users, Illustrator allows you to design layouts, logos for print, or vector-based images that can be imported into other programs, such as Photoshop, InDesign, or Macromedia Flash. Adobe also enables you to easily and quickly create files by saving Illustrator documents as templates (so that you can efficiently reuse designs) and using a predefined library and document size.

Illustrator CS2 even has support for 3D effects that allow you to create 3D shapes and wrap custom bitmap or vector artwork around those shapes. Or you can add three-dimensional bevels to shapes in an Illustrator document. You can add advanced lighting effects to shapes by adding multiple light sources; the brightness of each light source can be individually controlled. Check out Book III to discover some of the new features added to Illustrator CS2.

Illustrator also integrates with the other products in the Adobe Creative Suite by allowing you to create PDF documents easily within Illustrator. You can also use Illustrator files in Photoshop, InDesign, and Adobe's special effects program, After Effects. Illustrator, shown in Figure 1-2, allows you to integrate with third-party applications and suites, such as Microsoft Office, by allowing you to export Illustrator files to a format well suited for use with Office products.

Toolbox   Palettes

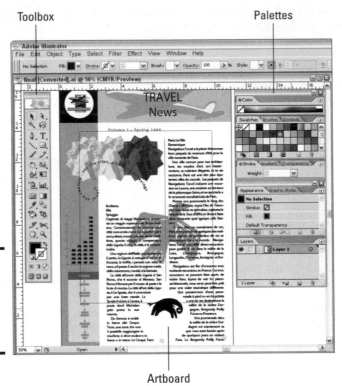

Figure 1-2:
Create
drawings
or detailed
layouts in
Illustrator.

Artboard

Here are some of the things you can create and do when using Illustrator:

✦ Create technical drawings (floor plans, architectural sketches, and so on), logos, illustrations, posters, packaging, and Web graphics.

✦ Add effects like drop shadows and Gaussian blurs to vector images.

✦ Enhance artwork by creating your own custom brushes.

✦ Align text along a path so that it bends in an interesting way.

✦ Lay out text into multicolumn brochures — text automatically flows from one column to the next.

✦ Create charts and graphs using graphing tools.

✦ Create gradients that can be imported and edited in other programs, such as InDesign.

✦ Create interesting gradients using the Airbrush tool.

✦ Create documents quickly and easily using the existing templates and included stock graphics in Illustrator.

✦ Distort images in exciting ways by creating warp and liquefy effects.

✦ Save a drawing in almost any graphic format, including Adobe's PDF, PSD, EPS, TIFF, GIF, JPEG, and SVG formats.

✦ Save your Illustrator files for the Web by using the Save for Web dialog box, which allows you to output HTML, GIF, JPEG, and even Macromedia Flash SWF files.

✦ Save Illustrator files as secure PDF files with 128-bit encryption.

Book III details how to illustrate and create interesting designs using the wide range of drawing tools and controls available in Illustrator. Some of these controls are described in the previous list.

Getting Started with Photoshop CS2

Photoshop, shown in Figure 1-3, is the industry-standard software for Web designers, video professionals, and photographers who need to manipulate bitmap images. Photoshop allows you to manage and edit images by correcting color, editing photos by hand, and even combining several photos together to create interesting and unique effects. Alternatively, you can use Photoshop as a painting program, where you can artistically create images and graphics by hand. Photoshop even includes a file browser that lets you easily manage your images by assigning keywords or allowing you to search the images based on metadata.

Photoshop also allows you to create complex text layouts by placing text along a path or within shapes. The text can be edited after it has been placed along a path and can even be edited in other programs (such as Illustrator CS2).

Sharing images from Photoshop is very easy to do. You can share multiple images in a PDF file, create an attractive photo gallery for the Web with a few clicks of the mouse, or upload images to an online photo service. You can preview multiple filters (effects) at once without having to apply each filter separately. Photoshop CS2 also supports various artistic brush styles, such as wet and dry brush type effects and charcoal and pastel effects.

You can even create Macromedia Flash vector animations by using ImageReady CS2, which is used for Web production and is part of Photoshop CS2. If you're accustomed to using Macromedia Flash, you will find basic functionality built into ImageReady that can help speed up your workflow between the two programs.

Toolbox Main menu Options bar Palettes Palette well

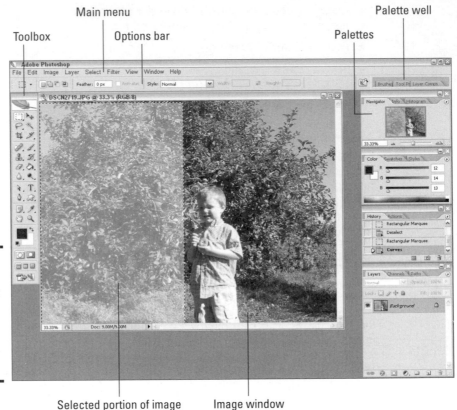

Figure 1-3:
Manipulate
and correct
photos or
create
graphics
with
Photoshop.

Selected portion of image Image window

Photoshop also has some great features for scanning. You can scan multiple images at once, and Photoshop is able to straighten each photo and save it as an individual file.

Book IV shows you the diverse capabilities of Photoshop. From drawing and painting to image color correction, Photoshop has many uses for print and Web design alike.

Working with Acrobat 7.0

Acrobat 7.0 Professional is found only in the Premium edition of Creative Suite 2 and is aimed at both business and creative professionals. It provides an incredibly useful and secure way to share and review the documents you create in your Adobe Creative Suite 2 applications.

Portable Document Format (PDF) is the file format used by Adobe Acrobat. It is used primarily as an independent method for sharing files. This allows for users who create files on either Macintosh or PC systems to share files not only with each other, but also with users of handheld devices or Unix computers. PDF files generally start out as other documents — whether from a word processor or a sophisticated page layout and design program.

While PDF files can be read on many different computer systems using the free Adobe Reader, users with the Professional or Standard version of Adobe Acrobat can do much more with PDF files. With your version of Acrobat you can create PDF documents, add security to them, use review and commenting tools, edit the documents, and build PDF forms.

Use Acrobat to perform some of the following tasks:

✦ Create interactive forms that can be filled out online.

✦ Allow users to embed comments within the PDF files to provide feedback. Comments can then be compiled from multiple reviewers and viewed in a single summary.

✦ Create PDF files that can include MP3 audio, video, or SWF files.

✦ Combine multiple files into a single PDF and include headers and footers, as well as watermarks.

✦ Create secure documents with encryption.

Book V is all about Acrobat and PDF creation. Check out this minibook if you intend to create or edit PDF documents.

Introducing GoLive CS2

GoLive CS2 is used to create professional Web sites quickly and efficiently, without the need to know or understand HTML (HyperText Markup Language). You can work with a visual authoring workspace (commonly known as a *Design view*), or you can work in an environment where you work with the code. You can also work with both modes side-by-side. GoLive enables you to set up entire Web sites of multiple pages on your hard drive, and then upload them to a Web server. It also allows you to create a bunch of formatting settings, such as CSS styles. GoLive streamlines the Web site creation process and makes it a lot quicker than writing HTML code by hand.

GoLive has built-in support for CSS (Cascading Style Sheets). CSS is a language that allows you to format parts of your Web pages, such as the color and style of text. CSS can also help you control the layout of the elements on your Web pages and offers a much more efficient way of controlling styles than does HTML. GoLive supports other Web standards, such as Section 501, XHTML, and SVG, enabling you to build Web sites for mobile devices and sites that must be standards-compliant and/or accessible.

You can use guides and grids to lay out the elements on your pages in a visual and hands-on way. A very simple Web page layout is shown in Figure 1-4.

GoLive allows you to incorporate layouts and elements for your Web sites that were created in other programs such as InDesign or Photoshop. The process of moving between the programs in Adobe Creative Suite 2 is quick and seamless. You can package up a page or series of pages from InDesign and move to GoLive to prepare the work for the Web. You can even import layered Photoshop files into GoLive.

Figure 1-4: Laying out Web pages using GoLive makes Web authoring easy.

Main menu

Inspector palette

Document window

Palettes

Finally, GoLive introduces a new tool called Co-Author. Co-Author enables you to design Web sites with templates, which allows your clients or Web site contributors to upload new content to the site without anyone having to actually build new pages.

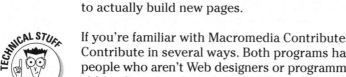

If you're familiar with Macromedia Contribute, Co-Author is quite similar to Contribute in several ways. Both programs have a similar purpose (allowing people who aren't Web designers or programmers to upload content to a site), although each software package has different ways of achieving that result. Both programs are approximately the same price, and have free trials available.

Go to Book VI to find out how to use GoLive to create exciting Web sites that include text, images, and multimedia. You'll be up and running in no time!

Integrating Software and Version Cue

With so many great pieces of software in a single package, it's only natural that you will want to start using the programs together to build exciting projects. You may want to design a book using InDesign, and then create a Web presence for that content in GoLive. Similarly, you may want to take a complex PDF file and make it into something that everyone can view online. Or you might create a layout design in Illustrator and integrate it into a page layout that you continue building in InDesign. All the tools in the Adobe Creative Suite are built to work together, and achieving the tasks described previously suddenly becomes much easier to do.

Benefiting from integration

Integrating software is typically advantageous to anyone. Integration allows you to streamline the workflow among programs and sometimes team members. If you wanted to create a Web site from an InDesign document, you would need to do a lot of preparation to get the file(s) ready to work with GoLive. However, tools exist that package up the files for you and prepare them for GoLive. If you wanted to prepare Photoshop files for the Web, you would also have to do a lot of manual work in order to prepare the documents. However, when you import a PSD file into GoLive, the layers are automatically translated into code and prepared for the Web.

Therefore, the integration features included in the Creative Suite do a great deal of the work for you. Tools exist so that you can import native files (such as Photoshop PSD files or Illustrator AI files) and take advantage of the better quality or more detailed information these file formats offer.

Using Version Cue

Version Cue is a new technology included with Adobe Creative Suite 2 and works with InDesign, Illustrator, Photoshop, and GoLive. Version Cue allows you to manage your files when you're working on a project. This software is particularly useful for file management if you're working with a team, because it helps you make sure that you're working with the most recent version of the file. Version Cue also allows you to add comments and notes about the files you're working on.

Version Cue allows you to save files, and view previews and search the contents of your files before opening them. Version Cue also helps control who is working on a file at any given time. If someone else is working on a file, the software will warn you that you're attempting to open a file that is currently being edited. Version Cue is a very useful and time-saving tool that you can take advantage of, no matter what kind of project you're working on.

Chapter 2: Using Common Menus and Commands

In This Chapter

✔ **Discovering common menus**

✔ **Using dialog boxes**

✔ **Encountering alerts**

✔ **Using common menu options**

✔ **Using contextual menus**

✔ **Using common shortcut commands**

✔ **Setting and changing preferences**

*W*hen you work with Adobe Creative Suite 2, you may notice that many menus, commands, and options are similar among its various programs. Discovering how to use menus and dialog boxes is essential to using the programs in Adobe Creative Suite 2.

You may already be familiar with using dialog boxes and menus from other software packages. You will quickly discover that the way you use these elements is pretty much the same for any program. Some of the specific keyboard shortcuts are the same across programs, even ones made by different software companies. This makes finding out how to use the commands and options very easy. This chapter provides an overview of some of the common menus, dialog boxes, options, commands, and preferences that exist in most or all of the programs in Adobe Creative Suite 2.

Discovering Common Menus

When you work with various programs in Adobe Creative Suite 2, you may notice that the menus in the main menu bar are the same. These menus often contain many of the same commands across programs. These menus are somewhat similar to other graphics programs you may have used before. Similar functionality makes it easy to find certain commands even when you're completely new to the software you're using.

Menus contain options and commands that control particular parts or functions of each program. You may have the option of opening a dialog box, which is used to input settings or preferences or to add something to a document. A menu may also contain commands that perform a particular action. For example, you may save the file as a result of selecting a particular command in a menu. Menus that commonly appear in the Adobe Creative Suite programs are

✦ **File:** Contains many commands that control the overall document, such as creating, opening, saving, printing, and setting general properties for the document. The File menu may also include options for importing or exporting data into or from the current document.

✦ **Edit:** Contains options and commands for editing the current document. Commands include copying, pasting, selecting, and options for opening preferences and setting dialog boxes that are used to control parts of the document. Spell checking and transforming objects are also common parts of the Edit menu.

✦ **View:** Contains options for changing the level of magnification of the document. The View menu also sometimes includes options for viewing the workspace in different ways, showing rules, grids or guides, and turning on and off snapping.

✦ **Window:** Contains options that are primarily used to open or close whatever palettes are available in the program. You can also choose how to view the workspace and save a favorite arrangement of the workspace, as well.

✦ **Help:** Contains the option to open the Help documentation that's included with the program. This menu may also include information about updating the software, registration, and tutorials.

Adobe Creative Suite on the Mac also has an additional menu that bears the name of the program itself. This menu includes options for showing or hiding the program on the screen, opening preferences, and opening documents that provide information about the software.

Figure 2-1 shows a menu in Photoshop that contains many common options to control the program. Notice that more menus are available in the program than are in the previous list. Each program has additional program-specific menus that are determined by the specific needs of whatever software you're using. For example, Photoshop has an Image menu that enables you to resize the image or document, rotate the canvas, and duplicate the image, among other functions. InDesign has a Layout menu that allows you to navigate the document, edit page numbering, and access controls for creating and editing the document's table of contents. What additional menus exist in each program is determined by what the software is designed to do; we discuss these menus where appropriate throughout the book.

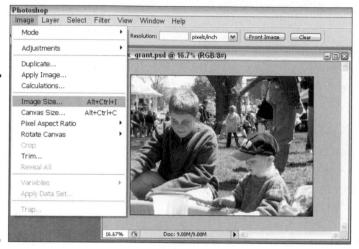

Figure 2-1:
Menus in
Photoshop
allow you to
choose and
control
many
options
in the
software.

Using Dialog Boxes

A *dialog box* is a small window that contains a combination of options formatted as drop-down lists, panes, text fields, option buttons, and check boxes that enable you to make settings and enter information or data as necessary. The dialog boxes enable you to control the software or your document in various ways. For example, when you open a new file, you typically use the Open dialog box to select a file to open. When you save a file, you use a Save As dialog box to select a location to save the file, name it, and execute the Save command.

Some dialog boxes also include tabs. These dialog boxes contain many settings of different types organized into several sections by using tabs. Dialog boxes typically have a button that executes the particular command and one that cancels and closes the dialog box without doing anything. A common dialog box is shown in Figure 2-2.

A dialog box in Windows is a lot like a dialog box you might find on the Mac. They perform similar functions and include the same elements to enter or select information. Some of the functions dialog boxes perform include the following:

✦ Save a new version of a file.

✦ Set up your printing options or page setup.

✦ Set up the preferences for the software you're using.

✦ Check spelling of text in a document.

✦ Open a new document.

Figure 2-2:
An example
of a dialog
box in
Illustrator
CS2.

When you have a dialog box open in the program you're using, the window pops up on the screen. Before you can begin working with the program again, you have to close the dialog box. You can close the dialog box either by making your choices and clicking a button (such as Save or OK) when you are finished, or by clicking the Cancel button to close the dialog box without making any changes. You cannot use the program you're working with until the dialog box is closed.

Encountering Alerts

Alerts are common on any operating system and in most programs. *Alerts* are similar to dialog boxes in that they are small windows that contain information. However, alerts are different from dialog boxes because you cannot edit the information in an alert. Alerts are designed to tell you something and give you one or more options. For example, you may encounter an alert that indicates you can't select a particular option. Usually there is an OK button to click to acknowledge and close the alert. You may have other buttons on the alert that will cancel what you were doing or open a dialog box. Figure 2-3 shows a typical alert.

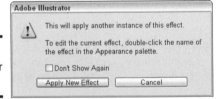

Figure 2-3:
An Illustrator
alert.

Alerts are sometimes used to confirm an action before it is executed. Sometimes these alert windows also offer the option (typically in the form of a check box) of not showing the alert or warning again. You may want to check this box if you repeatedly perform an action that shows the warning, and you don't need to see the warning each and every time.

Using Common Menu Options

Various menu options are typically available in each of the Creative Suite programs. Some of the options open dialog boxes. This is typically indicated by an ellipsis that follows the menu option, as shown in Figure 2-4.

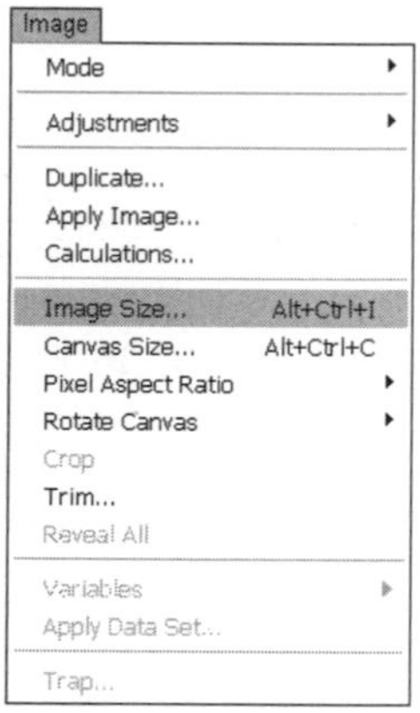

Figure 2-4:
If an ellipsis
follows
a menu
option,
a dialog
box opens.

The following menu options are found in several of the Adobe Creative Suite programs and perform similarly across programs:

✦ **New:** Creates a brand new document in the native file format. For example, in InDesign a new INDD file is created by choosing File➪New➪Document. You can sometimes choose what type of new file you want to create.

✦ **Open:** Opens a dialog box where you can choose a (supported) file on your hard drive or a disk to open.

✦ **Close:** Closes the current document. If you have unsaved changes, you're prompted to save those changes first.

✦ **Save:** Saves the changes you have made to the current document.

✦ **Save As:** Saves a new copy of the current document.

✦ **Import:** Imports a file into the current document, such as an image or sound file.

✦ **Export:** Exports the current data to a specified file format. You can sometimes select several different kinds of file formats to save the current data in.

✦ **Copy:** Copies the currently selected data onto the computer's Clipboard.

✦ **Paste:** Pastes the data from the Clipboard into the current document.

✦ **Undo:** Undoes the most recent thing you did in the program. For example, if you just created a rectangle, the rectangle is removed from the document.

✦ **Redo:** Redoes the steps that you applied the Undo command to. For example, if you removed that rectangle you created, the redo command adds it back to the document.

✦ **Zoom In:** Magnifies the document so that you can view and edit the contents closely.

✦ **Zoom Out:** Scales the view smaller so that you can see more of the document at once.

✦ **Help:** Opens the help documentation for the current program.

About Contextual Menus

Contextual menus are available in all kinds of programs; they're an incredibly useful, quick way to make selections or issue commands. Contextual menus include some of the most useful commands you may find yourself choosing over and over again. A *contextual menu* is similar to the menus that we describe in the previous sections; however, it's context-sensitive and opens when you right-click (Windows) or Control+click (Mac) something in the program. *Contextual* means that what options appear in the menu depends on what object or item you right-click (Windows) or Control+click (Mac). For example, if you open a contextual menu when the cursor is over an image, commands involving the image are listed in the menu. However, if you right-click (Windows) or Control+click (Mac) the document's background, you typically see options that affect the entire document instead of just a particular element within it. This means that you can select common commands specifically for the item that you've selected. Figure 2-5 shows a contextual menu that appears when you right-click (Windows) or Control+click (Mac) an object in InDesign.

Keep in mind that the tool you select in the toolbox may affect which contextual menus you can access in a document. You may have to select the Selection tool first to access some menus. If you want to access a contextual menu for a particular item in the document, make sure that the object is selected first before you right-click (Windows) or Control+click (Mac).

If you're using a Mac, you can right-click to open a contextual menu if you have a two-button mouse hooked up to your Mac. Otherwise, you would Control+click to open a contextual menu.

Figure 2-5:
Open a
contextual
menu in
Windows by
right-clicking
an object.

Using Common Shortcuts

Shortcuts are key combinations that enable you to quickly and efficiently
execute commands such as saving, opening, or copying and pasting objects.
Many of these shortcuts are listed in the menus discussed in the previous
sections. If the menu option has a key combination listed next to it, you
can press that key combination to access the command instead of using the
menu to select it. Figure 2-6 shows the shortcuts associated with a menu
item.

File	
New...	Ctrl+N
Open...	Ctrl+O
Browse...	Alt+Ctrl+O
Open As...	Alt+Shift+Ctrl+O
Open Recent	▶
Edit in ImageReady	Shift+Ctrl+M
Close	Ctrl+W
Close All	Alt+Ctrl+W
Close and Go To Bridge...	Shift+Ctrl+W
Save	Ctrl+S
Save As...	Shift+Ctrl+S
Save a Version...	
Save for Web...	Alt+Shift+Ctrl+S
Revert	F12

Figure 2-6:
Shortcuts
shown next
to their
associated
commands.

For example, if you open the File menu, next to the Save option is Ctrl+S
(Windows) or ⌘+S (Mac). Instead of choosing File⇨Save, you can press the
shortcut keys to save your file. This is a very quick way to execute a particular
command.

Some of the most common shortcuts in the Adobe Creative Suite are listed in Table 2-1.

Table 2-1	Common Keyboard Shortcuts	
Command	*Windows Shortcut*	*Mac Shortcut*
New	Ctrl+N	⌘ +N
Open	Ctrl+O	⌘ +O
Save	Ctrl+S	⌘ +S
Undo	Ctrl+Z	⌘ +Z
Redo	Shift+Ctrl+Z	Shift+⌘ +Z
Copy	Ctrl+C	⌘ +C
Paste	Ctrl+V	⌘ +V
Print	Ctrl+P	⌘ +P
Preferences (General)	Ctrl+K	⌘ +K
Help	F1 or sometimes Ctrl+?	F1 or sometimes ⌘+?

Many additional shortcuts are available in each program in the Creative Suite, and not all of them are listed in the menus. You can find these shortcuts throughout the documentation provided with each program. Memorizing the shortcuts can take some time, but the time you save in the long run is worth it.

Changing Your Preferences

Setting your preferences is important when you're working with new software. Understanding what the preferences can do for you gives you a good idea about what the software does as well. All the programs in the Adobe Creative Suite have different preferences; however, the way that the Preferences dialog box works in each program is the same.

The Preferences dialog box for each program can be opened by choosing Edit⇨ Preferences (Windows) or *Program Name*⇨Preferences⇨General (Mac). The Preferences dialog box opens, as shown in Figure 2-7.

The Preferences dialog box contains a great number of settings you can control by entering values into text fields, using drop-down lists, buttons, check boxes, sliders, and other similar controls. Preferences can be quite detailed; however, you don't have to know what each preference does or even change any of them. Most dialog boxes containing preferences are quite detailed in outlining what the preferences control and are therefore intuitive to use. Adobe sometimes includes a Description area near the bottom of the dialog box. When you mouse over a particular control, a description of that control appears in the Description area.

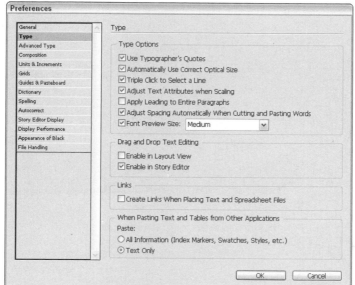

Figure 2-7: Click an item in the list on the left side of the InDesign Preferences dialog box to navigate between each section.

In some Preferences dialog boxes, the left side of the dialog box has a list box containing the different categories of preferences you can change. Alternatively, a Preferences dialog box may have a drop-down list, like the one from Photoshop shown in Figure 2-8. When you select an item from the list box or drop-down list, the dialog box jumps to the area you selected so you can modify various settings.

When you're finished changing the settings in that area, select a new area from the list box or drop-down list to change the settings for a different part of the program.

In some programs, not all the settings you can modify are in the Preferences dialog box. In Illustrator, for example, you can change your color settings by choosing Edit➪Color Settings to open the Color Settings dialog box, as shown in Figure 2-9. What is very useful about this dialog box is that when you mouse over particular drop-down lists or buttons, a description of that control appears at the bottom of the dialog box.

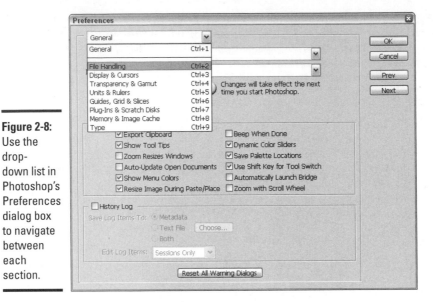

Figure 2-8:
Use the
drop-
down list in
Photoshop's
Preferences
dialog box
to navigate
between
each
section.

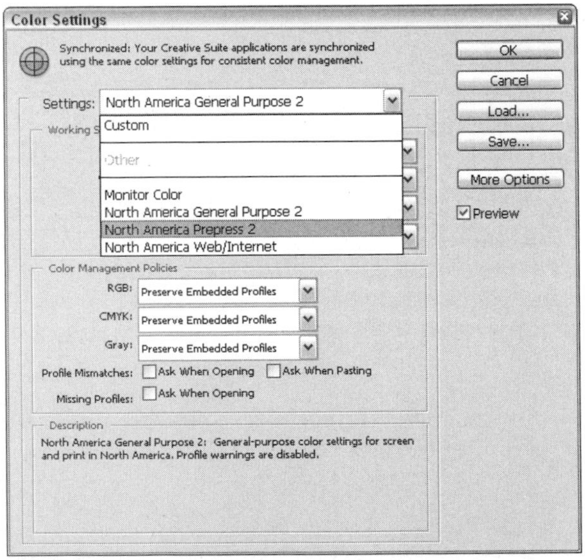

Figure 2-9:
Change
the color
settings in
Illustrator.

In many Adobe Creative Suite programs, you have an option for setting up
the main preferences for the overall document, such as setting up the page
dimensions, number of pages in the document, or the orientation (landscape

or portrait) of the pages. In GoLive and Photoshop, these kinds of options are available by choosing File➪Page Setup; in InDesign, Acrobat, and Illustrator, you choose File➪Document Setup. Figure 2-10 shows a Document Setup dialog box.

Figure 2-10:
The
InDesign
Document
Setup
dialog box.

Chapter 3: Using Common Palettes

In This Chapter

✔ Manipulating palettes in the workspace

✔ Discovering different kinds of palettes

✔ Getting to know the common palettes in Adobe Creative Suite 2

*P*alettes are an integral part of working with most of the programs in the Adobe Creative Suite because they contain many of the controls and tools that you use when you're creating or editing a document. The basic functionality of palettes is quite similar across the programs in the Adobe Creative Suite, and the purpose of all palettes is the same. Palettes offer you a great deal of flexibility in how you organize the workspace and what parts of it you use. What you use each program for and the level of expertise you have may affect what palettes you have open at a given moment. This chapter gives you an overview of how to work with the palettes you find in the Adobe Creative Suite.

Using Palettes in the Workspace

Palettes are small windows that contain controls such as sliders, menus, buttons, and text fields that you can use to change the settings or attributes of a selection or of the entire document. Palettes may also include information about a section or about the document itself. You can use this information or change the settings in a palette to modify the selected object or the document you're working on.

Whether you're working on a Windows machine or on a Mac, palettes are very similar in the way they look and work. Here are the basics of working with palettes:

✦ **Opening:** Open a palette in one of the Creative Suite programs by using the Window menu; choose Window and then select the name of a palette. For example, to open the Swatches palette (which is similar in many programs in the suite) shown in Figure 3-1, you choose Window⇨ Swatches.

Figure 3-1:
The
Swatches
palette
allows you
to choose
a color.

✦ **Accessing the palette menu:** Palettes have a flyout menu called the palette menu, shown in Figure 3-2. The palette menu opens when you click the arrow in the upper-right corner of the palette. The palette menu contains a bunch of options that relate to the tab currently selected when you click the palette menu. When you select one of the options in the menu, it may execute an action or open a dialog box. Sometimes there are very few options in a palette menu, but particular palettes may have a whole bunch of related functionality and therefore many options in the palette menu.

✦ **Closing:** If you need to open or close a palette's tab or palette, just choose Window⇨*Name of Palette's Tab*. You can close a palette the same way: select an open palette from the Window menu. Sometimes a palette contains a close button (an X button in Windows or the red button on a Mac), which you can click to close the palette.

✦ **Minimizing/maximizing:** All you need to do to minimize a selected palette is to click the minimize button in the title bar of the palette (if it's available). You can also double-click the tab itself (of an active tab) in the palette. This will either partially or fully minimize the palette. If it only partially minimizes, double-clicking the tab again will fully minimize the palette. Double-clicking the active tab when it's minimized maximizes the palette again.

You may also see what's called the *cycle widget* when a palette can be partially minimized and maximized. This is a small double-sided arrow that appears to the left of the palette's name on the tab. If you click this arrow, it progressively expands or collapses the palette.

Palettes that partially minimize give you the opportunity to work with palettes that have differing amounts of information. This simplifies the workspace while maximizing your screen real estate.

Most palettes contain tabs, which help organize information and controls in a program into groupings. Palette tabs contain a particular kind of information about a part of the program; a single palette may contain several tabs. The name on the tab usually gives you a hint about the type of function it controls or displays information about, and it is located at the top of the palette (or to the left of the palette when you're using side tabs), as shown in Figure 3-2.

Figure 3-2:
The name of
a palette is
located
within the
tab at the
top of
palettes (or
to the left of
the palette if
you're using
side tabs).

Click this button to see the palette menu

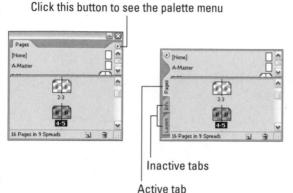

Inactive tabs

Active tab

To minimize a side tab (which we discuss further in the following section), you need to click in the gray area that surrounds the tab(s) in a palette. This collapses the side tab into the side of the workspace. To maximize a minimized side tab, click one of the tabs in the palette.

You can also minimize a side tab by clicking the active tab in a palette. If you click an inactive tab, the palette only switches to that tab in the palette so that you can work with it.

Working with Different Kinds of Palettes

The most common kind of palette contains tabs along the top of the palette (refer to Figure 3-1). A different way of arranging a palette is by changing it so that the tabs are arranged on the side (refer to Figure 3-2). InDesign allows you to either use top or side tab orientation. When you first open InDesign, you see palettes with the tab names to the left side of the palette. These palettes minimize and maximize into the side of the authoring environment. Also note that the palette menu button is located at the upper-left side of the palette, above the tabs.

Not all palettes can be turned into side tabs in a program such as InDesign that allows side tabs. For example, the Tools palette (or toolbox) in InDesign cannot be changed into a side tab. However, most palettes in InDesign can be changed into a side tab if you want. You can also change the orientation of side tabs. You can change a side tab into a regular tab and palette by dragging it away from the palette it's in. This changes the orientation of the side tab, which you can see because the outline of the palette changes orientation before you even release the mouse button. You can change the palette back into a side tab by dragging it into an existing side tab palette. Alternatively, you change a palette into a side tab by following these steps:

1. **Drag the tab to the far right of the InDesign workspace while pressing the mouse button.** *Don't release the mouse button.*

   You can see the outline of the tab when you drag it.

2. **Wait for the tab's outline to change into a vertical side tab orientation, and then release the mouse button.**

   The outline changes when the tab is within the *palette well,* which is a narrow vertical gray area on the far right of the workspace. When you release the mouse button, the palette changes into a side tab.

You can also find and arrange palettes above the workspace in Photoshop in the palette well. Only the tab portion of the palette is seen in Photoshop, without the actual palette window containing the tabs: It's actually part of the workspace itself, as shown in Figure 3-3.

If you're using a lower resolution or have a small monitor, you may not be able to see or use the palette well.

When you click the tab in the palette well, a menu-like palette opens that contains options for you to choose from or view. This is also shown in Figure 3-3. You can move other palettes into this palette well by clicking the tab and dragging the palette into this area. You will see a black outline around the palette well when you drag the tab over this region. If you release the mouse button while the area is highlighted, then the palette is added.

Palettes can be moved all around the workplace, and you can add or remove single tabs from a palette. Each palette snaps to other palettes, which makes it easier to arrange palettes alongside each other. Palettes can overlap each other as well. To snap palettes next to each other, drag the palette to a new location on-screen, as shown in Figure 3-4; you see a black outline around the palette where the tab will be placed.

You can separate tabs from a palette by clicking the tab and then dragging it outside the palette. You can also move a tab from one palette to another by dragging the tab from the original palette to the new palette; release the mouse button when you see a black outline around the new palette. Grouping similar tabs by moving them into a single grouped palette is a good idea — it makes accessing the different functions in your document a lot easier because you have less searching to do to find related functions for a task if similar palettes are grouped together.

Figure 3-3:
The tab resides above the palette well in Photoshop, and is not contained within a palette window.

You can also move side tabs in exactly the same way. Simply drag the tab to a new location or into a new palette. When you see a black outline around the new palette, release the mouse button and the tab is added to the new palette.

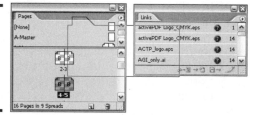

Figure 3-4:
To move a palette, just drag it to a new location.

You can hide all palettes by pressing the Tab key. Press the Tab key again to reveal all the palettes you have hidden.

You can save a particular layout as a workspace. All you need to do is choose Window➪Workspace➪Save Workspace. Type a name for your workspace into the Save Workspace dialog box. Your own workspace is saved and is available from the Window➪Workspace submenu.

Looking at Common Palettes

Many palettes are similar across programs in the Creative Suite. Although palettes do not have exactly the same content in each program, many are extremely similar. Figure 3-5 shows some of the most common palettes you find in the Adobe Creative Suite. You use these palettes in very similar ways, no matter what program or operating system you're using.

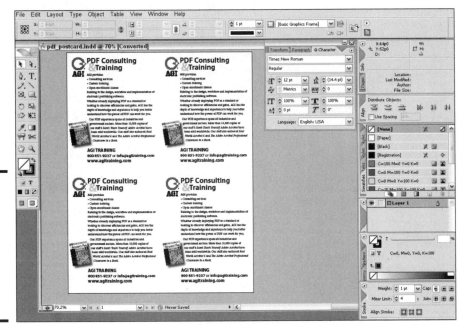

Figure 3-5: These palettes appear in most of the Adobe Creative Suite programs.

Acrobat does not contain numerous palettes like the other programs in the Creative Suite. Instead, Acrobat relies mainly (but not entirely) on a system of menus and toolbars filled with buttons and drop-down lists. In Acrobat, you can open dialog boxes that contain a bunch of settings that you can enter for your documents.

The following palettes are not available in *all* the programs in the Creative Suite; however, you find them in most programs:

✦ **Color:** The Color palette is used to select or mix colors in the current document. You can use different color modes and have several ways of mixing or choosing colors in the Colors palette.

✦ **Info:** The Info palette shows you information about the document itself or a particular selection you have made. The Info palette includes information on size, positioning, and rotation of selected objects. You can't enter data into the Info palette. It only displays information instead of accepting it, so you would have to use the Transform palette to make these modifications if necessary.

✦ **Swatches:** The Swatches palette can be used to create a library of swatches, which can be saved and imported into other documents or other programs. You can store colors and gradients that you use repeatedly in the Swatches palette.

✦ **Tools:** The Tools palette (commonly called the toolbox) is not available in all the Creative Suite programs, but it is a very important palette in the programs it does exist in. The toolbox is used to select tools such as the Pencil, Brush, or Pen tool that you use to create objects in a document.

✦ **Layers:** The Layers palette is used to display and select layers. The Layers palette also enables you to change layer order and helps you select items on a particular layer.

✦ **Align:** The Align palette enables you to align selected objects to each other or align them in relation to the document itself. This enables you to arrange objects in a precise way.

✦ **Stroke:** The Stroke palette allows you to select strokes and change the attributes of those strokes, such as the color, width/weight, style, and cap. The program you're using determines what attributes you can change.

✦ **Transform:** The Transform palette is used to display and change the shear (skew), rotation, position, and size of a selected object in the document. You can enter new values for each of these transformations.

✦ **Character:** The Character palette is used to select fonts, font size, character spacing, and other settings related to using type in your documents.

Chapter 4: Using Common Plug-Ins

In This Chapter

✔ Discovering the real purpose of filters and plug-ins

✔ Using common plug-ins and filters in Adobe Creative Suite 2

Many programs in the Adobe Creative Suite enable you to use plug-ins, filters, or extensions to change parts of the document. Even if you haven't used Photoshop, you're probably already familiar with some of the popular Photoshop filters, such as filters for adding special kinds of blurs, patterns, and color effects to images. Filters, plug-ins, and extensions are all pieces of software that you install or save on your computer that work as "add-ons" to existing programs. For example, a plug-in may enable you to integrate with a different program, or it may help add functionality to the program (such as the ability to create 3D text). Plug-ins may allow you to change the appearance of an object in your software, or add a 3D effect to a video file. This chapter shows you common plug-ins, extensions, and filters and how to use them in the Adobe Creative Suite.

Looking at Common Plug-Ins and Filters

Plug-ins are sometimes used for very similar tasks in several programs in the Adobe Creative Suite. Plug-ins are designed to enable a program to do extra things that it wouldn't otherwise be able to do. Or, if you are capable of replicating the task that the plug-in does, there is another advantage: Plug-ins and filters dramatically speed up the creative process. At the mere click of a button, you can add an amazing effect to your project that may have taken many hours to accomplish without the plug-in.

Additional filters and plug-ins for the programs in the Adobe Creative Suite are available or linked from the Adobe Web site. It's also very easy to find plug-ins on the Web for download as well. A search yields many results for these packages. A good place to start is at the Adobe Studio Exchange, located at `http://share.studio.adobe.com`, as shown in Figure 4-1. This site includes a wealth of tools that you can download and install for the Adobe Creative Suite.

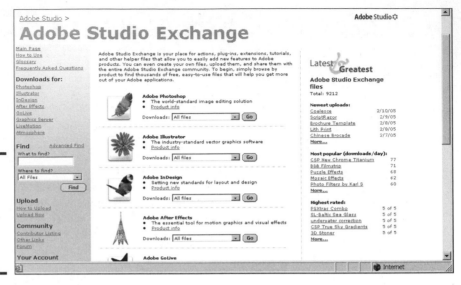

Figure 4-1:
Free plug-ins are located at the Adobe Studio Exchange.

Filters for Photoshop are probably the most common kind of add-on you will find online. Many filters do cost money; however, some filters are offered for free.

Plugging into InDesign

InDesign offers many filters for importing and exporting text. Plug-ins are available that enable you to work with PageMaker and for helping to import and paste in other content. Many plug-ins for InDesign are designed to help you with the following functions:

- ✦ Lay out spreads correctly for a printer.
- ✦ Create complicated indexes and tables of contents.
- ✦ Create cross-references within your documents.
- ✦ Create page previews and thumbnails of your documents.

Other filters created for InDesign can help you import certain content, such as text. A lot of the time, you will find that text formatting is lost when you import content into InDesign. Filters can help you retain this original formatting when you're importing text. These plug-ins and filters are just a small sample of what is available for InDesign. In all likelihood, many more plug-ins will be created for the software.

Installing plug-ins

Plug-ins can be installed in a few different ways. Sometimes they are installed using an executable file: You double-click the file on your hard drive and it automatically installs the software. This is a lot like installing any other program on your computer, such as the programs in the Adobe Creative Suite itself. Sometimes you're given individual files that need to be placed in a folder first. In this case, you need to find the Plug-Ins folder on your computer in the install directory of the program the plug-in or filter is for. For example, if your plug-in was for InDesign on Windows, you would need to find this directory:

```
C:\Program Files\Adobe\InDesign
    CS2\Plug-Ins
```

You would then copy and paste or move the plug-in file you downloaded into this directory on your hard drive. If your plug-in was for Photoshop on the Mac, you would need to find this folder on your hard drive:

```
Applications\Adobe Photoshop
    CS2\Plug-Ins
```

You would then copy and paste or move the plug-in file into this folder. If it is not clear how to install a plug-in, then the best thing to do is locate instructions for the software that explain how to install it on your computer. You can find instructions on the manufacturer's Web site, or instructions may be bundled with the plug-in file itself.

Adding on to Photoshop

Photoshop has a lot of plug-ins and filters already included with the program when you install it that give more functionality to the program. Not only can you find additional filters, but you can also find plug-ins to add new features that can inevitably add some interesting effects to your documents. You can also find a plug-in that installs a great number of filters into Photoshop. The kinds of filters and plug-ins you can find for Photoshop create the following effects:

✦ Remove blemishes and scratches from photos using special tools.

✦ Create 3D text, objects, and effects using several different plug-ins. Effects include drop shadows, bevels, and embosses that go beyond what is already available in Photoshop.

✦ Use special masking tools to create amazing effects.

✦ Liquefy an image, colorize an image, and perform other great image modification effects.

✦ Use one of thousands of special effects made by many companies to enhance, modify, and add to your images.

✦ Add a frame from a library to place around your favorite images.

These are only some of the many plug-ins (which are commonly a set of many filters bundled together) available on the market for Photoshop.

As you will quickly find out, many plug-ins have custom interfaces that you can use to make your settings. These interfaces include sliders, text fields, and buttons, and usually a thumbnail preview of how the filter is affecting the image. These interfaces vary greatly in style and features, but you'll discover that they are usually fairly intuitive and easy to use.

Using Illustrator plug-ins

You can find many tools to extend the capabilities of Illustrator. Plug-ins are available that enable you to create 3D forms from your drawings, while other programs take your 3D files and turn them into line drawings instead. Other plug-ins, ranging from simple to very complex, allow you to

✦ Create multi-page documents.

✦ Organize your font sets.

✦ Add common symbols (such as road signage) to your documents. The symbols are organized into libraries that you can use right in the Illustrator workspace.

✦ Import CAD files into a document.

✦ Create interactive documents.

✦ Handle patterns geared at creating textures and backgrounds.

The capabilities of Illustrator can be dramatically enhanced after you download and install a few plug-ins. Simple projects can become much more interesting or complex by merely entering a value and clicking a button.

Some fun things to download and install into Illustrator are custom brushes. This means that you can have a wider array of brushes available to work with when you create drawings and illustrations. "Styles" can also be installed into Illustrator and usually obtained for free. You can also download and install custom brushes for Photoshop.

Adding on capabilities to Acrobat

Acrobat has several plug-ins available that help speed up and diversify your project workflow. Some of the plug-ins available for Acrobat are designed to help you

+ Add stamps and watermarks to the documents.

+ Add features such as page numbering and watermarks.

+ Streamline productivity by offering solutions for batch processing.

+ Convert file formats to diversify what kinds of documents you can create from Acrobat.

+ Secure your PDF files with forms of encryption.

+ Work with and fix the PDF in prepress quickly and efficiently.

Many of the plug-ins available for Acrobat enable you to batch process the pages in a document. This means that all the pages are processed at one time. Many plug-ins for Acrobat help save you a lot of time when you're creating PDF files. Plug-ins are usually designed to be very easy to use and can thus save you from having to perform a tedious and repetitive task.

Plug-ins for Acrobat are available from the Adobe Web site, as well as numerous third-party Web sites.

Extending GoLive

GoLive offers you a quick and easy way to make Web pages, but you can add more tools to GoLive to diversify what the program can do. These extensions (essentially, plug-ins) also speed up the process of creating Web sites. Some of the available plug-ins are described in the following list. Extensions in GoLive can

+ Add e-commerce modules to a Web site automatically using GoLive.

+ Enable people who don't know how to edit Web pages to add their content to a live site.

+ Clean up the ugly HTML generated for a site designed and created using FrontPage.

+ Create menus for your Web pages.

+ Add PayPal to your Web site.

+ Use a PHP and JavaScript editor and/or tools right within GoLive to build dynamic Web sites.

GoLive also allows you to use actions in the program. *Actions* are premade JavaScript scripts that can be added to your Web sites for additional interactivity or interest. You can also use premade templates for your sites, many of which are available at `http://share.studio.adobe.com`. You can also find Actions for other programs such as Photoshop and Illustrator.

Templates, as shown in Figure 4-2, can be customized in GoLive so they are original and unique when you put the pages online. Actions and templates (as well as tutorials and more plug-ins) are available from the Adobe Studio Exchange. Go to `http://share.studio.adobe.com/axBrowseProductType.asp?t=2` to check out what's available for you to download.

Figure 4-2: Download free templates and store them in the Templates folder.

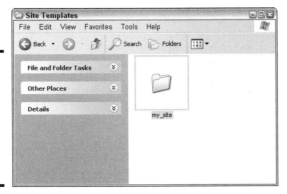

How to Use Filters

You can install plug-ins or filters into your Adobe Creative Suite programs. A filter can enhance an existing photo in a very exciting way. After you have installed a plug-in into Photoshop or Illustrator that includes a bunch of additional filters, you will want to check out what it can do to your photos. An example of this follows.

Install some filters for Photoshop (or Illustrator). After you have completed the installation and restarted your computer, if necessary, open Photoshop and locate the Filter menu option (the new filters are available in this menu). To use a filter, follow these steps:

1. **Choose an interesting photo that you want to apply an affect to and open the file in Photoshop.**

Choose a photo that has many colors or a lot of contrast to work with.

2. **Choose a filter from the Filter menu.**

Select a filter that you have installed from the Filter menu, as shown in Figure 4-3. If you haven't installed any plug-ins or filters, you can choose one that is already included in Photoshop, such as Filter⇨Blur⇨Motion Blur.

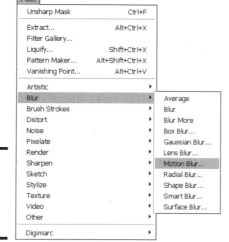

Figure 4-3:
Select a
filter from
the Filter
menu.

3. **Modify the filter's settings if necessary, and click the OK button to apply the effect.**

   Sometimes, you have a thumbnail preview to assess how the filter changes the image. For some filters and plug-ins, you even use a custom interface to manipulate the document. You can then change the settings accordingly until you're happy with the modifications that will be applied.

4. **Look at the image after you have chosen and applied the filter.**

   Your image is updated immediately, as shown in Figure 4-4. If you're unhappy with the results, you can either undo your changes by choosing Edit⇨Undo, or you can apply the filter again.

Filters add a great deal of interest and variety to a document. However, it is easy to go overboard when using filters and plug-ins. You can use filters in many different ways in the Adobe Creative Suite — and some of these ways (and some filters) are considered better than others. Going into filter overload is easy, particularly when you first start using them. This is okay when you're experimenting with filters; just make sure that you don't use too many filters on one part of an image when you're creating a final project. For example, if you bevel and emboss a particular letter in a few different ways, that character can become illegible. Similarly, adding a huge drop shadow can distract the eye from other parts of the text.

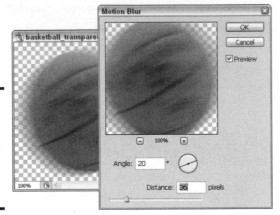

Figure 4-4:
Adding a
motion blur
to an image
adds a
sense of
movement.

The trick is knowing what you intend to accomplish with your document
before you actually go about creating it. If you set out to create your project
with a particular design in mind, you can sometimes achieve better results.
Try drawing out your ideas on paper first, writing down some notes about
what you want to achieve, and thinking about the plug-ins you want to use to
achieve it. Use one filter at a time, and make sure you like the results before
moving on to the next. The alternative is to continue adding filter upon filter
to achieve a particular result when you aren't quite sure what you're after or
how to get there. You can end up with a picture with too many filters applied
and an unpleasant result. With a clear idea of what you want out of a picture,
and what filters you need to achieve that effect, you'll use filters in a much
more successful way.

Chapter 5: Importing and Exporting

In This Chapter

✔ **Discovering the new Adobe Bridge application**

✔ **Importing content**

✔ **Importing from Adobe Creative Suite 2 programs**

✔ **Exporting publications and artwork**

✔ **Exporting from Adobe Creative Suite 2 programs**

*T*he capability to import and export content is important for much of the creative process you experience when using programs in the Adobe Creative Suite. You may want to import text composed by a designated writer into an InDesign document so that you can include the content in a page layout. Or you may want to import a 3D design into an Illustrator document so that you can use the image in a design. Importing is necessary in all kinds of circumstances during a typical workflow.

Exporting content from each program is sometimes necessary when you want to save the document as a different file format. You may want to do this for compatibility reasons: Your audiences, or those you're working with, need a different file format in order to open your work; or you may need to export to a different file format in order to import the work into a different program.

Discover the Adobe Bridge Application

Adobe has really done it with this functional standalone application. With Adobe Creative Suite 2, you not only get the integration of the Version Que workflow management system, but you get the Bridge application to help you pull all of your software functions together. It acts like a hub for the Creative Suite. For instance, by choosing to open files using the Bridge interface, you can browse and see previews of many of your Adobe files, as shown in Figure 5-1, and easily add and view metadata to your file, including important information such as keywords.

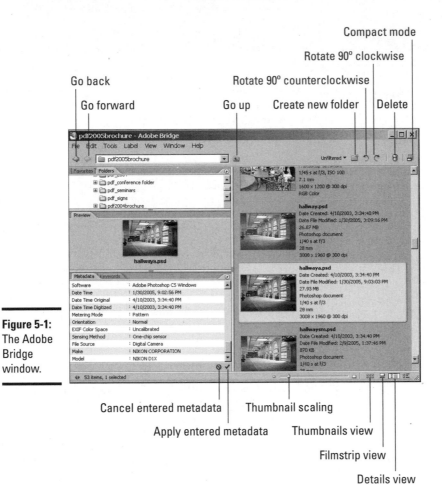

Compact mode

Rotate 90° clockwise

Rotate 90° counterclockwise

Go back

Go forward   Go up   Create new folder   Delete

Figure 5-1:
The Adobe
Bridge
window.

Cancel entered metadata   Thumbnail scaling

Apply entered metadata   Thumbnails view

Filmstrip view

Details view

Not only does the Bridge make a great deal of information accessible, you can use the Bridge as a central resource for all of your Help needs. Adobe even provides reasonably priced stock photos that you can access, search, and even pay for right in the Bridge software. Read on to see how the Bridge application can make your job easier.

Accessing the Bridge software

First, it is helpful to know where to locate the Adobe Bridge application. It should already be in your system if you went through a standard installation of the entire creative suite. Otherwise, you will have to go back and choose to install the Bridge software using your installation CDs.

After you install the Bridge software, you can open it in the following two
ways:

✦ Access the Bridge software using the directory system of your computer.
  Choose C:\Programs\Adobe\Adobe Bridge\Bridge (Windows) or Mac
  Hard Drive\Applications\Adobe Bridge\Bridge.

✦ Select the Bridge icon in the upper-right side of the control palettes of
  your Adobe Creative Suite Applications (see Figure 5-2).

Figure 5-2:
Access
Adobe
Bridge
from the
Creative
Suite 2
applications'
control
palettes.

Navigating the Bridge

To navigate the Bridge, simply use the Folders tab in the upper-right to
choose the folder you want to view. Watch in amazement as previews are
created and automatically replace the standard file format icon.

The Bridge may take a fair amount of time to build the preview the first time
you use it, so be patient. You can choose Tools➪Cache➪Export Cache to
save this data, or Purge it to free up file space.

Select an individual file by clicking it once (twice will open it), or select
multiple files by pressing Ctrl and clicking the mouse (Windows) or pressing
⌘ and clicking the mouse (Mac OS).

With one or more files selected, you can do the following:

✦ Relocate the file(s) to another location by dragging them to a folder in the Folders tab in the upper-right corner. Use the Bridge as a Central filing system. Using the commands in the File menu, you can create new folders, and delete or move files or groups of files.

✦ Read Metadata in the Metadata tab in the lower-left corner. This includes information such as Camera, Flash, F-stop, and more, as shown in Figure 5-3.

Figure 5-3:
The Metadata tab allows you to read and create important information about the selected file.

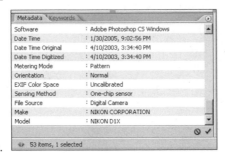

✦ Enter your own Metadata for any Metadata item listed with a pencil icon to the right. Use the Bridge to create and search for keywords and find detailed meta data about files.

Use Edit⇔Find to locate your files within the Bridge by using criteria such as Keywords, Description, Date Created, and more.

✦ Choose from many options such as Batch Rename and Contact Sheet. You can merge multiple images into one panoramic image by using the Photomerge command and others that you can find in the Tools menu (see Figure 5-4).

Figure 5-4:
Choose from many automated features under the Tools menu.

Color management

What a time-saver and production boost! The Color Settings that you use to have to set in each individual application can now be set across the board in all Creative Suite applications. Create consistent color choices in all of the Creative applications using the new synchronized color management controls that Adobe Bridge offers.

Choose Edit⇨Creative Suite Color Settings to choose a color management setting that will remain consistent through all of your Creative Suite applications, as shown in Figure 5-5. Read more about what these settings mean in Book IV, "Photoshop CS2."

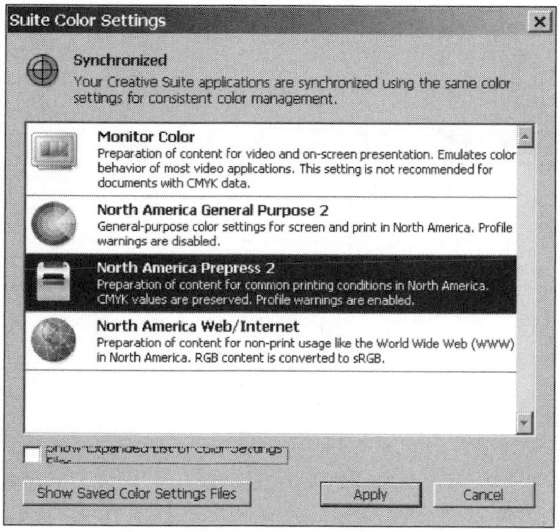

Figure 5-5:
Set one color management setting for all of the Adobe Creative Suite applications in the Bridge.

In summary, the Bridge offers more than can be covered in the scope of this minibook, but try to get in the habit of using this for placement of images, opening files, and organizing your directories.

Importing Files into a Document

Importing files works almost the same way, no matter what program you're working with. Importing content is more important in some programs than others. A program like InDesign relies on importing content into a document that is then incorporated into a page layout. However, in programs like Photoshop, importing content is much less important because you will frequently start out with editing an image you *open* in Photoshop. In this section, we take a look at importing content into each program.

Placing content in InDesign

Placing content in InDesign is a familiar task when you're creating a new layout. You need to import images and text for many of your layouts. When you choose File⇨Place, you can then select text or image files from your hard drive or network. You can also choose sound and video files that can be used when you're creating PDF documents for electronic distribution. After you choose a file to import, a new cursor icon appears when you place it over the page or pasteboard. To place the imported content, click on the page where you want the upper-left corner to be placed.

When you import different kinds of images, you're presented with the Place dialog box that allows you to select a variety of options for importing the selected content. However, to access additional settings to control how the content is imported into your document, you must remember to select the Show Import Options check box in the Place dialog box, shown in Figure 5-6.

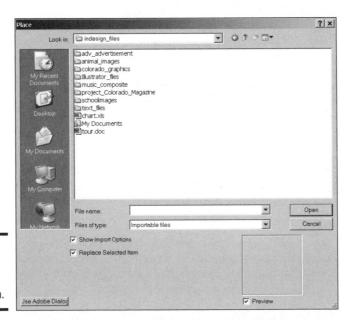

Figure 5-6:
The Place dialog box in InDesign.

Select a file and click the Open button. Another dialog box opens with options specific to the type of file you're importing. For example, if you're importing a bitmap image (say a JPEG), you can choose how you want the bitmap to appear, whether it contains a background or color management information, and other such options.

When you import text information, you may lose some text formatting that was made in the original file. Anything that InDesign doesn't understand won't be imported into the document. Column information, as well as margins, are also typically not retained when you import text. However, some plug-ins are available that help remedy the situation to some extent.

Adding content to a Photoshop file

In Photoshop, you can choose to open an image to work with, or you can import content into a document that is already open. Choose File➪Place to import PDF, AI, EPS, or PDP files. These files import onto a new layer in the document, and you can then use tools to manipulate the imported content, as shown in Figure 5-7.

Figure 5-7: Imported content is placed on a new layer in Photoshop, where you can manipulate it using your toolset.

As a default, your placed artwork in Photoshop maintains a connection back to the original. Double-click on the placed artwork layer to open and edit the original. After the file has been saved, the changes are immediately reflected back in Photoshop!

You can import photos from a camera or a scanner into Photoshop. In Windows, you can use Windows Image Acquisition (WIA) to import an image from either a digital photo or a scanner. To do so, you choose File➪Import➪ WIA Support. If you're importing content from a scanner, you may have an additional menu option. The menu option name may vary, but you can access it from the File➪Import submenu.

Placing files into Illustrator

Illustrator allows you to place images and other forms of data in a new document. You can import Photoshop, PDF, image, and vector files by choosing File⇨Place. The Place dialog box appears, allowing you to choose a file to import. Click OK (Windows) or Place (Mac) to import the file. An Import dialog box may appear at this point, depending on the type of file you are importing. This dialog box offers you several options for choosing a way to import the content into Illustrator. You can sometimes choose between flattening layers or retaining layers when you import a document containing layers.

EPS is a commonly used file format for saving vector drawings (although it can be used for other file types as well). Because this file format is used in many programs, you may find other people giving you these files to work with. To import an EPS document, you also choose File⇨Place. You should remember that EPS documents do not support transparency; after you import an EPS document into Illustrator, the file is converted to Illustrator objects.

You can also import text files into Illustrator. Microsoft Word, TXT, RTF, and Unicode, among other text documents, are all supported by Illustrator and can be imported by choosing File⇨Place. When you import the text file, you are prompted to choose the character set used for the text.

Not only can you use the Place command for importing files, but you can copy and paste from other programs. You can select part of an image in Photoshop and copy it onto the Clipboard by pressing Ctrl+C (Windows) or ⌘+C (Mac), and then pasting it into the Illustrator document. **Remember:** You should try and use the Place command whenever possible to avoid losing quality in the content you're importing. Also, transparency is not supported from one application to another when you copy and paste, but is when Place is used.

When you have particular plug-ins installed, you can import additional file types, such as CAD files.

Adding to Acrobat

Adobe Acrobat is primarily a tool for sharing completed documents — you will do most of your document construction and editing in other programs, such as InDesign or Illustrator. However, you can import several kinds of data into PDF documents, and there are some creative things that you can also place into PDF files as well.

✦ **Comments:** Probably the most useful and common items to import into an Adobe PDF file are comments made using the review and markup tools provided by Adobe Acrobat. By importing comments into a PDF file, you can consolidate suggestions and input from several reviewers (those editing a document) into a single document. This helps the reviewing process when many people are working on a single document. To import someone's comments into a PDF, choose Comments⇨Import Comments. If you are reviewing a document, you can also export only the comments rather than sending the document owner the entire PDF file.

✦ **Form data:** You can import form data into a PDF document by choosing Advanced⇨Forms⇨Import Data to Form. The data that you import can be generated by exporting the form data from another PDF form, or it can come from a delimited text file. This allows you to share form data between forms or from a database.

✦ **Trusted identities:** If you share digitally signed files or secured files with other Acrobat users, you can import the public version of their signature file into your list of trusted users with whom you share files. To import the identity of a user, choose Advanced⇨Trusted Identities and then click the Add Contacts button in the Manage Trusted Identities button that appears.

✦ **Multimedia files:** If you've ever had the urge to add a movie or sound file into your PDF documents, you're in luck. By using the Sound tool or Movie tool, you can identify the location on the page where you want the file to appear, and then choose whether to embed the multimedia file (compatible with Acrobat 6 or later) or create a link to the file (compatible with Acrobat 5 and earlier).

✦ **Buttons:** Creating buttons to turn pages, print a document, or go to a Web site makes your PDF files easier to use. Adding custom button images, such as pictures of arrows or a printer icon makes your document unique. Use the button tool to create the location of the button and then select the graphic file that will be used as the image on the button. The image file that you use must first be converted to a PDF graphic.

✦ **Preflight information:** If you are creating a PDF file that will be sent to a commercial printer for reproduction, you may want to preflight the book to check that it meets the specifications and needs of the printer. If your printer has supplied a preflight profile for Acrobat, you can import the profile to ensure that Acrobat checks for the things your printer has requested, such as certain font types or color specifications. Import a preflight profile by choosing Tools⇨Print Production⇨Preflight and in the Preflight window that opens choose Options⇨Import Preflight Profile.

Importing into GoLive

In GoLive, you can import several different kinds of files into a site you're creating. When you choose File⇨Import, you can choose from a submenu of the following options:

✦ **External Style Sheet:** Imports an external CSS (Cascading Style Sheet) into the site. This style sheet is then listed in the internal style sheets list.

✦ **From InDesign:** Imports a packaged site that was made using InDesign. If you plan to update the Web site, make sure you choose the option to copy the package into the site you're working on.

✦ **Photoshop Layers:** Imports layers from Photoshop and arranges them in the site.

✦ **Files to Site:** Imports files into your site, which are then listed under the Files tab.

✦ **Favorites as Site Externals:** Adds an e-mail address or a URL to your site. This imports the addresses from the favorites saved on your computer.

✦ **New Site from Site Locator:** Allows you to find a remote site on a server and access and edit the files locally in GoLive.

What is available in the File➪Import submenu depends on what you're currently working on or have selected. If you have an HTML page open, you see different options than if you have a GoLive site open, as shown in Figure 5-8.

Figure 5-8: Choosing to import when you have an HTML page forward (left) as compared to a site (right) provides different options in GoLive.

Exporting Your Documents

Exporting content from your Adobe Creative Suite documents is important if you're working with importing the content into another program, placing the document where it's publicly available and where it needs to be interpreted on other computers. Similarly, you may be working with a team of individuals who need your document to be readable on their machines when it's imported into other programs. Exporting your document as a different file format helps solve these issues, and the Adobe Creative Suite offers you the flexibility of allowing you to export your document as many different file formats.

Other programs sometimes accept native Adobe documents as files that you can import. For example, Macromedia Flash MX 2004 can import Illustrator AI files, Photoshop PSD files, and PDF documents.

Exporting from InDesign

InDesign enables you to export your pages or book as several file types. Most notably, you can export your layouts as a PDF document, which can be viewed by anyone who has the free Acrobat Reader installed. InDesign can also export to other image and vector formats, such as EPS and JPEG. An InDesign document can also export to SVG and XML, which is useful when you export something for the Web. InDesign has the very handy feature to package up your work for GoLive. By selecting File⇨Package for GoLive, it is possible to export a project you're working on and have it ready for page creation in GoLive. Notice in Figure 5-9 that elements from the packaged InDesign page can be dragged and dropped to the GoLive page.

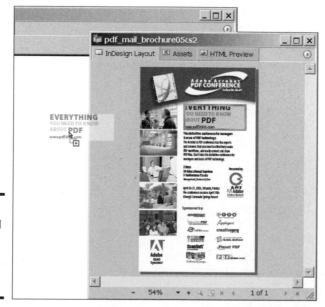

Figure 5-9:
A packaged InDesign file ready to layout in GoLive.

Exporting content from Photoshop

Photoshop can export paths in a document to Illustrator (an AI file). This means that your work in Photoshop is easy to manipulate after you open it using Illustrator. You have another option, though: If you choose to export your Photoshop file as a ZoomView document, the work is perfect for putting online and allows visitors to zoom into portions of the image.

Before visitors can zoom into your images, they must download and install the ZoomView Media Player on their system. Then several files are created, and you need to keep all the files together in order for this feature to work properly.

ImageReady, a program that comes with Photoshop, is where things are a bit more interesting. You can export a SWF file from ImageReady. An SWF file is an excellent format to export to, as the file is easily viewable online, and it can be imported into another SWF file or even a project (executable) file. ImageReady also allows you to export each layer as its own image file.

Exporting Illustrator files

Illustrator supports exporting to many different file formats. You can export files in a long list of image formats. Choose File⇨Export, and the Export dialog box opens. Click the Save as Type (Windows) or Format (Mac) drop-down list to view the exportable file formats, as shown in Figure 5-10.

Figure 5-10:
Illustrator
can export
documents
to many
different
supported
file formats.

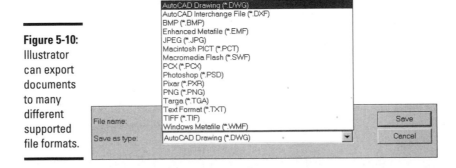

After you choose a file type to export to, a second dialog box may appear that allows you to enter a bunch of settings for the exported file.

Try choosing the Macromedia Flash SWF file format when you export a file. A second dialog box opens that includes many settings, such as options to generate an HTML page, save each layer as a separate SWF document, and preserve editability (when possible). The options that are available when you export a document depend on the type of file format to which you're exporting.

Exporting Acrobat content

Acrobat allows you to export certain parts of a PDF document that you're working on. For example, you may be using form data in one of your files. This means the data that is filled into a form made of text fields and so on. This data can be exported from Acrobat and then sent online, which is great because PDF documents tend to be rather large for the Web. Therefore, only a small amount of formatted data is sent online rather than a huge PDF file.

You can also export parts of an Acrobat document to use in other programs. Comments in a PDF can be exported to a Microsoft Word file that was used to create PDF. Acrobat allows you to do this by choosing Comments⇨Export Comments⇨to Word. You can also export comments to an AutoCAD file (assuming it was used to create the PDF). In both cases, you need the original document that was used to generate the PDF file in order to successfully import the comments.

Similarly, all comments from a PDF file can be exported using Comments⇨ Export Comments⇨to File and then imported into another version of the same document. You can use this option to consolidate comments from multiple reviewers, or overlay comments from a draft with a final version to confirm that all edits were completed.

Exporting GoLive content

In GoLive, you can export your sites so that they are prepared for publishing and ready to be placed on a live Web site. The site you're working on in GoLive is exported onto your hard drive before you put it somewhere on a server. Interestingly, your Web pages in GoLive can also be exported to a PDF file (see Figure 5-11). The HTML styles used in a site you're working on can be exported and saved as an XML document, which in turn can be reused if necessary. These files can then be imported into another GoLive project you're working on.

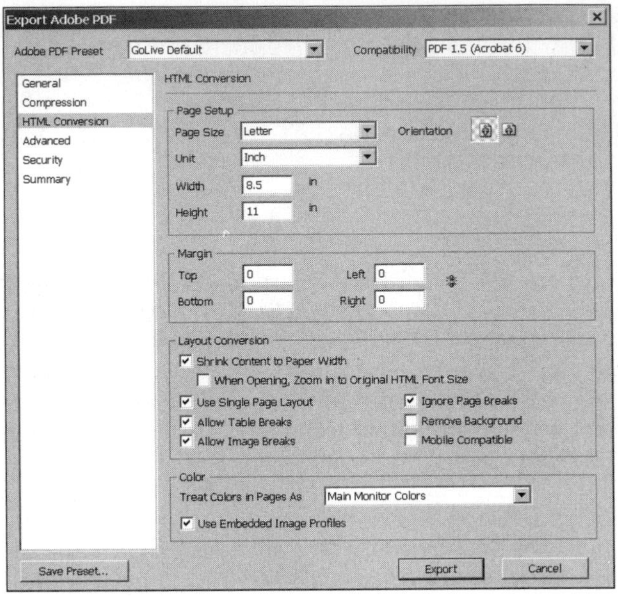

Figure 5-11:
You can export a Web page as a PDF document. This document can then be imported into many other Adobe Creative Suite 2 programs.

Chapter 6: Handling Graphics, Paths, Text, and Fonts

In This Chapter

✔ Using graphics in your documents

✔ Handling paths and their strokes

✔ Working with text and fonts

✔ Discovering page layout

Graphics, paths, text, and fonts are all integral parts of creating documents with the Adobe Creative Suite. You must know how to handle each element in your documents, and how to work with these elements together. Discovering the different ways you can work with images, text, and drawing is the fun part! Whether you're designing Web sites or creating a brochure's layout, you use these elements on their own or together, and it's likely you'll find out something new each time you work with them. A layout can include text, images, and drawings, but sometimes it will include more. If you're creating documents for the Web or you're creating PDF files with multimedia elements, you could be working with sound, animation, and video alongside text, images, and illustrations.

Using Graphics in Your Documents

Graphics are made up of many things. A graphic can be an image, a drawing, or a vector graphic. Graphics can be created manually by making marks on a page, or created electronically using software, such as the programs we are discussing in this book. Graphics can be displayed in many formats, such as on a computer screen, projected onto a wall, or printed in a magazine or book.

Computer graphics come in many forms, grouped by the way they are created electronically. Bitmap and vector graphics are formed in different ways to achieve the end result that you use in your documents.

Working with bitmap images

Bitmap images are pictures that are made up of many tiny squares, or *bits,* on an invisible grid. When these dots are next to each other, the picture is formed, depending on where and how the colors are arranged on the grid. The dots are also called *pixels*, and if you zoom in far enough, you can even see the blocky pixels that make up the image, as shown in Figure 6-1. At 400 percent zoom, notice how the image in Figure 6-1 is made of large squares; it becomes difficult to even figure out what the photograph is showing. However, when you look at most bitmap images at actual size, you don't even see any of the dots making up the picture.

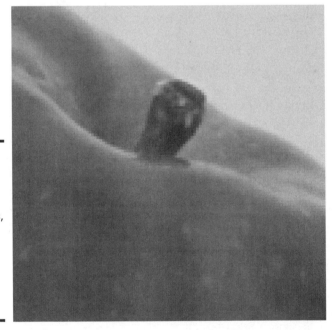

Figure 6-1:
This bitmap image is made up of many pixels, which you can see when you zoom in or resize the image.

Bitmaps are a great way to display photographs and apply effects to text. When you paint or create detailed graphics, you frequently use bitmaps. However, you should remember that you can lose some quality if you *scale* (change the size of) the image. Resizing the small pixels causes the image to lose definition and quality. Most problems occur when an image is enlarged. Common kinds of bitmap files are JPEG, GIF, TIFF, BMP, and PICT. You can read more about bitmapped images in Book IV, "Photoshop CS2."

The term *raster image* refers to these bitmap images as well. A *raster* is the grid on which all of those pixels are placed over the area of the graphic itself. *Rasterizing* an image means that you take a vector image (described in the following section) and change it into a bitmap (or raster) image.

Discovering vector graphics

A *vector image* (or graphic or drawing) is very different from a bitmap image. A vector image is created by a series of mathematical calculations or code that describes how the image should be formed. These calculations tell the computer how the lines should display and render on the page. Vector images are usually (but not always) a smaller file size than bitmap graphics. This is because the information required to make the calculations that create the vector image is usually smaller in file size than each pixel of a bitmap. Compression can lessen a bitmap's file size, but bitmaps are usually larger and slower to display than vectors.

For this reason, and also because vectors are great when it comes to scaling an image, as shown in Figure 6-2, these graphics are well suited for the Web.

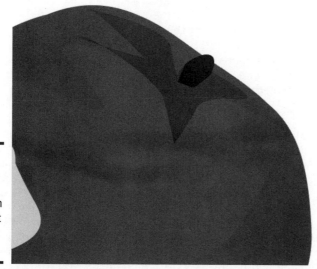

Figure 6-2:
This image of an apple is zoomed in to 400%, but no quality is lost.

Scaling is easy to do when you're using vectors because the program needs to modify the calculations only slightly to make the image larger or smaller. This means the file size won't change, and the scaling is very quick to accomplish. You can scale the image on a Web page to fill the browser window, whatever size it is, or make the image huge for a large banner you're printing. The quality won't degrade and the file size remains the same. Vectors aren't always perfect for the Web though. A bitmap is frequently the best way to display a photograph because if you change a bitmap image into a vector drawing (which is possible through the use of tools), you lose too much of the photograph's detail for many purposes. Also, certain effects such as drop shadows are best displayed as a bitmap image.

Working with Paths and Strokes

Paths are the vector lines and outlines that you create in a document. You can use paths to outline an image, separate areas of text, or be part of an illustration you create. You typically make paths with a Line tool, Pen tool, or the shape tools. You can use these tools to create paths of different shapes and sizes. You also can use tools to modify the color and size of *strokes* (the actual line that makes up a path).

You can also use paths to create clipping paths and paths for text. Clipping paths are used to mask (or *hide*) elements on a page. You define that mask using paths to create a shape for the area you need to hide. Clipping paths can even be saved in a file and imported into a different design pattern. A common workflow is to create an image in Photoshop CS2 with a clipping path and import that image into InDesign. InDesign can interpret the clipping path, meaning that you could remove the area you want to mask automatically.

When you want to create text that flows along a path, you begin by creating a new path and then use the Type on a Path tool to type text directly onto that path. For example, in Illustrator you would create a path using the Pen tool, and then select the Type on a Path tool in the toolbox. If you click the tool on the path you created, you can type new text along that path.

A *stroke* is the color, width, and style of the line that makes up the path you create. You might draw a line with the Pen tool, and the line making up that path is the stroke. However, that path can also have no stroke (represented as a diagonal line in the tools palette, which means you won't see the path itself. However, you may see a color or pattern filling that stroke (the *fill*), as shown in Figure 6-3.

Figure 6-3:
This path
does not
have a
stroke,
but it does
have a fill.

You can change the color, width, style (or *type*), and shape of a stroke using
controls and tools in the toolbox and the Stroke palette in Illustrator and
InDesign. This means that you can create dashed or solid strokes of different
patterns that are wide or narrow. Some of these kinds of strokes are shown
in Figure 6-4.

Figure 6-4:
Paths
that have
different
kinds of
strokes can
help you add
a creative
flair to your
InDesign
and
Illustrator
projects.

Adding Text

You may add text to your projects for different reasons. Text is frequently
used to educate and inform readers; text used this way is a lot different than
text used for artistic purposes only. For example, if you're creating an article,
you may place the text in columns on the page with a large title at the top.
Other times, you may use text as a creative element, or even as an object
instead of a letter. Alternatively, you may be laying out a Web page and use
the text for both a creative element in an animation, as well as the content
on pages that make up the Web site.

Text can be added to a document using the Text tool or by importing the text from another source, such as Microsoft Word. You can create a single line of text in a text field or create large blocks of text with or without columns. Text fields can be rotated and resized, and you can change the color, font face, orientation, and character size of the text.

Text can also be placed on a path, as we mention briefly in the earlier section, "Working with Paths and Strokes." This allows you to add text to your documents in a different way because you can draw a path and have the text follow it. This is particularly useful for headings on a page, footers, and artistic works that use text as one of the elements.

Using fonts

A *font* refers to the typeface of a set of characters. You can set the font to be a number of sizes, such as a miniscule size of 2 or a gargantuan size of 200. Fonts are given names, such as *Times New Roman* or *Comic Sans,* which you choose from when you add text to your document.

You may also hear about *glyphs,* which refer to an actual character itself. For instance, S is a glyph, which is different from the T glyph. A set of glyphs makes up a font. You can view glyphs in the Glyph palette in Illustrator (Window⇨Glyph), which is especially useful when you're using fonts like Wingdings that are exclusively made of pictures instead of the usual letters and numbers that make up your keyboard.

What fonts you use can make a huge difference to the look, feel, and style of your designs or documents. Whether you're working on a layout for a magazine article or creating a digital piece for an art gallery, the kinds of fonts you use determine a lot about the feel of the work.

Two major groupings for fonts exist and are illustrated in Figure 6-5:

✦ **Serif:** Characters have a small line that intersects the end of each line in a character, such as the little feet at the bottom of the "r" on the left side of Figure 6-5.

✦ **Sans-serif:** Characters do not have the small intersecting lines at the end of a line in a character.

Figure 6-5:
Spot the
difference!
A serif font
is on the
left, and a
sans-serif
font is on
the right.

Serif **Sans-serif**

What kind of fonts you use (serif or sans-serif) can help set the tone of a piece. Sometimes sans-serif fonts feel more modern, while serif fonts look more historical, formal, or literary in nature. This, of course, is all a matter of opinion and what you're used to seeing. Take a moment to look around the Web and your house to see how text is used in books, magazines, advertisements, and the newspaper. How text is commonly used greatly affects how other people view your work and react to the overall *feel* of the presentation. Finding a proper fit and an appropriate font is sometimes a challenging design task, but it can also be a lot of fun.

Types of fonts

Although you can find many free fonts on the Internet, you should be concerned about the quality of your finished product. Typically, those in the professional graphics industry will use Postscript fonts, which are more reliable when printing, as compared to TrueType fonts, which may reflow when outputting to different resolutions.

TrueType

Like other digital typefaces, the TrueType font file contains information such as outlines and character mappings (which characters are included in the font). Although available for both the Mac and Windows formats, there are slight differences in the TrueType fonts designed for each OS; therefore, Mac and Windows users cannot share TrueType fonts.

Postscript (Type 1)

 Postscript is a scaleable font system that is compatible with Postscript printers. It allows users to see fonts on the screen the same way they would be printed. Type 1 font files consist of two files — a screen font with bitmap information for on-screen display, and a file with outline information for printing the font. For high-end printing, both of the Type 1 font files must be included with the application file. Due to differences in their structure, Mac and Windows PostScript Type 1 fonts are not cross-platform compatible.

OpenType

 OpenType is font technology that was created in a joint effort between Adobe and Microsoft and is an extension of the TrueType font format that can also contain PostScript data. OpenType fonts are cross-platform — the same font file works under both Macintosh and Windows Operating systems. This digital type format offers extended character sets and more advanced typographic controls. Like TrueType, a single file contains all the outline, metric, and bitmap data for an OpenType font. Although any program that supports TrueType fonts can use OpenType fonts, not all non Adobe programs can access the full features of the OpenType font format at this time.

You can find the symbols, shown in Figure 6-6, in the Font menus of many of the Creative Suite 2 applications representing the type of font.

Figure 6-6:
The symbol
on the left
represents
the type
of font
in the list.

Text and fonts on the Web

Using text and fonts on the Web is a difficult task at times. When you use fonts in a Web page, system fonts are used to display text. You will usually specify a font or group of fonts to use on each page, and the fonts that are installed on the visitor's computer are used to display the text. The problem arises if you use (or want to use) fonts that are not installed on the visitor's computer. If you choose to use the Papyrus font and the visitor does not have that font, then a different one is substituted and the page looks completely different as a result.

When you're using GoLive to create Web pages or entire sites, you can set up a set of fonts that you want to use on each page. These fonts are similar in how they look, and if one of the fonts is not available, then the next font is used instead. Among the fonts in the set, at least one of them should be installed on the visitor's computer. This ensures that even if your pages don't look exactly like you planned, they will look very similar to your original layout. Figure 6-7 shows how similar the fonts in a font set appear on a page.

Figure 6-7:
Use font sets so if the font you specified isn't installed, a similar font is used instead.

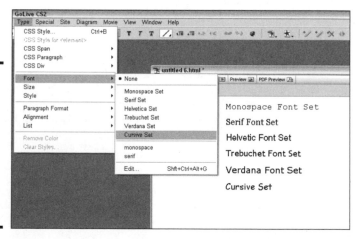

You can use Photoshop and Illustrator to create an image using any font installed on your computer and then save that image for the Web (File➪Save for Web). Then you can place that image in your Web page using GoLive. This option is best used for small amounts of text, say for buttons in a navigation bar, headings to separate areas of text, or a customized banner at the top of your Web page.

The Fundamentals of Page Layout

Page layout incorporates the many elements that we discuss in previous sections of this chapter, mainly text and images (and sometimes other forms of multimedia), to create a design on a page. When you're creating a page design, you must think about how people view a layout, such as how the eye moves across the page to take in the flow of information. How the elements are arranged and how much empty space is on a page between or around these elements needs to be considered. Two main kinds of page layout are discussed in this book: layout intended for print, and layout intended for the Web.

Both of these formats require you to work with many of the same elements. You will also probably create your content using the same programs. Image manipulation for the Web is frequently done using ImageReady or Photoshop. Photoshop is also the standard program for manipulating and correcting images intended for print. You can even design a page for print, but also put it online by using InDesign's Package for GoLive feature. The Package for GoLive feature makes putting page layout on the Web very easy because you only have to design and create the layout one time in InDesign, and then you can package the layout, do some modifications for the Web in GoLive, and place it online.

However, you have to make certain considerations when you put something online. Navigation, usability, file size, dimensions, and computer capabilities are considerations for the Web that aren't a concern when you're working for print. However, resolution, colors, and cropping (to name a few) are considerations of someone designing a piece for print, which aren't concerns for the Web.

Layout for print

When you design a page layout for print, you have to take into account the size and type of paper that will be used. Sometimes, you will create letterhead with certain elements on the page remaining the same, while other elements (the main content) differ from page to page. You can also create page layouts that serve as templates for a book, and use particular elements repeatedly in varying ways throughout the pages (such as bullets or sidebars). Page size, font size, and image resolution are all important considerations in print.

On-screen image resolution is measured in pixels per inch (ppi), which refers to the number of pixels that are within one inch on-screen. The printed resolution of an image is measured in dots per inch (dpi) — a dot of ink is printed for each pixel. A higher dpi means that the image is clearer with finer detail, which is very important for print. *Remember:* Printed images almost always use a higher resolution than on-screen images, so you may find that an image that is 4 x 4 inches on-screen (at 72 ppi) prints out at less than 1 x 1 inch (at 300 dpi). Read more about resolution in Book IV, "Photoshop CS2."

Templates are available for page layouts that take into consideration common dimensions of paper and help you lay out your content into a defined area. Many different kinds of templates are available online, and you can download them sometimes for free, but others are available for a small or modest fee depending on the template. For example, if you're creating a brochure, you may have to think about where the page will be folded, and how to orient your images and text so that they are facing the correct way when the brochure is read.

A few things to think about when you're laying out a page include the following:

✦ You should try to use a grid and snapping to align elements whenever possible. If certain elements on your page are not aligned, there should be a good reason for this.

✦ The eye will travel in the direction of the elements on the page. For example, if you have a picture of a person facing away from the center of a spread, the eye will travel in that direction. Make sure that the eye travels around the page, so all of the elements are seen. It's usually not good if the eye is led directly off the page.

✦ Try dividing your pages into thirds, which is called the *rule of thirds.* Parts of your layout should fall into these three areas.

Web page layout

Layout for the Web is quite different from layout for a document that you intend to print. However, many of the same issues arise in both print and Web layout, such as keeping your text legible and flowing across the page (or screen) in an intelligent way. In Web layouts, navigation and usability open up a few doors for things you should consider when planning a Web page:

✦ **Usability:** A usable site is accessible to most, if not all, of your visitors. This means that visitors can access your content easily because the text is legible, the file formats work on their computers, and they can find content on your site. Also, if the visitor has a challenge, such as a sight or reading disability, he or she can use software on the computer so the site is read or described aloud.

✦ **Size:** File size should always be kept to a minimum, which may mean changing your layout to accommodate for this. If many of the parts of your design require large images, you may need to change the design completely to reduce your file size. Also, you need to design the page with monitors in mind. If a visitor has his or her monitor set to a resolution of 800 x 600, then your site will scroll horizontally if it's designed any larger than 780 pixels wide. Most Web surfers dislike scrolling horizontally, so the dimensions of the visitor's display should be considered when designing sites.

✦ **Navigation:** Users have to navigate between pages on your site. To do so, you will need to create links to those pages by using buttons, text links, menus, and so on. Making that navigation easy to find and use takes some forethought and planning. Be sure that navigation is a big part of your plans when designing the layout of your site.

Not only do you have to think about usability and navigation, but you have to account for the different kinds of computers accessing the page, and how people from all over the world may be trying to access your page. If you need your page to be universal, you may need to translate it into different languages and use different character sets. (This is true of print, as well, if you're designing a page that requires a special character set other than the ones you regularly use.)

Because you may be using multimedia elements alongside text (such as images, video, animation, and so on), you're constrained to the dimensions and color limitations of a computer monitor and have to think about both file size and scrolling. There are many differences between preparing a layout for the Web and for print; however, you will find that you use many of the same tools for both (although you save or export your files in a different way), and a great deal of information crosses over between the two mediums.

Chapter 7: Using Color

In This Chapter

✔ **Checking out color modes and channels**

✔ **Using swatches**

✔ **Correcting color**

✔ **Choosing color for the Web**

*U*sing color in your documents is probably one of the most important considerations you can make in your projects. The colors you use, the mode that you use them in, and even the way you select colors make a difference in the way you create a document and the final output of that document. Even though you can create a document that looks the same on a monitor in different color modes, how that file prints onto paper is a different matter. Color is a very broad subject, and in this chapter you find out the basics of how color affects the projects you work on.

Figuring out what kinds of colors you're using is important, and this is greatly determined by what kind of output you have planned for the document. Different color modes are appropriate for work for the Web and work that you're having professionally printed. Monitors and printers have different modes for color, which means that you need to work with your files in different color modes (although this can be changed after you start working on a file if necessary). You may also find yourself in situations where very particular colors are required in your work. You may be working with specific colors that a company needs to match its logo, or creating an image that replicates how a building should be painted with specific colors of paint. You may need to use particular Pantone colors or color mixes, if not for the printing process, for the purpose of matching a client's needs.

In this chapter, we introduce you to the different color modes and how to use them. You discover new terminology, and how to find, mix, and add colors to your documents in the Adobe Creative Suite.

Looking at Color Modes and Channels

Several different color modes are available for use in the Adobe Creative Suite. When you start a new document in Photoshop and Illustrator, you can choose the color mode you want to work in. If you're working with print, generally you want to switch to CMYK mode right before the file is taken to the printers. If you're working on files that need to be displayed on a monitor, then RGB is a good choice. In Illustrator, you choose a color mode in the New Document dialog box, as shown in Figure 7-1. This narrows the choices in the swatches palettes as well as some other palettes, such as brushes and symbols to CMYK or RGB based colors. You can change it later in File⇨ Document Color Mode.

Figure 7-1: Choosing a color mode in Illustrator.

Using RGB

RGB (Red, Green, Blue) is the color mode used for on-screen presentation, such as an image displayed on the Web or a broadcast design for TV. Each of the colors displayed on-screen has a certain level (between 0 and 100 percent) of red, green, and blue to create the color. In a color mixer, you can either use sliders to set the level in values, as shown in Figure 7-2, or you can enter a percentage into a text field (such as in CMYK color mode).

Figure 7-2: Mixing colors in RGB mode.

Note the Cube and the exclamation point warnings on the color palette in Figure 7-2. These are warnings indicating that a color you have created is not totally suited for two models, Web colors and CMYK:

✦ Click the Web Cube icon to convert the selected color to the closest Web-safe color.

✦ Click the CMYK warning exclamation point to convert to a color that is suitable for the CMYK gamut. This is discussed in later chapters, but just know that you can make this adjustment in the Color Settings dialog box.

When you create a Web page, the color is represented as a hexadecimal number. A hexadecimal number starts with a pound sign (#) followed by three pairs of letters and numbers (A–F and 0–9), the first pair for red, the second pair for green, and the last pair for blue. The lowest value (the least amount of the color) in a hexadecimal number is 0 (zero), and the highest value (the greatest amount of the color) is F. For example, #000000 is black, #FFFFFF is white, #FF0000 is red, and #CCCCCC is a light gray. To see what a particular hexadecimal color looks like, check out the Webmonkey color code page at http://hotwired.lycos.com/webmonkey/reference/color_codes.

Working with CMYK

The RGB (Red, Green, Blue) color mode is the color standard for monitors and the Web, and CMYK — Cyan, Magenta, Yellow, and Key (or Black) — is the standard color mode for print media, particularly in commercial printing such as that done by a service provider. The CMYK color scheme is based on pigment (a substance used as coloring) color separation, and it describes how light reflects off pigments. When you work with this color mode, you create black by adding the maximum values of cyan, magenta, and yellow all at once. Different levels of gray can be created by combining equal, but not maximum, amounts of cyan, magenta, and yellow. White is simply the absence of all color. Many color printers you find today work using the CMYK color model and can simulate almost any color by printing two colors very close to each other; however, some at-home desktop printer models made by Epson, Hewlett-Packard (HP), and Canon use their own color systems to print your work.

Saving in grayscale

You have seen a lot of grayscale so far because that is how the pictures were printed in this book. *Grayscale* refers to when color images are displayed or printed in black and white. Grayscale refers to the different shades of gray that can be used when printing using only black ink on a white page. Halftone patterns are used to help simulate different color values. This is accomplished by adding dots to simulate shadows and gradients between colors. *Halftone patterns* are created when an image uses dots of varying diameter, or it uses many small dots in the same area to simulate different shades of gray.

Looking at color channels

When you work with an image in Photoshop, the image has at least one (but typically more) color channels. A *color channel* stores information about a particular color in a selected image. For example, an RGB image has three color channels: one that handles the reds (R), one for handling green information (G), and the last for information about the blues (B), as shown in Figure 7-3.

Click here to show or hide visibility

Figure 7-3:
This image contains red, green, and blue color channels.

In addition to each of the color channels, you can have an *alpha channel.* The alpha channel holds the transparency information about a particular image. If you're working with a file format that supports transparency, you can add and use the alpha channel to save alpha information.

In Photoshop, you can access the channels in your image by choosing Windows➪Channels. The Channels palette opens, and you can change how you view the image by toggling visibility of each icon. You can do this by clicking the eye icon next to each channel (refer to Figure 7-3).

Choosing Colors

When you create a document, you may have to consider what colors you use, or you could have the freedom to use an unlimited number of colors. If you print your documents, you can choose a specific set of colors to use. You may be restricted to only the two colors in a company logo, or you may have to print in grayscale. So finding the colors you need to use in each program is important, and then figuring out how to access those colors repeatedly in a document saves you a great deal of time.

Using swatches

Swatches are a good way to choose a color, particularly when you intend to print the document. The Swatches palette in the Adobe Creative Suite programs, shown in Figure 7-4, contains colors and sometimes gradients for you to use in a document. You can create libraries of swatches that contain colors that you can use repeatedly across several documents.

Figure 7-4:
The Swatches palette in Photoshop, which is similar to the Swatches palette in InDesign and Illustrator.

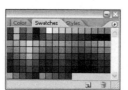

You can choose libraries of swatches (in Photoshop, choose one from the Swatches palette menu), or you can load and save swatch libraries. You can customize a swatch library by adding or deleting colors.

When printing your work professionally, it is advisable to work with *named colors* so that the service provider (commercial printer) knows exactly what inks to use when it outputs your work. An example of a named color is *Pantone 2747 M*. The best way to work with named colors is by using swatches to choose your colors. When you mix your own colors, you can end up working with unnamed colors. When a printing press looks at your documents, it's sometimes too difficult to determine exactly what color you want to print when the color is unnamed.

Mixing colors

A color mixer is found in the Color palette, shown in Figure 7-5, and this helps you choose colors. You can use the Eyedropper tool to choose a color, or you can enter values for each hue or percentages if you prefer that instead. You can use one of several different color modes in the programs that you use, which offers you a lot of flexibility for all of your projects.

Figure 7-5:
The Color
palette in
Illustrator,
which is
very similar
to that in
Photoshop
and
InDesign.

Click to open the palette menu

Follow these steps to choose a color in a specified color mode:

1. **In a program that has a Color palette, choose Window⇨Color to open the Color palette (if it's not already open).**

The Color palette is available in Photoshop, Illustrator, and InDesign.

2. **Click the Color palette menu to choose a new color mode.**

Open this menu by clicking the arrow button in the upper-right corner of the Color palette.

3. **Choose the RGB color mode from the palette menu that opens.**

The palette switches to RGB color mode.

4. **In the Color palette, click either the Fill box (solid square) or Stroke box (hollow square) to choose what color you want to change.**

If you click the Fill box, you can modify the color of a *fill* (the color inside a shape). If you click the Stroke box, then you can modify the color of a *stroke* (the outline of a shape or a line).

5. **Use the sliders in the Color palette to change the color values.**

You can also change the percentage values to the right of each slider.

6. **After you have chosen a color that you're happy with, return to your
document and create a new shape that uses that color.**

For instructions on how to create shapes in InDesign, see Book II.

Hold down the Shift key when adjusting any one color slider, and the other
color sliders will adjust proportionally to provide you with various tints
from your original.

Using Color on the Web

In the past, you had to be very conscious of what colors you used on the
Web. Some computer monitors were limited in the number of colors they
could display. Nowadays, color monitors are much more advanced and can
handle a full range of colors, so images on the Web are much more likely to
be properly displayed.

It doesn't have to do with color, but Macintosh and Windows computers
usually display your work differently because of gamma differences on these
machines. Generally speaking, colors on a Mac appear lighter, and colors on
a PC look darker. You can account for this difference by making a Mac version of your site, videos, and so on, look darker so both are the same (or
you can make the Windows version lighter), but these changes aren't usually
necessary.

Even though most computers can handle a full range of colors, you should
still take into account color limitations if you're designing a site specifically
targeted at old computers or a certain user base. Older computers
may handle only 256 colors, which means that any other colors used are
approximated, which can look bad. If it's likely that your site will be viewed
by users with older computers, consider the following:

✦ Use a Web-safe palette of 216 colors to design your Web sites so that you
specifically design with those older displays in mind and know what the
pages will look like. This number is 216 instead of 256 because the lower
number is compatible with both Mac and Windows computers. This
palette is usually called the *Web-safe palette* or *Web-safe RGB* and can be
accessed from the Swatches palette menu in Photoshop and Illustrator.

✦ Avoid using gradients whenever possible because they use a wide range
of colors (many unsupported in a limited Web palette).

✦ If a color is approximated because it cannot be handled by someone's
computer, that color is *dithered* — the computer tries to use two or more

colors to achieve the color you specified, causing a typically displeasing granular appearance. So a limited number of colors can have a negative affect on an image; notice the granular appearance on what should be the shadow of an apple in Figure 7-6.

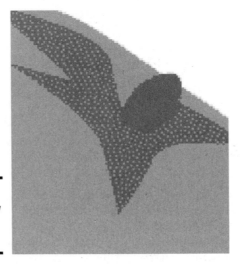

Figure 7-6:
The shadow
in the apple
is dithered.

If you keep the preceding elements in mind, you should be ready to start designing for the Web! Remember also that you don't have to worry about using the Web-safe palette if you're designing primarily for newer computers.

Chapter 8: Printing Documents

You can print documents in many ways with Adobe Creative Suite 2. Similarly, you can print many different kinds of documents. You can create anything from a CD-ROM sticker to a 300-page book to a T-shirt iron-on transfer using the programs you find in the Adobe Creative Suite. But whatever you're working on, it's a good idea to know the options that are available for printing your work. Knowing the kinds of printers you can work with, what to buy (and from where) in order to use them, and how to save your work helps improve the quality of the print job when you've finished your work.

Choosing Printers

When it comes to printers, you encounter hundreds of options at a great variety of prices. Printers can differ greatly when it comes to quality, cost of maintenance, and the speed at which the printer is able to print. Some inkjet printers excel at printing full-color photos but aren't great at printing text; a low-end or medium-end laser printer may print black-and-white documents at good speed and quality, but you can't print in color.

Using consumer printers

Currently, the most common type of consumer (home) printer is an inkjet printer. *Inkjet printers* work by spraying ink stored in cartridges onto a sheet of paper as it passes through the printer. This type of printer is common in households because it's the least expensive type of color printer. It's also versatile. You can walk into virtually any computer store and buy a color inkjet printer (which can print resumes, photos, and brochures) for a low price. The one drawback of inkjets is that they can be expensive to maintain in the long run. Depending on how much you print, you may need to replace the black or color cartridges pretty often, which can get costly and quickly exceed the cost of the printer itself.

Looking at professional printers

Professional printers typically have a more rounded feature set compared to consumer printers. Professional printers can either be inkjet or laser printers and can even perform multiple functions within the office. Not surprisingly, printers that have several roles within the office are often referred to as *multifunction* or *all-in-one* printers, and typically also include scanning, photo-copying, or faxing capabilities in addition to printing. These all-in-one units are great for small offices and home offices because they save the consumer some money while providing access to a variety of useful tools.

Laser printers have several benefits: They typically produce a higher quality printout and print pages faster than inkjet printers, as well as produce a clean, professional-looking document.

Factors to Consider when Choosing a Printer

Some common features to look for when purchasing a printer (either consumer or professional) are

+ **Speed:** Printers are rated in pages per minute (PPM). Low-end inkjet printers typically print about 12 or fewer PPM when printing black-and-white pages. When printing color documents, the number of pages printed per minute will be less.

+ **Color:** Almost all inkjet printers can print in color, but most laser printers print only in black and white. Color printers can be expensive to maintain because most inkjet printers have one cartridge for black ink and a second cartridge for colored inks. When one color runs out, you're forced to replace the entire cartridge, or all of the colors won't look right when you print the document. Color laser printers are available, although they are usually very expensive.

+ **Resolution:** Similar to monitors, a printer's quality can be rated in resolution. Higher resolution means images and text will appear crisper. Low-end or older inkjet printers may print only a maximum of 600 dpi (dots per inch), which is more than fine for text but may be low if you want to print high-quality photographs.

✦ **Connectivity:** You can connect a printer to your computer in three ways. Older printers typically connect to your system using a parallel (36-pin) port, whereas newer printers often offer both parallel and USB connections. The third way is to connect the printer to your network, although this option is usually seen only on professional printers.

✦ **Duplexing:** Another feature you may want to think about when considering professional printers is duplexing. *Duplexing* refers to the ability to print on both sides of a sheet of paper without you having to manually flip the piece of paper and put it back in the paper tray.

Printing in Color

While RGB (Red, Green, Blue) is the color standard for the Web, CMYK — Cyan, Magenta, Yellow, and Key (or Black) — is the standard in print. For information about using the RGB and CMYK color modes in Adobe Creative Suite 2, see Chapter 7 of this minibook.

Printing Your Work

When it comes to printing, countless options and settings can affect the final result of your document. Whether you're printing banners, business cards, T-shirt iron-on transfers, or lost cat posters, you must be aware of several things, such as paper quality, printer quality, and ink usage. You also have to decide whether to print the documents yourself at home or take them to a professional printing business to get the work done.

Choosing where and how to print

You can choose from a couple of options when it comes to printing your files. You can take your digital files to a printing service provider, which is an establishment that prints out electronic documents (such as FedEx Kinko's), or even print the files yourself at home on your inkjet or laser printer. Each option has several advantages and disadvantages. Depending on how many copies and the number of colors, having your files printed professionally can be cost prohibitive. Having your files printed by a professional print house, however, almost always means the print quality will be much better than if the document was printed on a low-end inkjet printer.

Naturally, if you're only printing flyers to distribute around the neighborhood, you may not need high-quality output and a home inkjet or laser printer would be more than adequate. However, it may be cheaper to print documents professionally than it is to print documents at home if you're going to go through large amounts of black ink or perhaps one or two cartridges of toner.

If you're using an inkjet printer, often you can get an average of 400–600 pages of black text before you need to replace a cartridge; a laser printer prints around 2,500–4,000 pages before you need to purchase new toner. Simply using a laser printer can save hundreds of dollars a year, depending on the number of pages you need to print and whether you need to print in color. If you need to print in color, many color laser printers are available (although they can be expensive). Entry-level color laser printers can cost around $500 (US dollars); some high-end color laser printers can cost more than $10,000. In comparison, black-and-white laser printers can cost as little as about $100. So unless you plan on doing lots of printing, outsourcing your printing to a service provider may be the best solution.

The kind of printer you use (such as a commercial or PostScript printer, or a low-cost household inkjet) will make a great difference in the quality of output. Some of your illustrations or layouts will look a lot better when printed commercially depending on what's in your document. More information on PostScript features can be found in Book II, "InDesign CS2," and Book III, "Illustrator CS2."

Looking at paper

Before printing your documents, you need to consider the type of paper that is best for the job. If you're printing on glossy paper, you need to make sure that the paper works with your printer type. Although most glossy paper works fine in inkjet or laser printers, some brands or types of paper may not. Always double-check paper when purchasing it to make sure it won't damage your printer. The kinds of printers supported by the type of paper will be listed on the paper's packaging. One benefit to using glossy paper is that it has a photo-paper-like finish, which can make your printouts appear to have a higher quality.

Using a good paper can result in photos that have richer colors and show more detail. When purchasing printer paper, here are some important characteristics to look out for:

✦ **Brightness:** Brightness, not surprisingly, refers to how bright the paper is. Higher numbers mean the paper looks brighter and cleaner.

✦ **Weight:** This refers to how heavy the paper is. Higher weights mean a thicker, more durable piece of paper.

✦ **Opacity:** Opacity refers to how translucent, or transparent, the paper is. If the paper is too thin, then too much light can pass through it; also, it may be possible to see the ink through the other side of the page (which can be a problem if you want to print on both sides of the sheet). Opacity relates to weight, in that a heavier sheet of paper would be thicker and allow less light to pass through it.

✦ **Texture:** This can provide dramatic differences between inkjet and laser printers. Inkjet printers spray ink onto a page, so having a slightly textured surface to print on can be beneficial because the texture allows ink to dry somewhat faster and bleed a little less, making the finished product look a little sharper. When using a laser printer, the opposite is true. Having a smooth, flat surface for the toner to transfer onto produces better results.

Remember that you may not always print on 8.5-x-11-inch paper (also referred to as Letter or A4). Many printers also allow you to print onto envelopes, labels, stickers, business cards, and even iron-on transfers. Iron-on transfers can be used to create your own T-shirts with your company logo or shirts with your face on the front. Some newer printers even allow you to print directly onto the surface of a CD-ROM. You can even purchase small printers that were designed solely to print standard-sized photographs.

Another important note is the difference in paper sizes globally. While the United States and Canada use inches to measure paper, the rest of the globe uses a metric system based on an ISO standard. The North American Letter format could be replaced by the ISO A4 format. The other differences between the U.S. and Canadian system from the ISO is that the ISO paper sizes always follow a set ratio, while the U.S. and Canadian system uses two different aspect ratios.

Saving files for a service provider

When working with a professional print service provider, you need to check to make sure which file formats they will accept. Almost all print service providers will accept files created using an Adobe program (Illustrator, Photoshop, InDesign, Acrobat, and so on), as well as files created using QuarkXPress, CorelDRAW, or other professional-level programs. You'll also need to confirm what version and operating system the service provider will accept, because it may be necessary to save your files so that they are compatible with whichever version of software the service provider uses.

You may have to export your work as a different file format, such as PDF, if your service provider doesn't accept InDesign files. To export to PDF in InDesign, choose File➪Export and select PDF from the Save as Type (Windows) or Format (Mac) drop-down list. When you click the Save button, the Export PDF dialog box appears, as shown in Figure 8-1. Read specifics about the settings in Book V.

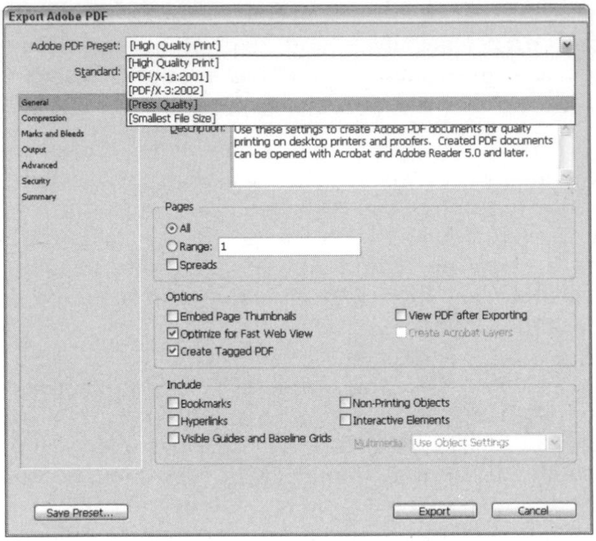

Figure 8-1:
Select from
various
presets to
export an
InDesign
file as a PDF
document.

If you have linked your graphics within your files instead of embedding them, you'll also want to use an uncompressed file format, such as EPS or TIFF. Using an uncompressed file format ensures that you aren't losing quality each time the image file is saved, which would happen if you used JPEG images.

Printing at home from Adobe Creative Suite 2

When you're ready to print your documents, you can access the Print dialog box and then specify a number of settings depending on what kind of printer you have installed. For this example, we assume that you have Acrobat Distiller (from Adobe Acrobat) installed on your system if you are printing from programs other than those from the Adobe Creative Suite, although the steps are similar for other printers that you may have installed.

To export a file as a PDF, follow these steps:

1. **Choose File⇨Print with Preview. This window provides many more options than the standard Print menu.**

In this case, we are using Photoshop on Windows, but you can use other programs in the same way such as Microsoft Word or Excel.

The Print dialog box opens, as shown in Figure 8-2.

The Print dialog box differs, depending on which program you're using. In this window, Photoshop allows you to change the scale of the image by entering a value in the scale text box, or selecting and dragging a handle on the preview image in the upper-left corner.

Figure 8-2:
The Print dialog box in Photoshop on a Windows system.

2. **When you have scaled the image to the paper, click the Print button.**

   You can select a printer from the list of installed local or network print-ers in the Print dialog box. If you have Adobe Acrobat installed, you will also notice that it's installed as a printer, allowing you to save your file as a PDF.

3. **Choose Adobe PDF from the Name drop-down list (Windows) or the Printer drop-down list (Mac).**

4. **Click the Properties button that's to the right of the Name drop-down list. You may need to click the Printer button on the Mac.**

   The Adobe PDF Document Properties dialog box opens on Windows, and another Print dialog box opens on the Mac if you had to click Printer. This allows you to define the PDF Page Size and Conversion Settings, among other settings.

When you want to print a document in Windows, click the Properties button to bring up the printer properties for the currently selected printer (see Figure 8-3).

The properties you can modify in this dialog box depend on both the printer you have and the printer drivers you have installed for the printer. If you have a printer that supports duplexing (double-sided printing), you can define whether duplexing is used, and any printer-specific settings you have.

Figure 8-3:
Depending on the printer that you select, you will have different options to choose from. These are Adobe PDF options.

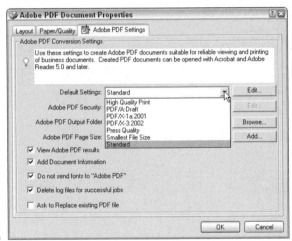

Most printers let you toggle between quality settings, such as Draft, Normal, and Best. Draft prints with the least amount of ink used, Normal prints with a medium amount of ink, and Best prints with the most ink but has the highest-quality output. If you're printing a quick sample page, you may want to set the quality to draft or normal to save on ink. Quality paper can cost $1 or more per page, in addition to $0.50 per page in the cost of ink if you're printing out quality photos — this can quickly drain your ink as well as your wallet!

Because most printers have custom interfaces for defining settings, you may need to consult your printer's documentation for detailed information on using the printer's features.

5. **Choose Standard (Windows) from the Default Settings drop-down list or PDF Options (Mac).**

Choosing Standard or PDF Options allows you to define settings such as page size, the version of Acrobat Reader the document is compatible with, and whether to auto-rotate pages. On the Mac, you can choose what happens when you finish creating the PDF and choose the type of PDF you create.

6. **Windows: Click the Edit button to the right of the Default Settings drop-down list.**

   The Standard — Adobe PDF Settings dialog box opens. When you change the default settings (some of which are described in Step 4), you will be alerted as to what version of the Acrobat Reader is needed to view the document you're exporting.

7. **Enter a name for the document in the Save As text field, and then click Print.**

   The document is exported and saved as a PDF file.

You can modify the security settings so that users must enter a password to view the PDF document.

Book II

InDesign CS2

The 5th Wave   By Rich Tennant

The new desktop publishing software not only lets Rags produce a professional looking greeting card quickly and inexpensively, but it also allows him to say it his way.

@RICHTENNANT

ARF!!
Whooof arf!

Arf, arf, arf

Contents at a Glance

Chapter 1: Introducing InDesign CS2

In This Chapter

✔ **Opening InDesign and creating new documents**

✔ **Looking at the workspace**

✔ **Making the workspace fit your needs**

✔ **Creating your first publication**

InDesign is one of the most sophisticated page layout programs available on the market. InDesign is used for page layout and print design: It has many features that allow you to manipulate text, tools that enable you to edit images and graphics, and the ability to integrate with other Adobe programs. (Chapter 8 of this minibook discusses integrating InDesign with other Adobe programs, such as Photoshop and Acrobat.) These features enable you to work quickly and efficiently with the other products described in this book and to create engaging publications.

This powerful application is also very easy to get started with. This minibook shows you how to use InDesign to make creative page layouts. In this chapter, you discover the InDesign interface and start your first publication.

Getting Started with InDesign CS2

InDesign is similar to other Adobe products when it comes to workspace layout and functionality. InDesign works with graphics and word processing programs so that you can use content that's created in a different piece of software and integrate it with InDesign to create a publication.

You can use InDesign to create a newsletter, brochure, advertisement, or even a book. These layouts may be for print, or you may want to keep them electronic and distribute your pages online. InDesign allows you to easily accomplish any of these tasks. See Figure 1-1 for an example of a page layout in InDesign that includes tables and columns of text.

InDesign documents are saved as .indd files on your hard drive, which are native InDesign documents. After you double-click an .indd document, the InDesign application starts and opens the selected file.

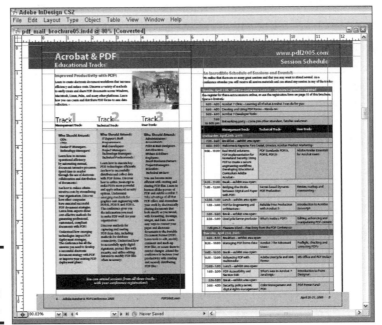

Figure 1-1:
A sample
page layout
in InDesign.

Opening InDesign

You can open InDesign in several different ways. Choose one of the following ways to open InDesign:

✦ **Double-click the InDesign icon on your desktop.**

✦ **Choose Start**➪**All Programs**➪**Adobe InDesign CS (Windows XP) or double-click the InDesign CS icon in your Applications folder (Mac).**

✦ **Find an InDesign document (*.indd) on your hard drive and double-click the document's title or icon.** InDesign starts up automatically and opens the document you chose.

About desktop publishing

Desktop publishing is when you use your computer to create page layouts for books, PDFs, newsletters, advertisements, brochures, and so on. Many different software applications enable you to publish printed work, and InDesign is one of the best you can use for desktop publishing.

A number of steps are required for desktop publishing (the ordering of the steps will likely vary depending on the content, the people you are working with, and other circumstances):

✔ **Design the page:** An early step is to design the layout of the page. This step may be accomplished by sketching with a pen or pencil on paper.

Page layout is the arrangement of graphics and text on a page. Page layout has a lot to do with graphic design. How you arrange text and graphics on a page takes knowledge of design, such as repetition, white space, alignment, flow, color, and contrast. Design is a large field of study, but you can also read about many of these principles in Book III and Book IV. You can create a page layout using anything from scissors and glue, to a desktop publisher, or even code such as HTML; however, this minibook covers using a computer and desktop publishing to create a page layout. See Chapter 4 of this minibook for more information on page layout and design.

✔ **Write the text:** You can create text for the document (sometimes the text content is referred to as a *story*), or have it supplied to you by someone else. Text can be composed right in InDesign using a tool such as the Story Editor (a tool in InDesign that allows you to write, edit and format text that you import into a document), or you can use a word processor such as Microsoft Word to create the text.

✔ **Gather images:** Use images that you have created, or perhaps find stock images for use in your layout. Remember that using stock images sometimes requires a fee, royalties, or credit to the artist.

✔ **File preparation:** You need to set up and prepare the file for printing. You can use the tools in InDesign to set up the file and prepare it for printing or exporting.

✔ **Printing or exporting:** The final step is to *print* the document or export it to a PDF, ebook, or Web page. You may be printing the document on a home printer or perhaps taking it to a commercial printing house.

Creating a new publication

When you open InDesign for the first time, you need to create a new InDesign document (also referred to as a *publication*). Just follow these steps to create a new publication:

1. **Choose File➪New➪Document.**

The New Document dialog box opens, as shown in Figure 1-2.

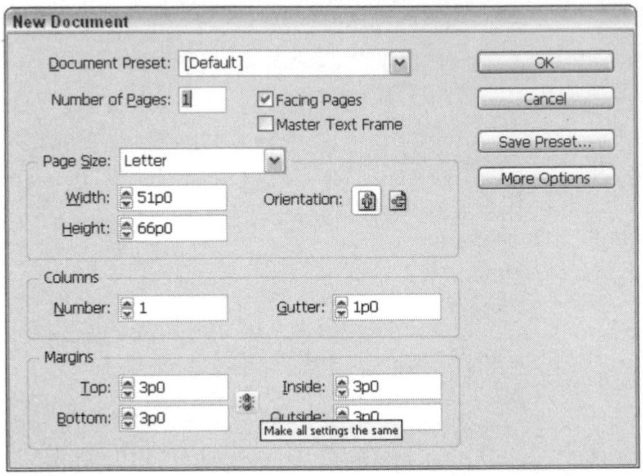

Figure 1-2:
The New Document dialog box allows you to make settings for the new file.

2. **Enter a value for the number of pages for the document in the Number of Pages text field.**

   This value can be between 1 and 9999. If you want a text frame on the master page, select the Master Text Frame check box.

   You can discover more about text frames in Chapter 3 of this minibook.

3. **Select the Facing Pages check box if you want the pages arranged as spreads.**

   With this option checked, the pages in your document are arranged in pairs, so you have *spreads,* which are facing or adjacent pages in a layout. For example, you would select this option if you're creating a publication that will be arranged like a book. If you deselect this option, pages are arranged individually.

4. **Choose a page size for the document from the Page Size drop-down list.**

   The page size should be set to the size of paper you intend to print on or display the content at. The Width and Height values below this drop-down list change, depending on the size you choose.

5. **Choose Portrait (vertical) or Landscape (horizontal) orientation for the orientation of the pages throughout the document.**

   Click the button on the left for Portrait, or the button on the right for Landscape. A portrait layout is narrow and tall, while a landscape layout is short and wide.

6. **Choose a number for the columns on the page.**

   This sets guides for columns where you plan to input text. You can also enter a value in the Gutter field (the *gutter* is the space in between each of the columns). For more information about using columns in page layout, see Chapter 4 of this minibook.

7. Choose values for the page margins.

Notice the Make All Settings the Same button in the middle of the four text fields where you enter the margin values. Click this button to set all margins to the same value.

If you see Top, Bottom, Inside, and Outside, you are specifying margins for a page layout that has facing pages (the Facing Pages check box is selected in the dialog box). If you see Top, Bottom, Left, and Right, you are creating a page layout without facing pages. The inside margins refer to the margins at the middle of the spread, and the outside margins refer to the outer left and right margins. The Inside setting can be set to accommodate the binding of a book.

8. When you're finished, click OK.

If you're going to use the same settings over and over, saving those settings as a preset is a good idea. Click the Save Preset button in the New Document dialog box after making your settings (before you click OK). Enter a name for the preset, and then click OK. After you save your settings, you can select the settings from the Document Preset drop-down list (at the top of Figure 1-2) whenever you create a new document.

After you click OK in the New Document dialog box, the new document is created with the settings you just specified.

We discuss margins, columns, orientation, and page size in further detail in Chapter 4 of this minibook.

Opening an existing publication

You may have InDesign files on your hard drive that you created or have saved from another source. To open existing InDesign documents (*.indd), follow these steps:

1. Choose File➪Open.

The Open dialog box appears.

2. Browse through your hard drive and select a file to open.

Select a file by clicking the document's title. To select more than one document, press Ctrl (⌘ on the Mac) while you click the filename.

3. Click the Open button to open the file.

The file opens in the workspace.

Looking at the document setup

If you need to change the size of your pages or the number of pages in a document that is already open in the workspace, you can make those changes in the Document Setup dialog box. To access and modify settings in the Document Setup dialog box, follow these steps:

1. Choose File⇨Document Setup.

The Document Setup dialog box opens, as shown in Figure 1-3. This figure shows how the Document setup dialog window appears with the More Options button selected.

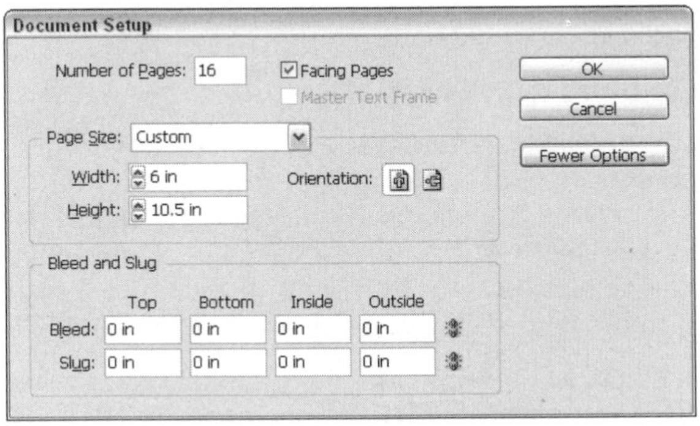

Figure 1-3: Change your current document settings even after creating the document.

2. Change the value in the Number of Pages text field if you need the number of pages in your document to be greater or less than the current value.

The number of pages in your document updates after you close this dialog box. You can also change this later by using Layout⇨Pages⇨ Insert Pages, or using the Pages palette.

3. Change the size of the page by selecting a new option from the Page Size drop-down list, or manually enter values into the Width and Height text fields.

You can also click the up and down arrows in the Width and Height text fields to choose a new value.

4. Change the page orientation by clicking the Portrait or the Landscape button.

The page orientation updates in the workspace after you exit this dialog box.

5. **Click OK when you're finished changing your document setup.**

   The modifications are applied to the currently open document.

A Tour of the Workspace

The InDesign workspace, or user interface, is designed to be intuitive and efficient. You will use several tools over and over again, so it's a good idea to keep them open and handy. Some of these tools are already open in the default user interface. The interface for Windows includes a toolbox, several palette groupings, the Control palette, and a large area for the pasteboard. Figure 1-4 shows how the InDesign workspace layout looks in Windows.

The Mac workspace is very similar to the Windows version. You will notice a difference in the main menu bar.

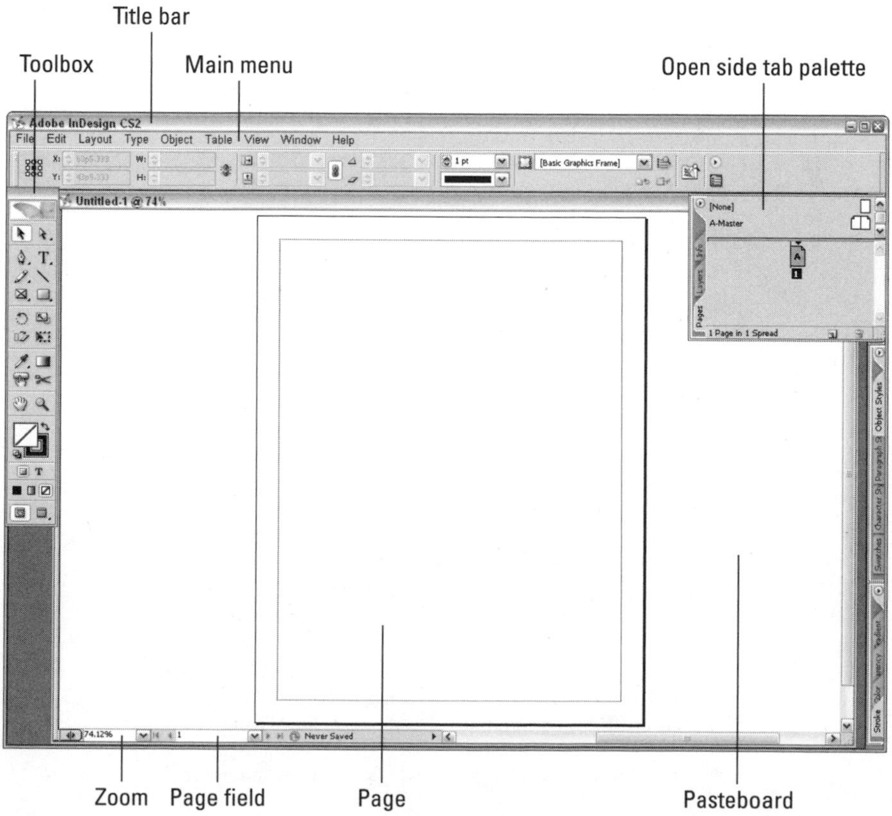

Figure 1-4:
The InDesign default user interface for Windows.

✦ **Page:** The main area of the InDesign workspace is called a page. A *page* is the area that is printed or exported when you're finished making a layout.

✦ **Master page:** You can define how certain text elements and graphics appear in an entire document (or just portions of it) using a master page. A master page is a lot like a template for your document because you can reuse elements throughout the pages. For example, if you have an element you want on each page (such as page numbering), you can create it on the master page. If you need to change an element on the master page, you can change it at any time, and your changes will be reflected on every page that the master page is applied to.

✦ **Spread:** A spread is referring to a set of two (or more) facing pages. You usually see spreads like these in magazines when you open them up and a design *spreads* across both pages.

✦ **Pasteboard:** The area around the page (and actually includes the page or spread as well) is called the pasteboard. The pasteboard can be used to store content until you're ready to lay it out on the page or spread you're working on. Pasteboards are not shared between pages or spreads. For example, if you have certain elements placed on a paste-board for pages 4 and 5, you cannot access these elements when you are working on pages 8 and 9.

Tools

The toolbox (also called the Tools palette) is where you find tools to edit, manipulate, or select elements in your document. Simply use your cursor and click a tool to select it. See Figure 1-5 for the default toolbox layout.

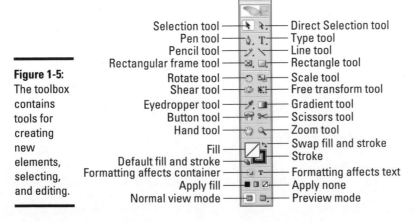

Figure 1-5: The toolbox contains tools for creating new elements, selecting, and editing.

Selection tool — Direct Selection tool
Pen tool — Type tool
Pencil tool — Line tool
Rectangular frame tool — Rectangle tool
Rotate tool — Scale tool
Shear tool — Free transform tool
Eyedropper tool — Gradient tool
Button tool — Scissors tool
Hand tool — Zoom tool
Fill — Swap fill and stroke
Stroke
Default fill and stroke
Formatting affects container — Formatting affects text
Apply fill — Apply none
Normal view mode — Preview mode

You can find out more about these tools and how to use them in the related chapters of this minibook. For example, we discuss the drawing tools in Chapter 2 of this minibook.

Using the tools in the toolbox, you can

+ **Create:** Create stunning new content on a page using drawing, frame, and text tools.

+ **Select:** Select existing content on a page to move or edit.

+ **View:** Move (pan) and magnify the page or spread.

+ **Edit:** Edit existing objects such as shapes, lines, and text. Use the Selection tool to select existing objects so that you can change them.

When a tool has a small arrow next to the button's icon, it means more tools are hiding behind it. When you click the tool and hold the mouse button down, a menu opens that shows you other available tools. Just move the mouse down this menu and release the button when the tool you want is highlighted. Figure 1-6 shows you what a menu looks like.

Figure 1-6:
Selecting
a hidden
tool from
a menu.

The layout of the toolbox can be changed to a single vertical or horizontal palette. To change the layout of the toolbox, follow these steps:

1. **Choose Edit⇨Preferences⇨General (Windows), or InDesign⇨Preferences⇨General (Mac).**

The Preferences dialog box opens.

2. **In the General Options section of the Preferences dialog box, choose Single Row from the Floating Tools Palette drop-down list (see Figure 1-7).**

Your other options are Single Column and Double Column.

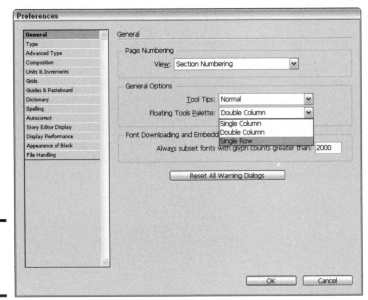

Figure 1-7:
Changing
the toolbox
layout.

3. **Click OK.**

The toolbox changes to a horizontal palette. If you want to switch back to the default, repeat these steps, but choose Double Column in Step 2.

Menus

The menus in the main menu bar are used to access some of the main commands and control the user interface of InDesign. They also allow you to open and close palettes used to edit and make settings for the publication.

InDesign menu commands are similar to most other applications you're probably familiar with, such as New, Open, and Save. The InDesign menus also include commands that are especially used for page layout, such as Insert with Placeholder Text. For more information on using menus, see Book I, Chapter 2. Remember to refer to the common commands and shortcuts that are also detailed in that chapter.

The InDesign main menu has the following options:

✦ **File:** This menu includes some of the basic commands to create, open, and save documents. It also includes the Place command to import new content, and many options to control document settings, exporting documents, and printing.

✦ **Edit (Windows) or InDesign (Mac):** You can access many commands for editing and controlling selection in this menu — such as copying and keyboard shortcuts. The Dictionary and spell check are found in this menu, too.

✦ **Layout:** This menu allows you to show and hide guides and grids. These options help you lay elements on the page accurately and aligned. The menu also allows you to navigate through the document's pages and spreads.

✦ **Type:** This menu allows you to select fonts and control characters in the layout. The many settings related to text can be accessed in this menu, which opens up the associated palette where you make the changes.

✦ **Object:** You can modify the look and placement of objects on the page using this menu. What options are available in this menu depend on what you have selected in the workspace, such as a text field or an image.

✦ **Table:** This menu enables you to create, set up, modify, and control tables on the page.

✦ **View:** You can modify the view of the page from this menu, including zooming in and out, and adding guides, rulers, or grids to help you lay out elements.

✦ **Window:** Use this menu to open and close palettes or switch between open documents.

✦ **Help:** This menu is where you can access the Help documents for InDesign and configure any plug-ins you have installed.

Palettes

In the default layout, you see a large area for the document, typically referred to as the page. To the right of the page are several *palettes* that snap (are *docked*) to the edge of the workspace. Palettes are used to control the publication and edit elements on your pages. *Docked* palettes are palettes attached to the edge of the user interface. Palettes can be maximized and minimized away from the main work area, moved around, or closed altogether.

Palettes in InDesign have a slightly different functionality than in other Adobe programs in the Creative Suite: You can make the tabs fit and slide in and out from the edge of the workspace horizontally instead of vertically. These new palettes are known as *side tabs,* as shown in Figure 1-8.

Click to open palette menu

Side tab

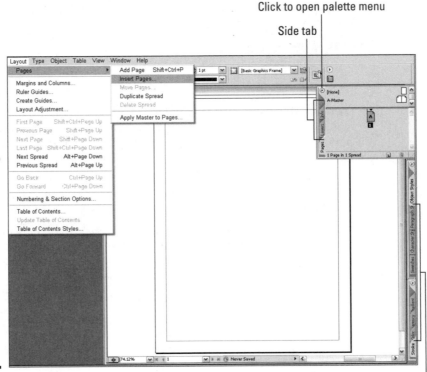

Figure 1-8:
Vertically oriented palettes are called side tabs; the palette menu is the small arrow in the upper-left corner of the palette.

Closed side tabs

To maximize a Side Tab palette (or group of palettes), simply click a tab in the group. The tab has the name of the palette on it. Then you can click any of the palette tabs in the group to see its contents. To minimize the palette group, simply click an *active* (open) palette tab. You can use these palette tabs to drag a palette to or from a group as well. The palette menu button is located in the upper-left corner of the palette (refer to Figure 1-8). Click and hold to view more options in the menu.

If you don't like Side Tabs, click the palette's tab and drag it away from the edge of the workspace. It changes into a regular palette. You can also drag any palette to the edge of the interface to change it into a Side Tab.

Even though some of the InDesign palettes perform different functions, similar palettes are grouped together depending on what they are used for. You can change the groupings by clicking and dragging a palette's tab into another grouping. You can change the size of a palette grouping by clicking and dragging the bottom edge of the palette. Mouse over the bottom edge of a palette until a double-ended cursor appears, and then click and drag the cursor to change the palette's size. (If you have changed the layout and cannot find this workspace, choose Window➪Workspace➪Default.)

Some of the palettes work intelligently when you're manipulating content on an InDesign page. If you work with a particular element, for example, the associated palette is activated. Throughout the later chapters of this mini-book, you discover these specific palettes as you create layouts. For now, we briefly show you two of the general InDesign palettes (the Control palette and the Pages palette).

**Book II
Chapter 1**

**Introducing
InDesign CS2**

Control palette

The Control palette is used to edit just about any element in InDesign, as shown for the Type tool in Figure 1-9. This palette is *context sensitive,* so it changes depending on what you have selected on a page. For example, if you have text selected on the page, it displays options allowing you to edit the text. If you have a shape selected, then it displays options allowing you to modify the shape.

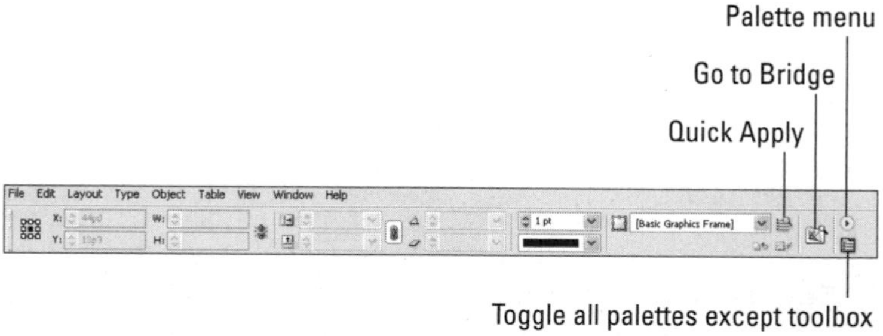

Palette menu

Go to Bridge

Quick Apply

Figure 1-9:
The Control palette as it appears when the Text tool is selected.

Toggle all palettes except toolbox

The Control palette also has a toggle that enables you to toggle the current relevant palette between open and closed; Figure 1-10 shows the Control palette when a stroke is selected, the palette menu allows you to select specific stroke options.

Figure 1-10:
The Control palette as it appears when a stroke is selected.

Pages palette

You can control pages by using the Pages palette, shown in Figure 1-11. This palette allows you to arrange, add, and delete pages in your document. You can also navigate between pages using this palette, which we discuss further in Chapter 4 of this minibook.

Figure 1-11:
The Pages palette allows you to arrange, add, and delete pages.

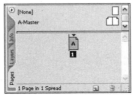

You can hide all the palettes that are open (including the Control palette) by pressing the Tab key; however, this shortcut only works when no elements on the page are selected. To make sure nothing is selected, click an empty part of the pasteboard before you press the Tab key.

Page controls

You can also control which spread you see and the magnification of the pages using a drop-down list at the bottom of the interface. Refer to Figure 1-4 to see where to access the page controls (the lower-left corner: Zoom and Page fields).

You can navigate through the document's pages using the left and right arrow buttons on either side of the page number. You can manually enter a value into the magnification text field and press Enter, or choose a preset value from the drop-down list.

Contextual menus

Contextual menus (or context menus) are menus that pop up when you right-click (Windows) or Control-click (Mac) the mouse. Contextual menus change depending on what you click. If you don't have any elements selected, the contextual menu will open for the overall InDesign document, allowing you to select options such as Zoom, Paste, Rulers, and Guides. If you have an element selected, you have options transforming, modifying, or editing the object.

Contextual menus are context sensitive (hence the name!). Remember to select an element on the page before you right-click to open the contextual menu. If you do not select the object first, the menu is for the document instead of for the object.

You can find out more about editing and transforming elements in Chapters 2 and 4 of this minibook.

Setting Up the Workspace

Workspace settings are important to know about because they help you create quality page layouts. Overall document settings enable you to show grids or use guides that help you align elements on the page. Grids and guidelines are pretty much the same thing, except that grids are designed to repeat across the page and be a specified distance apart. Neither guides nor grids will print when you print your document.

Showing and hiding grids and guides

Use *grids* when you need to align elements to the overall document. Elements in your layout can snap to a grid, which can help you align several elements or accurately space objects apart from each other. *Guides* can be placed anywhere on the page (and pasteboard) and are used to accurately position objects in your layout. This is different from grids, which cannot be freely placed just anywhere on the page. Objects can snap to guides just like they can snap to a grid.

The *document grid* is used for aligning elements on the page, and the *baseline grid* is used for aligning columns of text. To show the document grid, choose View⇨Show Document Grid; to show the baseline grid, choose View⇨Show Baseline Grid. You will immediately see the difference between these two kinds of grids. After you're done viewing grids, you can remove the grids by choosing View⇨Hide Document Grid or View⇨Hide Baseline Grid.

Figure 1-12 shows what grids look like on a page.

Book II
Chapter 1

Introducing
InDesign CS2

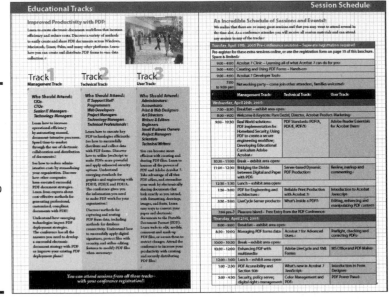

Figure 1-12:
You can show grids to help you lay out pages, and hide them to get an idea of what the layout will look like when it's printed.

To snap objects to a guide or the document grid, you must have snapping enabled. To enable snapping, choose View⇨Snap to Guides or View⇨Snap to Document Grid.

To create a guide and show or hide guides, follow these steps:

1. **Make sure rulers are visible by selecting View⇨Show Rulers.**

Rulers appear in the workspace. If you already have rulers visible, the option View⇨Hide Rulers is in the View menu. Do not hide the rulers.

2. **Move the cursor to a horizontal or vertical ruler.**

Make sure that your cursor is over a ruler.

3. **Click on the ruler and drag the mouse towards the page.**

A *ruler guide* shows on the page as a line.

4. **Release the mouse where you want the guide.**

You have just created a ruler guide!

5. **To hide the guide, choose View⇨Hide Guides.**

This hides the guide you created, but it does not delete it — so you can make it reappear easily in the next step.

6. **To see the guide again, choose View⇨Show Guides.**

The guide you created is shown on the page again.

You can find out more about the different kinds of guides and how to use them in page layout in Chapter 4 of this minibook.

You can control the color of the guides and grid in your preferences. Access the preferences by choosing Edit⇨Preferences⇨Grids. When the Preferences dialog box opens, you can change the color and spacing of the lines. Click Guides & Pasteboards in the list on the left to change the color settings for guides.

Snapping to a grid or guide

You can have elements on the page snap to a grid or a guide. Grid or guide snapping is very useful so that you don't have to try to eyeball the alignment of several elements to one another, because they are precisely aligned to a grid or guide. In fact, grids and guides are fairly useless unless you have elements snap to them! To make sure that this setting is enabled, choose View⇨Snap to Document Grid or View⇨Snap to Guides.

You can view a print preview of your document by clicking the Preview Mode button at the very bottom of the toolbox. When you click this button, all the object bounding boxes, guides, and the grid disappear.

Saving a custom workspace

You can rearrange palettes in InDesign in a particular order, layout, and quantity. You may never use particular palettes that are open by default, or you may always use ones that are closed by default. Oftentimes, you create a workspace that is just right for you, and you don't want to lose it after you shut down InDesign or your computer. Luckily, you can save your workspace so that when you return to InDesign, you can use the same work-space again.

To save a custom workspace, follow these steps:

1. **Have the InDesign workspace configured in the way you want to save it.**

This workspace will be saved as a custom workspace.

2. **Choose Window⇨Workspace⇨Save Workspace.**

The Save Workspace dialog box opens.

3. **Type a new name for the workspace into the Name text field.**

   When you finish, this name is displayed in the workspaces menu.

4. **Click the OK button.**

   The custom workspace is saved. To access your workspace, choose Window⇨Workspace⇨*Your Workspace* (where *Your Workspace* is the name you gave the workspace in Step 3).

You can delete the workspace if you no longer want it saved. Simply choose Window⇨Workspace⇨Delete Workspace.

Working with Publications

After you become comfortable getting around the InDesign workspace, you're ready to begin working with a new document. After you have started working on a document, it's important to find out how to import content from other programs and to save that document on your hard drive. A lot of the content you work with in InDesign is imported from other programs. Then the content is organized, modified, and integrated into a layout using InDesign. To begin, we show you the steps needed to import content and save new files.

We show you how to open new and existing documents earlier in the chapter; refer to the sections, "Creating a new publication" and "Opening an existing publication."

You may also be working with templates. *Templates* are layouts that you reuse by applying them to a document that requires a particular predesigned format. For example, a company may use a template for their official letterhead because every new letter requires the same page format and design. InDesign templates use the .indt file extension.

Importing new content

You can use many different kinds of content in an InDesign document because you can import many supported file types. InDesign enables you to import text, formatted tables, and graphics that help you create an effective layout. This ability makes integration with many different programs easy.

Follow these steps to import an image file into InDesign. (In this example, we import a bitmap graphic file.)

1. **Choose File⇨New⇨Document.**

   The New Document dialog box appears.

2. Review the settings and click the OK button.

A new document opens. Feel free to alter the settings before clicking the OK button, if necessary. You may want to change the Number of Pages setting, or change the orientation of the pages, but it is not necessary to do so.

3. Choose Edit⇨Place.

The Place dialog box opens, enabling you to browse the contents of your hard drive for supported files. If you select the Show Import Options check box, another dialog box opens before the file imports. Leave this option deselected for now.

4. Click the file you want to import, and then click the Open button.

Certain files, such as bitmap photo and graphic files and PDFs, show a thumbnail preview at the bottom center of the dialog box. See Figure 1-13 for an example of a file preview.

When you click the Open button, the Place dialog box closes, and your cursor becomes an upside-down L.

Figure 1-13:
The Place dialog box shows you a thumbnail of each file for several different file formats.

5. Click the page where you want the upper-left corner of the imported file (in this case, an image) to appear.

The image is placed on the page.

For general information on importing and exporting in the Adobe Creative Suite, check out Book I, Chapter 5. For more information on importing different kinds of file formats, such as text, images, and PDFs, refer to Chapters 3 and 4 in this minibook.

You can also import different kinds of file formats, such as text and Excel tables.

Viewing content

You can view elements in several different ways on your document's pages. Sometimes you need to see your drawings and images close up so that you can make precise edits, or you need to move the page around to see something that may extend past the workspace. InDesign offers the following ways to navigate your documents:

✦ **Scroll bars:** You can use the scroll bars to move the pages around. The scroll bars are located below and to the right of the pasteboard. Click a scroll bar handle and drag it left and right or up and down.

✦ **Zoom:** Zoom in or out from the document to increase or decrease the display of your document. Select the Zoom tool (the magnifying glass icon) from the toolbox and click anywhere on the page to zoom in. Press Alt (Windows) or Option (Mac) and click to zoom out.

✦ **Hand tool:** Use the Hand tool to move the page around. This is perhaps the best and quickest way to move your pages around and navigate the document. Select the Hand tool by pressing the Spacebar, and then click and drag to move around the pasteboard.

Saving your publication

Even the best computers and applications fail from time to time, so you don't want to lose your hard work unnecessarily. Saving your publication often is important, then, so that you don't lose any work if your computer or the software crashes, or the power goes out.

To save a file, choose File➪Save or press Ctrl+S (Windows) or ⌘+S (Mac).

Some people save different versions of their files. You may want to do this in case you want to revert back to an earlier version of the file. For example, you may decide to make a radical change to your page layout, but you want to keep an earlier version in case the radical change just doesn't work out.

Remember to choose File➪Save before proceeding if you want the current document to save the revisions you have made since you last saved the file. All new additions to the document will be made in the new version of the file.

To save a new version of the current document, and then continue working on the new document, follow these steps:

1. **Choose File⇨Save As.**

   The Save As dialog box opens.

2. **Choose the directory you want to save the file in.**

3. **In the File Name text field, enter a new name for the document.**

   This saves a new version of the file. Consider a naming scheme at this point. If your file is called `myLayout.indd`, you might call it `myLayout02.indd` to signify the second version of the file. Future files can then increase the number for each new version.

4. **Click the Save button when you are finished.**

   This saves the document in the chosen directory with a new name.

The File⇨Save As command is also used for other means. You may want to save your design as a template. After you create the template, choose File⇨Save As, and then choose InDesign 3.0 template from the Save as Type (Windows) or Format (Mac) drop-down list.

You can also choose File⇨Save a Copy. This saves a copy of the current state of the document you're working on with a new name, but you then continue working on the original document. Both commands are very useful for saving incremental versions of a project that you're working on.

To find out more about working with files, go to Chapter 7 of this minibook.

**Book II
Chapter 1**

**Introducing
InDesign CS2**

Chapter 2: Drawing in InDesign

Many of the tools that you find in the InDesign toolbox are used for drawing lines and shapes on a page. This means you have several different ways of creating interesting drawings for your publications. You can create anything from basic shapes to intricate drawings inside InDesign, instead of having to use a drawing program like Illustrator. Even though InDesign doesn't replace Illustrator (see Book III), which has many more versatile drawing tools and options for creating intricate drawings, InDesign is adequate for simple drawing tasks. In this chapter, you discover how to use the most popular InDesign drawing tools and also how to add colorful fills to your illustrations.

Getting Started with Drawing

When you're creating a document, you may want drawn shapes and paths to be a part of the layout. For example, you may want to have a star shape for a yearbook page about a talent show, or run text along a path. Whatever it is you need to do, you can draw shapes and paths to get the job done.

Paths and shapes

Paths can take a few different formats. They can either be open or closed, with or without a stroke:

✦ **Path:** The outline of a shape or object. Paths can be closed and have no gaps, or they can be open like a line on the page. Freeform paths can be drawn freely by hand, such as squiggles on a page.

✦ **Stroke:** A line style and thickness that you apply to a path. A stroke can look like a line, or like an outline of a shape.

Figure 2-1 shows the different kinds of paths and strokes that you can create.

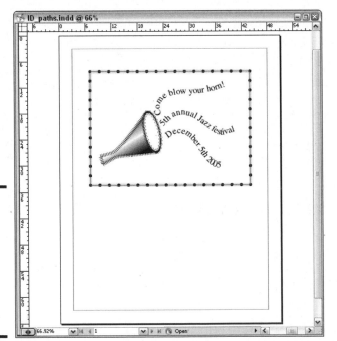

Figure 2-1: Some different kinds of paths and strokes made on a page in InDesign.

Paths contain points where the direction of the path can change. You find out more about points in the following section, "Points and segments." You can make paths by using freeform drawing tools, such as the Pen or Pencil tools, or by using the basic shape tools, such as the Ellipse, Rectangle, Polygon, or Line tools.

The shape tools create paths in a predefined way so that you can make basic geometric shapes, such as a star or ellipse. All you need to do is select the shape tool, drag the cursor on the page, and the shape is automatically drawn. Creating shapes this way is a lot easier than trying to manually create them using the Pen or Pencil tool! See Figure 2-2 for shapes drawn using the shape tools found in the toolbox.

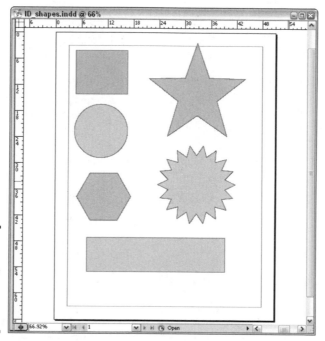

Book II
Chapter 2

Drawing in
InDesign

Figure 2-2:
You can
create many
shapes with
the basic
shape tools.

You can change shapes into freeform paths, like those drawn using the Pencil or Pen tools. Similarly, you can make freeform paths into basic shapes. Therefore, you don't need to worry about which tool you initially choose.

We created the stars and starburst shown in Figure 2-2 by double-clicking the Polygon tool and changing the options. Read more about the Polygon tool later in this chapter.

Points and segments

Paths are made up of points and segments:

✦ **Point:** Where the path changes somehow, such as changing direction. There can be many points along a path that are joined with segments.

Points are sometimes called *anchor points*. You can create two kinds of points:

- **Corner points:** These points have a straight line between them. Shapes like squares or stars have corner points.

- **Curve points:** These points are along a curved path. Circles or snaking paths have lots of curve points.

✦ **Segment:** A line or curve connecting two points — kind of like connect the dots!

Figure 2-3 shows corner points and curve points joined together by segments.

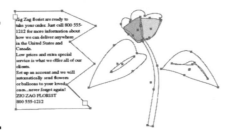

Figure 2-3:
Points are joined together by line segments.

Getting to Know the Tools of the Trade

This section introduces you to tools that you will probably use the most when creating drawings in your publications. When you draw with these tools, you are using strokes and fills to make designs. This section shows you what these common tools can do to help you create basic or complex illustrations in InDesign.

The Pencil tool

The Pencil tool is used to draw simple or complex shapes on a page. Because the pencil is a freeform tool, you can freely drag the Pencil tool all over the page and create lines or shapes, instead of having them automatically made for you like when you use basic shape tools. The pencil is a very intuitive and easy tool to use.

You find out how to use the pencil tool in the section "Drawing Freeform Paths," later in this chapter.

The Pen tool

The Pen tool is used to create complex shapes on the page. The Pen tool works together with other tools, such as the Add, Remove, and Convert

Point tools. The pen works by adding and editing points along a path, thereby manipulating the segments that join them.

Drawing with the Pen tool isn't easy at first. In fact, it takes many people a considerable amount of time to use this tool well. Don't get frustrated if you don't get used to it right away — the Pen tool can take some practice in order to get it to do what you want it to. You find out how to use the Pen tool in the "Drawing Freeform Paths" section, later in this chapter.

Get more practice with the Pen tool and creating paths in Book III, Chapter 4. Lucky for you, the Pen tool works generally the same in all the Adobe CS2 applications.

Basic shapes and frame shapes

Basic shapes are preformed shapes that you can add to a document by using tools in the toolbox. The basic shape tools include the Line, Rectangle, Ellipse, and Polygon tools.

You can also draw these shapes and turn them into *frames* (containers that hold content in your document) if you want. You may use a frame as a text frame, or as a graphic frame that is used to hold pictures and text. Draw a basic shape, and then convert the shape to a graphic or text frame by choosing Object⇨Content⇨Text or Object⇨Content⇨Graphic.

We discuss graphic and text frames in more detail in Chapters 3 and 4 of this minibook.

The Frame and Shape tools look the same and can even act the same. Both can hold text and images, but look out! By default, shapes created with the Frame tool have a 1 pt black stroke around them. Many folks don't see this on the screen but later discover that they have strokes around their text boxes when they print. Stick with the shape tools and you will be fine.

Drawing Shapes

InDesign allows you to create basic shapes in your document. You can easily create a basic shape by following these steps:

1. **Create a new document by choosing File⇨New.**

2. **When the New Document dialog box appears, click the OK button.**

A new document opens.

 3. **Select the Rectangle tool in the toolbox.**

The Rectangle tool becomes highlighted in the toolbox.

4. **Click anywhere in the page and drag the mouse diagonally.**

When the rectangle is the desired dimension, release the mouse button. You've created a rectangle.

That's all you need to do to create a basic shape. You can also use these steps with the other basic shape tools (the Line, Ellipse, and Polygon tools) to create other basic shapes. To access the other basic shapes from the tool-box, follow these steps:

1. **Click the Rectangle tool and hold down the mouse button.**

A menu with all the basic shapes opens.

2. **Release the mouse button.**

The menu remains open, and you can mouse over the menu items. The menu items become highlighted when the mouse pointer is over each item.

3. **Select a basic shape tool by clicking a highlighted menu item.**

The new basic shape tool is now active. Follow the preceding set of steps to create basic shapes using any of these tools.

To draw a square shape, use the Rectangle tool and press the Shift key while you drag the mouse on the page. The sides of the shape are all drawn at the same length, so you get a perfect square. You can also use the Shift key with the Ellipse tool if you want a perfect circle — just hold down Shift while you're using the Ellipse tool. Make sure you release your mouse before the Shift key for this constrain shape trick to work!

Creating a shape with exact dimensions

Dragging on the page to create a shape is easy, but making a shape with precise dimensions using this method requires a few more steps. If you want to make a shape that's a specific size, follow these steps:

1. **Select the Rectangle tool or the Ellipse tool.**

The tool is highlighted in the toolbox.

2. **Click anywhere on the page, but don't drag the cursor.**

This point becomes the upper-right corner of your Rectangle or Ellipse *bounding box* (the rectangle that defines the object's vertical and horizontal dimensions). After you click to place your corner, the Rectangle or Ellipse dialog box appears.

3. **In the Width and Height text fields, enter the dimensions you want the shape to be created at.**

4. **Click OK.**

The shape is created on the page, with the upper-right corner at the place where you initially clicked on the page.

Using the Polygon tool

A *polygon* is a shape that has many sides. For example, a square is a polygon with four sides, but the Polygon tool enables you to choose the number of sides you want for the polygon you create. When you're using the Polygon tool, you may not want to create a shape with the default number of sides. You can change these settings before you start drawing the shape.

To customize the shape of a polygon, follow these steps:

1. **Select the Polygon tool in the toolbox by selecting the Rectangle tool and holding down the mouse button until the menu pops up.**

The Polygon tool is highlighted after you select the tool.

2. **Double-click the Polygon tool in the toolbox.**

The Polygon Setting dialog box opens, as shown in Figure 2-4.

**Book II
Chapter 2**

**Drawing in
InDesign**

Figure 2-4:
The Polygon
Settings
dialog box.

3. **In the Number of Sides text field, enter the number of sides you want the new polygon to have.**

For example, enter **8** in the Number of Sides text field to create an octagon.

4. **If you want to create a star instead of a polygon, enter a number in the Star Inset text field for the percentage of the star inset you want the new shape to have.**

A higher percentage means the sides will be inset further towards the center of the polygon, creating a star. If you want a regular polygon and not a star, enter **0** in the Star Inset text field. If you want a star, enter **50%**, a starburst with about **25%**.

5. **Click OK.**

6. Move your cursor to the page and click and drag to create a new polygon or star.

Your new polygon or star appears on the page.

Figure 2-5 shows what a few different polygons and stars with different settings look like.

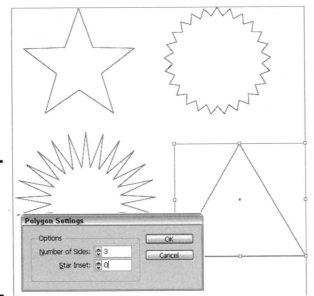

Figure 2-5: Change the star inset percentage and create different kinds of polygons.

Editing Basic Shapes

In this section, you find out how to edit basic shapes using several palettes in InDesign. This means you can create original shapes and craft exactly the kind of design you require in your page layout. You aren't stuck with the predetermined shapes, such as a square or oval: You can make these forms take on much more complicated or original shapes.

Changing the size using the Transform palette

You can change the size of a shape by using the Transform palette. Here's how:

1. With the Selection tool (the tool that's used to select objects), select the shape that you want to resize.

When the shape is selected, a bounding box appears around it. You can see a selected shape in Figure 2-6.

Bounding box

Selected object

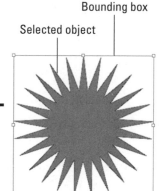

Figure 2-6:
A selected shape with a bounding box.

**Book II
Chapter 2**

Drawing in
InDesign

2. **Open the Transform palette by choosing Window⇨Object and Layout⇨Transform.**

   The Transform palette opens.

3. **Enter different number values in the W and H fields to change the size of the shape.**

   The shape changes size on the page automatically to the new size dimensions that you specify in the Transform palette.

Changing the stroke of a shape

You can also change the stroke of shapes you have created. The *stroke* is the outline that appears around the edge of the shape. The stroke can range from no stroke to a very thick stroke, and it's measured in point sizes.

Even if a shape has a stroke set to 0 points, it still has a stroke! You just can't see the stroke.

Follow these steps to edit the stroke of your shapes:

1. **Select a shape on the page.**

   A bounding box appears around the selected shape.

2. **Open the Stroke palette by choosing Window⇨Stroke.**

   The Stroke palette opens, as shown in Figure 2-7.

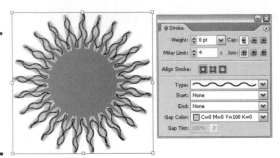

Figure 2-7:
Use the Stroke palette to change the shape's outline.

Note that you can quickly change many stroke attributes in the control palette as well!

3. Select a new width for the Stroke using the Weight drop-down list.

As soon as a value is selected, the stroke automatically changes on the page. This number is measured in points. You use some of the other options in the following exercise.

You can click in the Stroke text field and manually enter a numerical value for the Stroke width. The higher the number you enter, the thicker the stroke. You can also change the style of the stroke with the Stroke palette by following these steps:

1. With a basic shape selected, choose Window⇨Stroke to access the Stroke palette.

2. Choose Show Options from the palette menu, located on the upper-left corner of the palette.

If the options are already open, you see Hide Options in the menu instead, as shown in Figure 2-8. If that's the case, skip this step!

Figure 2-8:
Make sure the options are showing with the Stroke palette menu.

3. Choose a new line type from the Type drop-down list.

We chose Dashed. As soon as a value is selected, the stroke automatically changes, as shown in Figure 2-9.

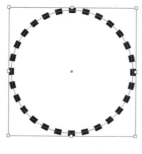

Figure 2-9:
The stroke now appears thick and dashed on this ellipse.

4. **Choose a new line weight from the Weight drop-down list.**

We chose 10 points. The ellipse automatically updates on the page.

Want to create custom dashes? Notice at the bottom of the Stroke palette that when a dash stroke is selected, you can define the dash and gap size. Enter one value for an even dash, or several numbers for custom dashes for maps diagrams, fold marks, and more!

Add special ends to the lines using the Start and End drop-down lists. For example, you can add an arrowhead or large circle to the beginning or end of the stroke. The Cap and Join buttons allow you to choose the shape of the line ends, and how they join with other paths when you are working with complex paths or shapes. For more information on creating and editing lines and strokes, see Book I, Chapter 6.

Changing the shear value

You can change the shear of a shape by using the Transform palette. *Skew* and *shear* are the same thing — it means that the shape is slanted, so you create the appearance of some form of perspective for the skewed or sheared element. This transformation is useful if you want to create the illusion of depth on the page. Follow these simple steps to skew a shape:

1. **With a basic shape selected, choose Window⇨>Object and Layout⇨ Transform.**

The Transform palette opens.

2. **Select a value from the Shear drop-down list (the drop-down list in the lower-right corner of the Transform palette), as shown in Figure 2-10.**

After selecting a new value, the shape skews (or shears), depending on what value you select. Manually entering a numerical value into this field also skews the shape.

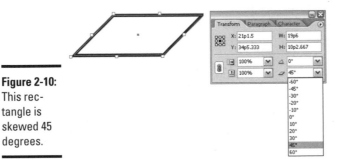

Figure 2-10:
This rectangle is skewed 45 degrees.

Rotating a shape

You can change the rotation of a shape by using the Transform palette. The process of rotating a shape is very similar to how you skew a shape (see the preceding section):

1. **With a basic shape selected, choose Window⇨Object and Layout⇨ Transform.**

   The Transform palette opens.

2. **Select a value from the Rotation drop-down list, as shown in Figure 2-11.**

   After selecting a new value, the shape automatically rotates, based on the rotation angle you specified. You can also manually enter a value into the text field.

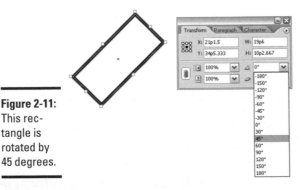

Figure 2-11:
This rectangle is rotated by 45 degrees.

These are only a few of the ways you can edit basic shapes in InDesign. You can edit shapes and manipulate their appearance in other ways. We cover some of these ways, such as editing fills, in the later section, "Using Fills."

Drawing Freeform Paths

Different tools can be used to draw paths. For example, you can use the Pencil tool to draw freeform paths. These kinds of paths typically look like lines, and the Pencil and Pen tools can be used to create simple or complex paths.

Using the Pencil tool

The Pencil tool is perhaps the easiest tool to use when drawing freeform paths (see Figure 2-12). Follow these easy steps to get started:

1. **Create a new Document by choosing File⇨New and clicking OK in the New Document dialog box that appears.**

2. **Select the Pencil tool in the toolbox.**

The Pencil tool is highlighted in the toolbox.

3. **Drag the cursor around the page.**

You have created a new path by using the Pencil tool.

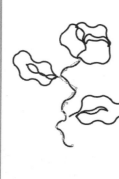

Figure 2-12: Paths created using the Pencil tool. The strokes are the wavy style.

Using the Pen tool

Using the Pen tool is different from using the Pencil tool. When you start out, the Pen tool may seem a bit complicated — but after you get the hang of it, using the Pen tool isn't too hard after all. The Pen tool uses points to create a particular path. These points can be edited in order to change the segments between them. This can take a bit of practice. To create points and segments on a page, follow these steps:

1. **Close any existing documents and create a new Document by choosing File➪New Document. Click OK in the New Document dialog box that appears.**

   A new document opens using the default settings.

2. **Select the Pen tool in the toolbox.**

   The Pen tool is then highlighted in the toolbox.

3. **Click anywhere on the page, and then click a second location. Ctrl-click (Windows) or ⌘-click (Mac) on an empty part of the Page to deselect the current path.**

   You have created a new path with two points and one segment joining them with the Pen tool. After you deselect the path, it means you can create a new path or add new points to the path you just created.

4. **Add a new point to the segment by hovering over the line and clicking.**

   A small + icon appears next to the Pen tool's cursor, as shown on the left in Figure 2-13. You can also do the same thing by selecting the Add Anchor Point tool (located in the menu that flies out when you click and hold the Pen icon in the toolbox).

Figure 2-13:
Adding a
point to a
path (left)
and creating
a curved
path (right).

5. **Repeat Step 4, but this time click a new location on a line segment and drag away from the line.**

   This creates a curved path, as shown on the right in Figure 2-13.

   The segments change and curve depending on where the points are located along the path. The point you created is called a curve point.

Editing Freeform Paths

Even the best artists sometimes need to make changes or delete parts of their work. If you have made mistakes or change your mind about a drawing you have made, follow the steps in this section to make your changes.

In order to change a path segment, you need to select a point with the Direct Selection tool (upper right of the toolbox). When a point is selected, it appears solid; unselected points appear hollow. You can see this difference in Figure 2-14.

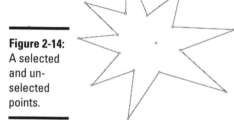

Figure 2-14:
A selected
and un-
selected
points.

All you need to do to select a point is use your cursor to click the point itself. Then you can use the handles that appear when the point is selected to modify the segments as follows:

1. **Select the Direct Selection tool from the toolbox, and then click a point.**

   The selected point appears solid and if a curve, could have handles extending from it, as shown in Figure 2-15.

Figure 2-15:
The Direct
Selection
tool and a
selected
point with
handles.

2. Select a handle end and drag the handle left or right.

The path changes, depending on how you drag the handles, as shown in Figure 2-16.

Figure 2-16:
Editing a corner point and editing a curved point.

A curved point and a corner point edit differently when you select and drag them. Curve points have handles that extend from the point, but corner points don't. However, you can edit a corner point without needing handles by dragging it in any direction. Figure 2-16 shows the difference between a corner point and a curved point when editing their shapes.

To understand how the Convert Point tool works the best, you should have a path that contains both straight and curved segments.

Follow these steps to change a corner point into a curved point and vice versa:

1. Select the Convert Direction Point tool.

This tool resides in a menu under the Pen tool in the toolbox. Hold the mouse button down over the Pen tool icon until a menu appears; select the Convert Direction Point tool from the menu.

2. Click a curved point with the Convert Direction Point tool.

The point you click changes into a corner point, which changes the path's appearance.

3. Click and drag a corner point with the Convert Direction Point tool.

The point is modified as a curved point. This changes the appearance of the path again.

As you can see, this tool is handy when you need to alter the way your path changes direction. If you need to manipulate a point in a different way, you may need to change its type by using the Convert Direction Point tool.

Making Corner Effects

You can use corner effects on basic shapes to customize the shape's look. Corner effects are great for adding an interesting look to borders. You can be very creative with some of the shapes you apply effects to or by applying more than one effect to a single shape.

Here's how to create a corner effect on a rectangle:

1. **Select the Rectangle tool and create a new rectangle anywhere on the page.**

Hold the Shift key when using the Rectangle tool if you want to create a square.

2. **With the Selection tool, select the shape, and then choose Object⇨ Corner Effects.**

The Corner Effects dialog box opens.

3. **Choose an effect from the Effect drop-down list and enter a value into the Size text field.**

To create the corner effect shown in Figure 2-17, we chose Fancy from the Effect drop-down list and entered **2** in the Size field.

4. **Click OK.**

The corner effect is applied to the shape.

**Book II
Chapter 2**

**Drawing in
InDesign**

Figure 2-17:
A corner
effect
changes
a dull
rectangle
into an
interesting
shape.

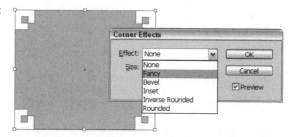

Using Fills

A fill is located inside a path. You can fill your paths and shapes with several different kinds of colors, transparent colors, or even gradients. Fills can help you achieve artistic effects, illusions of depth, or add interest to a page design.

You may have already created a fill! In the toolbox, there are two swatches: one for the stroke (a hollow square) and one for fill (a solid box). Refer to Figure 1-5 in Chapter 1 of this minibook to locate the Fill and Stroke boxes. If the Fill box contains a color, your shape will have a fill when it is created. If the Fill box has a red line through it, the shape is created without a fill.

Creating basic fills

You can create a basic fill in several different ways. One of the most common ways is to specify a color in the Fill swatch before you create a new shape. To create a shape with a fill, follow these steps:

1. **Open the Color palette by choosing Window⇨Color.**

The Color palette opens or becomes active in the workspace.

2. **Select a color in the Color palette.**

You can enter values into the CMYK fields manually or by using the sliders. Alternatively, you can use the Eyedropper tool to select a color from the color ramp at the bottom of the Color palette. For more information on color modes (such as CMYK and RGB color modes), refer to Book I, Chapter 7.

Use the Color palette menu to select different color modes if CMYK is not already selected. Click and hold the arrow button, and select CMYK from the Color palette menu, as shown in Figure 2-18.

Figure 2-18: Select a color mode in the Color palette menu.

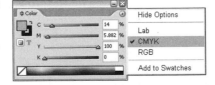

3. **When you are finished, click OK.**

The Fill box in the toolbox is updated with the new color you have selected in the Color palette.

4. **Create a new shape on the page.**

Select a shape tool and drag on the page to create a shape. The shape is filled with the fill color you chose.

As in the other Creative Suite 2 applications, you can create tints of a color built with CMYK by holding down the Shift key while dragging any color's slider. All color sliders will then move proportionally.

You can also choose to use color swatches to select a fill color by using the Swatches palette (choose Window⇨Swatches to open the Swatches palette). Create a new color swatch (of your present color) by clicking the New Swatch button at the bottom of the panel. Double-click the new swatch to add new color properties by using sliders to set CMYK color values or by entering numbers into each text field.

Perhaps you already have a shape without a fill, and you want to add a fill to it. Select the shape, and then choose a fill color for the Fill box in the toolbox. A new fill color is applied to the shape.

You can drag and drop a swatch color to fill a shape on a page, even if that shape isn't selected. Open the Swatches palette by choosing Window⇨ Swatches, and then drag the color swatch over to the shape. Release the mouse button, and the fill color is automatically applied to the shape.

Making transparent fills

Fills that are partially transparent can create some very interesting effects for the layout of your document. You can set transparency to more than one element on the page and layer those elements to create the illusion of depth and stacking.

Follow these steps to apply transparency to an element on the page:

1. **With the Selection tool, select a shape on the page.**

A bounding box appears around the selected shape.

2. **Open the Transparency palette by choosing Window⇨Transparency.**

The Transparency palette opens.

3. **Use the Opacity slider to change how transparent the shape appears.**

Click the arrow to open the slider, or click in the text field to manually enter a value using the keyboard. The effect is immediately applied to the selected shape.

The same transparency settings are applied to both fill and stroke. You cannot have separate transparency settings for a fill and a stroke when both of them are part of the same object. If you want this effect, use Adobe Illustrator for your object.

Looking at gradients

A *gradient* is the color transition from one color (or no color) to a different color. A gradient can have two or more colors in the transition.

Gradients can add interesting effects to shapes, including 3D effects, such as making a circle appear to be a rounded ball. Sometimes you can use a gradient to achieve glowing effects or the effect of light hitting a surface. The two kinds of gradients available in InDesign are radial and linear, as shown in Figure 2-19:

✦ **Radial:** A transition of colors in a circular fashion from a center point radiating outwards.

✦ **Linear:** A transition of colors along a straight path.

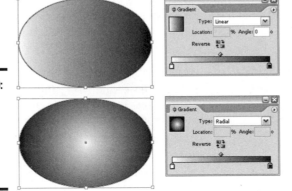

Figure 2-19: A linear gradient (top) and a radial gradient (bottom).

You can apply a gradient to a stroke a fill or even text. To apply a gradient to a stroke, simply have the stroke selected instead of the fill. Even though you can apply a gradient to the stroke of live text, you will create a printing nightmare . . . use these features sparingly!

Here's how to add a gradient fill to a shape:

1. **Using the Selection tool, select the object that you want to apply a gradient to, and then open the Swatches palette by choosing Window⇨Swatches.**

The Swatches palette opens.

2. **Choose New Gradient Swatch from the Swatches palette menu.**

The New Gradient Swatch dialog box opens, as shown in Figure 2-20. Note in Figure 2-19 that the gradient palette can also be used to create Gradients. Access it by choosing Window➪Gradient.

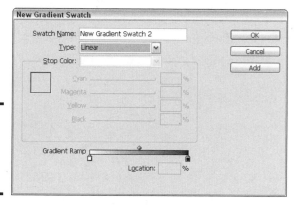

Figure 2-20: The New Gradient Swatch dialog box.

3. **Type a new name for the swatch into the Swatch Name field.**

Sometimes giving the swatch a descriptive name, such as what the swatch is being used for, is helpful.

4. **Choose Linear or Radial from the Type drop-down list.**

This option determines the type of gradient the swatch will create each time you use it. We chose Radial from the drop-down list.

5. **Manipulate the gradient stops below the Gradient Ramp to position each color in the gradient.**

Gradient stops are the color chips located below the Gradient Ramp. You can move the diamond shape above the Gradient Ramp to determine the center point of the gradient. You can select each gradient stop to change the color and move them around to edit the gradient. When the gradient stops are selected, you can change the color values in the Stop Color area by using sliders or by entering values in each CMYK text field.

You can add a new color to the gradient by clicking the area between the gradient stops. Then the new stop can be edited just like the others. To remove the gradient stop, drag the stop away from the Gradient Ramp.

6. **Click OK when you're finished.**

The gradient swatch is created and applied to the selected object.

To edit a gradient, double-click the gradient's swatch. This opens the Gradient Options dialog box, which allows you to modify the settings made in the New Gradient Swatch dialog box.

Removing fills

Even easier than creating fills is removing them:

1. **Select the shape using the Selection tool.**

A bounding box appears around the shape.

2. **Click the Fill box in the toolbox.**

3. **Click the Apply None button located below the Fill box.**

This button is white with a red line through it. The fill is removed from the selected shape, and the Fill box is changed to no fill.

Adding Layers

Layers are like transparent sheets that are stacked on top of one another. If you add layers to your drawings, you can create the appearance that graphics are stacked on top of one another. The Layers palette allows you to create new layers, delete layers you don't need, or even rearrange them to change the stacking order. Here's how you work with layers in InDesign:

1. **Open the Layers palette by choosing Window⇨Layers.**

The Layers palette opens, as shown in Figure 2-21. This palette allows you to create, delete, and arrange layers in the publication.

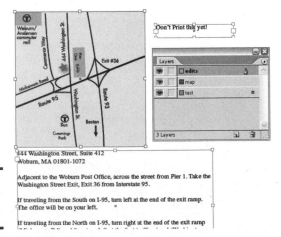

Figure 2-21: The Layers palette.

2. **Draw a shape on the page using a shape tool.**

Create the shape anywhere on the page. Create it large enough so that you can easily stack another shape on top of part of it.

3. **Create a new layer by clicking the Create New Layer button in the Layers palette.**

   A new layer is added in the Layers palette. The new layer is stacked on top of the currently selected layer and becomes the active layer.

   Double-click on a layer to give it an appropriate name, or even better yet hold down Alt (Windows) or Option (Mac OS) key and click the New Layer button to bring up the Layer options dialog box before the layer is created.

   Make sure that the layer you want to create content on is selected before you start modifying the layer. You can tell what layer is selected because the selected layer is always highlighted in the Layers palette. It is very easy to accidentally add content to the incorrect layer if you don't check this palette frequently. If you add an item to the wrong layer, you can always cut and paste items to the correct layer.

   Delete a layer by selecting it and clicking the Delete Selected Layers button (it looks like a trash can). Click the Eye icon to make the layer invisible. You can lock a layer by clicking the empty box next to the Eye (*visibility* or *show*) icon.

4. **Make sure a shape tool is still selected, and then create a shape on the new layer by dragging the cursor so that part of the new shape covers the shape you created in Step 2.**

   The new shape is stacked on top of the shape you created earlier. This is because the new shape is on a layer that is higher in the stacking order. Your layered shapes should look similar to what's shown in Figure 2-22.

Book II Chapter 2

Drawing in InDesign

Figure 2-22: Two shapes are layered on top of each other.

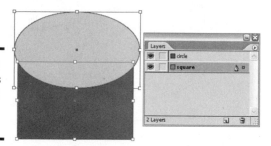

Stacking layers on top of each other allows you to create images that overlap. This can help you add a feeling of depth and height to your drawing in InDesign. Not only can you stack drawing objects, but you can also layer and arrange imported images and text. We cover this in more detail in Chapter 4 of this minibook. Layers are also used to help group similar objects in one place, making it easier to work with your publication files.

Chapter 3: Working with Text and Text Frames

In This Chapter

✔ Understanding text and frames in a publication

✔ Adding and importing text

✔ Exploring text frame options

✔ Modifying text frames

✔ Changing paragraph settings

✔ Editing with text editors and spell checking

✔ Working with tables

✔ Creating and editing text on a path

Most of your publications will contain text, so knowing how to use and modify text is very important in InDesign. Text is made up of characters, and the characters are styled in a particular font. If you're wondering about fonts, check out Book I, Chapter 6, where we explain more about fonts and font faces. Book III, Chapter 5 explains manipulating text in Illustrator.

This chapter explains how InDesign uses text in publications and gets you started editing and manipulating text in *text frames* — containers on the page that hold text content. The most important thing you can take away from this chapter is how to add text to your publication, and then change the text so that it looks how you want it to look when laid out on the page. In Chapter 4 of this minibook, you find out how to create effective layouts that contain both text and graphics so that your audience will be encouraged to read everything you have to say!

Understanding Text, Font, and Frames

Text is usually integral to a publication because it contains specific information you want or need to convey to an audience. Understanding some of the terminology that appears in the following pages is important: *Text* and *font* refer to similar things, although they're quite different from each other in the specifics:

✦ **Text:** The letters, words, sentences, and/or paragraphs making up content within the text frames in your publication.

✦ **Font:** The particular design forming a set of characters used for text. You can find thousands of styles of fonts to choose from and install on your computer for your use. Font is sometimes known as *type*. For more information on type, refer to Book III, Chapter 5.

Frames are like containers that are used to hold content. You can use the following two kinds of frames together in a publication:

✦ **Text frame:** Contains text in a publication. You can link text frames so that text flows from one text frame to another, and you can have text wrap around graphic frames.

✦ **Graphic frame:** A graphic frame holds an image that you place into your publication.

The nice thing about shapes and frames is that they automatically change to adapt to the content that is placed in them! Both the Frame tools and Shape tools can be used for text and graphics.

Find out how to use graphics in your publication in Chapter 4 of this minibook.

Creating and Using Text Frames

Text frames contain any text that you add to a publication. You can create a new text frame in many different ways. InDesign also allows you to add text to creative shapes that you draw, thereby changing them into text frames. Creating and using text frames in your publication is important because you will typically use a lot of text. Throughout this section, we show you how to create text frames in different but important ways using three different tools. (If you need a refresher on the InDesign tools, check out Chapter 1 of this minibook.)

Text frames are sometimes automatically created when you import text into a publication. You find out how to do this in the "Importing text" section, later in this chapter.

Creating text frames with the Type tool

You can use the Type tool to create a text frame. If you take the Type tool and click the page, nothing happens unless you've first created a frame to put text in. Here's how to create a text frame using the Type tool:

1. **Select the Type tool in the toolbox and place it over the page.**

The Type tool cursor appears, as shown in Figure 3-1. The cursor is an I-bar. Move the cursor to where you want the upper-left corner of your text frame to be.

**Book II
Chapter 3**

**Working with Text
and Text Frames**

Figure 3-1:
With the
Type tool
selected,
click and
drag to
create a
text frame.

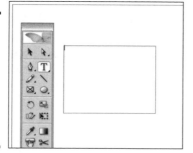

2. **Drag diagonally to create a text frame.**

When you click, the mouse has a cross-like appearance. When you drag, an outline of the text frame appears, giving you a reference to its dimensions (refer to Figure 3-1).

3. **Release the mouse button when the frame is the correct size.**

The text frame is created, and an insertion point is placed in the upper-left corner of the frame. You can start typing on the keyboard to enter text or import text from another source. (We cover this process in the later section appropriately named, "Importing text.")

Creating text frames with the Frame tool

You can use the Frame tool to create frames that are rectangular, oval, or polygonal. Then, after you've placed the frame on the page, you can turn it into a text frame or back into a graphic frame. To create a new text frame with the Frame tool, follow these steps:

1. **Choose the Frame tool from the toolbox and drag diagonally to create a new frame.**

   A new frame is created on the page.

2. **Select the Type tool and click inside of the frame.**

   The X across the frame disappears, and the frame is now a text frame instead of a graphic frame.

   An insertion point appears in the upper-left corner of the text frame. If you start typing, the frame fills with text.

3. **Choose the Selection tool and use it to move the text frame.**

   You can move the text frame to a new location if you click within the frame using the Selection tool and drag it to a new location. An outline of the frame moves with the cursor, as shown in Figure 3-2, so you can see where the text frame is placed when you release the mouse button.

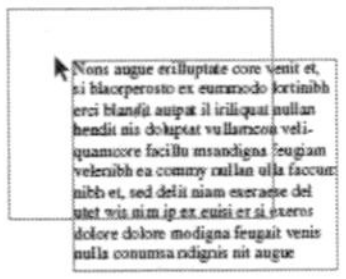

Figure 3-2:
An outline of the text frame shows where you're moving the frame.

Creating text frames from a shape

If you have an interesting shape that you've created with the drawing tools that we discuss in Chapter 2 of this minibook, you can easily change that shape into a text frame. You can then add text within the shape. Just follow these steps:

1. **With the Pen, Pencil, or a shape tool, create a shape with a stroke color and no fill.**

   A shape is created on the page that does not have a solid color for the fill. We used the Pencil tool to create a freeform shape for this example.

2. **Select the Type tool from the toolbox.**

The Type tool becomes active.

3. **Click within the shape you created in Step 1 and enter some text.**

This changes the shape into a text frame that you can enter text into. Notice how the text is confined within the shape as you type, as shown in Figure 3-3.

Figure 3-3:
A shape
converted
into a text
frame.

Adding Text to Your Publication

In the previous section's step lists, we show you how to add text simply by clicking in the text frame and typing new content. You can add text to your publications in other ways, which is particularly useful when you use other applications to edit documents containing text.

Importing text

In the previous section, we show you how to enter text directly into a text frame in InDesign. You can also import text that you have created and/or edited using other software, such as Microsoft Word, Microsoft Excel, or Adobe InCopy (used for word processing). Importing externally edited text is a typical workflow when creating a publication, as dedicated text editing software is frequently used to edit manuscripts before they go to layout. To import text into InDesign, follow these steps:

1. **Choose File➪Place.**

The Place dialog box opens. Choose an importable file (such as a Word document, InCopy story, or a plain text file) by browsing through your hard drive.

2. **Select a document to import and click the Open button.**

The Place Text icon replaces the cursor arrow. Move the cursor around the page to where you want the upper-left corner of the text frame to be created when the document is imported.

3. **Click to place the imported text.**

This creates a text frame and imports the story into InDesign.

If you select a text frame *before* importing text, the text is automatically placed inside the text frame — so, in this case, you wouldn't have to use the cursor to place the text. You can move the text frame anywhere on the page after the text is added, or resize the frame, if necessary.

Controlling text flow

Control the flow of the text by using these simple modifier keys while placing text:

✦ Choose File➪Place, select the text you want to import, and choose OK. Hold down the Shift key when clicking to place the text. The text is imported and automatically flows from column to column or page to page until it runs out. InDesign even creates the pages for you if you don't have enough ready.

✦ Choose File➪Place, select the text you wish to import and choose OK. Hold down the Alt (Windows) or Option (Mac OS). Then click and drag a text area (don't let go of that Alt or Option key!). You can continue clicking and dragging additional text frames and your text will flow from one text frame to another until you run out of copy!

If you check Show Import Options in the Place window, see Figure 3-4, a second window appears in which you can choose to Remove Styles and formatting from text and tables. This will then bring in clean, unformatted text for you to control.

Figure 3-4:
Check Show
Import
Options
to open a
second
window for
more control
on the text
import.

Adding placeholder text

Suppose you're creating a publication, but the text you need to import into the publication isn't ready to import into InDesign yet (perhaps it's still being created or edited). Instead of waiting for the final text, you can use placeholder text and continue to create your publication's layout. *Placeholder text* is commonly used to temporarily fill a document with text. The text looks a lot like normal blocks of text, which is more natural than trying to paste the same few words in over and over to fill up a text frame. However, placeholder text is actually not in any particular language at all because it's just being used as filler.

InDesign has the ability to add placeholder text into a text frame automatically. Here's how you do it:

Book II
Chapter 3

1. **Create a frame on the page by selecting the Type tool and dragging diagonally to create a text frame.**

   A text frame is created on the page with an insertion point active. If you create a frame using the Frame tool, remember to click the frame using the Type tool or choose Object⇨Content⇨Text to convert it into a text frame before moving on to Step 2.

2. **Choose Type⇨Fill with Placeholder Text.**

   The text frame is automatically filled with characters and words, similar to Figure 3-5.

Figure 3-5:
The text frame is filled with placeholder text.

Andover Happenings

Copying and pasting text

Another way to move text from one application into your publication is by copying and pasting the text directly into InDesign. If you select and copy text in another program, you can paste it directly into InDesign from your computer's Clipboard. Here's how:

1. **Highlight the text that you want to use in your publication and press Ctrl+C (Windows) or ⌘+C (Mac) to copy the text.**

When you copy the text, it sits on the Clipboard until it's replaced with something new. This means that you can transfer this information into InDesign.

2. **Open InDesign and press Ctrl+V (Windows) or ⌘+V (Mac) to create a new text frame and paste the text into it.**

A new text frame appears centered on the page with your selected text inside it.

You can also click in a text frame and press Ctrl+V (Windows) or ⌘+V (Mac) to paste text from the Clipboard directly into an existing frame. You can do the same thing with an image, as well.

All you need to do is double-click a text frame if you want to access, edit, type, or paste some text into it.

Looking at Text Frame Options

In the previous sections of this chapter, we show you how to create text frames and enter text into them. In this section, we show you how to organize text frames in your publication and achieve results you need. Controlling text frames so that they do what you need them to do is a matter of knowing how they work after you have text in them.

You're given a lot of control over the text in your publication. Changing text frame options allows you to change the way text is placed inside a frame. Changing these kinds of settings is sometimes important when you're working with particular kinds of fonts. (To read more about fonts, check out Book I, Chapter 6, where we discuss graphics, strokes, text, and fonts.)

The text frame contextual menu contains many options for the text frame. This menu allows you to perform basic commands, such as copy and paste, fill the text frame with placeholder text, make transformations, add or modify strokes, and change the kind of frame it is. Access the text frame's contextual menu by right-clicking (Windows) or Control+clicking (Mac) a text frame. You can also find most of these options in the Type and Object menus, as well.

Changing text frame options

To change text frame options that control the look of the text within the frame, follow these steps:

1. **Create a rectangular text frame on the page, select the frame, and choose Edit⇨Text Frame Options.**

You can also press Ctrl+B (Windows) or ⌘+B (Mac) or use the text frame's contextual menu to open the Text Frame Options dialog box.

You can tell that a text frame is selected when it has handles around its bounding box.

The Text Frame Options dialog box appears, shown in Figure 3-6, showing you the current settings for the selected text frame.

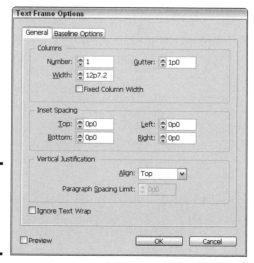

Figure 3-6:
The Text
Frame
Options
dialog box.

2. **Select the Preview check box to automatically view updates.**

Now any changes you make in the dialog box are instantly updated on the page. This means you can make your changes and see how they will look before you apply them.

3. In the Inset Spacing area of the dialog box, change the Top, Bottom, Left, and Right values.

These values are used to inset text from the edges of the text frame. The text is pushed inside the frame edge by the value you set, as shown in Figure 3-7 (for this example, we used 1p0). You can also indent your text, which we discuss in the section, "Indenting your text," later in this chapter. You can also choose how to align the text vertically (Top, Center, Bottom, or Justify) using this dialog box. You can align the text to the top or bottom of the text frame, center it vertically in the frame, or evenly space the lines in the frame from top to bottom (Justify).

4. When you're finished making changes in this dialog box, click OK.

The changes you made are applied to the text frame.

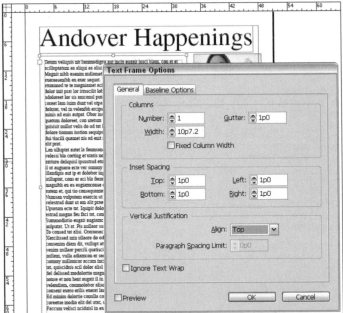

Figure 3-7:
The text frame's contents are inset 1 point on all sides.

Using and modifying columns

You can specify that the document contain a certain number of columns on the page when you create a new publication. This allows you to snap new text frames to the columns so that they are properly spaced on the page. You can even modify the amount of the *gutter,* which is the spacing between the columns.

You can also create columns within a single text frame by using the Text Frame Options dialog box (refer to Figure 3-6). You can add up to 40 columns in a single text frame. If you already have text in a frame, it's automatically divided amongst the columns you add. The following steps show you how to add columns to a text frame on a page:

1. **Create a rectangular text frame on the page.**

   Use the Text or Frame tool to create the text frame. Columns can be created in text frames that are rectangular, oval, or even freehand shapes drawn on the page.

2. **Select the text frame and enter some text.**

   You can type some text in, paste text copied from another document, or add placeholder text by choosing Text⇨Insert Placeholder Text.

3. **With the text frame still selected, choose Object⇨Text Frame Options.**

   The Text Frame Options dialog box opens. Be sure to select the Preview check box in the dialog box, which enables you to immediately view the changes your settings make to the frame on the page.

4. **In the Columns section, change the value in the Number text field.**

   In this example, we entered **2** in the Number text field. The selected text frame divides the text in the frame into two columns.

5. **Change the width of the columns by entering a new value in the Width text field.**

   The width of the columns is automatically set, depending on the width of the text frame you created. We entered **10** (picas) in the Width text field for this example. The text frame changes size depending on the width you set in this column. When you click in a different text field in the dialog box, the text frame updates on the page to reflect the new value setting. It should look similar to the text frame shown in Figure 3-8.

6. **Change the value in the Gutter text field.**

   The gutter value controls how large the space is in between columns. If the gutter is too wide, change the value in the Gutter text field to a lower number. We entered **0p5** in the Gutter text field for this example to change the gutter to half a point in width.

7. **When you're finished, click OK to apply the changes.**

   The changes are applied to the text frame you modified.

After you create the columns in the text frame, you can resize the frame by using the handles on its bounding box, which is detailed in the later section, "Resizing and moving the text frame." The columns resize as necessary to divide the text frame into the number of columns you specified in the Text Frame Options dialog box. If you select the Fixed Column Width check box in the Text Frame Options dialog box, your text frames will always be the width you specify, no matter how you resize the text frame. When resizing the text frame, the frame snaps to the designated fixed width.

Figure 3-8:
This text frame has two columns, with a gutter of 0p5.

You can also change the columns of a selected text frame using the control palette. The Number of columns box is in the upper-left corner, as shown in Figure 3-9.

Figure 3-9:
You can change the number of columns in a selected text frame using the Control palette.

Modifying and Connecting Text Frames on a Page

Making modifications to text frames and then connecting them to other text frames in a publication so that the story can continue on a separate page is vital in most publications. You will typically be working with stories of many paragraphs that need to continue on different pages in the document.

When you have a text frame on the page, you need to be able to change the size, position, and linking of the frame. You need to link the frame to other frames on the page so that the text can flow between them. This is important if you're creating a layout that contains a lot of text.

If you paste more text content than is visible in the text frame, the text still exists beyond the boundaries of the text frame — so if you have a text frame that is 20 lines tall, but you paste 50 lines of text in, the last 30 lines of text isn't cropped off. You need to resize the text frame, or have the text flow to another frame, in order to see the rest of the text you pasted in. You can tell that the frame has more content when you see a small plus sign (+) in a special handle on the text frame's bounding box.

**Book II
Chapter 3**

**Working with Text
and Text Frames**

Resizing and moving the text frame

When creating most layouts, you regularly resize text frames and move them around the document while you figure out how you want the page layout to look. You can resize and move a text frame by following these steps:

1. **Use the Selection tool to select a text frame on the page.**

   A bounding box with handles appears on the page. If the text frame has more text than it can show at the current size, a small handle with a red box appears on the bounding box. Therefore, this handle cannot be used to resize the text frame.

2. **Drag one of the handles to resize the text frame.**

   The frame automatically updates on the page as you drag the handles, as shown in Figure 3-10. Change the width or height by dragging the handles at the center of each side of the frame, or change the height and the width at the same time by dragging a corner handle.

   Shift+drag a corner handle to scale the text frame proportionally.

3. **When you're finished resizing the text frame, click the middle of a selected frame and move it around the page.**

   If you click within the frame once and drag it, you move the frame around the page. An outline of the frame follows your cursor and represents where the frame is placed if you release the mouse button. Simply release the frame when you're finished moving it.

Figure 3-10:
Resize a text frame by dragging the handles of the bounding box.

What's Inside?
Calender 2
School Activities 3
After School fun 3
Volunteer opportunities 4

If you're using guides or grids on the page, the text frame snaps to them. Also, if you opened a document with columns, the text frame snaps to the columns when you drag the frame close to the column guidelines. You can find out about guides, grids, and snapping in Chapter 4 of this minibook.

You can also use the Transform palette in order to change the location and dimensions of a text frame. If the Transform palette is not already open, choose Window➪Object and Layout➪Transform to open the palette, and then follow these steps:

1. **Change the values in the X and Y text fields.**

Enter **1** in both the X and Y text fields to move the text frame to the upper-left corner of the page.

The X and Y coordinates (location) of the text frame update to 1,1. A small square can be seen in the middle of the text frame. This is the reference point of the text frame, meaning that the X and Y coordinates you set match the position of this point of the text frame.

Change the reference point by clicking on any point in the reference point indicator in the upper left of the Control palette.

2. **Change the values in the W and H text fields.**

For this example, we entered **35** (picas) in the W and H text fields. The text frame's width and height changes to the dimensions you specify. Using the Transform panel to change the width and height is ideal if you need to set an exact measurement for the frame.

Not only can you resize and move text frames, you can also change their shape. Select a text frame and choose the Direct Selection tool from the toolbox. The corners on the text frame can then be selected and moved to reshape the text frame.

Threading text frames

Understanding how to thread text frames together is very important if you plan to build page layouts with a lot of text. *Threading* is when text frames are arranged so that the text in one frame continues on in a second text frame. This is useful for most layouts because you won't always be able to include all of your text in a single frame.

First, you should take a look at some of the terminology because Adobe has some special names it likes to use for text frames that are linked together. Figure 3-11 shows some of the icons that we refer to in the following list:

✦ **Flowing:** When text starts in one frame and continues in a second frame.

✦ **Threading:** When two text frames have text flowing from the first to the second frame, the text frames are considered to be threaded.

✦ **Story:** The group of sentences and paragraphs you have in a threaded text frame or frames.

✦ **In port:** An icon on the upper-left side of a text frame's bounding box that allows you to tell whether a frame is the first frame in a story or has text flowing in from another frame. An in port icon has a story flowing into it if it contains a small arrow; otherwise, the in port icon is empty.

✦ **Out port:** An icon on the lower-right side of the text frame's bounding box that allows you to tell whether a frame has text flowing out of it. The out port icon contains a small arrow if the frame is threaded to another frame; an empty out port icon signifies the frame is not connected to another text frame.

If a text frame is not connected to another frame and has *overset text* (more text than can be displayed in a text frame), the out port shows a small red + icon.

An out port with text flowing into another frame

Figure 3-11:
The in port
and the out
port depict
threaded
text frames.
A special
icon shows
if text
extends past
the text
frame and is
not threaded
to another
frame.

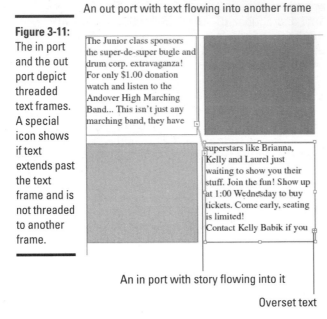

The Junior class sponsors the super-de-super bugle and drum corp. extravaganza! For only $1.00 donation watch and listen to the Andover High Marching Band... This isn't just any marching band, they have

superstars like Brianna, Kelly and Laurel just waiting to show you their stuff. Join the fun! Show up at 1:00 Wednesday to buy tickets. Come early, seating is limited! Contact Kelly Babik if you

An in port with story flowing into it

Overset text

Find a block of text that you want to thread (if you use a block of text that has formed sentences, as opposed to placeholder text, the process of connecting text and threading it through multiple frames is better illustrated), and then follow these steps:

1. **Copy some text onto the Clipboard, such as text from the InDesign help files, a page loaded in a Web browser window, or a document you have in Word, Notepad, or SimpleText.**

   It doesn't matter what kind of content you're pasting in. You only need to make sure the text is a few paragraphs long so that you have enough text to flow between frames.

   In Figure 3-11, you can see the text thread represented with a line connecting one text frame to another. InDesign will show you text threads if you choose View⇨Show Text Threads.

2. **Use the Type tool to create two text frames on a page.**

   The text frames can be above or beside one another, similar to the layout in Figure 3-12.

3. **Using the Text tool, click in the first text frame, which should be above or to the left of the second text frame.**

   A blinking insertion point appears in the first text frame, allowing you to enter or paste text into the frame.

The Junior class sponsors the super-de-super bugle and drum corp. extravaganza! For only $1.00 donation watch and listen to the Andover High Marching Band... This isn't just any marching band, they have

Figure 3-12: Two frames on the page; the first frame contains text.

4. **Press Ctrl+V (Windows) or ⌘+V (Mac) to paste the text into the text frame.**

The text you have copied on the Clipboard enters into the frame. If you have pasted enough text, you should see the overset text icon (a red +) on the lower-right side of the text frame, as shown in Figure 3-12. If you don't see the overset text icon, use the paste command a second time so that more text is entered into the frame.

5. **Click the overset text icon.**

The cursor changes into the loaded text icon. This icon means you can select or create another text frame to thread the story.

6. **Move the cursor over the second text frame and click.**

The cursor changes into the thread text icon when it's poised over the second text frame. When you click the second text frame, the two frames are threaded because the text continues in the second frame.

You can continue creating more frames and threading them. They can be threaded on the same page or on subsequent pages in the document.

You can *unthread* text as well, which means you are breaking the link between two text frames. You can rearrange which frames are used to thread text, such as changing what page the story continues on when it's threaded to a second text frame. Break the connection by double-clicking the in port or the out port icon of the text frame that you want to unthread. The frame is then unthreaded (but no text is deleted).

TIP

If you don't have multiple pages in your document, choose File↔Document Setup. Change the value in the Number of Pages text field to 2 or greater and click OK when you're finished. Now you can click through the pages using the Page Field control at the bottom of the workspace.

Adding a page jump number

If you have multiple pages, you can add a *page jump number* (text that notifies a reader where the story continues if it jumps to a text frame on another page) to an existing file. Before you start, make sure a story threads between text frames on two different pages, and then follow these steps:

1. **Create a new text frame on the first page and type** continued on page.

2. **Use the Selection tool to select the text frame you just created.**

3. **Move the text frame so that it slightly overlaps the text frame containing the story.**

You need to allow InDesign to know what text frame it's tracking the story from or to. You need to overlap the two text frames (and keep them overlapped), as shown in Figure 3-13, so that InDesign knows to associate these text frames (the continued notice text frame and the story text frame) with each other.

Figure 3-13: Slightly overlap the two text frames so the story can be tracked properly.

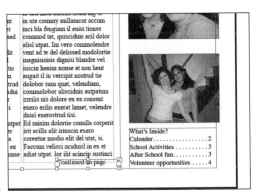

TIP

You can then *group* these two text frames, which means that they will move together. Choose Object↔Group with both text frames selected (Shift+click with the Selection tool to select both text frames).

4. **Double-click the new text frame (which contains the text "continued on page") to place the insertion point where you want the page number to be inserted.**

The page number will be inserted where you have the insertion point, so make sure there is a space after the preceding character.

5. Choose Type⇨Insert Special Character⇨Next Page Number.

A number is added into the text frame. This number is sensitive to where the next threaded text frame is, so if you move the second text frame, the page number automatically updates.

You can do the same thing for adding where a story is continued *from*. Repeat these steps, except when you get to Step 4, choose Type⇨Insert Special Character⇨Previous Page Number. See how this looks in Figure 3-14.

Figure 3-14:
A story is tracked so the reader is notified as to what page to turn to in a document.

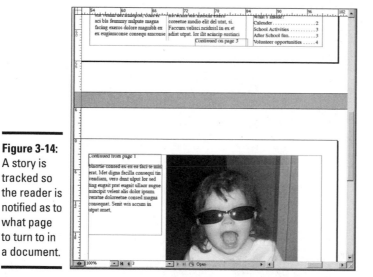

Understanding Paragraph Settings

You can change the settings for an entire text frame or a single paragraph in a text frame in several ways. You can use the Paragraph palette, shown in Figure 3-15, to make adjustments to a single paragraph or an entire text frame's indentation, justification, and alignment. Open the Paragraph palette by choosing Window⇨Type & Tables⇨Paragraph.

If you want the changes in the Paragraph palette to span across all the text frames you create, don't select any paragraph or text frame before making the changes but instead select the entire text frame or frames on the page first. Then, the selections you make in the Paragraph palette will affect all the paragraphs in the selected text frame(s) instead of just one paragraph. If you want the selections you make in the Paragraph palette to affect just one paragraph within a text frame, select that paragraph first and then make your changes.

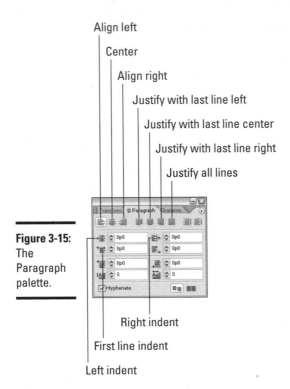

Align left
Center
Align right
Justify with last line left
Justify with last line center
Justify with last line right
Justify all lines

Figure 3-15:
The
Paragraph
palette.

Right indent
First line indent
Left indent

Indenting your text

You can indent a paragraph in a story using the Paragraph palette. Indentation moves the paragraph away from the edges of the text frame's bounding box. Here's how you modify indentation:

1. **Create a text frame on the page and fill it with text.**

You can fill the text frame by typing in text, copying and pasting text, or by inserting placeholder text by choosing Text⇨Fill with Placeholder Text.

2. **Make sure the insertion point is blinking in the text frame in the para- graph you want to change, or use the Selection tool to select the text frame. Then open the Paragraph palette by choosing Window⇨Type & Tables⇨Paragraph.**

The Paragraph palette opens, showing the text frame's current settings. Refer to Figure 3-15 to find out the name of each setting control.

3. **Change the value in the Left Indent text field and press Enter.**

For example, we entered **2p0** in the Left Indent text field to indent the text two points from the left edge of the text frame.

4. **Change the value in the First Line Left Indent text field and press Enter.**

We entered **1p0** in the First Line Left Indent text field to indent the first line of the selected paragraph a further 1 point from the left edge of the paragraph. Figure 3-16 shows the effects of changing the indentation settings on a selected paragraph.

If you want to change all the paragraphs in a story, then click the insertion point in a paragraph, and choose Edit➪Select All before changing your settings.

Figure 3-16:
Indentation changes how the paragraphs appear in a text frame.

> Sun protection
> Don't forget to pack the following items:
>   Sunglasses
>   Sunscreen
>   Hats
>
>   It has long been proven that you can stay healtheire and look younger when you have a plan of action when working in the sun.

**Book II
Chapter 3**

**Working with Text
and Text Frames**

Text alignment and justification

You can use the alignment and justification buttons in the Paragraph palette to format your text frames. Align helps you left, center, or right align the text with the edges of the text frames. Justification allows you to space the text in relation to the edges of the text frame. It also allows you to justify the final line of text in the paragraph. (Refer to Figure 3-15 to see the align and justify buttons in the Paragraph palette.)

To align and/or justify a block of text click one of the align and justify buttons. In Figure 3-17, the paragraph on top has been aligned to the right; the paragraph on the bottom has been aligned to the left and then justified.

Figure 3-17:
On top, a right-aligned paragraph; on bottom, a justified paragraph.

> Just got the summer job in the sun that you have been hoping for? Well all is great until you get such a sunburn that you can't believe you have to function. Learn the tips of the trade in the one-hour seminar being held at the Collins center this coming Friday, 1:00.
>
> You might look great now with a tan, but don't forget that you have to live in your skin for the next fifty or so years, take care of it, wear sunscreen and have fun! This message was sponsored by the parents with wrinkled skin foundation.

Saving a paragraph style

Ever go through all of the work of finding just the right indent, font, or spacing that you want in your copy, just to find that you have to apply those attributes one hundred times to complete your project? How about when you decide that the indent is too much? Wouldn't it be nice to change one indent textbox and have it update all other occurrences? You can do this by using Paragraph styles in InDesign. To create a paragraph style, follow these steps:

1. **Create a text frame, add some text, and apply a first line indent, any size.**

Select some of the text. Doesn't even have to be all of it.

2. **Choose Window⇨Type & Tables⇨Paragraph Styles.**

The Paragraph Styles palette opens.

3. **From the Paragraph Styles palette's menu, choose New Paragraph Style.**

The New Paragraph Style dialog box opens, as shown in Figure 3-18.

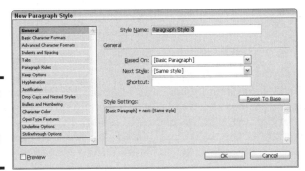

Figure 3-18:
The New Paragraph Style dialog box.

Note that every attribute, font, size, indent, etc. is already recorded in this unnamed style. You don't have to do anything at this point but name the style. Change the name from Paragraph Style 1 to something more appropriate like BodyCopy, and click OK. Your style has been created!

If you want to change an existing style the New Paragraph Style dialog box has several different areas in a large list on the left side. Select an item in the list to view and change the associated paragraph properties on the right side of the dialog box. This will update all usages of that paragraph style.

After you click OK, the dialog box closes, and the new style is added to the Paragraph Styles palette list. You can modify the settings by double-clicking the style name in the Paragraph Styles palette. You can apply the style to other text frames by selecting the frame and clicking the style in the Paragraph Styles palette.

 You can import paragraph styles from other documents or from a file on your hard drive. This is particularly useful when you need to use a particular set of styles for a template. To import paragraph styles, choose Load Paragraph Styles from the Paragraph Styles palette menu. A dialog box prompts you to browse your hard drive for a file. Select the file to load and click OK.

Editing Stories

Your publications will likely have a lot of text in them, and some of that text may need to be edited. InDesign has a built-in story editor for editing text. This can be useful if opening another text editor to make changes to the text isn't convenient or possible.

InDesign solidly integrates with another Adobe product called InCopy, which is a text editor that is similar to Microsoft Word, but has integration capabilities with InDesign for streamlined page layout.

Using the story editor

The InDesign story editor allows you to view the story outside tiny columns and format the text as necessary. To open the story editor to edit a piece of text, follow these steps:

1. **Find a piece of text that you want to edit and select the text frame with the Selection tool.**

   A bounding box with handles appears around the text frame.

2. **Choose Edit➪Edit in Story Editor.**

   The story editor opens in a new window right in the InDesign workspace.

3. **Edit the story in the window as necessary, and click the close button when you're finished.**

   Your story appears in one block of text. Any paragraph styles that you apply to the text in the story editor are noted in an Information pane at the left side of the workspace, as shown in Figure 3-19.

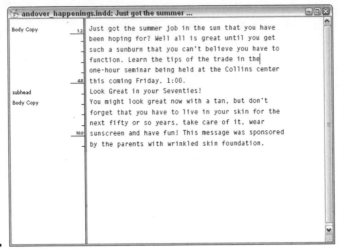

Figure 3-19:
Editing a
large block
of text is
usually
easier with
the story
editor than
when the
text is laid
out in text
frames on
a page.

Updating an InCopy story

If you create a story in InCopy, you can import the story into InDesign
and then continue to edit the story using InCopy. InDesign allows you to
update the file when it has been changed in InCopy. InDesign even alerts
you when the file has been changed and saved.

To update an InCopy story, follow these steps:

1. **Choose Edit⇨Place to import a new document into InDesign.**

   The Place dialog box opens, where you can find an InCopy (`*.incd`) file.

2. **Browse to an InCopy file, select the file, and then click Open.**

   The Place Text icon appears in place of the regular cursor. Click anywhere
   on the page to import the story into your publication. The InCopy story
   is placed on the page.

3. **Return to InCopy and modify the document you imported. Save the
   changes and return to InDesign.**

   A new Alert icon, as shown in Figure 3-20, appears above the text frame.
   The changes made are also noted when you mouse over the text frame
   with the InCopy story. When you place the cursor over the imported text,
   it alerts you that the document has been changed.

4. **Choose Edit⇨InCopy Stories⇨Update Story.**

   The InCopy story updates in InDesign. The edits you made to the story
   in Step 3 are now visible in InDesign.

Figure 3-20:
An alert
means that
you should
update
InDesign
to reflect
the new
changes
made in
InCopy.

Alert icon

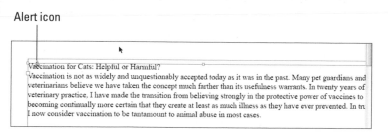

Book II
Chapter 3

Working with Text
and Text Frames

Checking for correct spelling

Typos and spelling errors are very easy to make. Therefore, it's important to check for correct spelling in a document before you print it or export it to a PDF. Here's how to check for spelling in InDesign:

1. **Choose Edit⇨Spelling⇨Check Spelling.**

2. **In the Check Spelling dialog box that appears (see Figure 3-21), choose a selection to search from the Search drop-down list, and then click the Start button.**

   The spell check automatically starts searching through the story or document.

3. **Either click the Skip button to ignore a misspelled word, or select a suggested spelling correction from the list in the Suggested Corrections pane and click the Change button. Choose Ignore All to ignore any more instances of that word.**

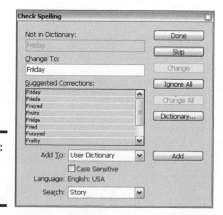

Figure 3-21:
The Check
Spelling
dialog box.

The spelling is corrected right in the text frame and moves on to the next spelling error.

4. **To stop the spell check, click the Done button; otherwise, click OK when InDesign gives you an alert that the spell check is done.**

Using dictionaries

New in this version, you can easily add words such as proper nouns to your dictionary by clicking the Add button to the right of the Add to: User Dictionary drop-down menu.

You can create a user dictionary, or you can add user dictionaries from previous InDesign versions, from files that others have sent you, or from a server. The dictionary you add is used for all your InDesign documents. Follow these steps to create your own custom dictionary:

1. **Choose Edit➪Preferences➪Dictionary (Windows) or InDesign➪ Preferences➪Dictionary (Mac OS).**

2. **From the Language menu, choose the language of your dictionary.**

3. **Click the New User Dictionary icon below the Language menu (see Figure 3-22).**

4. **Specify the name and location of the user dictionary and then click Save.**

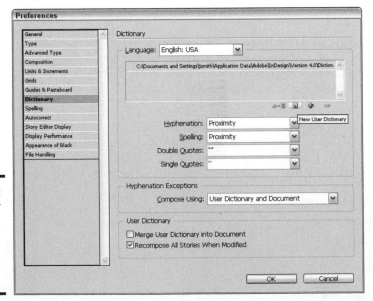

Figure 3-22: Create your own User dictionary to check spelling against.

Using Tables

A table is made of columns and rows, which divides a table into cells. You see tables every day on the television, in books and magazines, and all over the Web. In fact, a calendar is a table: All the days in a month are shown down a column, every week is a row, and each day is a cell.

You can use tables for many different things, such as listing products, employees, or events.

The following list describes the components of a table and how you can modify them in InDesign:

✦ **Rows:** Rows extend horizontally across the table. You can modify the height of a row.

✦ **Columns:** Columns are vertical in a table. You can modify the width of a column.

✦ **Cells:** Each cell is a text frame. You can enter information into this frame and format it like any other text frame in InDesign.

Creating tables

The easiest way to create a table is to have data ready to go. Mind you, this is not the only way, you see another method in a short bit. This is the most dynamic way of seeing what InDesign can do with tables.

1. **Create a text area and insert tabbed copy into it. The example used is dates for an event:**

Summer Events

June	July	August
1	2	3
4	5	6

Notice that the text was simply keyed in with the tab key pressed between each new entry. The text doesn't even need to be lined up.

2. **Select the text and choose Table➪Convert Text to Table.**

The Convert text to table options window appears.

3. **Click OK to accept the default settings.**

See Figure 3-23 for the results.

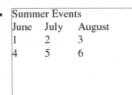

Figure 3-23:
Create
tables from
tab sepa-
rated text.

4. **To stretch the table in or out, hold down the Shift key and grab the outside right border. The cells proportionally accommodate the new table size.**

5. **Merge the top three cells by clicking and dragging across the entire top row. Choose Table⇨Merge cells.**

To create a new table without existing text, follow these steps:

1. **Create a new text frame using the Type tool.**

   The insertion point should be blinking in the new text frame you create. If it isn't or if you created a new frame another way, double-click the text frame so that the insertion point (I-bar) is active. You cannot create a table unless the insertion point is active in the text frame.

2. **Choose Table⇨Insert Table.**

3. **In the Insert Table dialog box that opens, enter the number of rows and columns you want to add to the table in the Rows and Columns text fields, and then click OK. In this example, 6 rows and 3 columns were entered.**

   A table similar to Figure 3-24 is added to the text frame.

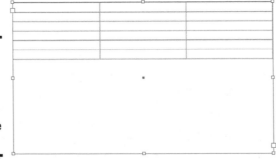

Figure 3-24:
A table
with rows,
columns,
and cells is
added to the
text frame.

Editing table settings

You can control many settings for tables. InDesign allows you to change the text, fill, and stroke properties for each cell or of the table itself. Because of this, you can create fully customized tables to display your information in an intuitive and creative way. In this section, we show you some of the basic options you have for editing your tables. To get started editing the table settings, follow these steps:

1. Select the table you want to make changes to.

A bounding box appears around the table when it's selected.

2. Choose Table⇨Table Options⇨Table Setup.

The Table Options dialog box opens with the Table Setup tab selected, as shown in Figure 3-25. The dialog box contains several tabs that contain settings you can change for different parts of the table.

The Table Setup tab allows you to edit the columns and rows, border, spacing, and how column or row strokes are rendered in relation to each other. For example, we changed the number of rows and columns, and changed the table border weight to a 3pt stroke.

3. Select the Preview check box at the bottom of the dialog box.

The Preview is activated so that you can view the changes you made on the page while you're using the dialog box.

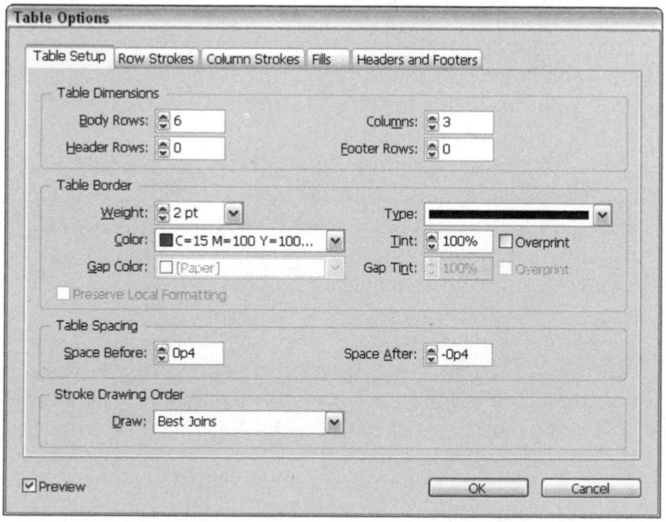

Book II
Chapter 3

Working with Text
and Text Frames

Figure 3-25:
The Table
Setup tab of
the Table
Options
dialog box.

4. Click the Row Strokes tab and change the options.

For this example, we selected Every Second Row from the Alternating Pattern drop-down list, changed the Table Border Weight to 2, and changed the Color property for the first row to C=15 M=100 Y=100 K=0 (This is the CMYK equivalent of Red.).

This causes every second row to have a red, 2-point stroke. You can also click the Column Strokes tab if you want to change the properties for column strokes. The two tabs work the same way.

5. Click the Fills tab and change the options.

For this example, we chose Every Other Column from the Alternating Pattern drop-down list, changed the Color property to the same CMYK equivalent of red, and left the Tint at the default of 20%. This changes the first row to a red tint.

6. Click OK.

The changes you made in the Table Options dialog box are applied to the table.

7. Click in one of the table cells so that the insertion point is blinking.

The table cell is selected.

8. Find an image that you can copy onto the Clipboard. Press Ctrl+C (Windows) or ⌘+C (Mac) to copy the image.

9. Return to InDesign and paste the image into the table cell by pressing Ctrl+V (Windows) or ⌘+V (Mac).

The image appears in the table cell, and the height and/or width of the cell changes based on the dimensions of the image. Make sure that the insertion point is active in the cell if you have problems pasting the image.

Not only can you change the table itself, but you can customize the cells within the table as well. Choose Table⇨Cell Options⇨Text to open the Cell Options dialog box. You can also make changes to each cell by using the Paragraph palette. Similarly, you can change the number of rows, columns, and their widths and heights using the Tables palette. Open the Tables palette by choosing Window⇨Type and Tables⇨Table.

InDesign allows you to import tables from other programs, such as Microsoft Excel. If you have a spreadsheet you want to import, use the File⇨Place command. The spreadsheet is imported into InDesign as a table that you can further edit as necessary.

Looking at Text on a Path

You can create some interesting effects using text on a path. Using the Type on a Path tool, you can have text curve along a line or shape. This is particularly useful when you want to create interesting titling effects on a page. To create text on a path, follow these steps:

1. Use the Pen tool to create a path on the page.

Create at least one curve on the path after you create it. Feeling uncomfortable using the Pen tool? In Chapter 2 of this minibook, we show you how to wield it with confidence.

2. Click and hold the Type tool to select the Type on a Path tool.

3. Move the cursor near the path you created.

When you move the cursor near a path, a + symbol appears next to the cursor (see top path in Figure 3-26). This means you can click and start typing on the path.

4. Click when you see the + icon and type some text onto the path.

An insertion point appears at the beginning of the path after you click, and you can then add text along the path. See how text along a path might look in the bottom of Figure 3-26.

Book II
Chapter 3

Working with Text
and Text Frames

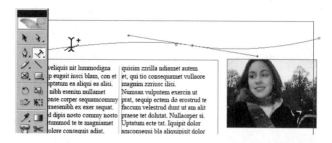

Figure 3-26:
Adding type
along a path.

You select type on a path as you would normally select other text: by dragging over the text to highlight it.

To change properties for type on a path, you can use the Type on a Path Options dialog box, which you access by choosing Type⇨Type on a Path⇨ Options. The Type on a Path Options dialog box, shown in Figure 3-27, allows you to use effects to modify how each character is placed on the path. You can also flip the text, change character spacing, and change how the characters align to the path in the Align drop-down list, or to the stroke of the path in the To Path drop-down list. Play with the settings to see how they affect your type. Click OK to apply your changes; to undo anything you don't like, press Ctrl+Z or ⌘+Z.

Figure 3-27:
The Type
on a Path
Options
dialog box.

Chapter 4: Understanding Page Layout

In This Chapter

- ✔ Working with image files
- ✔ Selecting images on the page
- ✔ Knowing page layout settings
- ✔ Using text and graphics in your layouts
- ✔ Working with pages
- ✔ Using master pages and spreads

In Chapters 1 through 3 of this minibook, we show you how to start a new document, create graphics using the drawing tools, and add stories and text to your publications. This chapter shows you how to put all those things together so that you can start creating page layouts. Interesting and creative page layouts help draw interest to the pictures and words contained within the publication. An interesting layout motivates more of the audience to read the text you place on a page. So that you can create layouts that intrigue the audience to spend some time with your publications, it is important that you grasp how to use the layout tools in InDesign.

Importing Images

You can add several kinds of image files to an InDesign document: Some of the most common kinds are JPEG, TIF, GIF, and PSD. Images are imported into graphic frames, which are instantly created when you add the image to the page.

InDesign allows you to make specific settings when importing an image, such as those for quality, linkage, and color management. You can make additional settings when you import an image using the Image Import

Options dialog box. We later show you how to change various import options, but for now, to import an image into InDesign (without changing the import settings), follow these steps:

1. Make sure that nothing on the page is selected.

If an object on the page is selected, click an empty area so that the element is deselected before you proceed.

2. Choose File⇨Place.

The Place dialog box opens, where you can browse through your hard drive for image files to import. This dialog box allows you to import various kinds of files into InDesign, not just images. You may be able to see previews for some of the images on your hard drive. If so, the thumbnail appears at the bottom of the Place dialog box in Windows, as shown on the left in Figure 4-1; on the right is the Place dialog box on a Mac.

Figure 4-1:
Importing an image with a preview.

3. Choose Images from the Files of Type drop-down list.

Only image files show when you browse through your hard drive. Uncheck Show Import Options if is it checked.

4. **Select the image that you want to import and click Open.**

The Place dialog box closes, and your cursor changes to the Place Graphic icon.

5. **Move the cursor to where you want the upper-left corner of the image to be placed on the page, and then click the mouse.**

The image is imported and placed into the publication as a graphic frame. You can now resize, move, and modify the image as necessary.

Don't worry if the image imports and is too large for the layout, or needs to be cropped — for more information about selecting graphic frames and modifying them, check out Chapter 5 of this minibook. To find out about importing and working with text and stories, refer to Chapter 3 of this minibook.

Book II
Chapter 4

Understanding
Page Layout

It is sometimes easier to create a graphic frame and then add an image to it. The graphic frame you create can be used as a placeholder until you import the image into your publication. Just make sure you have the graphic frame selected before you import the image into InDesign.

Accessing image import options

To open the Image Import Options dialog box, follow these steps:

1. **Choose File⇨Place.**

The Place dialog box opens.

2. **Select the Show Import Options check box.**

This check box is located at the lower-left corner of the Place dialog box.

3. **Select an image to import and click Open (Windows) or Choose (Mac).**

The Image Import Options dialog box opens, as shown in Figure 4-2.

Figure 4-2:
The Image Import Options dialog box contains additional settings for importing images.

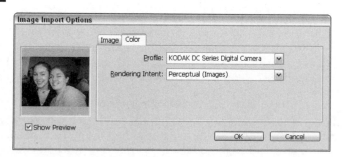

Importing PDFs

When you import PDF files, you can preview and crop the pages using the Place PDF dialog box (choose File➪Place). You can import only one page at a time, so you will need to use the forward and back buttons under the preview to select a page to place in the publication. Also, you cannot import any video, sound, or buttons, and you can't edit the PDF after it is imported into InDesign. The Place PDF dialog box, shown in Figure 4-3, offers the following options:

✦ **Crop:** You can crop the page you're importing using this drop-down list. You can choose between many options. Some of the options are unavailable because they depend on what is in the PDF you're importing. The hatched outline in the preview shows you the crop marks.

✦ **Transparent Background:** If you select this check box, the PDF background is made transparent so that elements on the InDesign page will show through. The PDF background is imported as solid white if this option is not selected.

Figure 4-3:
Choose
which page
you want to
import, as
well as other
options
when you
place a PDF.

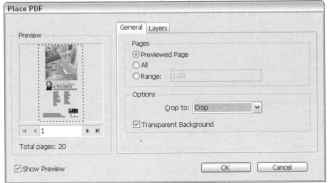

Linking and Embedding Images

You can either have your images linked to a publication or embedded within it. Instead of importing images or files directly into InDesign and embedding them, you can link the content to the file instead. Here's the difference between linking and embedding:

✦ **Linking:** The image that appears in the InDesign document is basically a preview of the actual image file stored on your hard drive. If the file you linked to your InDesign document is changed (the name and location must remain the same), the link breaks and the image no longer appears in your layout.

✦ **Embedding:** The image is copied into and saved within the publication itself. It doesn't matter where the file you imported is or if you alter that file because an embedded image is stored within the InDesign document itself.

When you print or export the publication you're working on, the information is added to the document from linked files (if you have any). This means you have to be careful to keep all your linked files together with the InDesign document, particularly if you send or save it to a different location. You can update the links for an image by selecting it in the Links palette and choosing Relink from the Links palette menu. You're prompted to find that file on your hard drive so that the file can be linked to the new location.

If you choose to use embedded images instead of linked images, be aware that your publication's file size increases because of the extra data that is being stored within it.

Images 48K or smaller are automatically embedded within the publication. If an imported image is larger than that, the file is linked. To find out what files are embedded or linked, you need to look at the Links palette. Open the palette by choosing Window➪Links, and see if you have any linked or embedded images listed in the palette. Figure 4-4 shows an icon signifying an embedded file; the other files are linked.

You can choose to embed a file using the Links palette menu. Click the triangle in the upper-right corner to access the menu and select Embed File if you want a linked file to be embedded within the document. Alternatively, choose Unembed from the Link palette menu to link a file instead of having it embedded in the document.

Book II
Chapter 4

Understanding
Page Layout

Figure 4-4:
Linked and
embedded
files in the
Links palette.

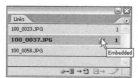

Setting Image Quality and Display

You can set different quality settings for how your images import and display in the workspace. This may help speed up your work (set at a lower quality), or give you a better idea of the finished print project (set at a higher quality). These settings are only applicable to how you see the images while using InDesign: They have no bearing over the final printed or exported product.

To change image display quality, choose Edit⇨Preferences⇨Display Performance (Windows) or InDesign CS⇨Preferences⇨Display Performance (Mac). You can then select one of the following settings from the Default View drop-down list:

✦ **Fast Display:** In order to optimize performance, the entire image or graphic is grayed out.

✦ **Typical Display (Default):** This setting tends to make bitmaps look a little blocky, particularly if you zoom in. The speed of zooming in and out is increased if you select this option. InDesign uses a preview that it has created (or was already imported with the file) to display the image on the screen.

✦ **High Quality Display:** The original image is used to display on-screen. This allows you to preview a very accurate depiction of what the final layout will look like, but you may find that InDesign runs slowly when you use the High Quality option.

Notice the difference between these different settings in Figure 4-5.

Figure 4-5:
From left to right: Fast Display, Typical Display, and High Quality Display.

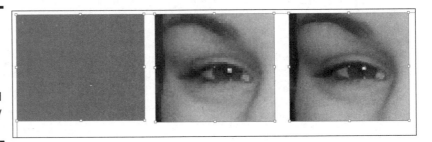

To change the display for individual images, select the graphic frame and choose View⇨Display Performance. Then choose one of the three options from the submenu.

Selecting Images

After you import an image into your document, you can select images in several different ways using the Selection or Direct Selection tools. This is useful when you want to select and edit just the graphic frame, or just the image inside of it.

To select and then edit an image on the page, follow these steps:

1. **Place an image on a page by importing it or pasting it into InDesign.**

The image is placed within a graphic frame, similar to what you see on top in Figure 4-6.

Figure 4-6:
The original image in a graphic frame (left); inside a frame that has been resized (center); in the process of being repositioned in the frame (right).

2. **Using the Selection tool, drag one of the corner handles on the graphic frame.**

The graphic frame is resized, but not the image. This means that the image appears to be cropped because you resized the graphic frame — but the image remains the same size within the frame, as shown in the center of Figure 4-6.

3. **Choose Edit⇨Undo or press Ctrl+Z (Windows) or ⌘+Z (Mac) to undo the changes to the image.**

The image returns to its original appearance on the page.

4. **Using the Direct Selection tool, drag one of the corner handles.**

The image inside the graphic frame resizes, but the graphic frame remains the same size.

5. **Click within the image and drag to move the image within the graphic frame bounding box.**

A hand appears when you move the cursor over the graphic; when you move the image just past the edge of the graphic frame boundaries, that part of the image is not visible anymore, as shown on the right of Figure 4-6.

TIP

When repositioning a graphic within a frame, click and hold. When you do so, the entire image appears (screened outside the frame area) as shown in the image on the right (Figure 4-6). This allows you to crop more effectively.

Resizing images and frames using the Control palette

Use the Options available in the upper right of the Control panel to quickly resize a graphic or a frame. See the buttons defined in Figure 4-7.

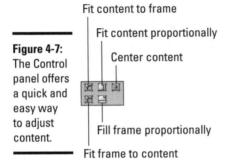

Fit content to frame

Fit content proportionally

Center content

Figure 4-7:
The Control panel offers a quick and easy way to adjust content.

Fill frame proportionally

Fit frame to content

Manipulating Text and Graphics in Layout

InDesign offers many tools that help you work with text and graphics together in a layout. From the tools in the toolbox to commands to palette options, InDesign offers you an immense amount of control over how graphics and text can be manipulated in a spread.

Page orientation and size

When you open a new document, you can set the page orientation and size. If you ever need to change your settings after you have created a document, choose File➪Document Setup and change the following options (note that these settings affect all the pages in your document):

✦ **Page Orientation:** Select either Landscape or Portrait. One of the first things you decide upon when you create a new document is how your pages will be oriented. A landscape page is wider than it is tall; a portrait orientation is taller than it is wide.

✦ **Page Size:** Choose from many standardized preset sizes, such as Letter, Legal, and Tabloid. Alternatively, you can set a custom page size for the document. Make sure that you properly set the page size so that it fits the kind of paper you need to print on.

Margins and columns

Margins, columns, and gutters help divide a page for layout and confine its dimensions:

✦ **Margin:** The guidelines that define an area between the edge of the page and the main printed area. Together, the four margins (top, bottom, left, and right) look like a rectangle around the perimeter of the page. Margins are not printed when you print or export the publication.

✦ **Column:** Columns divide a page into sections used for laying out text and graphics on a page. A page has at least one column when you start, which is between the margins. You can add additional column guides to this, which are represented by a pair of lines separated by a *gutter* area. Column guides are not printed when you print or export the publication.

✦ **Gutter:** The space between two columns on the page. A gutter prevents columns from running together. You can define the gutter's width in your settings; see Chapter 3 of this minibook for more information.

You can set margins and columns when you create a new document, which we discuss in Chapter 1 of this minibook. However, you can also modify margins and columns after the document has been created and specify different values for each page. You can also modify the gutter, which is the width of the space between each column. For more information on column guides, check out the next section, "Using guides and snapping." Figure 4-8 shows you how columns, margins, and gutters look on a page.

Margins and columns can be changed by setting new values in the Margins and Columns dialog box. Choose Layout⇨Margins and Columns to access this dialog box. Modifications can be made for each individual page.

Margins and columns are useful for placing and aligning elements on a page. These guides can have objects snap to them, enabling you to accurately align multiple objects on a page.

Using guides and snapping

We briefly mention guides in Chapters 1 and 3 of this minibook. Using guides when you're creating your page layouts is a good idea because guides help you more precisely align elements on a page and position objects in the layout. Aligning objects by eyeballing them is very difficult because quite often you can't tell if an object is out of alignment by a small amount unless you're zoomed in to a large percentage.

Make sure snapping is enabled by choosing View➪Grids and Guides➪Snap to Guides.

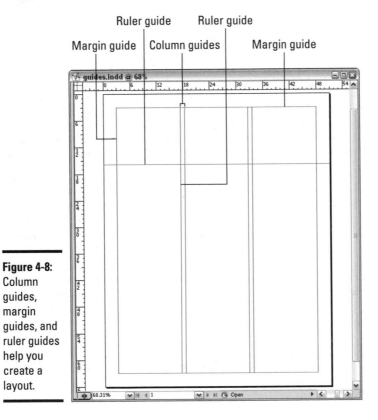

Figure 4-8:
Column guides, margin guides, and ruler guides help you create a layout.

Because guides are very useful in creating a layout, check out the following kinds available in InDesign (refer to Figure 4-8):

✦ **Column guides:** These guides are set when you open a new document in InDesign, as outlined in the previous section. Column guides evenly distribute the page into columns and can be used to align text frames in a document.

Column guides don't always have to be equally spaced the way they are originally placed on a page. You can drag columns to a new location manually. Simply click one of the column guides directly on a line and drag the line to a new location. The cursor changes to a double-ended arrow while you drag the column guide to a new location.

✦ **Margin guides:** Margin guides are the guidelines discussed in the previous section that define the area between the edge of the page and the main printable area.

✦ **Ruler guides:** Ruler guides are ones you manually define; they can be used to align graphics, measure an object, or specify the location of a particular asset you want to lay out. See Chapter 1 of this minibook for details about adding ruler guides to the workspace.

To find out how to show and hide grids and guides, refer to Chapter 1 of this minibook.

Snapping makes guides and grids useful. When you drag the object close to the grid, the object attaches to the guideline like it's a magnet. Getting an object aligned to a guide isn't easy or even possible to do by eyeballing it, so snapping is essential when using guides.

Locking objects and guides

You can lock elements such as objects and guides in place. This is particularly useful after you have carefully aligned elements on a page. Locking objects or guides prevents you from accidentally moving them from that position.

To lock an element, follow these steps:

1. Use a drawing tool to create an object on a page, and then select it using the Selection tool.

A bounding box with handles appears when the object is selected.

2. Choose Object⇨Lock Position.

The object is locked in position. Now when you try to use the Selection or Direct Selection tools to move the object, it will not move from its current position.

To lock guides in place, follow these steps:

1. **Drag a couple ruler guides onto the page by clicking within a ruler and dragging towards the page.**

A line appears on the page. (If rulers are not visible around the pasteboard, choose View⇨Rulers.)

2. **Drag a ruler guide to a new location if needed; when you're happy with the ruler guides' placement, choose View⇨Lock Guides.**

All guides in the workspace are locked. If you try selecting a guide and moving it, the guide remains in its present position. If you have any column guides on the page, these are locked as well.

Use layers in your publications for organization. Layers are a lot like transparencies that lay on top of each other, so they can be used for stacking elements on a page. For example, you may want to stack graphics or arrange similar items (such as images or text) onto the same layer. Each layer has its own color of bounding box. This helps you tell which item is on which corresponding layer. For more information on layers in general, refer to Book III, Chapter 7.

Merging Text and Graphics

When you have text and graphics together on a page, they should flow and work with each other in order to create an aesthetic layout. Luckily, you can work with text wrap to achieve a visual flow between text and graphics. In this section, you discover how to wrap text around images and graphics in your publications.

Wrapping objects with text

Images can have text wrapped around them. This is a typical feature of page layout in print and on the Web. Images can have text wrapping around them in many different ways, as shown in Figure 4-9.

You can choose different text wrap options by using the Text Wrap palette (see Figure 4-9), which you open by choosing Window⇨Text Wrap. The five buttons at the top of the palette are used to set what kind of text wrapping you want to use for the selected object. Below the buttons are text fields where you can enter offset values for the text wrap. The fields are grayed out if the option is not available.

(a) No text wrap

(b) Wrap around bounding box

(c) Jump object

(d) Jump column

Figure 4-9:
The different
ways to
wrap text
around
an object.

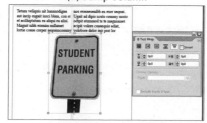

(e) Jump to next column

The drop-down list at the bottom of the Text Wrap palette is used to choose from various contour options. Choose from the following options to wrap text around an object's shape:

✦ **Wrap around Bounding Box:** Click this button to wrap text around all sides of the bounding box of the object.

Offset: Enter an amount to offset the text from wrapping around the object.

✦ **No Text Wrap:** Click this button to use the default setting or to remove any text wrapping from the selected object.

✦ **Wrap around Object Shape:** Click this button to wrap text around the edges of an object.

Contour Options: Select a contour from this drop-down list, which tells InDesign how the edges of the image are determined. You can choose from various vector paths or the edges to be detected around an object or image with transparency.

Top Offset: Enter a value for the top offset modifier to offset the text wrapping around the object.

✦ **Jump Object:** Click this button to have the text wrapping around the image jump from above the image to below it, with no text wrapping to the left or right of the object in the column.

✦ **Jump to Next Column:** Click this button to cause text to end above the image, and then jump to the next column. No text is wrapped to the left or right of the image.

Offset: Enter offset values for text wrapping on all sides of the object.

To add text wrapping to an object (a drawing or image), follow these steps:

1. **Create a text frame on the page.**

Add text to the text frame by typing, pasting text from elsewhere, or filling it with placeholder text. This text will wrap around the image, so make sure that the text frame is slightly larger than the graphic frame you will use.

2. **Using the Selection tool, select a graphic frame on the page and move it over the text frame.**

Bounding box handles appear around the edges of the image or graphic.

3. **Open the Text Wrap palette by choosing Window⇨Text Wrap.**

The Text Wrap palette opens.

4. **With the graphic frame still selected, click the Wrap around Object Shape button.**

   The text wraps around the image instead of hiding behind it.

5. **If you're working with an image that has a transparent background, choose Detect Edges or Alpha Channel from the Contour Options drop-down list.**

   The text wraps around the edges of the image, as shown in the third example in Figure 4-9.

Modifying a text wrap

If you have applied a text wrap around an object (as we show you how to do in the preceding section), you can then modify that text wrap. If you have an image with a transparent background around which you've wrapped text, InDesign created a path around the edge of the image; if you have a shape you created with the drawing tools, InDesign automatically uses those paths to wrap text around.

Before proceeding with the following steps, be sure that the object uses the Wrap around Object Shape text wrap (if not, open the Text Wrap palette and click the Wrap around Object Shape button to apply the text wrapping). Remember to choose Detect Edges if you're using an image with a transparent background.

To modify the path around an image with text wrapping by using the Direct Selection tool, follow these steps:

1. **Select the object using the Direct Selection tool.**

   The image is selected, and you can see the path around the object.

2. **Drag one of the anchor points on the path using the Direct Selection tool.**

   The path is modified according to how you move the point, as shown in Figure 4-10. (For more about manipulating paths, take a look at Chapter 2 of this minibook.) Notice how the text wrapping immediately changes, based on the modifications you make to the path around the object.

3. **Select the Delete Anchor Point tool from the toolbox and delete one of the anchor points.**

   The path changes again, and the text wrapping modifies around the object accordingly.

Figure 4-10:
Modify
the path
surrounding
the object
to change
how the
text wraps
around it.

You can also use the Offset values in the Text Wrap palette to determine the distance between the wrapping text and the edge of the object. Just increase the point values to move the text farther away from the object's edge.

Working with Pages and the Pages Palette

Pages are the central part of any publication. The page is where the visible part of your publication is actually created. Navigating and controlling pages is a large part of what you do in InDesign. The Pages palette allows you to select, move, and navigate through pages in a publication. When you use default settings, pages are created as *facing pages,* which means they are laid out as two-page spreads. Otherwise, pages are laid out individually. This is reflected, and can also be changed, in the Pages palette.

The Pages palette, which you open by choosing Window⊳Pages, also allows you to add new pages to the document, duplicate pages, or delete a page. The Pages palette, shown in Figure 4-11, contains two main areas: the master pages section (upper section) and the section containing the document's pages (lower section). To discover more about master pages and how they differ from regular pages in your document, refer to "Using Master Spreads in Page Layout" later in this chapter.

Navigate from page to page by using Ctrl+G (Windows) or ⌘+G (Mac). No dialog appears, this just highlights the page number in the lower-left corner of your document window. Just type the page number you want to jump to and press Enter or Return.

Document pages

Master pages

Selected spread

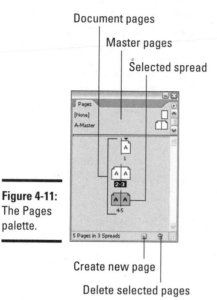

Figure 4-11:
The Pages
palette.

Create new page

Delete selected pages

Selecting and moving pages

Use the Pages palette to select a page or spread in your publication. Select a page by clicking the page. If you Ctrl+click (Windows) or ⌘+click (Mac) pages, you can select more than one page at a time; the darkened pages in the palette on the left of Figure 4-12 are selected.

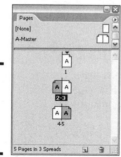
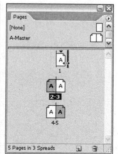

Figure 4-12:
Selecting
and moving
multiple
pages.

The Pages palette also allows you to move pages to a new position in the document. Select a page in the document pages area of the palette and then drag it where you want to move the page. A small line and changed cursor indicates where the page will be moved. You can move a page in between two pages in a spread; a hollow line (not shown in the figure) indicates where you're moving the page. If you move a page after a spread, a solid line appears (shown in the palette on the right in Figure 4-12). Release the mouse button to move the page to the new location.

Adding and deleting pages

You can also add new pages to the publication by using the Pages palette. To add a new page, follow these steps:

1. Open the Pages palette by choosing Window➪Pages.

The Pages palette opens.

2. Click the Create New Page button.

A new page is added to the document.

3. Select one of the pages in the Pages palette.

The selected page is highlighted in the pages palette.

4. Click the Create New Page button again.

A new page is added following the selected page.

To delete a page, select the page in the Pages palette and click the Delete Selected Pages button. The selected page is removed from the document.

Working with spreads

A *spread* is a layout that spans across two pages. Spreads are particularly common in magazines and can be the source of some very interesting page designs. InDesign automatically arranges pages into spreads by default when you create multiple-page publications. Open the Pages palette and take a look at how the pages in your publication are arranged.

When you need a spread of two pages that must stay together, you will want to create an *island spread*. To do so, follow these steps:

1. Select the spread in the Pages palette.

The selected pages are highlighted in the palette.

2. Choose Keep Pages Together from the Pages palette menu.

Brackets display around the spread, as shown in Figure 4-13. This means they will remain together, no matter whether you add or remove pages around them.

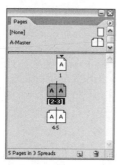

Figure 4-13:
The spread spanning pages 2 and 3 will always stay together.

You can even add three pages to a spread if you need to: All you need to do is drag a third page onto the spread you want to add it to.

Numbering your pages

When you're working with longer documents, adding page numbers before you print out or export the publication is a good idea. You don't have to do this manually: InDesign has a special tool that allows you to number pages automatically. This is particularly useful when you move pages around the document. You don't have to keep track of updating the numbering when you make these kinds of edits.

To number pages, follow these steps:

1. **Create a text frame on the page where you want the page number to be added.**

2. **Double-click the text frame so that the insertion point is blinking in the frame.**

3. **Choose Type⇨Insert Special Character⇨Auto Page Number.**

   The current page number appears in the text frame you selected. If you added the page number to a master page, then the master pages' letter appears in the field instead.

If you want page numbers to appear on all pages in the document, you need to add the text frame to a master page. Remember that page numbers are added only to the pages in your document associated with that master page. If you add the page number on a regular page in the document, it adds the page number only to that single page.

To modify automatic numbering settings, choose Layout⇨Numbering and Section Options. You can choose to have numbering start from a specific number or use a different style, such as Roman numerals.

Using Master Spreads in Page Layout

Master pages are a lot like templates that you use to format your page layouts. The settings, such as margins and columns, are applied to each layout that the master page is applied to. If you put a page number on a master page, then it also appears on each page that uses the layout. You can have more than one master page in a single publication, and you can choose which pages use a particular master page.

A master page or spread typically contains parts of a layout that are applied to many pages. It has elements that are used on many pages, such as page numbering, text frames to enter text into, background images, or a heading that's used on every page. The items you have on a master page cannot be edited on the pages assigned to it — you can edit those items on the master page only.

Master pages are lettered. The first master page is called the A-Master by default. If you create a second master page, it's then called the B-Master by default. When you create a new publication, the A-Master is applied to all of the pages you initially open in the document. You can add additional pages at the end that don't have a master applied to them.

Creating master pages and applying them to your publication enables you to create a reusable format for your publication, which can dramatically speed up your workflow when you put together documents using InDesign. So read on to find out how.

Creating a master spread

A new document is created with a master spread, which can be found in the Pages palette. However, you may need more than one master page or master spread for your document. You may have another series of pages that need a unique format. In this situation, you would need to create a second master page. You can create a master page or a master spread from any other page in the publication, or you can create a new one using the Pages palette.

To create a master page using a page in the publication, do one of the following:

✦ **Choose New Master from the Page palette's menu.**

   A blank master page is created.

✦ **Drag a page from the pages section of the palette into the master page section of the Pages palette.**

   The document page turns into a master page.

If the page you're trying to drag into the master pages section is part of a spread, you need to select *both pages in the spread* before you drag it into the master pages section. You can drag individual pages into the master page section only if they are *not* part of a spread.

Applying, removing, and deleting master pages

After you create a master page, you will want to apply it to a page. You can also remove a page from a master page layout as well as delete a master page altogether:

✦ **To add master page formatting to a page or spread in a publication:** In the Pages palette, drag the master page you want to use from the master page section on top of the page you want to format in the document pages section. When you drag the master page on top of the page, it will have a thick outline around it, as shown in Figure 4-14. Release the mouse button when you see this outline, and the formatting is applied to the page.

✦ **To remove any master page applied to a document page:** In the Pages palette, drag the None page from the master area in the Pages palette onto that document page. You may need to use the scroll bar in the master pages area of the Pages palette to find the None page.

✦ **To delete a master page:** In the Pages palette, select the unwanted master page, and then choose Delete Master Spread from the palette menu.

This action *permanently* deletes the master page — you cannot get it back — so think carefully before deleting a master page.

Book II
Chapter 4

Understanding
Page Layout

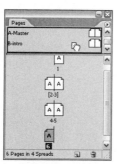

Figure 4-14:
Drag a
master page
on top of
a page to
apply the
formatting.

Chapter 5: Clipping Paths, Transforming Objects, and Alignment

In This Chapter

✔ **Transforming objects with the Transform palette and the Free Transform tool**

✔ **Rotating and scaling objects**

✔ **Shearing and reflecting objects**

✔ **Adding a clipping path**

✔ **Aligning objects in a layout**

In this chapter, you discover several different ways to manipulate and arrange objects on a page. You find out how to use the Transform palette and other tools in the toolbox to transform objects on page layouts. You can make the same transformation in many different ways in InDesign, so for each way you can transform an object, we show you a couple of different ways to get the same job done.

Aligning and/or distributing objects and images helps you organize elements logically on a page. In this chapter, you find out how to align objects using the Align panel. In Chapter 4 of this minibook, we touch on clipping paths when you have the option of placing images into the layout. This chapter provides more information about clipping paths. We show you how to create a new path to use as a clipping path for an image in your document.

Working with Transformations

Chapter 2 of this minibook shows you how to transform graphic objects by skewing them. You can manipulate objects in InDesign in many other ways. You can transform an object using the Object⇨Transform menu, the Transform palette, or the Free Transform tool.

Looking at the Transform palette

The Transform palette (shown in Figure 5-1) is extremely useful for changing the way an image or graphic looks, and also for changing the scale, rotation, or skew of the selected object. You can choose from a range of values for some of these modifiers or manually set your own by typing them in.

Reference point indicator

Rotating angle

Scale X   Palette menu

Figure 5-1:
The
Transform
palette
enables you
to change
a selected
object.

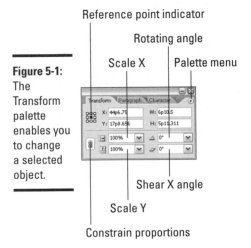

Shear X angle

Scale Y

Constrain proportions

The Transform palette offers the following information and functionality:

✦ **Reference point:** Indicates which handle is the reference for any transformations you make. For example, if you reset the X and Y coordinates, the reference point is set to this position.

✦ **Position:** Change these values to reset the X and Y coordinate position of the selected object.

✦ **Size:** The W and H text fields are used to change the current dimensions of the object.

✦ **Scale:** Enter or choose a percentage from the Scale X Percentage and Scale Y Percentage drop-down lists to scale (resize) the object on either of these axes.

✦ **Constraining proportions:** Click the Constrain Proportions button to maintain the current proportions of the object that's being scaled.

✦ **Shearing:** Enter or choose a negative or positive number to modify the shearing angle (skew) of the selected object.

✦ **Rotation angle:** Set a positive value to rotate the object clockwise; a negative value rotates the object counterclockwise.

When you are scaling, shearing, or rotating an object in your layout, it transforms based on the reference point in the Transform palette. For example, when you rotate an object, InDesign considers the reference point to be the center point of the rotation.

Click a new reference point square in the Transform palette to change the reference point of the graphic. This changes the reference point to the equivalent bounding box handle of the currently selected object.

You can access dialog boxes for each kind of transformation in the Object⇨ Transform menu. These dialog boxes have very similar functionality to the Transform palette, although they offer additional options, such as only affecting the path or frame and not modifying the content within.

Using the Free Transform tool

The Free Transform tool is a multipurpose tool that allows you to transform objects in different ways. Using the Free Transform tool, you can move, rotate, shear, reflect, and scale objects.

The different functions of the Free Transform Tool are represented in InDesign by different cursors, as shown in Figure 5-2.

Figure 5-2:
Different cursors indicate the ways you can use the Free Transform tool.

  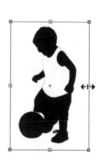 

   (a) Rotate   (b) Scale   (c) Scale   (d) Move

To move an object using the Free Transform tool, follow these steps:

1. **Use the Selection tool to select an object on the page.**

You can use an object that is already on the page, or create a new shape using the drawing tools. When the object is selected, you'll see handles around the edges.

2. **Select the Free Transform tool from the toolbox.**

The cursor changes to the Free Transform tool.

3. Move the cursor over the middle of the selected object.

The cursor changes its appearance to indicate that you can drag to move the object (refer to Figure 5-2). If you move the cursor outside the edges of the object, the cursor changes when the other tools, such as rotate, scale, and shear, become active.

4. Drag the object to a different location.

The object is moved to a new location on the page.

Rotating objects

You can rotate an object using the Free Transform tool or the Transform palette. Using the palette allows you to enter a specific degree that you want the object to rotate. The Free Transform tool lets you visually manipulate the object on the page.

To rotate an image using the Free Transform tool, follow these steps:

1. Select an object on the page using the Selection tool.

Handles appear around the edges of the object. You can rotate any object on the page.

2. Select the Free Transform tool in the toolbox and move it near the handle of an object outside of the bounding box.

The cursor changes when you move it close to the handle of an object. For rotation, you must keep the cursor just outside of the object.

3. When the cursor changes to the rotate cursor, drag to rotate the object.

Drag the cursor until the object is rotated the correct amount.

Alternatively, you can use the Rotate tool to spin an object by following these steps:

1. With the object selected, select the Rotate tool in the toolbox and move the cursor near the object.

The cursor looks similar to a cross hair.

2. Click the cursor anywhere on the page near the object.

The point the object rotates around is set on the page.

3. Drag the cursor outside of the object.

The object rotates around the reference point you set on the page. Hold the Shift key if you want to rotate in 45-degree increments.

You can also rotate objects using the Transform palette. Here's how:

1. Select an object on the page using the Selection tool.

The bounding box with handles appears around the selected object.

2. If the Transform palette isn't open, press F9 to open it.

The Transform palette appears.

3. Select a value from the Rotation angle drop-down list, or click the text field and enter a percentage.

The object rotates to the degree that you set in the Transform palette, as shown in Figure 5-3. Negative angles (in degrees) rotate the image clockwise, and positive angles (in degrees) rotate the image counterclockwise.

Figure 5-3:
Rotating an
object by
using the
Transform
palette.

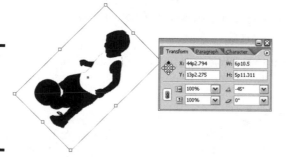

Scaling objects

You can scale objects by using the Transform palette (refer to Figure 5-1), the Scale tool, or the Free Transform tool. The Transform palette allows you to set exact width and height dimensions that you want to scale the object to, just like you can set exact percentages for rotating.

To scale an object by using the Free Transform tool or the Scale tool, follow these steps:

1. Select an object on the page.

A bounding box appears around the object.

2. Select the Free Transform tool or the Scale tool from the toolbox.

3. Move the cursor directly over a corner handle.

The cursor changes into a double-ended arrow, as shown in Figure 5-4.

Figure 5-4:
Use the double-ended arrow to scale the object.

4. **Drag outward to increase the size of the object; drag inward to decrease the size of the object.**

   If you want to scale the image proportionally, hold down the Shift key while you drag.

5. **Release the mouse button when the object is scaled to the correct size.**

To resize an object using the Transform palette, just select the object and enter new values into the W and H text fields in the palette. The object then resizes to those exact dimensions.

Shearing objects

Shearing an object means that you're skewing it horizontally, slanting it to the left or right. A sheared object may appear to have perspective or depth because of this modification. You use the Shear tool to create a shearing effect, as shown in Figure 5-5.

Figure 5-5:
The original image is on the left, and the sheared image is on the right.

Follow these steps to shear an object:

1. **Select an object on the page.**

   The bounding box appears around the object that is selected.

2. Choose the Shear tool in the toolbox.

The cursor changes so it looks similar to a cross hair.

3. Click anywhere above or below the object and drag.

The selected object shears depending on the direction that you drag. Press the Shift key as you drag to shear an object in 45-degree increments.

To shear objects using the Free Transform tool, click to select a side handle, and then hold down Ctrl+Alt (Windows) or ⌘+Option (Mac) while dragging. If you try this using a corner handle, it does not shear (it only scales!).

You can also enter an exact value into the Transform palette to shear an object. Select the object, and then enter a positive or negative value into the palette representing the amount of slant you want to apply to the object.

You can apply shear by using the Shear dialog box by choosing Object↔ Transform↔Shear. Using the Shear dialog box, you can shear the content separately from the path. If you want to shear only the path or frame, deselect the Shear Content check box. If you want the content to shear with the frame, make sure that the Shear Context check box is selected (which is the default setting).

Reflecting objects

You can reflect objects to create mirror images by using the Transform palette menu. The menu provides several additional options for manipulating objects.

Follow these steps to reflect an object:

1. Select an object on the page, and then open the Transform palette by pressing F9.

The object's bounding box and handles appear. The Transform palette shows the current values of the selected object.

2. Click the palette menu in the Transform palette.

The menu opens, revealing many options available for manipulating the object.

3. Select Flip Horizontal from the Transform palette menu.

The object on the page flips on its horizontal axis, as shown in Figure 5-6. You can repeat this step with other reflection options in the menu, such as Flip Vertical.

You can also reflect objects with the Free Transform tool by dragging a corner handle past the opposite end of the object. The object reflects on its axis.

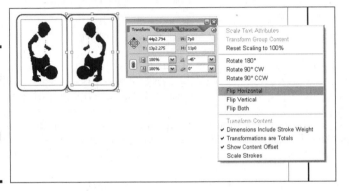

Figure 5-6:
Reflection is applied to this image that has been flipped on its horizontal axis.

Understanding Clipping Paths

Clipping paths allow you to create a path that crops out a part of an image based upon the path, such as removing the background area of an image. This shape can be one that you create using InDesign, or you can import an image that already has a clipping path because they are understood by InDesign. InDesign can also use an existing alpha or mask layer, such as one created using Photoshop or Fireworks, and treat it like a clipping path. Clipping paths are useful when you want to block out areas of an image and have text wrap around the leftover image.

You can create a clipping path right in InDesign using a drawing tool such as the Pen tool. You use the tool to create a shape, and then paste an image into this shape on the page. Here's how:

1. **Choose File⇨Place. Browse to locate an image.**

2. **Using the Pen tool, create a path right on top of the image. The path should be created so that it can contain the image. In Figure 5-7, the path is around the duck.**

3. **Using the Selection tool, click to select the image. Choose File⇨Cut.**

4. **Select the shape you created in Step 1 and choose Edit⇨Paste Into.**

The image is pasted into the selected shape that you drew with the Pen tool, as shown in Figure 5-8.

Figure 5-7:
A shape
drawn with
vector paths
is used as
a clipping
path.

Figure 5-8:
An image
pasted into
a pen path.

Arranging Objects on the Page

In other chapters of this minibook, we show you how to arrange objects on the page. However, you can arrange text or objects in a few other ways. This section covers the additional ways you can arrange objects, which gives you more control over the placement of elements in your document.

Aligning objects

You can align objects on a page using the Align palette (choose Window⇨ Object & Layout⇨Align), as shown in Figure 5-9. This palette gives you control over how elements align to one another or to the overall page. The align palette has many buttons to control selected objects. mouse over a button to see its ToolTip describing how that button aligns elements.

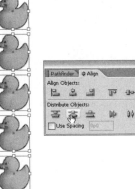

Figure 5-9: The Align palette allows you to control how you align elements on a page.

If you're not sure what each button does by reading the associated ToolTip, then look at the icon on the button. It's sometimes helpful in depicting what the align button does to the selected objects.

Here's how you align elements on the page:

1. **Select several objects on the page using the Selection tool. Hold the Shift key while clicking each object to select several objects.**

Each of the objects is selected as you click them on the page. If you don't have a few objects on a page, then quickly create a couple of new objects by using the drawing tools.

2. **Choose Window⇨Object and Layout⇨Align.**

The Align palette opens.

3. **Select the kind of alignment you want to apply to the selected objects.**

Try clicking the Align Vertical Centers button. Each of your selected objects aligns to the vertical center point on the page, as shown in Figure 5-10.

Figure 5-10:
The five bottom images are aligned to their vertical centers.

Distributing objects

In the preceding step list, we show you how to align a few objects on a page, which is easy enough. However, what if the objects that you're aligning are not distributed evenly? Maybe their centers are lined up, but there's a large gap between two of the images and a narrow gap between the other ones. In that case, you need to *distribute* objects as well as align them. You distribute objects on the page to space them relative to the page or each other in different ways. Here's how:

1. **Select objects on a page that are neither aligned nor evenly distributed (see the top row of images in Figure 5-11) by using the Selection tool while holding the Shift key.**

The objects are selected as you click each one. All of the objects you select will be aligned to each other on the page.

Book II
Chapter 5

Clipping Paths,
Transforming Objects,
and Alignment

Figure 5-11:
The three pictures in the bottom row are distributed evenly. The top row of images depicts how they were originally distributed.

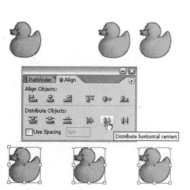

**2. If the Align palette is not open, choose Window⇨Object and Layout⇨
Align.**

The Align palette opens.

**3. Click the Distribute Horizontal Centers button (where the hand cursor
is pointing in Figure 5-11) on the Align palette.**

The selected objects are distributed evenly and aligned horizontally
on the page.

Chapter 6: Understanding Color and Printing

In This Chapter

✔ Using color in page layout

✔ Looking at color controls and models

✔ Discovering swatches and swatch libraries

✔ Understanding bleeding and trapping

✔ Looking at printing and preferences

Color is an important and complicated subject, especially in page layout; however, you probably already understand many of the concepts because the media bombards you with advertisements all the time. If you think about the advertisements you remember the most, this gives you an idea of the kinds of things that are successful in catching someone's attention. These ads often rely on color to relay an effective message. The success of printed ads greatly relies on *how* color is used in the layout. Color greatly enhances the message being relayed to readers. In this chapter, you find out some of the fundamental aspects of working with color and the basics on how to prepare a document for printing.

For more information on general subjects about color, refer to Book I, Chapter 7, which covers subjects such as color modes, inks, printers, and basic color correction across the programs in the Adobe Creative Suite.

Selecting Color with Color Controls

You have several different color modes and options when working in InDesign. Because color in print media can be quite a science, it's important to have a lot of control over how your documents print on the page. In Chapter 2 of this minibook, we show you how to add color to drawings with the Color palette. In this section, we cover using the Color palette to choose colors and apply them to the elements on your page. Swatches are used in many of the other chapters in this minibook.

It's a good idea to use swatches whenever possible because swatches use named colors that a service provider can match exactly. Swatches can be exactly the same in appearance as any color you choose that's unnamed, but a swatch establishes a link between the color on the page and the name of a color, such as a Pantone color number. You discover more about these kinds of color in the later section, "Using Color Swatches and Libraries."

You can use color controls for choosing colors for selections in the document:

✦ **Stroke color:** The Stroke color control allows you to choose colors for strokes and paths in InDesign. A hollow box represents the Stroke color control, as shown in Figure 6-1.

✦ **Fill color:** The Fill color control allows you to choose colors for filling shapes. A solid square box represents the Fill color control, which is also shown in Figure 6-1.

You can toggle between the Fill and Stroke color controls by clicking them. Alternatively, you can press X on the keyboard to toggle between selected controls.

✦ **Text color:** When you're working with text, a different color control becomes active. The Text color control is visible and displays the currently selected text color, as shown in Figure 6-2. Text can have both the stroke and fill colored.

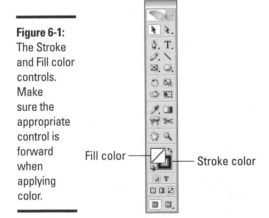

Figure 6-1: The Stroke and Fill color controls. Make sure the appropriate control is forward when applying color.

Fill color — Stroke color

To apply colors to selections, you can click the Apply color button below the color controls in the toolbox. Alternatively, you can select and click a color swatch.

REMEMBER

The default colors in InDesign are a black stroke and no color for the fill. Go back to the default colors at any time by pressing D. This works while on any tool except the Type tool.

Figure 6-2:
The Text
color
control is
active.

Understanding Color Models

You can use any of three kinds of color models in InDesign: CMYK, RGB, and LAB colors. A *color model* is a system used for representing each color as a set of numbers or letters (or both). The best color model to use depends on how you plan to print out or display your document:

✦ If you're creating a PDF that will be distributed electronically and probably won't be printed out, use the RGB color model. RGB is how colors are displayed on a computer monitor.

✦ You must use the CMYK color model if you're working with *process color:* Instead of having inks that match specified colors, four ink colors are layered to simulate a particular color. Note that the colors on the monitor may differ from what is actually printed. Sample swatch books and numbers can help you determine what colors you need to use in your document to match what will be printed in the end.

✦ If you know that the document needs to be printed by professionals who determine what each color is before it's printed, it doesn't matter whether you use RGB, Pantones, or LAB colors. You have to make sure you use named colors (predetermined swatches are a good idea) so that the service provider knows which color should be printed. In this case, you're using *spot colors,* which are mixed inks that match the colors you specify in InDesign.

For more information on color models and inks, check out Book I, Chapter 7. This chapter explains how colors are determined in the different color modes.

Using Color Swatches and Libraries

The Swatches palette and swatch libraries help you choose the colors. Swatch libraries help you use colors for specific publishing purposes. The colors you use in a document can vary greatly depending on what you're creating the document for. For example, one publication you make with InDesign may be for a catalog that only has two colors; another may be for the Web, where you have many colors available to you.

The Swatches palette

You can create, apply, and edit colors using the Swatches palette. In addition to solid colors, this palette also allows you to create and edit tints and gradients, and then apply them to objects on a page.

Choose Window⇨Swatches to open or expand the Swatches palette, as shown in Figure 6-3.

Figure 6-3:
The
Swatches
palette.

To create a new color swatch to use in your document, follow these steps:

1. **Click the arrow in the upper-right corner to open the Swatches palette menu; choose New Color Swatch.**

   The New Color Swatch dialog box opens.

2. **Type a new name for the color swatch, or leave the color named by color values. (The colors in the Swatches palette appear this way as a default.)**

   This name is displayed next to the color swatch when it is entered into the palette.

3. **Choose the color type from the Color Type drop-down menu.**

   Are you using a spot color (Pantone, for instance) or CMYK (color created from a combination of Cyan, Magenta, Yellow, Black)?

4. Choose the color mode.

Using the Color Mode drop down menu, select a color mode (see Figure 6-4). For this example, we use CMYK. Many of the other choices that you see are pre-built color libraries for various systems.

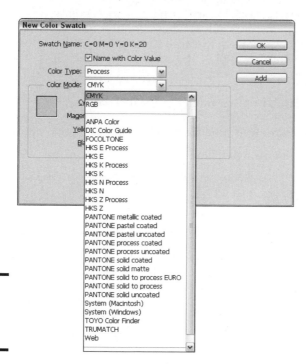

Figure 6-4:
Choosing
the color
mode.

5. Create the color using the color sliders.

Note that if you start with Black, you have to adjust that slider to the left to see the other colors.

6. Click OK or Add.

Click Add if you want to continue adding colors to your Swatches palette, or click OK if this color is the only one you are adding. The color(s) are added to the Swatches palette.

You can make changes to the swatch by selecting the swatch in the Swatches palette and then choosing Swatch Options from the palette menu.

Swatch libraries

Swatch libraries, also known as *color libraries,* are standardized sets of named colors that help you because they are the most commonly and frequently used sets of color swatches. This means that you can avoid trying to mix your own colors, which can be a difficult or tedious process to get right. For example, InDesign includes a swatch library for Pantone spot colors, and a different library for Pantone process colors. These libraries are very useful if you're working with either color set. (Refer to the earlier section, "Understanding Color Models," where we explain the difference between spot and process colors.)

To choose a swatch from a swatch library, follow these steps:

1. **Choose New Color Swatch from the Swatches palette menu.**

   The New Color Swatch dialog box opens.

2. **Select the color type you want to work with from the Color Type drop-down list.**

   Choose from Process or Spot Color types.

3. **Select a color library from the Color Mode drop-down list.**

   The drop-down list contains a list of color swatch libraries to choose from, such as Pantone Process Coated or TRUMATCH. After choosing a swatch set, the library opens and appears in the dialog box. For this example we chose the standard Pantone solid coated. If you are looking for the standard numbered Pantone colors, this is the easiest to choose from. The Pantone solid coated library of swatches loads.

4. **Pick a swatch from the library.**

   Type a Pantone number in the Pantone text box, if you have one. Most companies have set Pantone colors that they use for consistency. You can also scroll and click on a swatch in the library's list of colors as shown in Figure 6-5. Careful though, picking Pantone colors this way is rarely accurate, spending the money on the PANTONE(r) solid to process guide is a wise investment. Get more details about this guide at www.pantone.com.

5. **Click the Add button.**

   This adds the swatch to your list of color swatches in the Swatches palette. You can add as many color swatches as you like.

6. **When you're finished adding swatches, click the Done button.**

   After you add a new color, the swatch is added to the list of swatches in the Swatches palette and is ready to use in your project. Look in the Swatches palette to see the newly added colors.

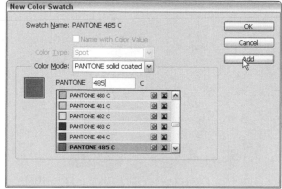

Book II
Chapter 6

Understanding
Color and Printing

Figure 6-5:
Choose a color from the swatch library and add it to the Swatches palette.

Printing Your Work

You can print your work from an InDesign document in many different ways, using many kinds of printers and processes. You can either use a printer at home or in your office, which are of varying levels of quality and design, or you can take your work into a professional establishment to print. Printing establishments (or service providers) also vary in the quality of production they can offer you.

This section looks at the different ways you can set up your document for printing, and the kinds of issues you may encounter during this process.

What is a bleed?

If you want an image or span of color to go right to the edge of a page, without any margins, you need to *bleed* off the edge of the document, This extends the print area slightly beyond the edge of the page into the area that will be cut as usual during the printing process. When you print your work, you can turn on crop and bleed marks to show where the page needs to be trimmed and to make sure the image bleeds properly. We cover this in the last section of this chapter, "Doing it yourself: Printing at home or in the office."

About trapping

When you print documents, the printer is seldom absolutely perfect when creating a printed page with multiple inks. The *registration* (which determines the alignment of the separate colors when printed) will most surely be off. This can potentially cause a gap between two colors on the page so unprinted paper shows through between them. To solve this problem, you use *trapping*. Trapping overlaps elements on the page slightly so that you don't have that gap in between the elements. The basic principle of trapping is to spread the lighter of the colors into the other, See Figure 6-6 for an example.

Figure 6-6:
Text on the
left as it
appears in
InDesign.
Text on the
right as it
appears
when
printed with
trapping
applied.

InDesign has built-in software for trapping. The settings you make are applied to the entire page. You choose settings in the Trap Presets palette. You can use the default settings, customize the trapping settings, or decide not to use trapping at all. To modify the default settings and then apply the customized settings, follow these steps:

1. Choose Window⇨Output⇨Trap Presets.

The Trap Presets palette opens, as shown in Figure 6-7.

Figure 6-7:
The Trap
Presets
palette.

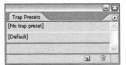

The Trapping presets in InDesign are document-wide, but you can assign individual trappings by using the Window⇨Attributes palette to over-print strokes on selected art only.

2. Double-click [Default] in the palette's list.

The Modify Trap Preset Options dialog box opens, as shown in Figure 6-8. The default settings are perfectly adequate for many printing jobs.

3. Change the trap preset options, if you know what is necessary, and then click OK to close the dialog box.

If you do not know what to change, you should investigate the options for a better understanding of how they work. You can also get settings from your print provider.

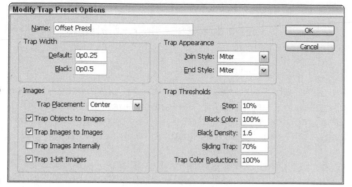

Figure 6-8:
The Modify
Trap Preset
Options
dialog box.

4. **In the Trap Presets palette, choose New Preset from the palette menu.**

   The New Trap Preset dialog box opens.

5. **Type an appropriate name for the new trap preset.**

   You see this name in the list of trap presets in the Trap Presets palette when it's opened. You might create a name for a printer that has different settings than another.

6. **Review and make any changes to the new preset in the dialog box.**

   You can change the presets in the following ways:

   • **Trap Width:** The Default value specifies the width of the trap for any ink that you use in the document, except for black. The value for black is entered into the Black text field.

   • **Images:** These settings control how InDesign handles trapping between elements on the document page and any imported graphics on it. Use the Trap Placement drop-down list to define how images trap to objects on the page. When you have bitmap images next to each other, select the Trap Images to Images check box.

   • **Trap Appearance:** These settings allow you to do some fine-tuning and change how the corner points appear in trapping. You can select how you want the corner points to appear with the Join Style drop-down list; you can select how you want end points to appear (overlapped or separated) from the End Style drop-down list.

   • **Trap Thresholds:** These settings allow you to control how InDesign traps the areas between two colors in your document. You can control whether InDesign traps two objects of similar colors (for example, how different do these colors have to be before InDesign starts trapping).

7. Click OK to create the trap preset.

The New Trap Preset dialog box closes, and the customized preset is added to the palette.

To assign a trap preset to a number of pages (or all of them), click the arrow in the upper-right corner of the Trap Preset palette and choose Assign Trap Preset from the palette menu. The dialog box that opens allows you to choose a trapping style and assign it to all pages or a range of pages. Click the Assign button to assign the preset before clicking the Done button.

There are also other ways to apply trapping to your document manually. This process goes beyond the scope of this book, but is worthwhile to look into if you want to fully realize what trapping is all about. Refer to *InDesign CS2 Bible* (written by Galen Gruman and published by Wiley Publishing, Inc.) for more information on trapping.

Taking your files to a service provider

If you're taking your file to a professional print service (service provider), you may have to save the `.indd` document as a different format. Even though they should, not all service providers will have InDesign on hand.

There are two major groups of printers: PostScript and non-PostScript. PostScript printers take files written in the PostScript language and read the files to print them. PostScript files describe the contents of each page and how they should look when printed. Most printers you find in a home or office are not PostScript printers.

If you're giving the file to someone to print, you can pass on your work in a few different ways. You can give the person printing the document your original InDesign document. Of course, he or she (or the business) must have a copy of InDesign on hand to open the file. Or you can send a PostScript file or PDF file to print. Sometimes, you have to ask what the preferred file type for opening and printing the document is. You're probably best off sending the original InDesign file (if you can) or a PDF. When you create a PDF, your documents should print accurately.

The *Preflight* feature is used to check for quality in your document, and tell you information about the document you're printing (such as listing the fonts, print settings, and inks that you're using). Using Preflight can help you determine whether your InDesign document has unlinked images or missing fonts before printing your document. Choose File➪Preflight to access the Preflight dialog box shown in Figure 6-9.

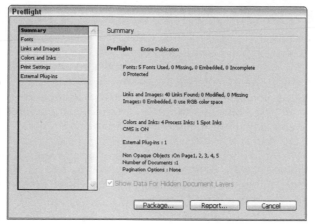

Figure 6-9:
The Preflight summary window, notice that it picked up on the images being RGB.

You can determine whether any elements associated with the file are missing, and then package it into a single folder to take the document to a service provider. Here's how:

1. **Choose File⇨Preflight.**

The Preflight dialog box opens. The Summary screen is open to begin with, and it shows you all the current images and fonts found in the document. Essentially, the summary is based on an analysis of the document.

2. **Click Fonts in the list on the left side of the dialog box.**

Any fonts in your document are listed in this screen. Select fonts on this list and click the Find Font button to discover where they're located on your hard drive. These fonts are directly saved into the package folder when you are finished.

3. **Click Links and Images in the list on the left side of the dialog box.**

The Links and Images screen lists the images within your document. You have to find the image, update it, and repair links before packing the file. If any images aren't properly linked, your document is incomplete and will print with pictures missing. Also, make sure that if you are sending your work to a professional printer, you have properly converted your images to CMYK. For your desktop printer, RGB should be fine.

4. **When you're finished, click the Package button at the bottom of the dialog box.**

Your document and all the associated files are saved into a folder. You're given the opportunity to name the folder and specify a location on the hard drive.

Doing it yourself: Printing at home or in the office

You have probably printed out other kinds of documents in the past, and perhaps you've even played with the printer settings. These settings depend on what kind of printer you're using and associated printer drivers you have installed on your system. Whatever operating system you work with, and whatever printer you use, you have some settings that control the printer's output. This section deals only with the more basic and common kinds of printing that you may perform at home or in the office.

Choose File⇨Print to open the Print dialog box, as shown in Figure 6-10. Many printing options are available in the list on the left side of the Print dialog box. Click an item, and the dialog box changes to display the settings you can change for the selected item.

Figure 6-10: The Print dialog box allows you to change settings in many different ways.

The options you're most likely to use when printing InDesign documents are as follows:

✦ **General:** Allows you to set the number of copies of the document you want to print and the range of pages to print. You can select the Reverse Order check box to print from the last to first page. Select an option from the Sequence drop-down list to print only even or odd pages instead of all pages. If you're working with spreads that need to be printed on a single page, select the Spreads check box.

✦ **Setup:** This screen is where you can define the paper size, orientation (portrait or landscape), and scale. You can scale a page so it is up to 1000% of its original size or as little as 1%. You can optionally constrain the scale of the width and height so that the page remains at the same ratio. The Page position drop-down list is useful when you're using paper that is larger than the document you have created. This option helps you to center the document on the larger paper.

✦ **Marks and Bleed:** The settings on this screen allow you to turn on or off many of the printing marks in the document, such as crop, bleed, and registration marks. For example, you may want to show these marks if you have a bleed extending past the boundaries of the page and need to show where to crop each page. This screen also shows a preview of what the page looks like when printed. You can also select options to print page information (such as filename and date) on each page.

✦ **Output:** This area allows you to choose how you're going to print the pages. For example, as a separation or composite, with which inks (if you are using separations), with or without trapping, and so forth. InDesign can separate and print your documents as plates (which are used in commercial printing) from settings you specify here.

✦ **Graphics:** This screen controls how graphics and fonts in the document are printed. The Send Data drop-down list controls bitmap images and how much of the data from these images is sent to the printer. The All option sends all bitmap data, the Optimized Subsampling option sends as much image data as the printer can handle, the Proxy option prints lower-quality images mostly to preview them, and the None option prints placeholder boxes with an X through them.

✦ **Color management:** In this area, you choose how you want color handled upon output. If you have profiles loaded in your system for your output devices, you can select them here.

✦ **Advanced:** Use this area to determine how you want images to be sent to the printer. If you do not have a clue about OPI, you can leave this setting at the default.

Flattening needs to be addressed if you used a drop shadow, feathered an object in InDesign, or applied transparency to any of your objects, even if they were created in Photoshop or Illustrator.

Use the preset Medium Resolution for desktop printers, and High Resolution for professional press output.

✦ **Summary:** This window does not allow for modifications, but provides you a good overview of all of your print settings.

After you make your settings, click the Save Preset button if you want to save the changes you have made. If you think you may print other documents with these settings repeatedly, using the Save Preset feature can be a great timesaver.

After you click the Save Preset button, the Save Preset dialog box opens, where you can enter a new name to save the settings as. The next time you print a document, you can select the saved preset from the Print Preset drop-down list in the Print dialog box.

Click the Print button at the bottom of the Print dialog box when you're ready to print the document.

Chapter 7: Exporting Your Work

You can export publications into several different kinds of file formats from InDesign, just as you can import various kinds of file formats. We touch on printing your files in Chapter 6 of this minibook, but in this chapter, we move a few steps forward and take a closer look at the different kinds of files you can create electronically with an InDesign document.

Exporting documents helps you import InDesign work into other software packages, which means that you can in turn save your work in even more formats. Exporting work also means that your documents can be displayed in different media (such as on the Web), making them accessible to a wider audience. Also, you may need to export your documents so that you can take them into a service provider to be printed. Therefore, understanding how to export and the main settings involved with each format can help your workflow greatly.

Understanding File Formats

What kind of file format you decide to export to depends on what you're going to use the file for. The first thing you want to do is figure out what you need your content to do. Does it need to be on a Web page, or do you need to send the file by e-mail? Do you need to import the content into a different program, such as Macromedia Flash or Adobe Illustrator? Do you need to take a particular kind of file somewhere else to print it out?

Exporting your files to a particular format is how you can take your content from InDesign and make it "portable" for integration or display purposes. You can choose from a range of formats, and you can control many settings to customize how the file is exported.

You can export a file in several different file formats from InDesign. You can export to image files (JPEG and EPS). You can also export to an InCopy story, XML files, SVG files, Adobe PDF format, and rich or plain text.

Different file formats are used for different purposes. Here are some of the things you can do with files exported from InDesign:

✦ **Image files:** Image files such as JPEG and EPS can be exported from InDesign and then imported into other software programs. You can export these images for use in print after being imported into a different graphics program, or you can use the images on the Web. It all depends on how you set up the document for export and the settings you use.

✦ **PDFs:** PDF (Portable Document Format) is a common format used extensively for distributing files, such as e-books, brochures, and so on. You may need to distribute the file to a wide audience or to a service provider for printing. Anyone who has installed the Adobe Reader (also known as Acrobat Reader) on his or her computer can view your document. PDF is also used for importing as an image or text into other programs, such as Macromedia Flash MX 2004.

✦ **InCopy stories:** InCopy is tightly integrated with InDesign and is used to create and edit text documents. Therefore, if you have InCopy, you can export to it when you want to extensively edit the text in your file. InCopy is used for word processing and is designed to integrate with InDesign for associated page layout. Read more about this application at `www.adobe.com/products/incopy`.

✦ **SVG files:** You can export as SVG (Scalable Vector Graphics), which is a file format that combines XML and CSS to display your files. SVG is a vector-based format that is also used for displaying content online through use of an oversized plug-in called SVG Viewer. You can download it for Mac or Windows platforms from `www.adobe.com/support/downloads/main.html` (look under the "Readers" section).

✦ **Text files:** Text files are a simple way to export your content. If you need the text from your document only to incorporate or send elsewhere, you can export as plain (Text Only), tagged, or rich text. If you need to send your document to someone who does not have InDesign, then exporting as text may be a good option.

After determining which file format you want to export your file as, take a look at how to export these files and the different kinds of settings you can control when doing so. The rest of this chapter shows you how to export different file types from InDesign.

We cover exporting InCopy stories in Chapter 8 of this minibook.

You can also export XML documents from InDesign. Although this goes beyond the scope of this book, you can find help on this in the InDesign documentation that comes with your software. If you're interested in XML and know how to make use of it, we encourage you to try this export option. Exporting XML can open the doors wide for what InDesign can offer to you, and it's a good way of putting data online.

Exporting Publications

You can export publications from the Export dialog box, shown in Figure 7-1. Access the Export dialog box by choosing File⇨Export. From this main Export dialog box, you can choose the file format, a name for the file, and a location to save it in. After specifying a name, location, and a format to export to for the new file, click Save, and a new dialog box opens where you can make settings specific to the file format you picked. We discuss some of the most common file formats that you're likely to use for export in the following sections.

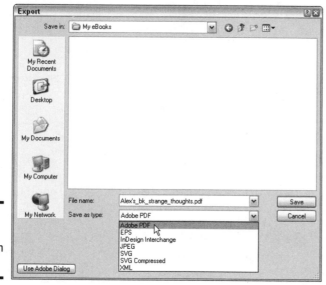

Figure 7-1:
The Export
dialog box in
InDesign.

Exporting PDF documents

InDesign allows you to export a PDF file of your document or book. If you choose to export a PDF document, there are many options available to customize the document you're exporting. You can control the amount of compression for the document, the marks and bleeds you have in InDesign, and security settings. Here's how you export a PDF:

1. **Choose File⇨Export.**

The Export dialog box opens.

2. **Choose a location in which to save the files and enter a new filename.**

Browse to a location on your hard drive using the Save In drop-down list if you're using Windows, and name the file in the File Name text field.

Name the file in the Save As text field on the Mac and choose a location using the Where drop-down list.

3. **Select PDF from the Save as Type (Windows) or Format (Mac) drop-down list.**

4. **Click Save.**

The Export PDF dialog box appears with the General options screen open, as shown in Figure 7-2.

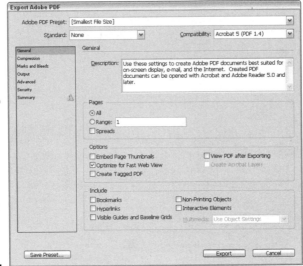

Figure 7-2:
The Export PDF dialog box contains many settings you can control to create your PDF.

5. **Choose a Preset.**

These presets are very good and easy to use. If you are familiar with Adobe Acrobat and the Adobe Distiller functions, they are the same. For more detailed information about what each setting does, see Book V, "Adobe Acrobat 7.0."

6. **Leave the Standard drop-down menu at None.**

Unless, of course, you know about PDF/X and know which form of it to select. The details of PDF/X are explained in Book VI, "Adobe Acrobat 7."

7. **Select a range of pages to export.**

You can choose to export all pages or a range of pages.

8. **Choose a compatibility setting for the PDF in the Options area.**

Compatibility settings determine what kind of reader is required to view the document. Setting compatibility to Acrobat 5 (PDF 1.4) ensures a wide audience can view your PDF. Some PDF readers may not be able to interpret certain features in your document if you choose compatibility for a higher version.

9. Choose whether to embed thumbnails, whether to optimize the document, and what kinds of elements to include in the file.

Other settings allow you to include bookmarks, links, and other elements in the file. Unless you've added any of these elements, you don't need to worry about selecting these options. You may want to embed thumbnail previews, but an Acrobat user can create their own thumbnails when the file is open as well.

Click Security in the list on the left of the Export PDF dialog box to open the Security screen, where you can specify passwords to open the document. You can also choose a password that is required to print or modify the PDF file.

10. Click the Export button to export the file.

The file is saved to the location you specified in Step 2.

You can choose a preset to export your work from the Preset drop-down list on the General screen. These presets automatically change the export settings for your document. For example, you can select Screen from the Preset drop-down list if you're displaying your work online, or select Print if you plan for the PDF to be printed on home printers. Select Press if you intend to have the PDF professionally printed.

Many professional printers want High Resolution PDFs sent to them with marks and bleeds. Talk to your printer before exporting. If you are lucky, they can send you their preset, or educate you as to how to create the proper preset yourself.

Exporting EPS files

From InDesign, you can export EPS files, which are useful for importing into other programs. EPS files are single-page graphics files, which means each exported InDesign page is saved as a separate EPS file. Here's how to export EPS files:

1. Choose File⇨Export.

The Export dialog box opens (refer to Figure 7-1).

2. Select a location on your hard drive to save the EPS files, enter a new filename, and select EPS from the Save as Type (Windows) or Format (Mac) drop-down list; click Save.

The Export EPS dialog box opens, as shown in Figure 7-3.

Book II
Chapter 7

Exporting Your
Work

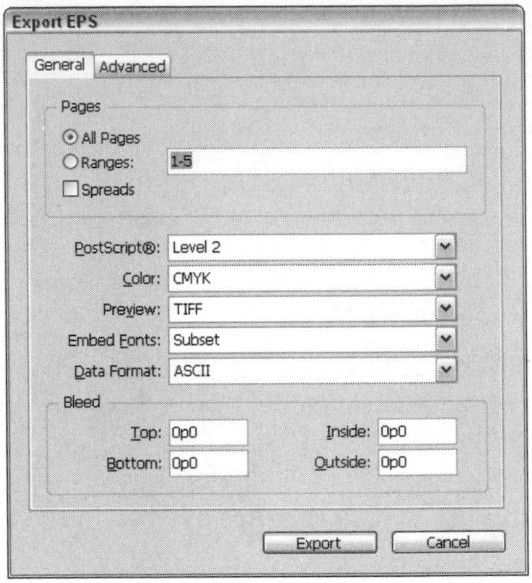

Figure 7-3:
The Export
EPS dialog
box.

3. Choose a page or range of pages to export.

Select the All Pages option to export all pages, or select the Ranges option and enter a range of pages. If you want spreads to export as one file, then select the Spreads check box.

If you're creating more than one EPS file (for example, exporting more than one page of your InDesign document), then the file is saved with the filename, an underscore, and then the page number. For example, page 7 of a file called `cats.indd` would be saved as `cats_7.eps` in the designated location.

4. From the Color drop-down list, select a color mode; from the Embed Fonts drop-down list, select how you want fonts to be embedded.

From the Color drop-down list, select Leave Unchanged to retain the color mode you're using for the InDesign document. You can also change the color mode to CMYK, Gray (grayscale), or RGB. For more information on color modes, flip to Chapter 6 of this minibook.

From the Embed Fonts drop-down list, select Subset to embed only the characters that are used in the file. If you select Complete, all the fonts in the file are loaded when you print the file. Selecting None means that a reference to where the font is located is written into the file.

5. Choose whether you want a preview to be generated for the file.

A preview (a small thumbnail image) is useful if an EPS file cannot be displayed. For example, if you're browsing through a library of images, you'll see a small thumbnail image of the EPS file; so whether or not you use the image or can open it on your computer, you can see what the file looks like. From the Preview drop-down list, you can select TIFF to generate a preview; select None if you don't want a preview to be created.

If you're exporting for a PostScript printer, set the compatibility by selecting Level 2 or Level 3 from the PostScript drop-down list. Level 2 and Level 3 are two different kinds of PostScript printers that are supported by InDesign. Each kind of printer is a different device, and has different kinds of capabilities. For example, setting the printer to Level 3 means your work prints quickly and at very high quality, but you need a Level 3 PostScript printer to use this setting.

6. Click the Export button to export the files.

The files are saved to the location you designated in Step 2.

Exporting JPEG files

You can export JPEG files from an InDesign document. You can export a single object on the selected page, or you can export entire pages and spreads as a JPEG image. JPEG files allow you to effectively compress full color or black and white images.

To export a JPEG image, follow these steps:

1. Select an object on a page, or make sure no object is selected if you want to export a page or spread.

2. Choose File➪Export.

The Export dialog box opens.

3. Type a filename, locate where you want to save the file on your hard drive, and select JPEG from the Save as Type (Windows) or Format (Mac) drop-down list; click Save.

The Export JPEG dialog box opens, as shown in Figure 7-4.

Figure 7-4:
The Export JPEG dialog box allows you to choose settings for the JPEG file.

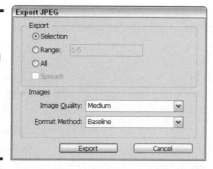

4. **If you want to export a page, select the Page option and enter the page number; if you want to export the currently selected object, make sure the Selection option is selected.**

   The selection option is available only if a selection was made in Step 1.

5. **Choose an image quality and format to export.**

   The Image Quality drop-down list controls the amount of compression used when you export the JPEG. The Maximum option creates an image with the highest file size and best quality, while the Low option creates a smaller file of lesser quality because it includes less image information.

   If you choose the Baseline format from the Format Method drop-down list, the entire image has to be downloaded before it displays in a Web browser. Select Progressive to show the image in a progressively complete display as it downloads in a Web browser.

6. **Click the Export button.**

   The file exports and saves to the location that you specified in Step 3.

Exporting SVG files

You can export to SVG using the Export dialog box (refer to Figure 7-1). You can export a spread, pages, or even a single element from a page of the InDesign document. Here's how you export an SVG file:

1. **Select an object on a page, or make sure no object is selected if you want to export a page or spread.**

2. **Choose File⇨Export.**

   The Export dialog box opens.

3. **Choose a location to save the files, enter a new filename, and select SVG from the Save as Type (Windows) or Format (Mac) drop-down list; click Save.**

   The SVG Options dialog box opens, as shown in Figure 7-5.

4. **Select a page, range of pages, spreads, or selection to export in the SGV Options dialog box.**

   If you have selected an object, select the Export Selection check box. Alternatively, you can select the Range option and enter values for a range of pages to export. If you chose to export pages, each page (or spread) is exported as a separate SVG file.

5. **Choose to use glyphs or a character set in the Fonts section.**

   If you don't plan to change text in the document, you can embed glyphs by selecting Only Glyphs Used from the Subsetting drop-down list.

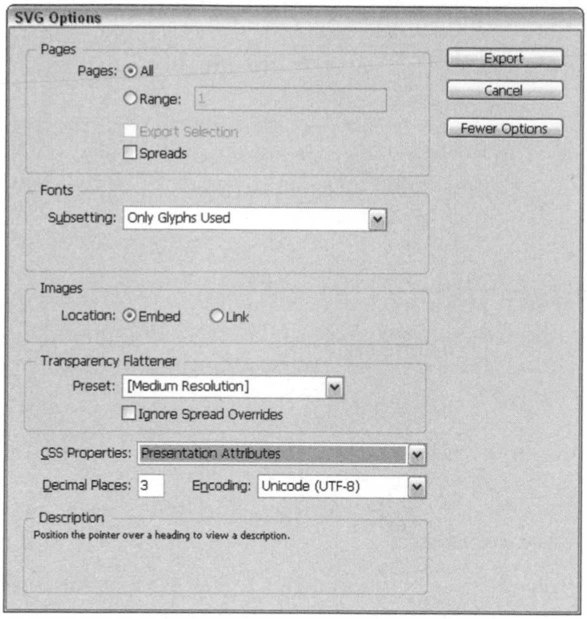

Figure 7-5:
The SVG
Options
dialog box.

A *glyph* is a single character. For example, N is a glyph, which is different from the P glyph, and a set of glyphs makes up a particular font. The Only Glyphs Used setting means that only the characters you use export in the document. Otherwise, you can choose to use a set of characters (such as Common English) to export, which means all the characters in the English or Roman characters are included for the fonts you use.

You can also choose not to embed characters at all, and use system fonts on the user's system. This means the user has to have the fonts you use installed on his or her system for the characters to display properly, or a default font is used as a replacement.

For more information on glyphs, refer to Book I, Chapter 6.

6. **Choose to embed or link to bitmap image files used in the Images section.**

If you select the Embed option, your bitmap images in the SVG file are larger when they export because the image is included within the file itself. If you select the Link option, then the SVG file is smaller but you have to make sure to include the bitmap images with the SVG files when you upload or send your work. InDesign converts your images into JPEG files, and saves them with the SVG file.

Use the Description area to discover more about each setting. Hover your cursor over a setting, and a description of the setting appears at the bottom of the dialog box.

7. Click the Export button to export the file.

The files are exported and saved to the location you designated in Step 3.

If you want to put your InDesign pages online, you can package the document for GoLive. GoLive is used for designing and creating Web pages. For more information on packaging InDesign pages for GoLive, read Chapter 8 of this minibook.

Exporting text files

You can export plain or rich text from an InDesign document, or as an InDesign tagged text format. These formats can be slightly different, depending on the text in your document.

To export text, follow these steps:

1. Select the Text tool from the toolbox and select some text within a text frame in your document.

You must have text selected in order to see text export options in the Export dialog box.

2. Choose File➪Export.

The Export dialog box opens (refer to Figure 7-1).

3. Enter a filename, select a location to save the file in, and select Text Only from the Save as Type (Windows) or Format (Mac) drop-down list; click Save.

The Text Export Options dialog box opens, as shown in Figure 7-6.

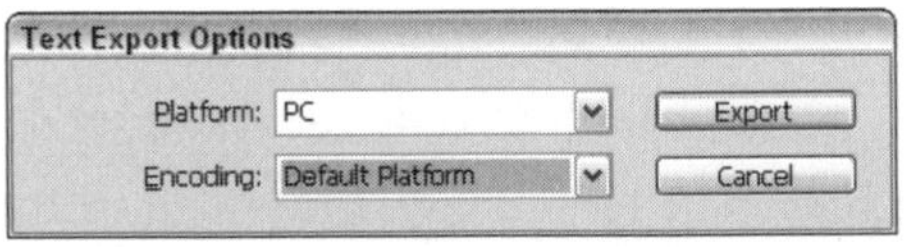

Figure 7-6:
The Text
Export
Options
dialog box.

Text Export Options

Platform: PC

Encoding: Default Platform

Export

Cancel

4. Choose a platform and encoding for the export.

Select either Windows or Macintosh from the Platform drop-down list to set the PC or Mac operating system compatibility. Select an encoding method for the platform you choose from the Encoding drop-down list; you can choose either Default Platform or Unicode.

Unicode is a universal character-encoding standard that is compatible with major operating systems. *Encoding* refers to how characters are represented in a digital format, and it is essentially a set of rules that determines how the character set is represented by associating each character with a particular code sequence.

5. **Click the Export button.**

The file exports and saves to the location that you specified in Step 3.

Chapter 8: Integrating InDesign

The Adobe Creative Suite and specifically in this chapter, InDesign, offer you a multitude of options to integrate all of the Creative Suite 2 applications. When you *integrate products,* you work on a single project using more than one piece of software.

When software products are built as a suite, it typically is an advantage to the user. Software designers create ways that the user can integrate the products to work together and give the user more power to maintain a workflow, check errors, and help with consistency in a project. This is true of the Adobe Creative Suite 2: By making the products work together, you can get some incredible results!

Using InDesign with Version Cue

Using Adobe Version Cue, you can keep a project organized and accessible from all of the creative suite applications. This is like an Aha! when you discover its capabilities. Many users do not jump right in because they have never experienced the convenience project management software provides, but we guarantee that you will love it.

Adobe Version Cue manages files you author in the following Adobe Creative Suite 2 components: Photoshop, InDesign, Illustrator, GoLive, and Acrobat 7. In Version Cue, you create projects, either new, blank projects that you save into, or new projects from existing work. You and other users can then access the projects through the Creative Suite applications. Version Cue manages files stored in projects, which keep all the files related to an assignment together in one place. This can even include non Adobe files, such as spreadsheets and invoices. Because Version Cue works in each Creative

Suite component, your design process isn't interrupted when you work on each file in a project.

You can use Version Cue to track changes to files as you work on them. You can even keep several versions of each file for future reference. By using Version Cue, multiple users can access files in a project, work on them and "lock out" anyone else who may want to work on the file at the same time. Benefit to this one: no changes being overwritten accidentally by another person on your team!

The following list is a quick look at what you can do with Version Cue:

✦ Create a new project and organize all your files into that single project

✦ Make your projects secure, private, or shared

✦ Create and manage different versions of a file

✦ Insert comments that you can refer to later

✦ Browse projects with comments, thumbnails, and information on each file contained within the project

✦ Back up projects

✦ Set and remove permissions on the project files (if you're working with the more advanced features of Version Cue)

✦ Add users to a project, who can work on and edit files

✦ Share projects among several users

New in this version of Version Cue, you can host PDF reviews from your computer. Any PDF file in a project can be reviewed. Automatic e-mail generation allows you to quickly invite users to the review.

You must have Version Cue CS2 installed on your system before you can use these features. Version Que is enabled in InDesign as a default. Verify that Version Cue CS2 is installed by following these steps:

1. **Choose Edit⬄Preferences⬄File Handling (Windows) or InDesign⬄ Preferences⬄File Handling (Mac OS).**

   The Preferences dialog box appears with the File Handling screen open, as shown in Figure 8-1.

2. **If the Enable Version Cue check box is not selected, click it and then click OK.**

   You must restart InDesign before your modifications take effect.

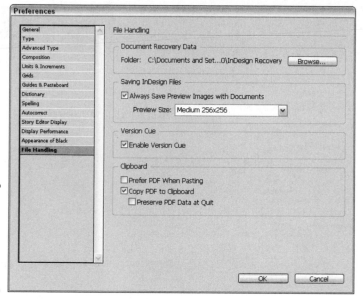

**Book II
Chapter 8**

Integrating InDesign

Figure 8-1:
Enable
Version
Cue in the
Preferences
dialog box.

Setting up a Project file

The scope of this book does not allow for a lot of detail in project management, but it would be helpful to see how to set up a project file and save to it. To set up a project folder, follow these steps:

1. **Launch Version Cue CS2 (Windows) in the Control Panel. If you are working on a Mac, choose Apple⇨System Preferences⇨Other⇨ Version Cue CS2.**

   In the Version Cue CS2 window select the Advanced Administration button. A login window appears.

2. **Use the standard Login:**

   Login: system

   Password: system

   The Version Cue interface, shown in Figure 8-2, makes it very easy to follow along to create a new project folder and assign users. Once you complete this process, you can start taking advantage of its benefits.

   If you want more help with setting up a project using Version Cue, launch the Adobe Bridge application. This resides in the same folder as your other Adobe Creative Suite applications. Click *Version Cue* in the left column and choose Help⇨Version Cue Help (see Figure 8-3).

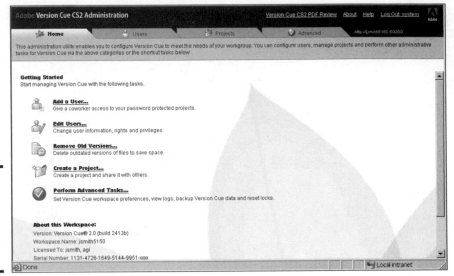

Figure 8-2:
The Version Cue interface is easy to work with.

Figure 8-3:
Access all Help files, including Version Cue, from the Adobe Bridge application.

3. **Select Create a project.**

4. **Select Blank Project, create a name (perhaps *test project*), and enter it in the Project Name text box.**

5. **Click the Save button.**

Adding a user to the project

To add a user to the project, simply follow these steps:

1. **Click the Users tab at the top of the Version Cue CS2 window.**

2. **Click New.**

3. **Choose an admin access level of System Administrator for yourself, and enter a name, login, and password.**

   Pick something easy to remember!

4. **Click the Save button, and close the Version Cue CS2 interface window.**

Next, you return to InDesign to save a file into the project folder.

Saving a file into a project

Return to InDesign and create a new document, or open an existing one that you want to save in a project file. To save the file into a project, follow these steps:

1. **Choose File⇨Save As.**

2. **In the Save As window, click the Use Adobe Dialog button.**

   The Save dialog appears, similar to the one shown in Figure 8-4.

3. **Select Version Cue from the panel on the left. You user name is now listed.**

Book II
Chapter 8

Integrating InDesign

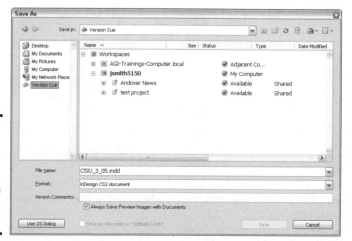

Figure 8-4:
The Save As dialog window when Adobe Dialog is selected.

4. Double-click your user name, and locate your project. Double-click the project and name and save your file.

This is just a start. Once you save into a project, you can save various versions, set up other users to share that file (remember that they are locked out if you are using it), and help you to keep entire projects organized . . . what fun!

Integrating InDesign with Acrobat

You can import, export, and create documents for creating PDF files using InDesign. These files can be further manipulated using Adobe Acrobat, or you can build in certain features using InDesign instead. In Chapter 7 of this minibook, you discovered more about exporting PDF files from InDesign. In this chapter, we look at some of the other ways that you can control PDF attributes right in InDesign. InDesign is one of the best ways to design and create PDF documents. With InDesign, you can add features and interactivity to a PDF in the following ways:

✦ Add clickable elements, such as hyperlinks and bookmarks

✦ Add buttons that perform actions

✦ Add movies (such as Flash SWF files or QuickTime movies) and sound files

In this section, we show you how to add some basic interactivity to a PDF file using InDesign by adding a movie file and creating a hyperlink. You can add an SWF file or an MOV file, depending on what you have available. These media files will not play while you're using InDesign. However, the files will play if you export the document to PDF or XML, or package the InDesign document for GoLive. To view a movie in a PDF file, double-click the movie.

You can add the following movie files to a PDF: SWF, MOV, AVI, and MPEG. And you can add these audio files: AIF, AU, and WAV.

You can add hyperlinks to link to another piece of text, a page, or a URL (a Web site address). To create a URL hyperlink in a PDF using InDesign, follow these steps:

1. Open a new document that includes some text in a text frame.

Choose a document that you want to add a hyperlink to.

2. Open the Hyperlinks palette by choosing Window⇨Interactive⇨Hyperlinks.

The Hyperlinks palette opens. Notice that the palette's menu contains several options, and there are buttons along the bottom of the palette that you can use to add new hyperlinks or delete links from the palette.

3. **Use the Text tool to select some text.**

   Select the text that you want to make into a hyperlink.

4. **Click the Create New Hyperlink button at the bottom of the Hyperlinks palette.**

   The New Hyperlink dialog box opens. Make sure that URL is selected in the Type drop-down list.

5. **Type a URL in the URL text field if necessary.**

   This is the Web page the URL links to. Make sure it is a complete URL, such as `http://www.yourdomain.com`. This field also accepts `mailto:` actions if you want to create an e-mail link. Simply enter an e-mail address, such as `mailto:you@yourdomain.com` in the URL text field.

Book II
Chapter 8

6. **Choose an appearance for the clickable text.**

   Under the Appearance section, you can choose to have a visible or invisible rectangle (whether you want a rectangle to appear around the link). Then you can choose the highlight, color, width, and style of your link.

7. **Click OK when you're finished.**

   The dialog box closes. When you export your document as a PDF, this text will be clickable. Clicking the text opens a browser window to the Web page you entered in the URL text field. Make sure that the Hyperlinks check box is selected in the Export PDF dialog box when you create the PDF file.

You can also select a URL that exists in your text frame. To do so, select the URL and right-click (Windows) or Control+click (Mac) the selected text. Choose Interactive⇨New Hyperlink Destination, and the dialog box opens where you can edit the link. Click OK and a hyperlink is created.

To add a media file to a PDF document using InDesign, follow these steps (remember that you need at least Acrobat Reader 6 to view the PDF and play the media file):

1. **Choose File⇨Place.**

   The Place dialog box opens, where you can choose a media file to import. Choose an SWF, MOV, AVI, or MPEG to import.

   You can import only SWF files created for the Flash 5 Player and earlier. You can't import files into InDesign created for Flash Player 6 or Flash Player 7.

2. **Click within the document window to place the media file on the page.**

   The Place cursor appears after you select a file to import into the document. Click where you want the upper-left corner to be situated on the page.

3. **Export the PDF file by choosing File⇨Export and choosing Adobe PDF from the Save as Type (Windows) or Format (Mac) drop-down list. Click Save.**

The Export PDF dialog box appears. Make sure that the Interactive Elements check box is selected in the Export PDF dialog box. In the Multimedia drop-down list, you can select the Embed option to include the movie in the PDF, increasing the file size, the Link option to create a link to the movie file in the PDF (you must have the file accessible to the PDF when you send it to someone or put it online), or the Use Object Settings option to use the settings already made in InDesign.

If you play the file in Acrobat Reader 6 or greater, the video plays when you double-click the frame.

Integrating InDesign with Photoshop

Many people create their designs in Photoshop (which we discuss thoroughly in Book IV), and then import the native PSD files from Photoshop 4 or greater right into InDesign. InDesign supports many of the features you can find in Photoshop, so you can have additional control over the designs after the image is imported into InDesign.

Here's a great new feature that you will be thrilled with. InDesign CS2 lets you import a layered Photoshop file and turn on and off the layers, or even choose a layer comp to be placed. Follow these steps:

1. **Have a layered Photoshop file ready to place.**

2. **In InDesign choose File⇨Place. Browse to the location of your layered image file, and check Show Import Options.**

A window similar to the one you see in Figure 8-5 appears.

3. **Click the Layers tab and turn off and on the visibility of the layers you wish to change, or select a saved layer comp from the Layer Comp drop down menu.**

Transparency support and clipping paths

Many Photoshop files use transparency. The transparency in the PSD files is imported and interpreted by InDesign. This is particularly useful when you have an established background or want to have an interesting text wrap around an image that you import from Photoshop. Basically, you can use the transparency as a *clipping path* in InDesign. Clipping paths are like hard-edged masks that hide parts of an image, such as a background that you don't want visible around a certain part of the image. (See Book IV, Chapter 3, for more about Photoshop clipping paths.)

Figure 8-5:
InDesign CS2 allows you to pick and choose the layers you want placed in native Photoshop files.

Alpha channels, paths, and masks that you create in Photoshop can be used in InDesign. InDesign recognizes these parts of the PSD, so you can use them when you're wrapping text around the image or when you want to create a clipping path. Alternatively, you can also use these parts to remove a background from the image. For example, if you have an image with one of these assets, you can use the Detect Edges feature in InDesign to detect the edges and wrap text around the image. (We explain text wrapping in Chapter 4 of this minibook.)

Photoshop spot colors in InDesign

If you're using spot colors in an image you import from Photoshop, those colors show up in the Swatches palette in InDesign. There is a chance that a color from your spot colors channel won't be recognized. If that's the case, the color is shown as gray instead. You can find more information on spot and process colors in Chapter 6 of this minibook.

The swatches imported with the Photoshop file can be used with other parts of your file. Simply use the swatches as you would any other swatch in InDesign. You cannot delete these swatches unless you remove the Photoshop file that you imported into InDesign. For more information about using the Swatches palette in InDesign, see Chapter 6 of this minibook.

Integrating InDesign with Illustrator

Illustrator (which we discuss at great length in Book III) is a tremendous drawing program that enables you to create complex drawings. Therefore, it is a great tool to use for creating illustrations bound for InDesign page layouts. Luckily, you have several ways to control your Illustrator artwork directly in InDesign, which we discuss in this section. You can import Illustrator 5.5 files and greater into InDesign and maintain the editability of the objects from the AI (Illustrator) file within InDesign. This means that you can edit the objects further after they are imported. Also, any transparency in the AI file is preserved when you import it, meaning that you can wrap text around the drawings you create.

You can also copy and paste graphics from Illustrator to InDesign, and then edit them directly in InDesign.

Integrating InDesign with InCopy

Adobe InCopy is text-editing software that enables writers to write and edit documents while layout is prepared separately. InCopy is similar to Microsoft Word in that you can make notes and comments, track changes, and use other similar editing features.

You may not have InCopy installed (it isn't part of the Adobe Creative Suite), but there are several important ways that you can integrate this Adobe software with InDesign that you shouldn't overlook. If you're extensively editing stories, you may want to consider using InCopy for writing the text and importing and editing it further using InDesign.

Using InCopy together with InDesign enables you to use a particular workflow because you can tell whether a file needs to be updated, or if it is currently being edited, by a series of icons that appear on the page in InDesign. The following sections show some of the ways that you can directly manipulate InCopy stories using InDesign.

Importing InCopy stories

Here are the steps for importing stories from InCopy:

1. **In InCopy, create and save a text file.**

    If you don't have a copy of InCopy, you can download a thirty day trial version from www.adobe.com.

2. **Return to InDesign, create a text frame, and keep it selected.**

3. **Choose File⇨Place.**

4. **Browse to locate your InCopy file. (InCopy files end with the file extension .incx.)**

    The InCopy story is placed into the text frame and in the Links palette, just like a graphic.

Updating InCopy stories

When a file is out of date, you need to update that story so that the most recent revisions are available to you for editing. You can update InCopy stories when you see an icon like the one shown in Figure 8-6.

Figure 8-6:
When an InCopy story is out of date, a warning icon appears in the text frame and the Links palette.

When you see the warning icon, you can follow these steps to update the InCopy story from InDesign:

1. **Choose the story listed in the Links palette.**

2. **Select the button Update Link in the bottom of the Links palette.**

The story updates and the icon disappears. You can now work with the up-to-date version of the story in InDesign.

Integrating InDesign with GoLive

The way InDesign handles HTML is not always the greatest. It certainly helps if you can edit HTML manually, or at least have some experience with an HTML editor to help you create Web pages from your InDesign content. If you decide to work with InDesign and GoLive together, you should use the Package for GoLive feature. (Head to Book VI for everything you ever wanted to know about using GoLive.)

Packaging an InDesign document for GoLive allows you to take InDesign documents (or even complete books) and package them up for further editing in GoLive CS2. This enables you to put InDesign documents on the Web and make them available to a wide audience. The document is exported in PDF and XML files that can be opened in GoLive.

To package a document for GoLive, follow these steps:

1. **With an InDesign document open, choose File⇨Package for GoLive.**

   The Package Publication for GoLive dialog box opens.

2. **Find a location on your hard drive for the package and enter a name for your folder in the Folder Name text field.**

   This assigns a name for the folder that will include all the packaged files for GoLive.

3. **Click the Package button (Windows) or the Save button (Mac).**

   The Package for GoLive dialog box appears and includes an option to view the package after you finish this process using GoLive or your Web browser.

4. **Select GoLive.exe from the View With drop-down list to view the package in GoLive (see Figure 8-7).**

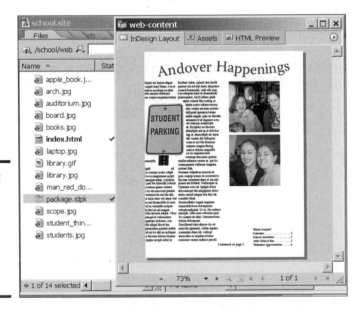

Figure 8-7: Your InDesign document opens for further editing in GoLive.

Book III

Illustrator CS2

The 5th Wave   By Rich Tennant

NATIONAL ENQUIRER
PHOTO IMAGING
WORKSHOP

"Remember, your Elvis should appear bald and slightly hunched.
Nice Big Foot, Brad. Keep your two-headed animals in the
shadows and your alien spacecrafts crisp and defined."

Contents at a Glance

Chapter 1: Discovering Illustrator CS2

In This Chapter

↙ What's new in Illustrator CS2

↙ Knowing when to use Illustrator

↙ Opening documents

↙ Creating new documents

↙ Checking out the tools

↙ Getting to know the palettes

↙ Changing views

↙ Zooming in and out

A dobe Illustrator goes hand in hand with the other Adobe products but serves its own unique purpose. Adobe Illustrator creates single-page artwork, not lengthy documents with repeated headers, footers, and page numbers, such as documents created in InDesign, and not artwork created out of pixels, such as images edited or created in Photoshop. Illustrator is generally used to create logos, illustrations, maps, packages, labels, signage, and more.

What's New in Adobe Illustrator CS2

Many of you may be new users, but there are plenty of Illustrator users who after months and years of trying to self teach, break down and buy a book to see how to better utilize the application. In either situation it is helpful to familiarize yourself with the new features implemented in Illustrator CS2; many are exciting features that simplify the illustration process for all skill levels of users.

Vector tracing

Some of you with a history of working in Adobe Illustrator may remember a small application from Adobe that allowed you to easily convert a *raster*, or bitmap image, into vector paths. This feature is now built directly into Illustrator. If you are not unfamiliar with the terms *vector*, *raster*, or *bitmap*, look for the sidebar, "Vector graphics," in this section.

You can use the vector tracing feature to take raster images in AI accepted formats, such as .psd, .tiff, .eps, .and .jpg, and trace-convert them into vector art. Discover more about this feature in Chapter 4 of this minibook.

Live Paint

The Live Paint bucket automatically detects regions composed of independent intersecting paths and fills them accordingly. The paint within a given region remains live and flows automatically if any of the paths are moved.

This paint bucket can also paint strokes as with fills. The color of a stroke flows as the intersecting regions change. For example, when you fill an intersection, the fill will change depending upon the position of the intersecting shapes. Why is this so great? Well, in the past you had to create a closed shape to control its fill. Using the Live Paint Bucket, you can scribble intersecting lines and then fill each loop with color. Read more about this feature in Chapter 8 of this minibook.

Vector graphics

Vector graphics are made up of lines and curves defined by mathematical objects called *vectors*. Because the paths (the lines and curves) are defined mathematically, you can move, resize, or change the color of vector objects without losing quality in the graphic.

Vectorgraphics are resolution-independent; that is, they can be scaled to any size and printed at any resolution without losing detail. On the other hand, bitmap graphics have a predetermined amount of pixels creating them, so you can't scale (resize) them easily — if you scale them smaller, you throw out pixels; if you scale them bigger, you end up with a blocky, jagged picture. The following figure shows the differences between an enlarged vector graphic on the left (notice the smooth edges) and an enlarged bitmap graphic on the right (note the jagged edges). Many companies have their logos created as vectors to avoid problems with scaling: A vector graphic logo maintains its high quality appearance at any size.

Control Palette

Yeah! Finally a control palette in Illustrator! This now makes Illustrator look more like other Creative Suite applications. The Control Palette is contextually sensitive and presents control options based on selected artwork. For more details about palettes, read on in this chapter.

Improved Photoshop Import options

Illustrator has added support for Photoshop Layer Comps on Import. If you have a Photoshop file with a number of saved Layer Comps, you will now be able to specify which Comp you want to import. Read more details about importing Photoshop images in Chapter 3 of this minibook.

Workspaces (It's about time!)

Illustrator will now let you save your palettes and location on screen to a named file. You may have used this feature in other Creative Suite applications. This chapter discusses workspaces and other palette options.

Spot-Color Rasters

With this feature, you can specify a spot-color raster, such as a drop shadow, and have the artwork generate the correct color separations. For those of you on the prepress end, this is going to make your life much easier. Read more about color in Chapter 8 of this minibook.

SVG 1.1 Support

This feature provides the ability to import and export to SVG 1.1 format, and include support for profiles that include Tiny, Basic, and Full. Read more about saving files in Chapter 12 of this minibook.

Offset Paths

This feature will provide the ability to offset stroke alignment around a path. It is now possible to offset the path to either be completely inside a path, or completely outside (the default is still to center the stroke across the path). Find these new options in the Stroke palette.

Underline and strikethough text

What . . . you never noticed that Adobe Illustrator didn't have these text attributes? Well, if you never needed them, this is not a big deal, but if you have been using a previous version of Illustrator and missed this feature, this newcomer is enormous.

Deciding When to Use Illustrator CS2

So how do you draw the line and decide when to create graphics in Illustrator rather than Photoshop? By using Illustrator, you gain the following benefits:

✦ **Illustrator can save and export graphics into most file formats.** By choosing to save or export, you can create a file that can be used in most other applications. For instance, Illustrator files can be saved as `.svg`, `.bmp`, `.tiff`, `.pdf`, `.jpg`, and even as a Flash `.swf` file, to name a few.

To save back to an older version of Illustrator prior to CS, you must choose File➪Export➪Legacy, Legacy (*.AI), or Illustrator Legacy (*.EPS). This is due to an improvement of the Illustrator Type Engine. Read more about type in Chapter 5 of this minibook.

✦ **Illustrator files are easily integrated into other Adobe applications.** Illustrator files can be saved in their native format and opened or placed in other Adobe applications, such as InDesign, Photoshop, and GoLive. Adobe Illustrator artwork can also be saved in the `.pdf` format (Acrobat Portable Document Format). This allows anyone using the free Acrobat Reader software to open and view the file, but editing capabilities are still maintained when the file is later opened in Illustrator.

✦ **Illustrator is resolution-independent.** Resolution of Illustrator vector artwork is not determined until output. In other words, if you print to a 600 dpi (dots per inch) printer, the artwork is printed at 600 dpi; print to a 2400 dpi printer and the artwork will print at 2400 dpi. This is very different from the bitmap images you create or edit in Photoshop, where resolution is determined upon creation of the artwork.

✦ **Illustrator has limitless scalability.** This means that you can create vector artwork in Illustrator and scale it to the size of your thumb or the size of a barn, and it will still look good. See the nearby "Vector graphics" sidebar for more information.

Opening an Existing Document

To familiarize yourself with the basics of Illustrator and what the work area looks like, jump right in by opening an existing document in Illustrator. If you don't have an Illustrator file already created, you can open one of the sample files that are packaged with the Illustrator application.

When you launch Illustrator CS2 for the first time, a Welcome screen appears, giving you various options, as shown in Figure 1-1. Click the Open Document icon, and then browse to locate a file to open. (Note that you can uncheck the "Show this dialog at startup" check box to not see the Welcome screen at launch.)

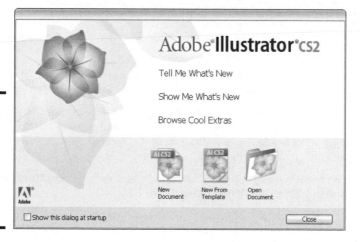

Figure 1-1:
The
Welcome
screen
appears
when you
launch
Illustrator.

If your preferences have been changed from the original defaults, the Welcome screen may not appear. To open a file in that case, choose File➪Open and select the file in the Open dialog box. The Open dialog box is used to open existing Adobe Illustrator files, or even files from other Adobe applications. For example, you could open the file named Cheshire Cat.ai in the Sample Art folder. The path to the file is C:\Programs\Adobe\Adobe Illustrator CS2\ Cool Extras\Sample Files\Sample Art\ (Windows) or Applications\Adobe Illustrator CS2\ Cool Extras\Sample Files\Sample Art\ (Mac).

Creating a New Document

To create a new document in Illustrator, follow these steps:

1. Choose File➪New.

The New Document dialog box appears, as shown in Figure 1-2. This dialog box enables you to determine the new document's size, units of measurement, color mode, and page orientation.

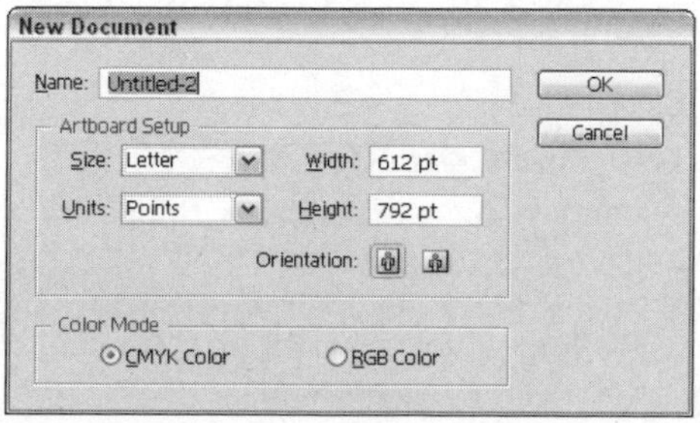

Figure 1-2:
The New
Document
dialog box.

Book III
Chapter 1

Discovering
Illustrator CS2

2. **Enter a name for your new file in the Name text field.**

   The name of the file can be determined now or when you save the document later.

3. **Set the size of the document page by choosing from the Size drop-down list or by typing measurements in the Width and Height text fields.**

   The size can be set from several standard sizes available in the Size drop-down list, or you can enter your own measurements in the Width and Height text fields. Note that several Web sizes are listed first, followed by other typical paper sizes.

4. **Select the type of measurement that you're most comfortable with by choosing from the Units drop-down list.**

   Note that your selection sets all measurement boxes and rulers to the increments you choose: points, picas, inches, millimeters, centimeters, or pixels.

5. **Pick the color mode by selecting the RGB or CMYK option:**

   - **RGB (Red Green Blue):** Select this color mode if your illustration will be displayed on-screen, such as artwork created for the Web.

   - **CMYK (Cyan, Magenta, Yellow, Black):** Select this color mode if your artwork will be printed on a printing press. CMYK colors are separated and printed on a press, with each of the four ink colors being applied after one another. This creates the illusion of many colors and is called four-color artwork.

6. **Last but not least, pick the orientation for the artboard.**

   You can choose between Portrait (the short sides of the artboard at the top and bottom) and Landscape (the long sides of the artboard on the top and bottom).

7. **When you're finished making your selections, click OK.**

   An Illustrator artboard appears. The *artboard* is your canvas for creating your artwork in Illustrator.

Don't worry if any of these settings need to be changed at a later point. You can change these settings by choosing File➪Document Setup and making changes in the Document Setup dialog box.

Taking a look at the document window

To investigate the work area and really get familiar with Illustrator, open a new document and take a look around. In the Illustrator work area, you have a total of 227 inches in width and height to create your artwork in. That's great, but it also leaves enough space to lose objects, too! The following list explains the areas that you will work with as you create artwork in Illustrator:

✦ **Imageable area:** The space inside the innermost dotted lines, which marks the printing area on the page. Many printers can't print all the way to the edges of the paper, so the imageable area is determined by the printer that you have selected in the Print dialog box. To turn off or on this dotted border, choose View⇨Hide/Show Page Tiling.

You can move the imageable area around on your page by using the Page tool. See the nearby sidebar, "The Page tool," for more on this tool.

✦ **Edge of the page:** The page's edge is marked by the outermost set of dotted lines.

✦ **Nonimageable area:** The space between the two sets of dotted lines representing the imageable area and the edge of the page. The nonimageable area is the margin of the page that can't be printed on.

✦ **Artboard:** The area bounded by solid lines that represents the entire region that can contain printable artwork. By default, the artboard is the same size as the page, but it can be enlarged or reduced. The U.S. default artboard is 8.5 x 11 inches, but it can be set as large as 227 x 227 inches. You can hide the artboard boundaries by choosing View⇨Hide Artboard.

✦ **Scratch area:** The area outside the artboard that extends to the edge of the 227-inch square window. The scratch area represents a space on which you can create, edit, and store elements of artwork before moving them onto the artboard. Objects placed onto the scratch area are visible on-screen, but they do not print. However, objects in the scratch area will appear if the document is saved and placed as an image in other applications.

TIP

**Book III
Chapter 1**

Discovering
Illustrator CS2

The Page tool

Use the Page tool to move the printable area of your page to a different location. For instance, if you have a printer that can only print on paper that is 8.5 x 11 inches or less, but you have a page size of 11 x 17, you can use the Page tool (a hidden tool accessed by holding down the mouse button on the Hand tool) to indicate what part of the page you want to print. Follow these steps to use the Page tool:

1. **When adjusting page boundaries, choose View⇨Fit in Window so that you can see all of your artwork.**

2. **Hold down on the Hand tool to select the hidden Page tool.**

The pointer becomes a dotted cross when you move it to the active window.

3. **Position the mouse over the artboard and click and drag the page to a new location.**

As you drag, the Page tool acts as if you were moving the page from its lower-left corner. Two gray rectangles are displayed. The outer rectangle represents the page size, and the inner rectangle represents the printable area of a page. You can move the page anywhere on the artboard; just remember that any part of a page that extends past the printable area boundary is not printed.

How the work area affects your artwork

Basically, the rules are simple: If you're printing directly from Adobe Illustrator, make sure that you choose the proper paper size and printer in the Print dialog box. Open the Print dialog box by choosing File➪Print. If you're creating artwork for another application, such as for a document you're creating in InDesign, the boundaries have no effect on what appears in the Illustrator file. Everything in Illustrator's scratch area will appear in the other application.

Tools Overview

As you begin using Adobe Illustrator, you'll find it helpful to be familiar with its tools. Tools are used to create, select, and manipulate objects in Illustrator. The tools should be visible as a default, but if not, you can access them by choosing Window➪Tools.

Table 1-1 lists the tools that we show you how to use throughout this minibook. Hover the cursor over the tool in the toolbox to see the name of the tool appear in a ToolTip. In parentheses on the ToolTip (and noted in the second column of Table 1-1) is the keyboard command that you can use to access that tool. When you see a small triangle at the lower-right corner of the tool icon, you know that there are additional hidden tools. Select the tool and hold the mouse button to see any hidden tools.

Table 1-1		Illustrator CS2 Tools	
Icon Covered	*Tool*	*What It Does*	*Chapter in This Minibook*
	Selection Tool (V)	Activates objects	Chapter 2
	Direct Selection (A)	Activates individual points or paths	Chapter 2
	Group Selection (A)	Selects grouped items	Chapter 2
	Magic Wand (Y)	Selects based upon similarity	Chapter 2
	Lasso (Q)	Freehand selection tool	Chapter 2
	Pen (P)	Creates paths	Chapter 4

Icon Covered	Tool	What It Does	Chapter in This Minibook
	Type (T)	Creates text	Chapter 5
	Line Segment (/)	Draws line segments	Chapter 4
	Shape Tool (M)	Creates shape objects	Chapter 3
	Paint Brush (B)	Creates paths	Chapter 4
	Pencil (N)	Creates paths	Chapter 4
	Rotate (R)	Rotates objects	Chapter 6
	Scale (S)	Enlarges or reduces objects	Chapter 6
	Warp (Shift+R)	Warps objects	Chapter 6
	Free Transform (E)	Transforms objects	Chapter 6
	Symbol Sprayer (Shift+S)	Applies Symbol instances	Chapter 10
	Graph Tool (J)	Creates graphs	
	Mesh (U)	Creates a gradient mesh	Chapter 10
	Gradient (G)	Modifies gradients	Chapter 10
	Eyedropper (I)	Copies and applies attributes	Chapter 7

(continued)

**Book III
Chapter 1**

**Discovering
Illustrator CS2**

Table 1-1 *(continued)*

Icon Covered	Tool	What It Does	Chapter in This Minibook
	Blend (W)	Creates transitional blends	Chapter 8
	Live Paint Bucket (K)	Applies color to strokes and fills	Chapter 8
	Live Paint Selection Tool (Shift+L)	Selects Live Paint Areas	n/a
	Slice Tool (Shift K)	Creates HTML slices	Chapter 12
	Scissors (C)	Cuts paths	Chapter 4
	Hand (H)	Navigates on the page	Chapter 1
	Zoom (Z)	Increases and decreases the on-screen view	Chapter 1

Checking Out the Palettes

Two groups of palettes and the toolbox appear by default when Adobe Illustrator is launched. Illustrator has more than two palettes; the palettes that you see as a default are docked together. To *dock* a palette means that, for organizational purposes, the palette is attached to another palette, a toolbar, or a side of the screen.

Palettes can be arranged to make them more helpful for production. You may choose to only have certain palettes visible while working. Here's the lowdown on rearranging palettes:

✦ To make the options on a palette's tab appear in the palette, click the tab.

✦ To move a palette, drag its title bar.

✦ To rearrange or separate a group of tabs in a palette, drag a palette's tab. Dragging a tab outside its palette creates a new palette window.

✦ To move a tab to another palette, drag the tab to that palette.

✦ To dock palettes so that you can move them together, drag a palette to the bottom of another palette.

✦ To move an entire docked palette group, drag the topmost palette's title bar.

Look out for those palettes, they can take over your screen! Some of the palettes, but not all, can be resized. Palettes that can be resized have an active lower-right corner (denoted by three small lines in the corner). To change the size of a palette, drag the lower-right corner of the palette (Windows) or drag the size box at the lower-right corner of the palette (Mac).

As you become more efficient, you may find it helpful to reduce the clutter on your screen by hiding all palettes except those that are necessary for your work.

You can access additional palette-specific options by clicking the arrow in the upper-right corner of the palette window; options appear in a palette menu.

You can also choose to save your palette configuration by choosing Window⇨ Workspace⇨Save Workspace.

Changing Views

When you're working in Illustrator, precision is important, but you also want to see how the artwork really looks. Whether for the Web or print, Illustrator offers several ways in which to view your artwork.

Preview and Outline views

By default, Illustrator shows the Preview view. This means that you see colors, stroke widths, images, and patterns as they should appear when printed or completed for on-screen presentation. Sometimes this can become a nuisance, especially if you have two thick lines and you're trying to create a corner point by connecting them. At times like this, or whenever you want the strokes and fills reduced to the underlying structure, choose View⇨Outline. You now see the outline of the illustration, as shown in Figure 1-3.

Figure 1-3:
Preview
view (left)
and Outline
view (right).

Pixel view

If you don't want to be surprised when your artwork appears in your Web browser, use the Pixel view. This view, shown in Figure 1-4, maintains the vectors of your artwork, but gives you a view showing how the pixels will appear when the image is viewed on-screen, as if on the Web.

Figure 1-4:
See how your artwork translates into pixels in the Pixel view.

Pixel view is great for previewing what your text will look like on-screen — some fonts just don't look good as pixels, especially if the text is small. Using Pixel view, you can go through several different fonts until you find one that is more readable as pixels.

Overprint view

For those of you in print production, the Overprint preview can be a real timesaver. Choose View➪Attributes to bring up the Attributes palette, which you can use to set the fill and stroke colors to overprint. This creates additional colors when printing and aids printers when trapping abutting colors.

Trapping is the slight overprint of a lighter color into a darker color to correct for press *misregistration*. When several colors are printed on one piece, the likelihood that they will be perfectly aligned is pretty slim! Setting a stroke to Overprint on the Window➪Attributes palette is one solution. With overprint selected, the stroke is overprinted on the touching colors. This mixing of color produces an additional color, but is less obvious to the viewer than a white space created by misregistration. Select Overprint to see the result of overprinting in Overprint view in Figure 1-5.

Figure 1-5:
Overprint view.

Navigating the Work Area with Zoom Controls

You can navigate the work area efficiently by using the Hand tool and the various zoom controls. You can change the magnification of the artboard in several ways, including using menu items, the Zoom tool, and keyboard commands. Choose the method you feel most comfortable with after you check them out in the following sections.

The Hand tool

Scroll around the document window by using the scrollbars or the Hand tool. The Hand tool gives you the ability to scroll by dragging. You can imagine you're pushing a piece of paper around on your desk when you use the Hand tool.

Hold down the spacebar to temporarily access the Hand tool while any tool (except the Type tool) is selected. Holding down the spacebar while the Type tool is selected will only give you spaces!

The View menu

Using the View menu, you can easily select the magnification that you want from a choice of four. Here are your choices:

✦ Zoom In

✦ Zoom Out

✦ Fit in Window (especially useful when you get lost in the scratch area)

✦ Actual Size (gives you a 100 percent view of your artwork)

The Zoom tool

Using the Zoom tool, you can click the document window to zoom in; to zoom out, Alt+click (Windows) or Option+click (Mac).

Double-click with the Zoom tool to quickly resize the document window to 100 percent.

Control what is visible when using the Zoom tool by clicking and dragging over the area that you want zoomed into.

Keyboard shortcuts

If you're not the type of person who likes to use keyboard shortcuts, you may change your mind about using them for magnification. They make sense and are easy to use and remember. Table 1-2 lists the most popular keyboard shortcuts to change magnification.

Table 1-2	Magnification Keyboard Shortcuts	
Command	*Windows Shortcut*	*Mac Shortcut*
Actual Size	Ctrl+1	⌘+1
Fit in Window	Ctrl+0 (zero)	⌘+0 (zero)
Zoom In	Ctrl++ (plus)	⌘++ (plus)
Zoom Out	Ctrl+− (minus)	⌘+− (minus)
Hand tool	Spacebar	Spacebar

The shortcuts in the following table require a little coordination to use, but they give you more control in your zoom. While holding down the keys, drag from the upper-left to the bottom-right corner of the area you want to zoom to. A marquee appears while you're dragging; when you release the mouse button, that selected area zooms up to the size of your window! The Zoom Out command doesn't give you that much control; it simply zooms back out, much like the commands in Table 1-2.

Command	*Windows Shortcut*	*Mac Shortcut*
Zoom In to Selected Area	Ctrl+spacebar+drag	⌘+spacebar+drag
Zoom Out	Ctrl+Alt+spacebar	⌘+Option+spacebar

Chapter 2: Using the Selection Tools

In This Chapter

✔ Anchor points, the bounding boxes, and selection tools

✔ Working with selections

✔ Grouping and ungrouping selections

✔ Constraining movement and cloning objects

You've probably heard the old line, "You have to select it to affect it." This is so true. When you're ready to apply a change to an object in Illustrator, you must have that object selected, or Illustrator won't know what to do. You'll sit there clicking a color swatch over and over again, and nothing will happen. Although it may sound simple to make selections, you'll find that it can become more difficult when working on complicated artwork.

Getting to Know the Selection Tools

Before delving into the world of selecting objects in Illustrator, you must know what the Selection tools are. So to begin this chapter, we take you through a quick tour of anchor points (integral to the world of selections), the bounding box, and of course the selection tools (yes, there are more than one).

Anchor points

To understand selections, you must first understand how Illustrator works with *anchor points*. Anchor points act like handles and can be individually selected and moved to other locations. Essentially, the anchor points are what you use to drag objects or parts of objects around the workspace. After you've placed anchor points on an object, you can then create strokes or paths from the anchor points.

You can select several anchor points at the same time (Figure 2-1) or only one (Figure 2-2). Selecting several anchor points at once enables you to move the entire object without changing the anchor points in relationship to one another. You can tell which anchor points are selected and active because they appear as solid boxes.

Figure 2-1:
Several
anchor
points
selected.

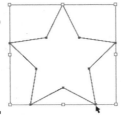

Figure 2-2:
One anchor
point
selected.

Bounding box

As a default, Illustrator shows a bounding box when an object is selected with the Selection tool (a bounding box is shown in Figure 2-1). This can be helpful if you understand its function, but confusing if you don't know how to use it.

By dragging on the handles, you can use the bounding box for quick transforms, such as scaling and rotating. To rotate, you pass the mouse cursor (without clicking) outside a handle until you see a rotate symbol, and then drag.

If the bounding box bothers you, you can turn off the feature by choosing View➪Hide Bounding Box.

Selection tools

Illustrator CS2 offers three main selection tools:

✦ **Selection tool:** Selects entire objects or groups. This tool activates all anchor points in an object or group at the same time, allowing you to move an object without changing its shape.

 ✦ **Direct Selection tool:** Selects individual points.

 ✦ **Group Selection tool:** Hidden in the Direct Selection tool in the toolbox, you use this tool to select items within a group. This tool adds grouped items as you click on an object in the order in which objects were grouped. This selection tool will become more useful to you as you find out about grouping objects in Illustrator.

You can select an object with the Selection tool using one of three main methods:

✦ Click the object's path.

✦ Click an anchor point of the object.

✦ Drag a marquee around part or all of the object's path. (In the later section, "Using a marquee to select an object," we further discuss using the marquee method.)

 Use the Magic Wand selection tool to select objects with like values, such as fill and stroke colors, based upon a tolerance, and stroke weight. Change the options of this tool by double-clicking on the magic Wand tool.

 Use the Lasso tool to click and drag around anchor points that you want to select.

Working with Selections

After you have an understanding about the basics of selections, you probably will be anxious to jump in and start with the selecting. So in this section, we introduce you to the basics: making a selection, working with anchor points and the marquee, making multiple selections, and, of course, saving your work.

Creating a selection

To work with selections, you need to actually have something on the page in Illustrator. Use the following techniques to make a selection:

1. **Create a new page in Adobe Illustrator (any size or color mode is okay).**

Alternatively, you can open an existing illustration; see Chapter 1 of this minibook for instructions.

2. If you're starting from a new page, create an object to work with. For example, select the Rectangle tool and click and drag from the top left to the lower right to create a shape.

Exact size doesn't matter, but make it large enough that you can see it. To start over, choose Edit⇨Undo, or press Ctrl+Z (Windows), or ⌘+Z (Mac).

As a default, all shapes start out having a black stroke and a white fill (see Figure 2-3). If yours is not black and white, press D, which changes the selected object to the default colors.

Figure 2-3:
Create a
rectangle to
practice
using the
Selection
tools.

3. Using the Selection tool, click on the object to make sure that it's active.

Note that all anchor points are solid, indicating that all anchor points are active, as shown in Figure 2-4.

Figure 2-4:
All anchor
points
activate
with the
Selection
tool.

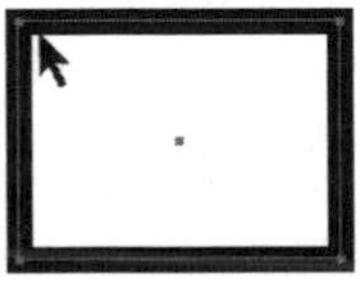

4. Click and drag the rectangle to another location.

All anchor points travel together.

5. To deactivate a selection, use one of these three methods:

- Choose Select⇨Deselect.
- Ctrl+click (Windows) or ⌘+click (Mac) anywhere on the page.
- Use the key command Ctrl+Shift+A (Windows) or ⌘+Shift+A (Mac).

Selecting an anchor point

When you have a selection to work with (see the preceding numbered list), you can deselect all the active anchor points, and then make just one anchor point active. Just follow these steps:

1. **Make sure that the object is not selected by choosing Select⇨Deselect.**

2. **Select the Direct Selection tool (the white arrow) from the toolbox.**

3. **Click on one anchor point.**

   Only one anchor point (the one you clicked on) is solid and the others are hollow, as shown in Figure 2-5.

Figure 2-5:
Only the selected anchor point becomes active with the Direct Selection tool.

4. **Click and drag that solid anchor point using the Direct Selection tool.**

   Only that one anchor point moves.

Using a marquee to select an object

Sometimes it's easier to surround what you want selected by dragging the mouse to create a marquee. Follow these steps to select an object by creating a marquee:

1. **Choose the Selection tool.**

2. **Click outside the object (we use a rectangle in this example) and drag over a small part of it, as shown in Figure 2-6.**

   The entire object becomes selected.

Figure 2-6:
Selecting an entire object with a marquee and the Selection tool.

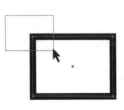

You can also select just one anchor point in an object by using the marquee method:

1. **Make sure the object is not selected by choosing Select⇨Deselect, and then choose the Direct Selection tool.**

2. **Click outside a corner of the object and drag over just the anchor point that you want to select.**

Notice that only that anchor point is active, as shown in Figure 2-7. This can be a sight-saver when you're trying to select individual points.

Figure 2-7:
Selecting individual anchor points with a marquee and the Direct Selection tool.

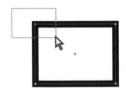

You can use this method to cross over just the two top points or side anchor points to activate multiple anchor points as well.

Selecting multiple objects

If you have multiple items on your page, you can select them by using one of the following methods:

✦ Select one object or anchor point, and then hold down the Shift key and click on another object or anchor point. Depending on which selection tool you're using, you will either select all anchor points on an object (Selection tool) or additional anchor points only (Direct Select tool).

You can use the Shift key to deactivate an object as well. Shift+click on a selected object to deselect it.

✦ Choose Select⇨All or use the key command Ctrl+A (Windows) or ⌘+A (Mac).

✦ Use the marquee selection technique and drag outside and over the objects. When you use this technique with the Selection tool, all anchor points in the objects are selected; with the Direct Selection tool, only the points that you drag over are selected.

Saving a selection

Spending way too much time trying to make your selections? Illustrator CS2 comes to the rescue with the Save Selection feature. After you have a selection that you may need again, choose Select⇨Save Selection, and name the selection. It now appears at the bottom of the Select menu. To change the name or delete the saved selection, choose Select⇨Edit Selection. This selection is saved with the document.

Grouping and Ungrouping

Keep objects together by grouping them. The Group function is handy in a situation when you're creating something from multiple objects like a logo, for instance. With the Group function, you can make sure that all the objects that make up the logo stay together when you move, rotate, scale, or copy it. Just follow these steps to create a group:

1. **If you aren't already working with an illustration that contains a whole bunch of objects, create several objects on a new page, anywhere and any size.**

   For example, select the Rectangle tool and click and drag on the page several times to create additional rectangles.

2. **Select the first object with the Selection tool, and then hold down the Shift key and click on a second object.**

3. **Choose Object⇨Group or use the keyboard shortcut Ctrl+G (Windows) or ⌘+G (Mac).**

4. **Choose Select⇨Deselect, and then click one of the objects with the Selection tool.**

   Both objects become selected!

5. **While the first two objects are still selected, Shift+click on a third object.**

6. **With all three objects selected, choose Object⇨Group again.**

   Illustrator remembers the grouping order. To prove that, deselect the group by choosing Select⇨Deselect and switch to the Group Selection tool. (Hold down the mouse button on the Direct Selection tool to access the Group Selection tool).

7. **Using the Group Selection tool, click on the first object, and all anchor points become active. Click again on the first object, and the second object becomes selected. Click yet again on the first object, and the third object becomes selected.**

   This tool activates the objects in the order that you grouped them. After you've grouped the objects together, you can now treat them as a single object.

To Ungroup objects, choose Object⇨Ungroup, or use the key command Ctrl+Shift+G (Windows) or ⌘+Shift+G (Mac). In a situation where you group objects twice (because you added an object to the group, for example), you would have to choose Ungroup twice.

Manipulating Selected Objects

In this section you can discover a few other cool things that you can do with selected objects.

Moving selected objects

When an object is selected, you can drag it to any location on the page, but what if you only want to nudge it a bit? To nudge an item one pixel at a time, select it with the Selection tool and press the left-, right-, up-, or down-arrow key to reposition the object. Hold down the Shift key as you press an arrow key to move an object by ten pixels at a time.

Constraining movement

Want to move an object over to the other side of the page without changing its alignment? Constrain something by selecting an object with the Selection tool and dragging the item, then hold down the Shift key before you release the mouse button. By pressing the Shift key mid-drag, you constrain the movement to 45-, 90-, or 180-degree angles!

Cloning selected objects

Use the Selection tool to easily clone (duplicate) an item and move it to a new location. To clone an item, simply select it with the Selection tool, and then hold down the Alt key (Windows) or Option key (Mac). Look for the cursor to change to two arrows (see Figure 2-8), and then drag the item to another location on the page. Notice that the original object is left intact and that a copy of the object has been created and moved.

Figure 2-8:
Look for the double arrow before dragging the clone.

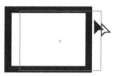

Constraining the clone

By Alt+dragging (Windows) or Option+dragging (Mac) an item, and then pressing Shift, you can clone the item and keep it aligned with the original. ***Remember:*** Don't hold down the Shift key until you're in the process of dragging the item; otherwise, pressing Shift will deselect the original object.

After you have cloned an object to a new location, try this neat trick where you create multiple objects equally apart from each other using the Transform Again command: Choose Object⇨Transform⇨Transform Again, or press Ctrl+D (Windows) or ⌘+D (Mac) to have another object cloned the exact distance as the first cloned object (see Figure 2-9). We discuss transforms in more detail in Chapter 9 of this minibook.

**Book III
Chapter 2**

**Using the
Selection Tools**

Figure 2-9:
Using the Transform Again command.

Using the Select Menu

Using the Select Menu you can gain additional selection controls, such as Select⇨Inverse, which allows you to select one object and then turn your selection inside out. Also the Select⇨ Select Same options which allows you to select one object and then select additional objects on the page based upon similarities in Color, Fill, Stroke, and other special attributes.

Chapter 3: Creating Basic Shapes

In This Chapter

✔ **Introducing rectangles, ellipses, stars, and polygons**

✔ **Resizing shapes after creation**

✔ **Tips for creating shapes**

Shapes, shapes, shapes . . . they're everywhere in Illustrator. Basic shapes such as squares, circles, polygons, and stars are used in all types of illustrations. With the right know-how and the right shape tools, you can easily create these shapes exactly the way you want. In this chapter, we show you how to use these tools to control a shape's outcome, how to create shapes based on precise measurements, and even how to change the number of points a star has.

The Basic Shape Tools

As a default, the only visible shape tool in the toolbox is the Rectangle tool. Click and hold down that tool and *voilà,* you have access to the Rounded Rectangle, Ellipse, Polygon, and Star tools, as shown in Figure 3-1. (Note that although you see the Flare tool in this menu, it isn't considered a basic shape.)

Rectangle

Ellipse Star

Figure 3-1:
The basic
shape tools.

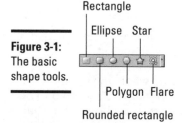

Polygon Flare

Rounded rectangle

You can tear off this tool set so that you don't have to find the hidden shapes in the future. Click and hold on the Rectangle tool and drag to the arrow on the far right. Wait until you see the pop-up hint (Tearoff) and then release the mouse button. These tools are now in a free-floating toolbar that you can drag to another location — ready to go!

Creating rectangles and ellipses

Rectangles and ellipses are the most fundamental shapes that you can create (see Figure 3-2). In this section, we discuss how to get them to be the size that you want. To create a rectangle shape freehand, select the Rectangle tool and simply click on the page where you want the shape to appear. Then drag diagonally towards the opposite side and drag it the distance that you want the shape to be in size and release the mouse button. You can drag up or down. You do the same to create an ellipse with the Ellipse tool.

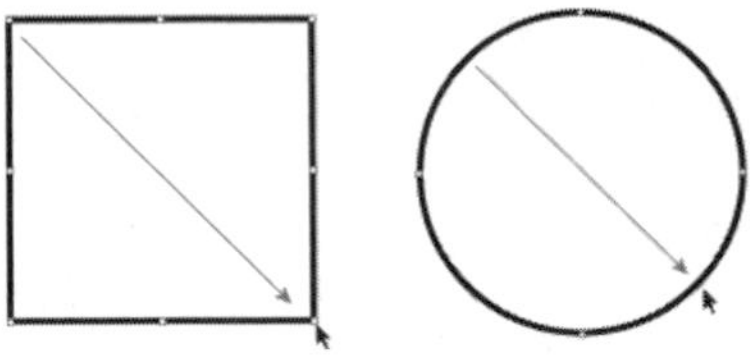

Figure 3-2:
Click and drag on a diagonal to create a rectangle or an ellipse.

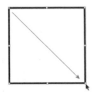

 After you create the shape, adjust its size and position by using the Selection tool. Reposition the shape by clicking on the selected object and dragging. Resize the object by grabbing a handle and adjusting in or out. To adjust two sides together, grab a corner handle. To resize your shape proportionally, Shift+drag a corner handle.

Using the Rounded Rectangle tool

The rounded rectangle can be created by using either of the following two methods:

✦ Freehand clicking and dragging to create the rounded rectangle shape.

✦ Clicking once on the artboard to bring up the Rounded Rectangle dialog box, where you can enter values to define the shape.

The difference between these two methods is that when you open the Rounded Rectangle dialog box (see Figure 3-3), you have the option to enter a value in the Corner Radius text field, which determines how much rounding is applied to the corners of the shape. The smaller the value, the less rounded the corners will be; the higher the value, the more rounded. Be careful, you can actually round a rectangle's corners so much that it becomes an ellipse!

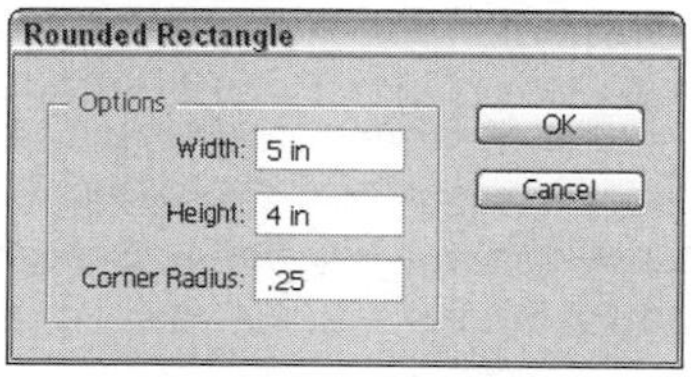

Figure 3-3:
Select the
Rounded
Rectangle
tool and
click once
on the
artboard to
customize
the size.

Using the Polygon tool

You create stars and polygons in much the same way as the rectangles and ellipses. Select the Polygon tool and click and drag from one corner to another to create the default six-sided polygon shape. You can also select the Polygon tool and click once on the artboard to change the Polygon tool options in the Polygon dialog box.

You can change the polygon shape by entering new values in the Radius and Sides text fields, as shown in Figure 3-4. The radius is determined from the center to the edge of the polygon. The value for the number of sides can range from 3 (making triangles a breeze to create) to 1000. Whoa . . . a polygon with 1000 sides would look like a circle unless it was the size of Texas!

**Book III
Chapter 3**

Figure 3-4:
Creating a
polygon.

Creating Basic
Shapes

Using the Star tool

To create a star shape, select the Star tool from the toolbox. (Remember that it may be hiding under other shape tools.) If you click once on the artboard to bring up the Star dialog box, you see three text fields in which you can enter values to customize your star shape:

✦ **Radius 1:** The distance from the outer points to the center of the star.

✦ **Radius 2:** The distance from the inner points to the center of the star.

✦ **Points:** The number of points that make up the star.

The closer together the Radius 1 and Radius 2 values are to each other, the shorter the points on your star. In other words, you can go from a starburst to a seal of approval by entering values that are close in the Radius 1 and Radius 2 text fields, as shown in Figure 3-5.

Figure 3-5:
Radius 1 and
Radius 2 are
farther from
each other
in the star
on the left.

Resizing Shapes

You often need a shape to be an exact size (for instance, 2 x 3 inches). After you create a shape, the best way to resize it to exact measurements is to use the Transform palette, shown in Figure 3-6. Have your object selected and then choose Window⇨Transform to open the Transform palette. Note that on this palette, you can enter values to place an object in the X and Y fields, as well as enter values in the Width and Height text fields to determine the exact size of an object.

Figure 3-6:
Use this
palette to
precisely
size a
shape.

In many of the Adobe Illustrator palettes, you may see measurement increments consisting of points, picas, millimeters, centimeters, or inches, and that can be confusing and maybe even intimidating. But you can control which measurement increments to use.

Show Rulers by choosing View⇨Show Rulers, or press Ctrl+R (Windows) or ⌘+R (Mac). Then right-click (Windows) or Control+click (Mac) on the ruler to change the measurement increment to an increment you're more familiar with. The contextual menu that appears allows you to change the measurement increment right on the document.

Alternatively, you can simply type the number followed by a measurement extension into the Width and Height text fields in the Transform palette (refer to Figure 3-6), and the measurement converts properly for you. The extensions that you can use are shown in the following table.

Extension	Measurement Unit
" or in	Inches
pt	Points
mm	Millimeters
cm	Centimeters
p	Picas

If you don't want to bother creating a shape freehand and then changing the size, select the shape tool and click on your page. An options dialog box specific to the shape you're creating appears, in which you can type values into the width and height text fields.

If you accidentally click and drag, you end up with a very small shape on your page. If this happens, don't fret. Simply get rid of the small shape by selecting it and pressing the Delete key, and then try again.

Tips for Creating Shapes

The following are simple tips to improve your skills at creating basic shapes in Illustrator:

✦ Press and hold the Shift key while dragging with the Rectangle or Ellipse tool to create a perfect square or circle. This trick is also helpful when you're using the Polygon and Star tools — holding down the Shift key constrains them so they're straight. See Figure 3-7.

Figure 3-7:
Use the
Shift key to
constrain
your shape.

✦ Create a shape from the center out by holding down the Alt (Windows) or Option (Mac) key while dragging (see Figure 3-8). Hold down Alt+Shift (Windows) or Option+Shift (Mac) to pull a constrained shape out from the center.

Figure 3-8:
Pull shapes
from a
center point.

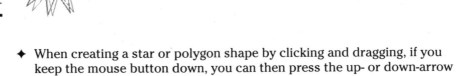

✦ When creating a star or polygon shape by clicking and dragging, if you keep the mouse button down, you can then press the up- or down-arrow key to interactively add points or sides to your shape.

Chapter 4: Using the Pen Tool and Placing Images

In This Chapter

✓ **Familiarizing yourself with the Pen tool**

✓ **Creating paths, closed shapes, and curves**

✓ **Creating template layers**

✓ **Placing images in Illustrator CS2**

You've seen illustrations that you know are made from paths, but how do you make your own? In this chapter, we show you how to use the Pen tool to create paths and closed shapes. Discover the tricks that make it easy! Have you ever tried to pat your head while rubbing your belly? If so, you will feel comfortable using the Pen tool. Not really, but we felt we should point out that using the Pen tool requires a little more coordination than other Illustrator tools. After you master the Pen tool, however, the possibilities for creating illustrations are unlimited. Read this chapter to build your skills with the most popular feature in graphic software, the Bézier curve.

Pen Tool Fundamentals

 You can use the Pen tool to create all sorts of things like straight lines, curves, and closed shapes, that you can then incorporate into illustrations:

✦ **Bézier curve:** Originally developed by Pierre Bézier in the 1970s for CAD/CAM operations, the Bézier curve (shown in Figure 4-1) became the underpinnings of the entire Adobe PostScript drawing model. A Bézier curve is one that you can control the depth and size of using direction lines.

✦ **Anchor points:** Anchor points are used to control the shape of a path or object. These are automatically created when using shape tools. You can manually create anchor points by clicking from point to point with the Pen tool.

✦ **Direction lines:** These are essentially the handles that you use on curved points to adjust the depth and angle of curved paths.

Figure 4-1:
The depth and direction of Bézier curves are controlled by direction lines.

✦ **Closed shape:** When a path is created, it becomes a closed shape when the start point joins the endpoint.

✦ **Simple path:** A *path* consists of one or more straight or curved segments. Anchor points mark the endpoints of the path segments. In the next section, we show you how to control the anchor points.

Creating a straight line

A basic function of the Pen tool is to create a simple path. You can create a simple, straight line with the Pen tool by following these steps:

1. Before you start, press D or click on the small black and white color swatches at the bottom of the toolbox.

This reverts you back to the default colors of a black stroke and a white fill. With black as a stroke, you can see your path clearly.

2. Click on the Fill swatch, located at the bottom of the toolbox, to make sure that it is forward, and then press the forward slash (/) key to change the fill to None.

The trick of pressing D to change the foreground and background colors to the default of black and white also works in Photoshop and InDesign.

3. Open a new blank page and select the Pen tool.

Notice that when you move the mouse over the artboard, the Pen cursor appears with an X beside it. This indicates that you are creating the first anchor point of a path.

4. Click on the artboard to create the first anchor point of a line.

The X disappears.

Don't drag the mouse, or you'll end up creating a curve instead of a straight segment.

5. **Click anywhere else on the document to create the ending anchor point of the line.**

   Illustrator creates a path between the two anchor points., Essentially, the path looks like a line segment with an anchor point at each end (see Figure 4-2).

Figure 4-2:
A path
connected
by two
anchor
points.

To make a correction to a line you created with the Pen tool (as described in the preceding steps), follow these steps:

1. **Choose Select⇨Deselect to make sure no objects are currently selected.**

2. **Select the Direct Selection tool from the toolbox.**

3. **Select one anchor point on the line.**

   Notice that one anchor point is solid and the other is hollow. This indicates that the anchor point you clicked is active (solid) while the other is not.

4. **Click and drag the anchor point with the Direct Selection tool.**

   The selected anchor point moves, changing the direction of the path while not affecting the other anchor point. And that's it. Seems rather simple, but this is the gist of using the Direct Selection tool, you make changes to a path without affecting other segments.

Use the Direct Selection tool (select by pressing A) to make any corrections to paths. Make sure that only the anchor point you want to change is active. If the entire path is selected, all anchor points are solid. If only one anchor point is selected, all but that one point will be hollow.

Creating a constrained straight line

In this section, we show you how to create a real straight line, meaning one that is on multiples of a 45-degree angle. Illustrator makes it easy; just follow these steps:

1. **Select the Pen tool and click anywhere on the artboard to place an anchor point.**

2. **Hold down the Shift key and click on another location to place the ending anchor point.**

   Notice that when you're holding the Shift key, the line snaps to a multiple of 45 degrees. ***Remember:*** Release the mouse button before you release the Shift key, or else the line will pop out of alignment.

You can get some practice creating constrained lines by trying to re-create the shape shown in Figure 4-3. We used ruler guides to more precisely place the anchor points with the Pen tool, but using guides isn't necessary to create this shape. Read more about guides in Chapter 6 of this minibook.

Figure 4-3:
Hold down the Shift key while creating a path to constrain it.

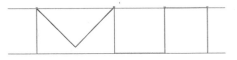

Creating a curve

You knew that it was coming: In this section, you discover how to use the Bézier path to create a curved segment. We won't guarantee that you'll love it — not at first anyway. But after you know how to use a Bézier path, you'll likely find it useful. To create a Bézier path, just follow these steps:

1. **Starting with a blank artboard, select the Pen tool and click anywhere on the artboard to place the first anchor point.**

2. **Now click some place else to place your ending anchor point, but don't let go of the mouse button. Drag the cursor until a direction line appears.**

   If you look real close, you see that anchor points are square and the direction lines have circles at the end, as shown in Figure 4-4.

Figure 4-4:
Creating a curved path.

3. **Drag the direction line closer to the anchor point to flatten the curve; drag farther away from the anchor point to increase the curve, as shown in Figure 4-5.**

4. **Release the mouse button when you're happy with the curve.**

Figure 4-5:
The directional line determines how the curve appears.

What you have created is an *open path,* a path that doesn't form a closed shape. We show you how to reconnect to the starting point of the path to make a closed shape in the next section.

To alter a curved segment after you have created it, follow these steps:

1. **Choose Select⇨Deselect to make sure no objects are currently selected.**

2. **Choose the Direct Selection tool and click on the last anchor point created.**

   If they're not already visible, the direction lines appear.

3. **Click precisely at the end of one of the direction lines; drag the direction line to change the curve. If you have a hard time selecting the anchor point, drag a marquee using the Direct Selection tool around it.**

Reconnecting to an existing path

Creating one segment is fine if you just want a line or an arch. But if you want to create a shape, you need to add more anchor points to the original segment. If you want to fill your shape with a color or a gradient, you need to close it, meaning that you need to eventually come back to the starting anchor point.

To add segments to your path and create a closed shape, follow these steps:

1. **Create a segment (straight or curved).**

   We show you how in the preceding sections of this chapter.

**Book III
Chapter 4**

**Using the Pen Tool
and Placing Images**

You can continue from this point, clicking and adding anchor points until you eventually close the shape. For this example, you deselect the path so that you can discover how to continue adding to paths that have already been created. This is extremely helpful when you need to make adjustments on existing artwork.

2. **With the Pen tool selected, move the cursor over an end anchor point on the deselected path.**

3. **To connect your next segment, click when you see the Pen icon with a forward slash indicating that you are connecting to this path.**

4. **Click someplace else to create the next anchor point in the path; drag the mouse if you want to create a curved segment.**

5. **Click to place additional anchor points, dragging as needed to curve those segments.**

Remember that you want to close this shape, so place your anchor points so that you can eventually come back around to the first anchor point.

Figure 4-6 shows a shape that is a result of several linked anchor points.

Figure 4-6:
Adding more anchor points to create a shape.

6. **When you get back to the first anchor point, move the cursor over it and click when the close icon (a small hollow circle) appears, as shown in Figure 4-7.**

The shape now has no end points.

Figure 4-7:
Click when the close icon appears.

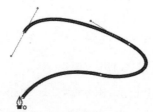

Controlling the curves

After you feel comfortable creating curves and paths, it's time to take control of those curves so that you can create them with a greater degree of precision. To control a curve, follow these steps:

1. **Create a new document, and then choose View⇨Show Grid to show a series of horizontal and vertical rules that act as guides. If it helps, use the Zoom tool to zoom into the document.**

2. **Using the Pen tool, click on an intersection of any of these lines in the middle area of the page to place your initial anchor point and drag upward.**

   Don't let go, but do not click when the direction line has extended up to the horizontal grid line above it, as shown in Figure 4-8a.

3. **Click to place the second anchor point on the intersection of the grid directly to the right of your initial point; drag the direction line down to the grid line directly below it, as shown in Figure 4-8b.**

   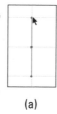

   If you have a hard time keeping the direction line straight, hold down the Shift key to constrain it.

4. **Choose Select⇨Deselect to deselect your curve.**

   Congratulations! You have created a controlled curve. In these steps, we created an arch that is going up, so we first clicked and dragged up. Likewise, to create a downward arch, you must click and drag down. Using the grid, try to create a downward arch like the one shown in Figure 4-8c.

Book III
Chapter 4

Using the Pen Tool and Placing Images

Figure 4-8:
Creating a
controlled
curve.

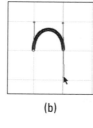
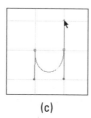

(a)   (b)   (c)

Creating a corner point

To change directions of a path from being a curve to a corner, you have to create a *corner point,* as shown on the right in Figure 4-9. A corner point has no direction lines and allows for a sharp direction change in a path.

Figure 4-9:
Smooth versus corner points.

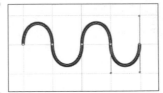
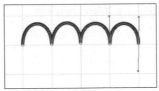

You can switch from the Pen tool to the Convert Anchor Point tool to change a smooth anchor point into a corner point, but that process is a bit time consuming. An easier way is to press the Alt (Windows) or Option (Mac) key (this temporarily changes the Pen tool into the Convert Anchor Point tool) while clicking on the anchor point.

To change a smooth anchor point into a corner point using the shortcut method, follow these steps:

1. **Create an upward arch.**

   We show you how in the preceding section, "Controlling the curves" (refer to Figure 4-8b).

2. **Hold down the Alt (Windows) or Option (Mac) key and position the cursor over the last anchor point (the last point that you created with the Pen tool).**

3. **When the cursor changes to a caret (that's the Convert Anchor Point tool), click and drag until the direction line is up to the grid line above, as shown on the left in Figure 4-10.**

Figure 4-10:
Making a smooth anchor point a corner point.

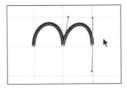

4. **Release the Alt (Windows) or Option (Mac) key and the mouse button, and then move the cursor to the grid line to the right, and click and drag down.**

The Hidden Pen Tools

Hold down on the Pen tool icon in the toolbox to access additional tools: the Add Anchor Point, Delete Anchor Point, and Convert Anchor Point tools, shown in the following table. In the preceding section, we show you how to create a corner point with the shortcut method, by pressing the Alt (Windows) or Option (Mac) key to access the Convert Anchor Point tool. You may feel more comfortable switching to that tool when you need to convert a point, but switching tools can be more time-consuming.

Icon	Tool
	Pen
	Add Anchor Point
	Delete Anchor Point
	Convert Anchor Point

Keep this in mind: Even though there is a hidden tool to delete and add anchor points, Illustrator will automatically do this as a default when you're using the Pen tool. When you move the cursor over an anchor point with the Pen tool, a minus icon appears. To delete that anchor point, simply click. Likewise, when you move the cursor over a part of the path that does not contain anchor points, a plus icon appears. Simply click to add an anchor point.

If you prefer to use the tools dedicated to adding and deleting anchor points, choose Illustrator⇨Preferences⇨General; in the Preferences dialog box that appears, deselect the Disable Auto Add/Delete check box. Then, when you want to add or delete an anchor point, select the appropriate tool and click on the path.

Creating a Template Layer

Throughout this chapter, we show you how the Pen tool works. So now we bet you're anxious to put this tool to use. So what we show you here is how to create a *template layer*. A template layer is a locked, dimmed layer that you can use to draw over placed images with the Pen tool, much like you would do with a piece of onion skin paper over the top of an image.

How is that done? Just follow these steps:

1. **Take a scanned image or logo and save it in a format that Illustrator can import from your image-editing program, such as Photoshop.**

   Typically, you save the image as an `.eps`, `.tif`, or native `.psd` (Photoshop file).

2. **Choose File⇨Place to open the Place dialog box, shown in Figure 4-11.**

Figure 4-11:
The Place
dialog box.

3. **In the Place dialog box, locate the saved image; then select the Template check box and click Place.**

   Selecting the Template check box tells Illustrator to lock down the scanned image on a layer. Essentially, that means it can't be repositioned or edited.

   After you click Place, a template layer is automatically created for you and another layer is waiting for you to create your path. The top layer that has been created is like a piece of tracing paper has been placed on top of the scanned image.

4. **Re-create the image by tracing over it with the Pen tool, as shown in Figure 4-12.**

Figure 4-12:
Tracing over
an image
placed on a
template
layer.

5. **When you're done, turn the visibility off the placed image by clicking the Visibility icon to the left of the template layer.**

You now have a path that you can use in place of the image, which is useful if you're creating an illustration of an image or are digitally re-creating a logo.

For more about layers, check out Chapter 7 of this minibook.

Keep practicing to get yourself more comfortable with clicking and dragging, flowing with the direction line pointing the way that you want the path to be created; everything will fall into place.

Placing Images

In the preceding section, you discover how to place an image as a template. But what if you want to place an image to be utilized in your illustration file? This is relatively easy, of course — simply choose File⇨Place.

Click once on an image to see the Link check box. If you keep the check box selected, the image is linked to the original file. This is good if you plan on referencing the file several times in the illustration (saves file space) or if you want to edit the original and have it update the placed image in Illustrator. This option is usually checked by those in the prepress industry who want to have access to the original image file. Just remember to send the image with the Illustrator file if it is to be output or used someplace other than on your computer.

If you uncheck the Link check box, the image is embedded into the illustrator file. This does keep the filing system cleaner, but doesn't leave much room to edit the original image at a later point. There are certain instances, like if you want an image to become a Symbol (see Chapter 10 of this minibook) that the image will have to be embedded, but most functions work with linked and unlinked files.

New in Illustrator CS2

New in Illustrator CS2, you can place a .psd (Photoshop) image that has saved Layer Comps from Photoshop and choose which layer comp set you want visible while placing in Adobe Illustrator CS2. See Figure 4-13.

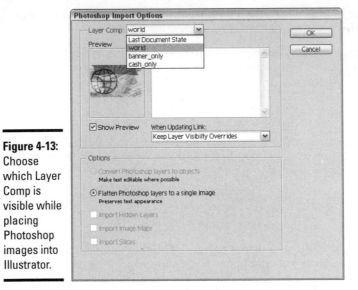

Figure 4-13:
Choose
which Layer
Comp is
visible while
placing
Photoshop
images into
Illustrator.

Layer Comps are a feature in Photoshop that allow you to set the visibility, appearance, and position of layers. It is a great organizational tool that can now be taken advantage of in other Adobe products. Read more in Book IV.

Chapter 5: Using Type in Illustrator

In This Chapter

✔ **Introducing the Type tools**

✔ **Getting to know text areas**

✔ **Manipulating text along paths and within shapes**

✔ **Assigning font styles**

✔ **Discovering the Character and Paragraph palettes**

✔ **Using the new Control palette for text controls**

✔ **Saving time with text utilities**

*O*ne of Illustrator's strongest areas, manipulating text, just got stronger with the release of Adobe Illustrator CS2, which was vastly improved in the previous CS version to use the same type engine as InDesign. Whether you're using Illustrator to create logos, business cards, or type to be used on the Web, this improvement leads to more professional capabilities and liberates you from time-consuming workarounds when you're simply trying to create good, clean type.

To help you take advantage of this strength, we begin this chapter by introducing you to the Type tools and showing you a few basic (and more advanced) tricks that you can do in Illustrator, typography-wise. We then move on to the other text tools, the Character and Paragraph palettes. We end the chapter by giving you a quick-and-dirty lowdown on the Illustrator text utilities. These utilities can save you loads of time, so don't skip that section.

Working with Type

We admit that this first section is a doozy, but type is important, and we don't want you to miss anything. After introducing you to the Type tools, we move on to the importance of understanding and creating text areas. After that, the fun begins! We show you all sorts of cool things you can do with type, from the simplest tasks of creating a line of text and dealing with text overflow to more complicated tricks such as placing text along paths and wrapping text around objects.

The Type tools

Figure 5-1 shows the Type tools with an example of what you can do with each one. Click and hold on the Type tool to see the hidden tools. The different tools give you the ability to be creative and also accommodate foreign languages.

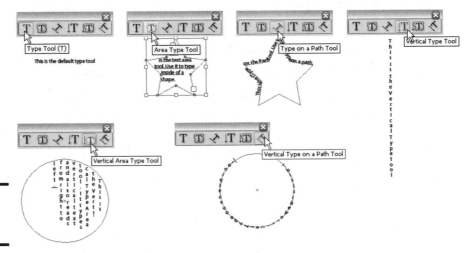

Figure 5-1:
The Type tools.

Creating text areas

A *text area* is a region that you define. Text, when inserted in this region, is constrained within the shape. To create a text area, click and drag with the Type tool.

As you create and finish typing in a text area, you may want to quickly click and drag a new text area elsewhere on your artboard. Unfortunately, if you are on the Type tool, Illustrator will not allow you to do this. You have two options to address this:

✦ Choose Select⇨Deselect, and then create another area.

✦ Hold down the Ctrl (Windows) or ⌘ (Mac) key to temporarily access the Selection tool, and click. When you release the Ctrl (Windows) or ⌘ (Mac) key, you will still be on the Type tool, and you can then create a new text area.

Creating a line of text

To create a simple line of text, select the Type tool and click on the artboard. A blinking insertion point appears. You can now start typing. Using this method, the line of type will go on forever and ever (even beyond the end of the Scratch area) until you press Enter (Windows) or Return (Mac) to start a new line of text. This is fine if you just need short lines of text, say for callouts or captions, but doesn't work well if you're creating a label or anything else that has large amounts of copy.

Many new users click and drag an ever-so-small text area that doesn't allow room for even one letter. If you do this, switch to your Selection tool and delete the active type area, and then click to create a new text insertion point.

Flowing text into an area

Select the Type tool and then drag on the artboard to create a text area. The cursor appears in the text area; text you type in automatically flows to the next line when it reaches the edge of the text area. You can also switch to the Selection tool and adjust the width and height of the text area using the handles.

Need an exact size for a text area? With the Type tool selected, drag to create a text area of any size. Then choose Window⇨Transform to view the Transform palette. Type an exact width in the W text field and exact height in the H text field.

Text overflow

Watch out for excess text! If you create a text area that's too small to hold all the text you want to put into it, a red plus sign appears in the lower-right corner, as shown in Figure 5-2. When Illustrator indicates to you that you have too much text for the text area, you have several options:

✦ Make the text area larger by switching to the Selection tool and dragging the handles.

✦ Make the text smaller until you don't see the overflow indicated.

✦ Link this text area to another. This is called *threading* and is covered later in this chapter in the "Threading text into shapes" section.

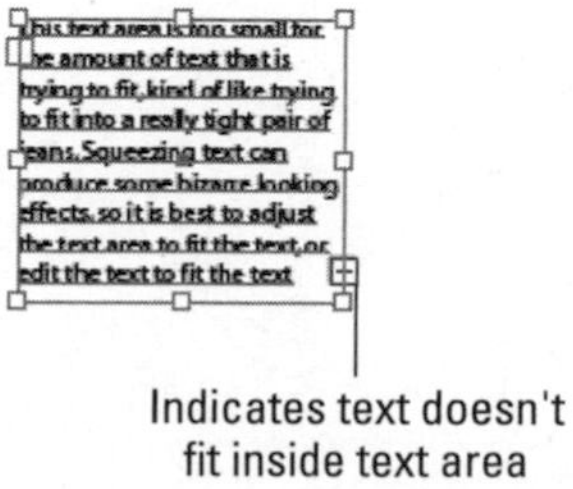

Figure 5-2:
Too much
text!

Indicates text doesn't
fit inside text area

**Book III
Chapter 5**

**Using Type in
Illustrator**

Creating columns of text with the Area Type tool

The easiest and most practical way to create rows and columns of text is to use the area type options in Adobe Illustrator. This feature lets you create rows and columns from any text area. You can just have rows, or you can just have columns, much like columns of text in a newspaper, or even both.

1. **Select the Type tool and drag to create a text area.**

2. **Choose Type⇨Area Type Options.**

The Area Type Options dialog box appears, as shown in Figure 5-3. At the end of this section, we provide a list explaining all the options in the Area Type Options dialog box.

3. **Enter the desired width and height in the Width and Height text fields.**

The Width and Height text fields contain the height and width of your entire text area. For example, we entered **325 pt** in the Width text field and **250 pt** in the Height text field.

4. **In the Columns area, enter the number of columns you want to create in the Columns Number text field, the span distance in the Columns Span text field, and the gutter space in the Columns Gutter text field.**

We entered **2** to create two columns in the Columns Number text field.

The *span* specifies the height of individual rows and the width of individual columns. The *gutter* is the space between the columns, and is automatically set for you.

5. **Click OK.**

When you create two or more columns of text using the Area Type Options dialog box, text flows to the next column when you reach the end of a column, as shown in Figure 5-4.

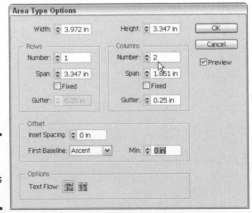

Figure 5-3:
The Area Type Options dialog box.

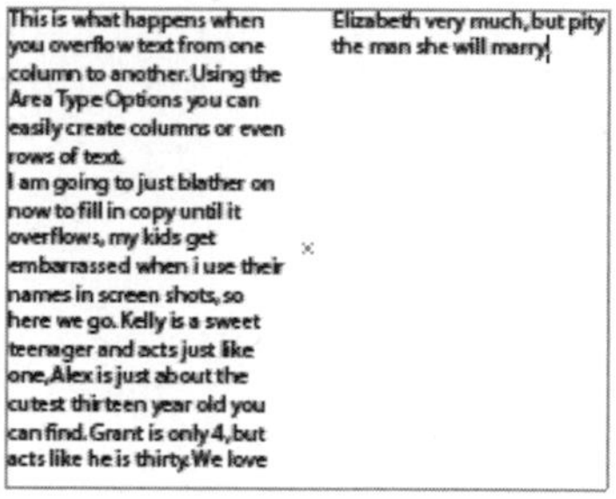

Figure 5-4:
One column
flows into
the next.

This is what happens when you overflow text from one column to another. Using the Area Type Options you can easily create columns or even rows of text.
I am going to just blather on now to fill in copy until it overflows, my kids get embarrassed when i use their names in screen shots, so here we go. Kelly is a sweet teenager and acts just like one, Alex is just about the cutest thirteen year old you can find. Grant is only 4, but acts like he is thirty. We love Elizabeth very much, but pity the man she will marry.

TIP

The following is a breakdown of the other options available in the Area Type Options dialog box (refer to Figure 5-3):

✦ **Width and Height:** The present width and height of the entire text area.

✦ **Number:** The number of rows and/or columns that you want the text area to contain.

✦ **Span:** The height of individual rows and the width of individual columns.

✦ **Fixed:** This check box determines what happens to the span of rows and columns if you resize the type area. When this check box is selected, resizing the area can change the number of rows and columns but not their width. Leave this option deselected if you want to resize the entire text area and have the columns automatically resize with it.

✦ **Gutter:** The empty space between rows or columns.

✦ **Inset Spacing:** The distance from the edges of the text area.

✦ **First Baseline:** Where you want the first line of text to appear. The Ascent option is the default and starts your text normally at the top. If you want to put a fixed size in, like 50 pts from the top, select Fixed from the drop-down list and enter **50 pt** in the Min text field.

Changing measurements

It doesn't matter what the preferred measurements are set at — Adobe Illustrator, Photoshop, and InDesign can all convert the measurements on the fly. If your preferences are set for inches and you want to use points, simply type **pt** after the value (for instance, **25 pt**) in the appropriate dialog box. The inches are converted into points! See Chapter 3 of this minibook for more details on using text fields to change measurements. If you want to change measurement systems for the future, choose Edit➪Preferences➪Units and Display Performance (Windows) or Illustrator➪Preferences➪Units and Display Performance (Mac). Remember to only change the measurements in the General drop-down list. Otherwise, you might type **12** for font size and end up with 12-inch tall text . . . yikes!

✦ **Text Flow:** The direction in which you read the text as it flows to another row or column. You can choose to have the text flow horizontally (across rows) or vertically (down columns).

Threading text into shapes

Create custom columns of text that are in different shapes and sizes by threading closed shapes together. This works with rectangles, circles, stars, or any closed shape, and can lead to some creative text areas.

1. **Create any shape, any size.**

For this example, we've created a circle.

2. **Create another shape (it can be any shape) someplace else on the page.**

3. **Using the Selection tool, select one shape and Shift+click the other to make just those two shapes active.**

4. **Choose Type⇨Threaded Text⇨Create.**

A threading line appears, as shown in Figure 5-5, indicating the direction of the threaded text.

Figure 5-5:
Threaded
text areas
flow from
one area
to another.

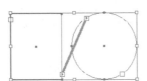

5. **Select the Type tool, click the top of the shape to start the threading, and start typing. Continue typing until the text flows over into the other shape.**

If you don't want the text to be threaded anymore, choose Type⇨Threaded Text⇨Remove Threading. This eliminates all threading from the text shapes. To remove one or more shapes from the threading but not all the shapes, select the shape you want to remove from the threading and choose Type⇨Threaded Text⇨Release Selection.

Wrapping text

Wrapping text is not quite the same as wrapping a present — it's easier! A *text wrap* forces text to wrap around a graphic, as shown in Figure 5-6. This feature can add a bit of creativity to any piece.

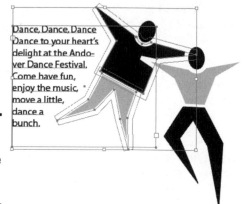

Figure 5-6:
The graphic
is forcing the
text to run
around it.

Follow these steps to wrap text around another object or group of objects:

1. **Select the wrap object.**

This is the object that you want the text to wrap around.

2. **Make sure that the wrap object is on top of the text you want to wrap around it by choosing Object➪Arrange➪Bring to Front.**

If you're working in layers (which we discuss in Chapter 7 of this mini-book), make sure that the wrap object is on the top layer.

3. **Choose Object➪Text Wrap➪Text Wrap Options.**

The Text Wrap Options dialog box appears, as shown in Figure 5-7, giving you the following options:

- **Offset:** Specifies the amount of space between the text and the wrap object. You can enter a positive or negative value.

- **Invert Wrap:** Wraps the text on the inside of the wrap object instead of around it.

4. **When you've finished making your selections, click OK.**

**Book III
Chapter 5**

**Using Type in
Illustrator**

Figure 5-7:
The Text
Wrap
Options
dialog box.

If you want to change the text wrap at a later point, select the object and choose Object➪Text Wrap➪Text Wrap Options. Make your changes and click OK.

If you want to unwrap text from an object, select the wrap object and choose Object➪Text Wrap➪Release Text Wrap.

Outlining text

Illustrator gives you the opportunity to change text into outlines or artwork. Basically, you change the text into an object, so you can no longer edit that text by typing. The plus side is that it saves you the trouble of sending fonts to everyone who wants to use the file. Turning text into outlines makes it appear as though your text was created with the Pen tool. You want to use this when creating logos that will be used frequently by other people or artwork that you may not have control over.

To turn text into an outline, follow these steps:

1. **Type some text on your page.**

For this example, just type a word (say, your name) and make sure that the font size is at least 36 pts. You want to have it large enough to see the effect of outlining it.

2. **Switch to the Selection tool and choose Type➪Create Outlines.**

You can also use the keyboard command Ctrl+Shift+O (Windows) or ⌘+Shift+O (Mac).

The text is now grouped together in outline form.

3. **If you are being creative, or just particular, and want to move individual letters, use the Group Select tool, or choose Object➪Ungroup to separate the letters, as shown in Figure 5-8.**

Figure 5-8: Letters become artwork when you create outlines of the text.

When you convert type to outlines, the type loses its hints. *Hints* are the instructions built into fonts to adjust their shape so that your system displays or prints them in the best way based on the size. Without hints, letters like lowercase *e* or *a* might fill in as the letter forms are reduced in size.

Make sure that the text is the approximate size it might be used at before creating outlines. Because the text loses the hints, try not to create outlines on text smaller than 10 pts.

Putting text on a path, in a closed shape, or on the path of a shape

Wow — that's some heading, huh? You have probably seen text following a swirly path or inside some shape. Maybe you think accomplishing such a task is too intimidating to even attempt. In this section, we show you just how easy these things are! There are Type tools dedicated to putting type on a path or a shape (refer to Figure 5-1), but we think you'll find that the key modifiers we show you in this section are easier to use.

Creating text on a path

Follow these steps to put type on a path:

1. **Create a path using the Pen, Line, or Pencil tool.**

   Don't worry if it has a stroke or fill applied.

2. **Select the Type tool and simply cross over the start of the path. Look for an I-bar with a squiggle to appear (this indicates that the text will run along the path) and click.**

   The stroke and fill of the path immediately change to None.

3. **Start typing, and the text runs on the path.**

4. **To reposition where the text falls on the path, choose Window⇨Type⇨ Paragraph and change the alignment in the Paragraph palette; alternatively, switch to the Selection tool and drag the I-bar that appears, as shown in Figure 5-9, to move the text freehand.**

TIP

Flip the text to the other side of a path by clicking and dragging the I-bar under or over the path.

Book III
Chapter 5

Using Type in
Illustrator

Figure 5-9: Using the Selection tool, drag the I-bar to another location.

Creating text in a closed shape

Putting text inside a shape can add some spunk to a layout. This feature allows you to custom-create a closed shape with the shape tools or the Pen tool and flow text into it. Follow these steps to add text inside a shape:

1. **Create a closed shape, a circle or oval, for instance.**

2. **Select the Type tool and cross over the closed shape. When you see the I-bar swell or become rounded, click.**

This indicates that the text insertion point will be inside the shape.

3. **Start typing, and the text is contained inside the shape.**

Text on the path of a closed shape

Perhaps you want text to run around the edge of a shape instead of inside it. Follow these steps to have text created on the path of a closed shape:

1. **Create a closed shape.**

A circle is a good one.

2. **Select the Type tool and cross over the path of the circle. Don't click when you see the I-bar swell up; hold down the Alt (Windows) or Option (Mac) key instead. The icon now changes into the squiggle I-bar that you see when creating text on a path. When the squiggle line appears, click.**

3. **Start typing, and the text flows around the path of the shape, as shown in Figure 5-10.**

Figure 5-10:
By holding down the Alt or Option key, you can flow text around a closed shape.

4. **To change the origin of the text or move it around, use the alignment options in the Paragraph palette or switch to the Selection tool and drag the I-bar to a new location on the path.**

You can drag the I-bar in and out of the shape to flip the text so that it appears on the outside or inside of the path.

Assigning Font Styles

After you have text on your page, you will often want to change it to be more interesting than the typical 12 pt Times font. Formatting text in Illustrator is not only simple but can be done in multiple ways. In the following list, we name and define some basic type components (see Figure 5-11):

✦ **Font:** A complete set of characters, letters, and symbols of a particular typeface design.

✦ **X height:** The height of type, based on the height of the small x in that type family.

✦ **Kerning:** The space between two letters. Often used for letters in larger type that need to be pulled closer together, like "W i." Kern a little to get the i to slide in a little closer to the W, maybe even going into the space that the W takes, as shown in Figure 5-12. This does not distort the text; it only increases or decreases the space between two letters.

✦ **Tracking:** The space between multiple letters. Designers like to use this technique to spread out words by increasing the space between letters. This does not distort text; it increases or decreases the space between the letters, as shown in Figure 5-13.

Pretty good tracking and kerning has already been determined in most fonts. You don't need to bother with these settings unless you're trying to tweak the text for a more customized look.

✦ **Baseline:** The line that type sits on. This does not include descenders, type that extends down, like lowercase *y* and *g*. You would adjust the baseline for trademark signs or mathematical formulas, as shown in Figure 5-14.

Figure 5-11:
Components
of type.

Figure 5-12:
The letters
before kern-
ing (left)
and after.

Figure 5-13:
A headline
with tracking
set at zero
(top) and at
300 (bottom).

AGI TRAINING

AGI TRAINING

Figure 5-14:
Adjust the
baseline for
characters
that need to
be above or
below the
baseline.

The Keyboard shortcuts for type shown in Table 5-1 work with Adobe
Illustrator, Photoshop, and InDesign.

Table 5-1	Keyboard Shortcuts for Type	
Command	*Windows*	*Mac*
Align left, right, or center	Shift+Ctrl+L, R, or C	Shift+⌘+L, R, or C
Justify	Shift+Ctrl+J	Shift+⌘ +J
Insert soft return	Shift+Enter	Shift+Return
Reset horizontal scale to 100%	Shift+Ctrl+X	Shift+⌘ +X
Increase/decrease point size	Shift+Ctrl+> or <	Shift+⌘ +> or <
Increase/decrease leading	Alt+↑ or ↓	Option+↑ or ↓
Set leading to the font size	Double-click the leading icon in the Character palette	Double-click the leading icon in the Character palette
Reset tracking/kerning to 0	Alt+Ctrl+Q	Option+⌘ +Q
Add or remove space (kerning) between two characters	Alt+→ or ←	Option+→ or ←
Add or remove space (kerning) between characters by 5 times the increment value	Alt+Ctrl+→ or ←	Option+⌘ +→ or ←

Command	Windows	Mac
Add or remove space (kerning) between selected words	Alt+Ctrl+\ or Backspace	Option+⌘ +\ or Backspace
Add or remove space (kerning) between words by 5 times the increment value	Shift+Alt+Ctrl+\ or Backspace	Shift+Option+⌘ +\ or Backspace
Increase/decrease baseline shift	Alt+Shift+↑ or ↓	Option+Shift+↑ or ↓

Using the Character Palette

To visualize changes that you're making to text and to see characteristics that are already selected, choose Window⇨Type⇨Character or press Ctrl+T (Windows) or ⌘+T (Mac), which brings up the Character palette. Click the triangle in the upper-right corner to see a palette menu of additional options. Choose Show options to show additional type attributes, such as baseline shift, underline, and strikethrough.

Pressing Ctrl+T (Windows) or ⌘+T (Mac) is a toggle switch to either show or hide the Character palette. If you don't see the Character palette appear at first, you may have hidden it by pressing the keyboard shortcut. Just try it again.

The following list explains the options in the Character palette (see Figure 5-15):

Book III
Chapter 5

Using Type in
Illustrator

✦ **Font:** Pick the font that you want to use from this drop-down list.

In this version, you can select the font name in the Character palette or Control panel and press the up or down arrow key to automatically switch to the next font above or below on the font list. Do this while you have text selected to see the text change live!

✦ **Set Font Style:** Pick the style (for instance, bold, italic, or bold italic) from this drop-down list. The choices here are limited by the fonts that you have loaded. In other words, if you have only Times regular loaded in your system, you won't have the choice to bold or italicize it.

✦ **Type Size:** Choose the size of the type in this combo box. Average readable type is 12 pt; headlines can vary from 18 pts and up.

✦ **Leading:** Select how much space you want between the lines of text in this combo box. Illustrator uses the professional typesetting method of including the type size in the total leading. In other words, if you have 12 pt and want it double-spaced, set the leading at 24 pts.

✦ **Kerning:** Use this combo box by placing the cursor between two letters. Increase the amount by clicking the up arrow or by typing in a value to push the letters further apart from each other; decrease the spacing between the letters by typing in a lower value, even negative numbers, or by clicking the down arrow.

✦ **Tracking:** Use the Tracking combo box by selecting multiple letters and increasing or decreasing the space between all of them at once by clicking the up or down arrows or by typing in a positive or negative value.

✦ **Horizontal Scale:** Distorts the selected text by stretching it horizontally. Enter a positive number to increase the size of the letters; enter a negative number to decrease the size.

✦ **Vertical Scale:** Distorts the selected text vertically. Enter a positive number to increase the size of the letters; enter a negative number to decrease the size.

Using horizontal or vertical scaling to make text look like condensed type often doesn't give good results. When you distort text, the nice thick and thin characteristics of the typeface also become distorted and can produce weird effects.

✦ **Baseline Shift:** Use baseline shift for trademark signs and mathematical formulas that require selected letters to be moved above or below the baseline.

✦ **Character Rotation:** Rotate just the selected text by entering an angle in this text field or by clicking the up or down arrows.

✦ **Rotate:** Text Character Rotation. Choose to rotate your selected text on any angle.

✦ **Underline and Strikethrough:** Finally! This simple text attribute was noticeably missing from previous versions, but now a type style you can choose.

✦ **Language:** Choose a language from this drop-down list. Note: The language you specify here is used by Illustrator's spell checker and hyphenation feature. We discuss these features in the later section, "Text Utilities: Your Key to Efficiency."

Figure 5-15:
The Character palette with options showing.

Using the Control Palette

New in CS2, you have access to a contextual Control panel (located across the top of the Adobe Illustrator work area as a default). With the text selected with the Type tool, you can use this as a quick and easy way to select fonts, size, alignment, color, and transparency.

Using the Paragraph Palette

Access the Paragraph palette by choosing Window⇨Type⇨Paragraph. In this palette are all the attributes that apply to an entire paragraph, including alignment and indents, which we discuss in this section, and also hyphenation, which we discuss later in this chapter. For instance, you can't flush left one word in a paragraph. When you click the Flush Left button, the entire paragraph flushes left.

Alignment

You can choose any of the following alignment methods by choosing the appropriate button on the Paragraph palette:

✦ **Flush Left:** All text is flush to the left with a ragged edge on the right. This is the most common way to align text.

✦ **Center:** All text is centered.

✦ **Flush Right:** All text is flush to the right and ragged on the left.

✦ **Justify with the Last Line Aligned Left:** Right and left edges are both straight, with the last line left-aligned.

✦ **Justify with the Last Line Aligned Center:** Right and left edges are both straight, with the last line centered.

✦ **Justify with the Last Line Aligned Right:** Right and left edges are both straight, with the last line right-aligned.

✦ **Justify All Lines:** This method is called *forced justification*, where the last line is stretched the entire column width, no matter how short it is. This alignment is used in many publications, but it can create some awful results.

Indents

You can choose from the following methods of indentation:

✦ **First Line Indent:** Indents the first line of every paragraph. In other words, every time you press the Enter (Windows) or Return (Mac) key, this spacing is created.

**Book III
Chapter 5**

Using Type in
Illustrator

To avoid first-line indents and space after from occurring, say if you just want to break a line in a specific place, create a line break or soft return by pressing Shift+Enter (Windows) or Shift+Return (Mac).

✦ **Right Indent:** Indents from the right side of the column of text.

✦ **Left Indent:** Indents from the left side of the column of text.

 Use the Eyedropper tool to copy the character, paragraph, fill, and stroke attributes. Select the text that you want to, and then select the Eyedropper tool and click once on the text which attributes you want to apply to the selected text.

By default, the Eyedropper affects all attributes of a type selection, including appearance attributes. To customize the attributes affected by these tools, double-click the Eyedropper tool to open the Eyedropper dialog box.

Text Utilities: Your Key to Efficiency

After you have text in an Illustrator document, you may need to perform various tasks within that text, such as searching for a word to replace with another word, checking your spelling and grammar, saving and creating your own styles, or changing the case of a block of text. You're in luck, because Illustrator provides various text utilities that enable you to easily and efficiently perform all these otherwise tedious tasks. In this section, we give you a quick tour of these utilities.

Find and replace

Generally, artwork created in Illustrator isn't text heavy, but the fact that Illustrator has a Find and Replace feature can be a huge help. Use the Find and Replace dialog box (choose Edit➪Find and Replace) to search for words that need to be changed, such as changing Smyth to Smith, or to locate items that may be difficult to find otherwise. This feature works pretty much like all other search and replace methods.

Spell checker

Can you believe there was a time when Illustrator didn't have a spell checker? Thankfully, it does now — and its simple design makes it easy to use. To use the spell checker, choose Edit➪Check Spelling, and then click the Start button in the dialog box that appears. The spell checker works much like the spell checker in Microsoft Word or other popular applications: When a misspelled word is found, you're offered a list of replacements. You can either choose to fix that instance, all instances, ignore the misspelling, or add your word to the dictionary.

If you click the arrow to the left of Options (see Figure 5-16), you can set other specifications, such as whether you want to look for letter case issues or have the spell checker note repeated words.

Note: The spell checker uses whatever language you specify in the Character palette. We discuss this palette in the earlier section, "Using the Character Palette."

Figure 5-16:
The spell checker offers additional options.

If you work in a specialized industry that uses loads of custom words, save yourself time by choosing Edit⇨Edit Custom Dictionary, and then add your own words. We recommend that you do so before you're ready to spell check a document so that the spell checker doesn't flag the custom words later (which slows you down).

Book III
Chapter 5

Using Type in Illustrator

The Hyphenation feature

Nothing is worse than severely hyphenated copy. Most designers either use hyphenation as little as possible or avoid it altogether by turning off the Hyphenation feature. Here are a few things that you should know about customizing your hyphenation settings if you decide to use this feature:

✦ **Turning the Hyphenation feature on/off:** Activate or deactivate the feature in the Hyphenation dialog box (see Figure 5-17); access this dialog box by choosing Window⇨Type⇨Paragraph, clicking the arrow in the upper-right of the Paragraph palette to access the palette menu, and then choosing Hyphenation from the list of options that appears. If you're not going to use the Hyphenation feature, turn it off by deselecting the Hyphenation check box at the top of the Hyphenation dialog box.

✦ **Setting specifications in the Hyphenation dialog box:** Set specifications in the dialog box that determine the length of words to hyphenate, how many hyphens should be used in a single document, whether or not to hyphenate capitalized words, and how words should be hyphenated. The Before Last setting is useful, for instance, if you don't want to have a word such as "liquidated" hyphenated as "liquidat-ed", type **3** in the Before Last text field, and Illustrator won't hyphenate words if it leaves only two letters on the next line.

✦ **Hyphenation Limit and Hyphenation Zone:** They're not diets or worlds in another dimension. The Hyphenation Limit setting enables you to limit the number of hyphens in a row. So, for instance, type **2** in the Hyphenation Limit text field so that there are never more than two hyphenated words in a row. The Hyphenation Zone text field enables you to set up an area of hyphenation based upon a measurement. For instance, you can specify 1 inch to allow for only one hyphenation every inch. You can also use the slider to determine whether you want better spacing or fewer hyphens. This slider works only with the Single-line composer (the default). See the later section, "The text composition method," where we discuss text composers.

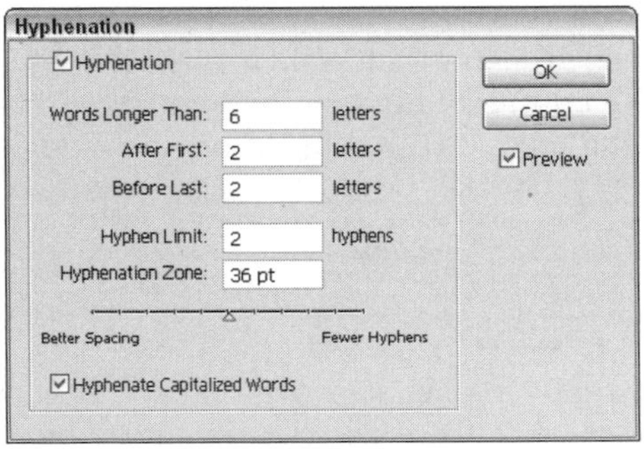

Figure 5-17:
Customizing hyphenation settings.

The Find Font feature

If you work in production, you'll love the Find Font feature, which enables you to list all the fonts in a file that contains text and then search for and replace fonts (including the font's type style) by name. You do so from the Find Font dialog box (see Figure 5-18), accessed by choosing Type⇨Find Font. Select the font that you want to replace from the Fonts in Document list. Next, select a font from the Replace with Font From list, Note that the font must already appear in the document. Click the Change button to replace the font (or click the Change All button to replace all instances of the font), and then click OK. That's it!

This cool feature enables you to replace fonts with fonts from the current working document or from your entire system. Select System from the Replace with Font From drop-down list to choose from all the fonts loaded in your system.

Figure 5-18:
The Find
Font
dialog box.

The Change Case feature

Doesn't it drive you crazy when you type an entire paragraph before discovering that you somehow pressed the Caps Lock key? Fix it fast by selecting the text and choosing Type➪Change Case and then choosing one of the following:

✦ **Uppercase:** Makes the selected text all uppercase.

✦ **Lowercase:** Makes the selected text all lowercase.

✦ **Title Case:** Capitalizes the first letter in each word.

✦ **Sentence Case:** Capitalizes just the first letter in the selected sentence(s).

The text composition method

New in Adobe Illustrator CS2, you can use the same type engine used by InDesign for high-quality text control. As a default, you're working in what is referred to as a single-line composer. Select Single or Every Line composer from the Paragraph palette menu. Read on to see what the different options include.

✦ **Single-Line Composer:** This option is useful if you prefer to have manual control over how lines break. In fact, this is the method that had been in place in the past. The single-line composer doesn't take the entire paragraph into consideration when expanding letter space and word spacing, so justified text can sometimes look odd in its entire form (see Figure 5-19).

✦ **Every-Line Composer:** The every-line composer is a very professional way of setting text; many factors are taken into account as far as spacing is concerned, and spacing is based on the entire paragraph. Using this method, you see few spacing issues that create strange effects, such as the ones on the left of Figure 5-19.

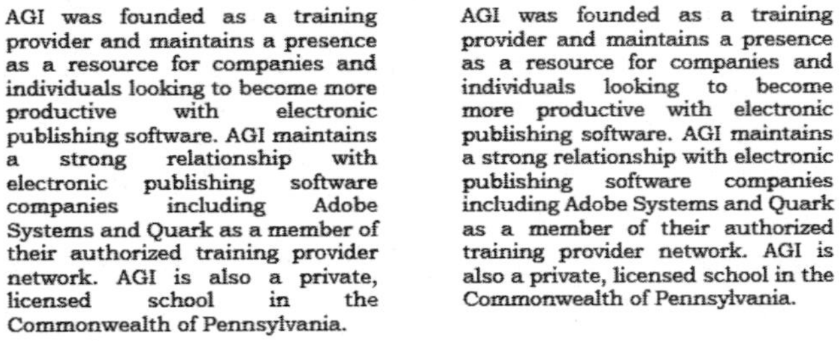

Figure 5-19:
A paragraph created using single-line composer (left) and every-line composer (right).

AGI was founded as a training provider and maintains a presence as a resource for companies and individuals looking to become more productive with electronic publishing software. AGI maintains a strong relationship with electronic publishing software companies including Adobe Systems and Quark as a member of their authorized training provider network. AGI is also a private, licensed school in the Commonwealth of Pennsylvania.

AGI was founded as a training provider and maintains a presence as a resource for companies and individuals looking to become more productive with electronic publishing software. AGI maintains a strong relationship with electronic publishing software companies including Adobe Systems and Quark as a member of their authorized training provider network. AGI is also a private, licensed school in the Commonwealth of Pennsylvania.

Text styles

A *text style* is a saved set of text attributes, such as font, size, and so on. Creating text styles keeps you consistent and saves you time by enabling you to efficiently implement changes in one step instead of having to select the text attributes for each instance of that style of text (say a heading or caption). So when you're finally happy with the way your headlines appear and the body copy looks, when your boss asks whether the body copy can be a smidgen smaller (okay . . . a smidgen?), you can confidently answer, "Sure!"

If you've created styles, changing a text attribute is simple. What's more, the change is applied at once to all text that uses that style. Otherwise, you'd have to make the attribute change to every occurrence of body text, which could take a long time if your text is spread out.

Illustrator offers two types of text styles:

✦ **Character styles:** Saves attributes for individual selected text. If you want just the word "New" in a line of text to be red 20 pt Arial, you can save it as a character style sheet. Then, when you apply it, the attributes apply only to the selected text (and not the entire line or paragraph).

✦ **Paragraph styles:** Saves attributes for an entire paragraph. A span of text is considered a paragraph until it reaches a hard return or paragraph break. Note that pressing Shift+Enter (Windows) or Shift+Return (Mac) is considered a soft return and paragraph styles will continue to apply beyond the soft return.

There are many ways to create character and paragraph styles, but we show you the easiest and most direct methods.

Creating character styles

Create a character style when you want individual sections of text to be treated differently from other text in the paragraph. So instead of manually applying a style over and over again, you create and implement a character style. To do so, open a document containing text and follow these steps:

1. **Set up text with the text attributes you want included in the character style in the Character and Paragraph palettes. Then choose Window⇨Type⇨Character Styles.**

   This opens the Character Styles palette.

2. **Select the text from Step 1 and Alt+click (Windows) or Option+click (Mac) the New Style button (dog-eared page icon) at the bottom of the Character Styles palette.**

3. **In the Character Styles Options dialog box that appears, name your style and click OK.**

   Illustrator records what attributes have already been applied to the selected text and builds a style for them.

4. **Now create another text area by choosing Select⇨Deselect and using the Type tool to drag out a new text area.**

   We discuss using the Type tool in the earlier section, "Creating text areas."

5. **Change the font and size to something dramatically different from your saved style and type some text.**

6. **Select some (not all) of the new text and then Alt+click (Windows) or Option+click (Mac) the style name in the Character Styles palette.**

   You Alt+click (Windows) or Option+click (Mac) to eliminate any attributes that were not a part of the saved style. The attributes of the saved character style are applied to the selected text.

When creating a new palette item (any palette) in Adobe Illustrator, InDesign, or Photoshop, we recommend that you get in the habit of Alt+clicking (Windows) or Option+clicking (Mac) the New Style button. This allows you to name the item (style, layer, swatch, and so on) while adding it to the palette.

Creating a paragraph style

Paragraph styles include attributes that are applied to an entire paragraph. What constitutes a paragraph is all text that falls before a hard return (you create a hard return when you press Enter [Windows] or Return [Mac]), so this could be one line of text for a headline or ten lines in a body text paragraph. To create a paragraph style, open a document that contains text or open a new document and add text to it; then follow these steps:

1. **Choose Window⇨Type⇨Paragraph Styles to open the Paragraph Styles palette.**

2. **Find a paragraph of text that has the same text attributes throughout it and put your cursor anywhere in that paragraph.**

   You don't even have to select the whole paragraph!

3. **Alt+click (Windows) or Option+click (Mac) the Create New Style button (the dog-eared icon at the bottom of the Paragraph palette) to create a new paragraph style; give your new style a name.**

   Your new style now appears in the Paragraph Styles palette list of styles.

4. **Create a paragraph of text elsewhere in your document and make its attributes different from the text in Step 2.**

5. **Put your cursor anywhere in the new paragraph and Alt+click (Windows) or Option+click (Mac) your named style in the Paragraph Styles palette.**

   The attributes from the style are applied to the entire paragraph.

Updating styles

When you use existing text to build styles, reselect the text and assign the style. In other words, if you put the cursor in the original text whose attributes were saved as a style, it does not have a style assigned to it in the Styles palette. Assign the style by selecting the text or paragraph and clicking on the appropriate style listed in the Styles palette. By doing this, you ensure that any future updates to that style will apply to that original text, as well as to all other instances.

To update a style, simply select its name in either the Character or Paragraph Styles palette. Choose Options from the palette menu, which you access by clicking the arrow in the upper-right corner of the palette. In the resulting dialog box (see Figure 5-20), make changes by clicking the main attribute on the left and then updating the choices on the right. After you do so, all tagged styles are updated.

Figure 5-20:
Updating a
paragraph
style.

Documents created in older versions of Adobe Illustrator (Version 10 or earlier) contain what is called *legacy text,* text using the older text engine. When these files are opened, you will see a warning dialog box, such as the one you see in Figure 5-21.

Figure 5-21:
Legacy text
warning.

Understand that if you click on the update button that any text on the document will most likely re-flow, causing line breaks, leading, and other spacing to change.

Click the OK button to update the file after it is opened. This locks down the text. If necessary, you can use the Type tool to click on a selected text area to update only the contained text. Another Warning dialog box appears that gives you the opportunity to Update the selected text, copy the Text Object, or cancel the text tool selection. This is the best way to see what changes are occurring so that you can catch any spacing issues right off the bat. See Figure 5-22 for samples of the three options in the warning dialog window.

Keep in mind, if you choose to Copy the Text Object, you can use the underlying locked copy to adjust the new text flow to match the old. Throw away the legacy text layer by clicking and dragging it to the trash icon in the Layers palette, or click on the visibility Eye icon to the left of the Legacy Text layer to hide it when you are finished.

Figure 5-22:
Original
text (left),
Updated
Text
(middle),
Text Object
copied
(right).

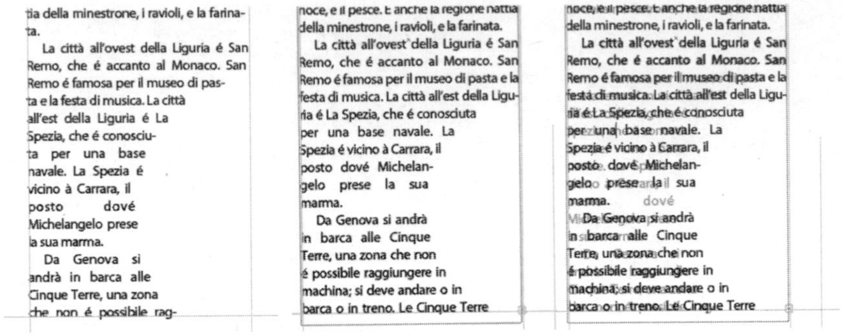

tia della minestrone, i ravioli, e la farinata.

La città all'ovest della Liguria é San
Remo, che é accanto al Monaco. San
Remo é famosa per il museo di pasta e la festa di musica. La città
all'est della Liguria é La
Spezia, che é conosciu-
ta per una base
navale. La Spezia é
vicino à Carrara, il
posto dové
Michelangelo prese
la sua marma.

Da Genova si
andrà in barca alle
Cinque Terre, una zona
che non é possibile rag-

noce, e il pesce. È anche la regione nattia
della minestrone, i ravioli, e la farinata.

La città all'ovest della Liguria é San
Remo, che é accanto al Monaco. San
Remo é famosa per il museo di pasta e la
festa di musica. La città all'est della Liguria é La Spezia, che é conosciuta
per una base navale. La
Spezia é vicino à Carrara, il
posto dové Michelan-
gelo prese la sua
marma.

Da Genova si andrà
in barca alle Cinque
Terre, una zona che non
é possibile raggiungere in
machina; si deve andare o in
barca o in treno. Le Cinque Terre

noce, e il pesce. È anche la regione nattia
della minestrone, i ravioli, e la farinata.

La città all'ovest della Liguria é San
Remo, che é accanto al Monaco. San
Remo é famosa per il museo di pasta e la
festa di musica. La città all'est della Liguria é La Spezia, che é conosciuta
per una base navale. La
Spezia é vicino à Carrara, il
posto dové Michelan-
gelo prese la sua
marma. dové
Da Genova si andrà
in barca alle Cinque
Terre, una zona che non
é possibile raggiungere in
machina; si deve andare o in
barca o in treno. Le Cinque Terre

Chapter 6: Organizing Your Illustrations

In This Chapter

✔ **Setting up the ruler**

✔ **Getting to know guides**

✔ **Placing paths and shapes**

✔ **Rearranging, hiding, and locking objects**

✔ **Masking objects**

You can know all the neat special effects in Illustrator, but if you don't have a strong foundation on the organization of your artwork, you may fall flat on your face when it comes to getting some of the features you love to work. So in this chapter, we focus on a few tricks of the trade when it comes to organizing your illustrations and workspace. Have fun exploring how to get your artwork to do what you want it to do.

Setting Ruler Increments

Using rulers to help you accurately place objects in your illustration sounds pretty simple (and it is), but not knowing how to effectively use the rulers in Illustrator can drive you over the edge.

To view rulers in Illustrator, choose View➪Show Rulers or press Ctrl+R (Windows) or ⌘+R (Mac).

When the rulers appear, they will be in the default setting of points (or whatever measurement increment was last set up in the preferences).

You can change the rulers' increments to the measurement system that you prefer in the following ways:

✦ Create a new document and select your preferred measurement units in the New Document dialog box.

✦ Right-click (Windows) or Control+click (Mac) the horizontal or vertical ruler. This displays a contextual menu from which you can pick a measurement increment.

✦ Choose Edit➪Preferences➪Units and Display Performance (Windows) or Illustrator➪Preferences➪Units and Display Performance (Mac) to bring up the Preferences dialog box.

Be *very* careful with this dialog box. Change ruler units only by using the General tab of the Preferences dialog box. If you change the units of measurement in the Stroke and Type tabs, you might end up with 12-*inch* type instead of that dainty 12-*point* type you were expecting! ***Remember:*** Setting the General Preferences changes the preferences for all future documents.

✦ Choose File➪Document Setup to change measurement units only for the document that you're working on.

Using Guides

Guides can make producing accurate illustrations much easier, and they can even go away when you're done with them . . . hmmm, sounds too good to be true. You can use two kinds of guides in Illustrator:

✦ **Ruler guides:** Straight line guides that are created by clicking on the ruler and dragging out to the artboard.

✦ **Custom guides:** Guides created from Illustrator objects, such as shapes or paths. Great for copying the exact angle of a path and replicating it, as shown in Figure 6-1.

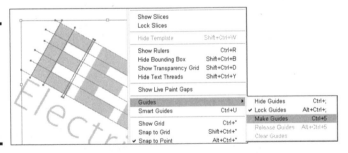

Figure 6-1: Create custom guides to turn paths and shapes into guides.

Creating a ruler guide

A ruler guide is the easiest guide to create. Click anywhere on the vertical or horizontal ruler and drag it to the artboard to create a ruler guide, as shown in Figure 6-2. By default, the horizontal ruler creates horizontal guides (no kidding), and the vertical ruler creates vertical guides. But, wait, there's more — you can Alt+drag (Windows) or Option+drag (Mac) to change the orientation of the guide. The vertical ruler then creates a horizontal guide and the horizontal ruler then creates a vertical guide.

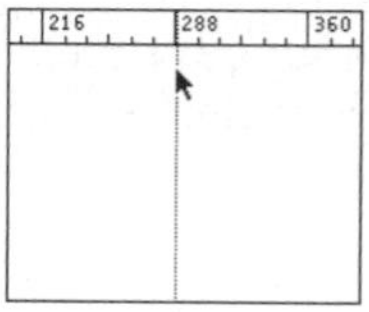

Figure 6-2:
Click directly
on the ruler
and drag
out a guide.

Creating a custom guide

Create a custom guide by selecting a path or shape and choosing View⇨
Guides⇨Make Guides. Whatever is selected turns into a non-printing guide.

Changing a path into a guide doesn't have to be permanent. Choose View⇨
Guides⇨Release Guides to turn guides back into paths.

As a default, guides are locked, which means that after you place them, they
won't move. That can be a problem if you misplaced a guide, but you can
easily rectify this by choosing View⇨Guides⇨Lock Guides. This will remove
the check mark beside Lock Guides in the menu and unlock the guides so that
you can move them around.

Using the Transform Palette for Placement

Placing shapes and paths precisely where you want them can be difficult for
those with even the most steady of hands. Save yourself aggravation by using
the Transform palette to perform such tasks as scaling and rotating objects.
On a more practical note, however, the Transform palette also enables you
to type in x, y coordinates. This way, you can position your objects exactly
where you want them.

In Adobe Illustrator and InDesign, the *Reference Point Indicator* icon is on the
left side of the Transform palette. Click the handle of the Reference Point
Indicator icon to change the point of reference. If you want to measure from
the upper-left corner, click on the indicator on the handle in the upper left.
Want to know exactly where the center of an object is? Click on the center
point in the indicator. The point of reference is the spot on the object that
falls at the x, y coordinates:

✦ **X coordinate:** Sets the placement of the selected object from left to right.

✦ **Y coordinate:** Sets the placement of the selected object from top to
   bottom.

**Book III
Chapter 6**

**Organizing Your
Illustrations**

Did you ever notice that Adobe Illustrator, which is based on PostScript, considers the lower-left corner the zero point? This can be confusing at first, but don't let it get you down. You can change the ruler origin if it really drives you crazy by following the steps in the next section.

Changing the Ruler Origin

 In Adobe Illustrator, InDesign, and Photoshop, you can change your *ruler origin*. This helps to define your measuring starting point and defines the part of the page that will print if you use manual tiling.

To change the ruler origin, follow these steps:

1. Move the pointer to the upper-left corner of the rulers where the rulers intersect, as shown in Figure 6-3.

Figure 6-3:
Click and drag where the rulers intersect to change the start point of the ruler.

2. Drag the pointer to where you want the new ruler origin.

As you drag, a cross hair in the window and in the rulers indicates where the new ruler origin will be placed.

You can put the original ruler origin back in place by double-clicking on the ruler intersection.

Object Arrangement

Just like stacking paper on your desk, new objects in Illustrator are placed on top of the existing objects. Change this order by using the Object➪Arrange choices.

The easiest choices are to bring an object to the front or send it to the back. The results of sending forward or backward can be a little unnerving if you don't know exactly in what order objects were created. Figure 6-4 shows an illustration that we rearranged using four of the available choices. Figure 6-5 shows the result of each choice.

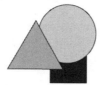

Figure 6-4:
The objects before rearrange-ment.

To change the stacking order, select the object(s) whose placement you want to change, and then choose one of the following:

✦ **Object⇨Arrange⇨Bring to Front:** Brings the selected object(s) to the top of the painting order. In Figure 6-5a, the square is brought in front of the other objects by using the Bring to Front command.

✦ **Object⇨Arrange⇨Bring Forward:** Brings the selected object(s) in front of the object created just before it, or one level closer to the front. In Figure 6-5b, the square is pulled up in front of the circle with the Bring Forward command.

✦ **Object⇨Arrange⇨Send Backward:** Moves the selected object(s) so that it falls under the object created just before it, or one level further to the back. In Figure 6-5c, the triangle is sent backward so that it is just under the circle.

✦ **Object⇨Arrange⇨Send to Back:** Pushes the selected object(s) to the bottom of the painting order. In Figure 6-5d, the triangle is placed on the bottom of the stack using the Send to Back command.

Book III
Chapter 6

Organizing Your
Illustrations

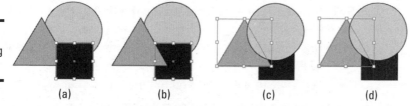

Figure 6-5:
Rearranging objects.

(a)   (b)   (c)   (d)

Hiding Objects

Seasoned Illustrator users love to use the Hide command. Use it when the object that you want to select is stuck behind something else, or when you need to select one object and another keeps activating instead.

A good opportunity to use the Hide command is when you're creating text inside a shape. In Chapter 5 of this minibook, we show you that as soon as you turn a shape into a text area, the fill and stroke attributes turn into None. Follow these steps for an example of when hiding a shape is useful:

1. **Create a shape.**

   For this example, we created a circle.

2. **Click the Fill color box at the bottom of the Illustrator toolbox, and then choose Window⇨Swatches.**

   The Swatches palette appears.

3. **In the palette, choose a color for the fill.**

   We've chosen yellow here. The stroke doesn't matter; we've set it to None.

   When changing your shape into a text area, the color you've chosen is going to disappear. To have the colored shape remain, you have to cheat the system.

4. **With your colored shape selected, choose Edit⇨Copy; alternatively, you can press Ctrl+C (Windows) or ⌘+C (Mac).**

   This makes a copy of your shape.

5. **Choose Edit⇨Paste in Back or press Ctrl+B (Windows) or ⌘+B (Mac).**

   This puts a copy of your shape exactly in back of the original.

6. **Choose Object⇨Hide or press Ctrl+3 (Windows) or ⌘+3 (Mac).**

   The copy of the shape is now hidden; what you see is your original shape.

7. **Switch to the Type tool by selecting the tool in the toolbox or pressing T.**

8. **With the cursor, cross over the edge of the shape to change it to the Area Type tool.**

   The Area Type tool enables you to type into a shape.

9. **When you see the type insertion cursor swell up (as shown in Figure 6-6), click on the edge of the shape.**

   The insertion point is now blinking inside the shape, and the fill and stroke attributes of the shape have been changed to none.

Figure 6-6:
The type insertion icon as it appears when positioned on the edge of a shape.

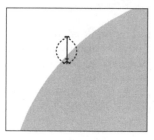

10. **Type some text (see Figure 6-7).**

Figure 6-7:
Type directly in your shape.

Oh
I love a sunny day!
Camp Jacuzzi 1984

11. **When you're finished entering text, choose Object⇨Show All, or press Ctrl+Alt+3 (Windows) or ⌘+Option+3 (Mac).**

Your colored shape reappears with the text in the middle of it! Use this process for creating custom text shapes with color. See Figure 6-8.

Figure 6-8:
The hidden shape reappears exactly where it was before.

Oh
I love a sunny day!
Camp Jacuzzi 1984

Use the Hide command anytime you want to tuck something away for later use. We promise that anything hidden in Illustrator won't be lost. Just use the Show All command, and any hidden objects are revealed, exactly where you left them. Too bad the Show All command can't reveal where you left your car keys!

Locking Objects

Locking items is handy when you're building an illustration. Not only does the Lock command lock down objects that you don't want to make changes to, but it also drives anyone who tries to edit your files crazy! In fact, we mention locking mainly to help preserve your sanity. There will be many times you need to make simple adjustments to another designer's artwork and you just can't, unless the objects are first unlocked. You can lock and unlock objects as follows:

✦ **Lock an object:** Choose Object➪Lock or press Ctrl+2 (Windows) or ⌘+2 (Mac) to lock an object so that you can't select it, move it, or change its attributes.

✦ **Unlock an object:** Choose Object➪Unlock All or press Ctrl+Alt+2 (Windows) or ⌘+Option+2 (Mac). Then you can make changes to it.

You can also lock and hide objects with layers. See Chapter 7 in this mini-book for more information about using layers.

Creating a Clipping Mask

Creating a clipping mask may sound complex, but it's actually very easy and brings together some of the items that we talk about in this chapter, such as arranging objects. A *clipping mask* allows a topmost object to define the selected shapes underneath it. This would be similar to you cutting a hole in a piece of paper and peering through it to the objects below, except that with a clipping mask, the area around the defining shape is transparent. Figure 6-9 shows two examples of clipping masks.

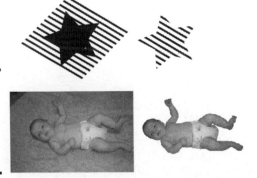

Figure 6-9: Examples of items using the clipping mask feature.

Some of you may remember what a film mask looked like. It was black to block out the picture and clear where you wanted to view an image, as shown in Figure 6-10.

Figure 6-10:
A conventional film mask.

The clipping mask feature uses the same principal as the conventional film mask; but the clipping mask is a whole lot easier to create and modify. To create a clipping mask, follow these steps:

1. **Choose File⇨Place, to place an image.**

    Masks work with objects created in Illustrator, as well as those placed (scanned or otherwise imported into Illustrator), but an example using a single placed image is less complicated.

2. **Create the item that you want to use as a mask by creating a shape or a closed path with the Pen tool.**

    For instance, in Figure 6-11, the circle is the mask (the photo underneath it is the placed image from Step 1). The circle is placed where the mask will be created. It does not matter what the shape's color, fill, and stroke are, these automatically change to None when you create a mask.

    Note: When creating a clipping mask, make sure that the object to be used as a mask is a closed shape and is at the top of the stacking order.

Figure 6-11:
The shape that will become the mask is positioned over the placed image.

3. Using the Selection tool, select both the placed image and the shape.

Shift+click to add an object to the selection.

4. Choose Object⇨Clipping Mask⇨Make.

Ta-da! The clipping mask is created, as shown in Figure 6-12. The masked items are grouped together, but you can use the Direct Selection tool to move around the image or the mask individually.

Figure 6-12:
The complete clipping mask.

5. To turn off the clipping mask, choose Object⇨Clipping Mask⇨Release.

You can also use text as a mask. Just type in a word, make sure that it is positioned over an image or other Illustrator object(s), select both the text and the object, and then choose Object⇨Clipping Mask⇨Make.

Chapter 7: Using Layers

In This Chapter

✓ **Creating new layers**

✓ **Using layers for selections**

✓ **Moving objects to layers**

✓ **Hiding and locking layers**

This chapter shows you just how simple it is to use layers and how helpful layers can be when you're producing complex artwork. Layers are similar to clear pages stacked on top of your artwork: You can place content (text, shapes, and so on) on a layer, lift up a layer, remove a layer, hide and show layers, or lock a layer so that you can't edit the content on it. Layers are an incredible feature that can help you

✦ Organize the painting (stacking) order of objects.

✦ Activate objects that would otherwise be difficult to select with the Selection or Direct Selection tool.

✦ Lock items that you don't want to reposition or change.

✦ Hide items until you need them.

✦ Repurpose objects for artwork variations. For example, business cards use the same logo and company address, but the name and contact information changes for each person. In this case, placing the logo and company address on one layer and the person's name and contact information on another layer makes it easy to create a new business card by just changing the name of the person.

Many Illustrator users don't take advantage of layers. Maybe these users don't understand the basic functions of layers, or maybe they think that layers are much more complicated than they really are. By reading this chapter, you'll be able to take advantage of layers in Illustrator.

Unlike in Photoshop, layers in Illustrator don't add an incredible amount of size to the file. Read on for more information about using layers.

Creating New Layers

When you create a new Illustrator document, you automatically have one layer to start with. To understand how layers work, create a new file and then follow these steps to create new layers and put objects on them:

1. **If the Layers palette isn't already visible, choose Window⇨Layers.**

   The Layers palette appears, as shown in Figure 7-1.

Target radio button

Active layer

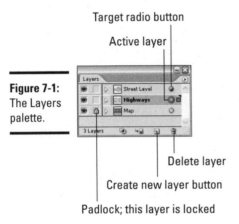

Figure 7-1:
The Layers
palette.

Padlock; this layer is locked

Create new layer button

Delete layer

2. **Create a shape anywhere on the artboard.**

   It doesn't matter what size the shape is, but make sure that it has a colored fill so that you can see it easily. For this example, we created a rectangle.

3. **Click the Fill color swatch at the bottom of the toolbox and select any color from the Swatches palette (choose Window⇨Swatches if the Swatches palette isn't visible).**

   The blue handle colors match the blue color selection square you see in the Layers palette when an object on that layer is selected. The color selection square to the right of the radio button signifies that something is active on this layer. If you choose Select⇨Deselect, the color selection square disappears.

   Also, notice now that you have a shape on this layer, an arrow appears to the left of the layer name. This indicates that you now have a *sublayer*, which is essentially a layer within a layer. Click the arrow to expand the layer and show any sublayers nested under it; sublayers are automatically created as you add objects. This helps when you're trying to make difficult selections.

4. **To make a new layer, Alt+click (Windows) or Option+click (Mac) the Create New Layer button at the bottom of the Layers palette.**

   The Create New Layer button looks like a dog-eared document (refer to Figure 7-1). By Alt+clicking (Windows) or Option+clicking (Mac), you bring up the Layer Options dialog box (shown in Figure 7-2), which allows you to name the new layer at the same time as you're creating it.

Figure 7-2:
Creating a
new layer.

5. **Enter a name for the new layer in the Name text field and click OK.**

   This automatically adds a new layer to the top of the stack in the Layers palette.

6. **Make a shape on the new layer that overlaps the shape you created in Step 2 (see Figure 7-3) and give the new shape a fill color different from the other shape's fill color so that you can see a contrast.**

   We named the new layer "circle" and created a circle on it.

Figure 7-3:
We created
a circle on
the circle
layer.

Do you see what happened to the selection handles? They change to a different color, indicating that you're on a different layer (refer to Figure 7-3). The different colors of the handles are for organizational purposes only and don't print.

You can also create a new layer by using the palette menu (triangle) in the upper-right corner of the Layers palette.

7. **Choose New Layer from the palette menu; the Layer Options dialog box appears, as shown in Figure 7-4.**

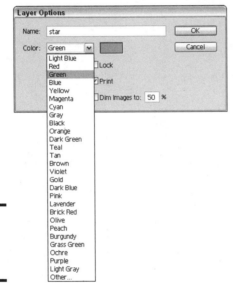

Figure 7-4:
The Layer
Options
dialog box.

8. **In the Layer Options dialog box, you can choose to change the color of the selection handles by selecting an option from the Color drop-down list as well as hide or lock the contents of the layer.**

9. **Enter a name for this new layer in the Name text field, click OK, and then create a shape on it.**

For this example, we named the layer "star" and used the Star tool to create a star.

10. **Again, change the fill color of your newest shape so that it's different from the fill colors of your other shapes.**

11. **Use the Selection tool to move your newest shape (in our case, the star) so that it overlaps the others slightly, as shown in Figure 7-5.**

12. **Rename the original layer by double-clicking the layer's name in the Layers palette, typing a new name, and then pressing Enter (Windows) or Return (Mac).**

In our case, it would make sense to rename the original layer as "rectangle" (that's nice and descriptive). You can open up the Options Dialog Box for any existing layer by choosing Options for Layer (Named Layer) from the palette menu in the Layers palette.

Congratulations! You have created new layers and now have a file that you can use to practice working with layers.

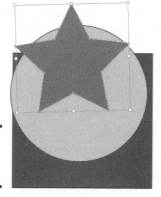

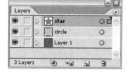

Figure 7-5:
Overlap the star slightly.

Using Layers for Selections

When you have a selected object on a layer, a color selection square appears to the right of the named layer. If you click the radio button directly to the right of the name, all objects are selected on that layer.

Sublayers each have their own radio button as well. If you have sublayers visible, you can use this same technique to select objects that may be buried behind others.

If you think that you will be selecting sublayers frequently, double-click the default name and type a more descriptive name.

Changing the Layer Stacking Order

In Chapter 6 of this minibook, we tell you about the Object⇨Arrange feature in Illustrator; with layers, this process gets just a little more complicated. Each layer has its own *painting order,* the order in which you see the layers. To move a layer (and thereby change the stacking order of the layers), click and drag that layer until you see the black insertion line where you want the layer to be moved.

As you add shapes to a layer, a sublayer is created, and it has its own little stacking order that is separate from other layers. In other words, if you choose to send an object to the back, and it is on the top layer, it will only go to the back of that layer, and still be in front of any objects on layers beneath.

Understanding how the stacking order affects the illustration is probably the most confusing part about layers. Just remember that for an object to appear behind everything else, it has to be on the bottom layer (and at the bottom of all the objects in that bottom layer); for an object to appear in front of everything else, it has to be on the topmost layer.

Moving and Cloning Objects

To move a selected object from one layer to another, click the small color selection square to the right of the layer's radio button, drag it to the target layer, and release. That's all there is to moving an object from one layer to another.

You can also *clone* items — that is, make a copy of it as you move the copy to another layer. Clone an object by Alt+dragging (Windows) or Option+dragging (Mac) the color selection square to another layer. A plus sign appears as you drag (so you know that you're making a clone of the object), as shown in Figure 7-6. Release when you get to the cloned object's target layer.

Figure 7-6:
Cloning a
selected
object to
another
layer.

Hiding Layers

On the Layers palette, notice that to the left of each layer is an eye icon. This is a *visibility* toggle button. Simply clicking this hides the layer (the eye disappears, denoting that this layer is hidden). Click the empty square (where the eye icon was) to show the layer again.

Alt+click (Windows) or Option+click (Mac) an eye icon to hide all layers but the one you click; Alt+click (Windows) or Option+click (Mac) again on the eye icon to show all the layers again.

Ctrl+click (Windows) or ⌘+click (Mac) the eye icon to turn just the selected layer into Outline view mode, as shown in Figure 7-7. In Outline view, all you see are the outlines of the artwork with no stroke widths or fill colors. The rest of your artwork remains in Preview mode, with strokes and fills visible. This is pretty tricky and helpful when you're looking for stray points or need to close paths. Ctrl+click (Windows) or ⌘+click (Mac) back on the eye icon to return the layer to Preview mode.

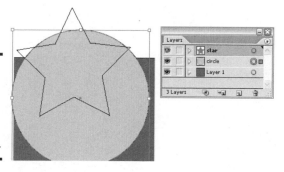

Figure 7-7:
Working with a selected layer in Outline view.

Locking Layers

Lock layers by clicking the empty square to the right of the Visibility (eye) icon (refer to Figure 7-1). A padlock icon appears so that you know the layer is now locked. Locking a layer prevents you from making changes to the objects on that layer. Click the padlock to unlock the layer.

Chapter 8: Livening Up Illustrations with Color

In This Chapter

✔ **Using the Swatch and Color palettes**

✔ **Working with strokes and fills**

✔ **Saving and editing colors**

✔ **Creating and using color libraries**

✔ **Assigning Pantone colors**

✔ **Discovering patterns**

✔ **Employing gradients**

✔ **Explore the Live Trace feature**

✔ **Using the new Live Paint feature**

*T*his chapter is all about making your brilliant illustrations come alive with color. Here we show you how to create new and edit existing colors, how to save custom colors that you create, how to create and use patterns and gradients, and even how to apply color attributes to many different shapes.

Choosing a Color Mode

Every time that you create a new file, you must choose whether the new document is to be in the RGB or CMYK color mode. Base the mode choice on how you plan to use the illustration:

✦ **CMYK:** If you're taking your illustration to a professional printer and the files will be separated into cyan, magenta, yellow, and black plates for printing, choose the CMYK color mode.

✦ **RGB:** If your final destination is the Web, color copier or desktop printer, or screen presentation, choose the RGB color mode.

The decision that you make affects the pre-made swatches, brushes, styles, and a slew of other choices in Adobe Illustrator. This all helps you to avoid sending an RGB color to a print shop. Ever see how that turns out? If your prepress person doesn't catch that the file isn't CMYK and sends an RGB file as separations (cyan, magenta, yellow, and black) to a printer, you could end up with a black blob instead of your beautiful illustration.

You can change the color mode at any time without losing information by choosing File⇨Document Color Mode.

Using the Swatches Palette

The Swatches palette, which you open by choosing Window⇨Swatches, is probably the easiest way to apply color. Although limited in choice, its basic colors, patterns, and gradients are ready to go. You can use the buttons at the bottom of the Swatches palette (shown in Figure 8-1) to show solid fills, gradients, and patterns.

Figure 8-1:
Click the buttons at the bottom of the Swatches palette to see individual choices.

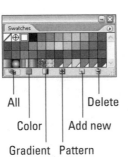

All   Delete

Color   Add new

Gradient Pattern

You may notice some odd color swatches, for instance, the cross hair and the diagonal line.

The cross hair represents the Registration color. Only use this when creating custom crop marks or printer marks. It looks like black, but is actually created from 100 percent of all colors. This way when artwork is separated, the crop mark appears on all color separations.

The diagonal line represents None. Use this if you want no fill or stroke.

Applying Color to the Fill and Stroke

Illustrator objects are created from fills (the inside) and strokes (border or path). Look at the bottom of the toolbox for the Fill and Stroke color boxes.

If you're applying color to the fill, the Fill color box must be forward in the toolbox. If you're applying color to the stroke, the Stroke color box must be forward.

In Table 8-1 are some keyboard shortcuts that can be a tremendous help to you when applying colors to fills and strokes.

Table 8-1	Color Keyboard Shortcuts
Function	*Keyboard Shortcut*
Switch the Fill or Stroke color box position	X
Inverse the Fill and the Stroke color boxes	Shift+X
Default (black stroke, white fill)	D
None	/
Last color used	<
Last gradient used	>
Color Picker	Double-click the Fill or Stroke color box

Try this trick , drag a color from the Swatches palette to the Fill or Stroke color box. This action applies the color to the color box that you dragged to. It doesn't matter which is forward!

To apply a fill color to an existing shape, drag the swatch directly to the shape. Select a swatch, hold down Alt+Shift+Ctrl (Windows) or Option+Shift+⌘ (Mac), and drag a color to a shape to apply that color to the stroke.

Changing the Width and Type of a Stroke

Access the Stroke palette by choosing Window➪Stroke. Like most Illustrator palettes, the options are initially hidden. Choose Show Options from the Stroke palette's palette menu to see more choices.

In the Stroke palette, you can choose *caps* (the end of a line) and *joins* (the end points of a path or dash) and also the *miter limit* (the length of a point). The Stroke palette also enables you to turn a path into a dashed line.

New in Illustrator CS2, you can choose the alignment of the path. In previous versions, any stroke amount that you applied was lined right up the center of the path. What this meant was that if you actually wanted a 5 pt stroke extending outside of a path, you had to set your stroke to 10 pt — but no more!

As you can see in Figure 8-2, you can choose, in the Stroke palette options, to align the stroke on the center (default) of a path, the inside of a path, and the outside of a path. Figure 8-3 shows the results.

Figure 8-2:
The Stroke Align options for strokes on paths.

Figure 8-3:
The Stroke Alignment options affect the placement of the stroke on a path.

This new feature is especially helpful when stroking outlined text. See Figure 8-4 to compare text with the traditional centered stroke, as compared to the new option for aligning the stroke outside of a path.

Figure 8-4:
The Stroke Align feature is especially helpful when stroking outlined text.

You cannot adjust the alignment of a stroke on text unless you change it to outlines first. Select the Selection tool, and then choose Type⇨Create Outlines, then the Align Stroke options will be enabled.

You can also customize the following aspects of a stroke in the Stroke palette:

✦ **Cap Options:** The endpoints of a path or dash.

- **Butt Cap:** Click this button to make the ends of stroked lines square.

- **Round Cap:** Click this button to make the ends of stroked lines semicircular.

- **Projecting Cap:** Click this button to make the ends of stroked lines square and extend half the line width beyond the end of the line.

✦ **Join Options:** How corner points appear.

- **Miter Join:** Click this button to make stroked lines with pointed corners.

- **Round Join:** Click this button to make stroked lines with rounded corners.

- **Bevel Join:** Click this button to make stroked lines with squared corners.

✦ **Dashed Lines:** Regularly spaced lines, based upon values you set.

To create a dashed line, specify a dash sequence by entering the lengths of dashes and the gaps between them in the Dash Pattern text fields (see Figure 8-5). The numbers entered are repeated in sequence so that after you have set up the pattern, you don't need to fill in all the text fields. In other words, if you want an evenly spaced dashed stroke, just type the same number in the first and second text fields, and all dashes and spaces will be the same length (say, 12 pts). Change that to 12 in the first text field and 24 in the next, and now you have a larger space between the dashes.

Book III
Chapter 8

Figure 8-5:
Setting up a
dash
pattern.

Using the Color Palette

The Color palette (access it by choosing Window➪Color Palette) offers another method for choosing color. It requires you to custom pick a color using values on the color ramp. As a default, you see only the *color ramp*, the large color well spanning the palette. To see the rest of the options in the Color Palette, choose Show Options from the Color palette's palette menu (click the triangle in the upper-right corner to access the palette menu).

Ever want to create tints of a CMYK color but aren't quite sure how to adjust the individual color sliders? Hold down the Shift key while adjusting the color slide of any color and watch how all colors move to a relative position at the same time!

As shown in Figure 8-6, the palette menu offers many other choices. Even though you may be in the RGB or CMYK color mode, you can still choose to build colors in Grayscale, RGB, HSB (Hue Saturation Brightness), CMYK, or Web Safe RGB. Choosing Invert or Complement from the palette menu takes the selected object and inverses the color or changes it to a complementary color. You can also choose the Fill and Stroke color boxes in the upper-left corner of the Color palette.

Figure 8-6:
Additional
options are
available in
the Color
palette
menu.

You will see the infamous cube and exclamation point in the Color palettes in most of Adobe's software. The cube warns you that the color you have selected is not one of the 216 non-dithering, Web safe colors, and the exclamation point warns you that your color is not within the CMYK print gamut. In other words, if you see the exclamation point in the Color palette, don't expect that really cool electric blue you see on-screen to print correctly — it might print as dark purple!

Click the cube or exclamation point symbols when you see them to select the closet color in the Web safe or CMYK color gamut.

Saving Colors

Saving colors not only keeps you consistent, but makes edits and changes to colors easier in the future. Any time you build a color, drag it from the Color palette to the Swatches palette to save it as a color swatch for future use. You can also select an object that uses the color and click the New Color button at the bottom of the Swatches palette (refer to Figure 8-1 to see this button). To save a color and name it at the same time, Alt+click (Windows) Option+click (Mac) the New Swatch icon. This opens the New Swatch dialog box where you can name and edit the color if you want. By double-clicking a swatch in the Swatches palette, you can open the options at any time.

A color in the Swatches palette is available only in the document in which it was created. Read the next section on custom libraries to see how to import swatches from saved documents.

Building and using custom libraries

When you save a color in the Swatches palette, you're essentially saving it to your own custom library. You can use Swatches palettes from one document in another by using the Libraries feature. Retrieve a Swatches palette created in another saved document by choosing Window⇨Swatch Libraries⇨Other Library. The Swatches palette you used in the other file is last on a very long list, so you may have to scroll down for quite a while. Locate the file that you want to import and choose Open. A palette appears with the name of the file that it is saved in, as shown in Figure 8-7. The colors in this palette cannot be edited. To use the colors in this palette, double-click a swatch or drag a swatch to your current document's Swatches palette.

Figure 8-7:
A custom library from the June_ schedule file.

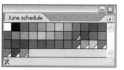

You can also choose Window⇨Swatch Libraries to access color libraries for Pantone colors, Web colors, and some neat creative colors, such as jewel tones and metals.

Adding Pantone colors

If you're looking for the typical Pantone Matching System numbered swatches, choose Window⇨Swatch Libraries⇨Pantone Solid Coated or Window⇨Swatch Libraries⇨Pantone Solid Uncoated (depending on what type of paper you plan to print the illustration on).

Colors for the Pantone numbering system are often referred to as PMS 485, or PMS 201, or whatever number the color has been designated. The numbered swatch can be located by typing the number into the Find text field of the Pantone palette, as shown in Figure 8-8. When that number's corresponding color is highlighted in the palette, click on it to add it to your Swatches palette. Many users find it easier to see colored swatches by using the List View. Choose List View from the palette menu.

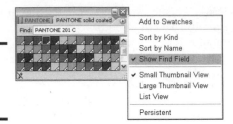

Figure 8-8:
Locating
Pantone
colors.

Editing Colors

Edit colors in the Swatches palette by using the Swatch Options dialog box (shown in Figure 8-9), which you access by double-clicking the color or by choosing Swatch Options from the Swatches palette menu.

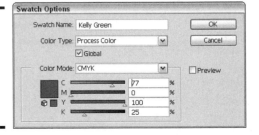

Figure 8-9:
Change a
swatch
color in the
Swatch
Options
dialog box.

Use the Swatch Options dialog box to

✦ **Change the color values:** Change the values in a color by using the sliders or by typing values into the color text fields. This is especially helpful if you were given a color build to match. Select the Preview check box to see results as you make the changes.

✦ **Use global colors:** If you plan on using a color frequently, select the Global check box. If the Global check box is selected and you use the swatch throughout the artwork, you only have to change the swatch options one time, and all instances of that color are updated.

One important option to note in the Swatch Options dialog box is the Color Type drop-down list. You have two choices here: Spot Color and Process Color. What's the difference?

✦ **Spot color:** A color that isn't broken down into the CMYK values. Spot colors are used for 1–2 color print runs or when precise color matching is important.

Suppose that you're printing 20,000 catalogs and decide to run only two colors, red and black. If you pick spot colors, the catalogs have to go through the press only two times: once for black and once for red. If the red were a process color, however, it would be created out of a combination of cyan, magenta, yellow, and black inks, and so the catalogs would need to go through the press four times in order to build that color. Plus, if you went to a print service and asked for red, what color would you get? Fire-engine red, maroon, or a light and delicate pinkish-red? But if the red you pick is PMS 485, your printer in Lancaster, Pennsylvania, can now print the same color of red on your brochure as the printer doing your business cards in Woburn, Massachusetts.

✦ **Process color:** A color that is built from four colors (cyan, magenta, yellow, and black). Process colors are used for multi-color jobs.

For example, you'd want to use process colors if you're sending an ad to a four-color magazine. The magazine printers certainly want to use the same inks they're already running and using a spot color would require another run through the presses in addition to the runs for the cyan, magenta, yellow, and black plates. In this case, you would take any spot colors created in corporate logos and such and convert them to process colors.

Choose the Spot Colors option from the Swatches palette menu to choose whether you want Spot colors changed to Lab or CMYK values.

✦ Choose Lab to get the best possible CMYK conversion for the actual spot color when using a color-calibrated workflow.

✦ Choose CMYK (default) to get the manufacturer's standard recommended conversion of spot colors to process. Results can vary depending upon printing conditions.

Building and Editing Patterns

Using patterns can be as simple or complicated as you want. If you become familiar with the basics, you can take off in all sorts of creative directions. To build a simple pattern, start by creating the artwork that you want to use as a pattern on your artboard — polka dots, smiley faces, wavy lines, whatever. Then select all the components of the pattern and drag them to the Swatches palette. That's it, you made a pattern! Use the pattern by selecting it as the fill or stroke of an object.

Patterns cannot be used in artwork that is then going to be saved as a pattern. If you have a pattern in your artwork and try to drag it into the Swatches palette, Illustrator will kick it back out with no error message. On a good note, text can be dragged right into the Swatches palette to become a pattern.

You can update patterns that you created or patterns that already reside in the Swatches palette. To edit an existing pattern, follow these steps:

1. **Click the pattern swatch in the Swatches palette and drag it to the artboard.**

2. **Deselect the pattern and use the Direct Selection tool to change its colors or shapes or whatever.**

   Keep making changes until you're happy with the result.

3. **To update the pattern with your new edited version, use the Selection tool to select all pattern elements and Alt+drag (Windows) or Option+ drag (Mac) the new pattern over the existing pattern swatch in the Swatches palette.**

4. **When a black border appears around the existing pattern, release the mouse button.**

   All instances of the pattern in your illustration are updated.

Cool little pattern extras

If you want to add some space between tiles, as shown in Figure 8-10, create a bounding box using a rectangle shape with no fill or stroke (representing the repeat that you want to create). Send it behind the other objects in the pattern and drag all objects, including the bounding box, to the Swatches palette.

Figure 8-10:
A pattern with a transparent bounding box.

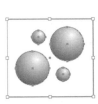 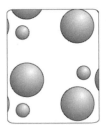

Transforming patterns

We cover transformations in detail in Chapter 9 of this minibook, but there are some specific transform features that apply to patterns. To scale a pattern, but not the object that it is filling, double-click the Scale tool. In the Scale dialog box that appears, type the value that you want to scale, but deselect all options except for Patterns, as shown in Figure 8-11. This works for the Rotate tool as well!

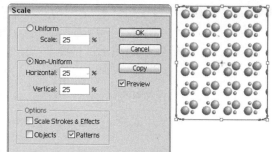

Figure 8-11:
Choose to
scale and
rotate only
the pattern,
not the
object it's in.

Working with Gradients

Create gradients for nice smooth metallic effects or just to add dimension to illustrations. If you are not sure which swatches are considered gradients, choose the Gradient button from the bottom of the Swatches palette.

Once applied, you can access the Gradient palette (shown in Figure 8-12) by choosing Window➪Gradient. Choose Show Options from the Gradient palette menu to see more options.

Book III
Chapter 8

Figure 8-12:
The
Gradient
palette.

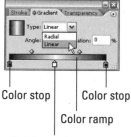

Color stop | Color stop

Color ramp

Gradient midpoint

Livening Up
Illustrations with
Color

On the Gradient palette, use the Type drop-down list to choose a Radial gradient (one that radiates from the center point) or a Linear gradient (one that follows a linear path).

Use the Gradient tool to change the direction and distance of a gradient blend as follows:

1. **Select an object and apply any existing gradient from the Swatches palette to its fill.**

2. **Choose the Gradient tool (press G), and drag in the direction that you want the gradient to go.**

   Drag a long path for a smooth, long gradient. Drag a short path for a short, more defined gradient.

To create a new gradient, follow these steps:

1. **With the Gradient palette options visible, click the gradient box at the bottom of the palette.**

   Two color stops appear, one on each end.

2. **Activate a color stop by clicking it.**

   When a color stop is active, the triangle on the top turns solid.

3. **Choose Window⇨Color Palette to access the Color palette, and then click the triangle in the upper-right corner to open the palette menu; choose RGB or CMYK colors.**

4. **Click the color ramp (across the bottom) in the Color palette to pick a random color (or enter values in the text fields to select a specific color) for the active color stop in the Gradient palette.**

   Repeat this step to select colors for other color stops.

To add additional color stops, click beneath the gradient slider and then choose a color from the Color palette. You can also drag a swatch from the Swatches palette to add a new color to the gradient. To remove a color stop, drag it off the Gradient palette.

Copying Color Attributes

 Wouldn't it be great if you had tools that could record all the fill and stroke attributes and apply them to other shapes? You're in luck — the Eyedropper tool can do just that! Copy the fill and stroke of an object and apply it to another object using the Eyedropper tool as follows:

1. **Create several shapes with different fill and stroke attributes, or open an existing file that contains several different objects.**

2. **Select the Eyedropper tool and click a shape that has attributes you want to copy.**

3. **Then Alt+click (Windows) or Option+click (Mac) another object to apply those attributes.**

Not only is this simple, but you can change the attributes that the Eyedropper applies. Do this by double-clicking the Eyedropper tool; in the dialog box that appears, select only the attributes that you want to copy.

The Live Trace feature

If you are looking for good source art to use to experiment with color, look no further than your own sketches and scanned images. New in CS2, you can automatically trace bitmap images using a variety of settings that range from black-and-white line art to vector art with multitudes of color that can be extracted from your image.

To use the Live Trace feature, follow these steps:

1. **Choose File⇨Place and select an image that you want to trace. This could be a logo, sketch, or even an image.**

2. **Choose Object⇨Live Trace⇨Tracing Options.**

   The Tracing Options window appears.

3. **Check the Preview checkbox and experiment with the various settings, as shown in Figure 8-13.**

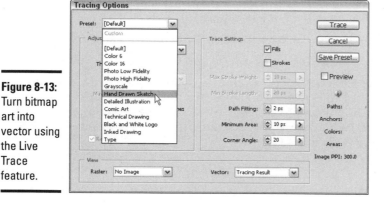

Figure 8-13: Turn bitmap art into vector using the Live Trace feature.

4. **When you find the setting that works best for your image, choose Trace.**

You can return to the Tracing Options window and change settings over and over again, until you find the best one.

The Live Paint Feature

Painting made easy! Don't worry about filling closed shapes, or letting fills escape out of objects with gaps into unwanted areas. With the new Live Paint feature, you can create the image you want and fill in regions with color. The new Live Paint bucket automatically detects regions composed of independent intersecting paths and fills them accordingly. The paint within a given region remains live and flows automatically if any of the paths are moved. If you want to give it a try, follow this nifty little exercise to put together an example to experiment with.

1. **Using the Ellipse tool, create a circle on your page. Make it large enough to accommodate two or three inner circles.**

2. **Press the letter D (just D, nothing else).**

   As long as you are not on the Type tool this reverts you back to the default colors of a black stroke and a white fill.

3. **Double-click the Scale tool and enter 75% in the Uniform Scale text box.**

4. **Press the Copy button and then click OK.**

   This produces a smaller circle inside of the original.

5. **Press Ctrl+D (Windows) or Cmd+D (Mac) to duplicate the transformation and create another circle inside of the last one.**

6. **Choose Select⇨All or Ctrl+A (Windows) or Cmd+A (Mac) to activate the circles you just created.**

7. **Make sure the Fill swatch is forward.**

   The Fill swatch is at the bottom of the toolbar.

8. **Use the Swatches or Color palette and choose any fill color.**

9. **Now the fun part! Select the Live Paint Bucket tool and move the cursor over the various regions of the circles. See how the different regions become highlighted? Click when you have the region activated that you want to fill. Now try it with other fill colors in different regions, as shown in Figure 8-14.**

Figure 8-14:
Experience newfound freedom when you paint objects with the Live Paint Bucket tool.

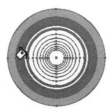

Got Gaps?

A companion feature to the new paint bucket is support for Gap Detection. With this feature, Illustrator is able to automatically and dynamically detect and close small to large gaps that may be part of the artwork. You can determine whether you want paint to flow across region gap boundaries by using the Gap Options dialog box under Object➪Live Paint➪Gap Options, as shown in Figure 8-15.

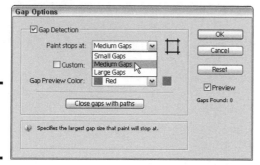

Figure 8-15: The Gap Options dialog box.

When you save a file with the Live Paint feature back to an older version of Illustrator, it is best to select the occurrences of Live Paint and choose Object➪Expand. When the Expand window appears, leave the options at their default and click OK. This breaks down the Live Paint objects to individual shapes, which older versions can understand.

Chapter 9: The Transform and Distortions Tools

In This Chapter

✔ Discovering transformation methods

✔ Putting the transform tools to work

✔ Becoming familiar with the liquify tools

✔ Distorting, warping, and otherwise reshaping objects

Transformations that you can give to objects in Illustrator include scaling, rotating, skewing, and distorting. In this chapter, we show you how to use the general transform tools as well as some of the neat Liquify and Envelope Distort features available in Illustrator.

Working with Transformations

With just the Selection tool, you can scale and rotate a selected object. Drag the bounding box handles to resize the object (as shown in Figure 9-1) or get outside a handle, and then, when the cursor changes to a flippy arrow (a curved arrow with arrowheads on both ends), drag to rotate the object.

Figure 9-1: Use the bounding box to resize or rotate a selected object.

If you want to scale proportionally, hold down the Shift key as you drag to resize. To rotate an object at 45 degree increments, hold down the Shift key while you're rotating.

When you use the bounding box to rotate a selection, the bounding box rotates with the object, but its handles show the object's original orientation, as shown in Figure 9-2. This can help you to keep track of the original placement but can also interfere when you're building additional artwork. To reset the bounding box so that it's straight at the new orientation, choose Object➪Transform➪Reset Bounding Box.

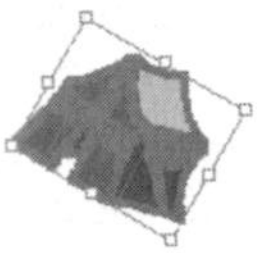

Figure 9-2:
The bounding box shows the original placement angle and can be reset to that angle.

When you scale, rotate, or use any other type of transformation in Illustrator, the final location becomes the *zero point*. In other applications, such as InDesign, you can rotate an object by any number of degrees (45 degrees, for example) and later enter 0 for the rotation angle in the Transform palette or in the Rotate dialog box to return the object to its original position. With Illustrator, if you enter 0 for the rotation angle to return a rotated object to its original position, the object will not change its position. To return the object to the previous position in Illustrator, you have to enter the negative of the number you originally entered to rotate the object, so you would enter –45 for the degree of rotation in this example.

Transforming an object

The Rotate, Reflect, Scale, and Shear tools all use the same basic steps to perform transformations. Read on for those basic steps, and then follow through some individual examples of the most often used transform tools. The following sections show five ways to transform an object: One for an arbitrary transformation and four others for exact transformations based on a numeric amount that you enter.

Arbitrary transformation method

This method is arbitrary, meaning that you're eyeballing the transformation of an object — in other words, you don't have an exact percentage or angle in mind, and you want to freely transform the object until it looks right. Just follow these steps:

1. **Select an object, and then choose a transform tool (the Rotate, Reflect, Scale, or Shear tool).**

2. **Click once on the artboard.**

   Be careful where you click because the click determines the point of reference, or *axis point*, for the transformation, as shown in Figure 9-3.

Figure 9-3: The first click creates the point of reference or axis point for the trans- formation.

Book III Chapter 9

The Transform and Distortions Tools

3. **Drag in one smooth movement.**

   Just drag until you get the transformation that you want.

Hold down the Alt (Windows) or Option (Mac) key when dragging to clone a newly transformed item while keeping the original object intact. This is especially helpful when you're using the Reflect tool.

Exact transformation methods

In the following methods, we show you how to perform transformations using specific numeric information:

✦ ***Exact transformation method 1: Using the tool's dialog box***

   1. **Select an object, and then choose the Rotate, Reflect, Scale, or Shear tool.**

2. **Double-click the transform tool in the toolbox.**

   A dialog box specific to your chosen tool appears. For this example, we selected and then double-clicked the Rotate tool to bring up the Rotate dialog box (see Figure 9-4).

Figure 9-4:
Double-click
a transform
tool to see
its options.

3. **Type an angle, scaled amount, or percentage in the appropriate text field.**

4. **Check preview to see the effect of the transformation before you click OK; click the Copy button instead of OK to keep the original object intact and transform a copy.**

✦ *Exact transformation method 2: Using the reference point*

   1. **Select an object, and then choose the Rotate, Reflect, Scale, or Shear tool.**

   2. **Alt+click (Windows) or Option+click (Mac) where you want the reference point to be.**

   3. **In the appropriate transform tool dialog box that appears, enter your values and click OK or the Copy button to apply your transformation.**

      This is the best method to use if you need to rotate an object an exact amount on a defined axis.

✦ *Exact transformation method 3: Using the Transform menu*

   1. **Select an object, and then choose a transform option from the Object⇨Transform menu.**

      The appropriate transform dialog box appears.

   2. **Enter your values and click OK or the Copy button.**

✦ *Exact transformation method 4: Using the Transform palette*

   Select an object and choose Window⇨Transform to access the Transform palette, as shown in Figure 9-5. While using this palette is probably the easiest way to go, it doesn't give you the option of specifying where you want your reference point to be or some other options that apply to the individual transform tools.

Figure 9-5:
Use the
Transform
palette to
scale, rotate,
and shear.

Using the transform tools

In this section, we show you how to use some of the most popular transform tools to create transformations.

The Reflect tool

Nothing is symmetrical, right? Maybe not, but objects that are not symmetrically created in Illustrator can look pretty off kilter. Using the Reflect tool, you can reflect an object to create an exact mirrored shape of it; just follow these steps:

1. **Open a new document in Illustrator and type some text or create an object.**

   If you want to reflect text, make sure that you use at least 60-point type so that you can easily see what you're working with.

2. **Select the Reflect tool (hidden under the Rotate tool) and click the object; if you're using text, click in the middle of the text's baseline, as shown on top in Figure 9-6.**

   This sets the reference point for the reflection.

3. **Alt+Shift+drag (Windows) or Option+Shift+drag (Mac) and release when the object or text is reflecting itself, as shown on the bottom in Figure 9-6.**

   This not only clones the reflected object or text, but also snaps it to 45-degree angles.

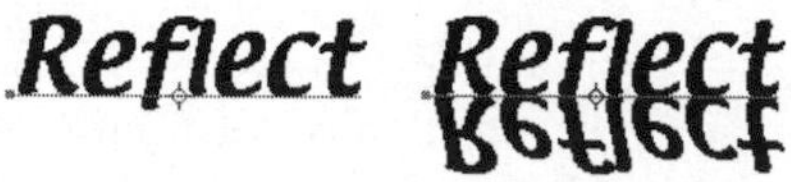

Figure 9-6:
Setting the
reference
point (top);
the com-
pleted
reflection
(bottom).

Reflect Reflect

Rotation example

Follow these steps to rotate objects around a circle so that they end up evenly spaced around the circumference of that circle:

1. **Create a circle sized to accommodate the additional smaller circles going around its circumference.**

   Hold down the Shift key as you drag; release the mouse button first to make a perfect circle.

2. **Change the Fill and Stroke boxes to None.**

   You won't be able to see the actual shape, but you can still see the selection.

3. **Choose View⇨Outline or press Ctrl+Y (Windows) or ⌘+Y (Mac) to change to Outline view.**

   This view shows everything in 1-point black strokes, no matter what the fill or stroke. (This is a great way to find shapes with no fill or stroke that you may have accidentally created!)

4. **Create a small circle on the path of the original circle at the very top, as shown in the following figure.**

   It doesn't matter where it is on the circle, but make sure that you give the new object a fill (you will see the fill on the Fill box, but it won't look filled until you return to the Preview view.)

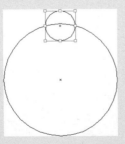

5. **Select the Rotation tool.**

6. **Alt+click (Windows) or Option+click (Mac) the center point of the large circle.**

   The Rotation dialog box appears, and the center point of the large circle is defined as the axis of rotation.

7. **Enter the degree of rotation for the smaller circles in the Angle text field.**

   Okay, so here's where you have to use a little math. (All the art majors start sweating.) A circle is 360 degrees, so divide that to find the perfect rotation to have the smaller circles evenly spaced around the circumference of the larger circle. If you want 10 circles, type 36 into the Angle text field (360÷10=36). If you want 20 circles, type 18 into the Angle text field (360÷20=18).

8. **Click the Copy button.**

9. **Use the Repeat Transform key command, Ctrl+D (Windows) or ⌘+D (Mac), and the circles repeat the exact same rotation around until you complete the circle, as shown in the following figure.**

10. **Press Ctrl+Y (Windows) or ⌘+Y (Mac) to return to the Preview view.**

    The center circle was just used to rotate around. Because it has no fill or stroke (and therefore is invisible), you can just leave it, or you can delete it if you want.

The Scale tool

Using the Scale tool, you can scale an object proportionally or non-uniformly. Most people like to be scaled non-uniformly, maybe a little taller, a little thinner, but on with the topic. Follow these steps to see the Scale tool in action:

1. **Create a shape and give it no fill and a 5-point black stroke.**

   For this example, we created a circle. See Chapter 3 of this minibook if you need a reminder on how to do this.

2. **Select your shape and double-click the Scale tool.**

   The Scale dialog box appears.

3. **Type a number in the Scale text field (in the Uniform section) and click the Copy button.**

   We entered 125 in the Scale text field to increase the size of the object by 125 percent.

4. **Press Ctrl+D (Windows) or ⌘+D (Mac) to repeat the transformation as many times as you want.**

   Each time you press Ctrl+D (Windows) or ⌘+D (Mac), the shape is copied and sized by the percent you entered in the Scale text field. This is especially handy with circles, creates an instant bull's-eye!

To experiment with the Scale tool, create different shapes in Step 1 and enter different values in Step 3. Remember that if you type 50% in the Scale text field, the object is made smaller; go over 100% — say to 150% for example — to make the object larger. Leaving the Scale text field at 100% has no effect on the object.

The Shear tool

The Shear tool enables you to shear an object by selecting an axis and dragging to set a shear angle, as shown in Figure 9-7. The axis will always be the center of the object unless you use method 1 or method 2 from the earlier section, "Exact transformation methods." Use the Shear tool in combination with the Rotate tool to give an object perspective.

Figure 9-7:
Create perspective using the Shear tool.

The Reshape tool

The Reshape tool enables you to select anchor points and sections of paths and adjust them in one direction. You determine that direction by dragging an anchor point with the Reshape tool selected.

 The Reshape tool works differently from the other transform tools. To use it, follow these steps:

1. **Select just the anchor points on the paths that you want to reshape. Deselect any points that you want to remain in place.**

2. **Select the Reshape tool (hidden under the Scale tool) and position the cursor over the anchor point that you want to modify; click the anchor point.**

   If you click a path segment, a highlighted anchor point with a square around it is added to the path.

3. **Shift+click more anchor points or path segments to act as selection points.**

   You can highlight an unlimited number of anchor points or path segments.

4. **Drag the highlighted anchor points to adjust the path.**

The Free Transform tool

 You use the Free Transform tool pretty much like you use the bounding box (see the earlier section, "Working with Transformations"). This tool is necessary only if you choose View⇨Hide Bounding Box but want free transform capabilities.

Creating Distortions

Bend objects, make them wavy, gooey, or spiky — you can do all of these things by creating simple to complex distortions with the liquify tools and Envelope Distort features.

The liquify tools

The liquify tools can accomplish all sorts of creative or wacky (depending on how you look at it) distortions to your objects. You can choose from seven liquify tools; even though we define these for you in Table 9-1, you really need to experiment with these tools to understand their full capabilities. Here are some tips:

✦ A variety of liquify tools are available by holding down the mouse button on the default selection, the Warp tool. If you use them frequently, drag to the arrow at the end of the tools and release when you see the ToolTip for Tearoff. You can then position the tools anywhere in your work area.

✦ Double-click any of the liquify tools to bring up a dialog box specific to the selected tool, as shown for the Warp tool in Figure 9-8.

✦ When a liquify tool is selected, the brush size appears. Adjust the diameter and shape of the liquify tool by holding down the Alt (Windows) or Option (Mac OS) key while dragging the brush shape smaller or larger. Add the Shift key to constrain the shape to a circle.

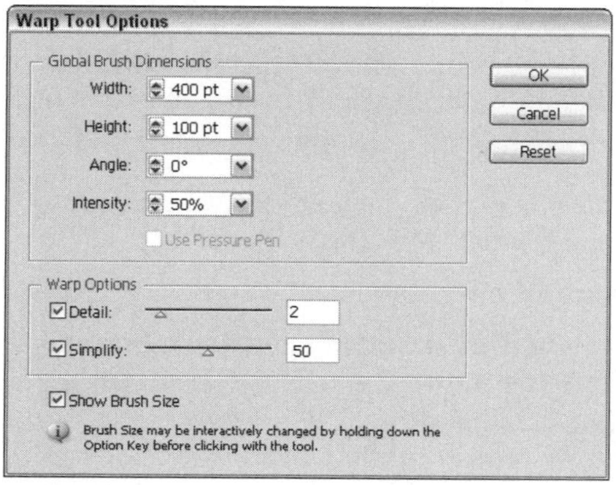

Figure 9-8:
The liquify
tools
options.

Warp Tool Options

Global Brush Dimensions

Width: 400 pt
Height: 100 pt
Angle: 0°
Intensity: 50%
☐ Use Pressure Pen

OK
Cancel
Reset

Warp Options
☑ Detail: 2
☑ Simplify: 50

☑ Show Brush Size

ⓘ Brush Size may be interactively changed by holding down the Option Key before clicking with the tool.

Table 9-1   **The Liquify Tools**

Tool Icon	Tool Name	What It Does
	Warp tool	The Warp tool (Shift+R) molds objects with the movement of the cursor. Pretend that you're pushing through dough with this tool.
	Twirl tool	Creates swirling distortions within an object.
	Pucker tool	Deflates an object.
	Bloat tool	Inflates an object.
	Scallop tool	Adds curved details to the outline of an object. Think of a seashell with scalloped edges.
	Crystallize tool	Adds many spiked details to the outline of an object, like crystals on a rock.
	Wrinkle tool	Adds wrinkle-like details to the outline of an object.

Using the Envelope Distort command

Use the Envelope Distort command to arch text and apply other creative distortions to an Illustrator object. To use the Envelope Distort command, you can either use a preset warp (the easiest method) or a grid or a top object to determine the amount and type of distortion. In this section, we discuss all three methods.

Using the preset warps

Experimenting is a little more interesting if you have a word or object selected before trying the different warp presets. To warp an object or text to a preset style, follow these steps:

1. **Select the text or object that you want to distort, and then choose Object⇨Envelope Distort⇨Make with Warp.**

   The Warp Options dialog box appears.

2. **Choose a warp style from the Style drop-down list, and then specify any other options you want.**

3. **Click OK to apply your distortion.**

Reshaping with a mesh grid

You can also assign a grid to the objects to give you the ability to drag different points and create your own custom distortion, as shown in Figure 9-9.

Figure 9-9:
Create your own custom distortion using a mesh grid.

Follow these steps to apply a mesh grid:

1. **Select the text or object that you want to distort, and then choose Object⇨Envelope Distort⇨Make with Mesh.**

   The Envelope Mesh dialog box appears.

2. **Specify the number of rows and columns that you want the mesh to contain, and then click OK.**

3. **To reshape the object, drag any anchor point on the mesh grid with the Direct Selection tool.**

To delete anchor points on the mesh grid, select an anchor point with the Direct Selection tool and press the Delete key.

You can also use the Mesh tool to edit and delete points when using a mesh grid on objects.

Reshaping an object with a different object

To form letters into the shape of an oval or distort selected objects into another object, use this technique:

1. **Create text that you want to distort.**

2. **Create the object that you want to use as the envelope (the object to be used to define the distortion).**

3. **Choose Object⇨Arrange to make sure that the envelope object is on top, as shown in Figure 9-10.**

Figure 9-10: Distort a selected object to the topmost object.

4. **Select the text and Shift+click to select the envelope object.**

5. **Choose Object⇨Envelope Distort⇨Make with Top Object.**

The underlying object is distorted to fit the shape of the top (envelope) object.

Chapter 10: Transparency and Special Effects Tools

In This Chapter

✔ **Finding out about the Gradient Mesh tool**

✔ **Getting to know the Blend tool**

✔ **Using the Symbol Sprayer Brush tools**

✔ **Discovering transparency, blend modes, and opacity masks**

This chapter is full of neat things that you can do using some of the more advanced features in Adobe Illustrator. These special effects tools can help you create art that really makes an impact: Discover how to make your art look like a painting with the Gradient Mesh tool, create morph-like blends with the Blend tool, become a pseudo-graffiti artist by trying out the Symbol Sprayer tool, and see what's underneath objects by using transparency!

The Mesh Tool

If you're creating art in Illustrator that requires solid colors or continuous patterns, you can achieve those results quite easily. But what if you're working on something that requires continuous tones, like a person's face? In that case, you would turn to the very handy Mesh tool that enables you to create the impression that you used paint and paintbrushes to create your illustration. Choose to blend one color into another and then use the Mesh tool to adjust where the blends occur and how dramatic the blends should be.

The Mesh tool can be as complex or simple as you want. Create intense illustrations that look like they were created with an airbrush, or just use it to give an object dimension, like the objects shown in Figure 10-1.

Figure 10-1:
Illustrations
can be as
complex or
simple as
you want
using the
Mesh tool.

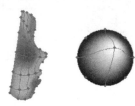

Figure 10-1:
Illustrations
can be as
complex or
simple as
you want
using the
Mesh tool.

We show you how to create a gradient mesh two different ways: First by clicking (which gives you a little more freedom to put mesh points where you want them) and then by manually setting the number of rows and columns in the mesh (which is a more precise method).

TIP

You can change the color in mesh points by choosing the Direct Selection tool and either clicking a mesh point and picking a fill color, or by clicking in the center of a mesh area and choosing a fill. Each gives you a very different result, as shown in Figure 10-2. To add a mesh point without changing to the current fill color, Shift+click anywhere in a filled vector object.

Figure 10-2:
Whether you
select the
mesh point
(left) or area
in between
mesh points
(right)
changes the
result of
painting.

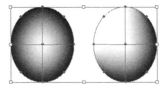

To create a gradient mesh by clicking, follow these steps:

1. **Deselect all objects by choosing Select⇨Deselect.**

2. **Select a fill color that you want to apply as a mesh point to an object.**

For example, if you have a red circle and you want a shaded white spot, choose white for your fill color.

3. **Select the Mesh tool (keyboard shortcut is U) and click anywhere in a filled vector object.**

   The object is converted to a mesh object.

4. **Click the object as many times as you want to add additional mesh points.**

To create a gradient mesh by setting the number of rows and columns, follow these steps:

1. **Select a bitmap or filled vector object.**

2. **Choose Object⇨Create Gradient Mesh.**

   The Create Gradient Mesh dialog box appears.

3. **Set the number of rows and columns of mesh lines to create on the object by entering numbers in the Rows and Columns text fields.**

4. **Choose the direction of the highlight from the Appearance drop-down list.**

   The direction of the highlight determines in what way the gradient flows (see Figure 10-3); you have the following choices:

   - **Flat:** Applies the object's original color evenly across the surface, resulting in no highlight.

   - **To Center:** Creates a highlight in the center of the object.

   - **To Edge:** Creates a highlight on the edges of the object.

Book III
Chapter 10

Transparency
and Special
Effects Tools

Figure 10-3:
The Flat
(left), To
Center
(middle), and
To Edge
(right)
highlight
directions.

5. **Enter a percentage of white highlight to apply to the mesh object in the Highlight text field.**

6. **Click OK to apply the gradient mesh to the object.**

The Blend Tool

 Use the Blend tool (located in the main Illustrator toolbox) to transform one object to another to create interesting morphed artwork or to create shaded objects. With the Blend tool, you can give illustrations a rendered look by blending from one color to another, or you can create an even amount of shapes from one point to another. Figure 10-4 shows examples of what you can do with this tool.

Figure 10-4:
Samples
of objects
using the
blend
feature.

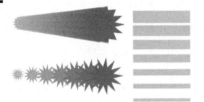

Creating a blend is not difficult at all, and as you get used to it, you can take it farther and farther, creating incredibly realistic effects with it. Follow these steps to create a simple blend from one sized rectangle to another, creating an algorithmic stripe pattern (a rectangle or one height blended to a rectangle of another height):

1. **Create a shape.**

   Size doesn't really matter for this example; you just want to make sure that you can see a difference in shapes when you blend. We're using a rectangle that's roughly 4 x 1 inches.

2. **Give your shape a fill and assign None to the stroke.**

   You can use other settings here, but we recommend keeping it simple if you're still new to working with blends.

3. **With the Selection tool, click on the rectangle and Alt+drag (Windows) or Option+drag (Mac) towards the bottom of the artboard to clone your shape; press the Shift key before you release the mouse button to make sure that the cloned shape stays perfectly aligned with the original shape.**

4. **Reduce the cloned shape to about half its original height by using the Transform palette (if the Transform palette isn't visible, choose Window⇨Transform).**

   Alternatively, you could drag the bottom-middle bounding box handle, as shown in Figure 10-5.

5. **In the Swatches palette (Window⇨Swatches), change the cloned shape's fill to a different color, but keep the stroke at None.**

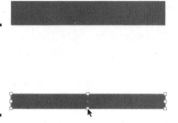

Figure 10-5:
Reduce the
size of the
cloned
shape.

Changing the color just helps you see the blend effect a little better.

6. **With the Blend tool, click the original shape, and then click the cloned shape.**

As a default, the Blend tool creates a smooth blend that transitions from one color to another, as shown in Figure 10-6. To change the blend effect, you need to experiment with the Blend Options dialog box.

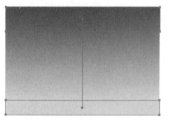

Figure 10-6:
A smooth
transition
is created
from one
rectangle to
the other.

You can change the way that a blend appears by using the Blend Options dialog box, shown in Figure 10-7, which you access by choosing Object⇨ Blend⇨Blend Options. From the Spacing drop-down list, change the blend to one of the following options:

✦ **Smooth Color:** The blend steps are calculated to provide the optimum number of steps for a smooth transition.

✦ **Specified Steps:** You can determine the number of steps in a blend by typing a number in the text field to the right of the drop-down list.

✦ **Specified Distance:** You control the distance between the steps in the blend by typing a number in the text field to the right of the drop-down list.

Figure 10-7:
The Blend
Options
dialog box.

You can also choose between two orientation options: Align to Page (orients the blend perpendicular to the X-axis of the page) or Align to Path (orients the blend perpendicular to the path). You will probably not see a difference when changing orientation unless you have edited the blend path.

TIP

You can easily access the Blend tool options by selecting a Blended object and double-clicking on the Blend tool in the toolbox.

If you are feeling adventurous, try changing a smooth blend (such as the one you create in the preceding steps) into a logarithmic blend. In the Blend Options dialog box, choose Specified Steps from the Spacing drop-down list and change the value to 5. This creates the blend in five steps instead of the 200 plus steps that may have been necessary to create the smooth blend.

Here are a few more tips to help you as you become more comfortable using blends:

✦ You can blend between an unlimited number of objects, colors, opacities, or gradients.

✦ Blends can be directly edited with tools such as the Selection tools, the Rotate tool, or the Scale tool.

✦ A straight path is created between blended objects when the blend is first applied. You can switch to the Direct Selection tool and edit the blend path by dragging anchor points.

✦ You can edit blends that you created by moving, resizing, deleting, or adding objects. After you make editing changes, the artwork is automatically reblended.

The Symbol Sprayer Tool

The Symbol Sprayer tool is a super tool that you must experiment with to understand its full potential. In a nutshell, however, what it does is work like a can of spray paint that, instead of spraying paint, sprays *symbols* — objects that, in Illustrator, can be either vector- or pixel-based. Each individual symbol is an *instance*.

Illustrator comes with a library of symbols ready for use in the Symbols palette (if the Symbols palette isn't visible, choose Window➪Symbols Palette). Use this palette as a storage bin or library to save repeatedly used artwork or to create your own symbols to apply as instances in your artwork, like blades of grass or stars in the sky. You can then use the Symbolism tools, described in Table 10-1, to adjust and change the appearance of the symbol instances.

Table 10-1		The Symbolism Tools
Button	*Tool Name*	*What It Does*
	Symbol Sprayer	Creates a set of symbol instances.
	Symbol Shifter	Moves symbol instances around. It can also change the relative paint order of symbol instances.
	Symbol Scruncher	Pulls symbol instances together or apart.
	Symbol Sizer	Increases or decreases the size of symbol instances.
	Symbol Spinner	Orients the symbol instances in a set. Symbol instances located near the cursor spin in the direction you move the cursor.
	Symbol Stainer	Colorizes symbol instances.
	Symbol Screener	Increases or decreases the transparency of the symbol instances in a set.
	Symbol Styler	Enables you to apply or remove a graphic style from a symbol instance.

**Book III
Chapter 10**

**Transparency
and Special
Effects Tools**

Press the Alt (Windows) or Option (Mac) key to reduce the effect of the Symbolism tool. In other words, if you're using the Symbol Sizer tool, you click and hold to make the symbol instances larger; hold down the Alt (Windows) or Option (Mac) key to make the symbol instances smaller.

You can also selectively choose the symbols that you want to effect with the Symbolism tools by activating them in the Symbols palette (shown in Figure 10-8). Ctrl+click (Windows) or ⌘+click (Mac) multiple symbols to change them at the same time.

Figure 10-8:
The Symbols palette.

Click to create new symbol

Just about anything can be a symbol, including placed objects and objects with patterns and gradients. If you're going to use placed images as symbols, however, Choose File➪Place and deselect the Linked check box in the Place dialog box.

To create a symbol, select the object and drag it into the Symbols palette or click the New Symbol button at the bottom of the Symbols palette. Yes, it's that easy. Then use the Symbol Sprayer tool to apply the Symbol instance on the artboard by following these steps:

1. **Select the symbol instance in the Symbols palette.**

Either create your own symbol or use one of the default symbols supplied in the palette.

2. **Drag with the Symbol Sprayer tool, spraying the symbol on the artboard (see Figure 10-9).**

And that's it. You can increase or reduce the area affected by the Symbol sprayer by pressing the bracket keys. Press] repeatedly to enlarge the application area for the symbol or [to make it smaller.

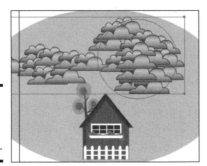

Figure 10-9: Using the Symbol Sprayer tool.

Note that you can access all sorts of Symbol Libraries from the Symbols palette menu. Find 3d, nature, maps, flowers, and even hair and fur symbol collections by selecting Open symbol library.

Want to store artwork that you frequently need to access? Simply drag the selected object(s) into the Symbols palette, or Alt+click (Windows) or Option+click (Mac) the New Symbol button to name and store the artwork. Retrieve the artwork later by dragging it from the Symbols palette to the artboard. In fact, you can drag any symbol out to your artboard to change or use it in your own artwork. To release the symbol back into its basic elements, choose Object➪Expand. In the Expand dialog box, click OK to restore the defaults.

Transparency

Using transparency can add a new level to your illustrations. The transparency feature does exactly what its name implies: It changes an object to make it transparent so that what's underneath that object is visible to varying degrees. You can use the Transparency palette for simple applications of transparency to show through to underlying objects, or you can use transparency for more complex artwork using *opacity masks*, masks that can control the visibility of selected objects.

Choosing Window⇨Transparency brings up the Transparency palette, shown in Figure 10-10, where you can apply different levels of transparency to objects. To do so, create an arrangement of objects that intersect, select the topmost object, and then change the transparency level of the object in the Transparency palette, either by moving the Opacity slider or by entering a value of less than 100 in the Opacity text field.

Figure 10-10:
The Transparency palette.

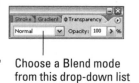

Choose a Blend mode
from this drop-down list

Blend modes

A blend mode determines how the resulting transparency will look. So to achieve different blending effects, you choose different blend modes from the Blend Mode drop-down list in the Transparency palette.

Truly, the best way to find out what all of these modes do is to create two shapes that are overlapping and start experimenting. Give the shapes differently colored fills (but note that many of the blending modes don't work with black and white fills). Then select the topmost object and change the blending mode by selecting an option from the Blend Mode drop-down list in the Transparency palette. You will see all sorts of neat effects and probably end up picking a few favorites.

We define each blend mode in the following list (but we'll say it again, the best way to see what each one does is to apply them — so start experimenting!):

✦ **Normal:** Creates no interaction with underlying colors.

✦ **Darken:** Replaces only the areas that are lighter than the blend color. Areas darker than the blend color don't change.

✦ **Multiply:** Creates an effect similar to drawing on the page with magic markers. Also looks like colored film you see on theater lights.

✦ **Color Burn:** Darkens the base color to reflect the blend color. If you're using white, there is no change.

✦ **Lighten:** Replaces only the areas darker than the blend color. Areas lighter than the blend color don't change.

✦ **Screen:** Multiplies the inverse of the underlying colors. The resulting color is always a lighter color.

✦ **Color Dodge:** Brightens the underlying color to reflect the blend color. If you're using black, there is no change.

✦ **Overlay:** Multiplies or screens the colors, depending on the base color.

✦ **Soft Light:** Darkens or lightens the colors, depending on the blend color. The effect is similar to shining a diffused spotlight on the artwork.

✦ **Hard Light:** Multiplies or screens the colors, depending on the blend color. The effect is similar to shining a harsh spotlight on the artwork.

✦ **Difference:** Subtracts either the blend color from the base color or the base color from the blend color, depending on which has the greater brightness value. The effect is similar to a color negative.

✦ **Exclusion:** Creates an effect similar to but with less contrast than the Difference mode.

✦ **Hue:** Applies the hue (color) of the blend object onto the underlying objects, but keeps the underlying shading, or luminosity.

✦ **Saturation:** Applies the saturation of the blend color, but uses the luminance and hue of the base color.

✦ **Color:** Applies the blend object's color to the underlying objects but preserves the gray levels in the artwork. This is great for tinting objects or changing their color.

✦ **Luminosity:** Creates a resulting color with the hue and saturation of the base color and the luminance of the blend color. This is essentially the opposite of the Color mode.

Opacity masks

Just like in Photoshop, you can use masks to make more interesting artwork in Illustrator. Create an opacity mask from the topmost object in a selection of objects or by drawing a mask on a single object. The mask uses the grayscale of the object selected to be the opacity mask. Black areas are totally transparent; shades of gray are semi-transparent, depending on the amount of gray; and white areas are totally opaque. Figure 10-11 shows the effect of an opacity mask.

Figure 10-11:
An opacity
mask takes
the topmost
object and
masks
underlying
objects.

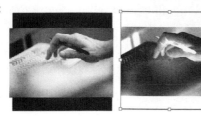

To create an opacity mask, follow these steps:

1. **Open the Transparency palette menu (click the arrow in the upper-right corner to access this menu) and choose Show Thumbnails.**

Also, be sure that the Blend Mode drop-down list is set to Normal.

2. **Create a shape anywhere on the artboard or open a document that has artwork on it.**

We're using a rectangle, but the shape doesn't matter. Make sure that the artwork has a fill. A solid color will help you see the effect.

3. **Open the Symbols palette (choose Window⇨Symbols Palette) and drag a symbol to the artboard.**

For this example, we're using the butterfly symbol.

4. **With the Selection tool, enlarge your symbol so that it fills up your shape (see Figure 10-12 on top).**

Figure 10-12:
Creating an
opacity
mask.

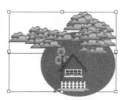 

5. **Select both the symbol and the shape, and then choose Make Opacity Mask from the Transparency palette menu.**

The symbol turns into a mask, showing varying levels of the underlying box through, depending on the original color value (see the bottom part of Figure 10-12). To delete an Opacity mask, choose Release Opacity Mask from the Transparency palette menu.

Click the right thumbnail (this is the mask) in the Transparency palette and a black border appears around it, indicating that it is active. You can move the items on the mask, or even create items to be added to the mask. It works just like the regular artboard, except that anything done on the mask side will only be used as an opacity mask. To work on the regular artboard, click the left thumbnail.

Chapter 11: Using Filters and Effects

In This Chapter

✓ Applying filters and effects

✓ Getting to know the Appearance palette

✓ Discovering graphic styles

✓ Making artwork 3D

✓ Playing with additional fills and strokes

*F*ilters and effects give you the opportunity to do jazzy things to your Illustrator objects, such as adding drop shadows and squiggling artwork. You can even use Photoshop filters right in Illustrator. In this chapter, we explain the difference between filters and effects (it's a very big difference); show you how to apply, save, and edit filters and effects; and give you a quick tour of the Appearance palette (your trusty sidekick when performing these tasks).

Working with Filters and Effects

Filters apply permanent changes to artwork. After you use the filter, the only way to remove the change is to undo your actions or choose Object⇨Expand and take it apart. This can be messy and not near as much fun as using an effect that is dynamically connected to the object. *Effects* are very different in that you can apply, change, and even remove effects at any time with the Appearance palette (Window⇨Appearance).

In Figure 11-1, we applied the drop shadow filter when the shape was a rectangle; then we applied the roughen filter. Notice that the drop shadow has no interaction with the original artwork. In contrast, in Figure 11-2, we applied the Roughen *effect,* and the rectangle's drop shadow changed to look like the new shape. In the Appearance palette, you can double-click an effect to change it, or even drag it to the trash can icon in the lower-right corner of the Appearance palette to remove it.

Figure 11-1:
A rectangle with the Drop Shadow and Roughen *filter* applied.

Figure 11-2:
A rectangle with the Drop Shadow and Roughen *effect* applied.

Understanding the Appearance palette

When you work using Illustrator's defaults, an effect is applied to an object, then another object is created and the effect applies to it as well! What if you don't want that effect applied? This is when a good working knowledge of the Appearance palette is necessary. If it isn't visible, choose Window⇨ Appearance to show the Appearance palette, as shown in Figure 11-3.

Figure 11-3:
The Appearance palette.

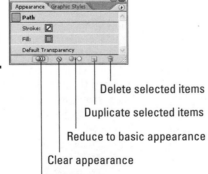

Delete selected items

Duplicate selected items

Reduce to basic appearance

Clear appearance

New art maintains appearance or
New art has basic appearance

To turn off effects so that they aren't automatically applied to any future objects, use any one of three buttons at the bottom of the Appearance palette:

✦ **New Art Maintains Appearance/New Art Has Basic Appearance:** With the New Art Maintains Appearance button selected, your new art maintains the effects that you have applied to the present object.

Click this button to switch to New Art Has Basic Appearance so that when you create the next object, colors are maintained but just a single fill and stroke are created.

✦ **Clear Appearance:** Click this button if you have a selected object and want the Fill and Stroke color boxes to be set to None.

✦ **Reduce to Basic Appearance:** If you have a selected object and discover that you applied unwanted effects, click this button to reduce it back to a single fill and stroke.

As a default, if you have no effects applied, you will see only a fill and a stroke listed in the Appearance palette. As you add effects, they are added to this list. You can even add additional strokes and fills to the list. Why would you do that? Because you can do incredible things with additional fills and strokes (which we show you later in this chapter).

Applying a filter

If effects are so great, why even use filters? Well, nothing can be all good. If you have lots of RAM (Random Access Memory) and you don't mind running through a few extra steps before printing (see Chapter 12 of this minibook), effects are the way to go. Most people don't mind, but you should see the alternative as well. Plus, some very useful Color filters are available that don't exist as effects — for instance, filters that take a full color illustration and change it to grayscale.

If you generally work in the CMYK color mode, you will come across filters and effects that are grayed out. These filters and effects can only be applied in the RGB color mode. Choose File➪Document Color Mode and change the document to RGB to use them.

Filters are not dynamically linked to the original object that they were created from.

To apply the Add Arrowhead Filter, follow these steps (which essentially just adds arrowheads to a path and is pretty straightforward):

1. **Create a new document, choose any color mode, and draw a path in your document.**

   If you haven't mastered the Pen tool yet (see Chapter 4 of this minibook), use the Pencil tool.

2. **To make it clear what is happening with the arrowheads, give the stroke a 3-pt stroke and make sure that there is no fill.**

   Using a 3-pt stroke enables you to see the stroke a little easier.

3. **Choose Filter➪Stylize➪Add Arrowheads.**

   The Add Arrowheads dialog box appears (see Figure 11-4).

Figure 11-4: Choose the arrowhead and the size.

4. **Choose to add an arrowhead to both the start and the end of the path by using the arrow keys to scroll through the selection.**

   Note that the Start arrowhead (top of Add Arrowhead dialog box) is the first point to be created; the End arrowhead (bottom of the dialog box) will be placed on the last point you create.

5. **Choose the size of the arrowhead by typing a number in the Scale text field.**

   You can go anywhere from 1 to 1000 percent, but typically an arrow is set at 50 percent. There is no preview available but this scales the arrowhead relative to the selected line stroke weight.

Note that if you used the Arrowhead Effect, instead of the filter the arrowhead would dynamically be linked to the stroke. Scaling and changing direction occur automatically as the stroke weight and direction are updated. See the next section for more information on Effects.

Applying an Effect

To apply the Add Arrowheads effect, choose Effects⇨Stylize⇨Add Arrowheads. Use the same settings that we describe in the preceding step list and then reposition some of the anchor points on the path by using the Direct Selection tool to see how the arrowhead applied with the effect moves with the direction of the path; the filter keeps the arrowhead in its original position.

Different from filters, the items under the Effect menu are dynamically linked to the object that they were applied to. Effects can be scaled, modified, and even deleted from the original object with no harm done to the original object.

Creating a drop shadow is a quick and easy way of adding dimension and a bit of sophistication to your artwork. The interaction between the object with the drop shadow and the underlying objects can create an interesting look. To add the Drop Shadow effect to an illustration, follow these steps:

1. **Select the object(s) that are to have the drop shadow applied.**

2. **Choose Effect⇨Stylize⇨Drop Shadow.**

3. **In the Drop Shadow dialog box that appears, select the Preview check box in the upper-right corner.**

   You will now see the drop shadow applied as you make changes.

4. **Choose from the following options (see Figure 11-5).**

   - **Mode:** Select a blending mode from this drop-down list to choose how you want your selected object to interact with the objects underneath. The default is Multiply, which works well — the effect is similar to coloring with a magic marker.

   - **Opacity:** Enter a value or use the drop-down list to determine how opaque or transparent the drop shadow should be. If it is too strong, choose a lower amount.

   - **Offset:** Enter a value to determine how close the shadow is to the object. If you're working with text or small artwork, smaller values (and shorter shadow) look best. Otherwise, the drop shadow may look like one big indefinable glob.

     The X Offset shifts the shadow from left to right, and the Y Offset shifts it up or down. You can enter negative or positive numbers.

   - **Blur:** Use blur to control how fuzzy the edges of the shadow are. A lower value makes the edge of the shadow more defined.

   - **Color and Darkness:** Select the Color radio button to choose a custom color for the drop shadow. Use Darkness to add more black to the drop shadow. Zero percent is the lowest amount of black and 100 percent is the highest.

**Book III
Chapter 11**

Using Filters and Effects

As a default, the color of the shadow is based upon the color of your object, sort of . . . the Darkness option has a play in this also. As a default, the shadow is made up of the color in the object if it is solid. Multicolored objects have a gray shadow.

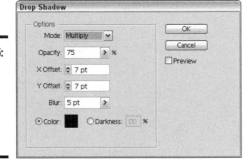

Figure 11-5:
The Drop
Shadow
dialog box
gives the
effect's
options.

Saving Graphic Styles

A *graphic style* is a combination of all the settings you choose for a particular filter or effect in the Appearance palette. By saving this information in a graphic style, you store these attributes so that you can quickly and easily apply them to other objects later.

Choose Window⇨Graphics Styles; in the palette that appears are thumbnails of many different styles that Adobe has provided to you as a default. Click any of these graphic styles to apply the style to an active object. Look at the Appearance palette as you click different styles to see that you're applying combinations of attributes, including effects, fills, and strokes. See Figure 11-6.

Figure 11-6:
The Graphic
Styles
palette
stores
combi-
nations of
attributes
like the ones
you see
listed in the
Appearance
palette.

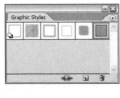 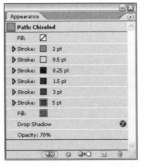

Find more styles by choosing the Graphic Styles flyout menu (click the arrow in the upper-right corner of the palette) and selecting Open Graphic Style Library.

You can store attributes as a graphic style in several ways; we show you two easy methods. If you have a combination of attributes already applied to an object, store them by doing one of the following:

✦ With the object selected, Alt+click (Windows) or Option+click (Mac) the New Graphic Style button at the bottom of the Graphic Style palette. Alt+clicking (Windows) or Option+clicking (Mac) allows you to name the style as it is added.

✦ Drag the selected object right into the Graphic Style palette. The palette stores its attributes, but you have to double-click the new style to name it.

After you store a graphic style, simply select the object that you want to apply the style to and then click the saved style in the Graphic Styles palette.

Creating 3D Artwork

All the effects in Illustrator are great, but this new feature is really swell. Not only can you add dimension by using the 3D effect, you can also map artwork (that is, wrap artwork around a 3D object) and apply lighting to the 3D object. This means that you can design a label for a jelly jar and actually adhere it to the jar to show the client!

Here are the three choices for the 3D effect:

✦ **Extrude and Bevel:** This uses the z-axis to extrude an object. For instance, a square becomes a cube.

✦ **Revolve:** Uses the z-axis and revolves a shape around it. You can use this to change an arc into a ball.

✦ **Rotate:** Rotates a 3D object created with the Extrude & Bevel or Revolve effects, or you can rotate a 2D object in 3D space. You can also adjust a 3D or 2D object's perspective.

To apply a 3D effect, you need to create an object appropriate for the 3D effect. Extrude and Bevel works great with shapes and text. If you want to edit an object that already has a 3D effect applied to it, double-click the 3D effect in the Appearance palette.

**Book III
Chapter 11**

**Using Filters and
Effects**

To apply a 3D effect, follow these steps:

1. **Select the object that you want to apply the 3D effect to.**

For this example, we're choosing Extrude and Bevel.

2. **Choose Effect⇨3D⇨Extrude and Bevel.**

Options for your chosen 3D effect appear. The Extrude and Bevel Options dialog box is shown in Figure 11-7.

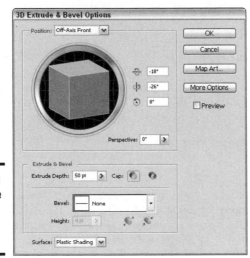

Figure 11-7:
The Extrude and Bevel Options dialog box.

3. **Select the Preview check box in the dialog box so that you can see results as you experiment with these settings.**

4. **Click the Preview pane (which shows a cube in Figure 11-7) and drag to rotate your object in space.**

It makes selecting the right angle fun, or you can choose the angle from the Position drop-down list above the preview. This is called positioning the object in space. You should never rotate a 3D object with the Rotate tool, unless you want some very funky results; use the Preview pane in this dialog box instead.

5. **If you want, use the Perspective drop-down list to add additional perspective to your object.**

6. **In the Extrude and Bevel section of the 3D Effects dialog box, choose a depth for your object and a cap.**

The cap determines whether your shape has a solid cap on it or whether it is hollow, as shown in Figure 11-8.

Figure 11-8:
Cap on (left) and cap off (right).

7. **Choose a bevel (edge shape) from the Bevel drop-down list and set the height using the Height drop-down list.**

   You have a choice of two ways to apply the bevel:

   • **Bevel Extent Out:** The bevel is added to the object.

   • **Bevel Extent In:** The bevel is subtracted from the object.

8. **Choose a rendering style from the Surface drop-down list, or click the More Options button for in-depth lighting options, such as changing the direction or adding additional lighting.**

9. **Click the Map Art button.**

   The Map Art dialog box opens. Use this dialog box to apply artwork to a 3D object.

10. **Using the Surface arrow buttons, select which surface you want the artwork applied to and then choose the symbol from the Symbols drop-down list, as shown in Figure 11-9.**

    The result is shown on the right in Figure 11-9.

Figure 11-9:
In the Map Art dialog box, select a surface and then a symbol to apply to the surface.

Points to keep in mind when mapping artwork:

✦ An object must be a symbol to be used as mapped artwork. You would simply need to select and drag the artwork that you want mapped to the Symbols palette to make it a selectable item in the Map Art dialog box.

✦ The light gray areas in the Preview pane are the visible areas based upon the object's present position. Drag and scale the artwork in this pane to get the artwork where you want it.

✦ Shaded artwork (the check box at the bottom of the dialog box) looks good but can take a long time to render.

Note: All 3D effects are rendered at 72 dpi (low resolution) so as not to slow down processing speed. You can determine the resolution by choosing Effect⇨Document Raster Effects Settings, or when you save or export the file. You could also select the object and choose Object⇨Rasterize. After the object is rasterized, it can no longer be used as an Illustrator 3D object, so save the original!

Applying Additional Fills and Strokes

Using the flyout menu in the Appearance palette, you can add additional fills and strokes. With this feature, you can put different colored fills on top of each other and individually apply effects to each one, creating really interesting and creative results.

Just for fun, follow along to see what you can do to a single object with the Appearance palette:

1. **Create a star shape.**

It doesn't matter how many points it has, or how large it is, just make it large enough to work with.

2. **Use the Window⇨Swatches palette to fill it with yellow and give it a black stroke.**

3. **Use Window⇨Stroke to make the stroke 1 pt.**

Notice that in the Appearance palette, the present fill and stroke are listed. Even in the simplest form, the Appearance palette helps track basic attributes. You can easily take advantage of the tracking to apply effects to just a fill or a stroke.

4. **Click Stroke in the Appearance palette.**

5. **Choose Effect⇨Path⇨Offset Path and in the Offset Palette dialog box that appears, change the Offset to –5pt and select the Preview check box.**

Notice that the stroke moves into the fill instead of on the edge, as shown in Figure 11-10.

Figure 11-10:
Choose to
just offset
the stroke
and not
the fill.

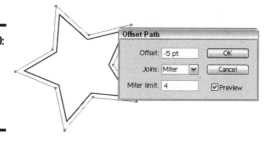

6. **Change the offset to something that works with your star shape and click OK.**

Depending on the size of your star, you may want to adjust the amount of offset up or down.

7. **From the flyout menu of the Appearance palette (see Figure 11-11), choose to add an additional fill to the star shape.**

This may sound ridiculous, but you can create some super effects with multiple fills.

Figure 11-11:
Add addi-
tional fills to
the same
object by
using the
Appearance
palette
menu.

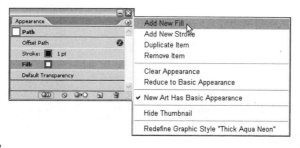

8. **Click Fill in the Appearance palette (the top one) and choose Effect⇨ Distort and Transform⇨Twist.**

**Book III
Chapter 11**

**Using Filters and
Effects**

9. **In the Twist dialog box that appears (see Figure 11-12), type** 45 **into the Angle text field and select the Preview check box.**

Notice how only the second fill is twisted? Pretty neat right? But wait, there's more!

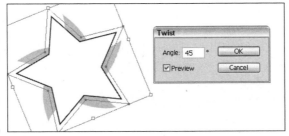

Figure 11-12:
Using
Effects to
twist just the
new fill.

10. **Click OK to exit the Twist dialog box.**

11. **Select the top Fill from the Appearance palette again.**

You always have to be sure that they are selected before doing anything that is meant to change just a specific fill or stroke.

12. **Then, using the Transparency palette (Window⇨Transparency), choose 50% from the Opacity slider or simply type 50% in the Opacity text field.**

Now you can see your original shape through the new fill!

13. **With that top fill still selected, change the color, or assign a pattern for a really different appearance, like the example shown in Figure 11-13.**

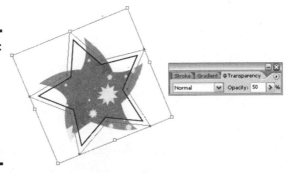

Figure 11-13:
The added
fill is made
slightly
transparent
and has a
pattern
applied to it.

You could go on for hours playing around with combinations of fills and strokes. Hopefully, this clicks and you can take it further on your own.

Chapter 12: Using Your Illustrator Image

In This Chapter

✔ **Saving Illustrator files**

✔ **Exporting files to other programs**

✔ **Preparing art for the Web**

✔ **Flattening transparency**

✔ **Printing from Illustrator**

So you have beautiful artwork, but you aren't sure how to get it off your screen. You could have a party and invite all interested clients to stand around your monitor and ooh and ah, or you could actually share or sell your artwork by putting it on the Internet or printing it.

In this chapter, we show you how to use your illustrations in a variety of workflows, from using Illustrator files in page layout programs, to exporting files for Photoshop (and other programs) and the Web. Hopefully, this chapter can help you really use your artwork and understand the saving and flattening choices available in Adobe Illustrator.

Saving and Exporting Illustrator Files

In this section, we show you how the general choices in the Save As dialog box (choose File➪Save As) differ and the benefits of each.

If you need a particular file format that is not listed in the regular Save As dialog box, choose File➪Export for additional choices. Using the File Export command, you can choose to save your files in any of the formats in the following table.

File Format	Extension
AutoCAD Drawing	`.dwg`
AutoCAD Interchange File	`.dxf`
BMP	`.bmp`
Enhanced Metafile	`.emf`
JPEG	`.jpg`
Macintosh PICT	`.pct`
Macromedia Flash	`.swf`
Photoshop	`.psd`
PNG	`.png`
Targa	`.tga`
Text Format	`.txt`
TIFF	`.tif`
Windows Metafile	`.wmf`

Many of these formats rasterize your artwork, meaning that they will no longer maintain vector paths and the benefits of being vector. Scalability is not limited, for instance. If you think that you might want to edit your image again later, be sure to save a copy of the file and keep the original in the `.ai` format.

The native Adobe Illustrator file format

If your workflow can handle it, the best way to save your file is as a native Illustrator `.ai` file. By workflow, we mean that you're working with Adobe applications such as Adobe InDesign for page layout, Adobe GoLive for Web page creation, Adobe Photoshop for photo-retouching, and Adobe Acrobat for cross-platform documents.

Understanding when it's best to use the `.ai` format is important. Saving your illustration as an `.ai` file ensures that your file is editable; it also ensures that any transparency is retained, even if you use the file in another application.

To save and use a file in the native Illustrator format, follow these steps:

1. **Make an illustration with transparency (50 percent transparent, for example) in Adobe Illustrator and choose File⊃Save As.**

2. **Select Adobe Illustrator Document (.ai) from the Save as Type drop-down list. Give the file a name and click Save.**

3. **Leave the Illustrator Native Options at the defaults and click OK.**

After you follow the preceding steps to prepare your Illustrator file, you can use the illustration in other Adobe applications:

✦ **Adobe Acrobat:** Open the Acrobat application and choose File➪Open. Locate the .ai file. Native Illustrator files open in Acrobat when you open them from within the Acrobat application.

✦ **Adobe InDesign:** Choose File➪Place. This method supports transparency created in Adobe Illustrator. (However, copying and pasting from Illustrator to InDesign does *not* support transparency.) See Figure 12-1.

Figure 12-1:
A native Adobe Illustrator file placed into InDesign — transparency is supported (left); artwork copied in Adobe Illustrator and pasted into InDesign — transparency is not supported (right).

✦ **Adobe Photoshop:** Choose File➪Place. That's it. Doesn't get much simpler, huh?

If you really want to go crazy with an Illustrator file in Photoshop, when you save the file in Illustrator, choose File➪Export and select the Photoshop (.psd) format from the Save as Type drop-down list. Choose a resolution from the options window. If you used layers, leave the Write Layers option selected.

In Photoshop, choose File⇨Open, select the file that you just saved in Illustrator as a `.psd`, and click Open. The file opens in Photoshop with all your layers intact.

✦ **Adobe GoLive:** Drag an image object onto the page from the basic section of the Objects toolbar. Click the Browse folder to the right of the Image Link text field and locate the native `.ai` file. The Save for Web dialog box appears (discussed later in this chapter); choose your settings, usually a GIF for images with lots of solid color. Make sure that you save the new Web image in your site folder with the rest of your site documents. See Book VI, Chapter 3 for more information about importing images in GoLive.

Saving Illustrator files back to previous versions

Not sure if you can call this a new feature, but saving back to older versions of Illustrator has come back around to the way it should be — accessible by choosing File⇨Save as.

When saving an `.ai` or `.eps` file, you can choose a version from the Version drop down menu. Keep in mind that any features specific to newer versions of Illustrator will not be supported in older file formats, so make sure you save a copy and keep the original file intact. Adobe helps you understand the risk of saving back to older versions by putting a warning sign next to the version drop down menu and showing you specific issues with the version you have selected in the Warnings window, as shown in Figure 12-2.

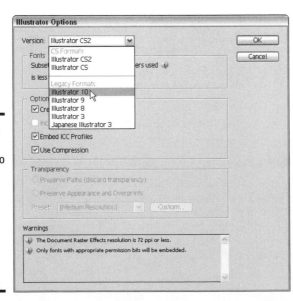

Figure 12-2: When you save back to older versions, warnings appear in the Illustrator Options window.

The EPS file format

EPS is the file format that most text editing and page layout applications accept; EPS supports vector data and is completely scalable. The Illustrator .eps format is based on PostScript, which means that you can reopen an EPS file and edit it in Illustrator at any time.

To save a file in Illustrator as an EPS, follow these steps:

1. **Choose File⇨Save As and select EPS (Encapsulated PostScript File) from the Save as Type drop-down list.**

2. **From the Version menu choose the Illustrator version you are saving to.**

3. **In the EPS Options dialog box that appears (shown in Figure 12-3), choose the preview from the Format drop-down list:**

   • **TIFF (8-bit Color):** A color preview for either Mac or PC.

   • **TIFF (Black & White):** A low resolution black and white preview.

4. **Select either the Transparent or Opaque option, depending on whether you want the non-image areas in your artwork to be transparent or opaque.**

5. **Set your Transparency Flattening settings. This will be grayed out if you have not used transparency in the file.**

   (See the "Flattening Transparency" section, later in this chapter, for more about this setting.)

6. **Leave the Embed Fonts (For Other Applications) check box selected to leave fonts you used embedded in the EPS file format.**

7. **In the Options section, leave the Include CMYK PostScript in RGB Files check box selected.**

8. **If you don't know which Adobe Postscript level you want to save to, leave this at the default.**

9. **Click OK to save your file as an EPS.**

The PDF file format

If you want to save your file in a format that supports over a dozen platforms and requires only the Acrobat Reader, available as a free download at www. adobe.com, choose to save in the PDF format.

If you can open an Illustrator file in Acrobat, why would you need to save a file in the PDF format? Well, for one thing, you can compress a PDF down to a smaller size; also, the receiver can double-click the file and Acrobat or Acrobat Reader will launch automatically.

**Book III
Chapter 12**

**Using Your
Illustrator Image**

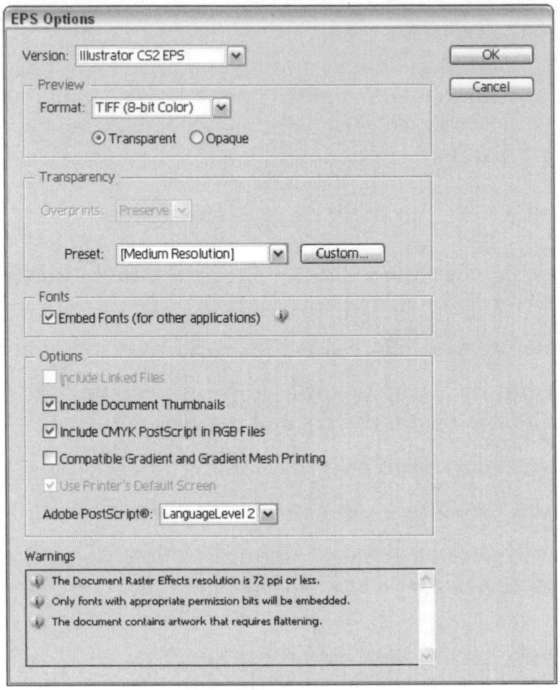

Figure 12-3: The EPS Options dialog box allows you to choose a preview as well as other important settings.

Depending on how you save the PDF, you can allow some level of editability in Adobe Illustrator. To save a file in the PDF format, follow these steps:

1. **Choose File⇨Save As; select Illustrator PDF (.pdf) from the Save as Type drop-down list, and then click Save.**

2. **In the Adobe PDF Options dialog box that appears, select one of the following options from the Preset drop-down list:**

   • **Illustrator Default:** Creates a PDF file in which all Illustrator data is preserved. PDF files created with this preset can be reopened in Illustrator without any loss of data.

   • **High Quality Print:** Creates PDFs for desktop printers and proofers.

   • **PDF/X-1a:2001:** This method is the least flexible delivery of PDF content data, but it can be very powerful. It requires that the color of all objects be in CMYK or spot colors. Elements in RGB or Lab color spaces or tagged with ICC profiles are prohibited. It also requires that all fonts used in the job be embedded in the supplied PDF file.

- **PDF/X-3:2002:** This method of creating a PDF has slightly more flexibility than the X-1a:2001 method in that color managed workflows are supported elements in Lab, and with attached ICC source profiles may also be used.

- **Press Quality:** Creates a PDF file that can be printed to a high resolution output device. The file will be large, but it will maintain all the information that a commercial printer or service provider needs to print your file correctly. This option automatically converts the color mode to CMYK, embeds all fonts used in the file, prints at a higher resolution, and uses other settings to preserve the maximum amount of information contained in the original document.

- **Smallest File size:** Creates a low resolution PDF suitable for posting on the internet or sending via email.

Before creating an Adobe PDF file using the Press preset, check with your commercial printer to find out what the output resolution and other settings should be.

- **Standard:** Don't pick a PDF/X standard unless you have a specific need or have been requested to. Through the Standard drop-down menu you can select the type of PDF/X file you wish to create.

- **Compatibility:** Different features are available for different versions, such as the ability to support layers in Version 6 or higher. If you want the most compatible file type choose Acrobat 5 (PDF 1.4). But if you want to take advantage of layers or need to preserve spot colors you must chose Acrobat 6 or higher.

3. Click Save PDF to save your file as a PDF.

If you want to be able to reopen the PDF file and edit it in Illustrator, make sure that you leave the Preserve Illustrator Editing Capabilities check box selected in the Adobe PDF Options dialog box. See Figure 12-4 for a look at the improved PDF save dialog window.

In the Adobe PDF Options dialog box, to the left of the preset choices are options that you can change to customize your settings. Scan through them to see how you can change resolution settings and even add printer's marks. Take a look at Book V on Acrobat to find out more about the additional PDF options.

Want a Press Quality PDF, but don't want to convert all of your colors to CMYK? Choose the Press settings, but then click on the Output options. In the Color section select No Conversion from the Color Conversion drop-down menu.

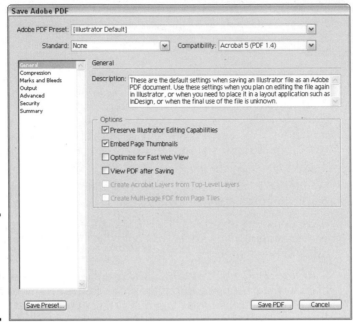

Figure 12-4:
Additional
PDF options
are available
in Illustrator
CS2.

Saving Your Artwork for the Web

If you need to save artwork for the Web, there is no better feature than Save for Web. The Save for Web dialog box gives you a preview pane where you can test different file formats before you actually save the file.

To save an Illustrator file that you intend to use in a Web page, just follow these steps:

1. **Choose File⇨Save for Web.**

   The Save for Web dialog box appears, showing your artwork on the Optimized tab.

2. **Choose a tabbed view: Original, Optimized, 2-Up, or 4-Up.**

   As a default, you will see the artwork in the Optimized view. This means that you're previewing the artwork as it will appear based upon the settings on the right. The 2-Up view is probably the best choice because it shows your original image versus the optimized version.

3. **Choose a setting for your file from the options on the right.**

   If you want to make it easy on yourself, choose a preset from the Settings drop-down list. Keep in mind these points:

- GIF is generally used for artwork with spans of solid color. GIF is not a lossy format. You can make your artwork smaller by reducing the number of colors in the image — hence the choices, such as GIF 64 No Dither (64 colors). The lower the amount of colors, the smaller the file size. You can also increase or decrease the number of colors in the file by changing the preset values in the Color text field or by using the arrows to the left of the Color text field.

- Dithering tries to make your artwork look like it has more colors by creating a pattern in the colors. It looks like a checkerboard pattern up close and even far away, as shown in Figure 12-5. It also makes a larger file size, so why use it? Most designers don't like the effect and choose the No Dither option.

- JPEG is used for artwork that has subtle gradations from one shade to another. Photographs are often saved in this format. If you have drop shadows or blends in your artwork, you should select this format. JPEG is a lossy file format, meaning that it will reduce your image to a lesser quality and can create odd artifacts in your artwork. You have choices such as High, Medium, and Low in the Settings drop-down list. Make sure that you choose wisely. You can also use the Quality slider to tweak the compression.

Figure 12-5: An example of dithering.

Book III
Chapter 12

Using Your Illustrator Image

4. **When you're satisfied with your chosen settings, save your file by clicking Save.**

When saving illustrations for the Web, you should keep the following points in mind, which will make the whole process much easier for you and anyone who uses your illustrations:

✦ **Keep it small:** Don't forget that if you're saving illustrations for a Web page, many other elements will be on that page. Try to conserve on file size to make downloading the page quicker for viewers using dial-up connections. Most visitors won't wait more than 10 seconds for a page to download before giving up and moving on to another Web site.

As you make your choices, keep an eye on the file size and the optimized artwork in the lower-left corner of the preview window. On average, a GIF should be around 10K and a JPEG around 15K. These rules aren't written in stone, but please don't try to put a 100K JPEG on a Web page!

You can change the download time by selecting the palette menu in the upper-right corner of the Save for Web dialog box and choosing Optimize to File Size to input a final file size and have Illustrator create your settings in the Save for Web dialog box.

✦ **Preview the file before saving it:** If you want to see the artwork in a Web browser before saving it, click the Preview in Default Browser button at the bottom of the Save for Web dialog box. The browser of choice appears with your artwork in the quality and size in which it will appear. If you have no browser selected, click and hold down the Preview in Default Browser button to choose Other, then browse to locate a browser that you want to use for previewing. Close the browser to return to the Save for Web dialog box.

✦ **Change the size:** Many misconceptions abound about size when it comes to Web artwork. Generally, most people view their browser windows in an area approximately 700 x 500 pixels. Depending on the screen resolution, this may cover the entire screen on a 14-inch monitor, but even viewers with 21-inch monitors with a high resolution often don't want to have their entire screen covered with a browser's window, so they still have a browser window area of around 700 x 500 pixels. When choosing a size for your artwork, use proportions of this amount to help you. For instance, if you want an illustration to take up about a quarter of the browser window's width, you should make your image about 175 pixels wide (700 __4 = 175). If you notice that the height of your image is over 500 pixels, you should whittle the height down in size as well, or your viewers will have to scroll to see the whole image (and it will probably take too long to download!).

Use the Image Size tab (shown in Figure 12-6) to input new sizes. As long as the Constrain Proportions check box is selected, both the height and width of the image will be changed proportionally. Click the Apply button to change the size but do not close the Save For Web dialog box.

✦ **Finish the save:** If you aren't finished with the artwork, but you want to save the settings, hold down the Alt (Windows) or Option (Mac) key and click the Remember button. (When you're not holding down the Alt or Option key, the Remember button is the Done button.) If you're finished, click the Save button and save your file in the appropriate location.

Figure 12-6:
Changing
the image
size.

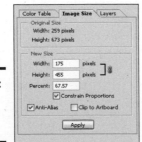

Flattening Transparency

You may find that all those cool effects that you put into your illustration don't print correctly. When you print a file that has effects such as drop shadows, cool gradient blends, and feathering, Illustrator turns transparent areas that overlap other objects into pixels and leaves what it can as vectors — this process is called *flattening*.

So what actually is flattening? Look at Figure 12-7 to see the difference between the original artwork (on the left) and the flattened artwork (on the right).

Figure 12-7: Artwork before and after flattening is applied.

Notice that in Figure 12-7, when the artwork was flattened, some of the areas turned into pixels. But at what resolution? This is why you want to know about flattening, so that you can determine the quality of art yourself — before getting an unpleasant surprise at the outcome.

Flattening a file

If you have taken advantage of transparency or effects using transparency (which we discuss in Chapter 10 of this minibook), follow these steps to get the highest quality artwork from your file:

1. **Make sure that you've created the artwork in the CMYK mode.**

   You can change the document's color mode by choosing File⇨Document Color Mode.

2. **Choose Effects⇨Document Raster Effects Settings.**

   The Document Raster Effects Settings dialog box appears, as shown in Figure 12-8.

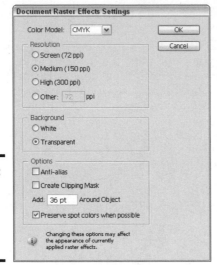

Document Raster Effects Settings

Color Model: CMYK

OK

Cancel

Resolution
- ○ Screen (72 ppi)
- ⊙ Medium (150 ppi)
- ○ High (300 ppi)
- ○ Other: 72 ppi

Background
- ○ White
- ⊙ Transparent

Options
- ☐ Anti-alias
- ☐ Create Clipping Mask
- Add: 36 pt Around Object
- ☑ Preserve spot colors when possible

ⓘ Changing these options may affect the appearance of currently applied raster effects.

Figure 12-8: Choosing the quality of your rasterized artwork.

3. Choose the resolution that you want to use by selecting an option in the Resolution area.

As a default, the rasterization setting is the Low (72 ppi) option, which is fine for the screen. Select the Medium (150 ppi) option for printers and copiers, and select the High (300 ppi) option for press.

4. Choose whether you want a white or transparent background.

If you select the Transparent option, you create an alpha channel. The alpha channel is retained if the artwork is exported into Photoshop.

5. You can generally leave the items in the Options section deselected:

- The Anti-Alias check box applies anti-aliasing to reduce the appearance of jagged edges in the rasterized image. Deselect this option to maintain the crispness of fine lines and small text.

- The Create Clipping Mask check box creates a mask that makes the background of the rasterized image appear transparent. You don't need to create a clipping mask if you select the Transparent option for your background.

- The Add Around Object text field adds the specified number of pixels around the rasterized image.

6. Click OK.

The next step is to set the transparency options in the Document Setup dialog box.

7. **Choose File⊄Document Setup; Choose Transparency from the drop-down menu in the upper left corner.**

   The Export and Clipboard Transparency Flattener Settings options appear. From the Preset drop-down list, select the Low, Medium, High, or Custom option. Select the Low option for on-screen viewing, the Medium option for printers and copiers, or the High option for press. Choose the Custom option if you want to control more of the settings yourself.

8. **Click OK.**

If you find yourself customizing the settings on a regular basis, choose Edit⊄Transparency Flattener Presets to create and store your own presets.

You can apply the flattening in several ways. Here are three simple methods.

✦ Select the object(s) that require flattening and choose Object⊄Flatten Transparency. Choose one of the default settings or a custom preset that you created from the Settings drop-down list and click OK.

✦ Choose File⊄Print and select Advanced from the list of print options on the left. Choose a preset from the Overprint and Transparency Flattener options. If you used the Attributes palettes to create overprints (for trapping used in high-end printing), make sure that you preserve the overprints.

   Note: Overprints will not be preserved in areas that use transparency.

✦ Choose File⊄Save As and choose Illustrator EPS. In the Transparency section of the EPS Options dialog box, choose a flattening setting from the Preset drop-down list.

Using the Flattener Preview palette

Want to preview your flattening? Use the Flattener Preview palette by choosing Window⊄Flattener Preview. Choose Show Options from the palette menu.

The Flattener Preview palette does not apply the flattening, but it gives you a preview based upon your settings. Click the Refresh button and choose to show options from the palette menu (see Figure 12-9). Test various settings without actually flattening the file. Experiment with different settings, and then save your presets by selecting Save Transparency Preset from the palette menu. The saved settings can be accessed in the Preset drop-down list in the Options dialog boxes that appear when you save a file as an EPS or in the Document Setup dialog box.

Click the Refresh button after making changes to update the preview.

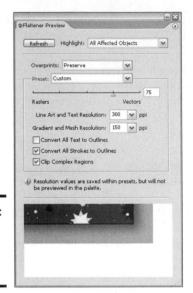

Figure 12-9:
The
Flattener
Preview
palette.

Zoom in on the artwork by clicking in the preview pane. Scroll the artwork in the preview pane by holding down the spacebar and dragging. Zoom out by Alt+clicking (Windows) or Option+clicking (Mac).

Printing from Illustrator

Printing from Illustrator gives you lots of capabilities, such as printing composites to separations and adding printer's marks.

To print your illustration, follow these steps:

1. **Choose File⇨Print.**

2. **In the Print dialog box that appears (see Figure 12-10), select a printer if one is not already selected.**

3. **If the PPD is not selected, choose one from the PPD drop-down list.**

    A *PPD* is a printer description file. Illustrator needs this to determine the specifics of the PostScript printer you're sending your file to. This setting lets Illustrator know whether the printer can print in color, the size paper it can handle, and the resolution, as well as many other important details.

4. **Choose from other options as follows:**

    Use the General options area to pick what pages to print. In the Media area, select the size of media that you're printing to. In the Options area, choose whether you want layers to print and any options specific to printing layers.

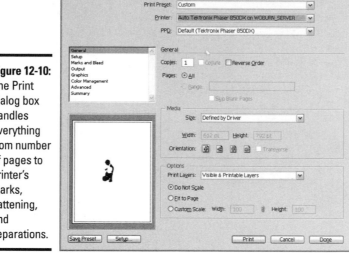

Figure 12-10:
The Print dialog box handles everything from number of pages to printer's marks, flattening, and separations.

5. **Click the Print button to print your illustration.**

And that's it. Printing your illustration can be really simple, but the following list highlights some basic things to keep in mind as you prepare your illustration for printing:

✦ **Printing a composite:** A *composite* is the full-color image, where all the inks are applied to the page (and not separated out onto individual pages, one for cyan, one for magenta, one for yellow, and one for black). To make sure that your settings are correct, click Output in the print options pane on the left side of the Print dialog box and select Composite from the Mode drop-down list.

✦ **Printing separations:** To separate colors, click Output in the print options pane on the left side of the Print dialog box; from the Mode drop-down list, choose the Separations (Host Based) option. Select the In-Rip Separations option only if your service provider or printer asks you to. Other options to select from are as follows:

   • The resolution is determined by your PPD, based upon the dpi in the printer description. You may have only one option available in the Printer Resolution drop-down list.

   • Select the Convert Spot Colors to Process check box to make your file 4-color.

   • Click the printer icons to the left of the listed colors to turn off or on the colors that you want to print (see Figure 12-11).

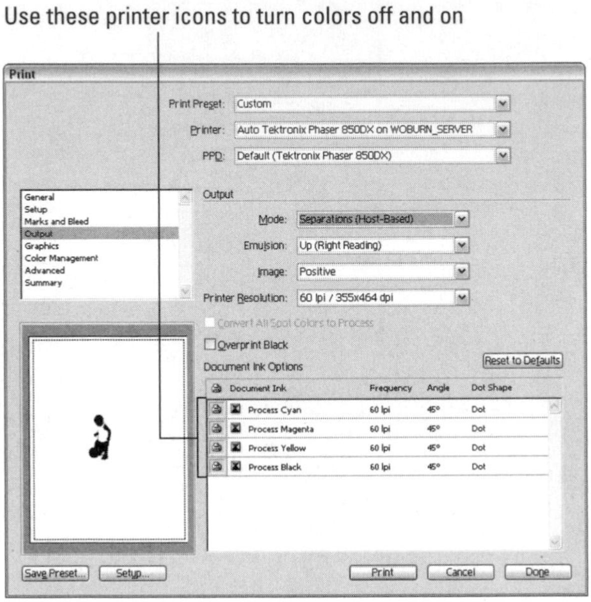

Use these printer icons to turn colors off and on

Figure 12-11:
Click the
printer icon
to the left of
the color to
keep it from
printing.
Click it again
to have it
print.

Printer's marks and bleeds: Click Marks and Bleeds in the print options
pane on the left side of the Print dialog box to turn on all printer's marks,
or just select the ones that you want to appear.

Specify a bleed area if you're extending images beyond the trim area of
a page. If you don't specify a bleed, the artwork will stop at the edge
of the page and not leave a trim area for the printer.

After you have created a good set of options specific to your needs, click
the Save Preset button at the bottom of the Print dialog box. Name your
preset appropriately; when you want to use that preset, select it from
the Print Preset drop-down list at the top of the Print dialog box for
future print jobs.

Book IV

Photoshop CS2

The 5th Wave   By Rich Tennant

"I'VE GOT SOME IMAGE EDITING SOFTWARE, SO I TOOK THE LIBERTY OF ERASING SOME OF THE SMUDGES THAT KEPT SHOWING UP AROUND THE CLOUDS. NO NEED TO THANK ME."

Contents at a Glance

Chapter 1: Photoshop CS2 Basics

In This Chapter

✔ **Getting familiar with Photoshop**

✔ **Getting to know the tools**

✔ **Palette organization**

✔ **Zooming**

✔ **Screen modes**

✔ **Cropping an image**

*N*avigating the work area in Photoshop can be slightly cumbersome at first, especially if you've never worked in a program that relies so heavily on palettes. In this chapter, we introduce you to Photoshop CS2 and show you how to do some basic tasks (such as opening and saving an image). We also introduce you to the work area, show you what the Photoshop CS2 tools are all about, as well as how to neatly organize and hide palettes. See how to zoom in and out of areas with keyboard commands and take advantage of underutilized features, such as new window and screen modes. The last thing we show you in this chapter is how to crop an image so that you can save only the important part of your images. This not only conserves file space but also processing time.

Getting Started with Photoshop CS2

Before delving into the nitty-gritty of Photoshop, read on to make sure you know how to get a file open in Photoshop and how to save it.

Opening an existing document

You rarely create a new file in Photoshop because you usually have a source image that you start with. This image may have been generated by a scanner, digital camera, or stock image library.

Open existing Photoshop images by choosing File➪Open, selecting the file in the Open dialog box, and then clicking the Open button. Photoshop can open a multitude of file formats, even if the image was created in another application, such as Illustrator or some other image editing program, but you have to open the image in Photoshop by choosing File➪Open. If you just double-click an image file in a directory (one that wasn't originally created in Photoshop, or from different versions), the image may open only in a preview application.

Creating a new file

If you're creating a new file, you may be doing so to create a composite of existing files, or to start with a blank canvas because you're super creative.

For whatever reason, note that when you choose File➪New, you have a multitude of basic format choices that range from basic sizes and resolutions, such as Letter, to multimedia, such as NTSC D1 Square Pix, 720 x 576 (with guides), that are prepared for on-screen presentation.

Keep in mind that you're determining not only size but resolution in your new file. If your new file is to contain images from other files, make sure the new file is the same resolution. Otherwise, you may get unexpected size results when cutting and pasting or dragging images into your new file.

Saving documents

Save an image file by choosing File➪Save. If you're saving the file for the first time, the Save As dialog box appears. Notice in the Save as Type drop-down list that there are plenty of choices for file formats. The different file formats are discussed in more detail in Chapter 9 of this minibook. You can always play it safe by choosing the Photoshop (PSD or PDD) file format. The native Photoshop format supports all features in Photoshop. Choosing some of the other formats may eliminate layers, channels, and other special features.

Many users choose to save a native Photoshop file as a backup to any other file formats. It's especially important to have a backup or original file saved as a native Photoshop file (PSD or PDD) as you increase in capabilities and start taking advantage of layers and the other great capabilities of Photoshop.

Getting to Know the Tools

Tools are used to create, select, and manipulate objects in Photoshop CS2. When you open Photoshop, the toolbox appears along the left edge of the workspace (see Figure 1-1). We discuss palettes and the palette well in the following section, "Navigating the Work Area."

Toolbox   Image window   Palettes   Palette well

Figure 1-1:
Your
Photoshop
tools
include the
toolbox,
palettes,
and the
palette well.

In the toolbox, look for the name of the tool to appear in a ToolTip when you hover the cursor over the tool. Following the tool name is a letter in parentheses, which is the keyboard shortcut command that you can use to access that tool. Using the Shift key in addition to the key command accesses any hidden tools. In other words, pressing P activates the Pen tool, and pressing Shift+P activates the hidden tools under the Pen tool in the order that they appear. When you see a small triangle at the lower-right corner of the tool icon, you know that this tool contains hidden tools.

Table 1-1 lists the Photoshop tools, what each is used for, and in what chapter you can find more about each.

Book IV
Chapter 1

Photoshop CS2
Basics

Table 1-1		Photoshop CS Tools	
Button	*Tool*	*What It Does*	*Where It's Covered in This Minibook*
[ ]	Marquee (M)	Selects image area	Chapter 3

(continued)

Table 1-1 *(continued)*

Button	Tool	*What It Does*	*Where It's Covered in This Minibook*
	Move (V)	Moves selections or layers	Chapter 3
	Lasso (L)	Makes freehand selections	Chapter 3
	Magic Wand (W)	Selects similar pixels	Chapter 3
	Crop (C)	Crops an image	Chapter 1
	Slice (K)	Creates HTML slices	n/a
	Spot Healing Brush (J)	Retouches flaws	Chapter 7
	Brush (B)	Paints foreground color	Chapter 7
	Clone Stamp (S)	Copies pixel data	Chapter 7
	History Brush (Y)	Paints from selected state	Chapter 7
	Eraser (E)	Erases pixels	Chapter 7
	Gradient (G)	Creates a gradient	Chapter 7
	Blur (R)	Blurs pixels	Chapter 7
	Toning (O)	Dodges, burns, saturates	Chapter 7
	Path Selection (A)	Selects paths	Chapter 4

Button	Tool	What It Does	Where It's Covered in This Minibook
T.	Type (T)	Creates text	Chapter 8
	Pen (P)	Creates paths	Chapter 4
	Vector Shape (U)	Creates vector shapes	Chapter 8
	Notes (N)	Makes annotations	n/a
	Eyedropper (I)	Samples pixels	Chapter 7
	Hand (H)	Navigates page	Chapter 1
	Zoom (Z)	Increases and decreases view	Chapter 1

Navigating the Work Area

Getting around in Photoshop isn't much different from getting around in Illustrator. Both programs make extensive use of palettes, for example. In the following sections, we cover the highlights on navigating around in Photoshop.

Docking and saving palettes

Palettes, palettes everywhere . . . do you really need them all? Maybe not just yet, but as you increase your skill level, you will take advantage of most (if not all) of the Photoshop palettes. The palettes give you easy access to important functions. Book I, Chapter 3 provides a lot of basic information about using palettes in the Adobe Creative Suite, so check out that chapter if you need a refresher on using palettes. We add only a few things here that are specific to using the palettes in Photoshop.

REMEMBER

As you work in Photoshop, keep in mind these two key commands: Press Tab to switch between hiding and showing the tools and palettes; press Shift+Tab to hide the palettes, leaving only the toolbox visible.

Book IV
Chapter 1

Photoshop CS2
Basics

On the far right of the *Options bar* (a toolbar that contains the options for each tool and appears across the top of the work area) is the *palette well*, which helps you organize and manage palettes. The palette well stores, or docks, palettes so that you can access them easily.

The palette well is available only when using a screen resolution greater than 800 x 600 pixels (a setting of at least 1024 x 768 is recommended). Dock palettes in the palette well by dragging the palette's tab into the palette well; release when the palette well is highlighted.

If you find that you're always using the same palettes, hide the palettes that you don't need and arrange your other palettes on-screen where you want them. Then follow these steps to save that palette configuration:

1. **Choose Window➪Workspace➪Save Workspace.**

2. **In the Save Workspace dialog box that appears, name the Workspace and click OK.**

3. **Any time you want the palettes to return to your saved locations, choose Window➪Workspace➪*Name of Your Workspace* (where *Name of Your Workspace* is the name you supplied in Step 2).**

Choose Window➪Workspace➪Reset Palette Locations to put the palettes back in the same order they were upon the initial installation.

Zooming in to get a better look

What looks fine at one zoom level may actually look very bad at another. You'll find yourself zooming in and out quite often as you work on an image in Photoshop. You can find menu choices for zooming in the View menu; a quicker way to zoom is to use the keyboard commands listed in Table 1-2.

Table 1-2	Zooming and Navigation Keyboard Shortcuts	
Command	*Windows Shortcut*	*Mac Shortcut*
Actual size	Ctrl+1	⌘ +1
Fit in window	Ctrl+0 (zero)	⌘ +0 (zero)
Zoom in	Ctrl++ (plus sign) or Ctrl+Spacebar	⌘ ++ (plus sign) or ⌘ +Spacebar
Zoom out	Ctrl+– (minus) or Alt+Spacebar	⌘ +– (minus) or Option+Spacebar
Hand tool	Spacebar	Spacebar

Here are a few things to keep in mind as you work with the Zoom tool to get a better look at your work:

✦ **100 percent view:** Double-clicking the Zoom tool in the toolbox puts you at 100 percent view. Do this before using filters to see a more realistic result of your changes.

✦ **Zoom marquee:** Drag from the upper-left to the lower-right of the area you want to zoom to. While dragging, a marquee appears; when you release the mouse button, the marqueed area zooms up to fill the image window. This gives you much more control than just clicking on the image with the Zoom tool. Zoom back out to see the entire image by pressing Ctrl+0 (Windows) or ⌘+0 (Mac). This fits the entire image in the viewing area.

If you have a dialog box open and you need to reposition or zoom to a new location on your image, you can use the keyboard commands without-out exiting the dialog box.

✦ **A new window for a different look:** Choose Window⇨Arrange⇨New Window to create an additional window for your front-most image. This is helpful when you want to see the entire image (say at actual size) to see the results as a whole, yet zoom in to focus on a small area of the image to do some fine-tuning. The new window is dynamically linked to the original window so that as you make changes, the original and any other new windows created from the original are immediately updated.

Press Ctrl+Tab (Windows) or ⌘+Tab (Mac) to cycle through open images.

Screen Modes

You have a choice of three screen modes in which to work. Most users start and stay in the default (standard screen mode) until they accidentally end up in another. The three modes are

✦ **Standard mode:** This is the typical view, where you have an image window open but can see your desktop and other images open behind.

✦ **Full screen mode with menu:** This view surrounds the image out to the edge of the work area with a neutral gray. This not only prevents you from accidentally clicking out of an image and leaving Photoshop, but also from seeing other images behind your working image.

✦ **Full screen mode, no menu:** This view is a favorite with multimedia types. It shows your image surrounded by black and also eliminates the menu items from the top of the window. Press Tab to hide all tools, and you have a very clean work environment.

With an image open, zoom back a little bit by pressing Ctrl+– (Windows) or ⌘+– (Mac) until you see the whole image, but it isn't taking up the entire screen. Press F to switch to the full screen mode with menu. We recommend working in the full screen mode with menu because in this mode, you can click outside the image and not exit Photoshop, and it gives you a helpful neutral gray background surrounding your image.

Press F again to switch to full screen mode without the menu. This puts a black background around the image, which is especially nice for presentations and showing off your work. Notice that in this mode, you have no menu at the top, so you better know your keyboard commands! If your palettes are visible, press Tab, and now your screen shows only the image.

Press F again to return to the default view, standard screen mode. You can also use the Screen Mode buttons at the bottom of the toolbox to switch between modes.

Cropping an Image

A simple but essential task is to crop your image. Cropping means to eliminate all that is not important to the composition of your image. This is especially important in Photoshop. Each pixel, no matter what color, takes up the same amount of information, so cropping eliminates unneeded pixels and saves on file size and processing time, so you want to crop your image before you start working on it.

You can crop an image in Photoshop CS2 in two ways: by using the Crop tool or by selecting an area with the Marquee tool and choosing Image⇨Crop.

To crop an image by using the Crop tool, follow these steps:

1. **Press C to access the Crop tool and drag around the area of the image that you want to crop to.**

2. **If you need to adjust the crop area, drag the handles in the crop bounding area.**

3. **When you're satisfied with the crop bounding area, double-click in the center of the crop area or press the Return or Enter key to crop the image.**

4. **If you want to cancel the crop, press the Esc key.**

Ever scan in an image crooked? When using the Crop tool, if you position the cursor outside any of the handles, a rotate symbol appears. Drag the crop's bounding area to rotate it and line it up as you want it cropped. When you press Return or Enter, the image is straightened out.

Chapter 2: Mode Matters

In this Chapter

- ✓ Discovering bitmap images
- ✓ Understanding Photoshop image modes
- ✓ Using color settings

*B*efore diving into using Photoshop, you must know what image mode you should be working in and how important color settings are. So no matter whether you're doing a one-color newsletter, a full-color logo, or something in between, this chapter can help you create much better imagery for both Web and print.

Working with Bitmap Images

You may have already discovered that Photoshop works a little differently than most other applications. In order to create those smooth gradations from one color to the next, Photoshop takes advantage of using pixels. *Bitmap images* (sometimes called *raster images*) are based on a grid of pixels. The grid is smaller or larger depending on the resolution that you're working in. The number of pixels along the height and width of a bitmap image are called the pixel dimensions of an image, which are measured in pixels per inch (ppi). The more pixels per inch, the more detail in the image.

Unlike *vector graphics* (mathematically created paths), bitmap images can't be scaled without losing detail. See Figure 2-1 for an example of a bitmap image and a vector graphic. Generally, it's best to use bitmap images at or close to the size that you need. If you resize a bitmap image, it can become jagged on the edges of sharp objects. On the other hand, you can scale vector graphics and edit them without degrading the sharp edges.

Bitmap   Vector

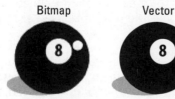

Figure 2-1:
Bitmap
versus
vector.

As shown in Figure 2-2, Photoshop has the capability to work on both bitmap and vector art (see the path line around the logo art and notice the text is not pixilated). It gives you, as a designer, incredible opportunities when combining the two technologies.

Figure 2-2:
A vector shape layer selected in a Photoshop image.

For information on changing and adjusting image resolution, see Chapter 5 of this minibook.

Choosing the Correct Photoshop Mode

Choose Image⇨Mode to see all the image mode choices you have to pick from. Selecting the right one for an image is important because each mode offers different capabilities and results. For instance, if you choose the Bitmap mode, you can work only in black and white . . . that's it. No shades of color, not even a gray. Most features are disabled in this Bitmap mode. This is fine if you're working on art for a black and white logo, but not for most images. If, instead, you work in the RGB mode, you have full access to Photoshop's capabilities. So read on to see what image mode is best for what you need. When you're ready to make your mode selection, have a file open and choose from Image⇨Mode. Read descriptions of each in the following section.

Along with a description of each image mode, we include a figure showing the Channels palette set to that mode. A *channel* is simply the information about color elements in the image. The number of default color channels in an image depends on its color mode. For example, a CMYK image has at least four channels, one each for cyan, magenta, yellow, and black information. Grayscale has one channel. If you understand the printing process, think of each channel representing a plate (color) that, when combined, creates the final image.

Bitmap

Bitmap mode, shown in Figure 2-3, offers little more than the ability to work in black and white. Many tools are unusable and most menu options are grayed out in this mode. If you're converting an image to bitmap, you must convert it to Grayscale first.

Figure 2-3: Bitmap mode is good for black-and-white images only.

Grayscale

Use Grayscale mode, shown in Figure 2-4, if you're creating black-and-white images with tonal values, specifically for printing to one color. Grayscale mode supports 256 shades of gray in the 8-bit color mode. Photoshop can work with Grayscale in 16-bit mode, which provides more information, but may limit your capabilities when working in Photoshop.

When you convert to Grayscale mode, you get a warning message confirming that you want to discard all color information. If you don't want to see this warning every time you convert an image to grayscale, select the option to not show the dialog box again before you click OK.

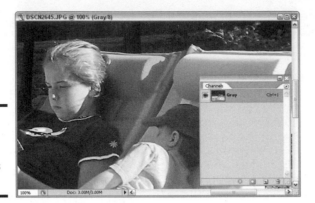

Figure 2-4:
Grayscale
contains
256 shades
of gray.

Duotone

Use Duotone mode (shown in Figure 2-5) when you're creating a 1-4 color image created from spot colors (solid ink, such as Pantone colors). You can also use the Duotone mode to create Monotones, Tritones, and Quadtones. If you're producing a two-color job, duotones create a beautiful solution to not having full color.

Figure 2-5:
In Duotone
mode, you
can use
Pantone
colors to
create the
image.

The Pantone Matching color system helps to keep printing inks consistent from one job to the next. By assigning a numbered Pantone color, such as 485 for red, you don't risk one vendor (printer) using fire engine red and the next using orange-red for your company logo.

To create a Duotone, follow these steps:

1. **Choose Image➪Mode➪Grayscale. Then choose Image➪Mode➪Duotone.**

2. **In the Duotone dialog box, choose Duotone from the Type drop-down list.**

   Your choices range from Monochrome (one-color) up to Quadtone (four-color). Black is automatically assigned as the first ink. But you can change that if you like.

3. **To assign a second ink color, click the white swatch immediately under the black swatch to open the Color Libraries dialog box, as shown in Figure 2-6.**

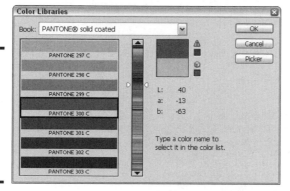

Figure 2-6: Click the white swatch to open the Color Libraries dialog box.

4. **Now comes the fun part: Type (quickly!) the Pantone or PMS number that you want to access, and then click OK.**

   There is no text field for you to enter the number in, so don't look for one, just type the number while the Custom Colors dialog box is open.

   Try entering **300** for an easy one. That selects PMS 300.

5. **You can already see that you have created a tone curve, but click the Curve button to the left of the ink color, as shown in Figure 2-7, to further tweak the colors.**

6. **Click and drag the curve to adjust the black in the shadow areas, perhaps to bring down the color overall; experiment with the results.**

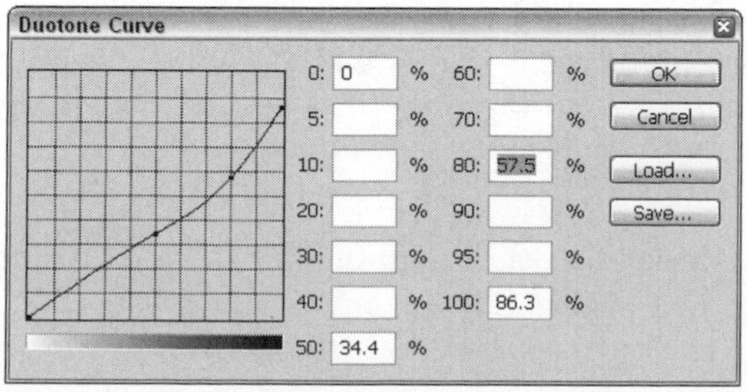

**Book IV
Chapter 2**

Mode Matters

Figure 2-7: Adjust the individual curves for a better Duotone.

7. (Optional) If you like your Duotone settings, store them by clicking the Save button.

Click the Load button to find your customized presets and to find preset Duotones, Tritones, and Quadtones supplied to you by Adobe.

Duotones must be saved in the Photoshop EPS format in order to support the spot colors. If you chose another format, you risk the possibility of converting your colors into a build of CMYK (Cyan, Magenta, Yellow, and Black.)

8. Click OK when you're finished.

Index color

You might not work in Index color, but you probably have saved a file in this mode. Index color mode (see Figure 2-8) uses a color look-up table (CLUT) in order to create the image.

Figure 2-8:
Index color uses a limited number of colors to create an image.

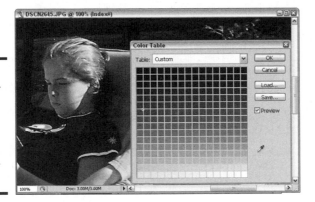

A *color look-up table* contains all the colors that make up your image, like a box of crayons used to create artwork. If you have a box of eight crayons and only those crayons are used to color an image, you have a color look-up table of only eight colors. Of course, your image would look much better if you used the 64-count box of crayons with the sharpener on the back, but that increases the size of the color look-up table, as well as the file size.

The most colors that can be in index mode is 256. When saving Web images, you often have to define a color table. We discuss the Save for Web feature (which helps you to more accurately save an index color image) in Chapter 9 of this minibook.

Choose Image➪Mode➪Color Table to see the color table making up an image (refer to Figure 2-8).

RGB

RGB (Red, Green, Blue), shown in Figure 2-9, is the standard format that you work in if you import images from a digital camera or you scan images on a scanner in RGB mode. For complete access to features, RGB is probably the best color mode to work in. If you're working on images for use on the Web, color copiers, desktop color printers, and on-screen presentations, you want to stay in the RGB mode.

If you're having your image printed on a press (for example, if you're having the image professionally printed), it must be separated. Do not convert images to CMYK mode until you're finished with the color correction and you know that your color settings are accurate. A good print service may want the RGB file so that they can do an accurate conversion. We discuss color settings later in this chapter.

Figure 2-9: RGB creates the image from red, green, and blue.

CMYK

CMYK (Cyan, Magenta, Yellow, Black), shown in Figure 2-10, is the mode used for final separations for the press. Use a good magnifying glass to look closely at anything that has been printed in color, and you may see the CMYK colors that created it. A typical four-color printing press has a plate for each color and runs the colors in the order of cyan, magenta, yellow, and then black.

Don't take converting an image into this mode lightly. You need to make decisions when you convert an image to CMYK, such as where the file is going to be printed and on what paper stock, so that the resulting image is the best it can be. Talk to your print provider for specifications that are important when converting to CMYK mode.

**Book IV
Chapter 2**

Mode Matters

Figure 2-10: You have four channels in the CMYK mode.

Lab color

Lab (Lightness, A channel, and B channel), shown in Figure 2-11, is a color mode that many high-end color professionals use because of its wide color range. Using Lab, you can make adjustments to luminosity (lightness) without affecting the color. In this mode, there is an L (Lightness or Luminosity) channel that can be selected and changed without affecting the A channel (green and red) and the B channel (blue and yellow).

Lab mode is also a good mode to use if you're in a color managed environment and want to easily move from one color system to another with no loss of color.

Figure 2-11: The Lab mode supports a wide range of color.

Multichannel

Multichannel is used for many things; sometimes you end up in this mode and you're not quite sure how. Deleting a channel from an RGB, CMYK, or Lab image automatically converts the image to Multichannel mode, as shown in Figure 2-12. This mode supports multiple spot colors.

Figure 2-12: A Duotone converted to Multichannel to individually adjust the colors.

Bit depth

New in Photoshop CS2, you have more functionality in 16-bit mode. Most of the time you work in 8-bit mode, which is more than likely all that you need.

Bit depth, also called *pixel depth* or *color depth,* measures how much color information is available to display or print each pixel in an image. Greater bit depth means more available colors and more accurate color representation in the digital image. In Photoshop, that increase in accuracy does also limit some of the features available, so don't use it unless you have a specific request or need for it.

To use 16-bit color mode, you also must have a source to provide you with that information, such as a scanner that offers a choice to scan at 16-bit.

Understanding Color Settings

Photoshop works dynamically with the settings that you choose from the Color Settings dialog box (Edit➪Color Settings [Windows] or Photoshop➪ Color Settings [Mac]). If the color settings are accurate, the image you see on-screen will closely resemble the printed image. Of course, the image on-screen can't exactly match the printed image, but using the Color Settings dialog box gives you better results than not having any direction. The correct color settings change many settings in Photoshop, from highlight and shadow settings to dot gain and previews.

Dot gain is the spread of ink on paper. This occurs with just about any paper stock, from a press as well as with a desktop printer. How dot gain is determined is by measuring with a densitometer the spread of ink at a 50 percent tint. For instance, if you print a tint of black and it comes off the press at 70 percent, you have a 20 percent dot gain. A dot gain for coated paper can range from 10 percent to 25 percent. Uncoated paper can gain much more.

Color settings attempt to give you a WYSIWYG (What You See Is What You Get) approach to working with images. If you're working with images that are going to the Web, you can set up Photoshop to preview colors as they might appear on a typical monitor.

For printing, color settings will adjust your image to accommodate for dot gain, as well as adjusting to the correct color gamut. *Gamut* is a range of colors within the capabilities of a particular device. In other words, your monitor might show a really great royal blue, but when printed, it turns purplish. That's because, though the royal blue is in the monitor's RGB color gamut, the same color is out of the CMYK printer's gamut. Your scanner has a gamut; so does your digital camera. Color settings help to adjust your image's colors, based upon the setting that you select.

CMYK color settings do not take effect until you choose Image➪Mode➪CMYK, and then based upon your settings, a color conversion takes place. That is why it is so important to *not* change to CMYK mode unless you have color settings accurately set. Changing the color settings after a file is in the CMYK mode will have no effect on the image.

By setting up your color settings correctly, you can see the changes on-screen. To get a better understanding of how powerful the Color Settings dialog box is, follow these steps:

1. **Choose Edit⇨Color Settings (Windows) or Photoshop⇨Color Settings (Mac).**

The Color Settings dialog box appears (see Figure 2-13).

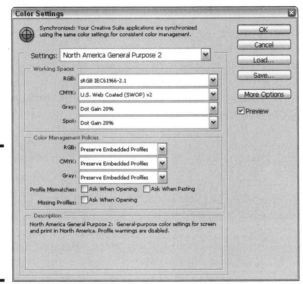

Figure 2-13: Use the Color Settings dialog box to make color more accurate.

2. **In the Settings drop-down list, choose North American Prepress 2.**

This is the generic setting that you can use if you're going to press. By selecting this preset, other selections are automatically made in the other drop-down menus.

3. **Select a paper stock, such as U.S. Sheetfed Coated (SWOP) v2, from the CMYK drop-down list.**

Other choices include, U.S. Web Coated (SWOP) v2 Coated, a shiny paper stock, usually coated with a clay-like substance. In this setting, *web* refers to a large press that would create publications with huge print runs (20,000 or more copies), such as magazines and catalogs. If you're printing brochures and smaller print runs, you're probably using Sheetfed press. For this example, choose the selection U.S. Sheetfed Coated (SWOP) v2.

If you know that you will more often use uncoated paper, such as your typical rough bond type of paper, choose U.S. Sheetfed Uncoated (SWOP) v2. This will make a difference in your results.

SWOP stands for Specifications Web Offset Publications. SWOP is a committee of people from the graphics arts industry that test and build specifications to make your job of supplying output to a printer a little easier. Read more at www.swop.org.

If you're not using color management, use the drop-down lists in the Color Management Policies section to set the RGB, CMYK, and Gray choices to Off.

4. **Next to Profile Mismatches, deselect the Ask When Opening check box so that annoying color management warnings won't pop up when you open images with embedded profiles; click OK.**

Using color management can truly be helpful. If it is important that your monitor is accurate to what will appear when printed, check out ColorSync at www.apple.com/colorsync.

5. **Using an RGB image, oversaturate an image (brighten it up) by choosing Image➪Adjustments➪Hue/Saturation.**

6. **Drag the Saturation slider over to the right to exaggerate and oversaturate the colors, and then click OK.**

Pretty awful, but you'll see where you're going with this in a minute.

7. **Press Ctrl+Y (Windows) or ⌘+Y (Mac) to toggle between what your file looks like in RGB mode and what it will look like when converted to CMYK.**

Photoshop is referring to the CMYK mode you selected in the Color Settings dialog box. Change your paper stock, and you might see even more of a difference.

You may notice, especially in blue areas, that the printed image isn't exactly what you see in the original RGB image. The title bar at the top of the document shows whether an image is in preview mode or not.

Using the key command Ctrl+Y (Windows) or ⌘+Y (Mac) or choosing View➪ Proof Colors is very helpful when you want to work in the CMYK preview, but you don't want to actually change the color mode of your image.

You can use View➪Proof Setup to change your preview to Macintosh RGB or Windows RGB. This is important if you're designing Web graphics on a Macintosh and you want to see what your images will look like on a PC (generally, images appear darker on the Windows platform). On the Mac, choose View➪Proof Setup➪Windows RGB to preview your images as they will appear on a PC. Now, every time you press Ctrl+Y (Windows) or ⌘+Y (Mac), the image appears as it will on the other platform.

Determining what settings to use

In most instances, you can get away with using the preset color defaults that Adobe Photoshop provides in the Settings drop-down list (in the Color Settings dialog box; refer to Figure 2-13); you just need to know what to choose. If you're printing images, stick with the U.S. Prepress defaults or whatever your printing service suggests.

A good service provider can click the Save button in the Color Settings dialog box to provide you with a `.csf` file that contains exactly the settings needed. If the printer supplies you with a file, click the Load button and locate it to apply the settings to your images.

Advanced and Web settings

Photoshop provides more advanced capabilities for those who understand printing and information about press settings.

Select Custom from the CMYK drop-down list in the Working Spaces section of the Color Settings dialog box (refer to Figure 2-13). In the Custom CMYK dialog box that appears, shown in Figure 2-14, lots of great options can be set up to match a printing service's press specifications. If you're a printer and get good results with your settings, you can save them and distribute them to customers.

Figure 2-14: If you have the printing knowledge, you can customize the CMYK settings.

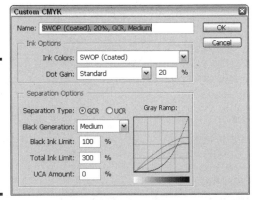

If your image is destined for the Web, in the Color Settings dialog box, choose Web Graphics Defaults from the Settings drop-down list. Going to the Web is much easier because you're staying within the RGB color mode.

Chapter 3: Creating a Selection

In This Chapter

- ✓ Discovering the selection tools
- ✓ Painting selections the easy way
- ✓ Giving transformed selections a try
- ✓ Feathering away
- ✓ Keeping selections for later use
- ✓ Using the new Vanishing Point feature

The most common ways to use Photoshop are to create compositions that might not actually exist and to retouch images to improve them. What you don't want is obvious retouching or a composition that looks contrived. (The exception is if you intend an image to be humorous, such as putting baby Joey's head on Daddy's body.)

That's where the selection tools come in. In this chapter, we show you several selection methods and how to use the selection tools to make your images look as though you *haven't* retouched or edited them. Even if you're an experienced Photoshop user, this chapter supplies a plethora of tips and tricks that can save you time and help make your images look absolutely convincing.

Getting to Know the Selection Tools

You create selections with the selection tools. Think of *selections* as windows in which you can make changes to the pixels. Areas that aren't selected are *masked,* which means that these unselected areas are unaffected by changes, much like when you tape around windows and doors before you paint the walls. In this section, we briefly describe the selection tools and show you how to use them. You must be familiar with these tools in order to do *anything* in Photoshop.

As with all the Photoshop tools, the Options bar across the top of the Photoshop window changes with each selection tool. The keyboard commands you read about in this section exist on the Options bar as buttons.

If you move a selection with the Move tool, pixels move as you drag, leaving a blank spot in the image. To *clone* a selection (that is, to copy and move the selection at the same time), Alt+drag (Windows) or Option+drag (Mac) the selection with the Move tool.

The Marquee tool

 The Marquee tool is the main selection tool; by that, we mean that you'll use it most often for creating selections. The exception, of course, is when you have a special situation that calls for a special tool, either the Lasso or Magic Wand tool (we discuss both of these a bit later in this chapter). Throughout this section, we describe creating (and then deselecting) an active selection area; we also provide you with tips for working with selections.

The Marquee tool includes the Rectangular Marquee (for creating rectangular selections), Elliptical Marquee (for creating round or elliptical selections), and Single Row Marquee or Single Column Marquee tools (for creating a selection of a single row or column of pixels). Access these other Marquee tools by holding down on the default, Rectangle Marquee tool.

To create a selection, select one of the Marquee tools (remember you can press M), and then drag anywhere on your image. When you release the mouse button, you create an active selection area. When you're working on an active selection area, whatever effects you choose are applied to the whole selection. To deselect an area, you have three choices:

+ Choose Select⇨Deselect.

+ Press Ctrl+D (Windows) or ⌘+D (Mac).

+ While using a selection tool, click outside the selection area.

How you make a selection is important because it determines how realistic your edits appear on the image. Read on for tips and tricks that you can use when creating both rectangular and elliptical selections:

+ Add to a selection by holding down the Shift key, and then drag to create a second selection that intersects the original selection (see the left image in Figure 3-1). The two selections become one big selection.

+ Delete from an existing selection by holding the Alt (Windows) or Option (Mac) key, and then drag to create a second selection that intersects the original selection where you want to take away from the original selection (on the right in Figure 3-1).

+ Constrain a rectangle or ellipse to a square or circle by Shift+dragging; make sure that you release the mouse button before you release the Shift key. Holding down the Shift key makes a square or circle only when there are no other selections. (Otherwise, it adds to the selection.)

✦ Make the selection from the center by Alt+dragging (Windows) or Option+dragging (Mac); make sure that you release the mouse button before the Alt (Windows) or Option (Mac) key.

✦ Create a square or circle from the center out by Alt+Shift+dragging (Windows) or Option+Shift+dragging (Mac). Again, make sure that you always release the mouse button before the modifier keys.

✦ When making a selection, hold down the spacebar before releasing the mouse button to drag the selection to another location.

Figure 3-1: Adding to and deleting from selections.

Fixed size

If you've created an effect that you particularly like, say changing a block of color in your image, and you would like to apply it multiple times throughout an image, you can do that. To make the exact same selection multiple times, follow these steps:

1. **With the Marquee tool selected, select Fixed Size from the Style drop-down list on the Options bar.**

You can also select Fixed Aspect Ratio from the Style drop-down list to create a proportionally correct selection, but not fixed to an exact size.

2. **On the Options bar, type the Width and Height values into the appropriate text fields.**

You can change ruler increments by choosing Edit⇨Preferences⇨Units and Rulers (Windows) or Photoshop⇨Preferences⇨Units and Rulers (Mac).

3. **Click the image.**

A selection sized to your values appears.

4. **With the selection tool, drag the selection to the location that you want selected.**

Shift+drag a selection to keep it aligned to a straight, 45-degree, or 90-degree angle.

Floating and non-floating selections

As a default, when you're using a selection tool, such as the Marquee tool, your selections are *floating*. This means that you can drag them to another location without affecting the underlying pixels. You know that your selection is floating by the little rectangle that appears on your cursor (see the left image in Figure 3-2). If you want to, however, you can move the underlying pixels. With the selection tool of your choice, just hold down the Ctrl (Windows) or ⌘ (Mac) key to temporarily access the Move tool; the cursor changes to a pointer with scissors, denoting that your selection is non-floating. Now, when you drag, the pixel data comes with the selection (as shown on the right in Figure 3-2).

Figure 3-2: The Float icon is shown on the left, and the Move icon is being used on the right.

Hold down Alt+Ctrl (Windows) or Option+⌘ (Mac) while using a selection tool and drag to clone (copy) pixels from one location to another. Add the Shift key, and the cloned copy is constrained to a straight, 45-degree, or 90-degree angle.

The Lasso tool

Use the Lasso tool for *freeform selections* (selections of an irregular shape). To use the Lasso tool, just drag and create a path surrounding the area to be selected. If you don't return to your start point to close the selection before you release the mouse button, Photoshop completes the path by finding the most direct route back to your starting point.

Just like with the Marquee tool, you can press the Shift key to add to a lasso selection, and press the Alt (Windows) or Option (Mac) to delete from a lasso selection.

Hold down on the Lasso tool to show the hidden Lasso tools, the Polygon Lasso and the Magnetic Lasso tool. Use the Polygon Lasso tool by clicking on a start point, and then clicking and releasing from point to point until you come back to close the selection. Use the Magnetic Lasso tool by clicking to create a starting point, and then hovering the cursor near an edge in your image. The Magnetic Lasso tool is magnetically attracted to edges; as you move your cursor near an edge, the Magnetic Lasso tool creates a selection along that edge. Click to manually set points in the selection; when you get back to the starting point, click to close the selection.

You may find that the Polygon Lasso and the Magnetic Lasso tools don't make as nice of a selection as you'd like. Take a look at the upcoming section, "Painting with the Quick Mask tool," for some tips on making finer selections.

The Magic Wand tool

The Magic Wand tool is particularly helpful when you're working on an image of high contrast or with a limited number of colors. What it does is select individual pixels of similar shades and colors. Select the Magic Wand tool, click anywhere on an image, and hope for the best — the Magic Wand tool isn't magic at all. You decide how successful this tool is. What we mean by that is that you control how closely matched each pixel must be in order for the Magic Wand tool to include it in the selection. You do this by setting the tolerance on the Options bar.

When you have the Magic Wand tool selected, a Tolerance text field appears on the Options bar. As a default, the tolerance is set to 32. When you click with a setting of 32, the Magic Wand tool selects all pixels within 32 shades (steps) of the color that you clicked. If it didn't select as much as you want, increase the value in the Tolerance text field (all the way up to 255). The amount that you enter really varies with each individual selection. If you're selecting white napkins on an off-white tablecloth, you can set this as low as 5 so that the selection doesn't leak into other areas. For colored fabric with lots of tonal values, you might increase the tolerance to 150.

Don't fret if you miss the entire selection when using the Magic Wand tool. Hold down the Shift key and click in the missed areas. If it selects too much, choose Edit⇨Undo (Step Backwards) or press Ctrl+Z (Windows) or ⌘+Z (Mac), reduce the value in the Tolerance text field, and try again.

Manipulating Selections

After you master creating selections, you'll find that working with the selections — painting, transforming, and feathering them — can be easy and fun.

Book IV
Chapter 3

Creating a Selection

Painting with the Quick Mask tool

If you have fuzzy selections (fur, hair, or leaves, for example) or you're having difficulty using the selection tools, the Quick Mask tool can be a huge help because it allows you to paint your selection uniformly in one fell swoop.

To enter into Quick Mask mode, create a selection, and then press Q (pressing Q again exits you from Quick Mask mode). You can also click the Quick Mask button at the bottom of the toolbox. If you have a printing background, you'll notice that the Quick Mask mode, set at its default color (red), resembles something that you may want to forget; rubylith and amberlith. (Remember slicing up those lovely films with Exacto blades before computer masking came along?) In Quick Mask mode, Photoshop shows your image as it appears through the mask. The clear part is selected; what's covered in the mask is not selected.

To create and implement a quick mask, follow these steps:

1. **Press Q to enter Quick Mask mode.**

2. **Press D to change the foreground and background color boxes the default colors of black and white.**

3. **Select the Brush tool and start painting with black in the clear area of the image in Quick Mask mode.**

   It doesn't have to be pretty; just get a stroke or two in there.

4. **Press Q to return to the Selection mode.**

   You're now out of Quick Mask mode. Notice that where you painted with black (it turned red in the Quick Mask mode), the pixels are no longer selected.

5. **Press Q again to re-enter the Quick Mask mode, and then press X.**

   This switches the foreground and background colors (giving you white in the foreground, black in the background).

 6. **Using the Brush tool, paint several white strokes in the red mask area.**

   The white strokes turn clear in the Quick Mask mode.

7. **Press Q to return to the Selection mode.**

   Where you painted white in the Quick Mask mode is now selected.

When in Quick Mask mode, you can paint white over areas you want selected and black over areas that you don't want selected. When painting in the Quick Mask mode, increase the brush size by pressing the] key. Decrease the brush size by pressing the [key.

In the Selection mode, your selection seems to have a hard edge; you can soften those hard edges by using a softer brush in the Quick Mask mode. To make a brush softer, press Shift+[and press Shift+] to make a brush harder.

Because the Quick Mask mode makes selections based on the mask's values, you can create a mask by selecting the Gradient tool and dragging it across the image in Quick Mask mode. When you exit Quick Mask mode, it looks as though there is a straight line selection, but actually the selection transitions as your gradient did. Choose any filter from the Filters menu and notice how the filter transitions into the untouched part of the image, as shown in Figure 3-3, to which we applied the new and improved Graphic Pen filter.

Figure 3-3:
Creating a gradient in the Quick Mask mode creates a transitional selection.

If you're working in Quick Mask mode, choose Window⇨Channels to see that what you're working on is a temporary Alpha Channel. See the later section, "Saving Selections," for more about alpha channels.

Transforming selections

Transform your selections by scaling, rotating, or otherwise distorting them. Follow these steps to transform a selection:

1. **Create a selection, and then choose Select⇨Transform Selection.**

- Drag the handles to make the selection larger or smaller. Drag a corner handle to adjust width and height simultaneously. Shift+drag a corner handle to size proportionally.

- Position the cursor outside of the bounding box to see the Rotate icon; drag when it appears to rotate the selection. Shift+drag to constrain to straight, 45-degree, or 90-degree angles.

• Ctrl+drag (Windows) or ⌘+drag (Mac) a corner point to distort the selection, as shown in Figure 3-4.

2. **Press Return, Enter, or double-click in the center of the selection area to confirm the transformation. Press Esc to release the transformation and return to the original selection.**

Figure 3-4:
Distort the selection using the Transform Selection feature. Use Ctrl/Cmd while grabbing a corner for more distortion.

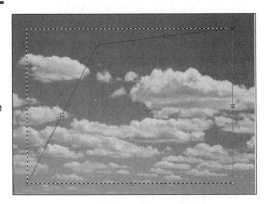

Feathering

Knowing how to make a selection means little if you don't know how to make it discreet. If you boost up the color using curves to the CEO's face, do you want it to appear like a pancake has been attached to his cheek? Of course not — that isn't discreet at all (or very wise). That's where feathering comes in. *Feathering* a selection blurs its edges, so as to create a natural-looking transition between the selection and the background of the image.

To feather an image, follow these steps:

1. **Create a selection.**

   For the non-feathered image shown on top in Figure 3-5, we used the Elliptical Marquee tool to make a selection. We then copied the selection, created a new, blank image, and pasted the selection into the new image.

   To create the feathered image on the bottom in Figure 3-5, we used the Elliptical Marquee tool to select the same area on the original image and went on to Step 2.

2. **Choose Select➪Feather.**

Figure 3-5:
On top, an image without feathering; on bottom, the same image with feathering applied.

3. **In the Feather dialog box that appears, type a value in the Feather Radius text field, and then click OK.**

For example, we entered **20** in the Feather Radius text field. (We then copied the selection, created a new image, and pasted the feathered selection into the new image to create the image on the bottom of Figure 3-5.) Voilà! The edges of the image are softened over a 20 pixel area, as shown on the bottom of Figure 3-5. This is also referred to as a *vignette* in the printing industry.

Book IV
Chapter 3

Creating a Selection

The results of the feathering depend upon the resolution of the image. A feather of 20 pixels in a 72 ppi (pixels per inch) image will be a much larger area than a feather of 20 pixels in a 300 ppi image. Typical amounts for a nice vignette on an edge of an image would be 20–50 pixels. Experiment with your images to find what works best for you.

This feathering effect created a nice soft edge to your image, but it is also useful when retouching images. Follow along for an example:

1. **Create a selection around a part of an image that you want to lighten.**

   This selection can be made with any of the selection methods.

2. **Choose Select➪Feather; in the Feather dialog box that appears, enter 25 in the Feather Radius text field and click OK.**

   If you get an error message stating, `No Pixels are more than 50% selected`, click OK and create a larger selection.

3. **Choose Image➪Adjustments➪Curves.**

4. **Click in the center of the curve to add an anchor point, as shown in Figure 3-6, and drag up to lighten the image.**

   This is lightening the midtones of the image.

Figure 3-6: Use curves to lighten the mid-tones in a selected area.

Notice how the lightening fades out so that there is no definite edge to the correction. You can have more fun like this in Chapter 6 of this minibook, where we cover color correction.

Saving Selections

The term *alpha channel* sounds pretty complicated, but it is simply a saved selection. Depending upon the mode you're in, you already have several channels to contend with. A selection is just an extra channel that you can call on at any time.

To create an alpha channel, follow these steps:

1. **Create a selection that you want to save.**

2. **Choose Select⇨Save Selection.**

3. **Name the Selection and click OK.**

   In the Channels palette is an additional named channel that contains your selection, as shown in Figure 3-7.

Figure 3-7:
An RGB image with an alpha channel (a saved selection).

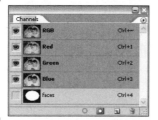

To load a saved selection, follow these steps:

1. **Choose Select⇨Load Selection.**

   The Load Selection dialog box appears, as shown in Figure 3-8.

Figure 3-8:
If you have a selection and then choose to load a selection, you have additional options.

2. **Select your named channel from the Channel drop-down list.**

   Notice in Figure 3-8 that if you have an active selection, and then choose to load a selection, that you have additional options. You can do the following with an active selection when loading a channel by selecting one of the following options:

   - **New Selection:** Eliminate the existing selection and create a new selection based upon the channel you select.

   - **Add to Selection:** Add the channel to the existing selection.

   - **Subtract from Selection:** Subtract the channel from the existing selection.

   - **Intersect with Selection:** Intersect the channel with the existing selection.

3. **Click OK.**

Alpha channels can also be recognized by other Adobe applications, such as InDesign, Illustrator, Premiere, and After Effects.

Try using the new Vanishing Point feature

This incredible new feature lets you preserve correct perspective in edits of images that contain perspective planes, such as the sides of a building. Follow these steps and have fun!

1. **Create a selection to confine edits to portions of the perspective planes.**

2. **Choose Filter⇨Vanishing Point.**

3. **Select the Create Plane tool and define the four corners of the plane surface.**

   Try to use a rectangle object in the image as a guide when creating the plane, as shown in Figure 3-9.

   After creating the plane, you can move, scale, or reshape the plane. Keep in mind that your results depend on how accurately the plane lines up with perspective of the image. If there's a problem with the plane, the grid will turn red or yellow. Position a corner node until the grid is blue; this indicates that the plane is proportionally valid.

   You can use your first Vanishing Point session for simply creating perspective planes and then clicking OK. The planes appear in subsequent Vanishing Point sessions when you choose Filter⇨Vanishing Point. This is especially useful if you plan to copy and paste an image into Vanishing Point and need to have a ready-made plane to target.

Figure 3-9:
Use an existing shape in the image to help you create a perspective plane.

4. **To make a selection, select the Marquee tool and drag in the plane.**

   You can use the Marquee tool options (Feather, Opacity, Heal, and Move Mode) at any time, either before or after making the selection. When you move the Marquee tool, the Stamp tool, or the Brush tool into a plane, the bounding box is highlighted, indicating that the plane is active.

   To clone a selection, select the Marquee or Transform tool and Alt+drag (Windows) or Option+drag (Mac OS) the selection to tear off a copy. The selection becomes a floating selection, which you can scale, move, rotate, or clone again using the Transform tool, or move or clone again using the Marquee tool. You can continue tearing off as many copies as you want. When you move a selection in a plane, the selection conforms to the perspective of the plane.

5. **Click OK.**

   To preserve the perspective plane information in an image, save your document in PSD, TIFF, or JPEG format.

If you create a new layer each time you use Vanishing Point, the results appear on a separate, editable layer. You can then use such layer features as opacity, layer styles, and blending modes. Putting the Vanishing Point results in a separate layer also preserves your original image.

**Book IV
Chapter 3**

Creating a Selection

Chapter 4: Using the Photoshop Pen Tool

In this Chapter

✔ **Putting shape layers to work**

✔ **Using a path as a selection**

✔ **Creating clipping paths**

The Pen tool is the ultimate method to make precise selections. You can also use it to create vector shapes and clipping paths (silhouettes). In this chapter, you discover how to take advantage of this super multitasking tool. This chapter also shows you how to apply paths made with the Pen tool as shapes, selections, and clipping paths. If you're interested in the fundamentals of creating paths with the Pen tool in Illustrator, check out Book III, Chapter 4, where we cover the Pen tool in depth.

We recommend that you use the Pen tool as much as you can to truly master its capabilities. If you don't use it on a regular basis, it will seem awkward, but it does get easier! Knowing how to effectively use the Pen tool puts you a grade above the average Photoshop user, and the quality of your selections will show it. Read Chapter 8 of this minibook to find out how to use the Pen tool to create layer masks and adjustment layers.

Using Shape Layers

As a default, when you start creating with the Pen tool, Photoshop automatically creates a *shape layer*, which is useful for adding additional elements, but is frustrating if you're attempting to create just a path with the Pen tool. Select the Pen tool and note the default setting on the left side of the Options bar. You can choose from the following options:

✦ **Shape:** Creates a new shape layer, a filled layer that contains your vector path.

✦ **Paths:** Creates a path only; no layer is created.

✦ **Fill Pixels:** Creates pixels directly on the image. No editable path or layer is created. This may not be useful to new users, but some existing users prefer to use this method because it is the only way to access the Line tool from previous versions.

Shape layers can be very useful when the goal of your design is to seamlessly integrate vector shapes and pixel data. A shape layer can contain vector shapes that can then be modified with the same features of any other layer. You can adjust the opacity of the shape layer, change the blending mode, and even apply layer effects to add drop shadows and dimension. Find out how to do this in Chapter 8 of this minibook. Create a shape layer using any of these methods:

✦ **Create a shape with the Pen tool.** With the Pen tool, you can create interesting custom shapes and even store them for future use. We show you how in the following section.

✦ **Use one of the Vector Shape tools shown in Figure 4-1.** Vector shapes are premade shapes (you can even create your own!) that you can create by dragging on your image area with a shape tool.

✦ **Import a shape from Illustrator.** Choose File➪Place to import an Illustrator file as a shape layer or path into Photoshop.

Figure 4-1:
The Vector Shape tools.

Creating and using a custom shape

Perhaps you like the wave kind of shape (see Figure 4-2) that has been cropping up in design pieces all over the place.

Figure 4-2:
A custom wave shape integrated with an image in Photoshop.

TECHNICAL STUFF

Importing shapes from Illustrator

In order to import an object from Illustrator into Photoshop, you must change your preferences in Illustrator. Choose Edit⇨Preferences (Windows) or Illustrator⇨Preferences (Mac); in the dialog box that appears, select File Handling & Clipboard. In the Clipboard on Quit section, select the AICB check box in the Copy As section.

Now when you choose Edit⇨Copy in Illustrator and then choose Edit⇨Paste in Photoshop, a Paste Options dialog box appears, giving you the option to paste the object as a path, shape layer, or fill.

You can create a wavy shape like that, too. With an image or blank document open, just follow these steps:

1. **Using the Pen tool, create a wavy shape, don't worry about the size of the shape.**

It's vector, so you can scale it up or down to whatever size that you need without worrying about making jagged edges. Just make sure that you close the shape (return back to the original point with the end point). As you create the shape, it fills in with your foreground color. Try to ignore it if you can; the next section shows you how to change the fill color, and Chapter 8 of this minibook covers how to change it to a transparent fill.

2. **With the shape still selected, choose Edit⇨Define Custom Shape, name the shape, and click OK.**

After you have saved your custom shape, you can re-create it at any time. If you don't like the shape, choose Windows⇨Layers to open the Layers palette, and then drag the shape layer you just created to the trash icon in the lower-right corner of the palette. If you'd like to experiment with your custom shape now, continue with these steps.

3. **Select the Custom Shape tool, click and hold on the Vector Shape tool to access the flyout menu, and then drag down to the last hidden tool.**

In the Vector Shape tool flyout menu are several shapes, as well as an amoeba-like shape at the end that represents custom shapes (refer to Figure 4-1).

When the Custom Shape tool is selected, a Shape pop-up menu appears on the Options bar at the top of the screen, as shown in Figure 4-3.

You have lots of custom shapes to choose from, including the one you've just created. If you just saved a shape, yours is in the last square; you have to scroll down to select it.

**Book IV
Chapter 4**

**Using the
Photoshop Pen Tool**

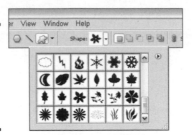

Figure 4-3:
The Options bar when the Custom Shape tool is selected.

4. **Select your custom shape; drag in the image area to create your shape.**

   You can make it any size that you want.

5. **To change the shape's size, choose Edit⇨Free Transform Path, press Ctrl+T (Windows) or ⌘+T (Mac), or grab a bounding box handle and drag.**

   Shift+drag a corner handle to keep the shape proportional as you resize it.

Because a shape is created on its own layer, you can experiment with different levels of transparency and blending modes in the Layers palette. Figure 4-4 shows shapes that are partially transparent. Discover lots of other features you can use with shape layers in Chapter 8 of this minibook.

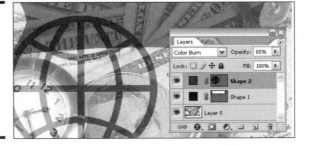

Figure 4-4:
Experiment with blending modes and opacity on shape layers.

Changing the color of the shape

When you create a shape with a shape tool, the shape takes the color of your foreground color. To change the color of an existing shape, open the Layers palette by choosing Window⇨Layers; notice that the Vector Shape tool creates a new layer for every shape you make. This can be a huge benefit when it comes to creating special effects because the shape layer is independent of the rest of your image. (Read more about using layers in Chapter 8 of this minibook).

To change a shape's color, double-click the color thumbnail, on the left in the shape layer. The Color Picker appears, as shown in Figure 4-5. To select a new color, drag the Hue slider up or down or click in the large color pane to select a color with the saturation and lightness that you want to use. Click OK when you're done.

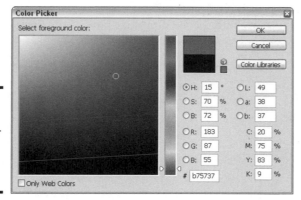

Figure 4-5: Using the Color Picker to assign a new fill color.

Editing a shape

Like Adobe Illustrator, Photoshop provides both a Path Selection tool and a Direct Selection tool. The Direct Selection tool is hidden under the Path Selection tool. To move an entire shape on a layer, choose the Path Selection tool and drag the shape.

To edit the shape, deselect the shape (while using the Path Selection or Direct Selection tool, click outside the shape). Then select the Direct Selection tool. With the Direct Selection tool, click individual anchor points and handles to edit and fine-tune the shape, as shown in Figure 4-6.

Figure 4-6: Edit individual anchor points with the Direct Selection tool.

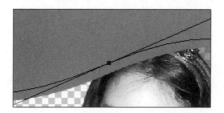

Removing a shape layer

Due to the fact that there are now multiple options with the Pen tool, you may find yourself unexpectedly creating a shape layer. Delete a shape layer by dragging the layer thumbnail to the Trash icon in the lower-right corner of the Layers palette.

If it is important to keep your path, but you want to throw away the shape layer, choose Window⇨Paths. Then drag the shape vector mask to the New Path icon, as shown in Figure 4-7. This creates a saved path. Now you can throw away the shape layer.

Figure 4-7:
Save a shape layer as a path before deleting if you just want the path.

Using a Path as a Selection

You can use the Pen tool to create precise selections that would be difficult to create with other selection methods. The Pen tool produces clean edges that print well and can be edited using the Direct Selection tool. Before using the Pen tool, make sure that you click the Paths button on the Options bar.

The Pen tool works relatively the same in Adobe Photoshop, Illustrator, and InDesign. Read Book III, Chapter 4 to see how to control the paths that you create in Illustrator and Photoshop; check out Book II, Chapter 2 for the basics of using the Pen tool in InDesign. In Photoshop, the only main difference is that you must Alt+click (Windows) or Option+click (Mac) on an anchor point if you're switching from a curved point to a straight path.

To use a path as a selection (this is extremely helpful when you are trying to make a precise selection), follow these steps:

1. **Using the Pen tool (make sure that the Paths button is selected on the Options bar), click to place anchor points; drag to create a curved path around the image area that you want selected; completely close the path by returning to the start point (see Figure 4-8).**

Use the techniques that we discuss in Book III, Chapter 4 to perform this step. A circle will appear before you click to close the path.

Figure 4-8:
Choose the Paths button to create a Pen path with no fill.

2. **Choose Window⇨Paths.**

In the Paths palette, you can create new and activate existing paths, apply a stroke, or turn paths into selections by clicking the icons at the bottom of the palette (see Figure 4-9).

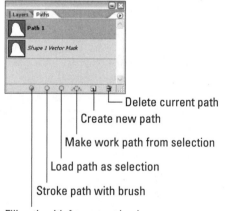

Figure 4-9:
Creating a closed path for a selection.

— Delete current path

Create new path

Make work path from selection

Load path as selection

Stroke path with brush

Fill path with foreground color

3. **Click the Load Path as Selection icon.**

The path is converted into a selection.

Use this quick and easy method for turning an existing path into a selection: Ctrl+click (Windows) or ⌘+click (Mac) the path thumbnail in the Paths palette.

Clipping Paths

If you want to create a beautiful silhouette that transfers well to other applications for text wrapping (see Figure 4-10), create a clipping path.

Figure 4-10:
The Paths
palette.

Creating a clipping path is easy when you have a good path! Just follow these steps:

1. **Use the Pen tool to create a path around the image area that is to be the silhouette.**

2. **In the Paths palette, choose Save Path from the palette menu (click the triangle in the upper-right corner of the palette to access this menu), as shown in Figure 4-11, and then name the path.**

Figure 4-11:
Create
silhouettes
with a
clipping
path to use
in other
applications.

3. **From the same palette menu, choose Clipping Path.**

4. **In the Clipping Paths dialog box, choose your path from the drop-down list if it is not already selected. Leave the Flatness Device Pixels text field blank unless you have a need to change it.**

The flatness value determines how many device pixels are used to create your silhouette. The higher the amount, the less points are created, thereby allowing for faster processing time. This does come at a cost though; set the flatness value too high and you might see (you would have to look really close) straight edges instead of curved edges.

5. **Choose File⇨Save As; in the Save as Type drop-down list, select Photoshop EPS. In the EPS Options dialog box that appears, accept the defaults and click OK.**

If you get PostScript errors when printing, choose Clipping Path from the palette menu and up the value to 2 pixels in the Flatness Device Pixels text field. Keep returning to this text field and upping the value until the file prints, or give up and try printing your document with another printer.

If you're placing this file in other Adobe applications, such as InDesign, it's not necessary to save the file as EPS; you can leave it as a Photoshop (.psd) file.

Chapter 5: Resolution Basics

In This Chapter

✔ Resolution basics

✔ Adjustments to file size

✔ Applying the Unsharp Mask filter to an image

Something as important as getting the right resolution for your images deserves its own chapter, but it isn't all that complex. In this chapter, you discover the necessary resolution for various uses of Photoshop imagery (from printing a high-resolution graphic to e-mailing a picture of your kids to Mom), how to properly increase the resolution, and how to adjust image size. Having the proper resolution is important to the final outcome of your image, especially if you plan to print that image. Combine the information here with using the correction tools that we show you in the next chapter, and you should be ready to roll with great imagery.

Creating Images for Print

To see the present size and resolution of an image in Photoshop, choose Image⇨Image Size. The Image Size dialog box appears, as shown in Figure 5-1.

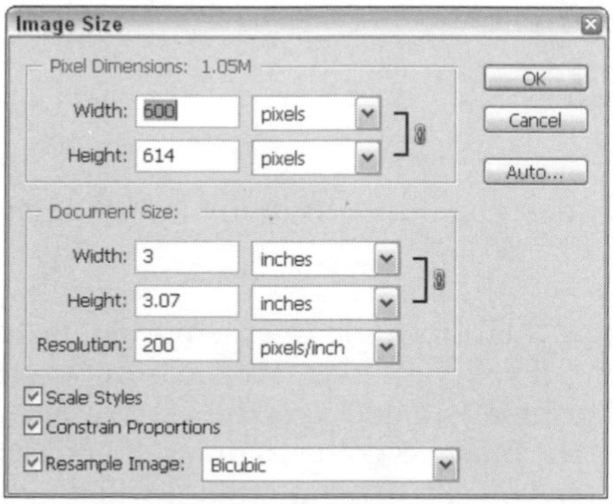

Figure 5-1:
Use the Image Size dialog box to change the pixel size or resolution of an image.

The Width and Height text fields in the Pixel Dimensions area of the Image Size dialog box are used for on-screen resizing, like for the Web and e-mail. The Width and Height text fields in the Document Size area show the size at which the image will print; the Resolution text field determines the resolution of the printed image; a higher value means a smaller, more finely-detailed printed image.

Before you decide upon a resolution, you should understand what some of the resolution jargon means:

✦ **dpi (dots per inch):** The resolution of an image when printed.

✦ **lpi (lines per inch):** The varying dot pattern that printers and presses use to create images (see Figure 5-2). This dot pattern is referred to as the lpi, even though it represents rows of dots. The higher the lpi, the finer the detail and the less of the dot pattern or line screen you see.

✦ **Dot gain:** The spread of ink as it is applied to paper. Certain types of paper will wick a dot of ink farther than others. For example, newsprint has a high dot gain and typically prints at 85 lpi; a coated stock paper has a lower dot gain and can be printed at 133–150 lpi and even higher.

Figure 5-2: The dot pattern used to print images is referred to as lpi.

Human eyes typically can't detect a dot pattern in a printed image at 133 dpi or higher.

So why do you need to know this? Deciding the resolution or dpi of an image requires backwards planning. If you want to create the best possible image, you should know where it will print *before* deciding the resolution. Communicate with your printer service if the image is going to press. If you're sending your image to a high-speed copier, you can estimate that it will handle 100 lpi; a desktop printer will handle 85 lpi to 100 lpi.

The resolution formula

When creating an image for print, keep this formula in mind:

$$2 \_ lpi = dpi \text{ (dots per inch)}$$

This means that if your image is going to press (using 150 lpi), have your image at 300 dpi. To save space, many designers use 1.5 x lpi and get pretty much the same results; you can decide which works best for you.

Changing the resolution

Using the Image Size dialog box is only one of several ways that you can control the resolution in Photoshop. Even though you can increase the resolution, you want to do this sparingly and avoid it if you can. The exception is when you have an image that is large in dimension size but low in resolution, like those that you typically get from a digital camera. You may have a top-of-the-line digital camera that produces 72 dpi images, but at that resolution, the pictures are 28 x 21 inches (or larger)!

Follow these steps to increase the resolution of an image with out depredating the quality:

1. **Choose Image⇨Image Size.**

   The Image Size dialog box appears, as shown in Figure 5-3.

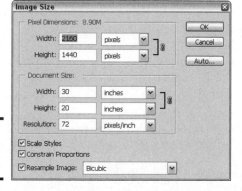

Figure 5-3:
The original
dimensions.

2. **Deselect the Resample Image check box.**

   This way, Photoshop won't add additional pixels.

3. **Enter the desired resolution in the Resolution text field.**

Notice in Figures 5-3 and 5-4 that Photoshop keeps the pixel size (the size of the image on-screen) the same, but the document size (the size of the image when printed) decreases when you enter a higher resolution.

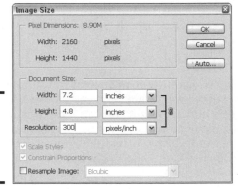

Figure 5-4: After increasing the resolution.

4. **If the image isn't the size that you need it to be, select the Resample Image check box and type the size in the Width and Height text fields in the Document Size section. (Note that it's best to reduce the size of a bitmap image, such as a digital photo, rather than increase it.)**

You can also deselect the Resample Image check box and essentially play a game of give and take to see what the resolution will be when you enter the size you want your image printed at in the Width and Height text fields in the Document Size area.

Images can typically be scaled from 50 percent to 120 percent before looking jagged (to scale by a percentage, select Percent from the drop-down lists beside the Width and Height text fields). Keep this in mind when placing and resizing your images in a page layout application, such as InDesign.

5. **Click OK when you're finished; double-click the Zoom tool in the tool-box to see the image at actual size on-screen.**

To increase the resolution *without* changing the image size, follow these steps (this is not the perfect situation because pixels that don't presently exist are created by Photoshop and may not be totally accurate. Photoshop tries to give you the best image, but you may have some loss of detail):

1. **Choose Image➪Image Size.**

2. **When the Image Size dialog box appears, make sure that the Resample Image check box is selected.**

Note that Bicubic is selected in the method drop-down list. This is the best, but slowest, method to reinterpret pixels when you resize an image. Using this method, Photoshop essentially looks at all the pixels and takes a good guess as to how the newly created pixels should look, based upon surrounding pixels.

3. **Enter the resolution that you need in the Resolution text field, click OK, and then double-click the Zoom tool to see the image at actual size.**

Determining the Resolution for Web Images

Did you ever have somebody e-mail you an image, and after spending 10 minutes downloading it, you discover that the image is so huge that all you can see on the monitor is your nephew's left eye? Many people are under the misconception that if an image is 72 dpi, it's ready for the Web.

Actually, pixel dimension is all that matters for Web viewing of images; this section helps you make sense of this.

Most people view Web pages in their browser windows in an area of about 640 x 480 pixels. You can use this figure as a basis for any images you create for the Web, whether the viewer is using a 14-inch or a 21-inch monitor. (Remember, those people who have large monitors set to high screen resolutions don't necessarily want a Web page taking up the whole screen!) If you're creating images for a Web page or to attach to an e-mail message, you may want to pick a standard size to design by, such as 600 x 400 pixels at 72 dpi.

To use the Image Size dialog box to determine the resolution and size for on-screen images, follow these steps:

1. **Have an image open and choose Image⇨Image Size.**

   The Image Size dialog box appears.

2. **To make the image take up half the width of a typical browser window, type 320 (half of 640) in the top Width text field, as shown in Figure 5-5.**

   If a little chain link is visible to the right, the Constrain Proportions check box is selected, and Photoshop automatically determines the height from the width that you entered.

3. **Click OK and double-click the Zoom tool to see the image at actual size on-screen.**

   That's it! It doesn't matter if your image is 3,000 or 30 pixels wide, as long as you enter the correct dimensions in the Pixel Dimension area, the image will work beautifully.

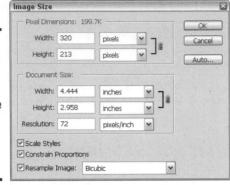

Figure 5-5:
Use propor-
tions of the
total width
to determine
how large
your image
will be
on-screen.

Some people may argue that an image at 300 dpi is larger in file size than the same file would be at 72 dpi; this isn't true! Take a look back at Figures 5-3 and 5-4; Photoshop gives the file size of an image at the top of the Image Size dialog box (right beside Pixel Dimensions). Though the dpi was increased in Figure 5-4, the file size remains the same (9.00MB).

Applying the Unsharp Mask Filter to an Image

When you resample an image in Photoshop, it can become blurry. A good practice is to apply the Unsharp Mask filter. This feature sharpens the image based upon levels of contrast, while keeping the areas that don't have contrasting pixels smooth. The Unsharp Mask filter is a great feature, but you have to set it up correctly to get good results. After resizing an image, choose Filter⇨Sharpen⇨Unsharp Mask to open the Unsharp Mask dialog box.

Here is the down-and-dirty method of using the Unsharp Mask filter:

1. **Choose View⇨Actual Pixels or double-click the Zoom tool.**

   When you're using a filter, you want to view your image at actual size to best see the effect.

2. **Choose Filter⇨Sharpen⇨Unsharp Mask.**

   In the Unsharp Mask dialog box that appears (see Figure 5-6), set these three options:

   - **Amount:** The Amount value ranges from 0–500. The amount that you choose has a lot to do with the subject matter; see Figure 5-7. Sharpening a car or appliance at 300–400 is fine, but do this to the CEO's 75-year-old wife, and you may suffer an untimely death because every wrinkle, mole, or hair will magically become more defined. If you're not sure what to use, start with 150 and play around until you find an Amount value that looks good.

- **Radius:** The Unsharp Mask filter creates a halo around the areas that have enough contrast to be considered an edge. Typically, leaving the amount between 1–2 is fine for print, but if you're creating a billboard or poster, you can increase the size.

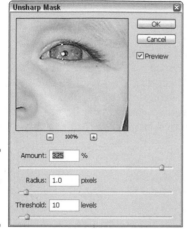

Figure 5-6:
The Unsharp Mask dialog box.

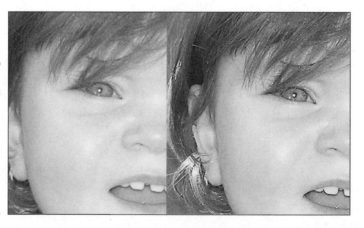

Figure 5-7:
The effect of the Unsharp Mask filter with the Amount value at 50 (left) and 250 (right).

- **Threshold:** This is the most important option in the Unsharp Mask dialog box. The Threshold setting is what determines what should be sharpened. If left at zero, you will see noise throughout the image, much like the grain that you see in high-speed film. Bring it up to 10, and this triggers the Unsharp Mask filter to apply only the sharpening when the pixels are ten shades or more away from each other. The amount of tolerance ranges from 1–255. Apply too much, and no sharpening appears; apply too little, and the image becomes grainy. A good number to start with is 10.

**Book IV
Chapter 5**

Resolution Basics

To compare the original state of the image with the preview of the Unsharp Mask filter's effect in the preview pane of the Unsharp Mask dialog box, click and hold on the image in the Preview pane; this shows the original stat of the image. When you release the mouse button, the unsharp mask is previewed again.

3. **When you've made your choice, click OK.**

   The image appears to have more detail.

Once in a while, stray colored pixels may appear after you apply the Unsharp Mask filter. Get in the habit of choosing Edit⇨Fade Unsharp Mask immediately after applying the Unsharp Mask filter. In the Fade dialog box, select the Luminosity blend mode from the Mode drop-down list, and then click OK. This applies the Unsharp Mask filter to the grays in the image only, thereby eliminating sharpening of colored pixels.

Chapter 6: Creating a Good Image

In This Chapter

✔ **Reading a histogram**

✔ **Setting up for the correction**

✔ **Creating a good tone curve**

✔ **Using an adjustment layer**

*W*ith all the incredible things you can do in Photoshop, it's easy to forget the basics. Yes, you can create incredible compositions with special effects, but if the people look greenish, it detracts from the image. Get in the habit of building good clean images before heading into the artsy filters and fun things. Color correction is not complicated, and if done properly, it will produce magical results in your images. In this chapter, you discover how to use the values you read in the Info palette and use the Curves dialog box to produce quality image corrections.

Reading a Histogram

Before making adjustments, look at the image's histogram to evaluate whether the image has sufficient detail to produce a high-quality image. In Photoshop CS2, choose Window⇨Histogram to show the Histogram palette.

The greater the range of values in the histogram, the greater the detail. Poor images without much information can be difficult, if not impossible, to correct. The Histogram palette also displays the overall distribution of shadows, midtones, and highlights to help you determine which tonal corrections are needed.

Figure 6-1 shows a good full histogram that indicates a smooth transition from one shade to another in the image.

Figure 6-1:
A histogram with lots of information.

Figure 6-2 shows that when a histogram is spread out and has gaps in it, the image is jumping too quickly from one shade to another, producing a poster-ized effect. *Posterization* is that cool effect of reducing multiple tonal values to a limited amount, creating a more defined range of values from one shade to another. Great if you want it, yucky if you want a smooth tonal change from one shadow to another.

Figure 6-2:
A not-so-good histogram.

So how do you get a good histogram? Make sure if you're scanning that your scanner is set for the maximum amount of colors. Scanning at 16 shades of gray will give you 16 lines in your histogram . . . not good!

If you have a bad histogram, we recommend that you rescan or reshoot the image. If you have a good histogram to start with, keep the histogram good by not messing around with multiple tone correction tools. Most professionals use curves . . . and that's it. Curves, if used properly, do all that adjusting the levels, brightness and contrast, and color balance, all in one step. Read more about curves later in this chapter.

Figure 6-3 shows what happens to a perfectly good histogram when someone gets a little too zealous and uses the entire plethora of color correction controls in Photoshop. Just because they're there doesn't mean that you have to use them.

Figure 6-3:
The his-
togram
as it goes
through too
many color
corrections.

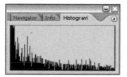

If you see a Warning sign appear when making adjustments, double-click anywhere on the histogram to refresh the display.

Key types

Don't panic if your histogram is smashed all the way to the left or right. The bars of the histogram represent tonal values. You can break down the types of images, based upon their values, into three key types:

✦ **High key:** A very light-colored image, such as the image shown in Figure 6-4. Information is pushed towards the right in the histogram. Color correction has to be handled a little differently for these images to keep the light appearance to them.

✦ **Low key:** A very dark image, such as the image shown in Figure 6-5. Information is pushed to the left in the histogram. This type of image is difficult to scan on low-end scanners because the dark areas tend to blend together with little definition.

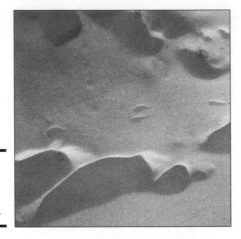

Figure 6-4:
A high key image is a light image.

Figure 6-5:
A low key image is a dark image.

✦ **Mid key:** A typical image with a full range of shades would be considered mid key, such as the image shown in Figure 6-6. These are the most common and easiest images to work with. In this chapter, we deal with images that are considered mid key.

Setting up the correction

To produce the best possible image, try to avoid correcting in CMYK mode. If your images are typically in RGB or LAB mode, keep them in that mode throughout the process. Convert them to CMYK only when you're finished manipulating the image.

Figure 6-6:
A typical image with a full range of values is a mid key image.

Don't forget! Press Ctrl+Y (Windows) or ⌘+Y (Mac) to toggle on and off the CMYK preview, so that you can see what your image will look like in CMYK mode without converting it!

Set up these items before starting any color correction:

1. **Select the Eyedropper tool. On the Options bar, change the sample size from Point Sample to 3 by 3 Average in the Sample Size drop-down list.**

   This gives you more accurate readings.

2. **If the Histogram palette isn't already visible, choose Window➪ Histogram.**

3. **If the Info palette isn't already visible, choose Window➪Info to show the Info palette so that you can check values.**

4. **Make sure that your color settings are correct.**

   If you're not sure how, Chapter 2 of this minibook gives you the lowdown.

Creating a Good Tone Curve

A tone curve represents the density of an image. To get the best image, you must first find the highlight and shadow points in the image. An image created in less-than-perfect lighting conditions could be washed out or have odd color casts. See Figure 6-7 for an example of an image with no set highlight and shadow. Check out Figure 6-8 to see an image that went through the process of setting a highlight and shadow.

Figure 6-7:
The image before setting highlight and shadow is too murky.

Figure 6-8:
The image after setting highlight and shadow is crisper.

To make the process of creating a good tone curve more manageable, we've broken the process into four parts:

✦ Finding the highlight and shadow

✦ Setting the highlight and shadow

✦ Adjusting the midtone

✦ Finding a neutral

Even though each part has its own set of steps, you must go through all four parts to accomplish the task of creating a good tone curve (unless you're working with grayscale images, in which case you can skip the neutral part).

Finding highlight and shadow

In the conventional (noncomputer) world, you would spend a fair amount of time trying to locate the lightest and darkest part of an image. Fortunately, you can cheat in Photoshop by using the Threshold feature:

1. **Choose Image➪Adjustments➪Threshold.**

The Threshold dialog box appears, as shown in Figure 6-9. Use this dialog box to determine which gray values in an image are shifted to white or black, somewhat like what a copier might do to a photograph. By dragging the triangle at the bottom of the Threshold dialog box, you can use threshold to find the lightest and darkest points of an image.

2. **Drag the triangle to the left (the last part of the image showing is the darkest part of the image); position your cursor over the darkest point and Shift+click.**

This drops a color sampler that is only visible to you (it doesn't appear in the printed image), as shown in Figure 6-9. You will use this color sampler later to set the shadow. The color sampler is simply a marker to define a location in your image. You'll reference it again later.

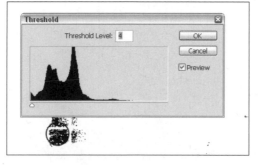

Figure 6-9: Shift+click the darkest area to leave a color sampler.

3. **Drag the triangle to the right to find the highlight of the image (it will also be the last part of the image showing); position the cursor over that area and Shift+click to leave a color sampler there as well, as shown in Figure 6-10. Don't click OK!**

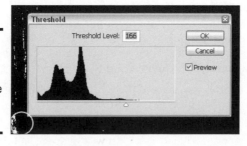

Figure 6-10: Shift+click the lightest area to leave a color sampler.

The reason why Auto Color, Auto Curves, and Auto Levels don't always give you the best result is because those features automatically pick the lightest point in the image as the highlight. This is not always necessarily good. If a specular highlight is picked as the highlight, your image will remain washed out because it is defining the bright point as the start of the tone curve. A *specular highlight* is a reflection off of metal, glass, jewelry, or even flames of candles, as shown in Figure 6-11. When looking for the lightest point on your image, select and deselect the Preview check box to make sure that you're not selecting a specular highlight. If you are, move the triangle slider more to the left to find the next lightest item.

Figure 6-11: An example of an image with lots of specular highlights.

4. Click Cancel to close the Threshold dialog box.

You don't really want this effect applied to your image, and you can use these color samplers in the next set of steps.

Setting the highlight and shadow

After you have found and marked the highlight and shadow of your image (see preceding steps), define them by using the Curves dialog box:

1. Choose Image⇨Adjustments⇨Curves.

The Curves dialog box appears; note the Eyedropper buttons in the lower-right corner (see Figure 6-12).

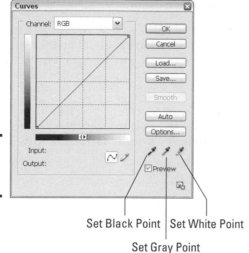

Figure 6-12:
The Curves dialog box.

Set Black Point | Set White Point

Set Gray Point

2. **Double-click the Set White Point button and input these typical values in the Color Picker dialog box (see Figure 6-13):**

   - Cyan (the C text field) = 5
   - Magenta (the M text field) = 3
   - Yellow (the Y text field) = 3
   - Black (the K text field) = 0

   If you're working on a grayscale image, you can just type **4** into the Black text field and leave the rest at zero.

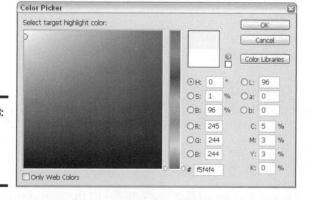

Figure 6-13:
Input the values into the CMYK text fields.

3. **Click OK to close the Color Picker dialog box, but leave the Curves dialog box open.**

   The values specified in Step 2 are typical for an image being printed on coated stock, but can also be used if your images are on-screen only. If you're going to press with your image, get the proper values from your print service provider.

4. **If your color settings are set up correctly, you won't have to change your black point settings. If you want to use typical values, double-click the Set Black Point button and enter the following values:**

   - Cyan (the C text field) = 65

   - Magenta (the M text field) = 53

   - Yellow (the Y text field) = 51

   - Black (the K text field) = 95

   If you're working on a grayscale image, just type **95** into the Black text field and leave the rest at zero.

5. **Choose the Set White Point Eyedropper (refer to Figure 6-12) and click on the color sampler that you created when you used the Threshold dialog box to find the lightest part of the image (see the preceding set of steps).**

6. **Choose the Set Black Point Eyedropper and click on the color sampler that you created to indicate the darkest part of the image (also in the preceding set of steps). Don't click OK!**

If you get really crazy results, you may have switched the shadow with the highlight and turned your image inside out (oops!). While the Curves dialog window is still open, reset the Curves dialog box by holding down the Alt (Windows) or Option (Mac) key; the Cancel button will change to the Reset button. Click the Reset button to return to the original values, and start over.

You have now set your highlight and shadow, but you're not quite done creating the tone curve. Keep the Curves dialog box open to adjust the midtone.

Adjusting the midtone

You may have heard the statement, "Open up the midtones." This essentially means that you're lightening the midtonal values of an image. In many cases, this is necessary to add contrast and bring out detail in your image.

To adjust the midtones, follow these steps:

1. **In the Curves dialog box, click the middle of the curve ramp to create an anchor point; drag up slightly.**

   This lightens the image, as shown in Figure 6-14. (If you're in CMYK mode, drag down to lighten the image.) Don't move a dramatic amount, and be very careful to observe what is happening in your Histogram palette (which you should always have open when making color corrections).

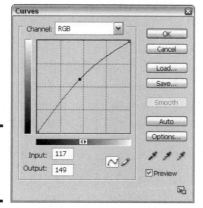

Figure 6-14:
Adjusting the midtones.

When the Preview check box is selected in the Curves dialog box (refer to Figure 6-14), the Histogram palette gives you a glimpse into how the corrections you're making will affect the histogram, as shown in Figure 6-15. Because you set highlight and shadow, and are now making a midtone correction, you will see the bars in the histogram spreading out. This is necessary to a point, and the reason why you don't click OK until *all steps* have been taken in the Curves dialog box.

Figure 6-15:
The existing histogram is in gray.

2. **To adjust the three-quarter tones (the shades around 75 percent), click halfway between the bottom of the curve ramp and the midpoint to set an anchor point.**

Use the grid in the Curves dialog box to find it easily. (In CMYK, the three-quarter point is in the upper section of the color ramp.) Adjust this up or down slightly to create contrast in the image. Again, keep an eye on your histogram!

3. **If you're working on a color image, don't click OK and keep the Curves dialog box open for the final step. If you're working on a grayscale image, your tonal correction is done. You can click OK.**

Finding a neutral

The last step in creating a tone curve only applies if you're working on a color image. The key to understanding color is knowing that equal amounts of color create gray. By positioning the mouse cursor over gray areas in an image and reading the values in the Info palette, you can determine what colors need to be adjusted.

1. **With your Curves dialog box still open, position it so that you can see the Info palette.**

If the Info palette is buried under another palette or a dialog box, choose Window⇨Info to hide it and then choose Window⇨Info again to bring it to the front.

2. **In the Info palette, look for the RGB values in the upper-left section.**

You'll see color values, and then forward slashes and more color values (see Figure 6-16). The numbers before the slash indicate the values in the image before you opened the Curves dialog box; the numbers after the slash show the values now that you have made changes in the Curves dialog box. Pay attention to the values after the slashes.

Pay attention
to these values

Figure 6-16:
Pay atten-
tion to what
is happening
to the num-
bers *after*
the forward
slashes.

3. **Position the cursor over something gray in your image.**

This could be a shadow on a white shirt, a counter top, a road, anything that is a shade of gray. Look at the Info palette. If your image is perfectly color balanced, the RGB values following the forward slashes should all be the same, as shown in the lower-left corner of Figure 6-17.

Figure 6-17: A neutral gray has close to equal amounts of red, green, and blue in it.

4. **If your color is not balanced, click the Set Gray Point Eyedropper in the Curves dialog box and click the neutral or gray area of the image.**

   The middle eyedropper (Set Gray Point) is a handy way of bringing the location that you click on closer together in RGB values, thereby balancing the colors.

5. **Now you can click OK; when asked if you want to save your color target values, click Yes.**

This concludes the fast track to color correction. Curves can be as complex or simple as you make them. As you gain more confidence using them, you can check neutrals throughout an image to ensure that all unwanted color casts are eliminated. You can even individually adjust each color's curve by selecting them from the Channel drop-down list in the Curves dialog box.

When you're finished with color correction, using the Unsharp Mask filter on your image is a good idea. Chapter 5 of this minibook shows you how to use this filter.

Using an Adjustment Layer

You may go through a curve adjustment only to discover that some areas of the image are still too dark or too light. If this is the case, you're better off using an *adjustment layer,* which is a layer that adjusts a selected area of your image, based upon a correction applied on the layer. By using an adjustment layer, you can turn off the correction or change it over and over again with no degradation to the quality of the image. You can apply an adjustment layer by following these steps:

1. **Select the area of the image that needs adjustments.**

   See Chapter 3 of this minibook if you need a refresher on how to make selections in Photoshop.

2. **Choose Select⇨Feather to soften the selection.**

   The Feather dialog box appears. If you're not sure what value will work best, enter **15** in the Feather Radius text field and click OK.

3. **If the Layers palette isn't visible, choose Windows⇨Layers; click and hold on the Create New Fill or Adjustment Layer icon (it looks like a half moon; see Figure 6-18) and select Curves from the menu that appears.**

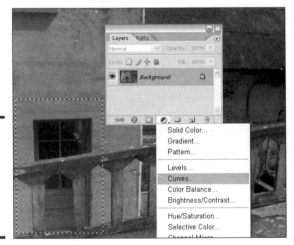

Figure 6-18: Apply a curve correction using an adjustment layer.

4. **In the Curves dialog box, click the middle of the curve ramp to create an anchor point; drag up or down to lighten or darken your selected area. Click OK.**

   Notice in the Layers palette (see Figure 6-19) that your adjustment layer, named Curves 1, has a mask to the right of it. The selected area is white; unselected areas are black.

5. **With your adjustment layer selected in the Layers palette, use the Brush tool to paint white to apply the correction to other areas of the image; paint with black to exclude areas from the correction.**

   You can even change the opacity using the Brush tool Options bar at the top to apply only some of the correction!

Figure 6-19:
Paint white
on the
adjustment
layer mask
to apply the
curve to
other areas.

Testing a Printer

If you go through all of the work of making color corrections to your images and you still get printed images that look hot pink, it may not be you! Test your printer by following these steps:

1. **Create a neutral gray out of equal RGB values (double-click the Fill color swatch in the toolbar).**

2. **Create a shape (for example, you could use the Ellipse tool to create a circle or oval), using your neutral gray as the fill color.**

3. **Choose File⇨Print and click OK to print the image from your color printer.**

   If you're seeing heavy color casts, you need to adjust your printer; cleaning or replacing the ink cartridge may fix the problem. Check out Chapter 9 of this minibook for more about printing your Photoshop files.

**Book IV
Chapter 6**

**Creating a
Good Image**

Chapter 7: Painting and Retouching Tools

In This Chapter

✓ Getting to know foreground and background colors

✓ Using the Swatches palette

✓ Introducing the Spot Healing Brush, Brush, Clone Stamp, History Brush, Eraser, and Gradient tools

✓ Discovering blending modes

This chapter shows you how to use the painting and retouching tools in Photoshop. If you're unsure about how good the painting you're about to do will look, create a new layer and paint on that. (See Chapter 8 of this minibook to find out how to create and use layers.) That way, you can delete the layer by dragging it to the trash if you make any horrible mistakes. Don't forget to make the Eraser tool your friend! You can also repair painting or retouching mistakes by Alt+dragging (Windows) or Option+dragging (Mac) with the Eraser tool selected to erase to the last version saved or history state.

Have fun and be creative! Because Photoshop is pixel-based, you can create incredible imagery with the painting tools. Smooth gradations from one color to the next integrated with blending modes and transparency can lead from super-artsy to super-realistic effects. In this chapter, you discover painting fundamentals, and we show you how to use retouching tools to eliminate wrinkles, blemishes, and scratches . . . don't you wish you could do that in real life?

The Painting Tools

Grouped together in the toolbox (shown in Figure 7-1) are the tools used for painting and retouching. In this chapter, we show you how the Spot Healing Brush, Brush, Clone Stamp, History Brush, Eraser, and Gradient tools work. You also discover ways to fill shapes with colors and patterns.

Figure 7-1:
The Painting and retouching tools in Photoshop CS2.

Changing the brush

As you click to select different painting tools, note the Brush menu, second from the left, on the Options bar, as shown in Figure 7-2. Click the arrow to open the Brush Preset Picker and scroll to choose the brush you want. Then use the Master Diameter slider to make the brush size larger or smaller.

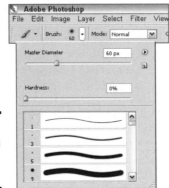

Figure 7-2:
The Brushes Preset Picker.

Choose from other brushes libraries using the palette menu (click the triangle in the upper-right corner of the Brushes Preset Picker). When you select an additional library, a dialog box appears, asking if you want to replace the current brushes with the brushes in the selected library, as shown in Figure 7-3. Click the Append button to keep existing brushes and add the library to the list, or click OK to replace the existing brushes.

Figure 7-3:
Click the Append button to add additional brushes.

Access the Brushes Preset picker as you're painting by right-clicking (Windows) or Control+clicking (Mac) anywhere in the image area. Double-click a brush to select it; press Esc to hide the Brushes palette.

Choosing foreground and background colors

At the bottom of the toolbox reside the foreground and background color swatches. The foreground color is the color that you apply when using any of the painting tools. The background color is the color that you see if you erase or delete pixels from the image.

Choose a foreground or background color by clicking the swatch. This opens the Color Picker dialog box. To use the color picker, you can either enter values in the text fields on the right, or you can slide the hue slider, as shown in Figure 7-4.

Hue slider

Figure 7-4:
Use the slider to the right to pick a hue, and then click in the color pane to select a color.

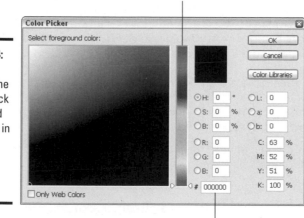

Hexidecimal color

Book IV
Chapter 7

Painting and Retouching Tools

Pick the hue (color) that you want to start with, and then click in the color pane to the left to choose the amount of light and saturation (grayness or brightness) you want in the color. Select the Only Web Colors check box to choose one of the 216 colors in the Web safe color palette. The hexadecimal value used in HTML documents appears in the text field in the lower right of the color picker.

Using the Swatches Palette

Use the Swatches palette to store and retrieve frequently used colors. The Swatches palette, shown in Figure 7-5, allows you to quickly select colors.

Figure 7-5:
The Swatches palette allows you to store and reselect colors.

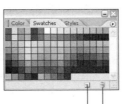

Add new swatch Delete selected swatch

The Swatches palette also gives you access to many other color options. By using the palette menu, you can select from a multitude of different color schemes, such as Pantone or Web-safe color sets. These color systems are converted to whatever color mode in which you are working.

To sample and then store a color for later use, follow these steps:

1. **To sample a color from an image, select the Eyedropper tool in the toolbox and click a color on the image.**

Alternatively, you can use any of the paint tools, the Brush tool for example, and Alt+click (Windows) or Option+click (Mac).

The color you click becomes the foreground color.

2. **Store the color in the Swatches palette by clicking the New Swatch button at the bottom of the Swatches palette (refer to Figure 7-4).**

Anytime you want to use that color again, simply click it in the Swatches palette to make it the foreground color.

The New Spot Healing Brush Tool

The Spot Healing Brush tool is destined to become everyone's favorite. Who wouldn't love a tool that can remove years from your face and any leftover teenage acne as well?

The Spot Healing Brush tool quickly removes blemishes and other imperfections in your images. Click on a blemish and watch it paint matching texture, lighting, transparency, and shading to the pixels being healed. The Spot Healing

Brush doesn't require you to specify a sample spot. The Spot Healing Brush automatically samples from around the retouched area.

The Healing Brush Tool

The Healing Brush tool can be used for repairs too, such as eliminating scratches and dust from scanned images. Figure 7-6 shows the miraculous effects of using the Healing Brush tool. The difference between the Spot Healing Brush Tool and the Healing Brush is that a sample spot is required before applying the Healing Brush. Follow these steps to use this tool:

1. **Select the Healing Brush tool in the toolbox (hidden tool of the Spot Healing Brush tool).**

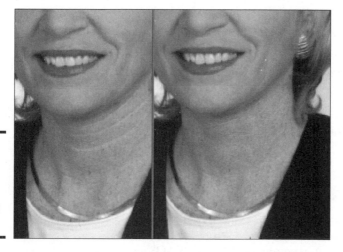

Figure 7-6: The before and after magic of the Healing Brush tool.

2. **Find an area in the image that looks good and then Alt+click (Windows) or Option+click (Mac) to sample that area.**

For instance, if you're going to eliminate wrinkles on a face, choose a wrinkle-free area of skin near the wrinkle. (Try to keep it relatively close in skin tone.)

3. **Position the mouse cursor over the area to be repaired and start painting.**

The Healing Brush tool goes into action, blending and softening to create a realistic repair of the area.

4. **Repeat Steps 2 and 3 as necessary to repair the blemish, wrinkles, or scratches.**

The Patch Tool

 Hidden behind the Healing Brush tool in the toolbox is the Patch tool. Use the Patch tool to repair larger areas, such as a big scratch or a large area of skin, by following these steps:

1. **Click and hold the Healing Brush tool to select the Patch tool; on the Options bar, select the Destination radio button.**

   You can either patch the source area or the destination. The preference is really up to you. We recommend taking a good source and dragging it over the location of the image that needs to be repaired.

2. **With the Patch tool still selected, drag to create a marquee around the source that you want to use as the patch.**

   The source would be an unscratched or wrinkle-free area.

3. **After you create the marquee, drag the selected source area to the destination that is to be repaired.**

   The Patch tool clones the selected source area as you drag it to the destination (the scratched area); when you release the mouse button, the tool blends in the source selection and repairs the scratched area!

 Make the patch look even better by choosing Edit➪Fade immediately after you apply the patch. Adjust the opacity until there are no tell-tale signs that you made a change.

The New Red Eye Tool

 So you finally got the group together and shot the perfect image, but "red eye" took over! Red eye is caused by a reflection of the camera's flash in the retina of your photo's subject(s). You'll see it more often when taking pictures in a dark room because the subject's iris is wide open. If you can, use your camera's red eye reduction feature. Or, better yet, use a separate flash unit that you can mount on the camera farther away from the camera's lens.

You will love the fact that red eye is extremely easy to fix in Photoshop CS2. Just follow these steps:

1. **Select the Red Eye tool (hidden behind the Spot Healing Brush tool).**

2. **Click on a red eye.**

   It should work immediately, but if you need to make adjustments to the size or the darkness amount, you can change options in the tool options bar at the top of your work area.

The Brush Tool

 Painting with the Brush tool in Photoshop is much like painting in the real world. What you should know are all of the nifty keyboard commands that you can use to be much more productive when painting. These are really great, so make sure you try them as you read about them. By the way, the keyboard commands you see in Table 7-1 work on all the painting tools.

Table 7-1	Brush Keyboard Shortcuts	
Function	*Windows*	*Mac*
Choose the Brush tool	B	B
Increase brush size	]	]
Decrease brush size	[	[
Harden brush	Shift+]	Shift+]
Soften brush	Shift+[	Shift+[
Sample color	Alt+click	Option+click
Switch foreground and background color	X	X
Change opacity by a given percentage	Type a number between 1 and 100	Type a number between 1 and 100

The Brushes palette

If you're really into the brushes, you have lots of great options available in the Brushes palette (choose Window⇨Brushes to open the palette).

You have the following choices of attributes, most of which have dynamic controls in the menu options that allow you to vary brush characteristics by tilting or applying more pressure to a stylus pen (if you're using a pressure-sensitive drawing tablet), among other things, as shown in Figure 7-7.

Note: A warning sign indicates that you don't have the appropriate device attached to use the selected feature, such as a pressure-sensitive drawing tablet.

The following options are available in the Brushes palette:

✦ **Brush Tip Shape:** Select from these standard controls for determining brush dimensions and spacing.

✦ **Shape Dynamics:** Change the size of the brush as you paint.

✦ **Scattering:** Scatter the brush strokes and control brush tip count.

+ **Texture:** Choose a texture from pre-existing patterns or your own.

Create a pattern by selecting an image area with the Rectangular Marquee tool. Choose Edit⇨Define Pattern, name the pattern, and then click OK. The pattern is now available in the Brush palettes Texture choices.

+ **Dual Brush:** Use two brushes at the same time.

+ **Color Dynamics:** Change the color as you paint.

+ **Other Dynamics:** Change the opacity and flow.

Figure 7-7: Setting the dynamic controls.

If you have been using Photoshop for several versions, you may notice that with Photoshop CS2, the attributes at the bottom of the Brushes palette are not necessarily new, but have been moved from their old positions on the Options bar. Here is what these attributes do:

+ **Noise:** Adds a grainy texture to the brush stroke.

+ **Wet Edges:** Makes the brush stroke appear to be wet by creating a heavier amount of color on the edges of the brush strokes.

+ **Airbrush:** Gives airbrush features to the Brush tools (there is no longer a standalone Airbrush tool as in previous versions of Photoshop). You can also turn on the Airbrush feature by clicking the Airbrush button, and adjusting the pressure and flow on the Options bar.

If you click and hold with the Brush tool out on the image area, the paint stops spreading. Turn on the Airbrush feature, and notice that when you click and hold, the paint keeps spreading, just like with a can of spray paint. You can use the Flow slider on the Options bar to control the pressure.

✦ **Smoothing:** Smoothes the path that you create with the mouse.

✦ **Protect Texture:** Preserves the texture pattern when applying brush presets.

In addition to the preceding options, you can also adjust the jitter of the brush. The *jitter* specifies the randomness of the brush attribute. At 0 percent, an element does not change over the course of a stroke; at 100 percent, a stroke will totally vary from one attribute to another. For instance, if you select Other Dynamics in the Brushes palette, and then change the Opacity Jitter to 100 percent, the opacity will vary from 0–100 percent while you're painting.

Saving presets

After going through all the available options, you may want to start thinking about how you will apply the same attributes later. Saving the Brush tool attributes will become very important to you as you increase in skill level.

All the Photoshop tools allow you to save presets so that you can retrieve them from a list of presets. The following steps show you an example of saving a Brush tool preset, but the same method can be used for all other tools as well:

1. **Choose a brush size, color, softness, or anything!**

2. **Click the Tool Preset Picker button on the left side of the Options bar.**

The preset menu for that tool appears.

3. **Click the triangle in the upper-right corner to access the flyout menu; choose New Tool Preset from this menu.**

The New Tool Preset dialog box appears, as shown in Figure 7-8.

4. **Type a descriptive name in the Name text field (leave the Include Color check box selected if you want the preset to also remember the present color), and then click OK.**

Your preset is created and saved.

5. **Access the preset by clicking the tool's Preset Picker button and choosing it from the tool's Preset Picker list, as shown in Figure 7-9.**

Figure 7-8:
Saving
the brush
attributes,
including
color.

Figure 7-9:
Choosing a
preset from
the Brush
Preset
Picker.

Each preset that you create is specific to the tool that it was created in, so you can have a crop preset, an eraser preset, and so on. After you get in the habit of saving presets, you'll wonder how you ever got along without them!

The Clone Stamp Tool

 The Clone Stamp tool is used for pixel-to-pixel cloning. It's different from the Healing Brush tool in that it does no automatic blending into the target area. The Clone Stamp tool could be used for removing a product name from an image, replacing a telephone wire that is crossing in front of a building, or to duplicate an item.

Here is how you use the Clone Stamp tool:

1. **With the Clone Stamp tool selected, position the cursor over the area that you want to clone, and then Alt+click (Windows) or Option+click (Mac) to define the clone source.**

2. **Position the cursor over the area where you want to paint the cloned pixels and start painting.**

   Note the cross hair back at the original sampled area, as shown in Figure 7-10. As you're painting, the cross hair follows the pixels that you're cloning.

 When using the Clone Stamp tool for touching up images, it's best to resample many times so as to not leave a seam where you replaced pixels. A good clone stamper Alt+clicks (Windows) or Option+clicks (Mac) and paints many times over until the retouching is complete.

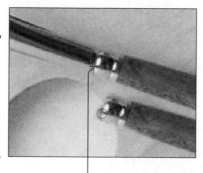

Figure 7-10:
A cross hair over the source target shows what you're cloning.

The cross hair shows what you are cloning

The History Brush Tool

Choose Window⇨History to see the History palette. You could work for weeks playing around in the History palette, but this section gives you the basics.

At the top of the History palette is a snapshot of the last saved version of the image. Beside the snapshot is an icon noting that it's the present History state, as shown in Figure 7-11.

Figure 7-11:
The brush icon indicates the source for the History Brush tool.

 This means that when you paint with the History Brush tool, it will paint back to the way the image looked at that state. By default, this is the last saved version, but you can click on the empty square to the left of any state in the History palette to make it the target for the History Brush tool.

In Figure 7-12, several filters were applied and the state was changed to erase back to the Graphic Pen filter.

Figure 7-12: An image painted back to a history state using the History Brush tool.

Use the History Brush tool to fix errors and to add some spunk to your images.

The Eraser Tool

 You might not think of the Eraser tool as a painting tool . . . but it can be! When you drag on the image with the Eraser tool, it rubs out pixels to the background color (basically, it paints with the background color). If you're dragging with the Eraser tool on a layer, it rubs out pixels to reveal the layer's transparent background (you can also think of it as painting with transparency).

The Eraser tool uses all the same commands as the Brush tools. You can make an eraser larger, softer, and more or less opaque. But even better, follow these steps to use the Eraser tool creatively:

1. **Open any color image and apply a filter.**

For example, we chose Filter⇨Blur⇨Gaussian Blur. In the Gaussian Blur dialog box that appeared, we changed the blur to 5, and then clicked OK to apply the Gaussian Blur filter.

2. **Select the Eraser tool and press 5 to change it to 50 percent opacity.**

You can also use the Opacity slider on the Options bar.

3. **Hold down the Alt (Windows) or Option (Mac) key to paint back 50 percent of the original image's state before applying the filter; continue painting in the same area to bring the image back to its original state!**

In Figure 7-13, you can see that the original sharpness of the image came back where we painted.

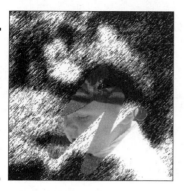

Figure 7-13: Alt+click or Option+click with the Eraser tool to bring back the image's original state.

Holding down the Alt (Windows) or Option (Mac) key is the key command to erase to the last saved version (or history state) of the image. This is an incredible tool for fixing little mistakes, or when you applied cool filters and you want to bring back some of the original image.

The Gradient Tool

Choose the Gradient tool and click and drag across an image area to create a gradient in the direction and length of the mouse motion. A short drag creates a short gradient, a long drag produces a smoother, longer gradient.

Using the Options bar, you can also choose the type of gradient that you want: Linear, Radial, Angle, Reflected, or Diamond.

As a default, gradients are created using the current foreground and background colors. Click the arrow on the gradient button on the Options bar to assign a different preset gradient, as shown in Figure 7-14.

Gradient preset picker

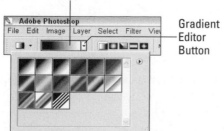

Gradient Editor Button

Figure 7-14: Choosing and editing gradients.

To create a gradient, follow these steps:

1. **Choose the Gradient tool and click the Gradient Editor button on the Options bar.**

   The Gradient Editor dialog box appears. At the bottom of the gradient preview, you see two or more stops. The stops are where new colors are inserted into the gradient. They look like little house icons. Use the stops on the top of the gradient slider to determine the opacity.

2. **Click a stop and click on the color swatch to the right of the word Color to open the color picker and assign a different color to the stop.**

3. **Click anywhere below the gradient preview to add additional color stops.**

4. **Drag a color stop off the Gradient Editor dialog box to delete it.**

5. **Click on the top of the gradient preview to assign different stops with varying amounts of opacity, as shown in Figure 7-15.**

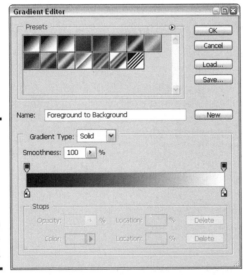

Figure 7-15: Assigning varying amounts of opacity using the stops on top of the gradient preview.

6. **When you're finished editing the gradient, name it, and then click the New button.**

   The new gradient is added to the preset gradient choices.

7. **To apply your gradient, drag across a selection or image using the Gradient tool.**

Blending Modes

Blending modes can be used to add some flair to the traditional opaque paint. Use blending modes to paint highlights or shadows that allow details to show through from the underlying image, or to colorize a desaturated image. You access the blending modes for paint tools from the Options bar.

You really can't get a good idea of how the blending mode will work with the paint color and the underlying color until you experiment. (That's what multiple undos are for!) Alternatively, you can copy the image you want to experiment with onto a new layer and hide the original layer; see Chapter 8 of this minibook for more about layers. The following list describes the available blending modes:

- ✦ **Normal:** Paints normally, with no interaction with underlying colors.

- ✦ **Dissolve:** Gives a random replacement of the pixels, depending on the opacity at any pixel location.

- ✦ **Behind:** Edits or paints only on the transparent part of a layer.

- ✦ **Darken:** Replaces only the areas that are lighter than the blend color. Areas darker than the blend color don't change.

- ✦ **Multiply:** Creates an effect similar to drawing on the page with magic markers. Also looks like colored film that you see on theatre lights.

- ✦ **Color Burn:** Darkens the base color to reflect the blend color. If you're using white, there is no change.

- ✦ **Linear Burn:** Looks at the color information in each channel and darkens the base color to reflect the blending color by decreasing the brightness.

- ✦ **Lighten:** Replaces only the areas darker than the blend color. Areas lighter than the blend color don't change.

- ✦ **Screen:** Multiplies the inverse of the underlying colors. The resulting color is always a lighter color.

- ✦ **Color Dodge:** Brightens the underlying color to reflect the blend color. If you're using black, there is no change.

- ✦ **Linear Dodge:** Looks at the color information in each channel and brightens the base color to reflect the blending color by increasing the brightness.

- ✦ **Overlay:** Multiplies or screens the colors, depending on the base color.

- ✦ **Soft Light:** Darkens or lightens the colors, depending on the blend color. The effect is similar to shining a diffused spotlight on the artwork.

✦ **Hard Light:** Multiplies or screens the colors, depending on the blend color. The effect is similar to shining a harsh spotlight on the artwork.

✦ **Vivid Light:** Burns or dodges the colors by increasing or decreasing the contrast.

✦ **Linear Light:** Burns or dodges the colors by decreasing or increasing the brightness.

✦ **Pin Light:** Replaces the colors, depending on the blend color.

✦ **Hard Mix:** Paints strokes that have no effect with other Hard Mix paint strokes. Use this when you want no interaction between the colors.

✦ **Difference:** Subtracts either the blend color from the base color or the base color from the blend color, depending on which has the greater brightness value. The effect is similar to a color negative.

✦ **Exclusion:** Creates an effect similar to but with less contrast than the Difference mode.

✦ **Hue:** Applies the hue (color) of the blend object onto the underlying objects but keeps the underlying shading or luminosity intact.

✦ **Saturation:** Applies the saturation of the blend color but uses the luminance and hue of the base color.

✦ **Color:** Applies the blend object's color to the underlying objects but preserves the gray levels in the artwork. This is great for tinting objects or changing their colors.

✦ **Luminosity:** Creates a resulting color with the hue and saturation of the base color and the luminance of the blend color. This is essentially the opposite of the Color mode.

Painting with color

This section provides an example of using the blending modes to change and add color to an image. A great example of using a blending mode is tinting a black and white (grayscale) image with color. You can't paint color in Grayscale mode, so follow these steps to add color to a black-and-white image:

1. **Open an image in any color mode and choose Image⇨Adjustments⇨ Mode⇨RGB.**

2. **If the image isn't already a grayscale image, choose Image⇨ Adjustments⇨Desaturate.**

   This feature makes it appear as though the image is black and white, but you're still in a color mode with which you can apply color.

3. **Choose a painting tool (the Brush tool, for instance) and, using the Swatches palette, choose the first color that you want to paint with.**

4. **On the Options bar, select Color from the Mode drop-down list, and then use the Opacity slider to change the opacity to 50 percent.**

   You could also just type **5**.

5. **Start painting!**

   The Color blending mode is used to change the color of the pixels, while keeping the underlying grayscale (shading) intact.

Another way to bring attention to a certain item in an RGB image (like those cute greeting cards that have the single rose in color and everything else in black and white) is to select the item you want to bring attention to. Choose Select➪Feather to soften the selection a bit (5 pixels is a good number to enter in the Feather Radius text field). Then choose Select➪Inverse. Now with everything else selected, choose Image➪Adjustments➪Desaturate. Everything else in the image looks black and white, except for the original item that you selected.

Filling selections

If you have a definite shape that does not lend itself to being painted, you can fill it with color instead. Make a selection and choose Edit➪Fill to access the Fill dialog box, shown in Figure 7-16. From the Use drop-down list, you can choose from the following options to fill the selection: Foreground Color, Background Color, Color (to open the color picker while in the Fill dialog box) Pattern, History, Black, 50% Gray, or White.

Figure 7-16:
The Fill
dialog box.

**Book IV
Chapter 7**

**Painting and
Retouching Tools**

If you have created a pattern for the Brushes palette, you can retrieve a pattern by using the Fill dialog box as well. Select History from the Use drop-down list to fill with the last version saved or the history state.

If you would rather use the Paint Bucket tool, which fills based upon the tolerance set on the Options bar, it is hidden in the Gradient tool.

To use the Paint Bucket tool to fill with the foreground color, simply click the item that you want to fill. This is not as exact as when you use the Fill dialog box, but it's good for filling solid areas quickly.

Chapter 8: Using Layers

In This Chapter

✔ **Discovering layers**

✔ **Using type as a layer**

✔ **Implementing layer masks**

✔ **Organizing your layers**

✔ **Pasting Smart Objects**

✔ **Playing with layer effects**

_L_ayers are incredibly helpful in production. By using layers, you can make realistic additions to an image that can be removed, edited, and controlled with blending modes and transparency. Unfortunately, to show you all the features of layers goes beyond what we can cover in this chapter. This chapter covers layer basics to get you started working with layers in Photoshop. We show you how to create composite images using easy layer features, just enough knowledge to get yourself into a pretty complex mess of layers! Even if you're an experienced Photoshop user, read on to discover all sorts of neat key commands that can help you in your workflow.

Have fun with layers, and don't worry if you mess up; you can always press F12 to revert the image to the state it was in at the last time you saved it.

Creating and Working with Layers

Layers make creating _composite images_ (images pieced together from many other individual images) easy because you can separate individual elements of the composite onto their own layers. Much like creating collages by cutting pictures from magazines, you can mask out selections on one image and place them on a layer in another image. When pixel information is on its own layer, you can move it, transform it, correct its color, or apply filters just to that layer, without disturbing pixel information on other layers.

The best way to understand how to create and use layers is to, well, create and use layers. The following steps show you how to create a new, layered image:

_1._ **Create a new document by choosing File➪New; in the New dialog box, select Default Photoshop Size from the Preset Sizes drop-down list,** select the Transparent option from the Background Contents area, and then click OK.

Because you select the Transparent option, your image opens with an empty layer instead of a white background layer. The image appears as a checkerboard pattern, which signifies that it is transparent.

If you don't like to see the default checkerboard pattern where there is transparency, choose Edit➪Preferences➪Transparency and Gamut (Windows) or Photoshop➪Preferences➪Transparency and Gamut (Mac). In the Preferences dialog box that appears, you can change the Grid Size drop-down list to None to remove the checkerboard pattern entirely. If you don't want to totally remove the transparency grid, you can change the size of the checkerboard pattern or change the color of the checkerboard.

When you open an existing document (say a photograph), this image will be your background layer.

2. **Create a shape on the new image.**

   For example, we created a red square by using the Rectangular Marquee tool to create a square selection; we then filled the selection with red by double-clicking the Foreground color swatch, selecting a red from the color picker, and clicking in the selection with the Paint Bucket tool.

3. **To rename the layer, double-click the layer name (Layer 1) in the Layers palette and type a short, descriptive name.**

   A good practice is to name your layers based on what they contain; for this example, we named the layer "square."

4. **Create a new layer by Alt+clicking (Windows) or Option+clicking (Mac) the New Layer button at the bottom of the Layers palette. In the New Layer dialog box that appears, shown in Figure 8-1, give your new layer a descriptive name, and then click OK.**

5. **Create a shape on the new layer.**

   We created a circle by using the Elliptical Marquee tool and filling the selection with yellow.

Figure 8-1:
Alt+click (Windows) or Option+ click (Mac) to create and name a layer at the same time.

The new shape can overlap the shape on the other layer, as shown in Figure 8-2.

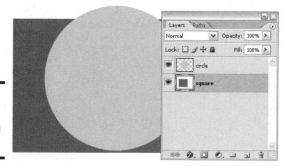

Figure 8-2: The circle overlapping the square.

Duplicating a layer

Perhaps you want to create a duplicate of a layer for your composite. This can be helpful for do-it-yourself drop shadows, as well as adding additional elements to an image, perhaps by adding more apples in a bowl of fruit.

 Alt+drag (Windows) or Option+drag (Mac) the square layer to the New Layer icon at the bottom of the Layers palette to duplicate it. Again, by holding down Alt (Windows) or Option (Mac), you can name the layer as you create it.

Selecting a layer

When you start working with layers, you may find yourself moving or adjusting pixels, only to discover that you accidentally edited pixels on the wrong layer. Select the layer that you plan to work on by clicking the layer name in the Layers palette. Unlike previous versions of Photoshop, Photoshop CS2 represents a selected layer by simply highlighting the layer in the Layer's palette. Don't bother looking for an indicator paintbrush icon in this version. Here are some tips to help you select the correct layer:

✦ Right-click (Windows) or Control+click (Mac) to see a contextual menu listing all layers that have pixel data at the point you clicked and to choose the layer that you want to work with.

✦ Get in the habit of holding down the Ctrl (Windows) or ⌘ (Mac) key while using the Move tool and when selecting layers. This temporarily turns on the Auto Select feature, which automatically selects the topmost visible layer that contains the pixel data that you clicked on.

✦ Press Alt+[(Windows) or Option+[(Mac) to select the next layer down from the selected layer in the stacking order.

✦ Press Alt+] (Windows) or Option+] (Mac) to select the next layer up from the selected layer in the stacking order.

Controlling the visibility of a layer

Hide layers that you don't immediately need by clicking the eye icon in the Layers palette, as shown in Figure 8-3. To see only one layer, Alt+click (Windows) or Option+click (Mac) the eye icon of the layer you want to keep visible. Alt+click (Windows) or Option+click (Mac) the eye icon again to show all layers.

Figure 8-3:
Show only one layer by Alt+clicking (Windows) or Option+ clicking (Mac) on the layer's visibility (eye) icon.

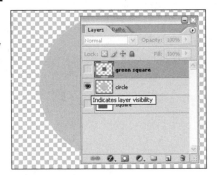

Rearranging the stacking order

Layers are like clear pieces of film lying on top of each other. Change the stacking order of the layers in the Layers palette by dragging a layer until you see a black separator line appear, shown in Figure 8-4, indicating that you're dragging the layer to that location. You can also use these great commands to help you move a layer:

Command	Windows Shortcut	Mac Shortcut
Move selected layer up	Ctrl+]	⌘+]
Move selected layer down	Ctrl+[	⌘+[

Figure 8-4:
Drag to rearrange the layer's stacking order.

Creating a Text Layer

When you create text in Photoshop, the text is created on its own layer. This simplifies the process of applying different styles and blending modes to customize the type, as well as repositioning the text.

To create a text layer, choose the Type tool and click on the image area. You could also click and drag to create a text area. The Options bar, shown in Figure 8-5, gives you the controls to change font, size, blending mode, and color of the text.

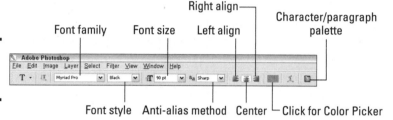

Figure 8-5: The Text tool options.

Warping text

When you click the Create Warped Text button on the Options bar, the Warp Text dialog box appears. This dialog box enables you to apply different types of distortion to your text, as shown in Figure 8-6. You can still edit text that has been warped. To remove a warp, click the Create Warp Text button again and select None from the Style drop-down list.

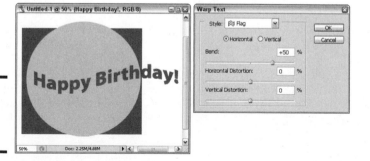

Figure 8-6: The Warp Text dialog box.

Fine-tuning text

For controls such as leading, baseline shift, and paragraph controls, click the Toggle the Character and Paragraph Palettes icon near the right end of the Options bar, as shown in Figure 8-7.

Figure 8-7:
The
Character
and
Paragraph
palettes in
Photoshop.

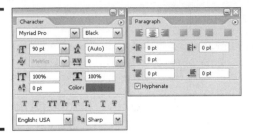

Use the keyboard commands in Table 8-1 to build text in Photoshop. Make sure that you have some text selected when you use these shortcuts.

Table 8-1	Helpful Typesetting Key Commands	
Function	*Windows*	*Mac*
Increase font size	Shift+Ctrl+>	Shift+⌘+>
Decrease font size	Shift+Ctrl+<	Shift+⌘+<
Increase kerning (cursor must be between two letters)	Alt+→	Option+→
Decrease kerning (cursor must be between two letters)	Alt+←	Option+←
Increase tracking (several letters selected)	Alt+→	Option+→
Decrease tracking (several letters selected)	Alt+←	Option+←
Increase or decrease leading (several lines selected)	Alt+↑ or Alt+↓	Option+↑ or Option+↓

To change the font, drag over the font family name on the Options bar, and then press the up-arrow key (↑) to go up in the font list or the down-arrow key (↓) to go down in the font list.

After you're finished editing text, confirm or delete the changes by clicking the buttons on the right of the Options bar.

If you would rather use key commands to confirm or delete your changes, press the Esc key to cancel text changes; press Ctrl+Enter (Windows) or ⌘+Return (Mac) to commit text changes (or use the Enter key on the numeric keypad).

Using Layer Masks

In this section, we show you how to create a layer mask from a selection or a pen path. A *layer mask* covers up areas of the image that you want to make transparent and exposes pixels that you want visible. Masks can be based upon a selection that you have created with the selection tools, by painting on the mask itself, or by using the Pen tool to create a path around the object you want to keep visible.

Creating a layer mask from a selection

You need to have two images open to follow these steps where we show you how to create layer masks from a selection:

1. **When combining images, choose Image⊅Image Size to make sure that the images are approximately the same resolution.**

Otherwise you might create some interesting, but disproportional, effects.

2. **Using the Move tool, click on one image and drag it to the other image window.**

A black border appears around the image area when dropping an image into another image window. This automatically creates new layer on top of the active layer.

Hold down the Shift key when dragging one image to another to perfectly center the new image layer in the document window.

3. **Using any selection method, select a part of the image that you want to keep on the newly placed layer. Choose Select⊅Feather to soften the selection (5 pixels should be enough).**

4. **Click the Layer Mask button at the bottom of the Layers palette.**

A mask is created off to the right of your layer, leaving only your selection visible, as shown in Figure 8-8. Note that the icon to the left of the visibility (eye) icon is now a mask icon.

Figure 8-8: A custom mask is created automatically from an active selection when you click the Layer Mask button.

5. **If you click on the Layer thumbnail in the layers palette, the layer icon to the left is now a paintbrush. Click on the mask thumbnail.**

   While the layer mask is active, you can paint on the mask.

6. **Press D to return to the default black and white swatch colors in the toolbox.**

7. **Select the Brush tool and paint black while the mask thumbnail is selected to cover up areas of the image that you want transparent. Press X to switch to white, and paint to expose areas on the image that you do want to see.**

   You can even change the opacity as you paint to blend images in with each other. See Figure 8-9.

TIP

To create a smooth transition from one image to another, drag the Gradient tool across the image while the layer mask is selected in the Layers palette.

Figure 8-9:
You can paint on a mask with shades of black and white to create an interesting transition from one image to another.

Creating a vector mask from a pen path

A *vector mask* masks a selection, but it does so with the precision that you can get only from using a path. The following steps show you another, slightly more precise, way to create a layer mask by using a pen path:

1. **Use the Pen tool and click from point to point to make a closed pen path. If you already have a path, choose Windows⇨Paths and click on a path to select it.**

See Chapter 4 of this minibook for more about working with the Pen tool.

2. **On the Layers palette, click the Layer Mask button and then click it again.**

Wow! A mask from your pen path! Anything that was not contained within the path is now masked out. Use the Direct Selection tool to edit the path if necessary. See Figure 8-10.

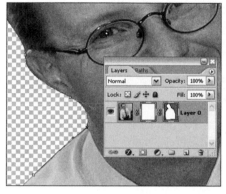

Figure 8-10:
A vector mask is created from an active pen path.

If you no longer want the layer or vector mask, drag the thumbnail to the trash can icon in the Layers palette. An alert dialog box appears, asking if you would like to discard the mask or apply it. Click the Discard button to revert your image back to the way it appeared before applying the mask, or click the Apply button to apply the masked area.

Layer Organization Tips

As you advance in layer skills, you will want to keep layers named, neat, and in order. In this section, we show you some tips to help you organize multiple layers.

Activating multiple layers simultaneously

Select multiple layers simultaneously by selecting one layer and then Shift+clicking to select additional layers. Notice in Figure 8-11 that the selected layers are highlighted. Selected layers will move and transform together, making repositioning and resizing easier than activating each layer independently.

Figure 8-11:
The high-lighted layers are selected.

Select multiple layers to keep their relative positions to each other and take advantage of alignment features. When you select two or more layers and choose the Move tool, you can take advantage of alignment features on the Options bar (see Figure 8-12). Select three or more layers for distribution options.

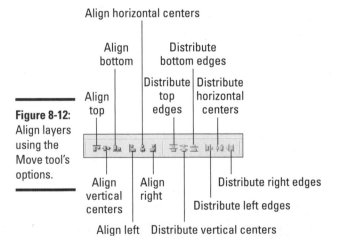

Figure 8-12:
Align layers using the Move tool's options.

Layer groups

After you start using layers, you will likely use lots of them, and your Layers palette will become huge. If you find yourself scrolling to navigate from one layer to another, take advantage of *layer groups,* which essentially act as folders that hold layers that you choose. Just like a folder you use for paper, you can add, remove, and shuffle around the layers within a layer set. Use layer sets to organize your layers and make the job of duplicating multiple layers easier.

To create a layer group, follow these steps:

1. **After creating several layers, Shift+click to select the layers that you want to group together in a set.**

2. **Choose New Group from Layers from the Layers palette menu, name the group, and then click OK.**

Pass through in the blending mode indicates that no individual blending modes are changed. Using the Blending Mode drop-down list in the Layers palette, you can change all the layers within a group to a specific blending mode, or you can use the Opacity slider to change the opacity of all layers in a group at once.

That's it, you have created a layer group, but you can still reorganize layers within the group or even drag in or out additional layers. You can open and close a layer group with the arrow to the left of the set name, as shown in Figure 8-13.

Figure 8-13: Our Funny man set when opened.

Duplicating a layer group

After you've created a layer group, you may want to copy it. For example, you may want to copy an image, such as a button created from several layers topped off with a text layer. The most efficient way to make a copy of that button is to create a layer group and copy the entire group. To copy an image made up of several layers that aren't in a layer group would require you to individually duplicate each layer — how time-consuming!

To duplicate a layer group, follow these steps:

1. **Select a group from the Layers palette.**

2. **From the palette menu, choose Duplicate Group.**

   The Duplicate Group dialog box appears.

3. **For the destination, choose the present document, any open document, or create a new document.**

   Be sure to give the duplicated set a distinctive name!

4. **Click OK.**

Using Layer Styles

Layer styles are wonderful little extras that you can apply to layers to create drop shadows, bevel and emboss effects, apply color overlays, gradients, patterns and strokes, and more.

Applying a style

To apply a layer style (for example, the drop shadow style, one of the most popular effects) to an image, just follow these steps:

1. **Create a layer on any image.**

   For example, you could create a text layer to see the effects of the layer styles.

 2. **With the layer selected, click and hold on the Layer Style button at the bottom of the Layers palette. From the menu options, choose Drop Shadow.**

   In the Layer Style dialog box that appears, you can choose to change the blending mode, color, distance spread, and size of a drop shadow. You should see it has already applied to your text. Position the cursor on the image area and drag to visually adjust the position of the drop shadow.

3. **When you're happy with the drop shadow, click OK to apply it.**

To apply another effect and change its options, click and hold on the Layer Style button in the Layers palette and choose the name of the layer style from the menu that appears, Bevel and Emboss, for instance. In the dialog box that appears, change the settings to customize the layer style and click OK to apply it to your image. For example, if you choose Bevel and Emboss from the Layer Styles menu, you can choose from several emboss styles and adjust the depth, size, and softness, as shown in Figure 8-14.

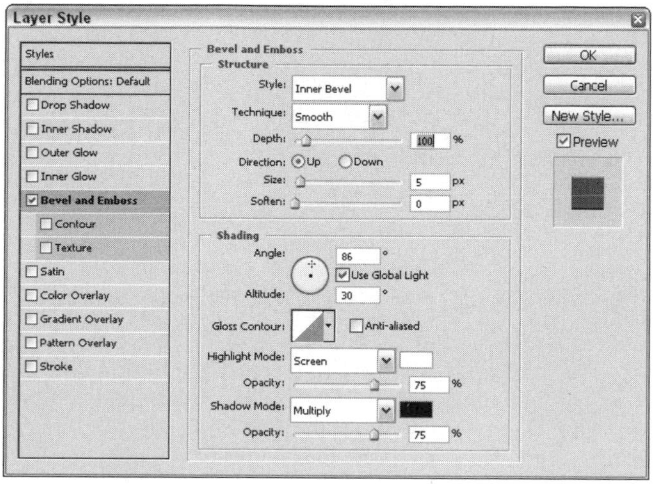

Figure 8-14:
Click the style to see available options.

Here are some consistent items that you see in the Layer Style dialog box, no matter what effect you choose:

✦ **Contour:** Use contours to control the shape and appearance of an effect. Click on the arrow to open the Contour flyout menu to choose a contour preset, or click the contour preview to open the Contour Editor (shown in Figure 8-15) and create your own edge.

✦ **Angle:** Drag the cross hair in the angle circle, or enter a value in the Angle text field to control where the light source comes from.

✦ **Global light:** If you aren't smart about lighting effects on multiple objects, global light will make it seem as though you are. Select the Use Global Light check box to keep the angle consistent from one layer style to another.

✦ **Color:** Whenever you see a color box, you can click on it to select a color. This color could be for the drop shadow, highlight or shadow of an emboss, or for a color overlay.

Book IV
Chapter 8

Using Layers

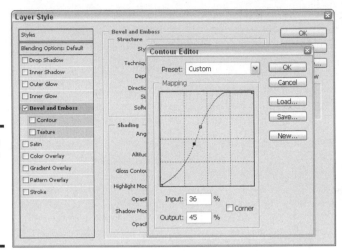

Figure 8-15: Create your own edge contour using the Contour Editor.

Creating and saving a style

If you come up with a combination of attributes that you like, click the New Style button in the upper right of the Layer Style dialog box. Name the style, and it is now stored in the Styles palette. After you click OK, you can retrieve the style at any time by choosing Window⇨Styles. If it helps, click the palette menu button and choose Small or Large List to change the Styles palette to show only the name of the styles.

After you have applied a layer style to a layer, the style is listed in the Layers palette, as shown in Figure 8-16. You can turn off the visibility of the style by turning off the eye icon, or even throw away the layer style by dragging it to the Layers palette's trash can icon.

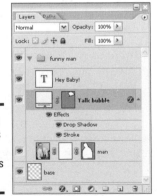

Figure 8-16: Layer styles are shown in the Layers palette.

Opacity versus fill

In the Layers palette, you have two transparency options, one for opacity and one for fill. Opacity affects the opacity of the entire layer, including effects. Fill, on the other hand, affects only the layer itself, but not layer styles. Figure 8-17 shows what happens when the Bevel and Emboss style is applied to text and the fill is reduced to 0 percent. It looks like the text was embossed onto the image. You can do lots of neat stuff with the Layer Fill feature!

Figure 8-17:
A text layer with layer styles applied, and the fill reduced to 0 percent.

New Smart Placement of Illustrator Images

Placing any image into a Photoshop file will create a new layer, but discover the new Smart feature available only in Photoshop CS2 — Smart Object pastes the art as a Vector Smart Object that can be scaled, transformed, or moved without degrading the image before it's placed into the Photoshop document. As the art is placed, its file data is embedded in the Photoshop document and the art is rasterized on a separate layer.

Follow theses steps to take advantage of Smart Objects in Photoshop:

1 **Open a file in Adobe Illustrator, select the art you want to copy, and choose Edit⇨Copy.**

   If you want to paste the Adobe Illustrator art as a Smart Object, path, or shape layer, be sure to turn on the PDF and the AICB (No Transparency Support) options in the File Handling & Clipboard preferences of Adobe Illustrator.

2. **In Photoshop, open the document into which you want to paste the Adobe Illustrator art, and choose Edit⇨Paste.**

3. **In the Paste dialog box, select how you want to paste the Adobe Illustrator art and then click OK. Figure 8-18 shows the Paste dialog box.**

Figure 8-18: Copy and paste from Illustrator for these placement options.

Smart Object: Pastes the art as a Vector Smart Object that can be scaled, transformed, or moved without degrading the image before it's placed into the Photoshop document. The file data is embedded in the Photoshop document and the art is rasterized on a separate layer. See Figure 8-19.

Pixels: Pastes the art as pixels that can be scaled, transformed, or moved before it is rasterized and placed on its own layer in the Photoshop document.

Path: Pastes the art as a path that can be edited with the Pen tools.

Shape Layer: Pastes the art as a new shape layer.

Figure 8-19: A Smart Object in the Layers palette.

4. **If you selected Smart Object or Pixels in the Paste dialog box, click Enter or Return to place the art.**

Merging and Flattening the Image

Merging layers combines several selected layers into one layer. *Flattening* is when you reduce all layers to one background layer. Layers can increase your file in size, thereby also tying up valuable processing resources. To keep file size down, you may choose to merge some layers or even flatten the entire image down to one background layer.

Merging

Merging layers is helpful when you no longer need every layer to be independent, like when you have a separate shadow layer aligned to another layer and don't plan on moving it again. Or when you combine many layers to create a composite and want to consolidate it to one layer.

To merge layers (in a visual and easy way), follow these steps:

1. **Turn on the visibility of only the layers that you want merged.**

2. **Choose Merge Visible from the Layers palette menu.**

That's it. The entire image is not flattened, but the visible layers are now reduced to one layer.

To merge visible layers onto a target (selected) layer that you create while keeping the visible layers independent, do this: Create a blank layer and select it. Hold down Alt (Windows) or Option (Mac) when choosing Merge Visible from the palette menu. That's it.

Flattening

If you don't have to flatten your image, don't! Flattening your image reduces all layers down to one background layer, which is necessary for certain file formats, but after you flatten an image, you can't take advantage of blending options or reposition the layered items. (Read more about saving files in Chapter 9 of this minibook.)

If you absolutely must flatten layers, keep a copy of the original, unflattened document for additional edits in the future.

To flatten all layers in an image, choose Layer➪Flatten Image, or choose Flatten Image from the palette menu on the Layers palette.

Chapter 9: Saving Photoshop Images for Print and the Web

In This Chapter

✔ Determining the correct file formats for saving

✔ Preparing your images for the Web

✔ Discovering the color table

A productive workflow depends on you choosing the proper format in which to save your Photoshop files. Without the correct settings, your file may not be visible to other applications, or you might delete valuable components, such as layers or channels. This chapter provides you with the necessary information to save the file correctly for both print and Web. We cover the file format choices before moving on to the proper use of the Save for Web feature (for saving in the GIF, JPEG, and PNG file formats).

Saving files in the correct file format is important not only for file size, but in support of different Photoshop features, as well. If you're unsure about saving in the right format, save a copy of the file, keeping the original in the PSD format (the native Photoshop format). Photoshop does this for you automatically when you choose a format in the Save As or the Save for Web dialog box that does not support some of the features you've used, such as channels or layers. A yield sign appears when a copy is being made. It's a good backup if you ever need to return to the original file.

Choosing a File Format for Saving

When you choose File➪Save for the first time (or you choose File➪Save As to save a different version of a file), you see at least 18 different file formats that you can choose from in the Save as Type drop-down list. We don't cover each format in this chapter (some are specific to proprietary workflows), but we do show you which formats are best for the typical workflow that you may face.

Wonderful and easy Photoshop PSD

If you're in an Adobe workflow (you're using Photoshop, InDesign, Illustrator, or GoLive), you can keep the image in the native Photoshop PSD format. By choosing this format, transparency, layers, channels, and paths are all maintained and left intact when placed in the other applications.

To maximize compatibility with previous versions of Photoshop and with other applications, choose Edit⇨Preferences⇨File Handling (Windows) or Photoshop⇨Preferences⇨File Handling (Mac). Choose Always from the Maximize PSD File Compatibility drop-down list. This saves a composite (flattened) image along with the layers of your document.

Creating a PDF presentation

Create a multipage PDF file or presentation by using Adobe Bridge (File⇨File Browse). From the Bridge menu, choose Tools⇨Photoshop⇨ PDF Presentation. Using the Browse button, choose files to add to the Source list. You can Ctrl+click (Windows) or ⌘+click (Mac) to select multiple files and add them to the Source list.

In the Output Options section, choose Multi-Page or Presentation PDF. If you choose Presentation, you're given the opportunity to set up slide show options, such as timing and transition effects. If you want to see the PDF immediately, make sure that you select the View PDF after Saving check box in the Output Options section.

Click Save, name the file, and click Save again. In the PDF dialog box that appears, choose any specific options that you want for the PDF (see Book V for more specifics on PDF settings), and click OK.

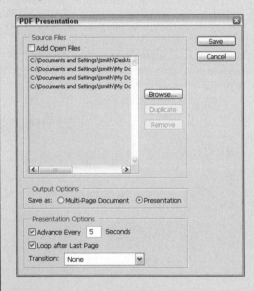

Leaving the Maximize PSD File Compatibility drop-down list set to Always creates a larger file. If file size is an issue, leave the drop-down list set to Ask, and only use the feature when you need to open the Photoshop file in older versions of Photoshop.

Photoshop EPS

Virtually every desktop application accepts the EPS (Encapsulated PostScript) file format. The EPS format is used to transfer PostScript-language artwork between various applications. It supports vector data, duotones, and clipping paths.

When you choose to save in the EPS format, an EPS Options dialog box appears. Leave the defaults and click OK.

Alter the settings in the EPS Options dialog box *only* if you're familiar with custom printer calibration, or you need to save your image to a specific screen ruling. Screen rulings (lpi) are usually set in a page layout application, such as Adobe InDesign or QuarkXPress.

Photoshop PDF

If compatibility is an issue, save your file in the Photoshop PDF (Portable Document Format) format. PDF files are supported by more than a dozen platforms when viewers use Acrobat or the Acrobat Reader (the Acrobat Reader is available for free at www.adobe.com). What a perfect way to send pictures to friends and family! Saving your file in the Photoshop PDF format supports your ability to edit the image when you open the file by choosing File⇨Open in Photoshop.

TIFF

TIFF (Tagged Image File Format) is a flexible bitmap image format that is supported by most image-editing and page-layout applications. TIFF supports layers and channels, but it has a maximum size of 4GB. We hope your files aren't that large!

DCS

The Photoshop DCS (Desktop Color Separation) 1.0 and 2.0 format is a version of EPS that enables you to save color separations of CMYK or multichannel files. Some workflows require this format, but if you have implemented spot color channels in your image, using the DCS file format is required to maintain them.

Choose the DCS 2.0 format unless you received specific instructions to use the DCS 1.0 format. This would be for reasons of incompatibility in certain workflows.

**Book IV
Chapter 9**

**Saving Photoshop
Images for Print and
the Web**

Saving for the Web

To access the maximum number of options for the GIF, JPEG, and PNG file formats, save your image by choosing File⇨Save for Web. The Save for Web dialog box appears, which allows you to optimize the image as you save it. This might sound like a big procedure, but it's just the process of making the image as small as possible while keeping it visually pleasing.

Saving images for the Web is a give-and-take experience. You may find yourself sacrificing perfect imagery to make the image small enough in size that it can be downloaded and viewed quickly by users. Read on to see how you can best handle creating Web images.

The following sections describe the differences between GIF, JPEG, and PNG. Choose the appropriate format based upon the type of image you're saving.

Having the image size correct before you save the file for the Web is a good practice. If you need to read up on resizing images, see Chapter 5 of this mini-book. But generally speaking, you want to resize the image to the right pixel dimensions, choose Filter⇨Sharpen⇨Unsharp Mask to gain back some of the detail lost when resizing the image, and then save the image for the Web.

JPEG

JPEG (Joint Photographic Experts Group) is the best format for continuous tone images (those with smooth transitions from one color to another, as in photographs), like the image shown in Figure 9-1.

Figure 9-1: Images with smooth transitions from one color to another make good candidates for the JPEG format.

The JPEG format is lossy, so you should not save a JPEG, open it, edit it, and save it again as a JPEG. Because the JPEG compression causes data to be lost, your image will eventually look like it was printed on a paper towel. Save a copy of the file as a JPEG, keeping the original image in the PSD format if you need to later edit the image, open the original PSD, make your changes, save the PSD, and then save a copy of the edited file as a JPEG.

The JPEG format does *not* support transparency, but you can cheat the system a little by using matting, which we discuss later in this chapter.

Saving a JPEG

A good image to save in the JPEG format would be a typical photograph or illustration with lots of smooth transitions from one color to the next. To save an image as a JPEG, follow these steps:

1. **Choose File➪Save for Web, and then click the 2-Up tab to view the original image (left) at the same time as the optimized image (right).**

2. **Choose one of the JPEG preset settings from the Settings drop-down list; you can choose Low, Medium, High, or customize a level in between the presets by using the Quality slider.**

3. **Leave the Optimized check box selected to build the best JPEG at the smallest size.**

   The only issue with leaving this check box selected is that some very old browsers won't read the JPEG correctly. (This is probably not an issue for most of your viewers.)

4. **Deselect the ICC Profile check box unless you're in a color-managed workflow and color accuracy is essential.**

   This dramatically increases the file size, and most people aren't looking for *exact* color matches from an image on the monitor . . . and it's scary if they are!

5. **Use the Blur slider to bring down some detail.**

   It's funny, but one JPEG that's the exact same pixel dimensions as another might vary in file size. This is because the more detailed an image, the more information is needed. So an image of lots of apples will be larger than an image the same size that has a lot of clear blue sky in it. The blur feature does blur the image (surprise!), so you might want to use this for only a Low Source image in GoLive. Read Book VI, Chapter 3 for more information on Low Source images.

6. **(Optional) Choose a matte color from the Matte drop-down list.**

   Because JPEG does not support transparency, you can flood the transparent area with a color that you choose from the Matte drop-down list. Choose the color that you're using for the background of your Web page by choosing Other and entering the hexadecimal color in the lower portion of the color picker.

7. **Click Save.**

**Book IV
Chapter 9**

Saving Photoshop
Images for Print and
the Web

PNG

PNG (Portable Network Graphics) is almost the perfect combination of JPEG and GIF. Unfortunately, PNG isn't yet widely supported . . . note, as well, that PNG-24 images have file sizes that can be too large to use on the Web.

PNG supports varying levels of transparency and anti-aliasing. This means that you can specify an image as being 50 percent transparent, and it will actually show through to the underlying Web page! You have a choice of PNG-8 and PNG-24 in the Save for Web dialog box. As a file format for optimizing images, PNG-8 does not give you any advantage over a regular GIF file.

PNG files are *not* supported by all browsers. In older browsers, a plug-in may be required to view your page. Ouch . . . by choosing PNG, you could shoot yourself in the foot because not all your viewers will be able to view the PNG.

Saving a PNG

If you're saving a PNG file, you have a choice of PNG-8 or PNG-24. The PNG-8 options are essentially the same as the GIF options, see the "Saving a GIF" section, later in this chapter, for details.

PNG-24 saves 24-bit images that support *anti-aliasing* (the smooth transition from one color to another). They work beautifully for continuous-tone images, but are much larger than a JPEG file. The truly awesome feature of a PNG file is that it supports 256 levels of transparency. In other words, you can apply varying amounts of transparency in an image, as shown in Figure 9-2, where the image shows through to the background.

Figure 9-2:
A PNG-24
with varying
amounts
of trans-
parency.

GIF

Supposedly, the way you pronounce GIF (Graphics Interchange Format) is based on the type of peanut butter you eat. Is it pronounced like the peanut butter brand (Jiff), or with a hard G, like gift? Most people seem to pronounce it like gift (minus the T).

Use the GIF format if you have lots of solid color, such as a logo like the one shown in Figure 9-3.

Figure 9-3: An image with large amount of solid color is a good candidate for the GIF format.

The GIF format is not lossy (does not lose data when the file is compressed in this format), but it does reduce the file size by using a limited number of colors in a color table. The lower the number of colors, the smaller the file size. If you have ever worked in the Index color mode, you're familiar with this process.

Transparency is supported by the GIF file. But generally GIFs don't do a good job with anything that needs smooth transitions from one color to another. This is because of its poor support of anti-aliasing. *Anti-aliasing* is the method that Photoshop uses to smooth jagged edges. When pixels transition from one color to another, Photoshop produces multiple color pixels to evenly blend from one pixel to another.

Because anti-aliasing needs to create multiple colors for this effect, GIF files are generally not recommended. In fact, when you reduce a GIF in size, you're more apt to see *banding*, as shown in Figure 9-4, because the anti-aliasing cannot take place with the limited number of colors available in the GIF format.

You can, of course, dramatically increase the number of colors to create a smoother transition, but then you risk creating monster files that take forever to download.

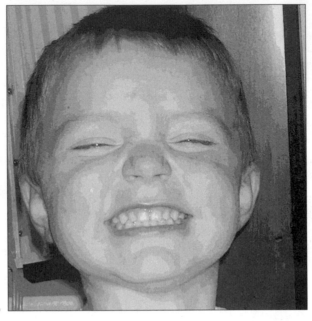

Figure 9-4:
The effect of banding occurs because of the limited number of colors in the GIF format.

Saving a GIF

When you choose File⇨Save for Web, you first see the available GIF format options. The GIF options may be more clear to you if you have an image (with lots of solid color) open for this.

To save a file for the Web as a GIF, follow these steps:

1. **Choose File⇨Save for Web.**

The Save for Web dialog box appears.

2. **At the top, click the 2-Up tab.**

This shows the original image on the left and the optimized image on the right. (Or top and bottom, depending upon the proportions of your image.)

In the lower portion of the display, you see the original file size compared to the optimized file size, as well as the approximate download time. This is important! Nobody wants to wait around for a Web page to load, most people won't wait more than ten seconds for the entire Web page to appear so try to keep an individual image's download time down to five seconds or less. Remember, all the images on a page can add up to one monstrous wait time for the viewer!

Change the download speed by choosing from the Preview menu (it's the arrow on the upper-right side of the Save for Web dialog box). The Preview menu isn't labeled, so look for the ToolTip to appear when you hover your cursor over the arrow icon.

3. **Choose GIF 32 No Dither from the Settings drop-down list.**

You might see a change already. Photoshop supplies you with presets that you can choose from, or you can customize and save your own.

Choose whether you want dithering applied to the image by selecting an option from the Specify the Dither Algorithm drop-down list. This is purely a personal choice. Because you may be limiting colors, Photoshop can use dithering to mix the pixels of the available colors to simulate the missing colors. Many designers choose the No Dither option.

Select the Preview in Default Browser check box at the bottom of the Save for Web dialog box to launch your chosen Web browser and display the image as it will appear with the present settings. If you have not set up a browser, click on the down arrow and choose Other from the drop-down menu. Browse to locate a browser that you wish to preview your image in.

How is the color table created? Based upon a color reduction algorithm method that you choose, the Save for the Web feature samples the number of colors that you indicate. If keeping colors Web safe is important, select the Restrictive (Web) option for the method; if you want your image to look better on most monitors, but not necessarily be Web safe, choose the Adaptive option.

4. **Use the arrows to the right of the Colors combo box or enter a number to add or delete colors from the color table.**

5. **If your image uses transparency, select the Transparency check box.**

Remember that transparency is counted as one of your colors in the color table.

6. **Select the Interlaced check box only if your GIF image is large in size (25K or larger).**

Selecting this option causes the image to build in several scans on the Web page, a low resolution image that pops up quickly to be refreshed with the higher resolution image when it is finished downloading. Interlacing gives the illusion of the download going faster but makes the file size larger, so use it only if necessary.

7. **Click Save.**

Now the image is ready to be attached to an e-mail message or used in a Web page.

**Book IV
Chapter 9**

**Saving Photoshop
Images for Print and
the Web**

Using the color table

When you save an image as a GIF using the Save for Web dialog box, you see the color table for the image on the right side of the dialog box. The color table is important because it not only allows you to see the colors used in the image, but also enables you to customize the color table by using the options at the bottom of the color table, as shown in Figure 9-5.

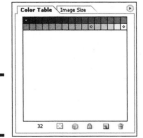

Figure 9-5:
The color table.

Customizing the color table

You may want to customize your color table by selecting some of your colors to be Web safe and locking colors so that they're not bumped off as you reduce the amount of colors. To customize a color table, follow these steps:

1. **If your image has only a few colors that you would like to convert to Web safe colors, choose the Eyedropper tool from the left of the Save for Web dialog box and click on the color, in either the Original or Optimized view.**

The sampled color is highlighted in the color table, as shown in Figure 9-6.

Figure 9-6:
Sample a color to make it Web safe.

2. **Click the Web Safe button at the bottom of the color table. A tooltip appears when you cross over this button with the text, Shifts/Unshifts selected colors to web palette.**

    A diamond appears, indicating that the color is now Web safe.

3. **Lock colors that you don't want to delete as you reduce the number of colors in the color table.**

    Select a color with the Eyedropper tool or choose it in the color table, and then click the Lock Color button. A white square appears in the lower-right corner, indicating that the color is locked (see Figure 9-7).

    If you lock 32 colors and then reduce the color table to 24, some of your locked colors will be deleted. If you choose to add colors, those locked colors will be the first to return.

Figure 9-7:
A white square indicates that the color is locked.

Matte

Matting appears as a choice in the JPEG, GIF, and PNG format options. Matting is useful if you don't want ragged edges appearing around your image. Matting looks for pixels that are greater than 50 percent transparent and makes them fully transparent; any pixels that are 50 percent or less transparent become fully opaque. See Figure 9-8 for an example of an image with and without matting applied.

Even though your image might be on a transparent layer, there will be some iffy pixels, the ones that aren't sure what they want to be . . . to be transparent or not to be transparent. Choose a matte color to blend in with the transparent iffy pixels by selecting Eyedropper, White, Black, or Other (to open the color picker) from the Matte drop-down list in the Save for Web dialog box.

**Book IV
Chapter 9**

Saving Photoshop Images for Print and the Web

Figure 9-8:
No matte
applied
(left); matte
applied
(right).

Saving settings

Whether you are saving a GIF, JPG, or PNG file, you probably spent some time experimenting with settings to find what works best for your needs. Save your selected options to reload at a later time by saving the settings. Do this by clicking the arrow to the right of the Preset drop-down list. Choose Save Settings from the menu that appears and give your settings a name. Your named, customized settings will then appear in the Settings drop-down list.

Book V

Acrobat 7.0

The 5th Wave   By Rich Tennant

"I couldn't say anything. They were in here with that program we bought them that encourages artistic expression."

Contents at a Glance

Chapter 1: Discovering Essential Acrobat Information

In This Chapter

✔ Discovering Acrobat and PDF files

✔ Knowing when to use PDF files

✔ Becoming familiar with the Acrobat workspace and tools

A dobe Acrobat 7.0 provides a variety of tools for sharing and reviewing documents. Although most of the Adobe Creative Suite applications can create PDF files, Adobe Acrobat allows you to create Portable Document Format (PDF) files from programs that are not part of the Creative Suite. In this chapter, we discuss why you may want to create PDF files, and acquaint you with the Adobe Acrobat tools and workspace. We show you how easy it is to navigate through PDF files using the navigational tools, tabs, and viewing options in Acrobat.

In the following chapters of this minibook, you can explore how to use Acrobat to create Adobe PDF files from documents produced in a variety of programs and discover ways to enhance your Adobe PDF files.

About Acrobat and PDF Files

Adobe Acrobat is used to create Adobe PDF files, review existing PDF files, and modify existing PDF files. But before we talk about how you create PDF files, we should look at why they are useful. When you work with programs in the Adobe Creative Suite, such as Adobe InDesign, and you want to share your work with colleagues or clients, you need to find a way to deliver the documents to them. Of course, you can always print your documents and send them via courier, the mail, or even fax. But all of these take time and do not provide for very easy collaboration.

Many people prefer to receive documents electronically, but there is a small problem: All the people with whom you need to share files probably do not have InDesign — or whatever part of the Adobe Creative Suite you're using. PDF provides a common file format that everyone can open to review your documents. PDF provides an application independent method for viewing your files regardless of what computer program was used to create them. The PDF file format also lets Mac users share their files with Windows users (and vice versa). In addition, Adobe Acrobat provides extensive tools for review, commenting and markup — making it easy to collaborate on a project without modifying the original document.

PDF files can be viewed on many different computer types, including Macintosh computers, Windows computers, UNIX computers, and even handheld computers such as those running the Palm OS. Because the software to view Adobe PDF files, the Adobe Reader, is free, you can be assured that those receiving your files don't need to purchase any special software. In fact, the odds are quite good that most users already have the free Adobe Reader as more than 500 million copies have been distributed.

PDF provides a true reproduction of original documents. The fidelity of PDF files is so good that the Internal Revenue Service uses this format to distribute tax forms online. Likewise, many banks, insurance agencies, and financial services firms use PDF as a method for distributing documents.

Although PDF files provide a high quality representation of an original file, they are more than just a picture of the document from which they were created. PDF files retain the high-quality appearance of text so that it prints clearly and is searchable. Logos and illustrations created using Adobe Illustrator retain the same high-quality appearance within a PDF file. PDF files also may contain the intricate details that are captured in bitmap images, such as those edited using Adobe Photoshop — but PDF files are able to keep both bitmap and vector information together in the same file, making them a great choice for distributing documents electronically. What this means for you is that you don't have to sacrifice quality to distribute a file electronically.

Adobe Acrobat is a tool for distributing documents; it is *not* a design tool. You don't use Acrobat to create new documents. But just because you don't design logos, brochures, and other documents with Acrobat, that doesn't make it any less useful than the other programs within the Adobe Creative Suite. Using Acrobat, you can

✦ Share documents with users who don't have the same software or fonts that you use.

✦ Review and mark up PDF files that others send you.

✦ Combine documents created in other programs. You can use Acrobat to merge PDF files that may have been originally created in different programs.

✦ Edit Adobe PDF files.

✦ Apply security to PDF files when you don't want them changed.

✦ Add interactivity to PDF files by infusing them with sounds, movies, and buttons.

✦ Create interactive forms, where you can collect information without requiring a user to print, write, and then fax or mail information back to you. You can do this electronically with PDF forms.

We cover these capabilities throughout the rest of this minibook.

When to Use Adobe PDF Files

So when does it make sense to use Adobe PDF files? Here are some examples:

✦ **When you've created a spreadsheet that includes numbers, formulas, and tables that you don't want others to edit:** Your recipients may have the same software you used to build the document, but you can keep them from editing the original spreadsheet file by distributing it as a PDF file.

✦ **When you've created a presentation that you want others to deliver, but you work on a PC and some of them use Macintosh systems:** By converting the document to PDF, you don't have to worry about typical issues that arise when sharing files between different computer types. For example, fonts are typically included within PDF documents and can be used on any computer systems with the free Adobe Reader or the complete Adobe Acrobat software.

In addition, by sending the presentation in PDF format rather than in the original presentation file format, you don't have to be concerned that the recipients may edit the file.

✦ **When you have a sensitive document that will be shared only with certain authorized colleagues:** If you have a document containing information that you don't want unauthorized persons viewing, you can add security to a PDF file by using Adobe Acrobat's security tools. Using these options, you can require users to enter a password to view the file, and you can limit other features, such as the ability to print or edit the document.

Introducing the Adobe Acrobat Workspace and Tools

To take advantage of all that Adobe Acrobat has to offer, you'll want to discover the workspace and tools Acrobat uses. Adobe significantly revised the interface to Acrobat in version 6, and version 7 includes even more changes.

The Acrobat workspace, shown in Figure 1-1, is divided into three areas: the document window, the toolbar well, and the navigation tabs (palettes). When you open a PDF document using Acrobat, you can use the toolbars, buttons, and tabs shown in Figure 1-1 to navigate and manipulate the PDF file. For example, a PDF file may contain multiple pages. You can use the buttons at the bottom of the document window to navigate through the document's pages:

✦ **Current page:** You can view the page information area at the bottom of a document to determine exactly how many pages are included in a document. Click in this area, enter a page number, and then press Enter (Windows) or Return (Mac) to view a specific page.

✦ **Previous page/Next page:** You can use these navigational buttons to skip forward or backward by one page.

✦ **First page/Last page:** You can click these buttons to jump to the first page or last page of a file.

✦ **Previous view/Next view:** You can use these navigational buttons to go to the last view you had displayed. For example, if you have been looking at the entire page of a PDF document, and then zoom-in on the file, you can use these buttons to toggle between the two views.

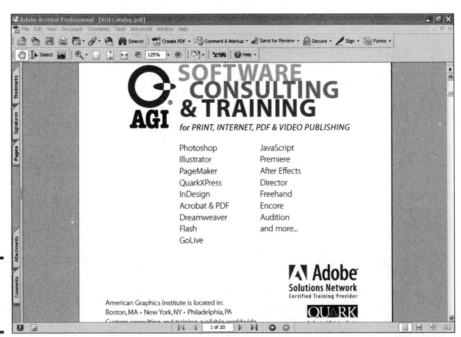

Figure 1-1:
The
Acrobat 7.0
workspace.

The Zoom tools

You can change the magnification used for viewing pages with the Zoom toolbar (refer to Figure 1-1). Using the toolbar, select from a preset magnification by choosing the drop-down list showing magnification percentages, or use the minus (–) and plus (+) symbols on either side of the magnification percent to increase or decrease the zoom level.

The Zoom In tool (a magnifying glass with a plus sign) is also located in the Zoom toolbar. You can use this tool to identify specific portions of a page that you want to magnify. Click and drag around a portion of the page where you want to increase the magnification. You can also click multiple times on an area to increase its magnification, but clicking and dragging a box with the Zoom In tool is generally a much faster way to focus on a portion of a page you want to view. The Zoom In tool can be changed to the Zoom Out tool (magnifying glass with a minus sign) by clicking and holding down on the tool, and then selecting the Zoom Out tool. The Zoom Out tool can be used to reduce the magnification of a page, but it is usually faster to choose a preset zoom percentage.

Adjacent to the Zoom tools are three page icons that you can use to change the page magnification to some commonly used magnifications:

✦ **Actual Size:** Use this button to quickly change the magnification to 100 percent.

✦ **Fit Page:** Use this to fit the current page within the available screen space on your monitor. For smaller documents, such as a business card, the magnification is increased. For larger documents, the magnification is decreased.

✦ **Fit Width:** Use this button to avoid scrolling from left to right when reading a document. The view is changed to fit the document's width in the available space, making it necessary to only scroll up and down on a page.

Acrobat also includes two more advanced tools for navigation in the Zoom toolbar, the Loupe tool and the Pan & Zoom window accessed by clicking and holding down the arrow to the right of the Zoom tool:

✦ **Loupe tool:** With the Loupe tool, you can click an area of the page that you want to magnify. The Loupe Tool window appears (see Figure 1-2), showing a portion of the page at an increased magnification. In the Loupe Tool window, you can increase or decrease the magnification by adjusting the slider left or right. You can change the area of the page being magnified by clicking a different portion of the page while the Loupe tool is selected.

✦ **Pan & Zoom window:** Using the Pan & Zoom window (see Figure 1-3), you can have a second view of the page you're presently viewing. You can use the Pan & Zoom window to navigate within a specific page without scrolling. For example, if you have a detailed technical drawing, you can increase your magnification considerably. Then use the Pan & Zoom window to move around the page to view different portions of the document.

Figure 1-2:
The Loupe
Tool window.

Figure 1-3:
The Pan &
Zoom
window.

Toolbars

Acrobat 7.0 makes many of its functions immediately accessible within a series of 16 toolbars plus the properties bar. You can use these toolbars to perform many of the same tasks that would typically require choosing an item from a menu. For example, you can search a PDF file by clicking a button on a toolbar instead of choosing Edit⇨Search. Less than half of the toolbars are visible when you initially start Acrobat. You can add to the toolbars by choosing View⇨Toolbars and then choosing the toolbars that you want to display, as shown in Figure 1-4. Similarly, you can remove toolbars that are currently visible by choosing View⇨Toolbars and clicking those you want removed. Toolbars that have a check mark next to their names are currently visible, while those with no check mark are not visible.

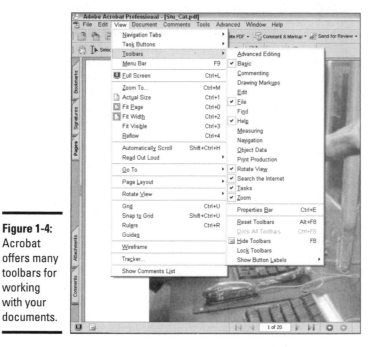

Figure 1-4:
Acrobat offers many toolbars for working with your documents.

You may want to customize the location of toolbars on your screen, making it easier to access the tools you need. Along the left edge of any toolbar is a serrated edge (refer to Figure 1-1). By clicking and holding onto this edge with your mouse, you can drag a toolbar to a new location on your screen. This new location can be within the same area holding the other toolbars, known as the docking area, or you can pull the toolbar anywhere in the Acrobat work area. If you pull a toolbar out of the docking area, it becomes its own independent floating toolbar. You can continue to reposition the toolbar or drag it back into the docking area when you've finished using it. You can also close a toolbar by clicking its Close Window button. Toolbars can also be placed along the left, right, and bottom of the Acrobat work area — turning any side of the Acrobat workspace into a docking area.

Although the flexibility of placing toolbars anywhere you like is useful, it may lead to a chaotic work environment. Instead of leaving toolbars all over your screen, you can have Acrobat clean up the workspace by choosing View➪ Toolbars➪Reset Toolbars.

Toolbars may contain either tools or buttons. For example, you choose the Zoom In tool to work on your document to increase your magnification. Buttons perform an immediate task, such as printing, saving, or applying security to a PDF document. In general, most of the task buttons are on the top row of the docking area, immediately below the menu bar, and most of the tools are on the bottom row — but you can move these toolbars. Some of the tools and task buttons also include additional options that are accessed through drop-down lists within the toolbars. For example, the Zoom In tool can be switched to the Zoom Out tool by clicking and holding on the tool.

Tools and buttons that contain additional choices are noted by the small triangle immediately to their right of the icon.

Viewing modes

Acrobat also provides four viewing modes that control how the entire document is displayed. You can choose which viewing mode is used by clicking the appropriate icon in the lower-right corner of the document window (refer to Figure 1-1). The viewing modes are

✦ **Single Page:** This mode displays only the current document page on-screen and does not show any adjoining pages. When you scroll to the top or bottom of the current page, other pages are not visible at the same time as the current page.

✦ **Continuous:** With this mode, you can see the current document page, and if you scroll to the top (or bottom) of the current page, the adjoining page is also visible. If you reduce your page viewing magnification, many document pages are visible.

✦ **Continuous-facing:** If you have a document with many pages containing text or pictures on their adjoining pages, you can use this mode to scroll from one pair of visible pages to the next. When the Continuous-facing view is selected, you can see adjoining page spreads. This option is identical to the Facing option, but it also shows pages above or below the spread you are presently viewing.

✦ **Facing:** Use this mode to see pages as a *spread,* where you can view both the left and right side of adjoining pages at the same time. When you have documents with pictures or text that spans a pair of pages, use this option to see the pages presented side-by-side in Acrobat. As with the Single Page mode, other pages that go before or fall after the spread are not visible — only the one pair of pages is visible on-screen, regardless of the magnification or scrolling.

Additional viewing options

Acrobat also has two options for changing your document display, both found in the lower-left corner of the document window.

✦ **Full Screen View:** You can use the Full Screen View option to hide all menus, toolbars, and other parts of the Acrobat interface. This option is useful if you want to focus on the document being displayed, not the program being used to view it. Use this, for example, if you have a converted PowerPoint file that is now a PDF document and you want to view the presentation using Acrobat.

✦ **Hide Toolbars:** With so many toolbars, they sometimes get in the way. Click this button to temporarily hide all your toolbars. A small mini toolbar appears adjacent to this tool, providing basic navigation tools when the other toolbars are hidden.

Navigation tabs

Acrobat offers a variety of tabs that are helpful when navigating through PDF documents. The term *tab* may be a bit misleading because similar options are called *palettes* in all the other Adobe Creative Suite programs. Regardless of the name, however, you'll use these to more easily get around PDF files. Later in this minibook, we show you how to add items to these tabs, such as bookmarks, which make your documents even easier for readers to navigate.

The navigation tabs are visible along the left side of your document window (refer to Figure 1-1). You can click the name of a tab to make it visible. For example, you can click the Pages tab (also called the Pages palette) to make visible thumbnails of each page; click a thumbnail to go to that page. You can also choose View⇨Navigation Tabs⇨Pages to access this tab. All the other navigation tabs are also available under the View⇨Navigation Tabs submenu. As with the toolbars, you can see which tabs are presently visible by the check mark adjacent to the tab's name in this submenu.

Many of the tabs have more advanced uses that we cover in later chapters of this minibook. In this chapter, we provide you with a brief understanding of how you can use the Pages tab to more easily navigate through a PDF document. Just do this:

1. **Make sure that the Pages palette is visible by clicking its tab.**

2. **Click any page thumbnail to navigate directly to that page.**

A dark border appears around the selected page.

In the lower-right corner of the page is a small red box — a very small red box. Depending on your present zoom level, you may already see the red bounding area representing the present view of the active page.

3. Drag this red box up and toward the left (in a diagonal movement) to focus the magnification on a smaller portion of the page, as shown in Figure 1-5.

4. When you're zoomed in on a page, click the page thumbnail on the spot that you want to see to change the area of the page shown in the document window.

Figure 1-5:
Drag the red box up in a diagonal movement to zoom in on the active page.

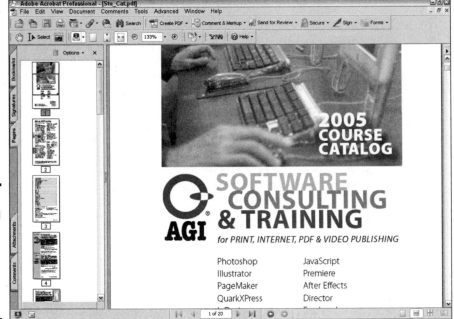

Chapter 2: Creating PDF Files

In This Chapter

- ✔ **Creating PDF files from Microsoft Word, Excel, and PowerPoint documents**

- ✔ **Creating PDF files from Adobe Creative Suite applications**

- ✔ **Creating PDF files from all other electronic formats**

- ✔ **Creating PDF files from paper documents and the Web**

You don't need Adobe Acrobat to create Portable Document Format (PDF) files from Adobe Creative Suite documents — this capability is built right into the Creative Suite application — but you do need Acrobat for creating PDF files from all other programs. Converting documents to the PDF format is a great way to share information. In this chapter, we discuss how to create Adobe PDF files from a variety of programs.

Creating PDF Files from Microsoft Office

Adobe Acrobat includes tools that make it easy to convert Microsoft Word, Excel, and PowerPoint files to PDF. These capabilities are much more robust for the Windows versions of these programs, so Macintosh users may find that not all of these options are available.

When you install Acrobat on your computer, it looks for Microsoft Office programs. If it locates Word, Excel, PowerPoint, or Outlook, it installs a utility called PDF Maker that helps convert Microsoft Office documents to PDF. This utility installs a PDF Maker toolbar that appears in these programs, allowing for one-click PDF creation.

You can tell whether PDF Maker has been installed for these Microsoft Office programs by looking for the Adobe PDF menu to the right of the Help menu, and the PDF Maker toolbar. If you don't see the Convert to PDF button and the Acrobat PDF menu, it's possible that Acrobat did not install PDF Maker. To gain access to the PDF Maker utility, you can reinstall Adobe Acrobat.

When you convert documents to Adobe PDF, the original file remains unchanged, so you'll have both the original file and a separate PDF document. The original document and the PDF are not linked, so changes to the original source file are not reflected in the PDF file.

PDF conversion options

Adobe PDF Maker provides a variety of controls over how PDF files are created. For example, you can have Acrobat create the file without asking you to confirm the location and name of the file each time you click the Convert to Adobe PDF button, and it will simply save the file in the same location as the original document. Similarly, you can choose to create PDF files that balance your need for quality and file size.

PDF Maker provides controls over the type of PDF file you create. This is because some PDF files may need to be of a higher quality for printing, and others may need to be smaller to allow for fast electronic distribution. For example, you may want to post a PDF document to a Web site, where you want to make the file small so that it can be quickly downloaded.

When working in Microsoft Word, Excel, or PowerPoint you can access the PDF Maker controls by choosing Adobe PDF⇨Change Conversion Settings. In the Acrobat PDF Maker dialog box that appears, you can then choose from a variety of settings that control how the PDF file is created. There are a number of options, but in this section, we focus on those options that are most useful for Microsoft Office users.

From the Conversion Settings drop-down list in the Acrobat PDF Maker dialog box, you can find these useful options that control how the PDF file is generated:

✦ **Standard:** Choose this option to create PDF files that will be printed on an office laser printer or distributed via e-mail. This setting meets the needs of most users — it provides some compression of graphics but they remain clear on-screen and look reasonably good when printed. In addition, this setting builds the fonts into the PDF file to maintain an exact representation of the document, regardless of where the file is viewed.

✦ **Smallest File Size:** With this setting, you can control the file size of the PDF documents you create. This setting provides significant compression of images and also reduces resolution. This causes graphics within the files to lose some clarity, and they may appear jagged.

In addition, fonts are not embedded in PDF files created with this setting. If the fonts used in the document are not available on a computer where a PDF created with the Smallest File Size setting is viewed, Acrobat uses a font substitution technology to replicate the size and shape of the fonts used in the document. This typically provides a similar appearance to the original document, but it is not always an exact match of the original file.

✦ **Press Quality:** If you need to provide PDF files to your commercial printer or copy shop, this is the setting to use when creating the PDF. When you use this setting, you create a PDF file that is designed for high-quality print reproduction. Along with including fonts in the PDF file, the graphics are not significantly compressed and they maintain a much higher resolution. Overall, these files tend to be larger than similar PDF files created using different settings, but the quality of the PDF file is more important than the file size when you're having the PDF professionally printed.

PDF conversion options from Microsoft Word and Excel

Although Microsoft Word and Excel are widespread standards on many corporate computers, they aren't always the best choice for distributing documents. Formatting of Microsoft Word documents and Excel spreadsheets changes depending on the fonts available on users' computers or even the printer they choose to print with. In addition, Microsoft Word and Excel files can be easily edited, and users can also copy and extract information from these files with very few limitations.

Converting a Word or Excel file to PDF overcomes these limitations and is quite straightforward. Choose from two methods:

✦ From inside Microsoft Word or Excel (make sure that the document you want to convert to an Adobe PDF file is open), simply click the Convert to PDF button in the main toolbar to convert the document.

✦ Alternatively, choose Adobe PDF⇨Convert to Adobe PDF.

No matter which method you choose, you must specify the location of the PDF file that is created and name the file.

Choose Adobe PDF⇨Change Conversion Settings and deselect the Prompt for PDF filename option so that PDF files are generated in one step, without having to input the name of the PDF file.

Not only can you create PDF files from Microsoft Office applications, but you can add other functionality into PDF documents. Choose Adobe PDF⇨ Change Conversion Settings and in the dialog box that appears, you can use the following settings:

✦ **Add Links:** This option automatically converts Word links, such as Web addresses, into PDF links that can be used when viewing the file in Acrobat or the Adobe Reader. Click the Word tab to access additional link options that can be built into PDF files created from Word, such as Table of Contents links.

✦ **Add Bookmarks:** With this option, you can add interactive bookmarks that make it easy to navigate the PDF file. Bookmarks are added based on Microsoft Word styles, such as text that is styled as Heading 1 or Heading 2. The bookmarks appear in the Bookmarks palette when viewing the PDF, making it easier to navigate the PDF file.

Converting PowerPoint files to PDF

You can convert your PowerPoint presentations to Adobe PDF documents using PDF Maker. This makes it easy to distribute electronic versions of presentations, without worrying that the file may be edited, or that the recipient may not have the same fonts that you used. From inside PowerPoint, click the Convert to Adobe PDF button to save the file as an Adobe PDF file (make sure that the presentation you're converting is open before you click the button!). You can also choose Adobe PDF⇨Convert to Adobe PDF from PowerPoint's main menu.

As with Word and Excel, you can choose Adobe PDF⇨Change Conversion Settings within PowerPoint to select options relating to the conversion. Along with the conversion settings that impact the quality of the resulting PDF file, there are two additional options you should select:

✦ **Save Slide Transitions in Adobe PDF:** With this option, you can have the slide transitions that were created in PowerPoint converted into PDF transitions that will be used when the presentation is delivered using Adobe Acrobat's Full Screen View option.

✦ **Convert Multimedia to PDF Multimedia:** Because Adobe PDF files are able to contain integrated sound and movie files, you can choose this option to have sounds and movies used in a PowerPoint file converted into the PDF document.

You can even use PDF as the method for delivering presentations that have been created using PowerPoint by choosing Window⇨Full Screen View after you've converted the file to PDF. You can also click the Full Screen option in the lower left corner of the document window. Press the Esc key to stop viewing the document in the Full Screen mode.

Creating PDF Files from Adobe Creative Suite Applications

Throughout this book, we discuss how to integrate the applications within the Adobe Creative Suite. So you won't be surprised to know that you can easily convert a Photoshop file, an Illustrator file, or an InDesign document to the PDF format. In this section, we show you how.

Converting Photoshop and Illustrator files to PDF

Both Adobe Photoshop CS2 and Adobe Illustrator CS2 can save documents directly in the Adobe PDF file format. To do this, simply choose File➪Save or File➪Save As. Then, from the File Type drop-down list, choose Adobe PDF (Illustrator) or Photoshop PDF (Photoshop). In these programs, you can create PDF files without Adobe Acrobat or Acrobat Distiller.

PDF files created from Photoshop or Illustrator can be viewed using Adobe Acrobat or Adobe Reader. But these PDF files can also be opened and edited by the same program in which they were created. For example, a logo created using Adobe Illustrator and saved as a PDF file from Illustrator can be opened and modified at a later time with Illustrator. The same file can also be viewed using either Adobe Reader or Adobe Acrobat software.

Converting InDesign documents to PDF

Like in Photoshop and Illustrator, the ability to convert InDesign documents to PDF is integrated into the application. Using Adobe InDesign CS2, you can choose File➪Export and select Adobe PDF from the File Type drop-down list. InDesign provides a significant number of options for controlling the size and quality of the resulting PDF file. Many of these options are similar to those available for PDF Maker for Microsoft Office, which we discuss earlier in this chapter.

In the Adobe InDesign Export PDF dialog box, you can choose from the Preset drop-down list at the top of the dialog box. The choices are many, but we list and describe here the most commonly used settings:

✦ **Smallest File Size:** Creates compact Adobe PDF files that are intended for display on the Internet or to be distributed via email. Use this setting to create PDF files that will be viewed primarily on-screen.

✦ **High Quality Print:** Creates Adobe PDF files that are intended for desktop printers and digital copiers.

✦ **Press Quality:** Use this setting to create PDF files that will be delivered to a commercial printer, for high quality offset print reproduction.

When creating PDF files to be used for high-resolution printing, be certain to select Marks and Bleeds in the list on the left in the Export PDF dialog box, as shown in Figure 2-1, and specify the amount of space items need to extend off the page (*bleed*). If you're delivering the file to a printing firm, they can provide you with guidance as to the value you should use for bleed and marks offset. A good rule to follow is to use at least .125 inches if you have items extending all the way to the edge of your document pages. Specify the value you want by entering the value in the Bleed and Slug section of the Marks and Bleeds tab. If the amount of bleed is to be the same on all four sides, type the value in the Top text field and then click the link icon to the right of the Top and Bottom Bleed text fields.

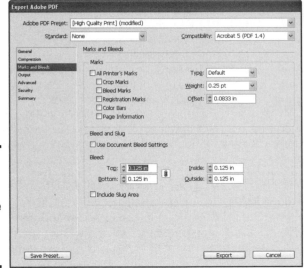

Figure 2-1:
Setting
the bleed
values in the
InDesign
Export PDF
dialog box.

Converting Other Electronic Documents to PDF

Adobe has made it quite easy to create PDF files from other Adobe Creative Suite applications and Microsoft Office programs, but you can also create PDF files from many other programs. When you installed the Adobe Creative Suite on your computer, you also installed a new printer, called the Adobe PDF printer, which is used to convert documents to Adobe PDF files. This printer captures all the same information that is normally sent to your printer and, instead of creating a piece of paper, the information is converted into an Adobe PDF file.

To create a PDF file from any program, choose File➪Print. In the Print dialog box, select Adobe PDF as the printer, as shown in Figure 2-2, and click OK (Windows) or Print (Mac).

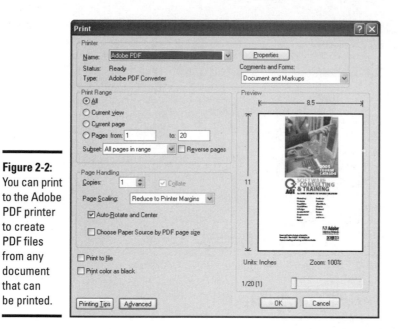

Figure 2-2:
You can print
to the Adobe
PDF printer
to create
PDF files
from any
document
that can
be printed.

To change the type of PDF file that is created, such as a smaller file for Internet Web posting, or a higher quality file for delivery to a commercial printer, do this:

✦ **Windows:** Click the Properties button in the Print dialog box to open the Adobe PDF Document Properties dialog box, shown in Figure 2-3. Here you can choose the PDF Settings you want to use to control the quality and size of the resulting PDF file.

✦ **Mac OS:** Choose PDF Options from the Copies and Pages menu and then choose the PDF Settings.

We discuss the settings earlier in this chapter, in the "PDF conversion options" section.

This process of navigating through the Print menu may appear strange, but it is probably the easiest way for Adobe to capture all of the same information that you would expect to see when you print your files. This provides an easy and standard method for generating PDF files from any program. In fact, you can even use this method for creating PDF files from Microsoft Office programs or other programs in the Adobe Creative Suite if you want.

Bookmarks and links are not exported if a PDF is generated using the Print menu option.

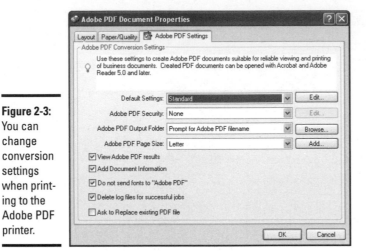

Figure 2-3:
You can change conversion settings when printing to the Adobe PDF printer.

Creating PDF Files from Paper Documents and the Web

PDF files do not need to start as electronic publishing files. Adobe Acrobat provides options for converting both paper documents and Internet Web pages into PDF format.

Converting paper documents to PDF

To convert paper documents into PDF, you need a scanner to digitize the information. If you expect to scan a large number of pages into PDF, you should consider purchasing a scanner with an automatic document feeder. There are also scanners that can scan both the front and backside of a document at the same time.

Unfortunately, we can't fully describe all the ins and outs of choosing a scanner to fit your needs, but Mark L. Chambers does a swell job of it in his book, *Scanners For Dummies* (Wiley Publishing, Inc.).

If a scanner is already hooked to the computer on which you use Acrobat, follow these steps to scan in a paper document and then convert it to PDF format:

1. **From the Acrobat main menu, choose File⇨Create PDF⇨From Scanner.**

The Create PDF from Scanner dialog box appears.

2. **Make sure that your scanner is turned on, put the document to be scanned into the scanner, and then click the Scan button.**

If necessary, continue to scan multiple pages into a single document.

When you're done scanning, the scanned page appears in Acrobat.

3. **Choose File⇨Save to save the PDF.**

If you have a PDF open and choose Create PDF from Scanner, a window appears giving you the opportunity to append the file (add to the existing file) or create a new PDF file.

The document opens in Acrobat.

If the pages need to be rotated, you can choose Document⇨ Rotate Pages. Some scanners from Fujitsu now automatically convert scanned documents to Adobe PDF files and automatically rotate them.

Use the Zoom In tool to increase the magnification of what you have just scanned. You can see that the text is jagged because it is a picture of the text. If you need the text to be searchable, use Document⇨Recognize Text Using OCR. This command makes the text you have just scanned searchable. Otherwise, you have only a picture of the text.

This is unlike text from electronic documents that you create by either PDF Maker or the Adobe PDF Printer. Both of these options create text that looks very clear, even when enlarged.

Converting Web pages to PDFs

By converting online content to Adobe PDF, you can capture contents from an Internet Web site. Because Web content can change rapidly, this allows you to capture something that may not remain online for a long period of time. Things such as news stories or competitive information can be converted from a Web site into PDF in a single click. And because PDF files can easily be combined with other PDF documents, you can merge information from a variety of sources, such as spreadsheets, word processing documents, and brochures.

If you want to convert only a single page and are using Internet Explorer, click the Convert Web Page to PDF button. This converts the current web page to a PDF. If you want to convert more than a single page, follow these steps from within Acrobat (not your Web browser):

1. **From the Acrobat main menu, choose File⇨Create PDF⇨From Web Page.**

The Create PDF from Web Page dialog box opens, as shown in Figure 2-4.

Figure 2-4: Converting Internet Web pages to PDF.

2. **In the URL text field, enter the URL for the Web site you're converting to PDF.**

3. **To capture additional pages that are linked from the main page you're capturing, select the Get Only radio button (selected by default) and enter the number of levels to be captured in the Levels text field and then select one of the following:**

- Select the Stay on Same Path check box if you want only URLs (pages) subordinate from the entered URL converted to PDF.

- Select the Stay on Same Server check box to download only pages that are on the same server as the entered URL.

Be cautious about selecting the Get Entire Site radio button instead of the Get Only radio button. The Get Entire Site option may take an enormous amount of time and not have any relevance to what you need.

4. **Click the Settings button to open the Web Page Conversion Settings dialog box and see accepted File types and change PDF settings (on the General tab), as shown in Figure 2-5.**

5. **On the Page layout tab of the Web Page Conversion Settings dialog box, make changes to page size, orientation, and margins.**

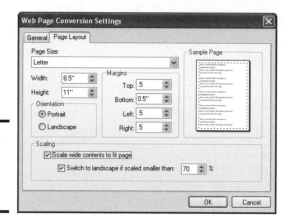

Figure 2-5:
Changing
file type
and PDF
settings.

6. **When you're done making changes in the Web Page Conversion Settings dialog box, click OK.**

7. **Back in the Create PDF from Web Page dialog box, click the Create button.**

   The Downloading Status window opens, showing the rate of download.

When the download is complete, the Web page (for the entered URL) selected appears as a PDF with existing hyperlinks (links to other pages within the site) left intact. When links on the converted Web page are selected, the viewer can open the page either in Acrobat or the Web browser.

Chapter 3: Adding Interactivity to PDF Files

In This Chapter

✔ Adding interactive bookmarks

✔ Creating and editing links

✔ Using buttons for easy navigation

*B*ecause many Adobe PDF documents are viewed online, it makes sense to make the documents easy for readers to navigate. Using Acrobat, you can design documents that are easier to navigate than their printed counterparts, adding rich interactive features that simply are not available with paper documents.

Rather than making readers scroll through a document to find what they want, you can add links within an index or table of contents, or you can add links to Web sites and e-mail addresses. Acrobat also includes features to build your own online table of contents (known as *bookmarks*), and you can add buttons that link to specific pages within a PDF document or that cause an action to occur when clicked, such as closing the document. We discuss all of these features in this chapter.

Adding Bookmarks to Ease PDF Navigation

One reason for distributing PDF documents is that it is convenient and cost-effective. But if users can't easily find the information they need, or they're unable to effectively understand how the contents of a file are structured, they may become frustrated or they may need to print the document, which defeats the purpose of electronic distribution.

A table of contents in a traditional, printed book does not work well with electronic PDF files. It requires you to constantly return to the page containing the contents, and then navigate to the page containing the data you need. But you can make your documents more user-friendly by adding bookmarks, which are the equivalent of a table of contents that is always available, no matter what page is being viewed in the document window.

Bookmarks provide a listing of contents that reside within a PDF file, or links to relevant external content. Bookmarks sit within a palette, and when you click the bookmark in the palette, you're taken to a specific destination in the PDF document (or possibly to an external file), much like a hyperlink. Acrobat technically calls the palette a pane, but all other Adobe Creative Suite programs call them palettes — so that's what we call them here. You can create bookmarks from existing text, or you can use your own text to describe the content, such as a chart or graphic.

By default, the Bookmarks palette resides along the left side of the Acrobat document window. Click the Bookmarks tab to make it appear; click the Bookmarks tab a second time to hide it. If the tab is not visible, choose View⇨Navigation Tabs⇨Bookmarks to make it appear.

Creating bookmarks that link to a page

By navigating to a page, and to a specific view on a page, you can establish the destination of a bookmark link. Have a PDF document open and just follow these simple steps:

1. **If the Bookmark tab is not visible, choose View⇨Navigation Tabs⇨ Bookmarks.**

   The bookmark pane appears on the left of the document window.

2. **In the document window, navigate to the page that you want as the bookmark's destination.**

3. **Set the magnification of the view that you want by using either the Zoom In or Zoom Out tools.**

   The zoom level that you are at when you create the bookmark is the view that viewers see when they click the bookmark.

4. **In the Bookmarks palette, choose New Bookmark from the Options menu, as shown in Figure 3-1.**

Figure 3-1: Choose New Bookmark to add bookmarks to a PDF.

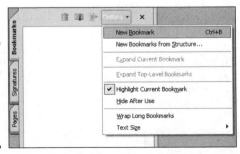

5. **The new bookmark appears in the Bookmarks palette as Untitled; change the name by typing something more descriptive.**

   Untitled is highlighted, so all you have to do to replace it is type the new name.

   If you leave the bookmark as Untitled but want to rename it later, you must click the bookmark and then choose Rename Bookmark from the Options menu in the Bookmark palette.

6. **Test your bookmark by scrolling to another page and view in the document window; then click your saved bookmark in the Bookmark tab.**

   The document window shows the exact location and zoom that you selected when you created the bookmark.

If you use the Select tool to highlight text that is a part of the bookmark destination, such as a headline or a caption, and then choose New Bookmark from the Options menu, the selected text becomes the title of the new bookmark. You can use this shortcut to avoid having to enter a new name for new bookmark titles. You can also press Ctrl+B (Windows) or ⌘+B (Mac OS) to quickly create a bookmark.

Creating bookmarks that link to external files

Although bookmarks are most commonly used to link to content within a PDF file, you can also use bookmarks to create links to other documents. To create a link to an external file, follow these steps:

1. **Choose New Bookmark from the Options menu in the Bookmarks palette.**

2. **Replace the Untitled bookmark entry that appears in the Bookmarks palette with an appropriate title for the bookmark.**

3. **Choose Properties from the Options menu at the top of the Bookmarks palette.**

   The Bookmark Properties dialog box appears. Using this dialog box, you can change a bookmark so that it links to any type of file. In this example, we use a PDF document but this could be a link to another PDF file, a Photoshop file, or even a Microsoft Excel file. Just remember that this creates a relative link. The linked file must travel with the PDF document in order for the link to work.

4. **In the Bookmark Properties dialog box, click the Actions tab and choose Open a File from the Select Action drop-down list, and then click the Add button.**

   The Select File to Open dialog box appears.

5. **Click the Browse button and choose a file to which the bookmark will navigate, and then click the Select button.**

6. **In the Specify Open Preference window, choose whether you want the linked file to open in a new document, then click OK.**

You have created a link to a page in another file. When the bookmark is clicked, the other document will open to the specified page.

It's important to note that the other file is not attached to the current document. If you distribute a PDF file containing the bookmarks to external files, you must distribute any external files that are referenced along with the source file; otherwise, the links will not work. In addition, the linked files need to be in the same relative location as the original documents — so don't change the name of the linked file or the folder in which it is located.

You can also create links to non-PDF files. Instead of choosing Go to a page in another document, you can choose Open a file to open a non-PDF file or choose Open a web link to access an Internet Web address.

Using bookmarks

Bookmarks are very intuitive to use, which makes them an attractive option to add to PDF files. After you click a bookmark, the action associated with it is performed, which typically navigates you to a certain page within the PDF file.

Unfortunately, the Bookmarks palette does not open automatically with a document, even when bookmarks are present within a file. To cause the Bookmarks palette to be displayed when a file is opened, do this:

1. **Choose File⇨Document Properties.**

2. **In the Document Properties dialog box that opens, select the Initial View tab, as shown in Figure 3-2.**

3. **From the Show drop-down list, choose Bookmarks Panel and Page, and then click OK.**

After the file is saved and then reopened, the Bookmarks palette is displayed whenever the document is opened.

Editing bookmarks

You can change the attributes of bookmarks so that they link to other locations by clicking to select a bookmark and then choosing Properties from the Options menu in the Bookmarks palette. In the Bookmark Properties dialog box (see Figure 3-3), you can choose the color and font type of the bookmark on the Appearance tab: To change the bookmark's font style, choose a style from the Style drop-down list; to change the bookmark's color, click the Color box and choose a color from the color picker.

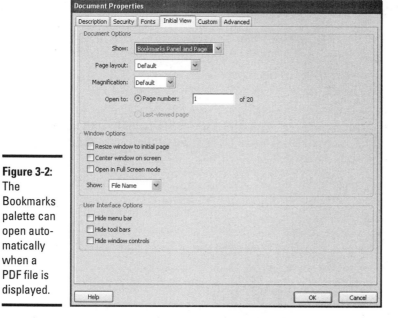

Figure 3-2:
The
Bookmarks
palette can
open auto-
matically
when a
PDF file is
displayed.

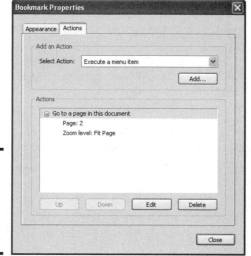

Figure 3-3:
Adding and
deleting
actions of
individual
bookmarks.

On the Actions tab of the Bookmark Properties dialog box, you can delete existing actions (in the Actions section of the Actions tab) by clicking to select an
action and then clicking the Delete button. Also, you can add additional actions
by choosing another action from the Add Action section, and then clicking
the Add button. This allows you to add more than one action to a bookmark.

Adding Interactive Links

When viewing a PDF file electronically, it is useful to add links for e-mail addresses, Web addresses, and even references to other pages. Links are attached to a region of a page, which you identify with the Link tool.

To add an interactive link to your PDF document, follow these steps:

1. **After locating an area of a page where you want to add a link, choose the Link tool from the Advanced Editing toolbar, and then drag around the region of the page to add a link.**

The Create Link dialog box appears, as shown in Figure 3-4.

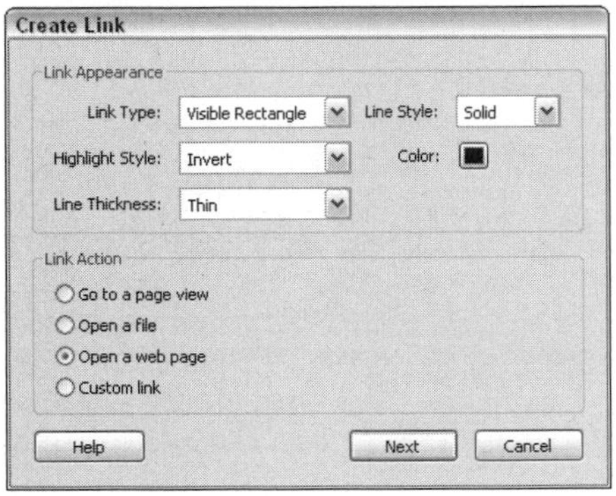

Figure 3-4:
You can add links to Web addresses, e-mail addresses, and other pages.

2. **Choose a Link Action:**

- **Go to a Page View:** This is the default, where you can scroll to the page that is the destination of the link.

- **Open a File:** Alternatively, you can choose to link to another file; click the Browse button to locate the file.

- **Open a Web Page:** If you choose this option, you're choosing to link to a Web address. In the Address text field, enter the complete address of the Web site to which the link should direct viewers. To create a link to an e-mail address, type **mailto:** followed by an e-mail address. Note that mailto: is all one word with no spaces.

- **Custom Link:** Use this option to choose from other types of links in the Link Properties dialog box.

The link is now created.

The Link tool is relatively simple to use, but you may prefer to create links from text in another way: Using the Selection tool, select the text, right-click (Windows) or Control+click (Mac) the selected text, and then choose Create Link from the contextual menu that appears.

Remember that you can also have links automatically transferred from your original Microsoft Office documents when using PDF Maker.

You can edit links by choosing the Link tool and double-clicking the link to open the Link Properties dialog box. While editing a link, you can change how it is presented in the Appearance tab. Make a link invisible or add a border to the link, such as a blue border that commonly is used to define hyperlinks. On the Actions tab of the Link Properties dialog box, you can add, edit, or delete actions, just as you can with bookmarks (see the preceding section).

Adding Buttons to Simplify Your PDF Files

Along with links and bookmarks, buttons provide another way to make your files more useful when they are viewed online. You can create interactive buttons entirely within Acrobat — designing their appearance and adding text to them. Or you can import buttons created in other Adobe Creative Suite applications, such as Photoshop and Illustrator. For example, you can create buttons that advance the viewer to the next page in a document.

 Buttons are added by using the Button tool that is on the Advanced Editing toolbar.

To add a button to your PDF document, follow these steps:

1. **Click the Button tool and click and drag to create the region where the button will appear.**

The Button Properties dialog box appears.

2. **In the General tab, you can enter a name for the button in the Name text field and provide a Tooltip in the Tooltip text field.**

A *ToolTip* is the text that is displayed whenever the mouse cursor is positioned over the button.

3. **In the Appearance tab, establish how your button will look:**

   • **Border Color/Fill Color:** Click the square to the right of the appropriate attribute in the Borders and Colors section of the Appearance tab, and then choose a color from the color picker, as shown in Figure 3-5.

- **Line Thickness and Style:** These options do not appear unless you change the border color from none (red diagonal line) to another selection.

- **Font Size/Font:** Change the size and font of the button text by making a selection from the Font Size and the Font drop-down lists.

- **Text Color:** Change the color of the text by clicking on the color square and choosing a color from the color picker.

Figure 3-5:
Modifying button properties.

4. **In the Options tab, shown in Figure 3-6, make these selections:**

- **Layout:** Use the Layout drop-down list to specify whether you want to use a label (text that you enter in Acrobat that appears on the face of the button) or whether you want an icon (an imported button graphic that you may have designed using Photoshop or Illustrator).

- **Behavior:** If you choose Push from the Behavior drop-down list, you can specify three separate looking buttons. You can use this to create different appearances for the button, so it changes based upon whether the mouse cursor is positioned over the button, and the button appearance can also change when it's being clicked.

- **State:** To specify the different appearances (see Behavior, discussed in the preceding paragraph), click the State on the left side of the Options tab and then choose the Label or Icon status for each state.

- **Label:** If you choose to use a label, enter the text for it in the Label text field.

- **Icon:** If you choose to use an icon, specify the location of the graphic file by clicking the Choose Icon button. Icon graphics must be saved as PDF files. You can create button icons in either Photoshop or Illustrator.

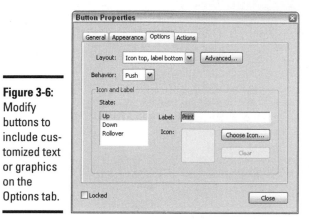

Figure 3-6:
Modify
buttons to
include cus-
tomized text
or graphics
on the
Options tab.

5. **In the Actions tab, you can choose an action from the Select Action drop-down list and then click the Add button.**

   Actions are applied to buttons similar to the way in which they are applied to links and bookmarks.

   • To choose actions that are a part of the menu commands, such as printing a document, closing a file, or navigating to the next or preceding page, choose the Execute Menu Item action, and then specify the command to be accessed.

   • You can also choose the activity that causes the action to occur, known as the *trigger*. The default trigger is Mouse Up, which causes the action to occur when the mouse button is depressed and then released. You can choose other actions, such as the mouse cursor merely rolling over the button without the need to click it.

6. **After you make all your changes in the Button Properties dialog box, click Close and you're done.**

Chapter 4: Editing and Extracting Text and Graphics

In This Chapter

✔ **Manipulating text with the TouchUp tools**

✔ **Modifying graphics with the TouchUp tools**

✔ **Pulling text and graphics out of PDFs for use in other documents**

You may assume that PDF files are mere pictures of your documents and can't be edited, but nothing is farther from the truth. Adobe Acrobat includes a variety of tools for editing both text and graphics. You can use these tools as long as the file has not been secured to prohibit editing. We introduce you to these great tools in this chapter. We discuss security, which allows you to limit access to these tools, in Chapter 6 of this minibook.

Editing Text

The tools for editing text and graphics are located on the Advanced Editing toolbar (shown in Figure 4-1) and also the TouchUp Toolbar. To display these toolbars, choose Tools➪Advanced Editing and then select either Show Advanced Editing Toolbar or Show TouchUp Toolbar.

Figure 4-1:
The Advanced Editing toolbar.

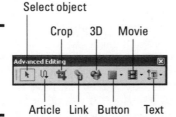

By default, the TouchUp Text tool is visible on the Advanced Editing toolbar. You can hold down on this tool's button to access the TouchUp Object tool and to switch between these two tools. Or hold down on the TouchUp Text tool and choose Show TouchUp Toolbar.

TIP

To make both the TouchUp Text and TouchUp Object tools visible at the same time, click and hold down the TouchUp Text tool button and choose the Show TouchUp Toolbar option. This displays the three TouchUp tools in their own separate toolbar. The TouchUp toolbar also includes a TouchUp Reading Order tool, which is used to correct the reading order or structure of the document. This tool is not used for changing the appearance of the document, so we don't discuss it in this chapter.

Using the TouchUp Text tool

As you might guess, the TouchUp Text tool is used for touching up — that is, *manipulating* — text. This can include changing actual text characters or changing the appearance of text. You can change the word "cat" to read "dog," or you can change black text to make it blue, or you can even change the Helvetica font to the Times font. When you change a PDF file, the original source document is not modified.

You have a few ways to accomplish text edits:

✦ Choose the TouchUp Text tool, click within the text that you want to change to obtain an insertion point, and then start typing the new text.

✦ Or insert the TouchUp tool into your text and press the Backspace or Delete key to delete text.

✦ Alternatively, you can drag, using the TouchUp tool, to highlight text and enter new text to replace what is currently in the file.

When changing text — whether you're adding or deleting — Acrobat tries to use the font that was specified in the original document. Sometimes this font is built into the PDF file, which means that it's *embedded* in the file. Other times, the font may not be available either because it hasn't been embedded or it's been embedded as a *subset* where only some of the characters from the font are included in the PDF file. In these cases, Acrobat may provide a warning message that "All or part of the selection has no available system font. You cannot add or delete text using the currently selected font."

Fortunately, you can change the font if you need to edit the text. However, when you change the font, the text may not retain the same appearance as the original document. In some instances, you may not have the exact same font on your computer as the font used in the PDF document, but you may have a similar font you can use without causing a noticeable change — most people won't notice the difference between Helvetica and Arial or between Times and Times New Roman. Fonts with the same name but from different font designers often look very similar. For instance, Adobe Garamond looks similar to ITC Garamond, even though they are two different fonts.

To change the font that is used for a word or range of words, follow these steps:

1. **Select the text with the TouchUp Text tool by dragging across it, right-click (Windows) or Control+click (Mac) the highlighted text, and then choose Properties from the contextual menu.**

   The TouchUp Properties dialog box appears, as shown in Figure 4-2.

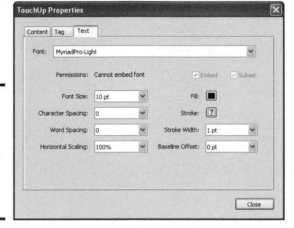

Figure 4-2:
Use the
TouchUp
Properties
dialog box
to change
text
attributes.

2. **In the Text tab, choose the typeface you want to use from the Font drop-down list, and make any other changes you want.**

   In this dialog box, you can also choose to change the size by selecting or typing a number into the Font Size drop-down list. In addition, you can modify the color by clicking the Fill color swatch.

3. **When you're satisfied with your changes, click the Close button to apply your changes to the selected text.**

Editing Graphics

You can also use the TouchUp Object tool to access editing software for modifying graphics. For example, you can use the TouchUp Object tool to select a graphic, bring the graphic into Photoshop, and then save the modified version back into the PDF file. In other words, you can edit the graphics used in PDF documents, even if you do not have access to the original graphic files.

To edit a photographic file from Acrobat in Photoshop, follow these steps:

1. **Right-click (Windows) or Control+click (Mac) on a photographic image with the TouchUp Object tool, and then choose Edit Image from the contextual menu, as shown in Figure 4-3.**

The image file opens in Adobe Photoshop.

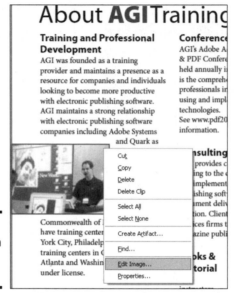

Figure 4-3: Selecting an image for editing.

2. **Using the many tools of Photoshop, make the necessary changes to the graphic, and then choose File⇨Save.**

When you return to the PDF file in Acrobat, the graphic is automatically updated in the PDF document.

If you have the original graphic file, it remains untouched — only the version used within the PDF file is modified. It isn't necessary to have the original graphic file to perform these steps.

You can also use Acrobat to edit vector objects from within PDF files, such as those created using Adobe Illustrator. Just follow these steps:

1. **Select the TouchUp Object tool, right-click (Windows) or Control+click (Mac) on a piece of vector artwork, and then choose Edit Object from the contextual menu (see Figure 4-4).**

Note that Acrobat displays Edit Object in the contextual menu if it detects a vector object, and it displays Edit Image if it detects a bitmap image. Acrobat also displays Edit Objects (note the plural) if you have more than one object selected. Use this to help determine exactly which objects will be edited. If you are editing a complex illustration, be sure to select all of its components by holding down the Ctrl (Windows) or ⌘ (MacOS) while clicking them with the TouchUp Object tool.

After choosing Edit Object, the object opens for editing using Adobe Illustrator.

2. Make the necessary changes in Illustrator, choose File⇨Save.

The graphic is updated in the PDF document.

Figure 4-4:
Use the Edit Object command to edit vector artwork, such as logos created using Adobe Illustrator.

Note that if Acrobat does not start Photoshop or Illustrator after choosing the Edit Image or Edit Object command, you may need to access preferences by choosing Edit⇨Preferences⇨Touch Up and then specify which programs should be used for editing images or objects.

You can also use the TouchUp Object tool to edit the position of text or graphic objects on a page. This includes the ability to relocate individual lines of text or to change the position of a graphic on a page. After you've selected an object with the TouchUp Object tool, you can simply drag it to a new location on the page.

Extracting Text and Graphics

Although editing text and graphics is helpful, you may need to take text or images from a PDF document and use them in another file. Fortunately, Acrobat also includes tools to make this a breeze. Of course, you should always make certain that you have the permission of the owner of a document before reusing content that is not your original work. You need the Basic toolbar for extracting text and graphics, so make sure it's visible. If it isn't, choose Tools⇨Basic⇨Show Basic Toolbar.

Extracting text

Make sure that the Basic toolbar is visible, and then follow these steps to extract text from a PDF file:

1. **With the Select tool on the Basic toolbar, drag to highlight text that you want to copy from the PDF file.**

2. **Right-click (Windows) or Control+click (Mac) the selected text and choose Copy to Clipboard from the contextual menu, as shown in Figure 4-5.**

   This is useful if you don't have access to the original source document, but you need to use the text from a PDF file.

Figure 4-5:
Copying text from a PDF file to reuse in other documents.

3. **Open another text-editing program, such as Adobe InDesign or Microsoft Word.**

   You can paste the copied text into a new document or a preexisting file.

4. **Insert your cursor in the document at the appropriate spot and choose File⇨Paste.**

   The text is pasted into the document, ready for you to use.

Text that is copied from a PDF file is no longer linked to the original document. Edits made to the extracted text are not reflected within the PDF file, and it is extremely difficult to have the extracted text reinserted into the PDF document. It is best to think of the extraction process as a one-way trip for the text, as it can be extracted but not reinserted.

You can also copy text within a table to the Clipboard or open it directly in a spreadsheet program, such as Microsoft Excel. And you maintain the table's formatting after it is extracted. Just follow these steps:

1. **With the Select tool (on the Basics toolbar), click and drag to select the text in the table. You can also position your cursor just outside the edge of the table, then draw a box around a table.**

   A border appears around the selected table.

2. **Right-click (Windows) or Control+click (Mac) and choose Open Table in Spreadsheet from the contextual menu, as shown in Figure 4-6.**

   The table is opened in Excel or whatever spreadsheet program you have installed on your computer.

   Alternatively, you can either save the table directly to a file or save a copy to the Clipboard to be later pasted:

   - To save the table directly to a file, choose Save Table As from the contextual menu.

   - To copy the table to the Clipboard so that you can paste it into other documents, choose Copy As Table from the contextual menu.

   And that's it. You can now use that table in another program.

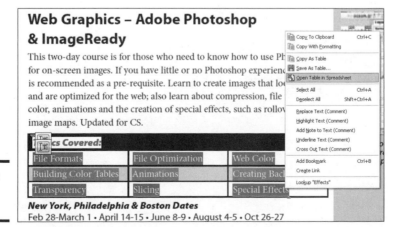

Figure 4-6:
Extracting
a table.

Extracting graphics

You can also extract graphics from PDF files, but extracting graphics is very different from editing them. We discussed editing graphics and vector objects earlier in this chapter. When editing graphics, you opened the original graphic file at its highest possible quality. Extracting graphics is different, as they are removed at the quality of the screen display resolution, which may be much lower quality than the original, embedded graphics.

With the Select tool, right-click (Windows) or Control+click (Mac) an image and choose Copy Image to Clipboard from the contextual menu (see Figure 4-7). The image is now available to be pasted into other applications.

You can also use the Snapshot tool to click and drag to create a picture of a certain area within a PDF file. This allows you to create what is commonly referred to as a "screen grab" of a section within a PDF file.

Figure 4-7: Copying an image to the Clipboard to paste into other applications.

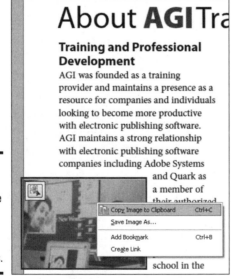

Chapter 5: Using Commenting and Annotation Tools

In This Chapter

✔ **Adding comments to PDF files**

✔ **Working with comments**

*O*ne of the fantastic features of Acrobat is the capability to mark up documents electronically using virtual sticky notes called *comments*. You can mark up text to indicate changes, and add annotations and drawing comments to a PDF file. The Acrobat commenting tools do not change the original file, and you can remove the comments at any time, so comments can be disabled for printing or viewing at any time. In this chapter, we describe these great features and show you how to put them to work for you.

Creating Comments

You can easily add annotations to PDF files, including stamps, text highlights, and electronic sticky notes. The review and commenting tools are spread across four palettes. You can access these toolbars by clicking the Comment & Markup button. This causes the Commenting toolbar to display, as shown in Figure 5-1. You can then choose to display the Highlighting toolbar by clicking and holding the arrow to the right of the Highlighter tool. You can display the Drawing Markups toolbar by choosing Tools⇨Drawing Markups⇨ Show Drawing Markups Toolbar, and from the Drawing Markups toolbar you can choose to display the Drawing toolbar by clicking the downward arrow to the right of the arrow tool and choosing Show Drawing Toolbar.

Figure 5-1: Acrobat's drawing, markup, and commenting tools.

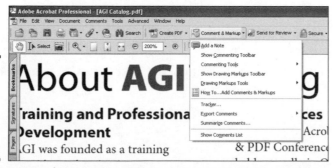

You can also access the review and commenting toolbars by choosing View⇨Toolbars and then choosing the appropriate toolbar from the available list. We discuss each of these toolbars throughout this section.

The Commenting toolbar

The Commenting toolbar, shown in Figure 5-2, provides five tools for adding comments to PDF documents, and a Show menu to help manage comments and the process of adding comments. We discuss these tools here.

Figure 5-2:
The
Commenting
toolbar.

The Note tool

Use the Note tool to add electronic sticky notes to your files. You can click on the location where you want the note to appear within a PDF document. An icon appears representing the note, along with a window where you can enter text. After entering text in the note, close the window so that the document is not hidden beneath it. You can change the icon and color used to represent the note by right-clicking (Windows) or Control+clicking (Mac) the note and choosing Properties from the contextual menu. In the Properties dialog box that appears, make the changes to the note icon or color, and then click Close.

The Text Edits tool

The Text Edits tool is actually six separate text commenting tools. Use these tools to cross out text, highlight text, underline text, add a note to selected text, replace the selected text, or create an insertion point showing where additional text should be inserted.

To use the Text Edits tool, follow these steps:

1. **Choose the Text Edits tool and drag to select text that requires a change or comment.**

2. **Click the arrow to the right of the Text Edits tool to access the drop-down list containing your six choices.**

3. Choose an option from the list of available editing choices.

Your selected text changes, depending on what you choose from the list.

After selecting the text that requires a comment, you can press the Delete or Backspace key to indicate a text edit to remove the text. Similarly, you can start to type, and Acrobat will create an insertion point. Also, if you right-click (Windows) or Ctrl-click (Mac OS) after selecting the text, you can select the type of edit or comment you want to insert from the contextual menu.

The Stamp tool

You can use stamps to identify documents or to highlight a certain part of a document. Common stamps include Confidential, Draft, Sign Here, and Approved.

The stamps are grouped into sections. Some of the stamps automatically add your default user name along with the date and time you applied them to the document; these are available under the Dynamic category in the Stamps menu. The more traditional business stamps, such as Confidential, appear under the Standard Business category. You can access each of the different categories by clicking on the arrow to the right of the Stamp tool in the Commenting toolbar, as shown in Figure 5-3.

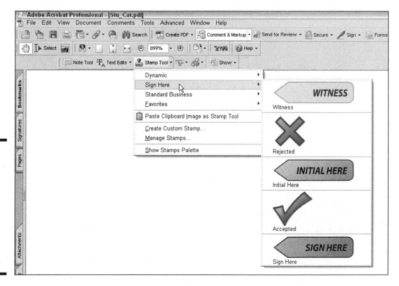

Figure 5-3:
The Stamp tool has many choices within different categories.

To apply a stamp to your document, follow these steps:

1. **Select the Stamp tool from the Commenting toolbar.**

2. **Click the arrow to the right of the stamp tool and, from the menu, choose the stamp you want to apply to the document.**

3. **Drag within your document at the location where you want the stamp to appear.**

The Highlight Text tool

The Highlight Text tool actually provides the same functionality and options that are available with the Text Edits tool, but this tool provides easy access to a function that you might use on a regular basis. You can use the Highlight Text tool to highlight, cross out, or underline text.

To highlight text, follow these steps:

1. **Select the Highlight Text tool from the Commenting toolbar.**

2. **Click and hold on the menu option arrow to the right of the Highlight tool and choose the comment that you want to appear when text is selected.**

   Choices include highlighting with a color, crossing out, or underlining text.

3. **Drag over the text that you want highlighted, crossed out, or underlined.**

   The text is now marked-up, reflecting the type of comment that you selected.

 You can have the Highlighting, Cross-out, and Underline tool appear in their own palette by clicking the Highlighting tool in the Commenting toolbar and then choosing Show Highlighting Toolbar.

The Attach File tools

Using the Attach File tools, you can attach an existing text file, sound file, or any file copied to the Clipboard from your computer (or computer network) and attach it to the PDF.

Follow these steps for file and sound attachments:

1. **Choose the Attach File tool from the Advanced Commenting toolbar.**

2. **Click and hold on the option menu arrow to the right of the Attach File tool to choose the type of file that you want to attach.**

3. **Click where you want the attachment noted.**

   The Add Attachment dialog box appears.

4. **In the Add Attachment dialog box, browse to the file that you want to attach and click the Select button.**

   An icon (either a paperclip for a text file or speaker icon for a sound file) appears on your document to denote that another file is attached.

   With the Attach Sound tool, you can either locate an existing sound file or share a verbal comment by using a microphone and recording a message directly into the PDF. The sound is added as a comment.

   REMEMBER

   The file(s) that you attach with the Attach File tools becomes embedded within the PDF file. The attached file remains in its original file format, even if the attached file is not a PDF file. For example, you can attach an Excel spreadsheet to a PDF document.

The Drawing Markups toolbar

Additional mark-up tools are available in the Drawing Markups toolbar (see Figure 5-4). Make the Drawing Markups toolbar visible by choosing Tools➪Drawing Markups➪Show Drawing Markups toolbar. This toolbar includes five tools that you can use to add expanded comments and annotations to your document. We show you how to use these tools here.

Figure 5-4:
The
Drawing
Markups
toolbar.

The Drawing tools

Use the drawing tools to add lines, ovals, rectangles, and other shapes to your PDF file. Select different shapes by clicking and holding on the menu option arrow to the right of the Drawing tool. These shapes can be used to call attention to specific portions of a document.

To add shapes to your document with the Drawing tool, follow these steps:

1. **Select the menu option arrow to the right of the Arrow tool (on the Drawing Markups toolbar) and choose a shape.**

2. **Drag on the document where you want the shape to appear.**

   The shape is created.

3. While the Drawing tool is selected, click the shape you created and drag the corner points to resize, if necessary.

4. After creating a shape, right-click (Windows) or Control+click (Mac) the shape and choose Properties from the contextual menu to change the color and thickness of the line values. You can also use the Properties toolbar to change the appearance of a selected comment.

The Drawing tools can be placed in their own separate toolbar by choosing Show Drawing MarkupsToolbar from the Comment & Markup menu in the toolbar, and then choosing Show Drawing Toolbar by clicking on the drawing menu tools. Note that there is both a Drawing Markup toolbar and Drawing toolbar.

The Text Box tool

When creating notes that you want to prominently display on a document, you can use the Text Box tool.

Follow these steps to add a text box to hold your comments:

1. Select the Text Box tool from the Drawing Markups toolbar.

   This provides a text field that is placed directly on the document.

2. Drag to add the comment.

3. Right-click (Windows) or Control+click (Mac) and choose Properties from the contextual menu to set the color of the text box that contains the note. You can also use the Properties toolbar to modify the selected text box.

4. Make your choices to modify the appearance of the text box, and then click Close.

The Pencil tool

With the Pencil tool, you can create freeform lines on your documents. These can be useful when trying to attract attention to a specific portion of a page. Just follow these steps:

1. Select the Pencil tool from the Drawing toolbar.

2. Click and drag to draw on your document.

3. Edit the color and thickness of lines created with the Pencil by right-clicking (Windows) or Control+clicking (Mac) on the line and choosing Properties from the contextual menu or use the Properties toolbar.

4. Make your choices and click Close.

By clicking and holding down on the Pencil tool, you can choose the Pencil Eraser tool. Use the Pencil Eraser tool to remove portions of lines that had previously been created with the Pencil tool.

Managing Comments

One of the most powerful features of PDF commenting is the ability to easily manage and share comments and annotations among reviewers. For example, you can determine which comments are displayed at any time, and you can filter the comments by author or by the type of commenting tool that was used to create the comment. In addition, you can indicate a response to a comment and track the changes that may have been made to a document based upon a comment. Also, comments from multiple reviewers can be consolidated into a single document.

Viewing comments

You can use any of several methods to see a document's list of comments:

✦ Click the Comments tab along the left side of the document window.

✦ Click and hold on the Show button in the Commenting toolbar, and choose Show Comments List from the menu that appears.

✦ Choose View⇨Navigation Tab⇨Comments.

No matter which method you use, the Comments List window that shows all the comments in the document appears along the bottom of the document window. You can see the author of each comment and any notes entered by reviewers. By clicking the plus sign to the left of a comment, you can view more information about it, such as what type of comment it is and the date and time it was created.

If you've clicked the plus sign to the left of the comment to expand the view, it changes to a minus sign, which can be clicked to return to the consolidated view showing only the author and the initial portions of any text from the note.

To the right of the plus sign is a check box that you can use to indicate that the comment has been reviewed or to indicate that a certain comment needs further attention. Use these check boxes for your own purposes; their status does not export with the document if you send the file to others, so they are for your own personal use only.

Changing a comment's review status

Acrobat makes it easy to indicate whether a comment has been reviewed, accepted, or has additional comments attached to it. To change the status of a comment, follow these steps:

1. **In the Comments List, Right-click (Windows) or Control+click (Mac) on a comment and choose Set Status⇨Review from the contextual menu.**

2. **Select Accepted, Rejected, Cancelled, or Completed, depending on what's appropriate to your situation.**

3. **Choose Comments⇨Show Comments List to see the entire list of comments and the status of each. You can also click the Comments tab to display the comments.**

   The comment you modified appears in the list, showing the new status you assigned to it.

Replying to a comment

You can also right-click (Windows) or Control+click (Mac) on a comment in the Comments List and choose Reply from the contextual menu to add a follow-up note to the comment. This way, new comments can be tied to existing comments. If your documents go through multiple rounds of review, this allows a secondary or final reviewer to expand on the comments from an initial reviewer. This also allows an author or designer to clearly respond to the suggestions from an editor.

Collapsing or hiding comments

Because the Comments List can become rather large, you can choose to collapse all comments so that only the page number on which comments appear is displayed in the list. To do this, click the Collapse All button in the upper left of the Comments List window; it has a minus sign next to it. To view all of the comments, click the Expand All button in the same location; this button has a plus sign next to it..

To hide all the comments within a document, click and hold the Show button on the Commenting toolbar and choose Hide All Comments. You can then click the Show button in the Comments toolbar and choose to show comments based upon:

✦ **Type of comment:** such as note, line, or cross out

✦ **Reviewer:** Such as Bob or Jane

✦ **Status:** Such as accepted or rejected

✦ **Checked status:** This can be checked or unchecked.

Use these filtering options to view only those comments that are relevant to you.

Sharing comments

You can share your comments with other reviewers who have access to the same PDF document by following these steps:

1. **Make sure that the Comments List is visible by clicking the Comments tab on the left side of the document window.**

2. **Select the comment that you want to export by clicking it (Shift+click for multiple selections).**

3. **From the Options menu on the far right side of the Comments List window, choose Export Selected Comments.**

The Export Comments dialog box appears.

4. **Browse to the location that you want the comments to be saved and give the saved file a new name.**

This creates a file that includes only the comments' information, and not the entire PDF file. You can share this with reviewers who have the same PDF file, and they can choose Import Comments from the Options menu in the Comments List window to add the comments into their document. You can use this method to avoid having to send entire PDF files to those who already have the document.

Summarizing comments

You can compile a list of all the comments from a PDF file into a new, separate document. To summarize comments, follow these steps:

1. **From the Options menu in the Comments List window, choose Summarize Comments.**

The Summarize Options dialog box appears.

2. **Create a listing of the comments with lines connecting them to their locations on the page by selecting the second radio button from the top of the list.**

In the Include section, you can choose which comments should be summarized.

3. **Click OK.**

This creates a new PDF document that simply lists all the comments, as shown in Figure 5-5.

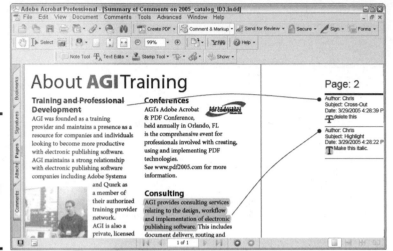

Figure 5-5:
Comments
after they
have been
summarized
on a new
PDF
document.

Enabling commenting in Adobe Reader

Acrobat 7 makes it easy to include users of the free Adobe Reader in a review process. To include Adobe Reader users in a review, choose Comments⇨ Enable for Commenting in Adobe Reader. After saving the file it can be shared with users of Adobe Reader, who can then use commenting and markup tools and save their comments into the file. It is necessary for a user of Adobe Acrobat 7 Professional to enable commenting in a PDF file before users of Adobe Reader can add comments to a file.

Chapter 6: Securing Your PDF Files

In This Chapter

✔ Finding out about security in Acrobat

✔ Using passwords

✔ Setting limits for editing and printing

You may think that because you've converted your documents to PDF that they are secure. This is not quite true, because Adobe Acrobat includes tools for changing text and images, and extracting them as well. For example, you can use the Select tool (which we discuss in Chapter 4 of this minibook) to select and copy a passage of text or graphics.

Applying security provides you with control over who is able to view, edit, or print the PDF documents you distribute. You can restrict access to certain features, which deters most users from manipulating your files. All Adobe applications recognize and honor security settings applied in Acrobat, but some software ignores Adobe's security settings, or can bypass them all together. For this reason, we recommend that you should share your most sensitive documents only when you've applied password security protection. This way the only users that can open a file are those who know the password.

In this chapter, we discuss using password protection to limit access to PDF files and show you how to limit what users can do within your PDF documents.

Understanding Password Security

By requiring users to enter a password to open and view your PDF files, you limit access to those files so that only certain users can view them. You can also apply security to limit access to certain Acrobat and Adobe Reader features, such as copying text or graphics, editing the file, and printing. Adobe calls this type of security *password security* because it requires a password to either open the document or to change the security that has been applied to the document.

Apply security options that limit the opening and editing of your PDF document to those who supply the proper password by using the Secure button on the Tasks toolbar. If the Secure button isn't visible, choose View➪Toolbars➪ Tasks.

Click and hold down on the Secure button in the Tasks toolbar and choose Secure this Document, which opens the Select a Policy to Apply dialog box, as shown in Figure 6-1.

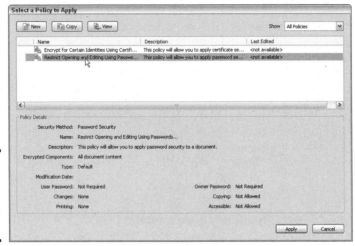

Figure 6-1:
The Select a Policy to Apply dialog box.

The Select a Policy to Apply dialog box is where you make your choices about the type of restrictions applied to a PDF document. Click the Restrict Opening and Editing Using Passwords option, and then click the Apply button. This causes the Password Security – Settings dialog box to appear.

In the Password Security – Settings dialog box, you choose an Acrobat version from the Compatibility drop-down list. The higher the version of Acrobat, the greater the level of security.

Your choice here is based on your needs for security and also the version of Acrobat or Adobe Reader that your audience will be using. In the following list, we explain the compatibility choices before showing you how to enable security in the following sections:

✦ **Acrobat 3.0 and Later:** If the users who receive your PDF files may have older versions of the software, you can choose Acrobat 3.0 and Later from the Compatibility drop-down list to ensure that they can work with the files you provide. This provides compatibility for users who may not have updated their software in many years, but the level of security is limited to 40-bit encryption. While this will keep the average user from gaining access to your files, it will not deter a determined hacker from accessing them.

✦ **Acrobat 5.0 and Later:** When sharing files with users who have access to Adobe Reader or Adobe Acrobat version 5.0 or 6.0, this option provides expanded security, increasing the security level to 128-bit. This makes the resulting PDF files more difficult to access. Along with the enhanced security, you can also secure the files while still allowing access to the file for visually impaired users. Earlier versions of security do not provide this option, but it is included when you choose either Acrobat 5.0 or Acrobat 6.0 compatible security.

✦ **Acrobat 6.0 and Later:** Along with the enhanced security offered with Acrobat 5.0 compatibility, this setting adds the ability to maintain plain text metadata. In short, this allows for information about the file, such as its author, title, or creation date, to remain visible while the remainder of the file remains secure.

✦ **Acrobat 7.0 and Later:** This includes all of the security options of Acrobat 6.0 compatibility and also allows you to encrypt file attachments that are a part of a PDF file. This also uses the Advanced Encryption Standard, which is a very high level of encryption making it unlikely that an unauthorized user could decrypt the file without the password.

Applying password security to your PDF documents

Selecting the Require a Password to Open the Document check box in the Password Security – Settings dialog box limits access to the PDF file to only those who know the password. The only practical way to open password-protected files, especially those secured with the most recent versions of Acrobat, is by entering the password. This provides a good incentive to use passwords that you can easily remember but are difficult for others to guess.

To apply password security to a file that users must enter to open the file, follow these steps:

1. **Have a PDF file open and then click and hold the Secure button on the Security taskbar and choose Secure this Document.**

The Select a Policy to Apply window opens.

2. **In the Select a Policy to Apply window, select the Restrict Opening and Editing Using Passwords option, and then click the Apply button.**

The Password Security – Settings window opens.

3. **Click the Require a password to open the document check box.**

Enter a logical password that will be required to open the file in the Document Open Password text field.

You can also add additional security settings, which we outline in the next section. Or you can use this as the only security to be applied to the document.

If this is the only security measure you apply to the document, authorized users are able to access the document by entering a password. Users with the password are also able to edit or print the document.

4. **Click the OK button.**

   Confirm the password, click OK again, and the dialog box closes.

5. **Save, close, and then reopen the PDF file.**

   A password dialog box appears asking for the proper password to be entered for access to this file. Now, every time a user accesses the file, this dialog box appears.

Limiting editing and printing

In addition to restricting viewing of a PDF file, you can also apply restrictions to editing and printing PDF files. In doing so, you restrict users from making changes to your document. Users will only be able to view the file.

To limit editing and printing of your PDF document, follow these steps:

1. **Have a PDF file open and then click and hold the Secure button on the Security taskbar and choose Secure this Document.**

   The Select a Policy to Apply window opens.

2. **In the Select a Policy to Apply window, select the Restrict Opening and Editing Using Passwords option, and then click the Apply button.**

   The Password Security – Settings window opens.

3. **In the Permissions area, select the checkbox labeled Use a password to restrict printing and editing of the document and its security settings.**

   Whew! This may win the prize for the longest name for a check box ever placed in a software program, but it allows you to require a password to edit the file or change the security settings.

   With this option selected, you can apply a password for access to features such as printing or editing. This password can be different than the password used to open the document — in fact, you don't even need to use a document open password if you don't want to, but it is a good idea to use both of these passwords for sensitive data.

4. **In the Permissions Password text field, enter a password.**

5. **Choose whether users are able to print the document by selecting from the Printing Allowed drop-down list.**

   The choices include low resolution or high resolution.

6. **To restrict editing, choose from the Changes Allowed drop-down list (see Figure 6-2).**

Figure 6-2:
Choose to restrict options such as printing and editing a PDF.

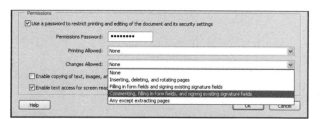

7. **If you want, enable the last two check boxes:**

- **Enable Copying of Text, Images, and Other Content:** Restrict the ability to copy and paste text and graphics into other documents by deselecting this check box.

- **Enable Text Access for Screen Reader Devices for the Visually Impaired:** When you choose Acrobat 5.0 or later compatibility, you can also select this check box to allow visually impaired users to have the PDF file read aloud to them.

  By choosing Acrobat 6.0 or Acrobt 7.0 and Later from the Compatibility drop-down list, you can choose Enable Plain Text Metadata to allow the files to be searched based upon their title, creation date, or author without providing access to the file itself. The Enable Plain Text Metadata is available *only* if you choose Acrobat 6.0 or Later from the Compatibility drop-down list.

Book VI

GoLive CS2

The 5th Wave
By Rich Tennant

"As a Web site designer I never thought
I'd say this, but I don't think your
site has enough bells and whistles."

Contents at a Glance

Chapter 1: Introducing GoLive CS2

In This Chapter

✔ **Discovering the Document window**

✔ **Getting to know objects**

✔ **Puttering around with palettes**

✔ **Inspecting the Inspector palette**

✔ **Setting GoLive preferences**

Adobe GoLive is a Web page and site management application that makes creating Web sites easy and fun. Because GoLive enables you to create Web pages and organize entire sites without putting a lot of thought into the code that creates them, designers can spend more time creating and less time figuring out HTML code. No matter what your goal or skill level, you can make interesting sites that function cleanly with simple links and images, up through intense interactive pages with JavaScript and dynamic content.

With proper planning (the first step in Web site creation), you can save hours, perhaps days, by taking advantage of GoLive site features such as templates, components, and snippets, to name a few.

In this chapter, you get your feet wet by working with a single page. This is to introduce you to the fundamentals of the GoLive workspace. Keep in mind that when working on actual pages that are part of a site, you work from a GoLive site window. This helps to keep links current. Discover how to use a site window in Chapter 2.

The Document Window

Before you get into the complexity of working in a site, discover the basics by working on a single page. This way, you can familiarize yourself with the work area and prepare to work on multiple pages in the future.

Creating a new page in the Document window

When you first launch GoLive, you see a Welcome screen. You can use this window to create a new page or new site, or open existing new pages and sites. Deselect the Show This Dialog at Startup check box if you don't want to see it each time you launch GoLive; then click New Document.

If the Welcome screen does not appear, choose File⇨New. The New window appears, as shown in Figure 1-1.

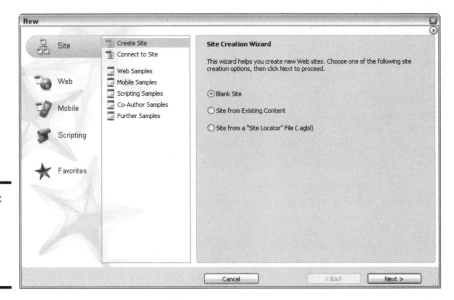

Figure 1-1:
The New window contains many options.

To create a blank page, choose Web⇨Pages⇨HTML page, and click OK. A new blank page appears.

Changing the Document window size

To view the page dimensions, click and hold on the arrow to the right of Web Layout View, at the base of the page window. Scroll to select Show⇨Page Dimensions, as shown in Figure 1-2. The page dimensions appear.

By default, pages are created at 619 x 368 pixels on Windows and 619 x 333 on Mac OS. This size of Web browser window is common for monitors between 14 and 17 inches. You can resize the window by dragging the lower-right corner, but understand that GoLive is not like any other application that lets you determine a page size. For instance, in Adobe InDesign, you create an 8.5-x-11-inch page, print that page, and it stays 8.5 x 11 inches. When you're creating Web pages, you generally have no control over the Web page's size at the viewers' end. (That is, unless you create an action that opens the browser window to a size that you specify, as we describe in Chapter 8 of this minibook.)

A note about monitor size

Have you heard the funny story of the haughty designer who stated that all the viewers of the site he was designing had 17-inch or better monitors, so to heck with designing for small monitors? It turns out that the designer got a frantic call from the CEO's executive secretary as soon as the Web site was posted because the technically illiterate man in charge had only a 14-inch monitor. The moral of the story: Remember that not everyone who will view your Web site has a large monitor and a fast Internet connection. Design your site to accommodate all your viewers.

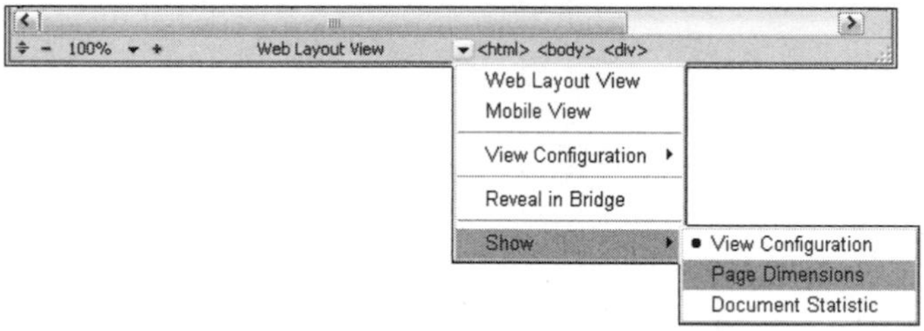

Figure 1-2:
Showing
page
dimensions.

The size you make your Document window is to keep you in check so that your design is appropriate and important items are not left off the page. Just because you may feel that most people have a 17-inch monitor by now, or even if you work on a company intranet site where everyone has 21-inch monitors, you should not design to the entire screen. Many viewers don't want the Web page taking up their whole screen, so they make their Web browser windows smaller. Going by the default size of 619 x 368 (333 on the Mac) pixels is actually a good way to go, even if it may appear small on your monitor.

You can customize the Document window as follows:

1. **Drag the lower-right corner to create the size window that you want to work with.**

   If you choose to always work in 650 x 400, drag the lower-right corner of the window to adjust to that size.

2. **Click the arrow to the right of the current window size in the center of the document bar at the bottom of the window to reveal a drop-down list.**

3. **Choose Settings.**

4. **When the Windows Settings dialog box appears, as shown in Figure 1-3, click OK.**

From now on, every time you create a new document, it will be 650 x 400, or whatever you sized the window to.

Figure 1-3:
Size your
Document
window and
then select
Settings to
set a default
window size
in GoLive.

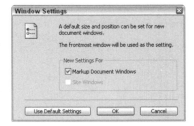

The Document modes

The Document window includes six modes (or views) in which you can choose to create your Web site. Each mode has a tab (located in the upper-left corner of the Document window); click the mode's tab to choose that mode. Following is a list of the six modes and how each is used:

✦ **Layout Editor:** This mode is much like working in a page layout application. In this view, you can type text, insert images, reorganize the layout, change styles, and much more.

Choose Window➪View to change the view of the Layout Editor to different browser displays. This is useful if you want to see how your page will appear in an older or different browser . . . even a different platform. Select the arrow next to Basic Profile to choose alternate browsers from a drop-down list, as shown in Figure 1-4. GoLive approximates the selected profiles' specifications and reflects the differences in your layout. You may or may not see a big difference if you're not implementing Cascading Style Sheets (which we discuss in Chapter 4 of this minibook), but you'll certainly appreciate seeing the restrictions of viewing your page on a small screen, such as one of the DoCoMo selections (phone browsers).

Figure 1-4:
Selecting
from saved
View
Config-
urations.

✦ **Frame Editor:** *Frames* are like panes that you use to display multiple Web pages in the same browser window. For example, you may have a frame that displays a heading or banner at the top of the browser window, and a large frame below that displays the page content. In order to use frames, you must create framesets and assign pages in the Frame Editor. Frames are discussed in more detail in Chapter 5 of this minibook.

✦ **Source Code Editor:** If you're into typing source code, you'll love the Source Code Editor in GoLive. As a default, it highlights tags, attributes, and values, as well as URLs and other media types. Color coding and other specifications can be changed; we discuss this further in the later section, "Understanding GoLive Preferences."

If you select an object or text in the Layout Editor, and then switch to the Source Code Editor, the code for the selected object is highlighted.

✦ **Outline Editor:** The Outline Editor is a neatly packaged source editor that is essentially a document tree that lets you open and collapse different parts of the source code as needed. You click and hold down the arrow to the right of a tag to show the available attributes in a pop-up menu, or you can type values for those attributes.

✦ **Layout Preview:** Click this tab to see a preview of your page. This will not be totally accurate all of the time, but can help give you a basic preview of how images and text and some scripts will work.

✦ **PDF Preview:** This view shows your page as a PDF (Portable Document Format). See your page as it would appear as a PDF and even test links by clicking the PDF Preview tabs. Choose File➪Export to save your file as a PDF page.

Introducing the Objects Palette

Working in GoLive has become more like working in any of the other Adobe applications. You have a toolbar across the top, palettes, and an Objects palette (also called objects toolbox) that can be viewed vertically like the toolbox in Photoshop or horizontally, like a palette.

To change between the vertical, default orientation, click the Separate Tools and Objects button in the lower left of the vertical Objects toolbar. Click the Join Tools and Objects button (on the right in the horizontally displayed Objects palette) to return the Objects palette to the default vertical display. Figure 1-5 shows the horizontal Objects palette.

The Objects palette has multiple categories of objects. To access the categories in the vertical display, click and hold the Palette options button and select the topic you want. If you are creating a form, for example, you select the Forms category. In the horizontal view, change categories by using the buttons at the top of the Objects palette.

Figure 1-5:
View the
Objects
palette
horizontally.

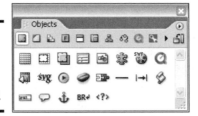

Table 1-1 shows a breakdown of the Objects palette buttons.

Table 1-1		Objects Palette Buttons
Button	*Name*	*Use It To . . .*
	Basic	Add objects such as layout grid, table, floating box, and plug-ins.
	Smart	Place native Adobe Illustrator, PDF, and Photoshop files into GoLive.
	CSS	Add liquid CSS formatting objects to your page.
	Forms	Add objects such as text boxes, check boxes, radio buttons, as well as objects such as hidden elements to get your CGI scripts to work correctly.
	Head	Add objects that belong in the head section of the HTML document, such as scripts, refresh code, meta tags, and keywords.

	Frames	Apply different framesets when using the Frame Editor tab on the Document window.
	Site	Organize your Site window by adding URLs, colors, font sets, and more.

Button	*Name*	*Use It To . . .*
	Diagrams	Preplan and present a Web site.
	QuickTime	Create or edit QuickTime movies in GoLive by dragging objects into a movie's timeline to add additional videos, transitions, and even Flash files.
	Movable Type	Support for Blogging software.
	SMIL	SMIL is an XML-compliant markup language that enables you to lay out and synchronize multiple streaming and static media tracks in a multimedia presentation for MMS (Multimedia Message Service)-compatible portable devices.
	TypePad Blog	Objects for creating Blogging sites.

Working with Palettes

Just like in most of the other Adobe applications, you can access palettes from the Window menu. If the palette is open but not visible, it comes to the front when you select it from the Window menu.

As a default, relevant palettes are grouped together, such as the Color and Swatches palette. Here are a few tricks for manipulating your palettes:

+ Separate palettes by dragging by a tab to a location outside of the group.

+ Add a tab to another palette by dragging the tab to the palette, forming a *palette group*.

+ Collapse a palette by dragging the tab to the side of the screen. The palette shows just the tab. Click to open it when needed.

If you find yourself working with the same palettes often and you want to save your palettes, first organize and show the ones you want, and then choose Window⇨Workspace⇨Save Workspace. In the dialog box that appears, enter a name for the workspace, and click OK. You can then access it by choosing Window⇨Workspace and then selecting the name you gave your customized workspace. Choose Window⇨Workspace⇨Default Workspace to return to the original GoLive palette configuration.

The Inspector Palette

The Inspector palette (Window⇨Inspector) in GoLive, shown in Figure 1-6, is the master controller of your object characteristics. If you drag an image object to your page, you use the image inspector to link to an image and apply other attributes, such as size, alignment, Alt text information, and so on.

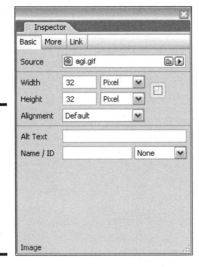

Figure 1-6:
The Inspector palette controls attributes and values of HTML objects.

A good way to see the Inspector palette in action is to open an existing page and click on different objects, such as an image, text, even the little page icon on the top right of the Document window to the right of Properties. (We discuss the page title further in Chapter 2 of this minibook.)

You discover more specifics about the Inspector palette as you read through the chapters in this minibook. The main thing to remember is that the Inspector palette should remain open at all times. In many applications, you open a specific dialog box to make changes and then close that dialog box;

in GoLive, the Inspector palette is contextual, so it changes with each object that you select. If you close the Inspector palette, use the keyboard command Ctrl+1 (Windows) or ⌘+1 (Mac) to reopen it.

Understanding GoLive Preferences

By choosing Edit➪Preferences (Windows) or GoLive➪Preferences (Mac), you can access the GoLive Preferences dialog box, shown in Figure 1-7. You could spend months studying just the preferences. In the likelihood that you have other things to do in the next few months, however, you can read the following list, which provides a description of the main preference.

**Book VI
Chapter 1**

**Introducing
GoLive CS2**

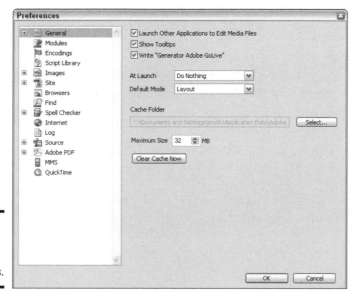

Figure 1-7:
Setting
GoLive
preferences.

As you look in the Preferences dialog box, select each preference (General, Modules, and so on) on the left to see all of its options on the right. After you change preferences, restart GoLive for them to take effect.

✦ **General:** This category of preferences contains fundamental preferences for working in GoLive.

   • **At Launch:** Use this drop-down list to turn off the Welcome screen (You can get tired of being welcomed!) or set GoLive to create a new page or do nothing when launched.

- **Default Mode:** Typically, you would want to open in Layout view and start working, but if not, select the view mode you prefer from the Default Mode drop-down list.

- **Write "Generator Adobe GoLive":** Deselect this check box if you don't want a meta tag giving GoLive credit for building your page. Of course, you want your customers to think that you hand-coded the site!

  Click the plus sign to the left of General in the list on the left of the Preferences dialog box for additional user interface options.

✦ **Modules:** In the Modules section, you can disable or enable selected modules and extend scripts as you need them. By deselecting unused modules, you can reduce the program's memory requirements to the minimum recommended of 24MB.

✦ **Encodings:** By default, all new pages created in GoLive include the UTF-8 encoding element in the head section. If necessary, choose another in the Encodings section.

✦ **Script Library:** Choose where you want scripts to be written, in the page or in a separate library, which you can name in this section.

✦ **Images:** Set up options for automatically creating rollovers, using like filenames and preferences for Smart Objects.

✦ **Site:** Set up personal preferences for site items in this section. Click the plus sign (PC) or arrow (Mac) to the left of Site for additional options. You can read about additional site features in Chapter 2 of this mini-book.

✦ **Browsers:** Use the Browsers preferences to edit your Preview in Browser button (discussed later in this chapter).

✦ **Find:** Set up Find preferences, such as source code search options and find window options.

✦ **Spell Checker:** Set up a dictionary in this section so that the spell checker recognizes custom terminology, proper names, and geography.

✦ **Internet:** Set up specific Internet options for connecting to your FTP site and the Internet in general.

✦ **Log:** Set the preferences for the log. If GoLive can't connect to the defined server, an error dialog appears.

✦ **Source:** If you tinker around in the source code, you will love the options in this section. Change the general appearance of the source code, or click the plus sign to the left of Source to apply themes and set preferences for enabling code completion.

✦ **Adobe PDF:** Set up specific options for creating PDFs from your Web pages in GoLive. These options will be your defaults, but they can be changed in the Inspector palette when you are in the PDF Preview mode.

✦ **MMS:** Choose or configure a device for Multimedia Messaging Services. MMS is based on Synchronized Multimedia Integration Language (SMIL). SMIL is an XML-compliant markup language that enables you to lay out and synchronize multiple streaming and static media tracks.

✦ **QuickTime:** GoLive includes a QuickTime editor. Choose options for scratch disks (memory while creating the movie) and workspace-related options in this section.

Preview in Browser

GoLive provides a Preview in Browser button on the toolbar (see Figure 1-8). Clicking this button allows you to preview a page in the browser of your choice while you're creating the page and without having to save the file. GoLive builds a temporary file for you.

You must be at a minimum screen resolution of 1024 x 768 to see all of the buttons on the GoLive CS2 toolbar.

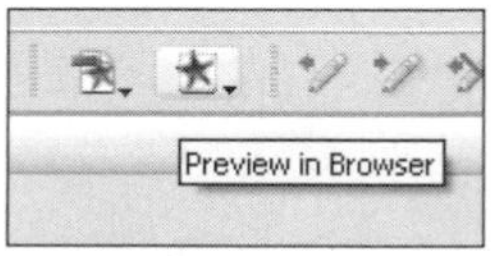

Figure 1-8:
The Preview in Browser button on the toolbar.

Preview in Browser

If you have not set up a browser previously, you must first *activate* the Preview in Browser button — that is, you must choose the browsers you want to use to preview your page. To do so, just follow these steps:

1. **Click and hold the Preview in Browser button and select Edit. The browser preferences window appears.**

2. **If you don't mind waiting quite some time, click the Find All button to locate all the browsers that are on your system.**

It may be more efficient to click the Add button in the lower right and browse to locate any Web browsers that you want to load pages into from GoLive.

As you load browsers, note the check box to the left of each browser name.

3. **Select only the check boxes for the browsers that you want GoLive to automatically launch when you click the Preview in Browser button.**

Live rendering gives you the ability to make changes and see them happen automatically in a preview. Select the Live Rendering check box to open a rendering window instead of a browser. You can also access live rendering by choosing File⇨Preview In⇨Live Rendering.

4. **Click OK.**

5. **To preview in the browsers you selected, click the Preview in Browser button on the toolbar, or click and hold to choose a browser that you loaded in the Browser Preferences, but did not select.**

If you check multiple browsers, all selected browsers launch your page.

Chapter 2: Creating a Web Site

*I*n this chapter, we show you the basics of putting a Web site together, from creating that first new, blank site, to adding files to Web sites, to playing (just a little bit) with HTML.

How Web sites are organized is important. Typically, the purpose of a Web site is to sell something — a product, service, or just a thought, like "Vote for me!" Without sound organization, a Web site may fail to sell to its visitors. Read these words slowly . . . *preplan your site.* Seriously, you will save an extraordinary amount of time if you just think ahead and plan out your site's organization. Think about the topics you want to cover and then organize your site as you would a high school essay project, planning out the topic sentence, subtopics, and so on. This can be a tremendous aid when you start mapping out which pages should be linked to others.

Web Site Basics

A *Web site* is a collection of related pages linked to one another, preferably in an organized manner. With the proper planning and an end goal in sight, you can easily accomplish the task of creating a great Web site. Figure 2-1 shows the general structure of a Web site. Web sites start with a main page (also called the home page), the central link to other pages in the site. The main page is also the page viewers see first when they type your URL in a browser. The main page is typically named `index.html`, but depending on your Internet service provider, it may be called `index.htm` or even `home.html`. Check with your provider to find the correct name.

Pages are linked together with *hyperlinks,* references that take viewers from one point in an HTML document to another or from one document to another. (You can read more about hyperlinks and how to create them in Chapter 6 of this minibook.)

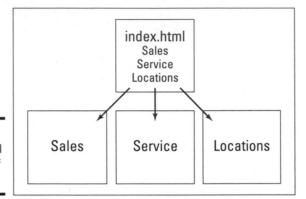

Figure 2-1:
The general
structure of
a Web site.

The following are terms that you should understand as you forge through the steps to create a Web site:

✦ **TCP/IP (Transmission Control Protocol/Internet Protocol):** Underlying protocols that make communication between computers on the Internet possible. TCP/IP ensures that information being exchanged goes to the right place, in a form that can be used, and gets there intact.

✦ **URL (Universal Resource Locator):** A standard for specifying the location of an object on the Internet, such as a file. The URL is what you type into a Web browser to visit a Web page, such as www.dummies.com. URLs are also used in HTML documents (Web pages) to specify the target of a link, which is often another Web page.

✦ **FTP (File Transfer Protocol):** Allows a user on one computer to transfer files to and from another computer over a TCP/IP network. FTP is also the client program the user executes to transfer files. You may use FTP to transfer Web pages, images, and other files to a host Web server when you publish your site.

✦ **HTTP (Hypertext Transfer Protocol):** The client-server TCP/IP protocol used on the World Wide Web for the exchange of HTML documents.

Starting a New Site

GoLive helps you manage your linked files by using a *site window*. This site window tracks links, manages changes, and even provides the tools necessary to get the latest pages transferred to your FTP server. You should always work in a site window in GoLive, even if you're just editing a single page. If you don't use a site file, you may find that strange problems quickly emerge when you upload the site from your computer to your ISP or Web host. Images may not be displayed in the browser, and links, rollovers, and other actions may not work as expected. Follow these steps to create a GoLive site:

To create a new, blank site, starting with a home page and default basic.css file, follow these steps:

1. **Choose File⇨New.**

   An options window appears, as shown in Figure 2-2, from which you can create new sites or pages.

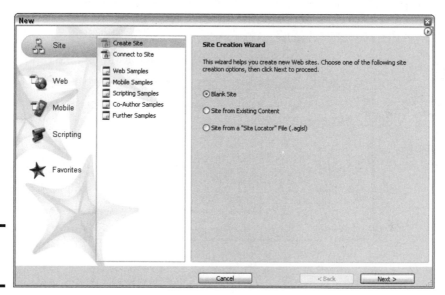

Figure 2-2:
The New
dialog box.

2. **Select Site⇨Create Site.**

3. **Select the Blank Site radio button and click Next.**

4. **In the Site Name and Location window, enter a name for the site.**

   The name you use here is also the name of the folder on your local computer containing the site, so make it easy to find by choosing an intuitive name. The name is for your organizational purposes only.

5. **Click the Browse button to locate a place on your hard drive that you want to store the site file, and then click Next.**

6. **A Using Version Cue window appears next.**

   In GoLive, you can create a single-user or a workgroup site (using the Version Cue system):

   • **Use Version Control.** Choose this option if you're working with a large group and aren't able to oversee every edit and change. Using Version Cue, you can set up the Web site with permissions, check files in and out, and check versions.

- **Don't Use Version Control.** Choose this option for a site that is tightly controlled and only updated by you or a few other people. Using this setting, one person keeps control of the editing.

If you are not sure what to choose, choose the Don't Use Version Control radio button, and click Next.

7. **In the Publish Server Options window, you can enter your ftp server location now or later. If you are just practicing, you want to choose the Specify Server Later radio button.**

8. **Click Finish.**

A site window appears with a blank index.html (see Figure 2-3).

9. **Double-click the index page to open the page and start creating.**

Read about importing files into this site and creating new files later in this chapter.

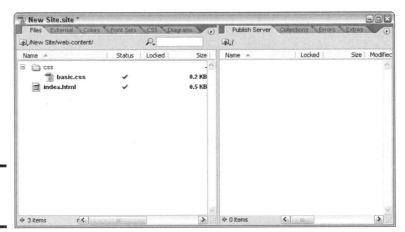

Figure 2-3:
The Site window.

Other options for creating a Web site

In the preceding steps, we show you how to create a new, blank Web site in GoLive. You have other options, though. You can import already existing Web sites, (either from a folder on your computer or from a server), into GoLive or create a site from a GoLive template.

Import from folder

If you have a site (pages, images, and so on) already created, but you want to turn it into a GoLive site, you can use this helpful option:

1. **Choose File⇨New.**

The New options window appears, waiting for your responses in order to generate a new GoLive site.

2. **Choose Site⇨Create Site.**

3. **Choose the Site From Existing Content radio button, and click Next.**

4. **In the Creating a Site From Existing Content window choose one of the following:**

- **From a Local Folder of Existing Files,** if you have the site resources, such as existing pages) already accessible on your computer.

- **By Downloading Files From a Remote Server,** if you plan on accessing through an ftp or http server.

- **By Connecting to a Project on a Version Control System,** if you already have started a Version Cue Project.

For this example, choose From a Local Folder of Existing Files, and click Next.

5. **The Selecting a Local Folder of Existing Files window appears. If you have an index file in the site already, click the bottom Browse button, locate the `index.html` file, and click Open.**

If you don't have a home page, GoLive creates a blank index.html by default.

6. **Click Next.**

The Specify Site Name and Location window appears. The site is named automatically with the folder name, but you can change it if you want.

7. **Click Browse to choose a location for this new site.**

To avoid organizational problems later, always save the site file alongside the folder you're doing the import on. To change the folder names to the default GoLive structure, choose Site⇨Convert Site to New Structure with the site window forward. This changes your Web site content folder to the generic name *web-content*.

8. **Click Finish to have the Site window appear with the files from the selected folder. Double-click to open pages from the Site window.**

Using Web Samples

Use this option to create a site from a base set of pages already created. GoLive provides you with some standard templates, but you can also create your own by saving site files into the Site Templates folder located in the GoLive Application folder. Follow these steps to create a new Web site from a template:

1. **Choose File⇨New.**

   The New options window appears, waiting for your responses in order to generate a new GoLive site.

2. **Select Site⇨Web Samples or one of the other site sample options.**

   In the Selecting a Site Sample for Copying window, a list generic Web sites appears.

3. **Select a site, and choose Next.**

   The Specifying a Site Name and Location window appears.

4. **In the Specifying a Site Name and Location window, provide your own name for this site, and choose Browse. Navigate to a location to save the site.**

5. **Choose Finish.**

6. **Double-click a page to start customizing the pages for your site.**

The Site window and toolbar

When you create a new site, the Site window appears (refer to Figure 2-3) that contains six tabs across the top, left side. Notice that the contextual toolbar (across the top) changes when you have the Site window forward instead of a page. The tools for keeping the site organized are included in the toolbar. (We discuss these tools where appropriate throughout this minibook.)

The tabs in the Site window are as follows:

✦ **Files tab:** The Files tab is the heart of the site. This tab lists your files and provides the organizational tools to create a clean site.

 If at any time files that you know were saved in the Site folder don't appear in the Files tab, click the Refresh button on the toolbar.

✦ **External tab:** This tab helps you inventory and manage all of the external references, such as external Web links and links to e-mail addresses, in your Web site.

✦ **Colors tab:** The Colors tab enables you to store and refer to colors used in your Web site. In this tab are swatches of the color and columns defining whether the color is presently being used, its HTML name and hexadecimal value, and whether it is Web safe.

✦ **Font Sets tab:** This tab lists the font sets used throughout the Web site.

✦ **CSS tab:** This tab lists any Cascading Styles used in this site.

✦ **Diagrams tab:** The Diagrams tab is useful for planning, mapping, and building Web sites. It shows a diagram of your site to illustrate the hierarchy of the pages and how they're interconnected by links. Refer to Figure 2-1 to see an example of a simple site diagram.

When GoLive created the site, it also created three folders and one `.site` file that are located in your main site folder:

✦ **`.site` file:** This is the actual Site window file. When you want to relaunch the Site window, you open this file. You have backups visible as well.

✦ **Web-content folder:** This folder contains the actual files creating your site. When you save images and other files from other applications, save them into this folder. Click the Refresh button when you return to GoLive to see the newly saved files in the Files tab of the Site window.

✦ **Web-Data folder:** This folder contains the folders that GoLive relies on to give you most of its dynamic and helpful features, such as components and templates. You discover how to use some of these features throughout the rest of this minibook.

✦ **Web-Settings folder:** This folder stores settings specific to your site for colors, fonts, and external links, to name a few.

**Book VI
Chapter 2**

Creating a Web Site

Adding files to your site

After you create a site, you likely want to load additional files (maybe images that you created before the site or pages from another site) into it by way of the Files tab. No matter what the files are, understand that GoLive does not *move* the selected files but merely *copies* them.

To import files into your site, follow these steps:

1. **Make sure that you have the Files tab of the Site window selected.**

2. **Choose File⇨Import Files to Site.**

The Add to Site dialog box appears.

3. **Select the file(s) that you want to add (select multiple files by Ctrl+clicking [Windows] or ⌘+clicking [Mac] the filenames), and click the Open button.**

The new files are added to your file list in the Site window.

Managing Your Web Site Files

When you're working on a site, keep in mind that you must save all pertinent files into the Web-content folder. Otherwise, they may get lost, or not make it to the server.

Opening files

To open files from the Site window, double-click the filename. If you want to open files outside the site (not in your Web-content folder), choose File⇨Open and browse to locate the files. If you open a file this way, be sure to read the next section, "Saving files," so that you can ensure that the file ends up in your main site folder.

Saving files

When saving files that were launched from GoLive by double-clicking them in the Site window, you can simply choose File⇨Save. If you're saving a new file or an existing file that has not been saved to your Web-content folder, choose File⇨Save As. In the Save As dialog box that appears, rename the file if you want, and click the Site Folder button in the lower portion of the dialog box. A pop-up menu appears; select Root to navigate directly to the Root (Main) site folder. Then click Save.

Click the New Folder icon at the top of the Save As dialog box to create a subfolder in the GoLive Site window. When you drag files into the subfolders, GoLive automatically updates the code so that you don't have broken links.

Naming files

Get in the habit right away of naming your files and folders correctly. Follow these rules to make sure that links and pages appear when they are supposed to:

✦ **Use lowercase for all filenames:** Some functions are case-sensitive, meaning they will not work if you don't get the capitalization right. Using all lowercase letters in filenames is an easy way to ensure you don't have broken links because you couldn't remember whether you initial-capped a filename or not. Some Web servers require filenames to be in lowercase, as well.

✦ **Don't use spaces in filenames:** If you need to separate words in a filename, use the underscore character instead of a space. For example, instead of `file new.html`, use `file_new.html` or even `filenew.html`.

✦ **Use only one dot, followed by the extension:** Macintosh users are used to having no naming restrictions, so this can be the toughest rule to adhere to. Don't name your files something like `finally.done. feb.9.jpg`. That is B-A-D for the Internet. Examples of dot-extensions are as follows: `.jpg`, `.gif`, `.png`, `.htm`, `.html`, `.cgi`, `.swf`, and so on.

✦ **Avoid odd characters:** Characters to avoid include dashes (-) or forward slashes (/) at the beginning of the filename. These mean other things to the Web server and will create errors on the site.

HTML Basics

The Web page itself is a collection of text, images, links, and possibly media and script. It can be as complex or simple as you want, both being equally effective if created properly. In this section, we show you how to create a page in GoLive and then investigate the HTML that creates it.

Choose File⇨New. In the New window, select Web⇨ Pages⇨HTML Page, and click OK. This creates a new, blank page in the Document window. It has no formatting until you add tables or layers (which we discuss in Chapters 5 and 7 of this minibook, respectively). When you type on the page in the document, text appears on the Web page. But there is much more to it than that; type some text (say, your name) on the page and click the Source Code tab (in the upper-left of the Document window; we discuss these tabs in detail in Chapter 1 of this minibook).

As you see in Figure 2-4, GoLive is working in the background to make your page work in Web browsers. Lots of code is created to help the Web browser recognize that this is HTML and which version of HTML it uses.

Figure 2-4:
The Source Code Editor as it appears after adding "This is text" to the page in the layout editor.

If you were to return to the Layout mode (the default mode) by clicking the Layout tab in the Document window, select your text and click the T button (Strong) on the toolbar across the top of the work area, you'd see the text turn bold. Click the Source Code tab to switch back to the Source Code Editor view, and you see that the `<strong>` tag was added before the text and the `</strong>` tag was added after the text.

HTML code, though easy, is just like any other language in that you must learn the syntax (the proper sequence and formation of the code) and vocabulary (memorize lots of tags). You don't have to have gobs of tape on your glasses to build good clean Web pages, but you should review the following HTML basics. If you're an experienced user, you know that by copying and pasting code, you can figure out a lot about HTML code. If you're a new user, copying and pasting code will help you understand what others have implemented on their pages and perhaps give you some ideas.

In general, HTML tags have three parts to them:

✦ **Tag:** The main part of the HTML information, for instance `<strong>` for strong or bold, `<font>` for the font tag, `<table>` for an HTML table, and so on. Most tags come in pairs, meaning that you must enter an opening tag (like `<p>`) and a closing tag (like `</p>`); refer to Figure 2-4.

For example, if you make text bold by adding the tag `<b>`, you need to tell it where to stop being bold by inserting a closing tag `</b>`. Otherwise, the text will continue to bold throughout the remainder of the page.

✦ **Attribute:** The part of the tag that can be changed. You can specify attributes for color, size, the destination of a link, and so on. For example, `bgcolor` is an attribute of the `<body>` tag that specifies what color the background of the Web page should be.

✦ **Value:** The actual color, size, destination of a link, and so on, in an attribute. For example, you can specify a hexadecimal number as the value for a color attribute. In Figure 2-4 on line 12, the value for the background color attribute (`bgcolor`) is `#ffffff` (white).

One last thing: *Nesting* is the order in which your tags appear. If a `<b>` tag is applied, it looks like this: `<b>This text is bold</b>`. Add an italic tag, and you have `<b><i>This text is bold and italic.</i></b>`. Notice the in-to-out placement of the tags; you work your way from the inside to the outside when closing tags. This is important to follow when hand coding or copying tags because it makes the HTML easier for yourself and other people to read and also gives you predictable results.

Chapter 3: Working with Images

In This Chapter

✔ **Putting images on a page**

✔ **Setting image attributes**

✔ **Creating image maps**

✔ **Creating rollovers**

✔ **Using Smart Objects**

This is sure to be a fun chapter. Adding images to a Web page makes the page more interesting. If you're creating a personal site, sharing images (say, your digital photographs or artwork you created in Illustrator) might be the entire point of your site. Images are also important for business and professional sites, because they can help communicate product information, company location, and maintain a consistent corporate look.

In this chapter, we show you several methods that you can use to get images on a Web page. We also show you how to use images as a background for your Web pages. You also discover how to use rollovers and Smart Images (which allow you to drop non-optimized images right into GoLive), and change optimization settings on the fly.

Putting Images on a Page

Placing images is not difficult, but you must think about which format images are saved in and how large the files are. (See Book IV, Chapter 9 for details on selecting the correct format and using the Save for Web feature in Photoshop.) Putting images on a Web page requires planning to make sure that sizes are exactly what you want them to be on the Web, unless you use Smart Objects. Make sure that you don't have too many images to keep the page loading quickly. Check the status of a page by choosing Special➪ Document Statistics when a page is forward. The Document Statistics dialog box appears (see Figure 3-1), where you can check how large the page is and approximate download times. Try to keep your page load time to about 10 seconds or less at 56 Kbps (the average speed of a dial-up Internet connection). Any slower than that, and your viewers are likely to go elsewhere.

Figure 3-1:
Check your
page's file
size and
download
time.

After you've placed an image inside a Web page, you can then resize it (not recommended), realign it, add space around it, or even use it as background; things we discuss later in this section. But first things first, right? you have to get the image in there first. So, to place an image inside a Web page, follow these steps:

1. **With a blank page open, make sure the Objects palette is forward by choosing Window⇨Objects or by pressing Ctrl+2 (Windows) or ⌘+2 (Mac).**

2. **In the Basic section of the Objects palette, either drag the Image icon (the icon with shapes on it) to the page where you want it placed or put your cursor where you want the image and double-click the Image icon.**

If you're not sure which is the image object, hover your cursor over the objects to see ToolTips, see Figure 3-2. The image object will be used to hold the image you select.

Note: Unless you're using tables, floating boxes, or the layout grid, the image follows the flow of the page's text. Read more about formatting pages in Chapter 5 of this minibook.

3. **Choose to link to an image on a page using one of these methods:**

- Click the Browse button on the basic tab of the Image Inspector palette, and locate the image you want to place.

- Use the Fetch URL button to the left of the link reference and drag to the image name in the Site window.

- Drag an image onto the page. You can do this with an image in your Site window, or from anywhere in your system, even from the desktop. Be very careful with this: We recommend that you choose File⇨Import and bring the image file into your Site window first to avoid linking problems later.

  If you cannot see both the image and the Site window at the same time, you can drag the Fetch URL button up to the Select Window button. This brings the Site window forward so that you can continue dragging to the filename.

Figure 3-2:
The Image
object.

Resizing an image

As a standard, Web images should not be resized in the layout. Not unless you're using Smart Images, which are discussed at the end of this chapter. The width and height are calculated and included in the code automatically, but if you absolutely must, you can enter different values in the Width and Height text fields in the Image Inspector palette, or you can drag the handles in the lower-right corner of the image to change its size.

If you change the size of an image, a warning icon appears in the lower right of the image. To revert the image back to its original saved size, click the Set to Original Size button on the Basic tab of the Image Inspector palette.

Aligning an image

As a default, images only allow text to run in one line off to the right of the image. To control the runaround of the text, change the alignment of the image by selecting an option from the Alignment drop-down list on the Basic tab of the Image Inspector, as shown in Figure 3-3.

Figure 3-3:
Change the
interaction
and
alignment of
text and
other
objects by
selecting an
alignment
attribute.

The Align drop-down list provides the following options:

✦ **Top:** Image aligns itself with the top of the tallest item in the line of text.

✦ **Middle:** Image aligns the baseline of the current line of text with the middle of the image.

✦ **Bottom:** Baseline aligns the bottom of the image with the baseline of the current line of text.

✦ **Left:** Aligns the image to the left, text flushes to the right of the image.

✦ **Right:** Aligns image to the right, text flushes to the left of the image.

✦ **Text Top:** Image aligns itself with the top of the tallest text in the line. This is usually (but not always) the same as `ALIGN=top`.

✦ **Abs Middle:** Aligns the middle of the current line with the middle of the image.

✦ **Baseline:** Aligns the bottom of the image with the baseline of the current line of text.

✦ **Abs Bottom:** Aligns the bottom of the image with the bottom of the current line of text.

Adding space around the image

You may want some space around the image to keep the text from butting right up to the image. On the More tab of the Image Inspector palette, enter values into the Hspace and Vspace text fields.

If you want space added only to one side of the image, open the image in Photoshop and choose Image⇨Canvas Size. In the Canvas Size dialog box that appears, click the middle left square in the Anchor section and add a value in pixels to your total image size. Click the right middle square to add the size to the left side of the image.

Gotta have that Alt text

We're guessing that you've probably seen *Alt text* a gazillion times; it's the text that appears before an image when a Web page is loading; it also appears as a ToolTip when you hover your mouse cursor over an image in a Web page. Alt text is helpful because it tells viewers something about the image before the image appears, but Alt text also is necessary for viewers who turn off their preference for viewing graphics, or for folks using a Web-reading program, like those for the visually impaired. US Federal regulations also require Alt tags for any work that is being done for federal agencies. They are also helpful for people with slow Internet connections.

To assign Alt text to an image, simply input it into the Alt Text field in the Basic tab of the Image Inspector palette. If you're adding Alt text for an image of a button, use a descriptive word that informs the viewer where the button will take them if they click it; for a photograph or other image, use Alt text to give a brief description of what the image shows.

Using an image as background

Creating backgrounds for Web pages is fun and can be pursued in more ways than most people think. You don't have to settle for an image repeating over and over again in the background; this feature offers many creative solutions. As a default, HTML backgrounds repeat the selected image until the entire screen is filled. If you're filling your background with a pattern, make sure that you create a pattern that has no discernable edges. (In Photoshop, choose Filter⇨Texture⇨Texturizer to see some good choices in the Texturizer dialog box.) Patterns that repeat are typically 100 x 100 pixels in size.

To utilize the default, repeated tiling for a background image to your advantage, follow these steps:

1. **In Photoshop, choose File⇨New to create a new image.**

2. **In the New dialog box that appears, create an image that's much wider than it is high, choose RGB, and choose 72 dpi, and then click OK.**

   For example, enter **2000** in the Width text field and **20** in the Height text field.

3. **Select a foreground and background color to create a blend; then with the Gradient tool, Shift+drag across the image area.**

4. **Choose File➪Save for Web and save the image as a JPEG into your site's Web content folder, and then close the image.**

See Book IV, Chapter 9 for more about the Save for Web feature.

5. **In GoLive, place the image as a background image in your Web page by using one of the following methods:**

- Drag the image from the Site window to the Show Page Properties icon in the upper right of the document window.

- Choose Page Properties by clicking on the page icon in the upper right of your GoLive page. In the Page Inspector palette, select the Image check box under Background, and then click the Browse button to locate an image.

Because browser windows are rarely opened more than 2000 pixels wide, your image is forced to repeat stacked on top of itself (rather than tiled across and down, as with a square image), producing an effect similar to what's shown in Figure 3-4.

To link to your background image, click and hold the Fetch URL button (to the right of the Image check box) and drag to the named image in the Site window. This is easier if you position the Site window so that you can view it at the same time as the page.

Figure 3-4:
The background image is so wide that it only repeats down the page.

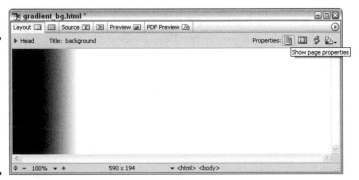

Creating Rollovers

A *rollover* is an area on a Web page that changes when a viewer passes the mouse cursor over it. Usually, a rollover is an image, such as a button, that becomes highlighted when the cursor passes over it. Simple rollovers are easy in GoLive, and you can even set them up so that GoLive automatically creates the rollover for you when you name your files correctly.

Follow these steps to take advantage of rollovers in GoLive:

1. **In Photoshop, create two or three images for the rollover, make sure that the images all have the same pixel dimensions.**

   One image is the *normal state* (what viewers see when the page is launched), another is the *over state* (what viewers see when they move the mouse cursor over the button), and the third is the *down state* (what viewers see when the button is clicked). All three are not necessary for a rollover, but you must have at least two images; the normal and over states.

2. **Save the files into the Web-Content of the Site folder.**

3. **Place the normal state image as you would any image.**

   See the earlier section, "Putting Images on a Page."

4. **Choose Window⇨Rollovers; in the palette that appears, click Over in the list of States.**

5. **Click the Create New Rollover Image button at the bottom of the Rollovers and Actions palette.**

6. **Using the Fetch URL button or the Browse button to the right of URL, locate the image that you created for the over state.**

7. **If you want to take it further and add another state, click Down in the list of states and click the Create New Rollover Image button again, this time locating the image that you saved for the down state.**

8. **When you're finished, check your rollover in the GoLive Preview tab, or click the Preview in Browser button on the toolbar to preview the page in a Web browser.**

If you choose Rollover Detection Settings from the Rollovers & Actions palette menu (shown in Figure 3-5), you can follow or create your own naming conventions to have GoLive automatically recognize your images as rollover states. In other words, if you name your images name_Base, name_Over, name_Down, *name* being whatever you decide to call the image file, the rollover is automatically created when the _Base file is placed! See other naming options and create your own using the Rollover Detection Settings window, as shown in Figure 3-6.

Book VI
Chapter 3

Working with Images

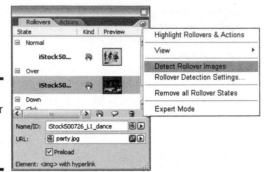

Figure 3-5:
The Rollover
& Actions
palette
menu.

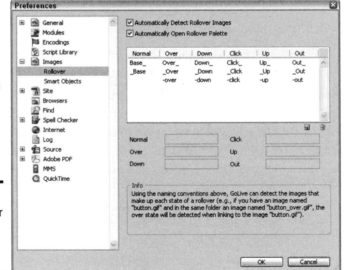

Figure 3-6:
The Rollover
Detection
Settings
window.

Working with Smart Objects

Smart Objects are one of those features that make you glad that you use the Adobe line of products. This feature enables you to drop native Photoshop, Illustrator, and PDF files right onto your Web page. GoLive automatically launches Save for Web in GoLive so that you don't have to open your image program to optimize images. Change optimization settings and image size as many times as you want right in GoLive with no degradation to the image because it always references the original image. That's the beauty of Smart Objects.

Follow these steps to create a Smart Photoshop Object (you use the same steps for the Smart Illustrator and PDF Objects):

1. **You can either drag a Photoshop file directly onto the page in GoLive, or click the Smart button in the Objects palette.**

   If the Objects palette isn't visible, choose Window➪Objects, or press Ctrl+2 (Windows) or ⌘+2 (Mac) and drag the Smart Photoshop Object to your page.

   If you drag your image onto the page, the Save for Web dialog box pops up immediately, waiting for you to make optimization selections.

   If you drag the Smart Photoshop Object to the page, you must then use the Source Browse button or the Fetch URL button to locate a Photoshop file (the file doesn't have to be a PSD file; it can be one of the many formats in which Photoshop can save, such as TIF or EPS). After the image is selected, the Save for Web dialog box appears.

2. **In the Save for Web dialog box, choose the appropriate optimization settings for your image.**

   Read in detail how to use the Save for Web dialog box in Book IV, Chapter 9.

3. **From the Site Folder drop-down list, select Root Folder to save the optimized graphic in the appropriate location in your site folder; click Save.**

   The Smart Object is placed, designated by an icon visible in the lower-right corner of the image, as shown in Figure 3-7. This indicates that the image is linked to a source and can be resized and reoptimized at any time.

Figure 3-7:
The icon in the lower right indicates that this is a Smart Object.

If you drag a corner handle to reduce the size of the image, a new image is generated from the original source image. Shift+drag a corner handle to maintain proportions. Drag the corner back out to increase the image and watch as GoLive regenerates a new optimized image based upon your settings!

Change settings by clicking the Settings button in the Smart Photoshop Image Inspector palette.

If the original image is updated, the Smart Image is updated as well. In other words, if you change the color of an object that is a source file for a Smart Object, GoLive recognizes that change and updates the placed, optimized image automatically.

Don't want the entire image? Crop your image right in GoLive by selecting the Crop tool on the Smart Photoshop Image Inspector palette. Then drag to make a crop selection. Adjust the crop size by using the crop handles and press Enter (Windows) or Return (Mac) to crop the image.

Take advantage of variables that enable you to change the content of a text layer saved in a Photoshop image. This cool feature enables you to create a button in Photoshop with a text layer on top, and change the text on the button to whatever you please in GoLive — you can reuse the original button created in Photoshop over and over, changing the text layer to customize the name of the button in GoLive. Just follow these steps:

1. **Create a Photoshop image; make its topmost layer a text layer.**

2. **In the text layer, type any word in the font face, size, and style that you want to use for the label on the button.**

3. **Save the file as a PSD (Photoshop document) and close the image; in GoLive, use the Smart Photoshop Object to place the image on a Web page.**

   As soon as an image with a top text layer is placed, the Variable Settings dialog box appears.

4. **Select the check box to the left (under Use) and type what you want the button to say in the large bottom text field; click OK when you're done typing.**

   After you click OK, the Save for Web dialog box appears, showing the button with the text you just changed in the Variable Settings dialog box.

5. **In the Save for Web dialog box, select the appropriate settings and choose to save the optimized image.**

   You can place an image using variables as many times as you want, by using additional Smart Objects from the Objects palette. Every time the image is selected, you can change the variable text. ***Warning:*** If you cut and paste a Smart Object using variables, you can't change the text independently from the original placed object.

If the original image is changed in Photoshop (text is resized, changed to another font, and so on), the Smart Objects in GoLive are updated, but the variable text remains as you set it in the Variable Settings dialog box! Think of the possibilities . . . one button created in Photoshop can be used as ten buttons in GoLive, each sporting different text! You can change the variable at any time by clicking the Variables button on the Smart Image Inspector palette.

**Book VI
Chapter 3**

**Working with
Images**

Chapter 4: Text and CSS

In This Chapter

✔ **Formatting and spell checking text**

✔ **Discovering font families**

✔ **Becoming familiar with CSS**

✔ **Helping viewers find your site**

Adding text to your Web page requires more than just typing on a page. You must carefully think about and plan your Web pages because you want search engines (and therefore viewers) to easily find relevant content that your Web site contains. In this chapter, we cover the fundamentals of text formatting for your Web pages; from the basics of font size and font family, to spell checking your text, to implementing Cascading Style Sheets (CSS).

Because you can assign type properties quickly and update all instances in a few easy steps with CSS, using CSS is viewed as the most efficient method of applying text attributes on a Web page. As you add all your great-sounding and dynamic-looking text to your Web pages, you'll also want to add keywords and meta tags that provide descriptions of your site's content. We discuss those topics in this chapter, as well.

Adding Text

To add text to your Web page, simply click on the page wherever you want the text to appear; this places an insertion point where you can start typing. You can add text right to the page, in a CSS layer, in the cell of a table, or in a layout text box when you use a Layout Grid. In Chapter 5 of this minibook, we show you how to integrate text with Layout Grids, tables, and frames.

Formatting text

Formatting text in GoLive can be as simple as formatting text in any other application. Using the Formatting toolbar that spans the top of the GoLive window, you can select text and apply character changes, including size, alignment, and color (see Figure 4-1).

Figure 4-1:
When a
page is in
front of the
site window,
the toolbar
contains
text
attributes.

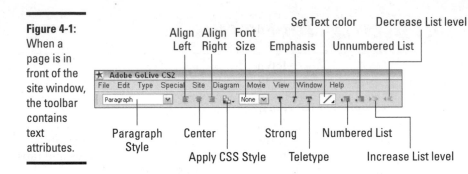

✦ **Paragraph style:** Use the Paragraph drop-down list on the Formatting toolbar to apply a style that affects an entire paragraph of text, even if you have selected only one character. These styles are generally added to headings and titles, and they help you process and organize copy in order of importance. Note that the Header tags also add extra space underneath the line. Later in this chapter, we show you how to change these default characteristics using Cascading Style Sheets (CSS).

Other choices include

• *None:* Removes the <p> and </p> tags from selected text.

• *Address:* Applies the <address> tag to a paragraph that contains the author's e-mail address.

• *Preformatted:* Lines up items such as text, using spaces, tabs, and paragraph returns. This choice changes your font to monospace to make all spaces even. It's not necessarily pretty!

✦ **Alignment:** You can click the alignment buttons on the toolbar to apply left, center, and right alignment. To revert to the default of left alignment, click the currently selected alignment button again.

✦ **Cascading Styles:** Apply an existing class style sheet or create a new style by clicking the Apply CSS Style button and choosing a class style from the list that appears. We show you how to create and apply style sheets later in this chapter.

✦ **Font Size:** Using the Font Size drop-down list, you can apply a fixed font size from 1–7 (seven being the largest). Or you can use the relative sizes indicated with the plus or minus signs, which resize the font larger or smaller according to the user's browser preferences for font size. If you leave the font size at None, it defaults to 3. Keep in mind that the browser preference of the viewer may be changed to a different default font size.

If you're planning to use Cascading Style Sheets, we recommend that you *do not* use the Font Size drop-down list because the font size attribute overrides any changes set with CSS.

✦ **Strong, Emphasis, and Teletype:** Simply click the Strong, Emphasis, or Teletype button to apply the Bold, Italic, or Teletype attributes to selected text. You can also assign these attributes to a style sheet later. Teletype creates evenly spaced text, which is useful if you're using spaces as an alignment tool, almost like a tab setting. In Figure 4-2, the text is set in teletype (pretty ugly, right?), and we chose Type⇨Paragraph⇨ Preformatted to apply formatting to the text so that the spaces and tabs don't vanish.

May	June	July
1	2	3
4	5	6

Figure 4-2:
Preformatted
teletype
text.

✦ **Color:** Assign a color to your text by selecting the text you want to change. Then click the bottom-right corner of the Set Text Color button on the toolbar. Choose a swatch library from the drop-down list that appears. If you select Web Named Colors from the drop-down list, for example, you would then release the mouse button, click again on the color button, and choose from the color palette at the top of the list.

You can select the Eyedropper tool to sample colors in GoLive or other applications. For instance, you can select the Eyedropper button in the Color palette, position the cursor over an open image in Photoshop, and click to sample the color for use in GoLive.

Notice that when selecting colors, you can add swatches to the Recent Color bar across the bottom of the Color palette. If you don't see recent colors, choose Show Recent Colors from the Color palette's menu.

✦ **Lists:** To create a list, use the automatic formatting features available from the Numbered and Unnumbered list buttons on the toolbar:

- *Numbered List:* Automatically numbers each additional line of text every time you press the Enter (Windows) or Return (Mac) key. To force the text to another line without adding the automatic numbering, press Shift+Enter (Windows) or Shift+Return (Mac).

- *Unnumbered list:* Automatically puts bullets in front of the listed items. As you advance in the use of Cascading Style Sheets, you can apply many more attributes to lists, including customizing the bullets.

- *Increase/Decrease list level:* Click the Increase List Level button to indent list items further inward. Click the Decrease List Level button to move list items back out. You can also use the Decrease List Level button to totally remove a line from being included in a list.

When you press the Enter or Return key, a `<p>` tag is automatically created in the HTML source code. This may create more space than you like between lines and create new list items. Pressing Shift+Enter (Windows) or Shift+Return (Mac) creates a `<br>` tag, essentially a line break or soft return.

Spell checking your text

Choose to spell check just the file that you have open or multiple files by choosing Edit⇨Check Spelling. As a default, only your front-most document is checked. But if you click on the Top Document button, you can choose to add files to checked (in the Check Spelling dialog box), you can add multiple files to the spell-checking task. Only pages with errors appear. If no pages appear, GoLive thinks that all is well on the spell-checking front.

Choosing and editing a font family

A *font family* is the typeface that you choose to display your text in. You don't have a huge choice in HTML, but the lack of typeface choice is not any restriction in GoLive. Keep in mind that what font the viewer sees on your Web page is based upon the availability of the fonts on his or her computer. This is another choice that you should be wary of because it creates a `<font>` tag that overrides any font family attributes in Cascading Style Sheets. To assign a font family, select the text to which you want to apply the font family, choose Type⇨Font, and then select the font family.

If you want to pick a standard family and let the viewer's browser choose the best appropriate font, use the choices listed in Table 4-1. These do not assign a specific font but choose from a variety of fonts that fall within the description.

Table 4-1	Font Families
Font Set Name	*Description*
Cursive	Generally have joining strokes or other cursive characteristics. Characters are partially or completely connected, and the result looks more like handwritten pen or brush writing than printed letters.
Monospace	The sole purpose of monospace fonts is to have each character maintain the same fixed width. The effect is similar to a manual typewriter and is often used to set samples of computer code.
Serif	Fonts with finishing strokes, flared or tapering ends. Serif fonts are typically proportionally spaced. They often display a variation between thick and thin strokes.
Sans-Serif	Fonts without the small serifs, or finishing strokes, at the ends of characters. Often considered to have a cleaner, more modern look than serif fonts, sans-serif fonts are frequently used for headlines. Sans-serif fonts include Helvetica, Verdana, and Trebuchet.

When a viewer opens a page referencing a font set, the text is displayed using the first available font in the font family. If the first font face on the list is not available, the next font face is referenced, continuing down the list in the font family until a font in the font set is found on the viewer's computer. If you choose Type⇨Font⇨Edit, the Font Editor dialog box appears (see Figure 4-3), containing the available font sets. Click the plus sign to the left of a set name to see which faces are included in each font set. Using the buttons at the bottom of the dialog box, you can select and delete faces or click an existing set and add additional faces to it. Click the arrow buttons to adjust the ranking of each font in the set.

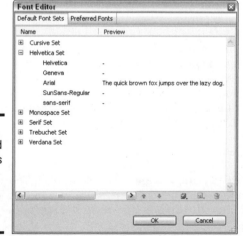

Figure 4-3:
You can add font families to existing sets or create new font sets.

Understanding Cascading Style Sheets

Using Cascading Style Sheets (CSS) is definitely the cleanest and most efficient method for creating Web sites. Style sheets are a powerful design tool that enables you to assign type properties quickly and update all instances in a few easy steps. The reason for the name Cascading Style Sheets is because there are certain *cascading rules* that apply when styles are used.

If you apply many different styles to a page, whether they are internally built on the page or linked to external style sheets, it's possible to have conflicts. This occurs when two (or more) styles assign different properties to the same element. For example, if you specify in an internal style sheet that anything bolded is blue but an external style sheet instructs the browser to display anything bolded as red, which style wins? The blue instruction from the internal style sheet wins. If conflicts occur in external style sheets, you can set the order of importance by using the up and down arrow. By default, the Web page's style sheet overrides the browser's default values.

There are several types of selectors that determine what defined style should be applied and where. In this section, we discuss three selectors: element, class, and ID.

Keep in mind that style sheets are not compatible with all browsers. Generally, the Internet Explorer and Netscape Navigator browsers (version 4x or higher) can display style sheets properly, as well as Opera and Safari. But even with the latest and greatest browser, some attributes may work in one browser but not in another. Always preview your pages in multiple browsers.

We definitely offer the quick-and-dirty course on CSS here. If you're interested in finding out more about this topic, check out *Cascading Style Sheets For Dummies* by Damon Dean (published by Wiley Publishing, Inc.).

The element selector

Using the element selector is the simplest and safest route for new users to CSS. This is because a page using element styles still has tags that older browsers understand, such as H1, H2, and so on. Using existing element tags on your page, you can choose to make all of your text tagged with `<H1>` blue or a certain size, or any number of additional character changes, many of which are not available through straight HTML.

To apply an element style to your page, follow these steps:

1. **To best see the results, create a page with lots of text. You can copy and paste text from another file; content is not important. Then select random words and click the Strong button in the main toolbar. This**

bolds the text and gives you a tag to which you can assign properties in this exercise.

2. **Click the Open CSS Editor button in the upper right of the page window.**

3. **When the CSS Editor window appears, click the Create a Style that Applies to Markup Elements button (<>) on the right side of the CSS editor.**

   For an Element style, you need to know the HTML tag that is used. The tag used for strong text is `<strong>`.

4. **For this example, type** `strong` **(the tag for strong) for the name on the left (replacing the word element) and press Enter (Windows) or Return (Mac).**

5. **Click the Font Properties tab (Figure 4-4), where you can see all of the font properties (color, size, and so on) available in the CSS Editor window.**

   As you click through the other tabs labeled in Figure 4-4, you can see that you have many properties that you can assign to text, backgrounds, and lists. We cover some of these throughout the rest of this section.

6. **Assign a color to the text using the Color drop-down list and change the size in the Size field (or choose from the Size drop-down list).**

   For size, enter a value such as **15**. The entered size defaults to pixels and fixes the font size so that it looks relatively the same on both Windows and Macintosh platforms.

7. **Change the font by clicking the Create New Font Family button (to apply an entire font family) or assign one font by clicking the Create New Font button.**

   As you're making these changes, you should notice immediate changes to the bold text on your page.

One of the many great things about using an element tag is the fact that if someone's browser can't read style sheets (this would have to be on a *very* old browser at this point), the visitor would still see the strong text. The text may not be as pretty as you want it to be, but at least it would still retain basic HTML formatting.

Click the Source Code Editor tab after creating this simple style sheet to see that only a small line of text, inside the `<style>` tag, was added in the Head section of the page. This code instructs the browser to change anything tagged with `<strong>` to use the properties following the selector name. By not selecting each string of text and using a `<font>` tag, you have saved lots of repetitive code in your document.

Text Properties   List Item and Other Properties

Selector
and
Properties

Margin and
Padding
Properties

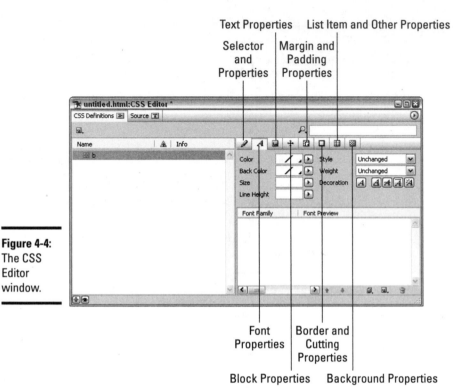

Figure 4-4:
The CSS
Editor
window.

Font
Properties

Border and
Cutting
Properties

Block Properties   Background Properties

TIP

Use the CSS Editor window to get rid of the underline beneath linked text by naming a new Element Style a (<a> is the tag for a hyperlink). On the Font Properties tab, click the No Text Decoration button. Links are no longer underlined!

The class selector

Giving your HTML page some class doesn't have to involve a huge makeover. By creating class selectors, you can create named styles for body, text, headlines, subheads, and so on. Essentially, it's like creating your own paragraph styles (see the earlier section, "Formatting text" where we discuss the default GoLive paragraph styles). By choosing a style from the CSS palette (Window⇨CSS) or by right-clicking (Windows) or Control+clicking (Mac) to bring up a contextual menu, styles can be applied to a selected word, paragraph, or even an entire page.

Follow these steps to create and then apply a class style:

1. **Have a page with text on it open and click the Open CSS Editor button in the upper-right corner of the document window.**

Block level versus inline

You may find that when you assign certain properties, you see varying results. That is because some properties that you select affect only block level elements as compared to inline elements. *Block level elements* apply to an entire paragraph, like the <H1> and <p> tags. Applying a style to these types of tags changes an entire paragraph of text. If you create an element style named H1 and change the line spacing, the space takes effect within the block-level element.

An *inline element* is one that does not apply to an entire paragraph but is used to apply formatting, such as the <b> tag to selected text only. If you choose to apply line spacing to the b element, the leading in paragraphs that contain the <b> tag will not be affected.

You'll eventually figure out which properties work with which tags, just keep this in mind so that you're not dumbfounded when some properties don't work as expected!

2. **In the CSS Editor window that opens, click the Create a New Class Style button (refer to Figure 4-4).**

   If you do not see the buttons for creating new styles on the right, click anywhere in a blank area on the left side of the CSS Editor window.

   You can change the .class that appears to any other name that you want, such as .headline or .description.

3. **Type a new name (under Name on the left side of the editor window) and press Enter (Windows) or Return (Mac) to finalize the name change and open the attributes area on the right.**

4. **Assign the properties by clicking the properties tabs and selecting the desired attributes (refer to Figure 4-4).**

   For instance, you can click the Margin and Padding Properties tab and type **10 px** in the Left text box to give your text a 10-pixel margin on the left side. You can preview the effect in the Inspector palette.

5. **Make another change, such as choosing a different color on the Font Properties tab, and then close the CSS Editor window.**

   Apply a few changes so that you can experiment, but also so that you can see a dramatic change when you apply the style to text.

6. **On your page, select one word and choose Window➪CSS to show the CSS palette (see Figure 4-5).**

   If you don't see the palette, it is probably docked at the bottom of the Colors palette.

Figure 4-5:
Apply a
Class style
using the
CSS
window.

You can also click the CSS button on the Formatting toolbar (refer to Figure 4-1) for the same options. You can reposition the CSS palette to make it more convenient.

7. **With one word highlighted, select the Inline check box to the right of your named class style (just the one selected word changes to the style that you created); select Block to apply your class style to the entire paragraph.**

Following are the options for applying class styles:

- **Inline Style:** Changes just the selected text to the style properties. This option uses a <span> tag to apply the style to only the selected text.

- **Block Style:** Creates a division that is disconnected from the normal flow of HTML. In other words, the style is applied to the entire paragraph, or up until a hard return. This uses a <div> tag to apply the style to the entire section.

- **<p>:** Similar to Block in that it formats an entire paragraph with a style. You don't need to select the entire paragraph; either place an insertion point in the paragraph or select a portion of it. This assigns the selected paragraph's <p> tag to the selected paragraph.

- **<body>:** Applies a style to the entire body of a page. If this option isn't listed in the CSS palette, you may be inside a floating box or table cell; if so, place an insertion point elsewhere on the page while in the Layout Editor.

- **Specific HTML tags (CSS palette):** Applies the style to a selected object, such as a table cell, image, or layer; for example, the <td> tag for a table cell, or the <img> tag for an image.

The ID selector

ID styles define unique style properties for just one element or selection on a page. Use this if you want one `<H1>` tag (or any existing tag for that matter) to be different from any other `<H1>` tag on that page.

Follow these steps to create and then apply an ID style:

1. **Have a page open and click the Open CSS Editor button in the upper-right corner of the document window.**

2. **Click the Create New ID Style (#), Create a Style that Applies to Unique Elements button.**

3. **Change the name (under Name on the left side in the window), leaving the # sign in front of the ID name and press Enter (Windows) or Return (Mac).**

   For this example, we've named the ID `#mystyle`.

4. **Select the properties by clicking the properties tabs to the right of the named style.**

5. **Select the text or element to which you want to apply the ID-selected style. You can also select text in the markup tree at the bottom of the Document window.**

6. **Choose Window ➪ Markup to open the Markup palette.**

7. **Click and hold the arrow to the right of the ID textbox and select the named ID style you created, as shown in Figure 4-6.**

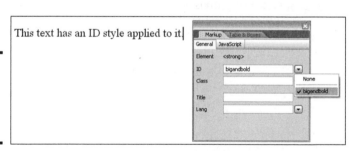

Figure 4-6:
Apply an ID style using the Markup window.

Creating an external style sheet

In the preceding sections of this chapter, we show you how to create styles directly on a page. What if you want to apply this style to multiple pages and also link the styles together so that in one change you can make the `<b>`

tagged elements navy and bold? You can do this using *external style sheets* and change one, two, or 400 pages at once!

You can create an external style sheet by choosing File⇨New. In the New options window choose Web⇨CSS⇨Basic CSS. You can also create the styles on a page, experiment with them, and then export them as an external style sheet. Follow these steps to export an internal style sheet:

1. **Have a document that contains style sheets open, such as an element style or class style that you created by following the steps in the preceding sections.**

2. **Choose File⇨Export⇨Internal Style Sheet; in the Export dialog box, enter a name for the style sheet and save it in the CSS folder in your Web-content folder.**

   After you export the style sheet, it's ready to be linked to other pages. Keeping the style sheet in the same folder as the other site elements is important because the style sheet will be linked to any other pages that use it.

To link a style sheet to other pages, follow these steps (see Online Help for additional methods):

1. **Open a page to which you want to apply an external style sheet.**

2. **Click the Open CSS Editor button in the upper-right corner of the document window, and then click the Create a Reference to an External Style Sheet File button (refer to Figure 4-4).**

3. **When (EmptyRefrence) appears as a listed item, click the Reference Browse button or the Fetch URL button to locate and link to the saved CSS style that you created.**

Apply an external style sheet to multiple files using this method:

1. **Have your external (`.css`) file saved in the same Site window as the pages to which you want to apply the style.**

2. **Ctrl+click (Windows) or ⌘+click (Mac) to select multiple pages in the File tab of the Site window.**

3. **Choose Window⇨CSS to open the CSS palette.**

4. **While the pages are selected, click and drag the Fetch URL button to point to the listed `.css` file in your Site window that you want to apply to the pages.**

Making Your Web Site Easy to Find

Knowing how to format your text to make your content look good is only part of adding text to Web pages. You also should know how to write the content to attract the most viewers. In GoLive, you can add keywords and a description to the Head sections. This ability helps viewers locate your Web site by using search engines, and also gives viewers a description of your site right in the search engine window.

Many search engines are out there; some use spiders to locate and catalog your information, and others are directories (meaning that you must submit information to these in order to be listed). For example, AltaVista (`www.alta vista.com`) is a search engine and Yahoo! (`www.yahoo.com`) is a directory.

You can build your page correctly, using correct titles, keywords, and *meta tags* (tags that contain valuable information for search engines, but aren't seen outside the source code), but that doesn't guarantee that your Web site will be included in search results. You should visit search engines and follow instructions on how to submit your URL to their databases to ensure that your Web site will show up in a potential visitor's search results. Some search engines or directories require payment, and that's not such a bad thing, either. Think of the payment as money spent for advertising, and the investment may be worth it. A good Web site for more information is `www.searchenginewatch.com`.

These three easy steps (which you can perform in no particular order) can make it much easier for viewers to find your Web site:

✦ **Choose a descriptive title for your Web pages:** If you create a new document, the default title is Untitled Page. Not very inviting to the user. Change the title by clicking the title on your document and typing a new name. This title is important; make it relevant to the content of the page. Also, the page title is what's listed when a visitor makes your Web page a Favorite or Bookmark, so keep the title concise. Don't waste space with a long title like, "Welcome to my really cool site about cars" because the title will probably truncate and list only "Welcome to my . . .".

✦ **Add keywords:** Open the Head section by clicking the arrow to the left of the word Head (upper left of the GoLive window). Write text for your pages using keywords throughout: If your keywords are viewed by search engines as being truly relevant to the page, you can pull your site up in rankings.

To add keywords to your page, have your Objects palette open, choose the Head category (by clicking and holding the Object's palette menu if it is displayed vertically or selecting the Head tab in the Objects palette if it's displayed horizontally); then drag the Keywords icon into the Head section of the GoLive page.

Enter keywords in the bottom text field of the Keywords Inspector palette, pressing Enter (Windows) or Return (Mac) after each entry.

Enter keywords in order of importance. Usually, search engines look for the first 10–15 keywords. Some may take more, but don't count on it.

✦ **Create a description of your Web page:** To add a description to your page, follow these steps:

1. **Click the arrow to the left of Head in the upper left of your document window.**

2. **Have the Head object in the Objects palette selected and drag the Meta object into the Head section.**

3. **Locate your inspector (Window⇨Inspector); then, using the attributes pop-up menu (the default id generic), choose the attribute description.**

4. **In the Content text field, replace the generic text with a short paragraph describing your page.**

Chapter 5: Layout Grids, Tables, and Frames

In This Chapter

✔ Understanding the new Layout Grid

✔ Discovering tables

✔ Finding out about frames

With no formatting structure, your text and images follow the flow of the HTML, with only the basic, default browser presentation of each. In Chapters 3 and 4 of this minibook, we show you how to align images and text (respectively), but aligning the image alongside the copy or exactly where you want it on the page may still be an elusive task.

In this chapter, we show you how to use the new Layout Grid, which consists of tables that you can use to build a grid or cell structure so that you can place elements exactly where you want them. You also see how you can use frames. Think of frames as individual windowpanes; a different page can be placed in each pane. There are positives and negatives to this way of adjusting the layout of a page. In Chapter 7 of this minibook, you discover how to use layers, the Cascading Style Sheet (CSS) alternative that enables you to position elements exactly where you want them on a page.

Working with the New Layout Grid

New in GoLive CS2, the Layout Grid creates formatting for your Web page using Cascading Style Sheets, or the standard table formatting.

What this means to you is that you can use new features related to CSS, including additional formatting controls.

Follow these steps to use a Layout Grid in GoLive:

1. **From the Basic section of the Object's palette, choose the Layout Grid object.**

2. Click and drag the Layout Grid Object to the page.

A Layout Grid of the default size of 200 pixels x 200 pixels appears. You can resize the grid by dragging the handles or by typing values into the Width and Height text fields of the Layout Grid Inspector.

 As a default the Layout Grid is created using CSS, hence the CSS stair icon in the upper right of the Layout Grid.

 If you would prefer to use coding based upon a traditional HMTL table, right+click (Windows) or Ctrl+Click (Macintosh) and choose Convert to a Table-Based grid from the contextual menu. The icon in the upper-right corner changes to a Table.

3. Add text to the Layout Grid by selecting the Layout Text box object from the Basic section of the Object's menu. Simply drag and drop it anywhere on the Layout Grid, and it sticks.

 Use the Standard Editing tool (top of the Objects palette) to grab the handles and reposition the text box.

4. Click inside of the Layout Text Box to see the cursor and start typing.

5. Place image objects on the Layout Grid by dragging and dropping them on the Grid, and then use the Image inspector to locate the image.

Placement is intuitive and natural when using a layout grid, much like using a page layout program like InDesign.

Working with Tables

When you think of a table, think of a grid that has multiple cells in it. Tables are used in HTML pages so that elements can be held in specific cells. You can change the colors of cells in tables, *span* or expand the cells (that is, combine them with other cells), and apply borders to them.

In many cases, you don't actually see the table because tables enable you to put content into row and column form without showing the table itself; in this case, the table is just a formatting tool. When you create a table, you can determine how many rows and columns it contains. You can also choose to span rows and columns to create unique tables, such as the one shown in Figure 5-1.

 To create a table, click the Basic Object button on the Objects toolbox. Then, either drag the Table object to your page or place your cursor where you want the table and double-click the Table object in the Object's palette. As a default, your table has three rows and three columns. You can add additional rows and columns if needed by using the Table Inspector (see Figure 5-2).

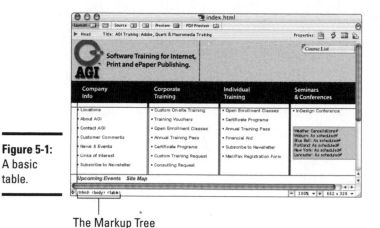

Figure 5-1:
A basic
table.

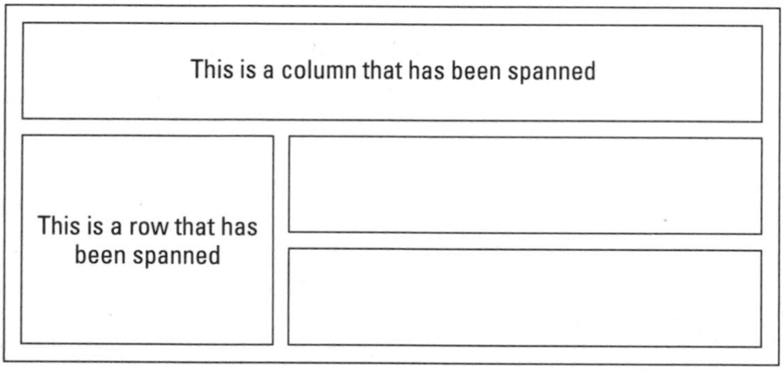

The Markup Tree

Figure 5-2:
We spanned
the rows
and
columns in
this table.

This is a column that has been spanned

This is a row that has
been spanned

When you first create a table, you can drag its right side, essentially just eye-balling as you go, to scale the table to the size you want. You can also choose a measurement from the Width and Height drop-down lists in the Table Inspector and enter exact pixel amounts or percentages in the Width and Height text fields (see Figure 5-3).

A pixel amount keeps the table to a fixed size, no matter how large the browser window is. Percentages resize the table as the browser window is made larger or smaller. In other words, if you choose the size to be 50 percent, the table always resizes itself to be half the size of the browser window. If you see red number values in the Table & Boxes palette, you messed up your math. Individual cells must add up to the size you made the table. Simply click the red value in the Table Inspector palette and GoLive solves your problem.

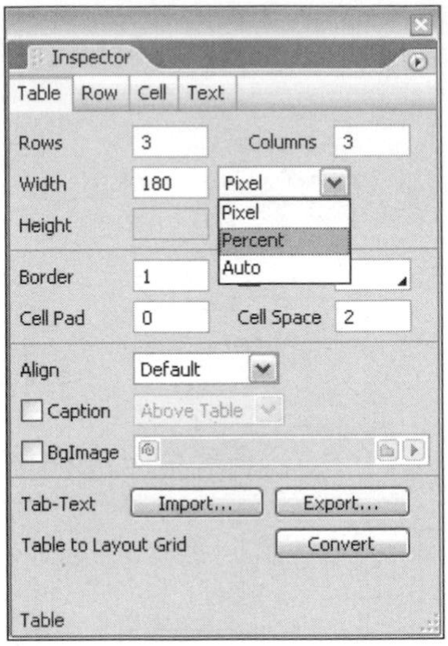

Figure 5-3:
The Table
Inspector
palette.

Throughout the rest of this section, we take you through all aspects of working with tables, from selecting tables and cells to manipulating rows and columns to changing a table's color to getting content into your tables.

Selecting a table and cells

Although this may sound absurd, you may have the most difficulty working with tables when you're trying to select a particular cell or table. We make this a non-issue for you, though, by showing you many cool techniques that you can use to get just what you want selected.

You may wonder why selection is so important. The contextual Inspector palette changes depending on what you have selected, so the options available to you (like changing the color and alignment of selected cells) are specific to your selection. If you have the wrong table or cell selected, you may not see the options you want. If this happens, then make sure that you have either a cell or table selected. Follow along for some table and cell selection tips:

✦ Select an entire table by positioning your cursor over its upper-left corner. When a square appears to the right of the cursor, click it and the entire table is selected.

✦ Use the Markup Tree in the lower-left corner of your Document window (refer to Figure 5-1). The markup tree is an incredible tool to use to select anything, but tables are extremely easy to select when using it. To use the Markup tree, just put your cursor inside a cell and then select `<td>` to select the cell that you're in, `<tr>` to select the entire row, or `<table>` to select the entire table.

The tag for table is `<table>` (difficult one to remember, right?), and each row is in a `<tr>` tag, which stands for *Table Row*. Each cell is in a `<td>` tag, which stands for *Table Data*.

✦ Insert your cursor into a table cell and Ctrl+Enter (Windows) or ⌘+Return (Mac) to select that cell; Ctrl+Enter (Windows) or ⌘+Return (Mac) again to select the table that the cell is in. If tables are nested (a table within a table), this technique continues to select outward with each Ctrl+Enter (Windows) or ⌘+Return (Mac).

✦ The most visual way to select a cell or table is to use the Table & Boxes palette. Choose Window⇨Table and Boxes, and an outline view of the table appears inside the Table palette, as shown in Figure 5-4. Simply click the cell that you want selected; click outside the cell, but still within the table on the Table palette, to select the table. If you have tables within tables, you can mouse over a nested table. When you see the cursor change to a nested table pointer, you click to zoom into a specific table or back out again.

**Book VI
Chapter 5**

**Layout Grids,
Tables, and Frames**

Figure 5-4:
Use the
Table
palette for
easy
selections.

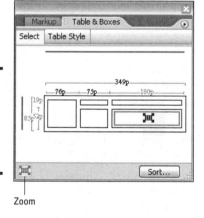

Zoom

✦ After selecting a cell, you can Shift+click other cells directly in the table to add them to the selection.

✦ With your cursor still in one cell, Ctrl+click (Windows) or ⌘+click (Mac) to select the cell. Press Ctrl+A (Windows) or ⌘+A (Mac) to select all of the cells. This is different from selecting the table because the Cell tab in the Inspector palette is still forward.

✦ Select an entire row or column by positioning the cursor outside the left side of a row or at the top of a column. When you see an arrow, click. This also works in the Table palette.

Manipulating rows, columns, and cells

After you create a table, you can change it to meet your needs. We briefly show you how in this list:

✦ **Adding rows and columns:** Use the Table Inspector (refer to Figure 5-3) to add rows and columns. Even if you have a cell selected within a table, you can click the Table tab of the Inspector palette to change the number of rows and columns.

Always determine the number of rows and columns before you change the width and height of a table; otherwise, you have to resize your table to get it back to where you had it.

This is a neat trick! Ctrl+drag (Windows) or ⌘+drag (Mac) the table object in the Object palette; while dragging, you can create your own custom number of rows and columns. When you release the mouse button, the table with your configuration appears where your cursor is.

✦ **Customizing rows and columns:** You can span columns and rows. When you *span* columns and rows, you connect two or more cells. Try this simple trick to span a row or column. Select the cell in the upper-left corner of a table and hold down the Shift key. Now press the right-arrow key on your keyboard (→). Notice that the cell now spans over the area of two columns.

To return to the original cell configuration, press Shift+←. You can also use Shift+↓ to span rows. If you don't like using keyboard commands, manually put spans in by using the Cell tab of the Table Inspector palette.

Customize rows and columns individually by Alt+dragging (Windows) or Option+dragging (Mac) the borders separating the rows and columns.

✦ **Changing the height and width of cells:** Something a little trickier is applying width and height to a table and cells. Tables and cells can be fixed to an amount based upon pixels or percentage, or left at Auto (refer to Figure 5-3). Auto is the default for the cells and can be a very *bad* thing.

Suppose that you have a table and you have left Cell Width in the Table Inspector palette set at Auto. When you put your cursor in the first cell to start typing, the cell automatically widens as you add text. Not good. (Choose Edit⇨Undo to fix this!) Go back to the Table Inspector palette and, on the Cell tab, change Auto in the Width drop-down list to Percent and type a number. Now when you type in the cell again, the cell does not expand unless it needs to accommodate text or objects larger than the size you designated.

Changing the backround color of a table or cells

You can change the color of an entire table, just its cells, or both. To change the background color of a table, select the table, click and hold the bottom-right corner of the color box in the Table Inspector (refer to Figure 5-3), and choose a color. You can also choose from the Color palette, which appears when you press Ctrl+3 (Windows) or ⌘+3 (Mac). If the Color palette is mini-mized, click the arrow in the title bar to show options. As long as the Color box is active, you can continue selecting colors and you'll see the results instantly. Use the same method to change the color of cells, except first select just the cells you want to color. Remember, a color assigned to a cell always overrides a color assigned to an entire table.

**Book VI
Chapter 5**

Layout Grids,
Tables, and Frames

To change your color library, click and hold the triangle in the lower right of the color box and then select a color library. Release the mouse and click and drag to choose a color from the palette at the top of the color list.

If you create a colored table but can't see the cells, it's because there must be an element inside a cell for it to show up. If you're designing a table but haven't yet put elements into its cells, select one cell and press Ctrl+A (Windows) or ⌘+A (Mac) to select all the cells. Right-click (Windows) or Control+click (Mac) and choose Insert⇨Nonbreaking Spaces from the menu that appears. This creates an empty space not visible to the viewer but that counts as an element, thereby allowing the color to be visible. This is the same result you get if you press Ctrl+spacebar (Windows) or Option+space-bar (Mac) in each cell separately.

Borders, spacing, and padding

In the Table tab of the Table Inspector palette (refer to Figure 5-3), you can define a border, cell spacing, and cell padding in pixels. You may want to change the border to 0 (zero) if you're using the table for formatting pur-poses only — that is, if you don't want the table itself visible; you just want your content arranged in rows and columns. Use *padding* to give you a margin around all sides of the cell; change *spacing* to change the size of cell walls. Figure 5-5 illustrates all three attributes used in a table.

Figure 5-5:
A table with border, cell padding, and cell spacing applied.

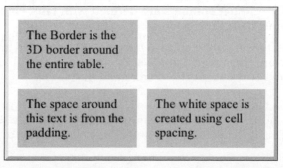

The Border is the 3D border around the entire table.

The space around this text is from the padding.

The white space is created using cell spacing.

Adding and importing content

Adding content to a table is easy — you just type directly into a cell for text or drag an image object into a cell. That's all there is to adding content to your table.

As a default, all elements center vertically inside a cell and are flush left. Change this on a cell-by-cell basis by selecting the cell (Shift+click to select multiple cells) and then changing the Vertical Alignment and Horizontal Alignment at the top of the Cell tab of the Table Inspector palette. Figure 5-6 illustrates various alignments.

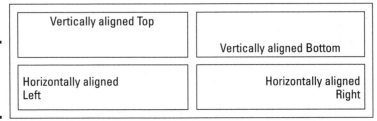

Figure 5-6:
Vertical and horizontal alignments.

Note: The Align buttons on the toolbar override the Vertical and Horizontal Alignment selected in the Cell tab of the Table Inspector palette.

To import content into a table, follow these steps (you'll love this if you're constantly updating table information):

1. **Drop the default table object onto your page.**

2. **Choose Special⇨Table⇨Import Tab Delimited Text.**

The Open dialog box appears.

3. **Browse to select a text document (`.txt`) from Excel or any other program that allows you to save as `.txt` or to export text — but don't click Open yet!**

4. **In the Col Separator drop-down list (at the bottom of the Open dialog box), choose whether columns are defined with tabs, commas, spaces, or semicolons; then click Open.**

As a default, tabs from the original text file are converted into columns and returns are converted into rows. Choose Special⇨Table⇨Export Tab-Delimited Text to export text from a table as well.

 After you build a table and add color, text, and images to it (just the way you want), you may notice that a margin appears in the upper left. Where's that coming from? This is the default margin for the HTML page. To butt the table up into the upper left of the page, select the Page Properties button in the upper right of your document window and set the Margin Width and Height to 0 (zero).

Introducing Basic Frames

To use frames or not to use frames, that is the question. Sure, frames are convenient, they make it easy to update one page without updating all, but what about issues with search engines and inexperienced Web surfers? Search engines don't find much content to index on a framed page, and sometimes new users end up stuck in individually framed documents and don't know how to get out. (And some Web browsers don't accommodate frames; see the "About noframes" sidebar, later in this chapter.) If you want to use frames, place some navigational path back to your home frameset for those viewers who end up in independent pages.

When using frames, you create a main page that contains nothing but a frameset. A *frameset* is much like a window with a page appearing in each pane (see Figure 5-7). Framed pages can contain targeted links. When a viewer clicks the link, the page that it is referencing opens within a frame specified by the Web page designer, thereby allowing you to have multiple pages open at once. Using frames can make updating pages easy. You can update one frame's page without affecting the other frames.

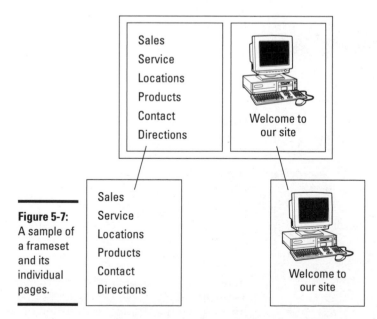

Figure 5-7:
A sample of
a frameset
and its
individual
pages.

Creating a frameset

To create a page that uses frames, choose File⇨New. Choose Web⇨Pages⇨ HTML Page and click OK. Click the Frame Editor tap at the top of the Document window. Select the Frame section of the Objects palette, also refered to as the Draggable Frame Objects.

Select a Frames object from the Object palette. There are many choices for framesets, including a single frame that can be added multiple times to customize your own layout. To apply a frameset, simply drag your choice into the GoLive page while in the Frame Editor.

When you create a frameset, GoLive pops up a dialog box that suggests that you change the doctype because you're applying frames; click OK. The doctype specifies, in the !DOCTYPE declaration, which Document Type Definition (DTD) to use when handling the document.

When a frameset is on the page, a series of empty references appears, one for each frame created. Individual frames can be deleted by pressing the Delete key or resized by dragging the frameset. Later in this section, we show you how to link pages into each of the sections in the frameset.

As shown in Figure 5-8, when you click on the Frameset, options that apply to the frameset are available in the Frameset inspector. If your inspector palette is not open, choose Window⇨Inspector.

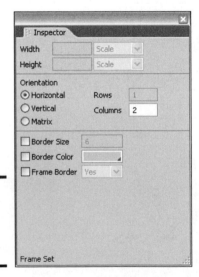

Figure 5-8:
The
Frameset
Inspector
palette.

Here are what the options in the Frameset Inspector palette are for:

✦ **Rows and Columns:** The values in the Rows or Columns text fields determine how many frames are displayed and what size they are. If you have both rows and columns, multiply the number in each text field to come up with the total number of frames.

✦ **Orientation:** Select either the Horizontal or Vertical radio button to arrange the frames in your frameset either horizontally or vertically. Select the Matrix radio button to create a frameset that has both rows and columns, defining a matrix.

✦ **Border Size:** The width of the border between frames; select the Border Size check box and type a size into the text field. Border size is set in pixels. If you enter 0 (zero), no border will show.

✦ **Border Color:** If you choose a border size of 1 or greater, you can choose a border color. Select the Border Color check box and click the color selection box to the right. Use the Color palette to choose a color.

✦ **Frame Border:** Choosing Yes from the Frame Border drop-down list gives your border a 3D appearance; selecting No means the border will be 2D.

✦ **Preview Set:** Allows you to preview the frameset in GoLive.

**Book VI
Chapter 5**

**Layout Grids,
Tables, and Frames**

To have a seamless frameset, where you have no evidence that the pages are separate, enter 0 in the Border Size text field, and select No from the Frame Border drop-down list.

Linking the pages

To have pages appear within the frameset, you must link each one to its specific location. Design your pages accordingly when using frames. You may have only a list running vertically (if it is going into a vertical frame) or a horizontal navigation bar (if it is going to be in a horizontal frame). In the Frameset Editor of the GoLive page, click the empty reference in the set that you want to link to, and then click the Frame tab at the top of the Inspector palette. Click the Browse button to the right of URL or use the Fetch URL button to link the already created page to the specific frame.

You can also drag a page from your Site window right into a frame to link it!

Links and framed pages

After you create your initial page, keep the viewer inside the frameset by *targeting* your links. A targeted link is one that you, as a designer, can control the destination of. For instance, you can direct a linked page to appear in a frame in the upper right of the page instead of opening up the page to take

About noframes

Some browsers are not capable of displaying frames. In these instances, you want to display some message to let the viewer know that the page uses frames, as well as a link to a non-framed page with the same information as the framed version.

To create a noframe message, simply click the Layout Editor tab and type a message on the page. This automatically appears in the `<noframes>` tag in the HTML source code. You may want to leave a polite message, like "Hey buddy! 'bout time you upgraded your browser...you know they're free!" and provide links to where they can update their browsers. More seriously, a link to a page not created with frames providing mailing and e-mail addresses, as well as other basic contact information, would be nice for these folks.

up the entire browser window. We discuss links in much greater detail in Chapter 6 of this minibook, but here we give you the link information that's specific to using frames. Before creating links, you must name each set. Note that when you click the Frame tab of the Inspector palette, it changes to show options that are specific to the selected frame, as shown in Figure 5-9.

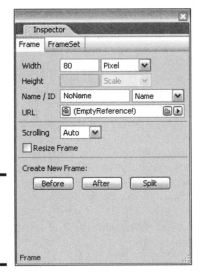

Figure 5-9:
The Frame Inspector palette options.

Look for these settings in the Frame Inspector palette:

✦ **Size:** Three choices are available in the Width or Height drop-down list:

• **Scale:** Automatically resizes the frame if the viewer resizes the browser window.

- **Pixel:** Enables you to set the size of the frame in pixels. You can't set all frames in a frameset in absolute pixel sizes. For instance, if you have a two-frame horizontal setup, you can have the top frame in pixels, but you must leave the bottom frameset to Scale. By setting one frame in the frameset to Scale, the frameset will adjust itself to accommodate the size of the browser window.

- **Percent:** Enables you to choose the percentage of the browser window that you would like the frame to take. For instance, you could set a left frame to 25 percent and a right frame to 75 percent. As the browser window is adjusted, the left frame will always fill a quarter of the whole window.

✦ **Name/ID:** This is important! You must name each frame in your frameset. Choose a descriptive name and type it into the Name field. For a two-frame horizontal layout, you can enter top and bottom as appropriate names, or something descriptive, such as navbar and description. Keep names in lowercase; frame names are case sensitive and won't work if you target a frame with an uppercase name when you typed it in lowercase.

**Book VI
Chapter 5**

**Layout Grids,
Tables, and Frames**

If one of your framed pages is a navigation tool with multiple links, you need to not only instruct the browser what page or location on a page should appear, but also which frame to have it appear in, which is the reason why you named the frames. Follow these steps to create a link that appears in a specified frame:

1. **Open a page in your frameset that has links.**

You can double-click right on the frame inside the frameset to open a page.

2. **Select the element that is going to be a link.**

3. **Press Ctrl+L (Windows) or ⌘+L (Mac) to create a link to (EmptyReference!).**

You could also click the Create Link button in the element's Inspector palette or toolbar.

4. **Use the Browse button or the Fetch URL button in the Inspector palette to replace (EmptyReference!) with a link to a specific file.**

5. **Specify the target frame by selecting the frame's name from the Target drop-down list in the Inspector palette, as shown in Figure 5-10.**

This specifies which frame your linked page will appear in. If your frameset is closed, you can type the name.

6. **Save the file and return to the page containing the frameset. Preview the entire frameset in the browser by clicking the Preview in Browser button on the toolbar.**

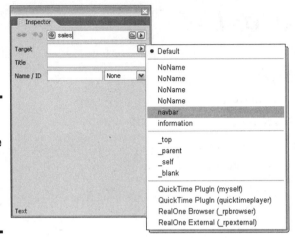

Figure 5-10:
Choose
which frame
will display
your linked
file by
specifying
a target.

If all your links are going to the same frame, you can switch back to the Layout mode of the frameset page and drag the Base object from the Head section of the Object's palette into the head section of your page. In the Base Inspector, leave Base blank, but assign the frame's name in the Target drop-down list. All links on the frameset page will be directed to the same frame, unless you specify otherwise.

Chapter 6: Links

*L*inks are a major component of any Web site. *Links* (short for *hyperlinks*) are navigational aids; viewers click links to go to other Web pages, a downloadable resource file, an e-mail address, or a specific spot on a Web page (known as an *anchor*). You must incorporate links on your Web site; otherwise, your viewers won't be able to navigate your site — not good! In this chapter, we show you how to add links easily and effectively with GoLive.

The Basics of Linking

As you create the first link from one of your Web pages to another, you have essentially created a Web site — it may be a small site, but it's a start. While you're still in the small site stage, here are a few things we recommend that you keep in mind as you add more pages and create more links, making your site ever bigger:

✦ Essentially, there are two kinds of links: internal and external. *Internal links* connect viewers to other parts of your Web site; *external links* connect viewers to other pages or content outside your site. We show you how to create each kind of link in this chapter.

✦ Before you start working with any pages that are to be linked, make sure that you are working with a site file open; otherwise, you won't have options available that make saving files to your site folder easier.

✦ Keep all files close at hand in your site folder (the folder that opens when you open a `.site` file). This will help you to avoid broken link issues later. Discover how to fix broken links in the later section, "Resolving Link Errors."

✦ To visualize your links, make sure your Site window is forward, click the Open Navigation View button in the Site toolbar, and click the Links tab. If your pages are collected on top of each other, click the plus sign to view the file hierarchy, as shown in Figure 6-1. Find out about organizing and keeping track of your links in the later section, "Managing Your Links with the External Tab."

Choose Window⇨View and click the Filter tab to narrow down the links that you are viewing in the Navigation Links window. In Figure 6-1, only URLs are checked.

✦ Resist the temptation to just add and add and add files into a site. Keep in mind what is happening to the ease of navigation for the viewer. Map out where you want content and follow that plan — you may also want to add a navigation bar to each page to make it easy for viewers to find the page they want to see on your site. If you don't carefully plan your site's navigation and manage the links, viewers could end up lost in dead ends all over the place.

Figure 6-1:
Click the
Open
Navigation
View button
on the Site
toolbar, and
then click
on links,
to get an
overview of
your site.

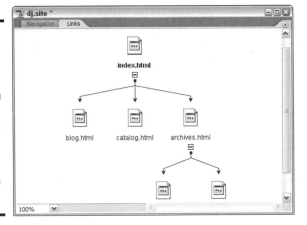

Implementing Internal Links

Internal links, an essential part of any user-friendly site, help your viewers easily and quickly navigate to other parts of your Web site. In this section, we show you how to create links in your own site and also how to create anchors.

Just a note of caution: If you need to change names of files after they have been linked anywhere, do so *only* within the GoLive Site window. Otherwise, you'll end up with broken links. Take a look at the "Resolving Link Errors" section, later in this chapter, to find out how to change the names of linked files without breaking the links.

Linking to pages in your own site

To manually create a link to other pages within your own site, follow these steps:

Book VI
Chapter 6

Links

1. **With a site open and the document window forward, select the element you want to make into a link.**

   You can create a link out of text or an image (say, a button image).

2. **Press Ctrl+L (Windows) or ⌘+L (Mac), or click the Create Link button on the toolbar or Inspector palette.**

   Press Ctrl+1 (Windows) or ⌘+1 (Mac) to open the Inspector palette if it isn't already open. This creates a link to an (EmptyReference!).

3. **Click the Browse button to the right of the text field containing (EmptyReference!), and in the Open dialog box that appears, locate the file inside your site folder that you are linking to.**

   The linked file name, and path to get to it, now appears in place of (EmptyReference!)

Here are two alternative methods for creating a link to other pages within your own site:

✦ With the site file open, select the element you're linking to, and then click the Fetch URL button and drag it to the file that you want to link. Remember, if your page is covering the Site window, you can click the Fetch URL button and drag to point at the Select Window icon on the toolbar. This brings the Site window forward so that you can point to the file you need.

   Try this great trick: Select the element that is to be the link and hold down the Alt (Windows) or ⌘ (Mac) key. An arrow with the Fetch URL icon appears. Drag and point it directly to the file that you want to link to.

✦ With the site file open, select the element you're linking to, and then click the palette menu to the right of the Browse button in the Inspector palette. The menu gives you the opportunity to open an Edit dialog box to show the full address, and also shows you recent links that you can select from (see Figure 6-2).

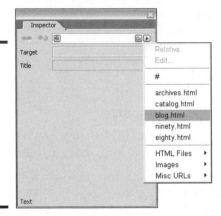

Figure 6-2:
The Inspector palette menu is useful for locating recently selected links.

Note: If you link to a file that is not inside your site folder, you get an Orphan File error. This is not critical; simply choose Errors from the Site window palette menu. Drag any files that are listed as orphan files from the right side of the Site window to the left side, placing them in the appropriate location in your Web-content folder. Doing this does not move the original files; it copies them into your Web-content folder.

Creating anchors

Anchors are a link to a specific section of a page, either on the same page as the link or on another page entirely. Anchors are especially handy for long pages that have a lot of text. You have probably seen and used anchors, for instance, when clicking a Back to Top button. They are extremely helpful to the viewer and should be implemented whenever necessary.

To create an anchor on the same page, follow these steps:

1. **Because anchors are most useful on pages with lots of text, open a text-heavy page (preferably one where you have to scroll a while to read it all in the browser).**

2. **Choose Window➪Objects or press Ctrl+2 (Windows) or ⌘+2 (Mac) to open the Object palette (if it isn't already open and visible).**

3. **From the Basic section of the Object palette, drag the Anchor object to the location on a page that you want the viewer to be navigated to.**

   If you really want to see the effect of using an anchor, put it somewhere near the bottom of your page.

4. **Select the Anchor object on the page, and in the Anchor Inspector palette, type a unique logical name in the Name/ID text box.**

Make the name simple and all lowercase. For example, for an anchor to the National Wildlife Park section of a long page, you might type **nwp**.

5. **Navigate to the location on the page that the link to the anchor will be (probably near the top of the page), and type the words that are to be linked, such as** Go To Wherever.

6. **Select the words you want to make into the link and create the link by pressing Ctrl+L (Windows) or ⌘+L (Mac).**

7. **Replace (EmptyReference!) in the Inspector palette with your anchor's logical name (the name you gave it in Step 4) preceded by the pound (#) sign.**

The pound sign must always be in front of a link to an anchor. So for the example anchor named in Step 4, you would enter **#nwp**.

8. **Test out the anchor in your browser to see the full effect.**

Frequently, you see anchors separated by the pipe sign (|). This type character can be created by pressing Shift+\. The backslash key is directly above the Enter (Windows) or the Return (Mac) key.

Anchors are also helpful when you want to have one page that lists links to specific locations on other pages of your site. So to take viewers from one page to a specific location on a totally different page, follow these steps:

1. **Drag the Anchor object from the Objects palette to the location you want as the final destination for the viewer on the target page.**

2. **Create a link on the other page.**

You can create a link on the other page by clicking the Create Link button or by using either of the two other methods we describe in the preceding section.

3. **Replace (EmptyReference!) in the Inspector palette with the name of the page the anchor is on and then the # sign followed by the anchor's name.**

Remember: Make sure there are no spaces in the anchor's name. For example, if the anchor for the National Wildlife Park is in the file named `parks.html`, you type **parks.html#nwp**.

Linking to a PDF file

To link to a PDF file instead of a Web page, you link to the name and location of the PDF file. If you link to a PDF file and the Acrobat PDF plug-in is loaded in the viewer's browser, the PDF is opened in the browser window. If the viewer does not have the Acrobat plug-in (free from `www.adobe.com`), the Save dialog box appears and you can browse to save the file to open with Acrobat or Reader at another time.

Book VI Chapter 6

Links

Implementing External Links

External links connect viewers to pages and content that isn't contained within your Web site, as well as to e-mail addresses or downloadable files. In the following sections, we show you how to create external links.

Linking to pages and files outside your Web site

To link to files outside of your Web site, follow these steps:

1. **Select the element that you want to become the link.**

2. **Create the link.**

   Use any of the three methods we discuss in the "Linking to pages in your own site" section to make the selected item into a link: Press Ctrl+L (Windows) or ⌘+L (Mac), click the Create Link button on the toolbar, or click the Create Link button in the Inspector palette.

3. **Replace (EmptyReference!) in the Inspector palette with the URL.**

   For instance, to go to Adobe.com from a link on your page, type **www.adobe.com**. GoLive automatically adds the `http://` to the front of the URL.

Linking to e-mail

Linking to an e-mail address opens a new mail message addressed to the address you specify as a link on the viewer's computer. This of course depends that the viewer has set up an e-mail program on his or her machine.

Follow these steps to add a link to an e-mail address:

1. **Select the element that you want to become the link to an e-mail address.**

2. **Create the link by selecting the Create Link button on the Inspector palette or the toolbar.**

3. **Replace (EmptyReference!) with the recipient's e-mail address and then press Enter (Windows) or Return (Mac).**

   GoLive automatically adds the `mailto:` protocol necessary for the e-mail link to work.

Managing Your External Links

When you link to external URLs, you lose just a little control because the Web pages that those links connect to may vanish or change, and there's nothing you can do about that. You can make your life easier, though, by getting to know the External tab of the Site window, on which you can inventory and manage the links to pages and files outside your Web site.

The External tab is most useful to you after you have a Web site that has one or two external links saved on a page. On the External tab, you can find all of your external references in the site by choosing Site➪Update➪Add Used➪ External Links. If they weren't already listed, all external references, including e-mail links, appear in the External tab, as shown in Figure 6-3.

**Book VI
Chapter 6**

Links

Figure 6-3:
The External tab of the Site window keeps track of all external links.

You can now use the External References tab of the Site window for many purposes:

✦ **Add an external reference without typing:** If you have a page open, you can now select an element and use the Fetch URL button in the Inspector palette and drag to point directly to a listed external reference. No more nasty typing!

✦ **Add external references:** Right-click (Windows) or Control+click (Mac) in the External References tab of the Site window and choose New URL from the contextual menu that appears. Add external references beforehand to make your job of linking to them easier when building pages.

✦ **Ensure external references are still active:** Choose Site➪Check External Links to have GoLive check URLs and make sure they are still active. If the link is no longer valid, a bug icon appears in the Status column to the right of the listed URL; if the link is valid, a check mark appears instead.

✦ **Change a URL and all of its linked references:** You can do this on the External References tab in just one step. Just select the link and change the name in the Inspector palette. When an alert dialog box appears stating that code on the listed pages is to be updated, click OK.

Resolving Link Errors

GoLive manages the source code and links to all of your files. If you change the name in the Site window, you get a dialog box allowing you to confirm the change and update the source code, as shown in Figure 6-4. If you change a linked file's name in your directory system, you essentially break the link, and a bug (yuck!) appears to the right of the HTML file in your Site window because GoLive was not able to track the change.

If you aren't sure which files are being used in your site, scroll past the Date Modified column in your Site window to show the Used column. A dot indicates whether the file has been used or not. To reorganize your files without breaking links, click the Files tab of the Site window and click the New Folder button on the Site toolbar, an untitled folder appears in the Files section of your Site window. Rename the folder and drag files to folders — without breaking links because GoLive keeps track of them for you!

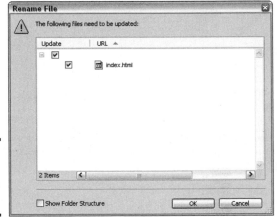

Figure 6-4:
The
Rename File
dialog box.

So that's the lowdown for preventing broken links. Here are several methods to exterminate bugs in the case of broken links:

+ Open a page with bugs and click the Show Link Warnings button (bug) on the toolbar. This highlights, in red, errors on your page. It could be that you have an empty space that is still linked to an outdated image or file. You will also get errors if you forget to replace (EmptyReference!) in the Inspector palette with a valid link.

+ From the Site window palette menu, choose Errors to see a list of all errors. Open the Missing Files folder and select each error. Then use the Inspector palette's Browse button or the Fetch URL button to link to the file in your system or to another file.

If you're not sure which file has the listed error, select the error and choose Window⇨Site⇨In and Out Links. This will show you links to and from the selected file.

✦ Orphans are created when you select files that aren't in your Web-content folder to be linked in your Web site. To eliminate orphans, simply choose Errors from the Site Window palette menu, and then open the Orphan Files folder. Select all orphans and drag them to an appropriate location on the left side (your site) to copy them to your Web-content folder, as shown in Figure 6-5.

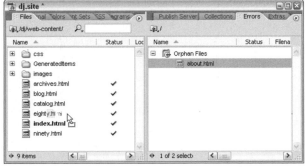

Figure 6-5: Moving orphans to your Web-content folder to fix broken links.

Chapter 7: Layers

In This Chapter

✔ Creating layers

✔ Customizing layers

✔ Making layers visible/invisible

✔ Working with animation

In this chapter, we show you how to use layers to format your pages. Using layers, you can precisely control the positioning and stacking order of any element on your page. Layers can contain elements, such as images and text, giving you the same control of the Web page layout that you have in a page layout program.

Layers actually utilize the id tag in cascading style sheets and are part of the CSS technology, making them efficient and much more controllable than a table is for formatting.

Creating Layers in GoLive

If you're familiar with Photoshop layers, you may think that GoLive layers work the same way, but that's not totally true. Understanding the concept of stacking one layer on top of another and moving layers independently of others can help you as you begin working with layers in GoLive. Choose Window➪Layers to see a list of all layers in the Layers palette, as shown in Figure 7-1. As you add layers, they appear in this palette. Use the Layers palette to select, lock, rename, or turn off and on the visibility of selected layers. You can even click the New Layer button at the bottom of the palette to create a new, empty layer.

Note: Clicking the eye icon does not make the layer invisible when you publish the site; this is just for working in GoLive. Read the "Hiding and Showing Layers" section, later in this chapter, to truly make a layer invisible. Hiding and showing layers is how you can create pop-up menus for your links.

To create a layer, click the Basic object on the Objects palette; this shows the objects included under the Basic heading. Drag the Layer object to your page. You can also put your cursor where you want the layer marker to appear and double-click the Layer object.

Denotes that a layer is locked

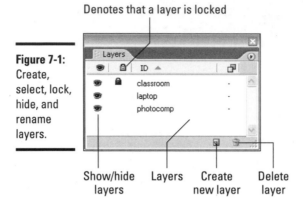

Figure 7-1: Create, select, lock, hide, and rename layers.

Show/hide layers   Layers   Create new layer   Delete layer

When a layer is placed on a page, it has two parts: a marker and the layer itself, as shown in Figure 7-2. Keeping the marker out of cells and other layers is important because the marker tells the browser the information necessary to display the layer properly. The marker is not visible when the page is viewed in a browser, so don't delete it.

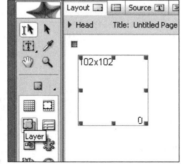

Figure 7-2: A layer and its marker.

Positioning elements with CSS layers is very different from positioning elements with tables. (We discuss tables in Chapter 5 of this minibook.) Don't mix tables and layers when formatting pages. In other words, don't expect that a layer perfectly lined up over a cell will stay in that position. Use layers for all of your formatting. Tables can still be used for data-specific information, such as charts and other items, but place the table inside a layer so that the positioning stays accurate in the browser.

Working with Layers

After you have layers in your site, you can do a lot of manipulating with these layers, from adding text and images to repositioning them to customizing a layer's colors. In the following list, we give you a quick-and-dirty rundown of these options:

✦ **Assigning a name:** As soon as you place a layer, use the Layer Inspector palette to name it properly. Just like in Photoshop, after you start using layers, they can become cumbersome and difficult to keep track of.

✦ **Adding elements to layers:** You can add elements such as text and images by dragging the object or inserting the cursor directly in the layer, just as if you were adding objects directly to a page.

✦ **Setting the position of a layer:** By positioning the cursor over the edge of a layer, you reveal a hand icon. When this hand (it looks more like a mitt) is visible, drag to reposition the layer.

Choose Layer Grid Settings from the Layers palette menu to change the setup of a grid, and then select the Snap and the Visible while Dragging options. If you selected the Visible while Dragging option, your grid appears as you reposition the layers.

✦ **Determining layer size:** You can grab the anchor points (handles) and change the width and height of the layer. For more precision, use the Layer Inspector palette and enter values for the top, right, bottom, and left (see Figure 7-3). As a default, only Top and Left are specified. You can also enter exact measurements for the width and height. Note in Figure 7-4 that as you change the size, the measurements are visible in the upper left of empty layers.

✦ **Adjusting stacking order:** Just as with other applications, the last layer created is at the top of the stacking order. Change this by changing the z-index in the Inspector palette. If you're a programmer by trade, you may recognize the term *z-index*; if not, understand that the lower the z-index, the closer to the page the layer is. If you set one layer at zero and another at five, the layer with the z-index of five is on top of the layer with the z-index of zero. If changing the z-index, make sure that you use intervals of five (0, 5, 10, 15, and so on). This way you can insert layers in between if necessary.

**Book VI
Chapter 7**

Layers

Figure 7-3:
Enter values for specific locations and sizes of layers.

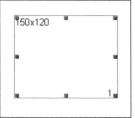

Figure 7-4:
The measurement values appear in the layer.

✦ **Importing Photoshop layers:** Choose File⇨Import⇨Import Photoshop Layers to open a Photoshop layered document and convert it to GoLive layers. This is an incredible feature that recognizes layered images and opens the Save for Web dialog box for each and every layer in Photoshop. The Photoshop named layer is retained, but avoid naming files starting with numbers in Photoshop because this can cause errors in the browser.

✦ **Aligning and distributing layers:** Say you want to use layers for columns of text, or you want images perfectly spaced apart from each other. You can do this by using the Align palette in GoLive. Select the layers you want to align and distribute by selecting one layer and Shift+clicking the other layers. To align layers to each other, click one of the buttons in the Align Objects section of the Align palette (see Figure 7-5). The Align to Parent section is used to align to the entire page.

Figure 7-5:
Use the
Align palette
to align and
distribute
layers.

To distribute the spaces in between the layers, click one of the buttons in the Distribute Objects section of the Align palette. Notice that there is a section for vertical spacing (up and down) and horizontal spacing (left to right).

As a default, the spacing for distribution is based upon the first and last layer position of the layers, but you can also define an exact amount of space between layers by selecting the Use Spacing check box at the bottom of the Align palette.

✦ **Customizing layers:** Using the Inspector palette, you can assign a color to the layer. This gives you the opportunity to create graphically interesting pages, much the same way that you would get by coloring cells in a table. To change the color of a layer, simply activate the color box in the Background section of the Layer Inspector palette, and then choose a color from the palette, as shown in Figure 7-6.

Double-click the color box in the Background tab of the Layer Inspector to open the standard color picker that you may be used to seeing in Photoshop.

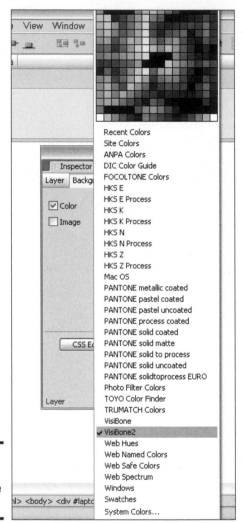

Figure 7-6:
Selecting a
color for the
layer.

You can also select a color from the Color palette. Remember that if you
click the Color box in the Inspector palette, a border appears around it.
As long as you see the border, the fill color is active; click a color in the
Color palette and the fill color changes immediately.

The layer is a Cascading Style Sheet element. For more customized
attributes, such as margins, position, and style attributes, choose the
CSS Editor in the upper-right of the toolbar and select the layer name in
the left side of the Editor.

Hiding and Showing Layers

Just *why* would you go through the trouble of creating a layer and then deselect the Visible check box on the Layer Inspector palette (refer to Figure 7-3)? It's not a silly question, but it brings up the topic of hiding and showing layers. For example, you can hide layers to keep the viewer from seeing their contents until they cross over or click on an element, triggering their visibility. You have probably experienced these interactions on Web pages; using layers is how it is done. Make the layer invisible and only turn the visibility on when a viewer requests it. This could be when they move the cursor over a button or click something.

Anything that involves creating JavaScript, such as a Hide/Show action, can be done using one of the many presupplied actions from GoLive. After you get the hang of creating actions, they're easy to implement.

Follow these steps to create a simple action for hiding and showing a layer:

1. **Create a layer and place an image on it.**

   This image should be something that you don't want viewers to see until they request the image by clicking a button or moving the cursor over a button or word.

2. **In the Layer Inspector palette, name the layer something appropriate, such as *product* or *ball*.**

   This name will have to be identified later when you create the Show/Hide action.

3. **Deselect the Visible check box in the Layer Inspector palette and position the layer in the middle of your page.**

4. **Using the Layer object, create a second layer and leave it at the top of the page.**

5. **Type some text on the second layer.**

   For example, type something like **See the product** or **Show the ball**, as shown in Figure 7-7. This text will be the trigger that turns the visibility of the first layer off and on. The ball layer is visible in the figure to show you the layout, but should not be seen if you are following this example.

6. **In the second layer's Inspector palette, add a descriptive name, like *text for product*, or *text for ball*.**

   You don't want it to get mixed up when you see a list of named layers.

7. **Select the text in the second layer by placing your cursor inside the layer and pressing Ctrl+A (Windows) or ⌘+A (Mac); then create a link by clicking the Create Link button on the toolbar or pressing Ctrl+L (Windows) or ⌘+L (Mac).**

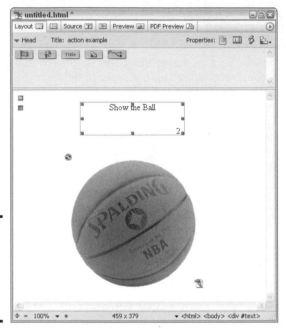

Figure 7-7:
Position the
second
layer at the
top of the
page.

8. **In the Text Inspector palette, replace (EmptyReference!) with the # sign.**

   This tells the browser not to go anywhere when the selected text is
   clicked.

   You're almost there! Now you create the actual Hide/Show action.

9. **With the linked text still selected, choose Window⇨Actions. Actions
   palette appears.**

   Notice the list of event triggers (on the left side of the palette) that can
   be selected to trigger an action.

10. **Select an action for your event trigger, and then click the Create new
    item button.**

    For this example, we chose Mouse Enter (this is the same as Mouse
    Over). See Figure 7-8.

11. **From the Action drop-down list at the bottom of the palette, select
    Multimedia⇨ShowHide.**

    The inspector changes to become a Show/Hide inspector.

12. **From the Layer drop-down list, choose your named layer (the one with
    the image). From the Mode drop-down list, choose Show (see Figure 7-9).**

    You're not done yet — you need to complete just a few more steps to
    hide the layer when the viewer moves the cursor off the text.

Figure 7-8:
Choose
from a list of
triggers to
make an
event occur.

Figure 7-9:
Choosing
the
ShowHide
action.

13. **With the text still selected, select another event trigger in the Actions palette and then click the Create new item button.**

We selected the Mouse Exit event trigger.

14. **From the Action drop-down list, choose Multimedia⟿ShowHide.**

15. **Choose the image layer from the Layer drop-down list, and choose Hide from the Mode drop-down list.**

Check your page in the Preview mode to see the actions. When you move the mouse cursor over the text, the image layer shows; when you move the cursor off the text, the image layer hides. If it doesn't work, verify that you followed the steps correctly, and that you don't have spaces in any file or folder names.

Making your Web site user-friendly for all

If you haven't heard of Section 508, you probably will. Section 508 contains the rules that make Web sites more accessible for the disabled; these rules apply to many government and corporate Web sites. Using layers is a good solution for columns of text because readers for the visually impaired can read the information in one paragraph. When using tables, the risk is that the reader will read one line of text and then progress to the next column to read the first line of the next column, and so on. Find out more about these rules by visiting `www.w3.org` and searching for Section 508.

Animation

There is a saying "Just because you can do it . . . doesn't mean that you should." This applies to animating layers. Yes, you can have your layer containing an airplane fly all over your page, but is it really necessary and effective, or just plain annoying to the viewer? These are decisions that you must make. In this section, you discover how to animate a layer and also how to use an action to trigger the animation.

Animating layers

In the first animation, you see how to make keyframes (layer positions at assigned times) by dragging the layer while the positioning is being recorded. If you're creating an animation for the first time, it will be less confusing if you have a new, clean page with only one layer in it to work with. Follow these steps to create an animation:

1. **Using the Layer object from the Basic section of the Objects palette, create a layer and put text or an image on it. Then select the layer.**

2. **Click the Timeline tab on the Layer Inspector palette.**

3. **Choose the shape of the animate path that you want to create.**

   - **None:** Makes the layer jump between the keyframes.

   - **Linear:** Makes the layer move in a straight line; this is the default path shape.

   - **Curve:** Creates a smooth curve between keyframes.

   - **Random:** Creates a zigzag path of random lengths between keyframes.

4. **Click the Record button.**

5. **Position the mouse cursor over the edge of the selected layer and when the hand appears, drag.**

Notice that a path is created as you drag the layer, as shown in Figure 7-10.

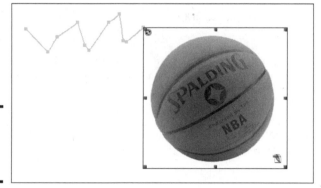

Book VI
Chapter 7

Layers

Figure 7-10:
The animation path.

6. **View the animation in the browser.**

Notice that it plays immediately as the browser window displays.

If you return to the Layout mode of the GoLive page, you see what looks like anchor points on your path. These are the keyframes you created when dragging the layer. Edit the position and time of the keyframes by using the Timeline Editor. To access the Timeline Editor, click the Open Timeline Editor button at the bottom of the Timeline tab of the Layer Inspector palette.

A timeline, like the one shown in Figure 7-11, appears. Each keyframe represents what position the layer is in at certain times. In the example shown, the second keyframe is at 15. Because the default of the animation is 15 FPS (frames-per-second), it will take one second to get to the keyframe's position.

Autoplay

Figure 7-11:
The second keyframe is at the 1-second mark.

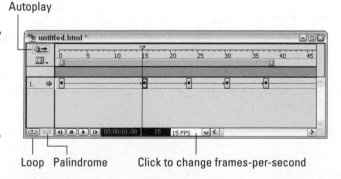

Loop   Palindrome   Click to change frames-per-second

Change the frame rate by selecting it from the bottom of the timeline. The higher the number, the faster the animation.

Change the timing by dragging the keyframe on the timeline. Change the position by selecting a keyframe and repositioning it manually, or by entering values in the Layer Inspector palette while the keyframe is selected.

You can click an individual keyframe and press the Delete or Backspace key to eliminate it.

As a default, the animation is set to automatically play. If you're planning to use this animation with an action, turn off autoplay by clicking the Autoplay button.

If you want to really get things going, you can also click the Loop button to play the animation over and over again, or even click the Palindrome button to play the animation forward and then backwards. Yow, the things that you can do!

An intermittent bug in Netscape 4.0 browsers may cause the content of an animated layer to temporarily disappear, especially if the content is an image. A workaround to avoid this bug is to insert a nonbreaking space on the animated layer by pressing Ctrl+spacebar (Windows) or Option+spacebar (Mac).

When you have multiple layers, they show up in the timeline but not with the name you created. Notice in Figure 7-11 that the selected layer shows up with an arrow to the right of the layer creation order. Keep this in mind when editing keyframes so that you don't accidentally edit the animation.

Creating an animation action

In this section, you discover some new keyboard commands to generate keyframes by using a different method.

Create an action to trigger an animation by following these steps:

1. **Create a new blank page.**

2. **Create a layer that you want to animate. Put an element such as text or an image on the layer.**

3. **With the layer selected, click the Timeline tab in the Layer Inspector palette. Click the Choose Open Timeline Editor button at the bottom of the palette.**

   The Timeline Editor appears.

4. **You have one keyframe representing the present position of the layer. Select the keyframe, and in the Layer tab of the Layer Inspector palette, type** -250 **in the Left text field.**

This puts the layer off the page.

5. **Position your mouse cursor on the same path as the existing keyframe at the 15 mark on the timeline (see Figure 7-12 Ctrl+click (Windows) or ⌘+click (Mac) to create your own keyframe. With this keyframe selected, in the Layer Inspector palette, type** 250 **in the Left text field.**

The layer appears.

Figure 7-12:
Add your own key-frame by Ctrl+clicking or ⌘+clicking on the timeline.

6. **Turn off Autoplay in the Timeline Editor by clicking the Autoplay button (refer to Figure 7-11 to see this button) and drag the current time marker back to the beginning in the Timeline editor.**

7. **Create another layer with text on it like,** *Click to see image*, **or whatever description you want.**

This is the trigger to make the animation occur.

8. **Select the text and create a link by pressing Ctrl+L (Windows) or ⌘+L (Mac). Replace (EmptyReference!) with the # sign.**

9. **Choose Window⇨Actions.**

10. **Select Mouse Click in the Events list and click the Create new item.**

11. **From the Actions palette menu, choose Multimedia⇨Play Scene. Select Scene 1 from the drop-down list.**

Preview the page in your browser to make sure your animation works correctly when you trigger it.

Create multiple scenes and rename scenes by clicking the Options button in the Timeline Editor.

Chapter 8: Forms

In This Chapter

✓ Creating forms for the Web

✓ Discovering form elements and functionalities

✓ Considering servers, input, and usability

✓ Labeling and grouping elements

✓ Putting a form to work

You use forms to provide your viewers with a way to enter information into your Web site. *Forms* contain such elements as buttons, boxes, and lists, and can be as complex or simple as you want. But you do need to follow certain rules when creating forms. In this chapter, you discover how to use many of the objects in the Form section of the Objects palette to put together a working form, how to link your form to CGI scripts (CGI stands for *Common Gateway Interface,* which is a standard for interfacing external applications with information servers, such as HTTP or Web servers), and even how to generate e-mail messages to the address of your choice.

Unfortunately, we don't have room to describe everything there is know to about forms in this chapter. So if you're looking for information about setting up secure forms for credit card transactions and the like, you'll need to contact your Internet service provider (ISP).

Starting a Form

In this section, we show you how to create a bare-bones form; what you need before you start adding buttons, text, or anything else to it. We get to all that fun stuff later.

To start a form, follow these steps:

1. Select the Form button on the Objects palette.

If this palette is not visible, choose Window⇨Objects or press Ctrl+2 (Windows) or ⌘+2 (Mac).

All the Form objects appear; we describe these in Table 8-1.

In order to create a working form, you must contain it within a Form object. The Form object is first in the form section of the Objects palette.

2. **Drag the Form object to your page, or place the insertion point where you want the Form object to appear, and double-click the Form object.**

3. **Name the form in the Name/ID textbox on the Form Inspector palette.**

   When using scripts, a form must be identified. Give the form a simple descriptive name, like *info,* in the Name/ID text field of the Form Inspector palette.

   All elements of a form must be contained inside this form object. This includes text fields, radio buttons, check boxes, and even the Submit and Reset buttons.

4. **Click once inside the Form object, and then select the Table object from the Basic Object palette. With the Table object selected, double-click. The table appears where the cursor had been. Customize the table to meet the needs of your form.**

   Dragging a table into the Form object is the best way to keep a neat tabular look to your form, as we've done with the form shown in Figure 8-1.

   You're ready to begin adding elements to your form, which we show you how to do throughout the rest of this chapter.

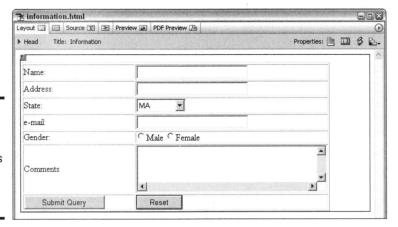

Figure 8-1:
A table in the Form object helps to organize your form elements.

Table 8-1		The Form Objects
Object	*Name*	*What It Does*
![F]	Form	The container for the form
![Submit]	Submit Button	Submits form information

Object	Name	What It Does
	Reset Button	Clears fields
	Button	A button that can be customized
	Form Input Image	Enables you to use an image for functions such as submitting the form
	Label	Inserts a visual label used to identify the purpose of form elements
	Text Field	Creates a text field for input
	Password	Enables viewers to enter a required password
	Text Area	Creates a text area for comments
	Check Box	Creates a check box; more than one check box can be selected in a list
	Radio Button	Creates a radio button; only one radio button can be selected in a list
	Popup	Creates choices in a drop-down list
	List Box	Creates choices in a list box
	File Browser	Inserts a file selection dialog box
	Hidden	Hidden tag that can be used for information when scripting
	Key Generator	Enables viewers to address an encryption algorithm for safeguarding transactions
	Fieldset	Inserts a bounding box that visually groups form elements

Adding Elements to the Form

After you have the skeleton of your form created (which we show you how to do in the preceding section), you can begin adding items to it: text fields, buttons, lists, and so on.

Locking down cells

To avoid the nasty movement of cells as you add text, follow these steps to lock down the cells:

1. **Select one cell by inserting the cursor and pressing Ctrl+Enter (Windows) or Ctrl+Return (Mac).**

2. **Choose Edit⇨Select All or press Ctrl+A (Windows) or ⌘+A (Mac) to select all the cells.**

3. **In the Cell Inspector palette, change the width from Auto to Pixels.**

   This stops the cell from automatically resizing as you type.

   It's okay if no value appears. By locking the cells to a pixel value, each cell is now defined and won't automatically resize.

Before you start adding form objects, create the text that defines the form objects that you're including in your form in the left column of the form's table, as shown in Figure 8-2. For example, if you're gathering user information, enter First Name, Last Name, Address, and so on; otherwise, enter whatever's pertinent.

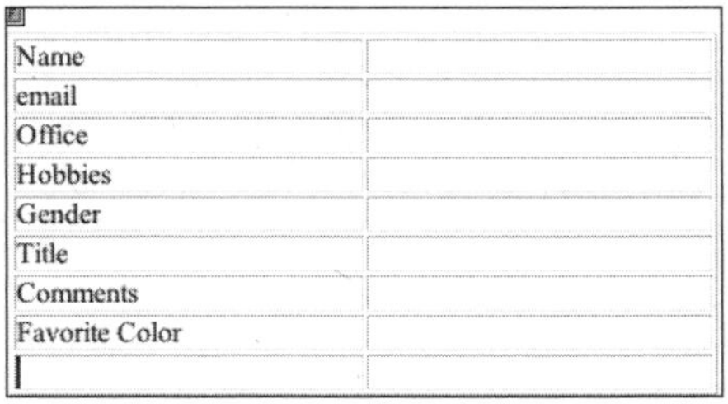

Figure 8-2:
Enter the
text for the
form in the
table cells.

Name	
email	
Office	
Hobbies	
Gender	
Title	
Comments	
Favorite Color	

Adding a text field

To add text fields to your form, start dropping Form objects into the appropriate table cells. Just drag a Text Field object from the Forms section of the Objects palette right into a cell that you want to be a text field; name the text fields as you go.

The Text Field object is probably the most common form element. It allows the user to enter virtually any type of information. Make the text field active by selecting it, and look at its Inspector palette. Each form element should be named, which helps to identify the fields when information is submitted. Change the name from textfieldName to *name*.

We discuss some of the other options at the bottom of the form Objects Inspector palette later in the next chapter, but two to focus on are the Visible and Max text fields. The visible characters define how large your text field is. The user can exceed the visibility value, but not the maximum value. You should probably put some value in the Max text field, such as 75, so a user can't accidentally paste the entire text of *War and Peace* into your text field.

+ **Readonly:** You can set individual HTML form elements to read-only status. Do this if you want to include text that must accompany the form. The text is included in the form, but the viewer cannot change the contents of the field.

+ **Disabled:** Use this check box in combination with a script to keep certain form elements inactive until they are triggered, such as a Submit button that does not work until all required text fields are filled in.

Adding a list box and its items

Use the List Box feature when you want to offer viewers a list of choices to select from. Drag the List Box object to the table cell where you want to put a list. The List Box needs to be named, of course, so give it an intuitive name in the Form List Box Inspector palette, as shown in Figure 8-3.

Customize your list in the Inspector palette as follows:

+ **Rows:** The number of visible rows. The list will scroll if you close this up or past the 4-row default.

+ **Multiple Selection:** You can give the user the ability to Ctrl+click (Windows) or ⌘+click (Mac) to select multiple items in the list box. In most cases, you just want the user to select one item, so you may want to deselect this check box.

+ **Label and Value:** The label is what the user sees; the value is information that you receive that the viewer is not aware of. In the Label column, select the word *First*. In the text field that appears at the bottom of the List Inspector palette, replace First with the text of your choice. Typically, the value is just a repeat of the label. In Figure 8-3, we entered Boston in place of First, and we entered IsCold as a value. Continue replacing the existing sample text (*Second* and *Third* and so on) with the text of your choice.

+ **Create New Item:** Add additional items to the list by clicking the Create New Item button at the bottom of the Inspector palette.

+ **Duplicate Selected Items:** You can also duplicate a selected list item by clicking the Duplicate Selected Items button at the bottom of the Inspector palette.

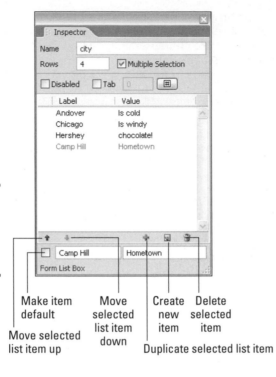

Figure 8-3:
The Form
List Box
Inspector
palette.

Make item default

Move selected list item up

Move selected list item down

Create new item

Delete selected item

Duplicate selected list item

✦ **Change list item order:** Change the order of the listed items by using the arrows at the lower-left corner of the Inspector palette.

✦ **Delete items:** Get rid of any unwanted list items by selecting the list item and clicking the Trashcan icon in the lower-right corner.

✦ **Set item as default:** If you want one list item to be the default (that is, it will always be the current selection in the list), select the check box to the left of the item at the bottom of the Inspector palette.

You use the Tab check box, pound sign (#) button, and Disabled check box to aid users in navigating your form; we discuss these in the later section, "Form Navigation."

Adding check boxes

Check boxes are intended to be used for selecting multiple items (such as hobbies). To add a check box to your form, follow these steps:

1. **Drag a Check Box object into the cell where you want to add a check box.**

A check box is placed right where you dragged to.

2. **Create a copy of the check box by selecting the Check Box object you just placed and Ctrl+dragging (Windows) or ⌘+dragging (Mac).**

   A plus sign appears while you're dragging to indicate that you're *cloning* (making a copy of) the check box. If you don't like the keyboard acrobatics, just copy and paste the check box.

3. **Insert the cursor after a check box, press the spacebar, and type the name of the check box.**

   If you're listing hobbies, you could list *Cooking*.

4. **Continue adding check boxes and labeling them until you have as many as you want.**

So now it looks like a working set of check boxes, but really nothing has been done to them to provide you with any significant information yet.

To make a check box useful, select one that you placed on a page and look at the Form Checkbox Inspector. (If it is not visible, choose Window⇨ Inspector.) Just like with all form elements, you need to type an appropriate name in the Name text field. Use a unique name to identify the contents of the check box.

Adding radio buttons

Radio buttons, as a default, allow only one selection in a group. This is used for selections like type of credit card, gender, title, and yes/no questions. Just follow these steps to add radio buttons to your form:

1. **Drag a Radio Button object into the cell where you want the radio button placed.**

2. **Copy it by selecting the Radio Button and Ctrl+dragging (Windows) or ⌘+dragging (Mac) it; or copy and paste it.**

   You always need at least two radio buttons.

3. **Place the insertion point to the right of each radio button you created and give each one a label.**

   Maybe *Male* and *Female,* maybe *Yes* and *No* — whatever you need.

   Essentially, you're done, unless you want to create multiple radio button selections. By creating a unique group name for each set of radio buttons, you can limit the viewer to one selection in each group; the rest of these steps show you how to do that.

4. **Select a Radio Button object and type a name in the Group text field in the Form Radio Button Inspector palette.**

   Create a logical group name, such as *creditcard* or *gender*. This way, when someone selects payment by Visa card, it doesn't deselect the selection that she is female.

5. **Select another Radio Button object.**

   Notice in Figure 8-4 that after you create a Group name, it appears in a pop-up menu to the right of the Group text field in the Inspector palette. In Figure 8-4, we selected Gender for the Group of the second radio button and changed the value to Female.

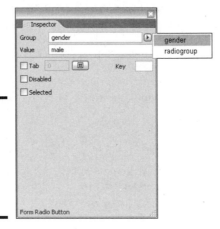

Figure 8-4:
After creating a group, it appears in the pop-up menu.

Adding a text area

A *text area* is different from a text field in that a text area gives the user the ability to submit comments (no matter how long-winded they may be), whereas the text field is for a specific piece of information, such as name, address, and so on. We discuss adding text fields in the earlier section, "Adding a text field."

Add a text area by dragging the Text Area object from the Objects palette into the cell that you want to use for comments. Make sure that you give the Text Area a descriptive name in the Name text field of the Form Text Area Inspector palette.

In the Element <textarea> Inspector palette, type the number of rows in the Rows text field to determine the maximum number of rows visible in the text area. In the Columns text field, type the number of characters to determine the width of the visible text area. You can also change this by grabbing the lower-right corner and adjusting the text area manually.

Change the Wrap features by using the drop-down list, if you like. Here are your options:

✦ **Off:** Tells the browser to ignore the Columns limit and prevents text entered into the text area from wrapping.

✦ **Virtual:** Wraps the text on-screen, but not when the data is processed.

✦ **Physical:** Wraps the text on-screen and when it's processed.

Using the pop-up object

Create an easy-to-use drop-down list by dragging the Popup object from the Objects palette to the target cell. Name the Popup object clearly to identify it later.

The Popup object is very similar to the List Box object. As a default, only one row appears, as is typical with drop-down lists; you can change this by entering a different value in the Rows text field (but understand that it's no longer a popup then; it becomes a list box.

Change the preset labels to the text that you want the user to select, and add additional labels by clicking the Create New Item button in the Form Popup Inspector palette.

Change the preset values to specific values that you want submitted with the form. Remember, the viewer does not see values.

Change the order in which labels appear by selecting the list item and clicking the up or down arrows.

Adding a Submit button

The form is no good to you unless you receive it, so you need to add a Submit button that viewers can click to send the form's information along its merry way. We further discuss this merry way at the end of this chapter (in the section, "Making a Form Work"). But for now, you just need to add a button that the viewer can click to complete the form.

Drag the Submit Button object to a cell in the lower-left of your form; that's generally where Submit buttons are. You don't have to put it there, of course, but that's likely where your viewers will look for it. This button is already labeled Submit, but you can change the name to *submitinfo*, or something else descriptive. As shown in Figure 8-5, you can select the Label check box in the Inspector palette and type your own button label in the text field, maybe something Like *Send Me Information,* or *Bug Off,* or whatever you want.

If you want to be nice, you can also include a Reset button by dragging the Reset object from the Object palette into a cell in the lower-right of your form (where viewers generally expect to find it). You can also type a different label for the Reset button in the Label text field in the Inspector palette.

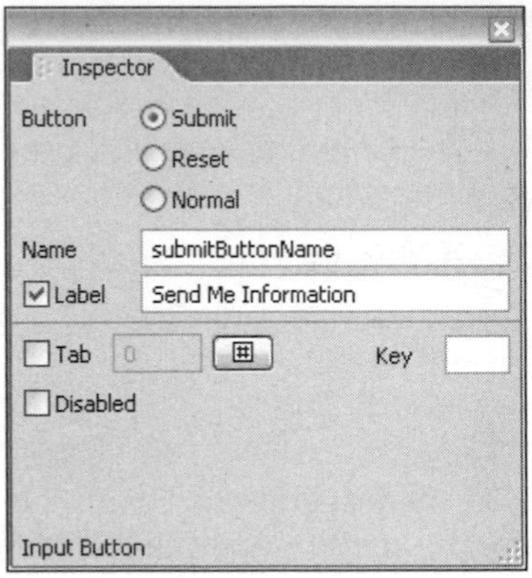

Figure 8-5: Change the label on a button by selecting the Label check box.

Form Navigation

When you complete the form's layout, there are yet two issues to consider before the form itself is complete: form navigation and making the form work. Figure 8-6 shows an example of a finished form to which we've added text fields, a list box, check boxes, and radio buttons; essentially all elements that you would add to a form (which we discuss throughout the earlier sections of this chapter). When you reach this point, it's time to think about how viewers will navigate through your form.

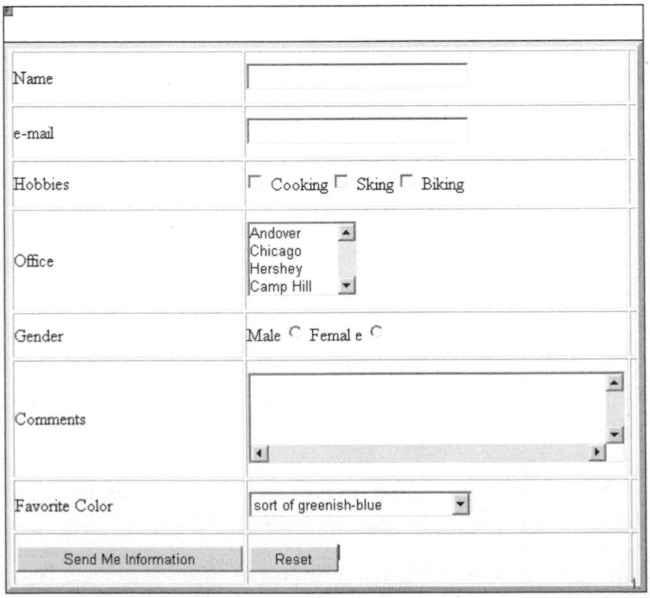

Figure 8-6: A finished form.

Refer to Figures 8-3 through 8-5 to see the Inspector palette; notice the Tab check box and a button next to it with the pound sign (#). You use these to set the tabbing order for the user. Viewers can press the Tab key to move from field to field in a form when filling it out. As a default, when a viewer presses the Tab key, the insertion point moves to the field on the right and then down to the left again.

You can manually enter a Tab value by selecting the Tab check box and then entering a value (1 is first in tabbing order), or you can use the # button to automatically record the order of your form field selections. This feature can sometimes go a little crazy, though, so you're taking your chances by using this button. Here's how it works:

1. **Make sure that the Tab check box is selected, select the form element that you want to be first in the tabbing order, and then click the # button located in the bottom half of the Form Element Inspector palette.**

The cursor changes into an arrow with a # sign next to it, and little gray boxes with question marks appear in the form fields, as shown in Figure 8-7.

2. **Click the first field and then click each field in the tabbing order you want to define.**

The fields are automatically numbered in the Tab text field.

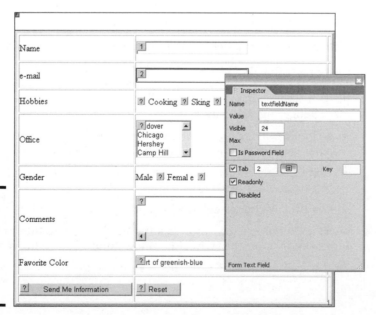

Figure 8-7:
Use the
button to
click and
select
tabbing
order.

If things get out of control while you're using this feature, or if you make a mistake, turn off the Tabbing # button by clicking it again, and then change the incorrect Tab value in the Tab text field in the Inspector palette.

Form Actions

So how do you know when you get the data submitted from a form that the e-mail address a viewer entered is really an e-mail address and not a phone number, or that the zip code has the proper amount of numbers? You can check this with form actions. You can also check the number of characters and general content of the information in the text field, such as whether the content is text or numbers. Read on for an example of how to use form actions.

To check the format of an e-mail address using form actions, follow these steps (in this example, we've selected the e-mail text field):

1. **Choose the Form object (the container for the entire form), click the little f in the upper-left corner of the Form object, and make sure that the Name/ID is *info*.**

   This name can be anything that you want; just remember it when creating the Action.

2. **Select the Text Field used for e-mail and make sure that it's named *email*.**

   Again, whatever the form element is called is okay; just remember it.

3. **With the e-mail Text Field object still selected, choose Window⇨Actions.**

   The Actions palette appears. In the list on the top-left side of the palette, you can choose from several events that cause an action to occur. The main ones that you might use for a form validator would be Key Focus, Text Change, and Key Blur:

   - **Key Focus:** Triggers an action when the field is selected, an insertion point is placed in the field, or when the viewer tabs to it.

   - **Text Change:** Validates entries when the viewer enters text and then selects another field.

   - **Key Blur:** Validates entries when the viewer tabs out of the field.

4. **Select a validator event and click the Create New Action button (the dog-eared icon on the right side of the Rollover & Actions palette).**

   For this example, we're using the Key Blur validator.

5. Choose Action➪Getters➪Field Validator.

The bottom of the Actions palette displays the options for this Action. This window does not show all options if it isn't opened to its full length. Click and drag the lower-right corner of the Actions palette to stretch it and show additional options.

6. In the Form Name text field, select the form name from the drop-down menu; in the Field Name text field, select the name of the text field from the drop-down menu.

In this example, we're using info and email, respectively.

7. Select a validation criterion from the Validation to Perform drop-down list.

You have plenty to choose from. For this example, we selected Field Is Proper E-mail Format.

8. Type a message in the Alert Message If Invalid Entry text field.

This is the message users see if the text they enter is not in the proper e-mail format. See Figure 8-8.

Test this out in the browser. Experiment with field validators' actions by following the same steps but choosing other field validators from the Validation to Perform drop-down list.

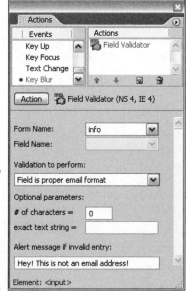

Figure 8-8:
Enter a message that will appear if the format is not correct.

Making a Form Work

So your form is dressed up but has nowhere to go. You can take care of that by adding an action to the Form tag that will send the form to you when the viewer clicks the Submit button (or whatever you've labeled this button). Select the F icon in the upper left of the Form object. Even if you've already assigned a Name/ID, the action is probably still referencing (EmptyReference!). Your form can either reference a script on your server or just an e-mail address:

✦ **E-mail:** If you replace the (EmptyReference!) with your e-mail address, use the Encode drop-down list to change the encoding to Text/plain and change the Method drop-down list to Post, and then the user can send you an e-mail directly. See Figure 8-9.

The user will get a security alert, which basically says that the submitted information is not secure. After the user closes the Alert dialog box, the form data is sent to your e-mail address. This is the cheap and sometimes ineffective method of getting a form to work. It only works if users have e-mail set up on the machine they submit the form from.

✦ **Server:** A much more reliable way to have forms sent is to replace the (EmptyReference!) with a path to a script residing on your server, such as `cgi-bin/sendinfo.pl`.

Showing how to write CGI scripts is outside the scope of this chapter, but you can find really good scripts online that you can modify for your own use. A favorite of ours is FormMail, which you can find at `www.script archive.com`. Download the instructions and post it in your cgi-bin folder or wherever you store scripts on your server. Ask your ISP if you need more specifics about the location and capabilities of your site.

Figure 8-9:
Having your
form sent
via e-mail.

Whether you're creating your own script, modifying one you found online, or building one at the request of someone else, you need to know how to insert *hidden tags,* the elements in the form that the viewer does not see, but that are read by the script. To insert a Hidden object, drag it from the Objects palette to any location within the Form object. Name the Hidden object according to the script requirements and enter values, such as a link to a Thank You page or an e-mail address.

Book VI
Chapter 8

Forms

Chapter 9: Multimedia

In This Chapter

✔ **Discovering plug-ins**

✔ **Adding animation to your site with Flash movies**

✔ **Adding sound to your site**

✔ **Adding video with QuickTime**

✔ **Adding graphics with SVG**

✔ **Using the generic plug-in**

*P*lug-ins open new capabilities for your Web page by utilizing other applications to do things like play a Flash or a QuickTime movie file. *Plug-ins* are mini applications that run within the browser and require special information such as MIME (Multipurpose Internet Mail Extensions), which allows Web browsers to interpret files that require plug-in technology. In this chapter, you discover how to make GoLive ready to accept files requiring plug-ins, as well as how to integrate Flash, RealVideo, QuickTime, and SVG files into your Web pages.

Always remember that as soon as you use files requiring plug-ins on your Web pages, you're also requiring each and every viewer to have that plug-in installed to access that file (such as an SWF movie file that requires the Macromedia Flash Player plug-in to play).

Loading Plug-Ins

Preset GoLive objects, shown in Figure 9-1, automatically provide the information needed to load files requiring plug-ins, such as Flash movies, RealAudio sound files, QuickTime movies, and SVG (Scalable Vector Graphics) files. A generic plug-in is also provided for files that require customized settings, such as you may need with specific sound files. Plug-ins in GoLive can also be customized in the Preferences dialog box by choosing Edit⇨Preferences⇨Plug-ins (Windows) or GoLive⇨Preferences⇨Plug-ins (Mac).

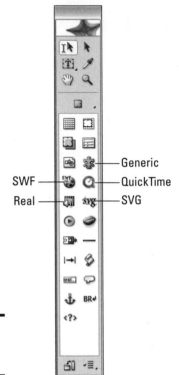

SWF

Real

Generic

QuickTime

SVG

Figure 9-1:
The Plug-in
objects.

Even though Plug-in objects are available on the Object's toolbar, you still need to have plug-ins loaded in GoLive to take advantage of previewing and additional options.

When you installed GoLive, a Plug-ins folder was created in the GoLive application folder. If you haven't already installed plug-ins, this folder is probably empty. Follow these steps to load plug-ins into GoLive:

1. **Quit GoLive.**

2. **Find your main browser application and open the Plug-ins folder within its application folder.**

In Windows, the Plug-ins folder is probably located via this path: `C:\Program Files\Internet Explorer\PLUGINS`.

On the Macintosh, finding the Plug-ins folder is a little more complicated. Follow these steps as an example:

1. Locate your Internet application (using Internet Explorer as an example): `MacintoshHD\Applications\Internet Explorer`.

You may notice that the browser launches when you double-click the browser icon, not opening a folder.

2. To show the contents of the browser application, Control+click the Internet Explorer icon and choose Show Package Contents from the contextual menu.

A directory window opens.

3. Locate the Plug-ins folder following this path: `Contents\MacOS\ Plug-ins`.

Note: Safari uses plug-ins located in this path: MacintoshHD\Library\ Internet Plug-ins.

3. Select all the plug-ins and copy them.

Right-click (Windows) or Control+click (Mac) and choose Copy from the contextual menu.

4. Open the GoLive Plug-ins folder and paste the plug-ins into the GoLive Plug-ins folder.

Right-click (Windows) or Control+click (Mac) and choose Paste from the contextual menu.

5. Open GoLive after you have copied the plug-ins into the GoLive Plug-ins folder.

If you don't have the necessary plug-ins, see Table 9-1 for the Web pages where you can download the latest versions of the plug-ins.

**Book VI
Chapter 9**

Multimedia

Table 9-1	Locating Plug-ins	
Plug-in Name	*Type of Files Played*	*URL*
QuickTime	`.mov`	`www.apple.com/quicktime`
Macromedia Shockwave Player	`.swf`	`www.macromedia.com/ shockwave`
RealOne Player	`.rm, .ram`	`www.real.com/player`
Adobe SVG Viewer	`.svg`	`www.adobe.com/svg/main. html`

Adding Flash Files to Your Site

If you have loaded the necessary plug-ins, you can start taking advantage of the plug-in options in GoLive. One of the ways you can use a plug-in is to add a Flash file to your Web page by following these steps:

1. **Have a page open to which you want to add a Flash file.**

2. **Select the Basic section of the Objects toolbar.**

3. **Drag the SWF object to your page.**

4. **Click the Browse button on the Plug-in Inspector palette to locate an SWF file.**

5. **If necessary, change the width and height on the Basic tab of the Inspector palette.**

When you select a plug-in using the SWF object, the MIME type is already specified. Note that on the More tab of the Inspector palette, URLs are specified that will automatically direct viewers to the Macromedia Web site for the plug-in if it isn't installed in their browsers or will direct browsers to a code base for additional information. You can also adjust the space surrounding the file by changing the values in the HSpace and VSpace text fields.

Click the Attributes tab to add custom attributes to the file. You can customize the following settings on the SWF tab of the Plug-in Inspector palette:

✦ **Autoplay:** Plays the Flash animation as soon as the page is loaded.

✦ **Loop:** Plays the movie in an endless loop.

✦ **Quality:** Plays the movie at the quality setting you select. Choose an appropriate setting based on the quality you want to achieve; there are noticeable differences between the Quality settings, so make sure that you test the final presentation and the time it takes to download.

✦ **Scale:** Adjusts the size of the Flash file by the entered amount. Entering 2, for instance, makes the Flash file twice the normal size. You can also choose Exact Fit and No Border from the drop-down list.

✦ **Plug-in:** Previews the Flash movie if you have loaded the plug-in into the GoLive Plug-ins folder.

Adding RealVideo Files

RealVideo is a streaming technology developed by Real Networks for transmitting live video over the Internet. Adding Real to your Web page is a little different from adding any other type of plug-in. Real controllers for displaying files can be customized to create unique consoles for the viewer.

Follow these steps to use Real files in GoLive:

1. **Drag the Real object from the Basic section of the Objects palette to your page.**

2. **Select the Basic tab of the Plug-in Inspector palette and click the Browse button to locate a RealVideo file.**

3. **Select the More tab for these options:**

   • **Page:** The Page text field in the More tab can be set up with an assigned Web page that gives a destination link for installation instructions.

   • **Code:** The Code check box is used to assign a destination link for any necessary code base. This control, like many others in the plug-ins, should be used only if you're familiar with the plug-in applications and what code base is needed.

   • **VSpace and HSpace:** Creates vertical and horizontal spacing around the Real file.

   • **Is Hidden:** Select the Is Hidden check box if this video is not to show up until triggered by an action or other script.

4. **Select the Real tab in the Inspector palette, as shown in Figure 9-2.**

**Book VI
Chapter 9**

Multimedia

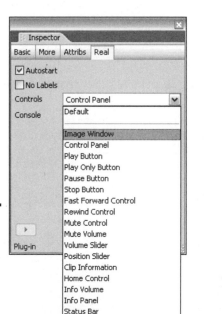

Figure 9-2:
Customize
the viewer
controls in
the Real tab
of the
Inspector
palette.

Customize the Real file by selecting from these options:

✦ **Autostart:** When selected, the RealVideo clip starts as soon as the page loads.

✦ **No Labels:** Select the No Labels check box to suppress the display of information such as title, author, and copyright.

✦ **Controls:** Select the controls for the RealVideo clip. You can define the console to group controls together.

You can assign only one control to each Real object. In other words, to set up Play and Stop controls, you need two Real objects. By using consoles, you can create unique sets of buttons arranged in a table. If Default is selected, the display will contain Play, Pause, Stop, Forward, and Rewind buttons, and Position and Volume controls.

✦ **Plug-in:** View the Real file in GoLive by clicking the Plug-in button.

Adding Movies with QuickTime

With all the increased bandwidth out there, using QuickTime files on Web pages has been more acceptable than ever. Do be nice to your viewers, though, and put movie files on their own page so that viewers can make a decision to play the movie if they like. Placing a QuickTime movie into your Web page is rather simple in GoLive; just follow these steps:

1. **Open a page and drag the QuickTime object from the Basic section of the Objects toolbar to the page.**

2. **Using the Plug-in Inspector palette, click the Browse button to locate a .mov file.**

Note that a MIME type is preassigned, as shown in Figure 9-3. The MIME type determines the rest of the basic settings.

Figure 9-3:
The Quick-Time MIME is assigned with the object.

3. **Select the More tab if advanced scripting requires the movie to be named. Adjust for extra space or padding around the movie by using the VSpace or HSpace fields.**

4. **On the QuickTime tab of the Inspector palette, shown in Figure 9-4, select from the following options:**

   • **Show Controller:** Shows users the playback controls.

     If you choose to show the controller, you must add 16 pixels to the height of the movie on the Basic tab; otherwise, the controller will be cut off.

   • **Cache:** Enables caching through the browser when the movie is played back. When a file is cached, it is stored temporarily in the memory of the viewer's computer, allowing the viewer to play the movie again without downloading it again.

   • **Autoplay:** Plays the movie automatically when the page loads.

   • **Loop:** Plays the movie on an endless loop. (Be aware that this might drive some viewers away!)

   • **Play Every Frame:** Plays all frames of a movie. Don't use this unless you have to. Playing all frames can cause playback problems with QuickTime movies, so the viewer gets a message that the movie could not download properly.

   • **Auto HREF:** Loads the URL listed in the HREF tab. You can use HREFs to change a page within a frameset while the movie is playing on another page in the same frameset.

**Book VI
Chapter 9**

Multimedia

Figure 9-4:
The Quick-
Time tab.

- **Kiosk Mode:** Disables Save commands, including drag-and-drop functionality.

- **BGColor:** Sets a background color for the movie. The background shows up only if the movie does not fill the specified size.

- **Volume:** Sets the sound volume for the movie; enter a value from 0 (mute) to 100 (full volume).

- **Scale:** Adjusts a movie's size by the entered scale amount. A setting of 2, for instance, makes the movie twice the normal size.

- **Palindrome:** Plays your movie forward and backward in an endless loop. The Loop check box must be selected to activate the Palindrome check box.

- **Don't Flatten:** Maintains references to movie assets, rather than flattening them into the movie file.

- **Enable JavaScript:** Enables JavaScript functions to control movies.

Adding High-Resolution Graphics with SVG

SVG (Scalable Vector Graphic) is an open-standard vector graphics language that allows the file to maintain vector capabilities. By using plain-text commands (XML), SVG enables you to design Web pages with high-resolution graphics that can contain complex elements such as gradients, animation, and filter effects. To find out more about this technology, visit `www.adobe.com/svg/main.html`.

Follow these steps to use the SVG plug-in:

1. **Select the SVG object from the Basic section of the Objects toolbar and drag it to your page.**

2. **Click the Browse button on the Basic tab of the Inspector palette to select an `.svg` file.**

3. **Click the More tab of the Inspector palette to see the Page and Code text fields.**

   The Page and Code text fields can be predefined to prompt the viewer to visit a Web page where they can download the SVG Viewer if they don't have the plug-in installed and to access code-based information if needed.

   The More tab also allows you to add space around the SVG file by entering values in the VSpace and HSpace text fields.

New in GoLive CS2 you can edit your SVG files right in GoLive. To Edit an SVG file in GoLive, Choose File > Open and locate the .svg file.

When you edit an SVG file, the document window displays a preview of the SVG file on the left, and a layer view on the right. The layer view shows layers as they appear in the file in Adobe Illustrator, see Figure 9-5.

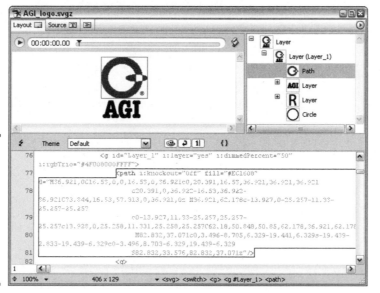

Figure 9-5: The SVG editor in GoLive, with the split view turned on to see the source code.

In the preview, you can magnify objects with the Zoom tool and select objects with the Hand tool. When you select objects in either the preview or layer view, GoLive highlights related code in the Source and Outline editors. Revise this code to change object properties such as position and scaling. To see the preview and layer view with code, click the Show/Hide Split Source button in the lower-left corner of the document window.

Using Generic Plug-Ins

For file formats that don't have a specific plug-in object, you can use the Generic Plug-in object. Unlike the QuickTime, Flash, Real, and SVG icons, a generic plug-in is not configured in the Inspector palette. You must be familiar with the necessary settings to get the plug-in to work correctly. It's good to know that many of the MIME settings are available from the MIME drop-down list in the Inspector palette.

If you're an advanced user and you know the proper MIME type and extension for the plug-in, you can also add the plug-in in the Plug-ins section of the Preferences dialog box by choosing Edit⇨Preferences⇨Plug-ins (Windows) or GoLive⇨Preferences⇨Plug-ins (Mac).

Chapter 10: Publishing Your Web Site

In This Chapter

✔ Preparing to publish your site

✔ Exporting your Web site

✔ Working with connections and networks

✔ Getting your Web site live

✔ Synchronizing your site

*I*n this chapter, you discover how to take a site and get it up and running by publishing it on a Web server (or *publish server,* as GoLive calls it). First we show you how to export a site to collect data, and then how to upload your site directly from the GoLive Site window to your publish server. Before starting, there are a few things you need to have prepared. Talk to your ISP (Internet Service Provider) to get the answers to these questions:

✦ What is your username and password?

✦ Do you need to specify a directory, or will your username and password be enough to determine access to folders on the publish server?

✦ Should you connect in Passive mode? (This is necessary if the FTP server is protected by a firewall.)

With answers in hand, you can easily publish a site with the GoLive tools. No more running dog for you Macintosh users! GoLive keeps you organized and up-to-date by synchronizing files, while making it visually apparent where files are located in your file hierarchy.

Keep in mind that as your site grows, organization is critical. Build folders as necessary and make sure that the directory paths are the same on your local server and the publish server.

Clean Up after Yourself!

You were told this as a child, and it still applies. Before moving files, make sure that you clean up your site. Get rid of old files you no longer use and check for any orphan files and broken links. A great feature to help you along the way is the Clean Up Site feature.

 First, click the Open Site Settings dialog button from the Site toolbar. In the Site Settings dialog box that appears, select Clean Up Site in the list on the left. Select the Site Specific Settings check box to see the options shown in Figure 10-1.

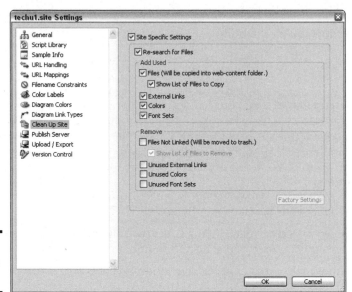

Figure 10-1:
Cleaning up
a site.

The Clean Up Site options include the following:

✦ **Re-search for Files:** Re-scans and updates any files that are loaded in your Web-content folder.

✦ **Add Used:** Lists files that are not in your Web-content folder. You can choose to copy these files over into your site.

The Add Used options also re-scan external references, colors, and font sets. These are added to the specific tabs in your Site window.

✦ **Remove:** Choose to remove unused files (a list is opened so that you can uncheck items before deleting) and unused external references, as well as colors and font sets. These options are deselected by default so that you don't accidentally remove files that you need later.

To clean up the site after setting the Clean Up Site options, choose Site➪Update➪Clean Up Site. If applicable, lists of files to be added and removed appear.

Keep in mind that when you throw anything away, the default is to place the item into the GoLive Trash folder. If you find that you need the file later, choose the Extras tab from the Site window, and then click Site Trash. Inside that folder are items that were thrown away while working in GoLive. If you delete from this folder, the items are deleted to your system Trash or Recycle Bin.

Exporting Your Web Site

You may choose to export your GoLive site for a variety of reasons, including to back up a site, strip the site of selected code, or to transfer the files to someone else. As with the other site features in GoLive, you must have the Site window forward to access the Site menu items and toolbar.

Keep in mind that exporting a site is for collecting data for the pages and other information in your Web site; it's not the same as saving a site that includes a site file, Web-content, Web-data, and Web-settings folders.

Follow these steps to export a site:

1. **Have the Site window forward in the site that you want to export.**

2. **Choose File➪Export➪Site.**

   The Export Site Options dialog box appears, shown in Figure 10-2, offering the following options:

   • **Hierarchy:** If you haven't been totally organized while building your site, here is your opportunity to rectify that. You can choose to leave the files organized as they are in your site, or organized into separate pages and media folders. Get this: GoLive will actually read the extension of a file and figure out for you what is a page and what is an image. The Flat option puts all files loose in one folder. Read on to see how you can change the folder names that GoLive uses.

   • **Honor "Publish" State Of:** This is a neat little feature. You might have original Photoshop files that you don't want uploaded to the server. Or for that matter, it can apply to any folder or file that you want to contain in your Site window but not upload.

The publish state is important! Your original artwork files (typically in Photoshop format) often are gigantic in file size (at least by Web graphics standards). If you just put everything up on your publish server, you'll use up a lot of space for files that aren't even used in your Web site. Doing this can put you over your allocated storage space very quickly and cause other headaches. Bottom line: Be disciplined about what you upload to your publish server; only put the files online that your site actually uses.

Define the publish state by selecting a folder or a file in the Site window. In the Inspector palette, choose from one of three options in the Publish drop-down list: *Never* to ensure that the folder or file will never be uploaded when using the automatically upload features in GoLive; *Always* to ensure that the folder or file will always be published to the server when using GoLive's upload features; or *If Referenced* to ensure that the folder or file will be uploaded only if it is referenced in the Web site, meaning that a link has been created to it.

- **Export Linked Files Only:** This options leaves any unused files behind. You can tell what is used and what is not by looking at the Used column in the Site window, as shown in Figure 10-3.

- **Export Linked Files That Are Not Part of the Site:** Use this option to export orphan files that may be linked, but are not imported into the Web-content folder. Read more about Orphan files in Chapter 6 of this minibook.

- **Don't Show Again:** Check this so that you don't get this dialog box again. You can always change your preferences by choosing Edit⇨ Preferences⇨Site⇨Upload/Export (Windows) or GoLive⇨Preferences⇨ Site⇨Upload/Export (Mac).

- **Strip Options:** Click the Strip Options button to have the GoLive script removed (sure you hand-coded it all!) or change options for other information to be stripped. Keep your original site intact if you plan on stripping out bunches of code at export. Otherwise, you may not have the wonderful GoLive features available to you when you open the pages again.

3. **After making your selections, click the Export button to browse to a location and save the new exported site.**

The site has been copied with your selected options to the location you selected.

Figure 10-2:
The Export
Site Options
dialog box.

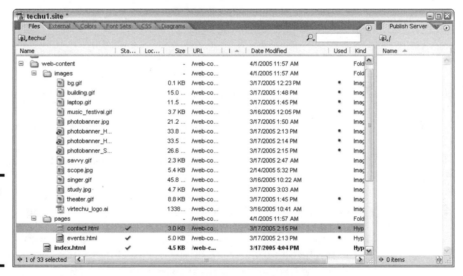

Figure 10-3:
The dot
indicates
that the file
is used.

If you want to change your export options, to change folder organization or names, just follow these steps:

1. **Click the Site Settings button in the Site toolbox.**

The Site Settings dialog box appears, as shown in Figure 10-4.

2. **Select Upload/Export in the list on the left.**

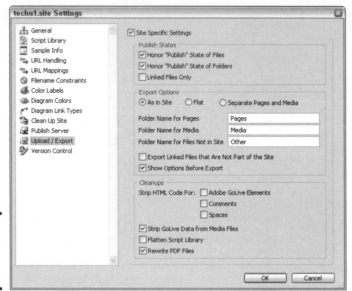

Figure 10-4:
The Upload/
Export
settings.

3. **Select the Site Specific Settings check box.**

   You can now set some of the same options as in the Export Site Options
   dialog box, but you can also change the folder names (get rid of that
   nasty initial cap!) and set up preferences if you're using the cleanup
   options when you're exporting a site.

4. **Click OK when you're satisfied with the export settings.**

Connections and Networks

 Connect to your publish server by clicking the Connect to Publish Server
button on the Site toolbar. If you have not set up your server settings, an
alert appears that gives you the opportunity to set them up now. You can
also click the Open Site Settings button to set your FTP settings beforehand.

Setting up your connection

Follow these steps to set up a connection to your publish server:

1. **Make sure that the computer you're working on has an active Internet
   connection.**

   This should be obvious, but you just never know what kind of things can
   be missed by overly intelligent users!

2. **Make sure that the Site window is forward and click the Open Site Settings dialog button on the Site toolbar.**

   The Site Settings dialog box appears (refer to Figure 10-5).

3. **Select Publish Server in the list on the left, and then click the New Server button in the Publish Server Options pane to the right.**

4. **Enter a name or description in the Nickname text field.**

   This is a name that you can use to describe the site, such as, "My cool Web Site," "Family Site," or something logical like your company's name.

5. **Leave the Protocol drop-down list set for FTP, unless you're told otherwise by your ISP.**

6. **Type in the server name supplied by your ISP.**

7. **If you were given a directory path, add it to the Directory text field.**

   Many times, you only have access from your ISP to certain folders based upon your username and password. In that case, you don't need to enter a directory path.

8. **Enter your username in the Username text field.**

   This is also supplied by your ISP.

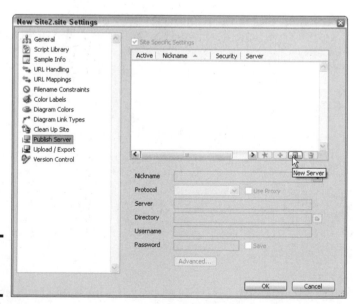

Figure 10-5:
Setting up
a server.

9. **Type in the password. If you don't want to type a password into the Password text field every time you update your Web site, select the Save check box.**

10. **Click OK.**

You can also set up and edit server connections as you create a new site or by choosing Site⇨Publish Server⇨Set Up Server.

Your Web site — live!

So now you have everything cleaned up and ready to go . . . or you're anxious and just want to get this site posted. Follow these steps to post your site to an FTP server:

1. **Have the site open that you want to post.**

Make sure that the Site window is forward.

2. **Click the Connect to Publish Server button.**

Pending that you have a connection, and that your settings are correct, you see your FTP server appear in a Publish Server tab on the right of the Site window, as shown in Figure 10-6.

3. **Slide the divider bar in the middle to adjust the size of the two sides of the window.**

4. **On the right side of the window (in the Publish Server tab), locate the folder that has been designated by your ISP as the directory for your Web site.**

Figure 10-6:
The local server is on the left, publish server on the right.

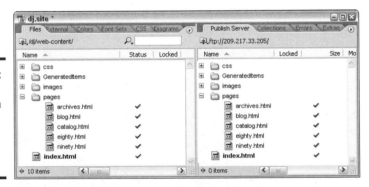

5. **Select Site⇨Publish Server⇨Upload All. This uploads all new files.**

If you are feeling pretty comfortable with the filing system, you can also select files from the left side of the window (in the Files tab) and drag them to the appropriate server location on the right. Be careful! You must keep the files in the same named directories because you want the paths to remain accurate on the server.

That's it . . . your pages are live on the server. Verify by launching your browser and navigating to your designated URL.

If you have files already loaded, use the GoLive synchronization features to make sure that the server files are the latest and greatest. See the next section for details.

Book VI
Chapter 10

Publishing Your Web Site

Synchronizing Your Site

After you have your site up on the server, you will probably be making lots of revisions. Save yourself the worry over whether the files on the server are the latest and greatest by synchronizing your site.

First of all, before you attempt to synchronize your Web site, make sure that the dates and times are accurate. You may have updated files outside of GoLive, and probably don't want to waste time uploading files that aren't necessary. To check sync times, choose Site⇨Publish Server⇨Sync Modification Times⇨All. This sets the modification times of local and remote files as "synched." So the local site version equals the publish server version.

You can also choose just selected files by choosing Site⇨Publish Server⇨Synch Modification Times⇨Selection.

Follow these steps to take advantage of synchronizing in GoLive:

1. **Synchronize the site by clicking the Synchronize with Publish Server button on the Site toolbar.**

GoLive scans and presents options to update selected files on the server. Missing files are listed as grayed out files on either side of the Site window. See Table 10-1 for the symbols you cycle through when selecting the check boxes to the right of the listed files.

If a Conflict icon appears, it means that the file was changed on the server and the local server.

2. **Using the check box options, make sure that you make a decision as to whether you should send this file to the server or download it to your computer from the publish server.**

3. **Click OK to complete the synchronization process.**

Table 10-1		Synchronization Symbols
Symbol	*Name*	*Function*
	Skip	Excludes file from synchronization
	Upload	Uploads file to server
	Download	Downloads the file from the server
	Delete	Deletes from the server and local site

 You can publish modified files by clicking the Upload Modified Files button on the Site toolbar. Use the Upload Modified Files button to only choose the files that have been modified, based upon the modified dates on the files.

 Click the Download Newer Files button to have GoLive download newer files from the publish server into your site.

You can also choose Site⇨Publish Server for other methods and options to upload and download only selected files.

Thoughts to Keep in Mind

Many a site has been ruined by users opening a page from the server and working on live pages. It's tough to resist when making small changes, but if the changes involve links to images and other local URLs, you will surely wreak havoc on your site. Save yourself the aggravation; if you're not sure that you're working on the latest page, drag it from the server to the appropriate folder in the File tab of the Site window.

 GoLive won't let you copy over the page that has been designated as your home page (the index.html page, for example). To copy over your original home page, choose another .html file in the Files tab of the Site window. Select the Home Page check box on the Pages tab of the File Inspector palette. This turns off the Home Page option for your index page. Now you can copy over the index.html page. Just make sure to designate the page as being your home page again when you're finished editing the file and you're ready to replace the file on the publish sever.

GoLive displays an error message, shown in Figure 10-7, when you have not entered the settings correctly in the Site Settings dialog box. If this error

GoLive displays an error message, shown in Figure 10-7, when you have not entered the settings correctly in the Site Settings dialog box. If this error message appears, make sure that your settings are accurate. Also, check with your ISP to see if an exact directory path is necessary or if Passive mode should be changed.

Figure 10-7:
Your
settings
aren't
accurate.

Index

H

halftone patterns, 75–76
Hand tool
  Illustrator, 254, 257
  InDesign, 112
  Photoshop, 403
Hard Light blend mode, 366, 482
Hard Mix blend mode, 482
harsh lighting effect, 482
Head button, 580
head section, Web pages, 580
Healing Brush tool, 471
Help menu, 20, 103
Help option, 24
Hidden object, 663
Hide command, 316–317
hiding/showing. *See also* clipping; masks
  Acrobat interface, 525
  artboard boundaries, 251
  Bookmarks tab, 540
  bounding boxes, 260
  Brushes palette, 469
  Character palette, 299
  color channels, 76
  comments, Acrobat, 564–565
  comments in PDF files, 564–565
  dotted border, 251
  elements on a page, 64
  GoLive layers, 653–655
  guides and grids, 103, 107–109
  imageable area border, 251
  images, 316–317
  layers, 327, 488, 653–655
  palettes, 35, 106, 255, 403
  toolbars, 525
  tools, 101, 403, 405
high key, 453
Highlight Text tool, 560
highlighting, comments in PDF files, 560
highlights
  finding, 456–458
  setting, 458–460
histograms, 451–453
History Brush tool, 402, 477–478

Horizontal Scale option, 300
hosting reviews of PDFs, 232–233
HTML
  attributes, 596
  basics, 595–596
  inspecting, 582–583
  nesting, 596
  overview, 595–596
  tags, 596
  values, 596
HTTP (Hypertext Transfer Protocol), 588
hue, 482
Hue blend mode, 366, 482
human eye, and resolution, 444
hyperlinks. *See* links
hyphenation, 303–304
Hyphenation utility, 303–304

I

ID selector, 619
illustrations. *See* drawing; Illustrator;
    images
Illustrator. *See also* drawing; images
  Area Type tool, 290–292
  arranging objects, 314–315
  artboard, 251
  Baseline Shift option, 300
  blend modes, 365–366
  Blend tool, 254, 360–362
  Bloat tool, 353
  Character Rotation option, 300
  Clear Appearance button, 371
  clipping mask feature, 318–320
  Color blend mode, 366
  Color Burn blend mode, 366
  Color Dodge blend mode, 366
  color models *See also* colors
    choosing, 329–330
    CMYK, 329
    RGB, 329
  creating PDFs from, 531
  Crystallize tool, 353
  custom guides, 312–313
  Darken blend mode, 365
  Difference blend mode, 366

BUSINESS, CAREERS & PERSONAL FINANCE

0-7645-9847-3   0-7645-2431-3

Also available:
- Business Plans Kit For Dummies
  0-7645-9794-9
- Economics For Dummies
  0-7645-5726-2
- Grant Writing For Dummies
  0-7645-8416-2
- Home Buying For Dummies
  0-7645-5331-3
- Managing For Dummies
  0-7645-1771-6
- Marketing For Dummies
  0-7645-5600-2

- Personal Finance For Dummies
  0-7645-2590-5*
- Resumes For Dummies
  0-7645-5471-9
- Selling For Dummies
  0-7645-5363-1
- Six Sigma For Dummies
  0-7645-6798-5
- Small Business Kit For Dummies
  0-7645-5984-2
- Starting an eBay Business For Dummies
  0-7645-6924-4
- Your Dream Career For Dummies
  0-7645-9795-7

HOME & BUSINESS COMPUTER BASICS

0-470-05432-8   0-471-75421-8

Also available:
- Cleaning Windows Vista For Dummies
  0-471-78293-9
- Excel 2007 For Dummies
  0-470-03737-7
- Mac OS X Tiger For Dummies
  0-7645-7675-5
- MacBook For Dummies
  0-470-04859-X
- Macs For Dummies
  0-470-04849-2
- Office 2007 For Dummies
  0-470-00923-3

- Outlook 2007 For Dummies
  0-470-03830-6
- PCs For Dummies
  0-7645-8958-X
- Salesforce.com For Dummies
  0-470-04893-X
- Upgrading & Fixing Laptops For Dummies
  0-7645-8959-8
- Word 2007 For Dummies
  0-470-03658-3
- Quicken 2007 For Dummies
  0-470-04600-7

FOOD, HOME, GARDEN, HOBBIES, MUSIC & PETS

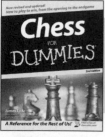

0-7645-8404-9   0-7645-9904-6

Also available:
- Candy Making For Dummies
  0-7645-9734-5
- Card Games For Dummies
  0-7645-9910-0
- Crocheting For Dummies
  0-7645-4151-X
- Dog Training For Dummies
  0-7645-8418-9
- Healthy Carb Cookbook For Dummies
  0-7645-8476-6
- Home Maintenance For Dummies
  0-7645-5215-5

- Horses For Dummies
  0-7645-9797-3
- Jewelry Making & Beading For Dummies
  0-7645-2571-9
- Orchids For Dummies
  0-7645-6759-4
- Puppies For Dummies
  0-7645-5255-4
- Rock Guitar For Dummies
  0-7645-5356-9
- Sewing For Dummies
  0-7645-6847-7
- Singing For Dummies
  0-7645-2475-5

INTERNET & DIGITAL MEDIA

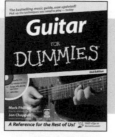

0-470-04529-9   0-470-04894-8

Also available:
- Blogging For Dummies
  0-471-77084-1
- Digital Photography For Dummies
  0-7645-9802-3
- Digital Photography All-in-One Desk Reference For Dummies
  0-470-03743-1
- Digital SLR Cameras and Photography For Dummies
  0-7645-9803-1
- eBay Business All-in-One Desk Reference For Dummies
  0-7645-8438-3
- HDTV For Dummies
  0-470-09673-X

- Home Entertainment PCs For Dummies
  0-470-05523-5
- MySpace For Dummies
  0-470-09529-6
- Search Engine Optimization For Dummies
  0-471-97998-8
- Skype For Dummies
  0-470-04891-3
- The Internet For Dummies
  0-7645-8996-2
- Wiring Your Digital Home For Dummies
  0-471-91830-X

* Separate Canadian edition also available
* Separate U.K. edition also available

Available wherever books are sold. For more information or to order direct: U.S. customers visit www.dummies.com or call 1-877-762-2974.
U.K. customers visit www.wileyeurope.com or call 0800 243407. Canadian customers visit www.wiley.ca or call 1-800-567-4797.

SPORTS, FITNESS, PARENTING, RELIGION & SPIRITUALITY

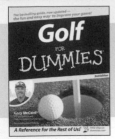

0-471-76871-5

0-7645-7841-3

Also available:

- Catholicism For Dummies
  0-7645-5391-7
- Exercise Balls For Dummies
  0-7645-5623-1
- Fitness For Dummies
  0-7645-7851-0
- Football For Dummies
  0-7645-3936-1
- Judaism For Dummies
  0-7645-5299-6
- Potty Training For Dummies
  0-7645-5417-4
- Buddhism For Dummies
  0-7645-5359-3

- Pregnancy For Dummies
  0-7645-4483-7 †
- Ten Minute Tone-Ups For Dummies
  0-7645-7207-5
- NASCAR For Dummies
  0-7645-7681-X
- Religion For Dummies
  0-7645-5264-3
- Soccer For Dummies
  0-7645-5229-5
- Women in the Bible For Dummies
  0-7645-8475-8

TRAVEL

0-7645-7749-2

0-7645-6945-7

Also available:

- Alaska For Dummies
  0-7645-7746-8
- Cruise Vacations For Dummies
  0-7645-6941-4
- England For Dummies
  0-7645-4276-1
- Europe For Dummies
  0-7645-7529-5
- Germany For Dummies
  0-7645-7823-5
- Hawaii For Dummies
  0-7645-7402-7

- Italy For Dummies
  0-7645-7386-1
- Las Vegas For Dummies
  0-7645-7382-9
- London For Dummies
  0-7645-4277-X
- Paris For Dummies
  0-7645-7630-5
- RV Vacations For Dummies
  0-7645-4442-X
- Walt Disney World & Orlando
  For Dummies
  0-7645-9660-8

GRAPHICS, DESIGN & WEB DEVELOPMENT

0-7645-8815-X

0-7645-9571-7

Also available:

- 3D Game Animation For Dummies
  0-7645-8789-7
- AutoCAD 2006 For Dummies
  0-7645-8925-3
- Building a Web Site For Dummies
  0-7645-7144-3
- Creating Web Pages For Dummies
  0-470-08030-2
- Creating Web Pages All-in-One Desk
  Reference For Dummies
  0-7645-4345-8
- Dreamweaver 8 For Dummies
  0-7645-9649-7

- InDesign CS2 For Dummies
  0-7645-9572-5
- Macromedia Flash 8 For Dummies
  0-7645-9691-8
- Photoshop CS2 and Digital
  Photography For Dummies
  0-7645-9580-6
- Photoshop Elements 4 For Dummies
  0-471-77483-9
- Syndicating Web Sites with RSS Feeds
  For Dummies
  0-7645-8848-6
- Yahoo! SiteBuilder For Dummies
  0-7645-9800-7

NETWORKING, SECURITY, PROGRAMMING & DATABASES

0-7645-7728-X

0-471-74940-0

Also available:

- Access 2007 For Dummies
  0-470-04612-0
- ASP.NET 2 For Dummies
  0-7645-7907-X
- C# 2005 For Dummies
  0-7645-9704-3
- Hacking For Dummies
  0-470-05235-X
- Hacking Wireless Networks
  For Dummies
  0-7645-9730-2
- Java For Dummies
  0-470-08716-1

- Microsoft SQL Server 2005 For Dummie
  0-7645-7755-7
- Networking All-in-One Desk Reference
  For Dummies
  0-7645-9939-9
- Preventing Identity Theft For Dummies
  0-7645-7336-5
- Telecom For Dummies
  0-471-77085-X
- Visual Studio 2005 All-in-One Desk
  Reference For Dummies
  0-7645-9775-2
- XML For Dummies
  0-7645-8845-1

HEALTH & SELF-HELP

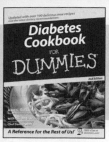

0-7645-8450-2

0-7645-4149-8

Also available:
- Bipolar Disorder For Dummies
  0-7645-8451-0
- Chemotherapy and Radiation
  For Dummies
  0-7645-7832-4
- Controlling Cholesterol For Dummies
  0-7645-5440-9
- Diabetes For Dummies
  0-7645-6820-5* †
- Divorce For Dummies
  0-7645-8417-0 †

- Fibromyalgia For Dummies
  0-7645-5441-7
- Low-Calorie Dieting For Dummies
  0-7645-9905-4
- Meditation For Dummies
  0-471-77774-9
- Osteoporosis For Dummies
  0-7645-7621-6
- Overcoming Anxiety For Dummies
  0-7645-5447-6
- Reiki For Dummies
  0-7645-9907-0
- Stress Management For Dummies
  0-7645-5144-2

EDUCATION, HISTORY, REFERENCE & TEST PREPARATION

0-7645-8381-6

0-7645-9554-7

Also available:
- The ACT For Dummies
  0-7645-9652-7
- Algebra For Dummies
  0-7645-5325-9
- Algebra Workbook For Dummies
  0-7645-8467-7
- Astronomy For Dummies
  0-7645-8465-0
- Calculus For Dummies
  0-7645-2498-4
- Chemistry For Dummies
  0-7645-5430-1
- Forensics For Dummies
  0-7645-5580-4

- Freemasons For Dummies
  0-7645-9796-5
- French For Dummies
  0-7645-5193-0
- Geometry For Dummies
  0-7645-5324-0
- Organic Chemistry I For Dummies
  0-7645-6902-3
- The SAT I For Dummies
  0-7645-7193-1
- Spanish For Dummies
  0-7645-5194-9
- Statistics For Dummies
  0-7645-5423-9

Get smart @ dummies.com®

- **Find a full list of Dummies titles**
- **Look into loads of FREE on-site articles**
- **Sign up for FREE eTips e-mailed to you weekly**
- **See what other products carry the Dummies name**
- **Shop directly from the Dummies bookstore**
- **Enter to win new prizes every month!**

Separate Canadian edition also available
Separate U.K. edition also available

Available wherever books are sold. For more information or to order direct: U.S. customers visit www.dummies.com or call 1-877-762-2974. U.K. customers visit www.wileyeurope.com or call 0800 243407. Canadian customers visit www.wiley.ca or call 1-800-567-4797.

Do More with Dummies

Instructional DVDs • Music Compilations
Games & Novelties • Culinary Kits
Crafts & Sewing Patterns
Home Improvement/DIY Kits • and more!

Check out the Dummies Specialty Shop at www.dummies.com for more information!

WILEY